THE ENGINES OF EUROPEAN INTEGRATION

THE ENGINES OF EUROPEAN INTEGRATION

DELEGATION, AGENCY, AND AGENDA SETTING IN THE EU

Mark A. Pollack

OXFORD

UNIVERSITY PRESS

OXFORD
UNIVERSITY PRESS

Great Clarendon Street, Oxford OX2 6DP

Oxford University Press is a department of the University of Oxford.
It furthers the University's objective of excellence in research, scholarship,
and education by publishing worldwide in

Oxford New York

Auckland Bangkok Buenos Aires Cape Town Chennai
Dar es Salaam Delhi Hong Kong Istanbul Karachi Kolkata
Kuala Lumpur Madrid Melbourne Mexico City Mumbai Nairobi
São Paulo Shanghai Taipei Tokyo Toronto

Oxford is a registered trade mark of Oxford University Press
in the UK and in certain other countries

Published in the United States
by Oxford University Press Inc., New York

British Library Cataloguing in Publication Data

Data available

Library of Congress Cataloging in Publication Data
Pollack, Mark A., 1966-
The engines of European integration: delegation, agency, and
agenda setting in the EU / Mark A. Pollack.
p. cm.
Includes bibliographical references.
1. European Union. 2. European communities. I. Title.
JN30 .P656 2002   341.242'2–dc21   2002038196
ISBN 0-19-925118-5 (hbk.)
ISBN 0-19-925117-7 (pbk.)

1 3 5 7 9 10 8 6 4 2

Typeset by Newgen Imaging Systems (P) Ltd., Chennai, India
Printed in Great Britain
on acid-free paper by
T. J. International Ltd., Padstow, Cornwall

For my parents

CONTENTS

Conclusions

LIST OF FIGURES

LIST OF TABLES

ACKNOWLEDGEMENTS

One of the (many) potential pitfalls of a career in political science is a tendency to apply theoretical concepts to one's personal life. In the years before the writing of this book, for example, I have seen political scientists use the concept of 'free riding' with reference to graduate students who join study groups but bank their best comments for seminars; 'nested games' with reference to the convoluted career plans of colleagues; and, of course, 'battle of the sexes' used, usually inaccurately, with reference to just about anything.

In that context, generic principal-agent models of delegation—in which one or more individuals, the principal(s), delegate powers to one or more other individuals, the agent(s)—are particularly perilous, since principal-agent relationships are ubiquitous in many areas of political, economic, and social life. Nevertheless, as I point out in Chapter 1 of this book, principal-agent models are not generally designed to serve as broad theories of political life, but rather as mid-range theories that isolate, problematize, and investigate particularly common and important principal-agent relationships like that between EU member governments and their supranational agents. As a corollary, not every social relationship is a principal-agent relationship, and indeed the vast majority of people whom I would like to thank in these acknowledgements are neither my principals nor my agents, but practitioners, colleagues, and friends without whose support this book would have been impossible.

For detailed comments and criticisms on papers and draft chapters leading up to the book, I would like to thank Karen Alter, Michael Barnett, Derek Beach, Jim Caporaso, Jeff Checkel, Joe Jupille, Amie Kreppel, Bert Kritzer, John Peterson, Thomas Risse, George Ross, and a number of anonymous referees. For correspondence, discussions, and hard questions, I am grateful to Jean Blondel, Lisa Conant, Gráinne de Búrca, Bruno De Witte, Beth DeSombre, Fabio Franchino, Simon Hix, Liesbet Hooghe, Christian Joerges, Gary Marks, Margaret McCown, Jürgen Neyer, Johan P. Olson, Martin Rhodes, Wayne Sandholtz, and Daniel Verdier. I am also grateful to Andreas Maurer and the Federal Trust for permission to reproduce Figure 4.1, which originally appeared in Maurer's 1999 book, *What Next for the European Parliament?*; to Catherine Divry for her tireless help in reproducing said figure; and to Michael Mosser, who provided valuable research assistance for several of the cases in Chapters 5 and 6. Other useful comments on earlier drafts were provided by audiences at the 1995 meeting of the European Union Studies Association, the University of Washington, the University of California at Irvine, the University of California at Berkeley, the Fletcher School of Law and Diplomacy, the ARENA programme at the University of Olso, the European University Institute, and the University of Siena.

Alec Stone Sweet and Helen Wallace were invaluable in their practical as well as moral support in the completion of the manuscript. My graduate advisers Stanley Hoffmann, Peter Hall, and Andrew Moravcsik all appear to regard the job of adviser as continuing indefinitely without a statute of limitations, and I am extremely grateful for their continuing advice and support.

In Chapter 1, I argue that researchers should if at all possible minimize reliance on interviews in favour of hard primary sources, particularly—as in the case of nearly all of my interviews—when they are granted on the basis of a promise of anonymity, making one's findings difficult if not impossible for other scholars to replicate. Nevertheless, as a supplement to hard primary sources, interviews remain an invaluable source of information for qualitative research on the European Union, and I would like to thank the many officials of the European Commission, the European Parliament, the Court of Justice, and the various EU member states who have shared their views with me over the past six years in the research for this book.

I have also been fortunate to have enjoyed financial and logistical support during the research and writing of the book, and would like to acknowledge in particular the support of the German Marshall Fund of the United States; the European Union Center and the Center on World Affairs and the Global Economy (WAGE) at the University of Wisconsin-Madison; and the BP Chair in Transatlantic Relations at the European University Institute, which provided funding and an ideal setting for the completion of the manuscript.

At Oxford University Press, I would like to thank my editor Dominic Byatt as well as Amanda Watkins, Gwen Booth, Zofia Stemplowska, and Valerie Shelley for their support and professionalism. Special thanks to Michael James, whose careful copy-editing vastly improved a manuscript which I had previously, and wrongly, regarded as 'finished'. One of the standard pieces of received wisdom about university presses is that they are stodgy and slow-moving; in fact, OUP was as efficient as any press I have ever worked with, and spent most of its time waiting for me to deliver manuscripts and proofs. I'm pleased to consider myself an OUP author.

On a personal note, I would like to thank my wife Rita Krueger and my son Cameron for their support and especially for their patience in the final phases of writing this book; I promise them that, if we ever get to live in Tuscany or somewhere comparably glorious again, I will *not* spend our weekends writing. Finally, I thank my parents, who missed the final stages of writing in Florence but put in decades of hard time before that, and to whom I dedicate this book. Like many of the concepts in this book, it is difficult to operationalize and measure the contribution of caring parents to an endeavour like this one, except to say that it's big, and I know it when I see it.

Mark Pollack

Florence
July 2002

INTRODUCTION

THEORY, HYPOTHESES, AND RESEARCH DESIGN

Introduction

The European Union (EU) is composed of its member states. The governments of those member states have signed and ratified successive Treaties outlining the objectives and institutions of the Union, starting with the European Coal and Steel Community of 1951 and continuing through the creation and institutional elaboration of today's European Union. As in any international organization, the member governments of the EU have assigned to themselves the central role in the governance of the Union. Member governments dominate both the European Council—the semi-annual summit meetings at which government leaders set the broad strategic direction of the Union—and the Council of Ministers, which has historically been, and remains, its pre-eminent legislative body. At the same time, however, the EU's member governments have created and allocated increasing powers and discretion to a number of supranational organizations, including the executive Commission, the European Court of Justice (ECJ), and a European Parliament (EP) which now acts as a co-legislator with the Council in a growing number of areas. Although clearly the creation, or agents, of the member governments, these supranational organizations possess powers and preferences distinct from those of their member-state principals, and they have frequently been posited by both practitioners and academic observers as the embodiment of the project of European integration, and indeed as the 'engines' or 'motors' of the integration process.

For the purposes of this book, the existence and activities of supranational organizations like the Commission, Court, and Parliament raise two sets of questions about the European Union and international organizations more generally. First, we can ask why, and under what conditions, do states create, delegate powers and allocate discretion to supranational agents, both within Europe and in international politics more generally. What functions do these and other organizations perform for the states that create them? How much discretion do member governments allocate to these organizations in the performance of their delegated powers? Do member governments deliberately design institutions to keep their supranational agents accountable, and, if so, how do they choose those institutions?

A second set of questions, by contrast, focuses on the post-delegation activities of supranational agents. Put simply, we can ask whether supranational institutions *matter*—that is, whether they deserve the status of an independent causal variable—in the politics of the European Union and other international organizations. Do these organizations have their own preferences, distinct from those of the states that created them? And, if so, how and under what conditions can supranational organizations act autonomously and influence outcomes in international relations? Put most simply, are supranational organizations 'the engines of integration'?

These are among the most important and hotly disputed questions in both the international relations literature on European integration as a *process*, and the comparative politics literature on the European Union as a *polity*. For international relations scholars, the role of supranational organizations has been one of the principal points dividing the two traditional schools of thought, with neo-functionalists generally asserting, and intergovernmentalists generally denying, any important causal role for supranational organizations in the integration process. By and large, however, neither neo-functionalism nor intergovernmentalism has generated testable hypotheses regarding the conditions under which, and the ways in which, supranational institutions exert an independent causal influence on the process of European integration.[1]

More recently, an increasing number of scholars have approached the EU using the tools of comparative politics, asking not about the process of integration but rather about the operation of the EU as a polity or a political system.[2] For these scholars, the EU's supranational organizations, as well as the central role of the intergovernmental Council of Ministers, raise questions about the democratic accountability and legitimacy of the Union. In this view, EU governance is often seen as remote and democratically unaccountable, with a growing number of appointed, non-majoritarian actors like the Commission, Court, and European Central Bank supervised largely by indirectly elected ministers in the Council and by a directly elected but relatively weak European Parliament.[3]

In this book, I present and test a theory of supranational delegation, agency, and agenda setting, drawn largely from the new institutionalism in rational choice theory. Although the empirical subject of the book is the supranational organizations of the European Union, the theoretical approach and many of the methodological tools used in the book are drawn from the rational choice study of American political institutions, and the implications of these theories extend beyond the EU to other domestic and international political systems. Specifically, the book draws upon principal-agent models of delegation of powers by legislative *principals*—such as Congressional representatives in the American case, or national governments in the case of international relations—to executive or judicial *agents*—such as regulatory agencies or courts in the American case, or supranational organizations in international relations. Such delegation, it is argued, offers potentially significant advantages to principals, reducing the transaction costs of policy-making by providing policy-relevant information and allowing principals to commit credibly to their agreements. Yet delegation also creates the potential for losses, if and in so far as the agents thus empowered possess policy preferences distinct from those of the principals and use their delegated powers to pursue those preferences. In the American context, therefore, analysts have derived and tested numerous hypotheses about the conditions under which legislative principals are likely to delegate greater or lesser power and discretion to their agents, and about the variable ability of agents to pursue their own policy preferences within the limits of discretion set down by their principals.[4]

To simplify only slightly, the contemporary rational-choice literature on American political institutions is traceable to Kenneth Shepsle's pioneering work on the role of institutions in the US Congress. Beginning with the observation by Richard McKelvey (1976), William Riker (1980), and others that in a system of majoritarian decision-making policy choices are inherently unstable, 'cycling' among multiple possible equilibria, Shepsle argued that Congressional institutions, and in particular the committee system, could produce 'structure-induced equilibrium' by ruling some alternatives as permissible or impermissible and by structuring the voting and veto power of various actors in the decision-making process. In more recent work, Shepsle and others have turned their attention to the problem of 'equilibrium institutions', namely, how actors choose or design institutions to secure mutual gains, and how those institutions change or persist over time.[5]

Shepsle's innovation and the subsequent development of the rational-choice approach to Congressional institutions have produced a number of theoretical offshoots with potential applications in comparative as well as international politics. For example, Shepsle and others have examined in some detail the 'agenda-setting' power of the Congressional committees that are the linchpin of his structure-induced equilibrium, specifying the conditions under which agenda-setting committees could influence the outcomes of certain Congressional votes.[6] Shepsle's 'distributive' model of Congressional committees has, however, been challenged by Keith Krehbiel and other scholars, who agree that committees possess agenda-power but argue that the committee system serves an 'informational' rather than distributive function by providing members with an incentive to acquire and share policy-relevant information with other members of Congress.[7] In another offshoot, students of the Congress have developed principal-agent models of Congressional delegation of authority to regulatory bureaucracies—and later to courts—and the efforts of Congress to control those bureaucracies.[8] More recently, Epstein and O'Halloran (1994; 1999*a*,*b*) and others have pioneered a 'transaction cost approach' to the design of political institutions, arguing that legislators deliberately and systematically design political institutions to minimize the transaction costs associated with making public policy.[9]

Although originally formulated and applied in the context of American political institutions, I argue, these approaches are applicable in other comparative and international political contexts, and I attempt in this book to generate and test hypotheses about the delegation of power to supranational organizations and the efforts by those organizations to influence political outcomes in the European Union. For the purposes of analysis, I divide the problem of supranational influence into three subsets of questions.

First, I examine the *delegation* stage, asking about the types of functions that member-state principals are likely to delegate to supranational organizations and the conditions under which they will allocate greater or lesser discretion to such agents. Legislative principals, I argue, delegate powers to agents in order to reduce the transactions costs associated with the adoption and implementation of policies. More specifically, executive and judicial agents may solve problems of incomplete information (by providing policy-relevant information to legislators) and credible commitments (by monitoring legislators' compliance with their agreements and by providing independent regulation of powerful economic actors). In line with this transaction-cost approach to delegation, I predict that member-state principals will delegate four key functions to their supranational agents, namely: (1) monitoring compliance; (2) solving problems of 'incomplete contracting' among principals; (3) adopting credible, expert regulation of economic activities in areas where the principals would be either ill-informed or biased; and (4) setting the legislative agenda so as to avoid the endless 'cycling' that might otherwise result if the principals retained that power for themselves.

In addition to the functions delegated to agents by legislative principals, a growing number of scholars in American politics have examined the conditions under which principals will allocate greater or lesser *discretion* to agents in the performance of these functions. As we shall see, these theorists generally predict that the discretion of an actor will vary across one of two explanatory variables. First, in keeping with the informational rationale for delegation, in which agents are assumed to provide policy-relevant information for their legislative principals, Epstein and O'Halloran (1999*a*) and others argue that the discretion of a given agent will vary as a function of the complexity or 'inherent uncertainty' of an issue area, with agents generally being allocated greater discretion in areas of scientific and technical complexity. A second, overlapping hypothesis has been put forward by students of independent central banks, regulatory agencies, and courts, who argue that delegation is driven primarily by a concern among the principals to commit themselves credibly to a certain line of policy where those principals would otherwise be tempted to renege on their agreements. In this view, legislative principals are likely to delegate the most extensive discretion to their agents in those issue areas where, because of time-inconsistency problems or the existence of concentrated costs and diffuse benefits, the credibility of legislative commitments would otherwise be in question.

Second, I examine the extent to which, and the conditions under which, supranational agents are able to take advantage of their discretion to pursue their own policy preferences—for example, by seeking to advance the process of European integration beyond the lowest-common-denominator preferences of the EU member governments. Faced with the threat of such supranational activism, I argue, member-state principals adopt both administrative procedures and oversight mechanisms in order to limit supranational discretion; yet these control mechanisms are themselves costly and are unlikely to be perfectly effective in preventing agents from pursuing their own preferences. In this context, I argue that the autonomy and influence of a given supranational organization depends primarily upon the efficacy and credibility of various control mechanisms established by member-state principals, and that these vary both across organizations and over time, leading to varying but predictable patterns of supranational autonomy and influence.

Third and finally, I turn to the problem of agenda setting, or the ability of an agent to influence decision-making processes among its legislative principals. Here, I distinguish between formal or procedural agenda setting on the one hand and informal or substantive agenda setting on the other. With regard to formal agenda setting, I demonstrate that the agenda-setting power of an agent such as the Commission relies fundamentally on its exclusive power to propose legislation and on the decision rules governing the adoption and amendment of draft legislation; put simply, the formal agenda-setting power of an agent is greatest when it possesses the sole right to propose legislation and when it is easier to adopt draft legislation than to amend it. By contrast with such formal agenda setting, informal agenda setting—often referred to as 'political entrepreneurship'—does not rely upon any particular decision rules but rather on the agent's ability to construct 'focal points' in intergovernmental bargaining, or to match policy proposals to pressing policy problems in an environment of uncertainty and imperfect information. Such informal agenda setting, I argue, offers supranational agents the prospect of influencing the course of European integration even in the absence of formal agenda-setting powers, but only under a highly restrictive set of assumptions about the distribution of information and entrepreneurial skills between supranational agents and the member governments they serve.

I. Research Design

Unfortunately, testing such hypotheses empirically is far more difficult than it might appear at first blush, and the principal-agent literature is replete with methodological warnings about the difficulties of distinguishing between obedient servants and runaway bureaucracies. In essence, the problem is that agents such as the Commission may *rationally anticipate* the reactions of their principals as well as the probability of sanctions, and adjust their behaviour to avoid the costly imposition of sanctions. If this is so, then agency behaviour which at first glance seems autonomous may in fact be subtly influenced by the preferences of the principals, even in the absence of any overt sanctions. Indeed, as Weingast and Moran (1983) point out, the more effective the control mechanisms employed by the principals, the less overt sanctioning we should see, since agents rationally anticipate the preferences of the principals and the high probability of sanctions for shirking, and adjust their behaviour accordingly. Studies of agency autonomy that rely on the frequency of sanctioning are therefore likely to run into the methodological problem of *observational equivalence*, namely, that the absence of sanctions is consistent with both the obedient servant and the runaway bureaucracy scenarios, each of which predicts, albeit for different reasons, the rarity of sanctions.

Faced with these methodological obstacles, an increasing number of scholars have opted to concentrate their empirical analyses not on the behaviour of the agent and its autonomy from the preferences of its principals but on the *delegation* stage, where principals make their strategic decisions about the powers delegated to agents and the control mechanisms established to limit their autonomy. In a recent contribution, for example, Epstein and O'Halloran (1999*a*) focus their attention entirely on the Congressional decision to delegate, testing hypotheses about the conditions—such as divided government—under which Congress might be expected to delegate greater or lesser discretion to the bureaucracy. More generally, Huber and Shipan (2000) have argued that, while hypotheses about agency typically require laborious case studies that provide no 'black and white' answers to questions about agency and control, hypotheses about delegation are more amenable to rigorous quantitative testing, and therefore offer a more promising subject for empirical research.

In this book, and notwithstanding Huber and Shipan's lucid methodological warning, I examine *both* the delegation stage—at which member-state principals create supranational organizations, delegate powers to them, and establish more-or-less restrictive control mechanisms to limit their discretion—*and* the actual behaviour of supranational agents in the day-to-day conduct of their executive, judicial, and legislative (agenda-setting) powers. Although causally related, these two stages raise very different methodological challenges, and thus the two parts of the book utilize distinct research designs and methods to answer the questions posed in each.

II. Delegation and Discretion

The first part of the book is devoted to the analysis of *delegation and discretion*, that is, the functions delegated to supranational organizations, the conditions under which those organizations are allocated more or less discretion, and the nature of the control mechanisms established by member states to fix the precise level of discretion across issue areas and over time. These chapters examine both the general or 'horizontal' powers delegated to supranational organizations in the EU's constitutive Treaties and the issue-specific or 'sectoral' powers delegated in both primary (Treaty) and secondary legislation. This analysis suggests that principal-agent models are quite successful in predicting the functions delegated to the Commission and the Court of Justice, which are indeed devoted to monitoring compliance, filling in the details of incomplete contracts, regulating economic activity, and setting the legislative agenda—but that these models are less successful in explaining delegation to the European Parliament, where democratic legitimacy rather than credible commitments or the provision of policy-relevant information appears to have been the primary motivation for delegation by member governments.

In terms of the conditions under which member states allocate discretion to supranational agents, I argue that member governments do indeed delegate powers and discretion to the Commission and the Court in order to reduce the transaction costs of EU policy-making. Specifically, I argue that the delegation of discretionary powers to the Commission and the ECJ is motivated largely, although not exclusively, by the demand for credible commitments by EU member governments. As we shall see, EU member governments have delegated extensive powers of monitoring, enforcement, and the completion of incomplete contracts to the Commission and the Court, thereby increasing the credibility of member states' commitment to their agreements. In addition, the member governments have delegated regulatory powers to the Commission in areas such as competition policy and international trade, where individual governments would otherwise face a temptation to renege rather than impose concentrated costs on important domestic constituents. By contrast, the hypothesis that member governments delegate powers to enjoy the benefits of agency expertise receives little support: By comparison with the member governments themselves, EU supranational agents are thinly staffed and enjoy little scientific or technical expertise, which is primarily provided at the EU level by committees of member-government representatives; and delegation to the Commission is not concentrated in scientific and technical areas or in the area of foreign policy, where we would expect policy-relevant expertise to be most in demand. Instead, I find that much of the delegation in areas such as agricultural and fisheries policy is motivated neither by credible commitments concerns nor by a demand for technical expertise, but rather by a concern for the *speed and efficiency* of decision-making. As we shall see, legislative decision-making in the Council of Ministers and the European Parliament is generally an agonizingly slow process, generating significant transaction costs for the member governments; hence, in areas such as the Common Agricultural and Fisheries Policies that require extensive day-to-day management, delegation of powers to the Commission offers speedy and efficient decision-making, with the option of reasserting control when and if the Commission strays too far from member-state preferences.

III. Agency and Agenda Setting

In the second part of the book, I undertake the very different task of testing principal-agent hypotheses about the conditions under which supranational agents *matter*, in the sense of acting autonomously from the principals and using their discretion to pursue their own policy preferences for 'more Europe'. Unfortunately, the aforementioned 'law of anticipated reactions' means that, in the European Union as in the United States, legislative overruling and other sanctions against supranational agents are extremely rare, and quantitative studies of supranational behaviour suffer from the same problem of observational equivalence mentioned earlier in the US context.

The primary methods used in these chapters, therefore, are qualitative, employing a carefully chosen set of six case studies and incorporating process tracing in order to multiply the observable implications of theory and observe hypothesized causal mechanisms at work within each case (King, Keohane, and Verba 1994). Specifically, I adopt three criteria for the selection of the case studies in the second part of the book. First, I select cases that provide considerable variation across the hypothesized independent variable, namely, the control mechanisms established by member states to limit supranational discretion in specific issue areas. Given the byzantine nature of the EU's decision rules, it has not proven possible to include every possible variant of member-state oversight and agenda-setting procedures; the analysis here therefore focuses on three categories of cases: (1) supranational agenda setting, where a Commission initiative requires a positive endorsement from a qualified majority of EU member governments; (2) supranational authority with member-state oversight, in the form of advisory or management committees, which in theory provide the Commission with greater discretion vis-à-vis the member governments; and (3) Treaty interpretation by the European Court of Justice, which can be overturned only by a unanimous decision of the member states to amend the Treaties. *Ceteris paribus*, we should see supranational influence increase as we move from the first to the third of these categories.

Second, I select cases which include both market liberalization and social regulation, which will allow us to determine whether the EU's supranational organizations are biased towards either liberalization or regulation, as suggested by several recent analyses.

Third and finally, I select cases which feature an open dispute or conflict between supranational organizations and one or more member governments. Although such cases do not qualify as a representative sample of all supranational behaviour, much of which is mundane and uncontroversial, they nevertheless present the advantage of revealing conflicting preferences among the various actors and illuminating the conditions under which member states are able—or unable—to rein in their agents. The resulting selection of cases is outlined in Table I.1, and discussed in greater detail in the chapter summaries below.

TABLE I.1. *Case selection, by issue area and decision rules*

Decision rules	Type of issue area	
	Market liberalization	Social regulation
Agenda setting (QMV to approve)	External trade policy (Uruguay Round: Blair House Accord)	Social policy (Working Time Directive)
Oversight committee (advisory or management)	Merger control (de Havilland merger)	Structural Funds (RECHAR case)
Treaty interpretation (unanimity to overturn)	Free movement of goods (*Cassis de Dijon*)	Equal opportunities (*Barber*)

IV. Plan of the Book

In the first chapter, I lay out in detail the theoretical argument summarized above, generating specific hypotheses about the functions delegated to supranational agents; the conditions under which greater or lesser discretion is allocated to such agents; and the conditions under which supranational actors like the Commission or the Court of Justice are able to pursue their distinct preferences, within the limits of their statutory discretion. I also point out, however, that the rational-choice approach is not the only possible approach to such questions, and I outline briefly a competing approach drawn from sociological institutionalism, emphasizing the possibility that actors behave according to a 'logic of appropriateness' rather than the 'logic of consequentiality' emphasized by rational-choice theorists. A final section discusses the research design, methods, and sources employed in the subsequent, empirical chapters.

   In the second and longest chapter of the book, I examine the record of delegation to the Commission throughout the EU's history, focusing in turn on Treaty-based delegation and on secondary legislation. The analysis here includes an examination of delegation and control mechanisms across 35 issue areas, each of which is coded to determine the extent of delegation and the extent and types of control mechanisms established to limit Commission discretion. Almost without exception, I argue, the member states delegate to the Commission precisely the functions hypothesized by principal-agent models, including most notably monitoring compliance, setting the legislative agenda, and laying down expert and credible market regulations. By the same token, however, the Commission is closely monitored by member governments, which have adopted a carefully designed and calibrated system of appointment and censure mechanisms, 'comitology' or oversight committees, and administrative law and judicial review by the ECJ, each of which is examined in detail. The choice of such instruments, I demonstrate, varies systematically by issue area, with the Commission being particularly constrained in politically sensitive areas such as taxation, public health, industrial relations, criminal law, and foreign affairs, and least constrained in the areas of competition policy, international trade, and other core areas of the internal market.

By contrast, Chapter 3 on the Court of Justice demonstrates that the ECJ has been delegated extraordinarily broad powers to interpret EU Treaties and secondary legislation and that this broad delegation has been accompanied by significant discretion, which Majone (2000) argues is necessary in order for the Court to settle disputes regarding the interpretation of the EU's 'incomplete contract'. Specifically, the chapter examines the comparatively small range of control mechanisms available to member governments vis-à-vis the ECJ—for example, the power of appointment and the threats of unilateral non-compliance or legislative reversal of Court judgments—and reviews evidence suggesting that the Court has indeed pursued an integrationist agenda with little regard to the preferences of powerful member states or to the likelihood of legislative overruling. However, the chapter also notes that—perhaps in response to this record of successful judicial activism—member governments have recently been more reluctant about delegating extensive new powers to the Court, which enjoys no jurisdiction in the area of Common Foreign and Security Policy and only partial jurisdiction in the area of Justice and Home Affairs, where member governments have adopted a byzantine system of safeguards to limit the reach of the Court into their domestic legal systems.

By contrast with the Commission and the Court—both of which are non-majoritarian institutions that have been delegated the functions hypothesized by principal-agent analysis, and subjected to the same kinds of constraints observed in the US case—the European Parliament is shown in Chapter 4 to be an outlier in terms of principal-agent analysis. Specifically, an empirical analysis of Treaty-based delegation demonstrates that the Parliament has been delegated a primarily legislative role—but *not* the right of initiative, which rests with the Commission—and that the issue-specific pattern of delegation differs sharply between the Commission and the Parliament, which enjoys little say in the areas such as competition policy and external trade where the Commission enjoys the greatest amount of discretion. While this emphasis on the democratic character of EU decision-making might seem to support the view that member governments behave according to a 'logic of appropriateness', a closer examination of the patterns and process of delegation to the EP suggests that member governments do indeed calculate the likely consequences of delegation to the EP, and refrain from delegating powers in areas where they believe that the EP would move political outcomes away from their collective preferences.

The second part of the book provides a shift in empirical focus and methods from the delegation stage to the actual behaviour of supranational organizations and their ability to use their discretion to advance the integration process. In Chapter 5, I begin by examining three cases of market liberalization representing a range of control mechanisms in the areas of external trade, competition policy, and the free movement of goods within the Union. The first case study examines the Commission's powers as the Union's chief negotiator in the area of external trade, where it enjoys the power to set the EU agenda by negotiating agreements with third countries that can subsequently be accepted by a qualified majority among the member governments. The case focuses specifically on the Commission's controversial 'Blair House' agreement on agricultural policy with the United States, and traces the member-state reaction to this agreement, and the subsequent debate over the extension of the Commission's trade powers to the 'new areas' of intellectual property and services. The second case study examines the area of competition policy, with a special focus on the 1989 Merger Regulation, which delegated to the Commission the power to review European-wide mergers, with minimal oversight by member governments. Specifically, I review the Commission's landmark decision to reject the proposed merger between the Canadian aircraft manufacturer de Havilland and the Franco-Italian consortium ATR, and the subsequent controversy regarding the renewal and extension of the Commission's powers in the area of merger control. The third case study examines the role of the European Court of Justice in the interpretation of the Treaty provisions on the free movement of goods within the EU, with a special focus on the Court's 1979 ruling in *Cassis de Dijon*, which established the principle of 'mutual recognition' of national regulations within the EU, and the 1991 *Keck and Mithouard* decision in which the Court retreated from the more far-reaching implications of *Cassis*. Taken together, these three case studies suggest that the Commission and the Court have indeed been activist in their mission to establish a single European market, but also that their successes have been limited as a function of the mechanisms established by member governments to control their discretion.

The cases in Chapter 6 mirror those of Chapter 5 in terms of decision rules, but in three areas of social regulation: workplace regulation, regional policy, and the principle of equal pay for men and women. The first case, the Working Time Directive of 1993, examines the Commission's agenda-setting powers in the area of health and safety in the workplace, which the Commission interpreted broadly to include regulation of the maximum working time allowable by law. Although this Directive was successfully adopted by a qualified majority on the basis of a Commission proposal, it was subsequently challenged before the ECJ by a disgruntled British government, which argued that the Commission had overstepped its mandate; the resulting legal and political controversy is examined in detail. The second case concerns the Commission's executive powers in the implementation of the Structural Funds, which were expanded considerably in the 1988 reform of the Funds to ensure careful financial control over expenditure in the various member states. Specifically, the chapter examines the controversy between the Commission, which insisted on upholding the principle of 'additionality' of EU funding, and the United Kingdom government, which protested against the 1991 Commission decision to withhold EU funding from a UK project which failed to meet these criteria. Although the Commission prevailed in its immediate conflict with the government of Prime Minister John Major, the member governments later responded by limiting the Commission's discretion in the subsequent review of the Structural Funds in 1993. Third and finally, the chapter examines the Court's interpretation of the equal pay provisions of the Treaties, and in particular the 1991 *Barber* ruling, which controversially extended the principle of equal pay for equal work to occupational pension schemes and to the pensionable age of women and men. Although the Court was successful in its expansive interpretation of the Treaty, the limits of ECJ discretion were revealed when the member states adopted an unprecedented and legally binding protocol to the 1992 Maastricht Treaty, limiting the retroactive effect of the Court's decision. Taken together, these three cases suggest that, in addition to their efforts to liberalize the European market, the Commission and the Court have also pursued a consistent policy of expanding the range of EU social regulation, but that their success in doing so has varied systematically with the control mechanisms established by member governments to limit supranational discretion.

The final chapter summarizes the empirical findings of the book, and looks beyond these cases to the growing 'agencification' of the European Union and global politics. With regard to delegation, I argue that EU member states have delegated functions to the Commission and the Court of Justice which correspond closely to the functions predicted by principal-agent models, but that delegation to the European Parliament fits poorly with the predictions of the model, and appears to be driven by concerns over democratic legitimacy rather than credible commitments or the provision of information. With regard to discretion, the empirical evidence presented in the book suggests that member governments make systematic choices about the powers delegated and the control mechanisms adopted to limit supranational discretion both across issue-areas and over time; and that credible commitments, together with an ongoing concern about the speed and efficiency of decision-making, explain the decisions by member governments to allocate discretion to the Commission and the Court.

With respect to the agency and agenda-setting activities of supranational agents, the evidence analysed in the book suggests that, despite their internal complexity and diversity, the EU's supranational agents generally behave like unitary actors with a preference for further integration, and the discretion of these agents to realize their preferences varies systematically with the institutional control mechanisms established by member governments in the initial acts of delegation. Specifically, principal-agent models allow us to explain the substantial difference in discretion observed, in this book and in many other studies, between the Commission and the Court of Justice, as well as the variable autonomy and agenda-setting power of the Commission across issue areas and over time.

In the second section of the conclusion, I look beyond the Commission, Court, and Parliament to consider the implications of this analysis for a Europe, and a world, which rely increasingly on delegation to non-majoritarian organizations. Within the EU, I examine the debate over the European Central Bank, which has arguably displaced the ECJ as the most independent and influential supranational organization in the European Union, as well as the recent proliferation of European agencies such as the European Environment Agency and the European Medical Evaluation Agency, which promise to bring efficiency and credible regulation to the European level but raise now-familiar issues about democratic accountability. Looking beyond the European Union, I consider the questions of delegation, agency, and agenda setting among other international organizations, including the

United Nations Secretariat, the World Bank, and the International Monetary Fund, as well as the various international courts and tribunals established within organizations such as the World Trade Organization and the North Atlantic Free Trade Agreement.

In the third and last section of the conclusion, I turn from the positive findings and implications of this study to the normative questions raised by the increasing delegation of powers to international organizations, many of which are only weakly accountable to democratic electorates in their various member states. I examine three possible approaches—parliamentarization, deliberation, and constitutionalization—to dealing with the 'democratic deficit' inherent in governance by supranational organizations, and I opt for the third of these options, which I suggest holds the greatest promise for reconciling the benefits of delegation with the normative desirability of democratic accountability. Whatever our normative evaluation of delegation to supranational agents, however, I suggest that the principal-agent approach laid out in the book offers a generalizable and testable theoretical framework within which to problematize and analyse the role of these actors, for good or ill, in international politics.

CHAPTER 1

Delegation, Agency, and Agenda Setting in the European Union

The primary argument in this book is that the member governments of the European Union delegate power and discretion to the European Commission and the Court of Justice in order to reduce the transactions costs of EU decision-making, and that they deliberately design and tailor a wide range of control mechanisms to limit agency discretion and maximize the benefits of delegation across issue areas and over time. Once created, however, supranational agents develop their own distinct preferences, generally for greater integration, and they pursue these preferences as 'engines of integration', albeit within the bounds of the discretion allocated to them in the original act of delegation.

In this chapter, I lay out in greater detail the theoretical argument of the book, as well as the research design and methods used in the subsequent, empirical chapters. The chapter is divided into five parts. In the first, I examine the decision by a group of principals to delegate authority to an agent, and I derive hypotheses about the functions likely to be delegated to agents and the conditions under which principals will allocate greater or lesser discretion to those agents. In the second part of the chapter, I turn to the supranational agents themselves, putting forward hypotheses about the preferences of supranational agents and the conditions under which they might be able to influence policy outcomes in ways that depart from the preferences of their principals. Third, I discuss both formal and informal agenda setting, and the very different conditions under which we would expect each type to occur. Fourth, I briefly summarize an alternative approach to the problems of delegation, agency, and agenda setting, drawn from sociological institutionalism, and derive some competing hypotheses from this approach. The fifth and final section discusses the research design, methods, and sources used in the book's substantive chapters.

I. Delegation and Discretion

Delegation: A Functionalist Approach

Generally speaking, the delegation of powers by à group of *principals*—such as domestic legislators or member governments—to an *agent*—such as a regulatory agency or a supranational organization—is a special case of the more general problem of institutional choice or institutional design: Why do a group of actors collectively decide upon one specific set of institutions rather than another to govern their subsequent interactions? The basic approach of rational choice theory to this problem of institutional choice is *functionalist*: that is to say, institutional choices are explained in terms of the functions that a given institution is expected to perform, and the effects on policy outcomes it is expected to produce, subject to the uncertainty inherent in any institutional design. As Keohane (1984: 80) argues:

In general, functional explanations account for causes in terms of their effects . . . So for example, investment is explained by profit, as in the statement, 'The increased profitability of oil drilling has increased investment in the oil industry.' Of course, in the temporal sense investment is the cause of profit, since profits follow successful investment. But in this functional formulation the causal path is reversed: effect explains cause. In our example, this inverse link between cause and effect is provided by the rationality assumption: *anticipated* profits lead to investment.

This functionalist approach to institutional design—and to the delegation of powers to an agent by principals—has been adopted by students of American Congressional politics and public bureaucracy, and more recently by students of international relations. Within American politics, a growing literature examines the *transaction costs* involved in the making of public policy, which make it difficult for re-election-minded members of Congress to produce efficient policies and satisfy their constituents. Some of these transaction costs are *informational*; that is to say, Congressional legislators are confronted with a complex policy environment, and often require technical information and expert advice in order to craft effective public policies. In order to produce the necessary information, therefore, legislators design political institutions that employ policy experts, and create incentives for those experts to provide policy-relevant information for legislators.[1]

Not all transaction costs are informational, however. Another central concern is the problem of *credible commitment*; that is to say, a group of legislators may find that it 'pays' electorally to commit themselves to certain kinds of policies, but that they cannot credibly bind themselves or their successors to maintain those policies in the future. For this reason, legislators may often delegate powers to bureaucratic agents—such as Congressional committees, regulatory agencies, or independent central banks—who, because of their independence and their insulation from day-to-day electoral pressures, are more able to commit themselves to maintaining a given policy in the future.[2]

Similarly, in Keohane's functional theory of international regimes, states agree to adopt certain institutions primarily to lower the transactions costs of international cooperation, thereby overcoming some basic collective action problems that might otherwise prevent cooperation under anarchy. International regimes, in this view, facilitate cooperation among states both by reducing the transactions costs of international negotiations *ex ante*, and by monitoring compliance and identifying transgressors *ex post*. Indeed, much of the literature on international institutions in recent years has focused precisely on the question of which institutions are able to reduce transaction costs, monitor compliance, and allow states to commit themselves credibly to their international agreements.[3]

In both the American and international cases, then, institutions serve to lower transaction costs and facilitate mutually advantageous cooperation among rational egoists by providing policy-relevant information and credibly committing them to their agreements. In both cases, moreover, principals decide to delegate powers to an agent, not for its own sake, but because that agent will reduce the transaction costs of policy-making either by producing expert information for the principals or by allowing the principals to commit themselves credibly to their agreed course of action. More specifically, principal-agent models of delegation have identified four key functions or powers that principals may or should delegate to their agents. These functions are: (1) monitoring compliance with agreements among the principals; (2) solving problems of 'incomplete contracting'; (3) adopting credible, expert regulation of economic activities in areas where the principals would be either ill-informed or biased; and (4) setting the parliamentary agenda so as to avoid the endless 'cycling' of policy alternatives that might otherwise result from the possession of agenda-setting power by the principals themselves. Let us consider each of these functions, very briefly, in turn.

Monitoring Compliance
Consider a typical collective action problem in which a group of actors—be they medieval traders, vote-trading Congressmen, or sovereign states—would enjoy mutual benefits from cooperation, but are

prevented from doing so by concerns about non-compliance by their would-be partners. If we assume further that each actor has only incomplete information about the compliance of other actors, or indeed of what constitutes compliance or transgression in the first place, then this uncertainty is likely to act as a significant transaction cost inhibiting cooperation and exchange among these actors. In other words, actors may find themselves unable to commit credibly to the mutually advantageous agreements because of the incentives for non-compliance and the lack of monitoring and enforcement mechanisms.

In this context of collective action under imperfect information, a group of principals may choose to create an agent to monitor individual compliance, and provide such information to all participants, in effect 'painting scarlet letters' on transgressors. In such cases, institutional actors—such as private 'law merchants' in medieval marketplaces or international secretariats in contemporary international relations—can monitor the behaviour of each actor and make this information available to all the actors, thereby reducing transactions costs and encouraging mutually beneficial cooperation. Furthermore, these organizations need not be given the power to enforce agreements through sanctions, but need provide only enough information about compliance to facilitate decentralized sanctioning by the principals themselves.[4]

Incomplete Contracting

Any institutional agreement—whether it be an economic exchange between two private actors, a logrolling trade of votes among legislators, or the establishment of a common market among sovereign states—can be theorized as a contract. In such a contract, the various parties to the agreement pledge to behave in certain ways—to deliver a product, vote as promised on the legislative floor, or refrain from interfering with free trade—in the future. However, as Williamson (1985) has pointed out, all but the simplest contracts are invariably incomplete in that they do not spell out in explicit detail the precise obligations of all the parties, in all conceivable circumstances, throughout the life of the contract. The main reason for this is once again uncertainty, or incomplete information, about future conditions, which makes the specification of future responsibilities impossible or at least prohibitively costly. Hence, rather than attempting to write a complete contract that would anticipate all possible contingencies,

... the contracting parties content themselves with an agreement that *frames* their relationship—that is, one that fixes general performance expectations, provides procedures to govern decision making in situations where the contract is not explicit, and outlines how to adjudicate disputes where they arise. (Milgrom and Roberts 1990: 62)

These various procedures may, but need not, involve the creation of an agent. For example, if the contract in question is simple and the number of contracting parties is small, the parties may simply choose to lay down rules governing the elaboration and amendment of the agreement and the arbitration of disputes, but leave it to the parties themselves to undertake these activities. Alternatively, where uncertainty is great and future decision-making is expected to be time-consuming and complex, the parties may choose to delegate these activities to an agent, such as an executive or a court, which can impartially interpret the agreement, fill in the details of an incomplete contract, and adjudicate any disputes that might arise.

Regulation, Information, and Credibility
A third function delegated to agents concerns the promulgation of detailed implementing regulations governing economic or other activities. Examples of such delegation to regulatory agencies are legion, covering a wide range of regulatory bodies and activities, including financial regulations, environmental protection, international trade, and competition or antitrust policy. Explanations for this type of delegation are similarly varied, emphasizing variously the importance of information or of credible commitments. Perhaps the classic explanation of delegation to regulatory agencies is the complexity and the technical nature of much economic regulation, which is simply too detailed and too complex to be undertaken by legislative principals on the floor of the US House or Senate, in the American example, or in multilateral diplomatic negotiations, in the case of international relations. In this sense, regulatory agencies or bureaux provide policy-relevant expertise and promulgate detailed regulations, reducing the informational demands and the workloads of legislative principals.

By contrast with this informational rationale, a second explanation of regulatory delegation emphasizes once again the importance of credible commitments. In this view, legislative principals delegate regulatory authority to independent agencies in order to establish the *credibility* of such regulation among constituents and market actors, if and in so far as the principals themselves would have difficulty in credibly promising to apply regulations consistently to concentrated and powerful constituents. In the US case, for example, Congressmen might be reluctant to adopt and enforce regulatory rules imposing concentrated costs on their constituents, and their threats to do so would therefore lack credibility among economic actors. Similarly, in the classic case of regulation to secure credible commitments, legislators have a strong incentive to delegate monetary authority to an independent central bank which would be insulated from political pressures to stimulate the economy—thereby creating inflationary pressures—prior to elections.[5]

The importance of credible commitments has also been emphasized by students of international institutions. In cases where national activities produce negative externalities—for example, trans-boundary pollution or distortion of international competition through state aids to industry—each member state has a rational incentive to regulate its own national industries leniently, leading to weak and non-credible regulation and a proliferation of trans-boundary externalities. National regulation in such cases is, in other words, a Prisoner's Dilemma in which no state can credibly commit itself in advance to the rigorous application of international regulations, and the result is regulatory failure. In this context, delegation of authority to a supranational agent, which unlike member states has a rational incentive to regulate national firms impartially and rigorously, can overcome the Prisoner's Dilemma and produce credible regulation, thereby improving the behaviour of private actors and minimizing the production of trans-boundary externalities (Gatsios and Seabright 1989; Majone 1996; 2001; Moravcsik 1998).

Formal Agenda Setting, or the Power to Propose
Formal agenda setting consists in the ability of a given actor to initiate policy proposals for consideration among a group of legislators, such as Congressmen on the floor of the US House and Senate, or member governments meeting within an international institution. The power of a formal agenda setter is, as we shall see below, greatest when her proposals are easier to adopt than to amend. In such cases, any actor with an exclusive right to initiate policy proposals could strategically select the proposal closest to her own preferences that could also secure the necessary majority among the legislators.

Despite this potentially dictatorial power of a formal agenda setter, there are two important reasons why a group of principals might choose to delegate this authority to an agent. First, as McKelvey (1976), Riker (1980), and others have pointed out, any majoritarian system in which each and every legislator had the right to initiate proposals would encourage an endless series of proposals from disgruntled legislators who had been in the minority in a previous vote. In such a system, no decision would be an equilibrium, and the result would be endless cycling among alternative policy proposals. Thus, *any* legislature would have a rational incentive to develop rules governing which actors can initiate proposals, and when (Shepsle 1979; Kiewiet and McCubbins 1991: 23–4).

Second, given the power of agenda setters to influence the outcome of legislative choices, legislative principals might choose to allocate agenda control deliberately so as to bias legislative outcomes in particular directions. In the so-called 'distributive model' of Congressional committee formation, for example, individual Congressmen have collectively created a system which divides legislative activity into a series of issue areas or jurisdictions, and delegates agenda-setting power within each jurisdiction to the relevant Congressional committee. Membership of such committees is then allocated to interested members on the basis of seniority. Such a system not only eliminates the problem of cycling but allows Congressmen to self-select onto committees that are of particular importance to their constituents and exert particular influence over legislative outcomes in those areas (Shepsle 1979; Weingast and Marshall 1988). By contrast, a second view of Congressional committees, the 'informational model', depicts Congressional representatives attempting to make policy in the face of a complex policy environment which generates considerable uncertainty. In this view, Congressional committees are designed primarily to provide policy-relevant information to floor voters, and the agenda-setting powers of such committees constitute an incentive for committee members to acquire and accurately convey such information to the full chamber (see for example Krehbiel 1991). Although these two schools differ about the motives underlying the decision to delegate power to Congressional committees, they agree that such committees may enjoy considerable power to influence final outcomes on the floor of Congressional chambers.

In sum, the transaction-cost approach to delegation predicts that the functions delegated to supranational actors will not be random but will rather be concentrated in four key functions: monitoring compliance, filling in incomplete contracts, providing expert and credible regulation, and setting the formal agenda for legislation. In the case of the European Union, we should therefore find the member governments that constitute the collective principals of the Union delegating these four types of functions to the Commission, Court, and Parliament. Such a pattern of delegation would support the hypothesis that member-state principals are indeed motivated primarily by a desire to minimize the political transaction costs of international cooperation. A random pattern of delegation, by contrast, or a pattern in which authority is systematically delegated for functions other than those specified above, would suggest that member states are motivated by concerns other than the minimizing of transaction costs.

Discretion: Institutional Design to Reduce Agency Costs

Thus far we have hypothesized that, under certain conditions, member-state principals might be expected to delegate authority to supranational agents. However, this initial act of delegation immediately raises another problem. What if the agent thus empowered has preferences systematically distinct from those of its principals, and uses its delegated powers to pursue its own preferences at the expense of the preferences of the principals? As McCubbins and Kiewiet (1991: 5) summarize the problem:

Delegation . . . entails side effects that are known, in the parlance of economic theory, as agency losses. There is almost always some conflict between the interests of those who delegate authority (principals) and the agents to whom they delegate it. Agents behave opportunistically, pursuing their own interests subject only to the constraints imposed by their relationship with the principal.

Agency losses come in two forms: slippage and shirking (McCubbins and Page 1987: 410–11). Slippage occurs when constraints or incentives provided by the principals induce the agent to behave in ways systematically different from those preferred by the principals. Shirking, on the other hand, occurs when an agent pursues preferences of its own rather than, or to the detriment of, the preferences of the principals. This shirking, or 'bureaucratic drift', thus emerges as the primary source of agency losses and the central problem of principal-agent analysis.

Agency shirking is a problem insofar as the agent has both an incentive and the ability to pursue its own preferences rather than those of its principals. As Terry Moe argues, these incentives and abilities can be quite considerable:

A new public agency is literally a new actor on the political scene. It has its own interests, which may diverge from those of its creators, and it typically has resources—expertise, delegated authority—to strike out on its own should the opportunities arise. (Moe 1990: 121, quoted in Pierson 1996)

The importance in this context of information, and of asymmetrically distributed information in particular, can scarcely be overstated. In any principal-agent relationship, information about the agent and its activities is likely to be asymmetrically distributed in favour of the agent, making control or even evaluation by the principal difficult.

Thus, for example, the agent is likely to have better information than the principal about its own expenditure of effort and performance, its budgetary needs, the technical requirements of a specific budgetary proposal, and so on. Without some means of acquiring the necessary information to evaluate the agent's performance, therefore, the principal seems to be at a permanent disadvantage, and the likelihood of agency losses seems large.

Principals, however, are not helpless in the face of these disadvantages. Rather, when delegating authority to an agent, principals can also adopt various control mechanisms that can rectify, or at least mitigate, the informational asymmetries in favour of the agent through various forms of monitoring, and constrain or shape the incentives of the agents through the use of positive and negative sanctions. These control mechanisms can be divided into two broad categories: *ex ante* administrative procedures and *ex post* oversight procedures. Administrative procedures define more or less narrowly the scope of agency activity, the legal instruments available to the agency, and the procedures to be followed by it. By contrast, oversight procedures consist of the various institutional mechanisms that principals can use to (1) monitor agency behaviour, thereby correcting the informational asymmetry in favour of the agent, and (2) influence agency behaviour through the application of positive and negative sanctions. Among the formidable array of sanctions at the disposal of legislative principals are control over appointments, control over budgets, and the possibility of overriding agency behaviour through new legislation (McCubbins and Page 1984; Weingast and Moran 1983).

If these control mechanisms were costless, one would expect principals to adopt the full range of administrative and oversight procedures in all cases in order to minimize or eliminate agency losses. These mechanisms, however, are not costless. As Kiewiet and McCubbins (1991: 27) succinctly state, 'Agency losses can be contained, but only by undertaking measures that are themselves costly'. Strict administrative controls, for example, such as narrowly defining the scope and flexibility an agent possesses in the execution of its functions, tend to produce rigid and inefficient policies. Oversight procedures may similarly consume considerable resources, and sanctions may impose costs upon principals as well as agents, as we shall see presently. In addition, both types of oversight, by limiting the autonomy of agents from their principals, also limit their credibility as independent regulators. There are, in other words, two types of agency problems: the *agency losses* resulting from slippage and shirking, and the *agency costs* of control mechanisms to minimize agency losses.

Given these agency costs of delegation, under what conditions will principals agree to allocate more or less *discretion* to their agents? Note here that the term 'discretion', as used by American students of delegation, refers not to the behaviour of the agency but rather to characteristics of the *act of delegation*—that is, a constitution, treaty, legislation, or other type of contract—that establishes the parameters of acceptable agent behaviour.

In an early formulation, McCubbins, Noll, and Weingast (1989) defined discretion as the set of agent decisions that no political coalition among the principals could overturn, given the voting rules for legislative overruling and the distribution of preferences among the principals. More recently, however, Epstein and O'Halloran (1999a: 26) have suggested that an agent's discretion depends not only on the threat of *ex post* legislative overruling but also on the establishment of explicit *ex ante* legislative provisions, including both administrative procedures and the specification of a range of acceptable policy outcomes.[6] Thus discretion, in Epstein and O'Halloran's view, can be measured by first examining the extent of delegation in any given act, but then taking into account all of the possible constraints that principals might impose upon their agents. The net of these delegation and constraint ratios, then, provides a measure of *discretion* which, in the American case, demonstrates considerable variation across issue areas and over time.[7]

This range of variation in the discretion allocated to regulatory agencies in turn directs our attention to the delegation decision as a question of institutional choice. In delegating to agents, principals do not simply delegate powers; they also attempt to choose the 'right' institutions to minimize agency losses at an acceptable cost to themselves. However, as Huber and Shipan (2000: 9) point out, the 'right' institutions may vary considerably depending upon the nature of the political environment: 'One size does not fit all.' Rather, they argue, the institutional design of control mechanisms can be considered as a *dependent variable*, which in turn reflects other factors of the political environment, which are the independent variables for the purpose of explaining institutional choice.

Over the past half-decade, rational choice scholars have put forward a wide range of hypotheses about the specific aspects of the political environment that might be expected to influence the decision by principals to allocate discretion to regulatory agents; but two factors already mentioned—the demand for policy-relevant expertise and the demand for credible commitments—have been singled out by various authors as the most important motivations for delegation and the most important determinants of agent discretion. Both of these factors are discussed here primarily with reference to delegation in the US Congress, but these same factors can be extended beyond the US case to the EU case, and to comparative and international politics more generally.

Imperfect Information and the Demand for Policy-Relevant Expertise

The existence of imperfect information—or, more specifically, legislators' need for policy-relevant information—is perhaps the most important transaction cost cited by rational choice scholars as justification for the delegation of powers from legislators such as the US Congress to regulatory agencies such as the Environmental Protection Agency or the Food and Drug Administration. The argument here is straightforward: the empirical world is inherently uncertain, and legislators face constant demands for policy-relevant information about the state of the world: for example, the effect of a given policy on the natural environment, or the safety requirements for civil aviation.[8] Under such circumstances, legislators may find it useful to delegate power to a regulatory agency, which is assumed to provide policy-relevant expertise and thereby improve the quality of regulation while reducing the workload of legislators and their staffs. This core assumption—that regulatory agencies are created and delegated powers largely in order to provide expert, policy-relevant information to legislators—is central to the analyses of many recent studies (Bawn 1995; 1997; Epstein and O'Halloran 1994; 1999*a*, *b*; Huber 1998). In the view of these and other authors, legislative principals should delegate greater discretion to regulatory agencies as a function of the uncertainty inherent in any given issue area.[9]

Credible Commitments and the Demand for an Independent, Credible Regulator

Despite the importance of imperfect information in principal-agent models, transaction cost theorists have offered a second, analytically distinct rationale for delegation, stressing the need for legislators to establish the credibility of their agreements and policies. More specifically, students of regulatory bureaucracies and especially independent central banks have suggested that legislative principals might face difficulties establishing the credibility of their commitment to specific policy choices over time, for several overlapping reasons. First, a group of principals, having agreed to cooperate in the adoption of some policy, may find themselves with a rational incentive to renege on their agreement if their cheating is unlikely to be discovered. Furthermore, if all the actors understand this incentive to cheat, the credibility of each actor will be suspect, and mutually advantageous agreements will go unrealized.

Second, the nature of politics as a game played *over time* points to two generic obstacles to credible commitment: *time inconsistency*, which occurs when a legislator's or government's optimal long-run policy differs from its short-run policy, so that these actors face a rational incentive in the short run to renege on their long-term commitments; and *ill-defined political property rights*, which occur when a group of legislators or a government faces the prospect of eventually being replaced in office by other actors with different preferences, who might then overturn their preferred policies. In both these cases, legislators and governments may enjoy a rational incentive to delegate powers—and very substantial *discretion*—to independent bodies charged with the adoption and maintenance of certain policies, even in the face of pressures to renege from the principals or their successors (Majone 2001). The classic example of such a disjunction between short-term and long-term preferences arises in the area of monetary policy, where legislators and governments may have a long-term preference for anti-inflationary monetary policies, but may simultaneously find themselves unable to commit to such policies because of the short-term temptation to reduce interest rates and stimulate the economy on the eve of an election (Huber 2000).

Third and finally, a group of legislative principals may find that these problems are particularly acute in specific issue areas where policies generate diffuse benefits for the public at large but impose concentrated costs on potentially important constituents. For example, Congressional legislators may find it politically efficient to adopt a rigorous antitrust policy against business cartels and concentrations or to close inefficient and expensive military bases, but in each case individual legislators would be tempted to be lenient faced with protests from concentrated interests—for example, large firms or military bases—in their own constituencies.[10] In this view, an independent regulator or central bank insulated from political pressures would enjoy greater credibility vis-à-vis political constituencies and markets, and legislators would benefit by delegating significant discretion to such non-majoritarian organizations. If this view is indeed correct, we should expect legislative principals to delegate powers, not only in issue areas marked by relative uncertainty but also in issue areas characterized by concentrated costs and diffuse benefits.

To sum up, the credible commitments view argues that principals deliberately delegate substantial discretion to agents in order to establish and maintain the credibility of their own commitments where problems of non-compliance, time inconsistency, or concentrated costs and diffuse benefits would otherwise undermine that credibility. In recent years, this argument has been applied to the European Union by Andrew Moravcsik (1998), who explicitly rejects the informational rationale for delegation, arguing instead that member governments delegated powers in the various constitutive treaties of the EU primarily to establish the credibility of their mutual commitments by monitoring compliance and filling in the details of the treaties that form the central, but incomplete, contracts of the Union.[11]

Giandomenico Majone goes further, arguing that there are not one but in fact 'two logics of delegation': one logic informed by the demand for policy-relevant expertise, in which principals delegate executive functions to agents within relatively constraining control mechanisms; and a second logic, guided by the demand for credible commitments, in which principals deliberately insulate their agents—or 'trustees', in Majone's term—so that the agents may implement policies to which their principals could not credibly commit. At the extreme, Majone suggests, such a 'fiduciary relationship' may lead principals to undertake a 'complete, and in some cases irrevocable' transfer of their 'political property rights' in a given issue area in favour of their trustees (Majone 2001: 113). Majone's model for such delegation is the independent central bank discussed above, but he argues that fiduciary relationships are not limited to monetary policy but extend to any area in which trustees perform the function of ensuring credible commitments. In the case of the EU, Majone argues, such trustee relations include the general powers of interpretation and enforcement granted to the ECJ in the treaties, as well as the Commission's power to set the agenda for Council legislation, enforce the provisions of the Treaties, and regulate member-state and firm behaviour in areas such as competition policy (Majone 2001: 114–15). By and large, Majone argues, member states have delegated powers in EU treaties primarily for the purpose of establishing credible commitments, and therefore grant considerable if not complete discretion to supranational agents in those Treaties. By contrast, the Council delegates implementing powers to the Commission in secondary legislation 'to reduce the costs and improve the quality of decision-making in the Council,' and accordingly design comitology rules that limit Commission discretion (Majone 2001: 115).

Majone's analysis is correct in distinguishing among two rationales for delegation—one informational, the other based on credibility of commitments—and it has the virtue of generating a specific, testable hypothesis: that EU member states will delegate extensive discretion to the Commission and other agents in the Treaties in order to secure their credible commitment to European integration, while secondary delegation will be motivated by demands for information and efficiency and be accompanied by substantially lower levels of discretion. In doing so, however, Majone too readily dichotomizes the two logics of delegation, which are not as diametrically opposed as he suggests. As we have seen, the transaction-cost approach to delegation is broad enough to encompass both the informational and the credibility rationales for delegation and the accompanying decision by principals to delegate more or less discretion to their agents. Principals may indeed delegate considerable discretion to their agents, and deliberately insulate them from political pressure in order to increase the credibility of their commitments, but concerns about shirking—say, in the form of embezzling central bankers, corrupt regulators or activist judges—remain even for Majone's trustees, which is why principals often provide constraining mandates and at least some sort of oversight mechanisms even in 'fiduciary' relationships. Furthermore, as Epstein and O'Halloran (1999a) point out, the informational and credibility rationales for delegation are not mutually exclusive but may overlap, so that delegation in a given area may reflect a demand for either expert information or credible commitment or both. Finally, as an empirical matter, it is worth noting that Majone's scenario of a complete and irrevocable transfer of political property rights is a theoretical limiting condition (Delegation = 1) which is rarely if ever realized in practice. Even in the areas of extensive, Treaty-based delegation to agents such as the European Court of Justice (see Chapter 3) or the European Central Bank (see Conclusion), member-state principals often specify a detailed and constraining mandate and required administrative procedures, and retain the ultimate right to revise the Treaties in response to shirking. In sum, Majone is correct to point to the importance of credible commitment alongside informational rationales for delegation; but this point is consistent with—indeed, is a central element in—the transaction-cost approach outlined above.

In addition to the demand for policy-relevant information and credible commitments, some rational-choice analysts point to a third factor that may, *ceteris paribus*, explain variation in the willingness of legislative principals to delegate powers and discretion to an agent: the extent of *conflicting preferences* either (1) among multiple principals or (2) between principals and agents. In the first case, the existence of conflicting preferences among multiple principals is assumed to reduce the desirability of delegation in so far as such conflicts complicate subsequent efforts to punish shirking by an agent (McCubbins and Page 1997; Moravcsik 1998: 75; Huber 2000). In the second and more intuitively obvious case, the existence of conflicting preferences between principals and agents increases the likelihood of significant agency costs and therefore decreases the desirability of delegation for the principals. In their study of Congressional delegation to regulatory bureaucracies, for example, Epstein and O'Halloran (1999*a*), begin with the assumption that the president nominates the heads of independent regulatory agencies, and that divided government therefore serves as a proxy for conflicting preferences among Congressional legislators on the one hand and regulatory agents on the other hand; and they do indeed find that Congress delegates less authority and less discretion to the executive branch during periods of divided government.[12]

Although systematic analyses of institutional choices for delegation are still relatively rare, empirical studies of Congressional delegation by Epstein and O'Halloran (1999*a*), Bawn (1995; 1997), and Huber (1998) suggest that Congressional legislators do indeed systematically delegate powers and allocate more or less discretion to regulatory agencies across issue areas, and that these institutional choices vary with at least some elements of the political environment. The promise of such studies, and their ability to measure delegation, discretion, and their relationship with various features of the institutional environment, can best be illustrated through a brief discussion of Epstein and O'Halloran's ambitious book.

Epstein and O'Halloran (1999*a*) begin by creating a formal model which generates a set of nine hypotheses about the degree of discretion likely to be delegated to agents under varying circumstances, the most important and generalizable of which are the presence of conflicting preferences between the President and Congress—that is, divided government—and the degree of uncertainty in any given issue area, for which they derive two distinct measurements. In order to test these hypotheses, Epstein and O'Halloran use an updated version of Mayhew's (1991) set of significant postwar legislation. For each of the 257 laws in their data-set, the authors adopt quantitative measures of: *delegation*, that is, the percentage of major provisions that delegate powers to an executive agent; *constraints*, an ordinal scale ranging from 1 to 14 and comprising the presence or absence of any of 14 distinct control mechanisms; and *discretion*, defined as the net of the delegation index and the constraints index. After defining and operationalizing these concepts in quantitative terms, Epstein and O'Halloran provide a full chapter of descriptive statistics demonstrating that Congressional decisions about delegation and discretion vary systematically across issue areas and over time. In later chapters, they analyse the correlation between their measurement of the dependent variable discretion and their key independent variables, including divided government and uncertainty, finding that these factors do indeed appear to influence the Congressional decision to delegate powers and discretion to executive agencies.[13]

To sum up this section, then, principal-agent analysts have hypothesized that legislative principals will not select identical degrees of discretion for all agents and in all issue areas: one size does not fit all. Rather, it has been argued, the degree of discretion allocated to agents should vary as a function of the uncertainty inherent in a given issue area, which provides an incentive to principals to delegate in order to acquire information, and the difficulty of establishing credible commitments, which provides an incentive for principals to delegate in order to establish their commitment to a given line of policy over time. In addition, the degree of policy conflict may also influence delegation decisions, with principals being most likely to delegate discretion where the degree of conflict is low both among the principals and between principals and their agents. However, testing such hypotheses has proven in practice to be a substantial methodological challenge, as we shall see below.

II. Agency and Accountability

In the previous section, I introduced the literature on delegation, including an extended discussion of the initial decision to delegate powers to an agent and allocate a given amount of discretion to that agent through the use of administrative and oversight mechanisms. Throughout this discussion, however, we have black-boxed two central questions. First, what do agents—in our case, supranational agents like the Commission, the Court of Justice, and the European Parliament—*want*? More precisely, how can we characterize the preference functions of supranational agents in the EU, and how would we expect them to behave if they did enjoy some degree of discretion in their behaviour? Second, if we assume that supranational agents do have preferences distinct from those of their member-state principals, under what conditions are they able to act on those preferences and influence policy outcomes?

What Do Supranational Agents Want?

Typically, principal-agent models of delegation begin with the assumption that agents have preferences distinct from those of their legislative principals, and that these agents, if left free to 'shirk', will act on those preferences and thereby move legislative outcomes away from the original intent of the principals who created them. Within the employer-employee relationship, for example, the employee as an agent is often presumed to want to maximize her income while minimizing the effort she puts into her job. The problem of shirking, in this situation, is essentially synonymous with a lack of productivity among workers, and the solution generally consists in the use of a manager to monitor and sanction such behaviour or the use of incentives to encourage workers to remain productive even when their behaviour is not monitored.

Moving from the employer-employee relationship to a political relationship between a group of legislators and their agent, however, introduces the possibility that agents might drift from the principals' collective preferences, not out of an aversion to work, but rather because these agents possess distinct *policy preferences* which they might attempt to pursue at the expense of the collective preferences of the principals. In the US case, for example, the Environmental Protection Agency is typically considered to possess relatively 'green' preferences for a high level of environmental protection, and the agency is assumed to maximize these green preferences in policy terms within the limits of control by a President and Congress whose commitment to environmental protection may fluctuate considerably over time (Wood 1988). More generally, rational-actor models of regulatory agencies generally assume that such agencies are unitary actors with exogenously given and fixed utility functions which they attempt to maximize within the constraints of the principal-agent relationship.

In previous studies of the EU's supranational agencies, a number of scholars—not all in the rational-choice tradition—have adopted a similar set of assumptions about the Commission and other supranational organizations as 'competence-maximizers' who seek to increase both their own competences and more generally the competences of the European Union. In this view, the issue space of the European Union is theorized along a single salient dimension—namely integration, or the balance between centralized European powers on the one hand and national autonomy on the other hand—and the EU's supranational organizations are placed toward the integrationist end of the spectrum.[14] This view of the Commission and other supranational organizations as competence maximizers is summarized most succinctly by Ross (1995: 14), who argues that supranational organizations like the Commission seek 'more Europe'. There are a number of reasons why such organizations might exhibit pro-integrationist or competence-maximizing preferences, including self-selection for integrationist personnel in European organizations (Bonham 1978); socialization of personnel once they arrive within the organization (cf. Mancini 1991); or simply bureaucratic politics (Peters 1992). Whatever the source of their preferences, it has been widely assumed among otherwise competing theories that the Commission, Court, and European Parliament have all pursued a broadly integrationist agenda throughout the history of the European Union; and it is this assumption of the EU supranational agents as unitary, rational, competence-maximizers that serves as the starting point for the analysis in this book.

Nevertheless, various EU scholars have over the past decade questioned the image of the Commission and other supranational agents as unitary rational actors with a one-dimensional set of preferences defined in terms of more or less integration. The literature on the Commission, for example, frequently begins with the observation that the organization is in fact a 'multi-organization', divided into a 'political' level composed of the Commissioners and their *cabinets* and an 'administrative' level composed of an ever-changing number of Directorates-General (DGs), each with its own sense of mission and organizational culture (Cram 1994). Furthermore, each of these very different DGs cultivates a distinct network of governmental and non-governmental actors who share its preferences and may often act at cross-purposes to the preferences of other DGs or of the Commission as a whole. Indeed, such authors often question whether it makes sense to speak of 'the Commission' as a whole, given the diversity of preferences within the organization and the arguably porous boundaries between the Commission as an organization and its governmental and non-governmental interlocutors.[15] Similar observations also apply to the European Court of Justice and most obviously to the European Parliament, where partisan differences among members are central to the organization and shape its procedures.

As an empirical matter, it is unquestionably correct that the Commission is composed of hundreds of bureaucratic sub-units and thousands of individuals; that these sub-units and individuals often have distinct policy preferences; and that internal Commission politics is frequently depicted as a haven of bureaucratic politics and intra-organizational struggle. Nevertheless, the question for our purposes is not whether the Commission and other organizations are genuinely unitary actors with monolithic preferences—of course, they are not—but rather whether these organizations behave with sufficient coherence vis-à-vis member governments and other organizations so that we can, for the purposes of analysis, treat them as unitary actors. This question, as March and Olsen point out, has no clear empirical answer, and depends upon the questions we ask and the level of analysis at which we examine the policy process:

The argument that institutions can be treated as political actors is a claim of institutional coherence and autonomy. The claim of coherence is necessary in order to treat institutions as decision makers. From such a point of view, the issue is whether we wish to picture the state (or some other political institution) as making choices on the basis of some *collective* interest or intention (e.g. preferences, goals, purposes), alternatives, and expectations. There is no necessary answer to the question unless we impose one. Whether it makes pragmatic theoretical sense to impute interests, expectations and other paraphernalia of coherent intelligence to an institution is neither more nor less problematic, a priori, than whether it makes sense to impute them to an individual. The pragmatic answer appears to be that the coherence of institutions varies but is sometimes enough to justify viewing a collectivity as acting coherently. (March and Olsen 1984: 738–9)

Similarly, in rational-choice models of EU decision-making, Tsebelis and others argue that, in so far as the Commission, Court, and Parliament typically vote by simple majority with no restrictive rules for amendments, each agent can be represented simply in terms of the preferences of the median voter in each organization.[16] For our purposes, then, the question to be asked in this book is not whether the Commission is a monolithic block with uniform preferences, but whether the Commission—and the Court of Justice and the Parliament—generally behave coherently and predictably according to a set of shared organizational preferences. To the extent that we see these organizations presenting a coherent and consistent position vis-à-vis the outside world, the unitary-actor assumption is defensible despite the multiplicity of voices within each organization.

A second dissenting argument arises from Simon Hix's (1994) argument that the politics of the European Union can be theorized in terms of a left-right cleavage as well as the more familiar cleavage between national independence and European integration. As Hix points out, most analyses of the European Union—including the rational choice approaches outlined above—have traditionally analysed the main events, and indeed the minutiae, of EU history in terms of whether these events increased or decreased the level of supranational integration in the EU. Yet such an emphasis on integration per se tells us little or nothing about the implications of European integration for domestic policies, including the traditional left-right conflict between free-market liberals and more interventionist Christian or social democrats. Indeed, Hix (1998) argues that the EU political system is a two-dimensional political space, with an 'integration' dimension and 'left-right dimension' neither of which is reducible to the other, and he examines the nature of partisan contestation in such a two-dimensional space (see also Hix and Lord 1997). Liesbet Hooghe and Gary Marks (1997) go further, positing the history of European integration as a contest between a centre-right neo-liberal project seeking to insulate markets from political interference and a centre-left project of regulated capitalism seeking to reimpose regulatory controls from the European level.

Hix's argument about the importance of the left-right dimension is particularly striking if we compare the literature on delegation within the US with the nascent literature on supranational organizations in the EU. In the former case, the salient dimension of political conflict, both among principals and between principals and agents, is typically assumed to be the partisan, left-right dimension. In Weingast and Moran's (1983) early article, for example, different political parties are assumed to have distinct preferences regarding regulatory outcomes, and the authors use a switch in party control of the relevant Congressional oversight committee to test their hypotheses about the sources of Congressional control. A similar logic is evident Epstein and O'Halloran's (1999*a*) analysis, which again places partisan competition at centre stage by focusing primarily on the implications of divided government for decisions to delegate authority and discretion to regulatory bureaucracies. By contrast, the rational-choice models put forward by EU scholars have focused almost exclusively on the integration dimension, on the assumption that this dimension is the most important source of inter-institutional cleavages between the Council, Commission, Court, and Parliament—all of which, it should be pointed out, represent a range of political party affiliations (Kreppel 1999). For this reason, and despite Hix's warning, I continue to focus in this book on the integration dimension as the primary source of potential conflicts between member-state principals on the one hand and their supranational agents on the other.

The left-right issue does, however, raise one final question regarding the preferences of supranational actors like the Commission, Court, and Parliament. Even if we assume that the EU supranational organizations share a collective preference for 'more Europe', might these same organizations embody a systematic bias toward the right or left, that is towards a neo-liberal project of liberalizing markets on the one hand or a regulated-capitalism project of EU-level social regulation on the other? In light of these arguments about supranational agents as 'multi-organizations' whose preferences may vary systematically along the left-right as well as the integration dimensions, I recast the most common assumptions about the preferences of supranational actors in the form of a hypothesis, namely, that supranational agents are characterized by a common preference for greater competences for themselves and for the European Union as a whole, including *both* the liberalization of the European internal market *and* the reimposition of social regulations from the European level, and that these organizations represent their preferences consistently vis-à-vis other actors despite the presence of internal conflicts within each organization.

Controlling Agents: Administrative and Oversight Procedures

If we assume that supranational agents do indeed have a preference for 'more Europe', under what conditions are those agents likely to act on those preferences rather than implementing strictly and faithfully the preferences of the member states that created and empowered them? This question is, of course, a specification of a more general question about the ability of multiple principals to control agents, and has been the subject of an extensive literature, most notably in the study of American regulatory agencies, which has in turn informed the scant work on supranational agency in the European Union. Much of this literature can be said to fall into one of two schools, depending on their positions regarding the autonomy of US regulatory agencies from their Congressional creators.

The first position, variously dubbed the 'abdication hypothesis' (Kiewiet and McCubbins 1991) or the 'runaway-bureaucracy thesis' (McCubbins and Schwartz 1987), argues that the US Congress, as a collective principal, effectively abdicates its policy-making responsibilities to various regulatory agencies, which become the central figures in regulatory policy-making, entirely unconstrained by their Congressional principals. In this view, regulatory agencies and other agents possess an incontrovertible informational advantage over their legislative principals, whose oversight procedures are lax and ineffective, leaving agents free to 'run amok' in their pursuit of their own policy preferences.[17] The runaway-bureaucracy thesis has had a number of advocates among students of American regulatory agencies and among both critics and advocates of European integration, who typically attribute considerable independence to both the Commission and the ECJ.

Largely in response to this runaway-bureaucracy school, a 'Congressional dominance' school arose during the 1980s and early 1990s among rational choice scholars who argued that, rather than abdicating control to runaway bureaucracies, legislative principals in the US Congress retain perfect or nearly perfect control over the actions of their agents through the use of the administrative and oversight mechanisms described above (Weingast and Moran 1983; McCubbins and Schwartz 1987; Weingast and Marshall 1988). Thus, for example, Weingast and Moran (1983) argued forcefully that regulatory bureaux such as the Federal Trade Commission do not run amok but are instead clearly responsive to the preferences of Congressional oversight committees, even in the absence of any overt intervention by those committees. Similarly, in the case of the European Union intergovernmentalist scholars have argued that member-state principals both create and control their supranational agents, whose actions invariably reflect the preferences of all the principals or of a subset of the most powerful principals. In an early study of the European Court of Justice, for example, Geoffrey Garrett boldly argued that 'the principles governing the decisions of the European Court of Justice . . . are consistent with the preferences of France and Germany' (Garrett 1992: 558).

However, as Terry Moe (1987) points out in an important critique of the Congressional-dominance view, theorists in this school tend to presuppose the perfect efficacy of agency-control mechanisms without theorizing explicitly how these mechanisms might work, their costliness to principals as well as agents, and the ability of agents to take advantage of conflicting preferences among multiple principals. Moe therefore argues for a theory that explicitly models the control relationship, including the costs and difficulties of employing control mechanisms whose efficacy is simply assumed in the Congressional-dominance literature. In response to Moe's critique, a growing number of scholars have formulated more detailed formal models of principal-agent relationships in political life, and undertaken empirical studies of the types of administrative and oversight procedures established to minimize agency costs.

Administrative Procedures

Administrative procedures are generally set out in the legislation delegating authority to an agent, and identify the scope of delegation, the instruments available to the agent—regulation, economic incentives, direct provision of public goods, and so forth—and the procedures that the agent is required to follow in carrying out its delegated functions. All else being equal, the autonomy of an agent should be greatest when the scope of delegation is wide, the choice of instruments is broad, and the procedural requirements are minimal. By contrast, the ability of a principal or principals to control agency behaviour should be greatest where the scope of delegation and the range of available instruments is narrow and where the procedural requirements governing agency action are most detailed and constraining.

In the United States, which has been most extensively studied by rational-choice students of delegation, procedural requirements are set out both in specific legislation delegating powers to regulatory agencies and in a 'horizontal' instrument, the Administrative Procedure Act of 1946, which lays down general procedural requirements for US government agencies.[18] As McCubbins, Noll, and Weingast argue in a pair of classic articles (1987; 1989), such procedural requirements can produce policy choices in accordance with the preferences of the principals—even where the principals themselves may be uncertain of their preferred policy! Procedural requirements induce such behaviour by an agent in two ways. First, they require the agent, when formulating a policy, to disclose information to all interested parties, thereby decreasing the informational asymmetry between the agent and its sponsors, and facilitating 'fire-alarm' monitoring of agency behaviour (see next section). Second, and perhaps more importantly, administrative procedures may require the agent to consult, and take into account the preferences of, the most important political constituents of the principals, such as producer groups or environmental interests, effectively 'stacking the deck' in favour of these actors in subsequent agency activities. Furthermore, these procedures, in so far as they are made explicit in the legislative mandate of the agency, can then be enforced by the courts through judicial review—although, as the authors also note, this use of judicial review also creates the additional possibility of shirking by the court as well as the original agent (McCubbins, Noll, and Weingast 1987: 272).

However, lest it be thought that administrative procedures and judicial review are anathema to agents, McCubbins, Noll, and Weingast (1987: 273–4) point out that procedures such as advance notification and consultation with politically relevant groups can also be in the interest of the agent in so far as they allow the agent to avoid drifting into politically dangerous territory and thereby incur costly sanctions from the principals. In addition, as Majone (1996) points out, widespread consultation and the construction of 'policy networks' can strengthen the position of an agent vis-à-vis principals by providing the agent with independent sources of information. From the perspective of the agent, therefore, administrative procedures may be costly and cumbersome, but they are also a source of technical and political information, and a means to avoid the possibly higher cost of sanctioning by the principals. We should, therefore, expect agents to pursue some degree of advance notification and consultation, although the precise procedures chosen by an agent are likely to be less formal, produce a shorter paper trail, and be more or less biased in favour of certain constituents than the ones selected by principals.

The Variety of Oversight Procedures: Police Patrols

The essence of *ex post* oversight procedures is that they allow principals to (1) *monitor* the activity of their agents to determine the extent of agency losses and (2) *sanction* their agents in the light of the information thus provided. The first part of this definition refers to the (partial) correction of informational asymmetries in favour of the agent, while the second refers to the ability of principals to apply positive or negative sanctions and thus to reward agents for appropriate behaviour and punish shirking. Both aspects, however, present principals with considerable challenges.

In a seminal article, Mathew McCubbins and Thomas Schwartz argue that oversight mechanisms come in two basic types. The first type, which they call 'police-patrol oversight', involves active monitoring by the principals of some sample of the agency's behaviour 'with the aim of detecting and remedying any violations of legislative goals and, by its surveillance, discouraging such violations' (McCubbins and Schwartz 1987: 427). Such procedures might include public hearings, field observations, and examination of agency documents and reports. In the case of the US Congress, such monitoring is often carried out by Congressional committees or subcommittees; similarly, as we shall see in Chapter 2, the member governments of the EU have established oversight committees of member-state representatives who meet and review Commission behaviour under the rubric of 'comitology'. According to McCubbins and Schwartz, police-patrol procedures may be effective in assessing agency conformity with legislative intent in at least a cross-section of agency activities, but only at a high cost to the principals. In the case of multiple principals, moreover, police-patrol oversight may be thought of as a public good—in the sense that a single principal, having expended resources in oversight activities, cannot exclude other principals from the benefit of those activities—and is thus likely to be under-supplied.

By contrast, a second type of oversight mechanism, which McCubbins and Schwartz call 'fire-alarm oversight', requires less centralized involvement by the principals, who instead rely on third parties—citizens, firms, organized interest groups—to monitor agency behaviour and, if necessary, seek redress through appeals to the agent, to the principals, or through judicial review. Such fire-alarm oversight mechanisms, they concede, are likely to produce patterns of oversight that are biased in favour of alert and well-organized groups, but from the perspective of the principals they have the dual advantage of focusing on violations of importance to their political constituents and of externalizing the costs of monitoring to third parties (McCubbins and Schwartz 1987: 426–34). As Moe (1987: 485) points out, however, fire-alarm oversight covers only a subset of agency behaviour, namely, those activities that are likely to mobilize politically powerful groups to protest. Outside this subset, which may potentially be quite small, agency behaviour may be essentially uncontrolled.

Finally, in a variation on third-party oversight, principals can effectively monitor their agents through the use of institutional checks, in which a number of agents are established with conflicting sets of incentives or organizational goals. In such a system, one agent, for example an auditor, may be charged with monitoring the activities of another agent and reporting this information to the principals; or it may be given the power to veto or block the activities of another. In the American context, examples include the establishment of the Congressional Budget Office, which effectively double-checks the budgetary estimates formulated by the Office of Management and Budget within the executive branch. If and in so far as member-state principals are concerned with bureaucratic drift in the EU, we should expect to see similar use of institutional checks in the European Union.

Multiple Principals

Even if we assume that legislative principals are able to monitor their agents through a combination of police patrols, fire alarms, and institutional checks, these principals may nevertheless find the imposition of sanctions to be costly, difficult, and only partially effective. The central problem, as McCubbins, Noll, and Weingast (1987; 1989) point out in the US case, arises in cases where agents are supervised by *multiple principals*, who may not share identical policy preferences. In the American political system, for example, sanctions against a bureaucratic agency often require coordinated effort by the President, the House of Representatives, and the Senate, which may be controlled by different parties and/or have different institutional stakes in the issue at hand. Under these circumstances, where any effort to sanction the agent requires a unanimous agreement among the principals, agents may exploit conflicting preferences among their principals to avoid the imposition of sanctions. Specifically, if any of the three principals is made better off by the agent's shirking, then that principal will block the application of sanctions—allowing the agent to pursue its own preferences without the risk of sanction.

Applying this analysis beyond the US case suggests four more general points about the use of police-patrol monitoring, sanctioning, and the potential zone of discretion of any given agent. First, and most obviously, the model draws our attention to the possibility of *conflicting preferences* among multiple principals and the ability of an agent to exploit those conflicts to avoid the application of sanctions and expand its zone of discretion.

Second, the ability of an agent to exploit conflicting preferences among the principals also depends crucially on the *decision rules* governing the application of sanctions against the agent, or the adoption of new legislation. In the McCubbins, Noll, and Weingast model, the decision rule governing the application of sanctions is unanimity among the three institutional actors—Senate, House, President—since any of the three can veto any application of sanctions. Put differently, it is not only the conflict of interest among the principals but also the decision rule governing the application of sanctions that determine the agent's ability to exploit conflicts among the principals. *Ceteris paribus*, the agent's room for manoeuvre is greatest when the decision rule for the application of sanctions is most demanding—for example, unanimity—and correspondingly less when sanctions can be adopted by a super-majority, simple majority, or a minority among the principals.

Third, however, the ability of principals to sanction a shirking agent also depends on what Fritz Scharpf (1988) calls the 'default condition' in the event of no agreement among the principals. If the default condition is the status quo—that is, the continuation of existing institutions and policies unchanged—Scharpf argues that these institutions and policies are likely to persist indefinitely, rigidly unchanging in the face of an ever-changing policy environment, a phenomenon Scharpf calls the 'joint-decision trap'. Extending Scharpf's argument to principal-agent relations, we can argue that a status quo default condition makes any type of sanctioning more difficult since it privileges the existing delegation of authority to the agent, thereby increasing the agent's autonomy. By contrast, a default condition under which the agent's mandate expires and must be re-authorized privileges would-be reformers among the principals, who may demand amendment of the agent's mandate as the cost of re-authorization; this should, *ceteris paribus*, limit the autonomy of the agent.

Fourth and finally, the use of *ex post* oversight and sanctioning means that an agent's discretion is established *not* by the preferences of the original principals in the original act of delegation but rather by the preferences of their successors at any given time. Thus, by contrast with administrative procedures, in which the specific policy preferences of the original principals may be 'hard-wired' into the act of delegation, oversight procedures facilitate the responsiveness of agents to legislative principals whose preferences may change substantially over time.

The Difficulties of Sanctioning

For all of these reasons, multiple principals are likely to run into difficulties agreeing on sanctions to punish agents that pursue their own agendas at the expense of at least some of the principals. Furthermore, even where principals are in agreement regarding the nature of the agency's behaviour, they may find that the most frequently mentioned sanctions—such as dismissing agency personnel, cutting agency budgets, overruling the agency with new legislation, or simply refusing to comply with agency decisions—are ineffective means of control. Let us consider each of these sanctions, very briefly, in turn.

The first and most frequently mentioned sanction against an errant agent is simply to dismiss, or refuse to reappoint, agency personnel perceived to be drifting from the preferences of the principals. This is perhaps the simplest and most attractive sanction available to principals, but its availability varies depending upon the provisions for appointment, dismissal, and reappointment in the initial act of delegation. In many principal-agent relationships, agency personnel may serve at the pleasure of the principals or they may serve short, renewable terms, facilitating the effective application of sanctions. In other cases, by contrast, principals have deliberately insulated agents from political control to enhance the credibility of their respective policies. In such cases, the leaders of certain agencies, central banks, or courts are expressly placed beyond the reach of the principals to maximize their independence and/or credibility vis-à-vis third parties; such leaders typically serve long terms of office, in some cases for life, and can be dismissed by their legislative principals only in case of criminal prosecution or medical or psychological incapacity (Majone 2001). At lower levels, moreover, bureaucrats may be protected by civil service statutes that place their independence and their jobs beyond the reach of political actors.

A second possible sanction, that of cutting agencies' budgets in response to shirking, is widely cited in the 'Congressional dominance' literature, which posits that, through its power of the purse, Congress determines the very existence of an agency, and therefore has considerable leverage over its behaviour. As Moe (1987: 487) points out, however, the use of budgetary cuts as a means of sanctioning is a blunt instrument:

A fundamental problem here is that budgets play two roles—one that shapes the incentives of bureaucrats, one that provides a financial foundation for programmatic behavior—and these may work at cross-purposes. Suppose, for example, that a committee wants substantially higher levels of regulatory enforcement but the agency refuses . . . If the committee slashes the agency's budget as punishment, on the other hand, it is simultaneously denying the agency the very resources it needs to comply with the committee's wishes. There is no clear solution. The budget is simply not a very dependable control mechanism.

These difficulties of using the budget to constrain agents may, however, be mitigated by creating multiple agents, which may then compete for resources and authority in any given issue area.

A third option in response to an objectionable decision by a bureaucratic agency or a court consists of overruling such a decision through new legislation by the principals, who may also choose to restrict the agent's mandate. The adoption of such legislation, however, may itself involve significant transaction costs; indeed, delegation to regulatory agencies is most likely precisely where the transaction costs of direct regulation by legislators are high. For this reason, students of American politics have argued that agents will enjoy greater discretion in so far as legislators face high transactions costs in adopting new legislation, either because of relatively demanding decision rules, which in the US case requires agreement among the Senate, the House, and the President, or because of conflicts among the principals which inhibit agreement on new regulation (McCubbins, Noll, and Weingast 1987; 1989; Epstein and O'Halloran 1999a, b). Moving beyond the US case, Cooter and Ginsburg (1996) have argued that judicial discretion varies cross-nationally as a function of the number of 'veto points' that must be overcome in order to adopt new legislation.

Similarly, in the EU case a number of scholars have suggested that the discretion of supranational agents is determined, at least in part, by the relative ease with which member-state principals are able to adopt new primary or secondary legislation to reverse the effects of a Commission or Court decision, which may vary significantly both across issue areas and over time. As we shall see, this threat of legislative overruling is particularly important vis-à-vis the Court, for which very few other potential control options exist; by contrast, the Commission can be overruled more easily through comitology than through new legislation in most of its implementation duties, and is subject to a wide range of other control mechanisms. A thorough discussion of the threat of legislative overruling is therefore left to Chapter 3, which is devoted entirely to the Court.[19]

Taken together, the hypotheses put forward in this and the previous section suggest that the discretion of an agent—and therefore its ability to move policy outcomes towards its own ideal point—depend upon the administrative and oversight procedures established by its principals. More specifically, the growing literature on legislative delegation to agencies suggests that the zone of an agent's discretion—and therefore the ability of supranational agents to pursue an integrationist agenda that goes beyond what member governments would collectively have decided—is a function of the *ex ante* and *ex post* control mechanisms established by member governments to control supranational agency in a given area. It is this set of hypotheses that will be tested in detail in the second half of the book.

III. Agenda Setting, Formal and Informal

In this third section of the chapter, I focus in detail on one particular aspect of principal-agent relations, namely, the role of an agent in setting the agenda for its legislative principals. The analysis here is complicated, however, by the fact that analysts use the term 'agenda setting' to refer to two distinct types of activities. For the sake of analytic clarity, I therefore distinguish between 'formal' and 'informal' agenda setting, both of which are derived from studies of legislative politics in the US Congress. Formal agenda setting, I argue, consists of an agent's right to set the *procedural* agenda for its legislative principals by placing before them proposals that can be more easily adopted than amended, thus structuring and limiting the choices available to legislators and the range of possible legislative outcomes. By contrast, informal agenda setting is the ability of a 'policy entrepreneur' to set the *substantive* agenda for a group of legislators, not through her formal powers but through her ability to define issues and present proposals that can rally consensus among the final decision makers. In each case, I specify the assumptions underlying each model of agenda setting, and the most important conditions under which agents might be expected to enjoy formal and informal agenda-setting powers, respectively.

Formal Agenda Setting

The concept of formal agenda setting arises from the American literature on Congressional politics, which points out that Congressional committees enjoy considerable 'agenda setting' and 'gatekeeping' powers by virtue of their ability to draft legislation for consideration on the floor of each legislative chamber. The agenda-setting power of a policy initiator in such models depends upon several key variables, including: the institutional rules governing who may propose legislation for consideration; the rules governing voting among legislators;

and the rules governing amendments to the agenda-setter's proposals. Let us consider each of these factors briefly, with empirical reference both to the American context and to the EU context that will be examined in greater detail later in this book.

The first and most obvious condition for the influence of an agenda setter is the institutional rules governing the power to propose legislation and to control the agenda of a legislative body such as the US Congress or the EU Council of Ministers. In the context of the US Congress, this power to propose is typically wielded by Congressional committees and is widely considered to be the source of their disproportionate influence within their respective jurisdictions. Not only must members on the floor of Congress negotiate and vote based upon texts submitted by Congressional committees, but these committees also retain 'gatekeeping' power in so far as they may choose to *withhold* legislative proposals from the floor if they prefer the status quo to any legislation likely to emerge from a floor vote. In the case of the European Union, the treaties have traditionally granted the sole 'right of initiative' for most legislation to the Commission, although in recent years the Commission has had to share this power with member governments in the so-called second and third 'pillars' of the EU, concerned with Common Foreign and Security Policy and with Justice and Home Affairs respectively. However, within most areas of the EU's first 'pillar', dealing with the Internal Market, Economic and Monetary Union, and other common policies, the Commission retains its sole right of initiative and its gatekeeping power vis-à-vis the member governments in the Council of Ministers (see Chapter 4).

The right to propose, however, is not sufficient to ensure formal agenda-setting power. The influence of an agenda setter will, *ceteris paribus*, be greatest where the voting rule is some form of majority vote and where the agenda setter's proposal is difficult to amend: in other words, where it is easier to adopt the agenda setter's proposal than to amend it. Consider, for example, a vote in the US Congress in which a Congressional committee (1) enjoys the exclusive right to propose a bill in a given area, (2) to be decided on the floor by simple majority vote, and (3) subject to a 'closed rule' for amendments, which requires a straight up-or-down vote on the floor with no amendments allowed. In such cases, McKelvey (1976) and others have demonstrated, agenda setters have quasi-dictatorial powers to select policy proposals which maximize their own gain while at the same time commanding the assent of a bare majority of legislators on the floor.

Not surprisingly, a number of factors may mitigate this dictatorial power of formal agenda setters, including variation in both the voting and the amendment rules. Thus, for example, where the voting rule is not some form of majority but unanimity, each legislator retains the ability to veto legislation that does not at least leave her better off than the status quo. In such cases, the agenda setter loses its ability to 'push through' its proposals by majority vote, and with it much, if not all, of its formal agenda-setting power.

Variation in the amendment rule is equally important. At the opposite extreme from the 'closed rule' for amendments is the 'open rule', where amendments to committee drafts are allowed without restriction and by simple majority vote. In such cases, the power of an agenda setter is severely diminished, since its proposals can be amended just as easily as they can be adopted. In fact, of course, closed rule and an 'anything can happen' open rule constitute the extremes on a continuum: between these extremes we find 'germaneness rules' governing the types and number of amendments allowed; 'rules of recognition' governing the order in which amendments are recognized and voted upon; and open amendment rules coupled with more demanding voting rules for amendments than for the agenda setter's proposal.

In the case of the US Congress, this analysis suggests that the agenda-setting power of a given committee on a given piece of legislation depends upon the jurisdiction of that committee, which may in some cases be shared with other committees; the voting rule on the floor, which is typically simple majority; and the amendment rules, which may vary from closed to open rules or anything in between. Furthermore, as Cox and McCubbins (1993) have pointed out, these characteristics are well known to members on the floor, to the majority leadership, and to the members of the rules committees, all of whom struggle to secure a set of rules that will maximize their likelihood of success in any given piece of legislation.

In the case of the European Union, we would expect the agenda-setting power of the Commission to vary depending upon its right of initiative—exclusive in most of the first pillar, shared with member states in the second and third pillars; the voting rules within the Council of Ministers, which typically votes by either unanimous or qualified-majority vote; and the rules governing amendment of legislation, which typically require a unanimous decision among the member states in Council, except for provisions decided in 'conciliation' between the Council and Parliament.[20]

Informal Agenda Setting

Formal agenda setting, however, does not exhaust the claims made in the empirical literature for the influence of the European

Commission.[21] A number of students of EU politics have argued that, even where the decision rule among member states is unanimity, the Commission might nevertheless 'set the agenda' by constructing 'focal points' for bargaining in the absence of a unique equilibrium or by putting forward policy proposals and matching those to pressing policy problems in an environment of uncertainty and imperfect information.

Thus, for example, Garrett and Weingast (1993), starting from the same basic assumptions as theorists of formal agenda setting, have suggested that under certain conditions an informal agenda setter, such as the European Court of Justice in their empirical example, might have an independent causal influence on legislative decisions, even where the traditional conditions for formal agenda setting are absent, and even in the presence of perfect information among legislators. In cases where a single coordination problem features multiple equilibrium solutions, with no 'objective' means of choosing among competing solutions, they argue, an informal agenda setter can put forward a proposal that serves as a 'constructed focal point' around which bargaining can converge. Note that the ability of an agenda setter to construct such a focal point does not depend on its formal powers of initiative or on any particular set of voting or amendment rules. Rather, the key to constructing such focal points is the provision of an idea or a solution around which bargaining can converge and in the absence of which no equilibrium position could be found. Thus, while retaining the formal assumption of instrumental rationality, Garrett and Weingast's model represents a significant departure from models of formal agenda setting.

A more radical departure is made by John Kingdon (1984), who explicitly rejects the assumptions of comprehensive rationality and perfect information, opting instead for a modified version of the 'garbage-can model' of organizational decision-making in which actor preferences are loosely defined, information is incomplete, and actor participation in decision-making varies across issue area and over time. By contrast with the assumption of comprehensive rationality, which begins with the identification of a problem followed by a search for alternative solutions and a decision among these alternatives, Kingdon's garbage-can model separates the policy process into three separate 'streams': (1) the identification of problems, (2) the proposing of specific policies or policy alternatives, and (3) politics, within which political changes—for example, in the composition of Congress, the presidency, or the national mood—suggest attention to certain agenda items rather than others. All three of these streams, he suggests, operate simultaneously, each according to its own particular logic. At certain times, Kingdon suggests, these streams—the rise of a particular problem to prominence, the existence of serious policy proposals, and the right political climate for their adoption—are combined or 'coupled'. This coupling creates a 'policy window' for the adoption of new policies, when a given agenda item has been identified in the problem stream, feasible policy alternatives have been proposed in the policy stream, and the chances for the adoption of policy in the politics stream are particularly propitious. At this window, Kingdon suggests, stands a *policy entrepreneur*, ready to propose, lobby for, and 'sell' a policy proposal to a decision-making body like the US Congress.

Applying Kingdon's view to the EU, we are faced with the stark observation that the EU's supranational institutions enjoy no monopoly on informal agenda setting, which depends more on expertise and persistence than on the formal right to propose or amend policies. Kingdon lists three characteristics of the successful policy entrepreneur: (1) the person must be taken seriously, as an expert or leader; (2) the person must be known for her political connections or negotiating skills; and (3) the successful entrepreneur must be persistent and wait for the opening of a policy window. In this context, Moravcsik (1995; 1999) has argued convincingly that member governments are fully capable of acting as entrepreneurs, providing the requisite combination of expertise, negotiating skills, and persistence, with little or no input from supranational actors. Nor do supranational organizations enjoy a unique incentive to influence the Union's political agenda: in Kingdon's model, policy entrepreneurs can be motivated by a variety of motives, including material gain, bureaucratic territoriality, or ideological motives. The Commission and other EU organizations may possess all of these incentives, but so may the EU member governments, as well as private actors operating within and across the member states.[22]

More specifically, the informal agenda-setting powers of a supranational organization such as the Commission would seem to be greatest under four conditions. First, the influence of a supranational agent should be greatest where information is imperfect, uncertainty about future developments is high, and the asymmetrical distribution of information between the agent and the principals favours the former. Thus, as Wayne Sandholtz (1992) suggests in his study of Commission entrepreneurship and the ESPRIT programme for research and development, member states in a rapidly changing and highly technical policy environment may settle around a Commission proposal as a constructed focal point because uncertainty about the effects of alternative proposals provides no clear basis for choice. By contrast, however, Moravcsik (1998; 1999) argues that national governments generally command greater bureaucratic and informational resources than even the largest supranational agencies, and that Commission contributions to intergovernmental deliberation are generally redundant, if not counter-productive, and usually causally insignificant.

Second, as Garrett and Weingast (1993) suggest in their discussion of constructed focal points, the influence of an informal agenda setter should be greatest when the distributional consequences of alternative policy proposals are the smallest. Where alternative proposals have clear and significant distributional consequences among the principals, by contrast, an agenda setter's proposals will be less important than the distribution of preferences and power among the principals.

Third, supranational influence is likely to be greatest when the transactions costs of negotiating alternative policies and the costs of waiting are both high. In such cases, a supranational entrepreneur may influence policy outcomes by constructing focal points for principals who might otherwise encounter high costs in reaching an agreement among themselves, particularly if those principals are impatient to reach an agreement.

Fourth and finally, the influence of supranational entrepreneurs in the EU has been hypothesized to vary with their ability to mobilize 'latent' sub-national actors to support their proposals and lobby member governments to do likewise. For example, a number of studies of Commission entrepreneurship in the formulation and 'selling' of the ESPRIT programme and the 1992 internal market programme emphasize the importance of such mobilizing activities.[23]

By and large, the existing literature on supranational entrepreneurship in the European Union is in agreement on the importance of these various factors—imperfect information, supranational expertise, low distributional consequences, high transactions costs of member-state bargaining, and the ability of supranational entrepreneurs to mobilize latent transnational coalitions—in determining the ability of the Commission and other supranational organizations to influence the outcome of intergovernmental bargains. However, these same authors differ sharply about the extent to which these conditions are fulfilled. To simplify only a little, neo-functionalists generally argue that the Commission sits at the centre of a large transnational network with access to information from all corners of Europe and the legitimacy that comes from being a neutral mediator acting on behalf of

'Europe' as a whole; by contrast, intergovernmentalists argue that the Commission rarely possesses any significant informational advantage over member governments, and that its claims to neutrality are effectively dismissed by governments which regard the EU's supranational organizations as partisan in their preference for further integration.[24]

In empirical terms, much of the debate over informal agenda setting in the EU has focused on the role of the Commission, and to a lesser extent the Parliament, in the periodic intergovernmental conferences (IGCs) that have renegotiated the terms of the 1957 Treaties of Rome. Scholarly claims for supranational influence in IGCs range from Wayne Sandholtz's (1992) argument that Commission entrepreneurship is a 'necessary but not sufficient condition' for successful EC reform to Moravcsik's (1998; 1999) claim that member governments are quite capable of negotiating institutional reforms without supranational proposals, mediation, or mobilization, and in fact that supranational attempts to influence the course of intergovernmental bargaining are most often redundant or even counter-productive. If we examine this debate through the lens of principal-agent analysis, we can see that the question of supranational agenda setting in IGCs is not a binary question of influence or no influence, as it has often appeared in the debate between neo-functionalists and intergovernmentalists, but a question of predicting the *conditions* under which supranational organizations like the Commission, Court, and Parliament are likely to be able to set the agenda for the member states. The prediction of principal-agent analysis in this case is clear: by contrast with the everyday legislative process in the EU, intergovernmental conferences provide supranational organizations with *no formal agenda-setting powers at all*: not only do member governments take the final decision on the contents of the treaty, as they do in everyday legislation, but the proposals of the Commission, the Parliament, and the Court have no special status in the negotiations; the Parliament and the Court are excluded from the negotiations entirely; and none of the supranational organizations possesses the *ex post* power of assent over the outcome. Thus, to the extent that they might wish to influence the outcome of the conference, each of these organizations would have to behave as a political entrepreneur, identifying problems and proposing solutions that might rally a unanimous consensus among the governments participating in the conference. Their ability to do so, however, is dependent on the existence of *imperfect information* and the existence of either *unclear preferences* among the member states or an *asymmetrical distribution of information in favour of supranational organizations*. These criteria are clear and demanding—and they have been met to varying degrees across various IGCs.

Neo-functionalists and other students of supranational entrepreneurship most frequently point to agenda-setting activities of the Delors Commission in devising the '1992' internal market programme and in proposing a number of draft provisions that served as the basis for the negotiation of the Single European Act of 1987. In that instance, the Commission succeeded in setting the substantive agenda for the collective decision of the member governments, which signed on to Lord Cockfield's internal market programme as it stood and accepted Delors's proposal of a package deal linking the completion of the internal market with a limited programme of institutional reform (Zysman and Sandholtz 1989; Ross 1995; Moravcsik 1998). Several years later, Delors, working together with the EU's central bank governors, influenced the provisions on Economic and Monetary Union in the 1992 Maastricht Treaty, although in this instance the Commission's influence was limited by the strong preferences and immense bargaining power of both the Bundesbank and the German government of Chancellor Helmut Kohl (Dyson and Featherstone 1999; Moravcsik 1998).

In the 1991 intergovernmental conference on political union, by contrast, the institutional preferences of the member governments were much clearer, the negotiations were more protracted, and the Commission played a less central role in defining the terms of the negotiations, which were dominated by the larger member governments and the Council presidency, supported by the Legal Service of the Council Secretariat. Delors, moreover, was widely perceived to have overreached in his political union proposals, leading the member states to discard the Commission proposals as the basis for negotiation. Jean-Charles Leygues, a member of Delors's cabinet, aptly summarized the Commission's respective positions in the 1985 and 1991 intergovernmental conferences:

Before we could count on being ahead of other people strategically. We knew what we wanted and they were less clear, partly because they didn't believe that anything much would follow from the decisions we asked them to make. Now they know that we mean business and they look for all the implications of our proposals. There are huge numbers of new things on the table and it will be much tougher going from now on. (Quoted in Ross 1995: 137)

The same insight applies to the 1997 Treaty of Amsterdam, the preparations for which began some two years in advance, with extensive participation of both governmental and non-governmental actors,

including the EU's supranational agents. At first glance, these circumstances would seem to have provided the Commission, the Court, and
the Parliament with a unique opportunity to set the agenda for the
IGC. By comparison with past IGCs, the Commission, the
Parliament, and (to a lesser extent) the Court were given numerous
opportunities to participate in the preparation and negotiation of the
Amsterdam Treaty. During the first half of 1995, all three organizations presented reports on the working of the Maastricht Treaty in
preparation for the IGC, and the EP was later invited to participate
alongside the representatives of the Commission and the member
governments in the work of the Reflection Group appointed to prepare the agenda of the conference. Throughout the IGC itself, moreover, the Commission and parliamentary representatives are widely
considered to have behaved in a sophisticated and pragmatic manner,
putting forward proposals which, while still in the integrationist and
competence-maximizing mode of earlier Commission and EP proposals, were moderate and realistic (Petite 1998; McDonagh 1998).
Put simply, the Commission, the Court, and the Parliament had
learned from previous IGCs that grandiose federalist proposals would
simply be ignored by the member states, and that only practical proposals capable of garnering the unanimous agreement of the member
states would be taken seriously by the conference. In the language of
rational choice theory, all of the EU's supranational organizations
behaved strategically rather than sincerely in their proposals to the
1996 IGC.

Yet, if the Commission, the Court, and the Parliament approached
the 1996 IGC with greater pragmatism and sophistication than in past
IGCs, they did so in an information-rich context relatively uncon-
ducive to entrepreneurial agenda setting. *Pace* scholars such as Lord
and Winn (1998), who argue that member-state preferences were
unclear and malleable at Amsterdam, the member governments of the
EU had years of advance notice regarding the approach of the 1996
IGC, and therefore possessed relatively good information about the
workings of the Maastricht Treaty and their own preferences about
the new treaty. As Moravcsik and Nicolaidis (1998) demonstrate
based on figures provided by the European Parliament, member governments had remarkably clear and stable *preferences* over the outcome of the treaty, even if they waited in some cases until the end
game of the negotiations to present specific negotiating *positions* on
secondary issues. In this information-rich context, the opportunities
for entrepreneurial agenda setting by supranational organizations
were correspondingly weak, as predicted by principal-agent analysis,

and most scholars and participants agree that the key entrepreneurial and brokering roles were played, not by the Santer Commission or the EP but rather by the member governments themselves, most notably the Irish and Dutch presidencies with the support of the Council Secretariat.[25]

Summing up this section, then, I have hypothesized that the formal agenda-setting power of a supranational agent such as the Commission depends upon three primary variables: its right of legislative initiative, the voting rules for the adoption of new legislation among legislative principals, and the rules governing the application of amendments. I therefore predict that, *ceteris paribus*, formal agenda-setting power will be greatest where the Commission possesses the sole right of initiative and where its proposals can be more easily adopted (for example, by qualified majority) than amended (that is, by unanimity). These predictions, moreover, do *not* depend upon any further assumptions about uncertainty, imperfect information, unclear preferences, or high transactions costs of bargaining among member-state principals. By contrast, the informal agenda-setting power of the Commission and other supranational organizations depends precisely upon the assumption that member states' information is incomplete, that the transaction costs of intergovernmental bargaining are high, and that supranational organizations can influence policy outcomes through the provision of otherwise unavailable information, mediation, or mobilization of transnational coalitions. The extent to which these conditions are fulfilled in EU politics will be the subject of empirical investigation later in this book.

IV. An Alternative Approach: Sociological Institutionalism

The rational-choice, principal-agent model put forward above provides a comprehensive and internally consistent approach to the problem of delegation, agency, and agenda setting in the European Union; yet, as Huber and Shipan (2000) point out, rational-choice analysis is not the only possible approach to such questions. Indeed, an increasing number of scholars both inside and outside EU studies have recently proposed an alternative approach drawn from sociological institutionalism, with very different assumptions and very different implications for questions of delegation, agency, and agenda setting in the EU and beyond.

Although sociological approaches to domestic and international institutions are diverse, we can nevertheless specify two basic assumptions about actors, their preferences, and their interaction with institutions that link together otherwise diverse sociological approaches, and distinguish those approaches from the rational choice approach put forward above. First, and most basically, sociological institutionalists generally reject the rationalist conception of actors as utility-maximizers acting according to a 'logic of consequentiality' in favour of March and Olsen's (1989: 23–4, 160–2) conception of a 'logic of appropriateness'. In this view, actors confronting a given situation do not consult a fixed set of preferences and calculate their actions in order to maximize their expected utility, but rather look to socially constructed roles and institutional rules and ask what sort of behaviour is appropriate in that situation.

A second point, closely related to the first, has to do with the origins of actor preferences and the interactions of those preferences with institutions. For sociological institutionalists, preferences are not fixed and exogenous but rather mutable and, above all, *endogenous* to institutions, which inform actors not only about their incentives and ideal strategies but about their core preferences. In the case of the EU, the claim often put forward by sociological and constructivist scholars is that 'membership matters' in so far as participation and socialization in EU institutions may alter the preferences and even the identities of both national and supranational elites involved in the process of European integration (Sandholtz 1993; Risse 1996; Lewis 1998*a, b*; Christiansen, Jorgensen, and Wiener 1999).

Although sociological institutionalists have yet to put forward a fully developed theory of delegation, agency, and agenda setting comparable to the one set out above, the sociological approach to institutions does have clear implications for the delegation of powers as a matter of institutional choice, for the day-to-day workings of supranational EU institutions, and for the prospects of formal and informal agenda setting by supranational actors.

First, with regard to institutional choice and delegation, sociological institutionalists would reject the rationalist model of institutional choice in which actors with fixed preferences over outcomes bargain over the choice of institutions designed to produce optimal 'policy streams'—subject to uncertainty—over time. Rather, sociological institutionalists would argue that powers are delegated to supranational actors such as the Commission, the Court, and the Parliament not as a result of functional logic and a calculation of the expected utility of such calculations but rather because such delegation is widely accepted as legitimate or appropriate. In a recent article on central bank independence, for example, Kathleen McNamara (2002) questions the functional argument in favour of delegating extensive discretion to central banks, noting that the economics literature is inconclusive regarding the supposed benefits of independent central banks in controlling inflation. Rather, McNamara suggests, the spread of central bank independence as an organizational form is an example of a broader phenomenon called 'institutional isomorphism', in which particular institutions are adopted and spread not—or not necessarily—as a result of functional analysis but rather because these institutions come to be seen as legitimate or appropriate in public discourse. If this view is correct, we should expect principals not to calculate carefully the consequences of individual acts of delegation but rather to turn to widely recognized and legitimate institutional templates which may or may not be suited to the context and the requirements of individual issue areas.

Second, to move from institutional choice to the day-to-day working of institutions, sociological institutionalists would dispute the rationalist premise that member-state principals and supranational agents operate with fixed preferences and that institutions serve only to structure the incentives of the actors. Rather, sociological institutionalists theorize institutions as a forum for communicative interaction among actors, who are socialized within common norms and engage in persuasion and deliberation, and in the process 'discover' their own preferences. This difference in views about the workings of institutions is most stark in the analysis of 'comitology', the EU network of policy-making by committees examined in detail in Chapter 2. Where rational choice theorists approach such comitology committees as instruments of political control by member governments over supranational agents, sociologically oriented scholars see these same committees as forums for deliberation in which decision-making is generally consensual and the distinction between member-state and Commission representatives often breaks down in the common search for the 'best' solution to a given policy problem (Joerges and Neyer 1997*a*, *b*). If this view is correct, we should see member governments using comitology committees not as instruments of control over the bureaucracy but rather as arenas within which governmental and supranational actors deliberate collectively in search of the optimal solution to a given policy problem.

Third and finally, sociological institutionalists put forward very different hypotheses regarding the prospects for formal and informal agenda setting. As we have seen, rational choice approaches generally assume fixed preferences among both principals and agents, and generally good if not perfect information about those preferences in highly institutionalized settings such as the European Union. Accordingly, rational choice scholars generally emphasize the importance of formal agenda-setting powers, and are relatively sceptical about the prospects for informal agenda setting, which rely on a highly restrictive set of assumptions about the existence of uncertain actor preferences and poor information. By contrast, scholars in the sociological institutionalist tradition assume that actors do *not* approach decisions with fixed preferences, but may change or discover their preferences as a result of socialization, learning, or persuasion.[26] The European Union, moreover, has frequently been put forward as a particularly promising arena for such socializing or 'constitutive' effects of institutions, within which national and supranational elites meet regularly, engaging in processes of socialization into European attitudes, collective preference formation, and persuasion rather than the hardball bargaining among fixed preferences that are the stuff of rational-choice analyses. Informed by such assumptions about the fluidity and malleability of actor preferences, sociological institutionalist and constructivist students of the EU tend to be much more optimistic about the prospects for informal agenda setting, with highly motivated supranational entrepreneurs putting forward innovative proposals in a 'garbage can' setting in which member governments may have weak preferences and be open to persuasion by an actor such as the Commission.[27]

In sum, although none of the scholars mentioned above has offered a comprehensive theory of delegation, agency, and agenda setting—nor do I attempt to formulate such a theory here—collectively these works offer a fairly consistent and coherent competing approach to examining the origins and workings of EU institutions, and a competing set of hypotheses against which the rational choice approach in this book can be tested.

V. Research Design, Methods, and Plan of the Book

Thus far, I have reviewed the rational choice literature regarding delegation of authority to supranational agents, and the autonomy and agenda-setting power of those agents vis-à-vis their member-state principals. Unfortunately, testing such hypotheses empirically is far more difficult than it might appear at first blush. In essence, the problem is that agents such as the Commission may *rationally anticipate* the reactions of their principals as well as the probability of sanctions, and adjust their behaviour to avoid the costly imposition of sanctions.

If this is so, then agency behaviour which at first glance seems autonomous may in fact be subtly influenced by the preferences of the principals, *even in the absence of any overt sanctions*. Indeed, as Weingast and Moran (1983) point out, the more effective the control mechanisms employed by the principals, the less overt sanctioning we should see, since agents rationally anticipate the preferences of the principals and the high probability of sanctions for shirking, and adjust their behaviour accordingly. Studies of agency autonomy that rely on the frequency of sanctioning are therefore likely to run into the methodological problem of *observational equivalence*, namely, that the absence of sanctions is consistent with both the obedient servant and the runaway bureaucracy theories, each of which predicts, albeit for different reasons, the rarity of sanctions.

Faced with these methodological obstacles, an increasing number of scholars have opted to concentrate their empirical analysis not on the behaviour of the agent but on the delegation stage, where principals make their strategic decisions about the powers delegated to agents and the control mechanisms established to limit their autonomy. Huber and Shipan, for example, argue that existing principal-agent analyses of regulatory bureaucracies have forced scholars to reconsider their views about the existence or absence of Congressional control over bureaucrats. Such studies, however,

are not without their drawbacks. One problem is that these studies tend to focus on the presence or absence of political control itself: either legislators control bureaucratic behavior or they do not. From the perspective of transaction cost theory, either claim is plausible and neither is likely verifiable . . . To validate an argument about the expected level of political control, one would have to establish that the actual level of control is consistent with the predicted level, given the transaction costs and the political institutions that are present. None of the theories we have discussed approaches a level of specificity that could serve as relevant for such tests. Even if they did, it would be difficult to imagine a data set that could be used to test such predictions. Not surprisingly, most existing evidence for the theories has involved case studies, which, while illuminating, can hardly be viewed as definitive. (Huber and Shipan 2000: 35)

For this reason, Huber and Shipan argue, scholars are increasingly turning away from direct studies of agency behaviour, focusing instead on the delegation stage:

A significant feature of the more recent research is its focus on variation in instruments of control as dependent variables. This represents a turn away from questions about the degree of control, which dominated much of the early literature. This change is sensible. If the question is, 'Do legislatures control bureaucracies?' the answer is always somewhere in the gray area. Consequently, although it may be possible to establish empirically whether decision making is affected by present or past legislative preferences, it is much more difficult to make black or white claims about the presence or absence of control, and thus about the validity of particular theoretical arguments. Not surprisingly, then, empirical tests that focus on the instruments of control have proven easier to undertake. (Huber and Shipan 2000: 41)

Although such analyses of the delegation stage do not provide a direct measure of bureaucratic autonomy, they *do* allow us to test hypotheses about the conditions under which principals will delegate powers and discretion to agents.

In this book, and notwithstanding Huber and Shipan's lucid methodological warning, I examine *both* the delegation stage—at which member-state principals create supranational organizations, delegate powers to them, and establish more-or-less restrictive control mechanisms to limit their discretion—*and* the actual behaviour of supranational agents in the day-to-day conduct of their executive, judicial, and legislative or agenda-setting powers. Although causally related, these two stages do indeed raise very different methodological challenges, and thus the two parts of the book utilize distinct research designs and methods to answer the questions posed in each.

Measuring Delegation and Discretion

The first part of the book is devoted to the analysis of delegation: the functions delegated to supranational organizations, the conditions under which those organizations are allocated more or less discretion, and the control mechanisms established by member states to fix the precise level of discretion in any given case. In this part of the book, the first methodological challenge consists of operationalizing the *dependent variables*, notably the *functions* delegated to various supranational organizations and the degree of *discretion* allocated to these organizations across issue areas and over time. In previous studies of delegation in the United States, the unit of analysis has typically been the individual law as an act of delegation, and such laws have been coded for statistical analysis in terms of both the extent of powers delegated and the presence or absence of various control mechanisms that might be expected to limit an agent's discretion (see for example Epstein and O'Halloran 1994; 1996; 1999*a*, *b*). In the case of the European Union, however, such an analysis is complicated by the fact that the EU's member governments have delegated powers through two distinct means. First, parallel to delegation in US Congressional legislation, the EU's Council of Ministers, often in cooperation or co-decision with the European Parliament, has delegated powers to the Commission in individual pieces of legislation that specify the Commission's powers of implementation as well as the administrative procedures and the various types of oversight committees designed to supervise the implementation process. These individual pieces of legislation provide us with a large number of discrete acts of delegation and control, and have served as the basis for several quantitative studies of discretion in EU secondary legislation.[28] Second, in addition to this day-to-day legislation, member-state principals have also chosen to delegate ever-increasing powers to supranational organizations in successive treaties, beginning with the 1950 Treaty of Paris and continuing with the Treaties of Rome (1957), Luxembourg (1970, 1975), the Single European Act (1986), Maastricht (1992), and Amsterdam (1997).

In Chapters 2, 3, and 4, therefore, I analyse systematically the delegation of powers to the Commission, the Court, and the European Parliament respectively, examining both the *functions* delegated to each organization and variation in the *discretion* enjoyed by each agent vis-à-vis the member governments. Specifically, in the case of the Commission, I follow Epstein and O'Halloran (1999*a*) and Franchino (2001) in the operationalization and coding of Commission discretion across issue areas in both primary and secondary legislation, and I focus in detail on the design and use of three specific control mechanisms: appointment and censure; judicial review of Commission acts; and the comitology system of police-patrol oversight. For the Court of Justice, I examine the functions delegated to the Court in the treaties; analyse in comparative perspective the various mechanisms—most notably the appointment process, the threat of legislative overrule, and the threat of non-compliance—that set the limits on judicial discretion; and consider the decision by the member states to limit explicitly the jurisdiction of the ECJ in the second and third pillars of the European Union. For the Parliament, finally, I examine the functions delegated to the EP, noting their poor fit with the predictions of the model, and characterize the development of the Parliament's legislative and other powers both across issue areas and over time.

Similar challenges arise when we attempt to measure the *independent variables* hypothesized by transaction-cost theorists to influence the delegation decision, most notably *uncertainty* and the demand for *credible commitments*. Measuring the inherent uncertainty, or informational intensity, of an issue area is a difficult and contentious process since the actual complexity of an issue area is impossible to measure directly, and the various proxies proposed by various scholars may in fact measure factors other than the issue-specific demand for information. In the various studies cited above, for example, a variety of measures of informational intensity, complexity, and uncertainty have been proposed, including the number of laws cited in a given bill (Krehbiel 1991); the number of Congressional committee meetings or hearings in a given issue area (Epstein and O'Halloran 1999*a*: 206–11); and, in the case of the EU, the length of a given piece of legislation (Franchino 2000*b*), the number of provisions calling for the adoption of 'detailed rules', the presence or absence of 'action plans' in a given area, and the presence or absence of committees in a given piece of legislation (Franchino 2001). However, of these other measures a number are inapplicable in the context of the EU or risk measuring factors other than information. For example, while Franchino's use of word count as an indicator of informational intensity seems plausible at first glance, it is striking that other studies of delegation— for example, Huber, Shipan, and Pfahler (2001)—employ the same measure as an indicator of *discretion* on the equally plausible grounds that longer legislation is, *ceteris paribus*, more detailed and hence more constraining to an implementing agent than shorter legislation. Similarly, the presence of action plans in a given area of EU policy *might* be a measure of informational complexity, but it might equally well measure the Commission's effort to prepare the ground for future legislation in a controversial area by laying down a track record of 'soft law' in that area (Cram 1997: 107–11). In short, attempts to measure informational intensity or uncertainty in quantitative terms invariably encounter a *proxy problem* in the sense that scholars are driven to rely on proxy indicators that provide precise numbers for statistical analysis, but at the risk of measuring something *other* than uncertainty.

For this reason, I resist developing quantitative proxies for uncertainty, relying instead on a broad classification of scientific and technical issues, together with foreign and defence policies, as the most likely to require extensive technical expertise.[29] If demand for policy-relevant expertise is an important motivation for member-state delegation to the Commission or other supranational agents, we should see such delegation clustering in these issue areas, and we should also see the member states allocating sufficient budgets and personnel to the Commission so as to provide this expertise. On the other hand, if delegation takes place largely outside these issue areas, or if the member governments do not provide a sufficient budget and staff for the

Commission to provide technical expertise in this area, then the informational rationale for delegation would not be supported.

Measuring the demand for credible commitments is equally challenging. Clearly, the demand for credible commitments arises when legislators face an incentive to renege on their commitments, either to each other (as in a legislative logroll or an international agreement modelled as a Prisoner's Dilemma) or to market actors subject to government regulation (as in monetary or antitrust policies). Nevertheless, authors like Majone (2001) and Moravcsik (1998) have generally not specified clear criteria for identifying what sorts of issues are likely to create a 'credibility crisis' for legislators and hence a demand for delegating substantial discretion to independent agents. As with uncertainty, we therefore face the challenge of recognizing a demand for credible commitment when we see it. Majone (2001) suggests that credibility problems arise when legislators are faced with problems of time inconsistency and ill-defined political property rights, but he makes no effort to operationalize these terms empirically or demonstrate that they vary systematically across issue areas. Similarly, Moravcsik (1998) argues that delegation of powers, as well as 'pooling' of sovereignty through qualified majority voting, is a mechanism whereby governments pre-commit themselves to specific policies on which they might later be tempted to renege. Specifically, he suggests that 'pooling and delegation are therefore most likely to be found in limited domains, such as specific issue-areas, implementation, enforcement, and secondary legislation, where a large number of smaller decisions over an extended period, each uncertain, take place within the broader context of a previous decision'. Moravcsik (1998: 76) goes on to identify the setting of commodity prices, monetary policy, and antitrust policy as issue areas that require 'constant adaptation to new economic or political circumstances'. However, Moravcsik does not make clear how we might distinguish these specific issue areas from other issue areas like agriculture, telecommunications, securities markets, or defence, which also call for constant adaptation and many individual decisions. Finally, Moravcsik (1998: 76) does not generate specific hypotheses about the extent of supranational *discretion* beyond the general claim that 'the credibility explanation predicts an inverse correlation between the scope and extent of delegation'.

In light of these weaknesses in the previous literature, I employ two indicators of credible commitments in this book: the first functional and the second based on the distribution of costs and benefits by issue area. With regard to the former, there appears to be general agreement in the literature on the US Congress as well as in the work of Majone and Moravcsik that certain delegated *functions* seem to be particularly associated with the alleviation of credibility problems. First, and most importantly, monitoring compliance with agreements is central to the credibility of any domestic or international agreement; although such delegation obviously includes an informational component, it should therefore count as evidence for the credible-commitments view. Second, the filling in of incomplete contracts by judicial rule-making or arbitration is another commonly cited means of increasing the credibility of a contract, which would otherwise be left more vague and less constraining for the principals and should therefore also count as support for a credible-commitments motivation.

By contrast, the other two functions specified above may count in favour of either an informational or a credible-commitments rationale for delegation. With regard to legislative agenda setting, American Congressional scholars such as Shepsle and Weingast have long identified the delegation of agenda-setting powers to committees as a means to enforce logrolling bargains among individual Congressmen, who might otherwise face the temptation to renege; but these views have been questioned by Krehbiel (1991) and others, who argue that Congressmen delegate powers to committees in order to benefit from their policy expertise. Similarly, with regard to the EU, Majone (2001) argues that member states delegated agenda-setting power to an integrationist Commission in order to increase the credibility of their common commitment to the European project; Nugent (2000) and others, however, have emphasized the Commission's informational role as an expert actor capable of producing legislative proposals that take into account the preferences and practices of all EU member states.

With regard to regulation, finally, it is commonplace to note that the delegation of regulatory powers can be designed either to take advantage of agency expertise in the face of technical uncertainty or to insulate regulators from political pressures to increase the credibility of regulation—or both, since the categories of information and credible commitments are not mutually exclusive but overlapping. In sum, delegation of the first two functions—monitoring and enforcement and the filling in of incomplete contracts—should qualify as support for the credible-commitments view of delegation; by contrast, delegation of agenda-setting and regulatory powers may provide support for either view, or both, requiring a closer analysis of the motivations of the principals.

A second means of analysing the importance of credibility as a motive for delegation is to examine the pattern of variation across issue areas. In recent years, a number of scholars have suggested that credible commitments should be particularly problematic for issue areas or policies that impose concentrated costs and generate diffuse benefits—the logic being that directly elected legislators will face temptations to make exceptions for politically powerful constituents, and that regulators in such areas should therefore remain politically insulated from such pressures. If this is the case, we should expect to see greater delegation of powers to agents, and greater discretion for those agents, in policies that impose concentrated costs and generate diffuse benefits, including trade liberalization, antitrust policy, environmental and consumer protection, and defence. By contrast, we should expect to see legislative principals retain regulatory powers in areas where benefits can be carefully targeted onto concentrated constituencies and costs are diffused, such as taxation policy, agriculture, and other pork-barrel spending programmes. In the US setting, Epstein and O'Halloran find support for this view in their analysis of Congressional delegation. According to Epstein and O'Halloran (1999a: 201–3), 'Legislators closely guard policy-making authority in those areas that afford them an opportunity to target benefits to particular constituents', such as taxation and social security. By contrast, legislators are more prone to delegate powers in areas where benefits are widely dispersed, making it hard to claim credit to individual constituents, and costs are concentrated, making delegation attractive as a means of shifting blame; examples include defence, foreign affairs, and selective service (the Draft). With regard to the EU, this view would predict extensive delegation of executive powers in legislation featuring concentrated costs and diffuse benefits, and minimal delegation in areas where benefits can be narrowly targeted to constituents.

Measuring Agency and Agenda Setting

In the second part of the book, I attempt to test principal-agent hypotheses about the conditions under which supranational agents matter, in the sense of acting autonomously from principals or exerting influence on their decisions through their agenda-setting powers. The empirical challenge in this part of the book is to overcome the law of anticipated reactions, measuring not only the activity but the autonomy and influence of supranational organizations vis-à-vis their member-state principals. The difficulties of measuring supranational autonomy becomes clear when we examine the previous literature on both the European Court of Justice and the Commission. For example, in response to Burley and Mattli's (1993) claims that the

European Court of Justice has independently fostered the development of a supranational constitution for the EC, Garrett and others
have argued that the Court's independence was only apparent, and
that the judges actually rationally anticipated the responses of the
most powerful member states and adjusted their rulings accordingly
(Garrett 1992; Garrett and Weingast 1993; Garrett, Kelemen, and
Schulz 1998). Similarly, students have differed in their interpretation
of the comitology system of committees overseeing the Commission
and the remarkable rarity of negative opinions by these committees.
According to Gerus (1991), for example, the management and regulatory committees for agriculture issued some 1,894 opinions on
Commission actions during 1990—not a single one of which was negative! At first glance, the remarkably low rate of committee referrals
to the Council would seem to suggest that committee oversight is per-
functory, and the Commission largely independent in its actions.
However, as Gerus points out, rational anticipation of committee
action by the Commission may mean that the Commission is effectively controlled by the member governments, despite the startling rarity of sanctions against it. As one Commission official explained, having
one's proposal referred from a committee to the Council can cast a long
shadow over the career prospects of a young *fonctionnaire*—a powerful incentive to rationally anticipate a proposal's reception in the
relevant committee.[30]

The point here is not that the Commission and other supranational
organizations enjoy no autonomy from the member governments, but
rather that such autonomy cannot be easily ascertained from quantitative measures of legislative sanctions, which seem to be as rare in the
EU as in the United States. Furthermore, in so far as quantitative
measures might prove useful to test hypotheses about legislative control, many of the quantitative methods and indicators used by scholars
in American politics are unavailable to students of the European
Union. First and foremost, students of American politics have relied
on the party affiliation of individual actors—and in particular on the
critical event of turnover in the partisan control of the Congress or
the presidency—to test predictions about Congressional control of the
bureaucracy. In their early study of the Federal Trade Commission
(FTC), for example, Weingast and Moran (1983) focused on the effects
of a change in party control in the relevant Congressional oversight
committee, showing that a shift in the majority party correlated with
a shift in the FTC's case load consistent with the predictions of their
model; Wood (1988), by contrast, used a change in party control of
the presidency to test hypotheses about presidential control of the

bureaucracy, and demonstrated that the Environmental Protection Agency retained some degree of autonomy despite the forceful efforts of the Reagan Administration to eviscerate enforcement of environmental laws.[31] In the EU, however, the partisan composition of member-state principals does not shift as frequently or as readily—nor, more importantly, is it clear that left-right party conflicts are relevant to many of the issues at stake in EU policy making. Thus, while it is in theory possible to measure the partisan balance among member governments in the Council of Ministers and determine the effect of shifts in party control on delegation decisions or Commission policy outputs, the effects of such changes are likely to be far more muted than in the United States, where party cleavages are more salient and sharp partisan shifts are more common than in the EU. In addition to being able to rely on party as a simple indicator of actor preferences, students of American politics also benefit from other statistical indicators such as roll-call voting,[32] which is of course available and in increasing use among students of the European Parliament, but which remains unavailable for most votes in the Council of Ministers, where deliberations are generally secret and voting records are not consistently made available to the public.

The primary methods used in these chapters, therefore, are qualitative, using a carefully chosen series of six *case studies* and incorporating *process-tracing* in order to multiply the observable implications of theory and observe hypothesized causal mechanisms at work. The use of case studies is, to some extent, a second-best solution in the absence of reliable statistical data on member-state control over supranational agency behaviour. However, the use of case studies does not preclude the careful selection of cases for variation across the hypothesized independent variables. Specifically, I adopt three criteria for the selection of the six case studies in the second part of the book.[33]

First, and most importantly, I select cases that provide considerable variation across the hypothesized independent variable, namely, the decision rules governing the adoption or overturning of supranational decisions. Given the byzantine nature of the EU's decision rules, it has not proven possible to include every possible variant of agenda setting and oversight procedures; the analysis here therefore focuses on three categories of cases: (1) supranational agenda setting, where a Commission initiative requires a positive endorsement from a qualified majority of EU member governments; (2) supranational authority with member-state oversight in the form of advisory or management committees, which in theory provide the Commission with greater discretion vis-à-vis the member governments; and

(3) treaty interpretation by the European Court of Justice, which can be overturned only by a unanimous decision of the member states to amend the treaties. *Ceteris paribus*, the model sketched above predicts that supranational autonomy and influence should be weakest in the first category and increase across each of the other two categories as the thresholds to member-state sanctioning or overruling increase.

Second, I select cases that include both market liberalization and social regulation, which will allow us to determine whether the EU's supranational organizations are biased towards either liberalization or regulation, as suggested above.

Third and finally, I select cases which feature an open dispute or conflict between supranational organizations and one or more member governments, which may or may not result in a sanctioning of the organization and a change in its behaviour. The risk of focusing on such conflicts is that they are, after all, extremely rare, since agents like the Commission typically seek to avoid open conflict with, and sanctioning by, their member-state principals. In this sense, the empirical cases examined in this book, and in most previous studies of Commission autonomy, are clearly not a representative sample of all Commission behaviour, the overwhelming bulk of which is undertaken quietly and with little controversy. Despite this risk, focusing on conflicts between member governments and their supranational agents has the advantage of revealing the conflicting preferences among the various actors and illuminating the conditions under which member states are able—or unable—to rein in their agents.[34] Such incidents of open conflict are, furthermore, hard or critical cases for the principal-agent model presented above, according to which supranational agents like the Commission should enjoy the greatest autonomy where member-government preferences are weak or uncertain, and not where they are directly opposed by one or more member governments. Hence, if we find that agents like the Commission enjoy some independent causal influence in cases of open conflict, it is likely that such agents should enjoy as much or greater influence in other, less high-profile cases where member governments have less information or only weak preferences. Finally, it is worth noting, such cases do not constitute selection on the dependent variable, since they were chosen only on the basis of the presence of conflict and *not* on the basis of the final outcomes which, as we shall see, vary considerably across the cases. The resulting selection of six cases is outlined in Table I.1, and these cases are considered in Chapters 5 and 6.

In addition to this selection of cases across the hypothesized independent variable, the case studies in the second part of the book also benefit from the use of process tracing *within* each case, which in this context serves two distinct purposes. First, it serves to disaggregate a single 'case' into a larger number of independent observations (King, Keohane, and Verba 1994). Specifically, the process-tracing approach adopted in the chapters of this book disaggregates each case into a number of principal-agent interactions, beginning with the initial decision by member states to delegate powers to a supranational agent. In most of these cases, moreover, the sequence of interactions involves not only an act of delegation and subsequent agent behaviour, but rather a series of principal-agent interactions at various levels, culminating in the acceptance of the agent's actions by member states, or its overturning, or the expansion or retrenchment of the agent's mandate.

Process-tracing also serves a second function, which is to capture the presence or absence of hypothesized causal mechanisms in operation. In the first part of the book, for example, I hypothesize that member governments will rely on 'comitology' oversight committees to monitor Commission actions and sanction excessive activism on the Commission's part. The case studies in the second part of the book, in turn, examine not only the final outcome of each case but whether member-state oversight committees were indeed used to perform a monitoring function, and whether member governments used, or attempted to use, these committees to sanction the Commission when it took controversial decisions on the implementation of EU law. Similarly, the analysis above suggested that the threat of new legislation or treaty revision is a potentially important source of member-state leverage over the Commission and the Court, and the case studies will allow us to assess whether in fact new legislation or treaty amendments are contemplated or used against an overly activist Commission and Court.

Finally, before we proceed to the empirical analysis, a few words about sources are in order. First, I have tried to rely, as far as possible, on what Moravcsik (1998: 80) calls 'hard primary sources', with a strong preference for contemporary official documents available for citation and replication by other scholars. The reader will therefore encounter in the notes of the following chapters a large number of official Commission documents—or COM docs, in the Brussels lingo—as well as European Court judgments, European Parliament reports and resolutions, and Directives, Regulations, and Decisions of the Commission, Council, and Parliament. In practice, however, such documents generally do not provide an accurate indication of actors' sincere preferences, since the latter typically go unrecorded—as in the case of Council negotiations or comitology committee meetings—or are distorted by strategic considerations in the formulation of official negotiating positions. I therefore supplement official documents through the use of interviews with key officials from EU supranational organizations and member governments, which are a rich source of behind-the-scenes information about actor preferences and principal-agent interactions that are not captured on the official record. By the same token, however, such interviews are subject to the usual problems that actors may not remember correctly or may misrepresent events after the fact; in addition, most interviews conducted for this book were agreed to on condition of anonymity, making a full citation and replication by other scholars impossible. For both of these reasons—and despite the general openness and honesty with which I was greeted by a wide range of European and national officials in Brussels over the past five years—I have attempted not to rely exclusively on interviews in support of my empirical claims, and to provide corroborating and publicly available evidence wherever possible. In addition, I have relied rather heavily on a third source of primary documents, namely, the journalistic reports of insider publications such as *Agence Europe* and *European Report*. Moravcsik (1998: 81) rightly warns scholars against excessive reliance on 'soft' primary sources, including public statements of politicians, memoirs, and newspaper articles, which often provide a forum for inaccurate and self-justifying claims by politicians without necessarily providing the detailed information needed to test hypotheses. Used with care, however, and as a supplement to hard primary sources, journalistic sources can provide additional details regarding the preferences and interactions of key actors, particularly in the case of insider publications like *Agence Europe* and *European Report*, which offer detailed, day-by-day analyses of EU negotiations with comparatively little attention to the public pronouncements of major politicians.

This brings me to a second and final observation regarding the use of secondary sources, especially previous studies of EU politics by other scholars. Here again, Moravcsik (1998), Lustick (1996), and others rightly warn that the conclusions of secondary studies should not be treated as primary sources, both because those conclusions may themselves be the result of a selective reading of the primary document base and because reliance on secondary sources may encourage selection bias by researchers naturally attracted to those secondary sources that support their own arguments. Nevertheless, for our purposes here it is impossible to ignore the increasing number of quantitative and qualitative empirical studies of principal-agent relations in the EU published during the last half-decade by scholars such as Rhys Dogan, Fabio Franchino, Jonas Tallberg, Susanne Schmidt, Alec Stone-Sweet and Tom Brunell, George Tsebelis, Geoffrey Garrett, and Bernadette Kilroy, among others. While I do not always agree with the methods and findings of these authors, their findings are highly relevant to the hypotheses laid out in this chapter, and it would be impossible to write a book about EU supranational organizations without reviewing their findings, criticizing them where appropriate, and giving intellectual credit where credit is due.

PART I

DELEGATION AND DISCRETION

CHAPTER 2

The Commission as an Agent: Delegation of Executive Power in the European Union

In Chapter 1, I elaborated a principal-agent model of delegation to, and agency and agenda setting by, supranational actors. In this chapter, I turn to the empirical study of delegation and discretion to the European Commission, examining both the functions delegated to the Commission and the patterns of delegation and discretion allocated to the Commission in primary and secondary EU legislation. Specifically, I utilize both qualitative and quantitative data to test two hypotheses specified in Chapter 1. First, my principal-agent model predicts that member states will delegate certain types of *functions* to supranational agents, namely, monitoring compliance, filling in incomplete contracts, setting the legislative agenda, and providing expert and credible regulation. In this chapter, I therefore analyse the functions delegated to the Commission in both primary (treaty) and secondary legislation, which I argue fit closely the functions predicted by the theory. Second, I test the hypotheses derived from Epstein and O'Halloran (1994; 1996; 1999*a, b*), Huber and Shipan (2000) and others, that agency *discretion*—defined as a function of the control mechanisms set down in an act of delegation—varies systematically across issue areas as a function of the demand for (1) expert information and (2) credible commitments. I also test Majone's (2001) hypothesis that delegation in the treaties is motivated primarily by a desire to secure credible commitments, and therefore features extensive discretion to EU organizations; while delegation in secondary legislation is motivated primarily by informational concerns, and is accordingly accompanied by the more extensive use of control mechanisms and thus lower levels of supranational discretion.

In the first part of this chapter, I examine patterns of delegation and discretion to the Commission, focusing in turn on (1) the historic role of delegation and discretion in the creation of the original institutions of the European Coal and Steel Community; (2) the functions delegated and the nature of the control mechanisms adopted in the general provisions of the EC and EU treaties; (3) issue-specific variation in the executive powers delegated, and the discretion allowed, to the Commission in the treaties; and (4) similar cross-issue variation in delegation and discretion in secondary legislation.

In the second part of the chapter, I examine the design and the workings of specific control mechanisms, with particular emphasis on (1) the procedures for the appointment, censure, and reappointment of the Commission; (2) the 'comitology' system of police-patrol oversight by committees of member-state representatives; and (3) the use of administrative law and judicial review by the European Court of Justice and the Court of First Instance. This analysis, together with the analysis of delegation and discretion across issue areas, suggests that these mechanisms are indeed chosen by member governments with precision and discrimination, and are used systematically to monitor and (rarely) to sanction the Commission in the conduct of its executive powers.

A disclaimer is in order. Throughout the chapter, the theoretical and empirical emphasis is on the institutional design of delegation to the Commission, and the control mechanisms established by member governments to limit its discretion. By contrast, I make no effort to undertake a comprehensive examination of the internal workings of the Commission, which has been examined in detail by a number of excellent books in recent years, including Nugent (1997; 2000), Cini (1996), Page (1997), Edwards and Spence (1995), and Stevens and Stevens (2000). In addition, a number of books provide detailed analyses of the Delors Commission, including most notably Ross's (1995) brilliant insider account, as well as Grant (1994), Endo (1999), and Drake (2000). I make no attempt here to summarize the results of these studies or to develop any theory of internal Commission politics, touching upon the internal structure and politics of the Commission only in so far as these are relevant to the analysis of its delegated functions and its discretion.

I. Delegation and Discretion

What powers, or functions, do the member governments of the European Union delegate to the European Commission, both in the treaties and in secondary legislation? To what extent, and in what ways, do member governments attempt to curtail the discretion of the Commission through the use of various control mechanisms? How does the discretion of the Commission vary between primary and secondary legislation, and across issue areas? Does such variation in delegation and discretion correspond to aspects of the political environment, such as uncertainty or the need for credible commitments? In this section, I seek to answer these questions through a detailed examination of the record of delegation and discretion to the Commission. Although the primary approach of the chapter is functional, I begin with an historical examination of delegation and discretion in the creation of the European Coal and Steel Community, on which the later EC and EU institutions were modelled; subsequently, I examine systematically the patterns of delegation and discretion in the general provisions of the contemporary EC and EU treaties, as well as the delegation of executive powers to the Commission in primary and secondary legislation.

Delegation and Discretion in the Creation of the EU Institutions

Most recent works on the European Union begin with the establishment of the European Economic Community in the Rome Treaties of 1957, and go on to study the successive amendments to those treaties, culminating in today's European Union. However, as Berthold Rittberger (2001) has recently argued, the basic institutional structure of today's European Union was in fact laid down, not by the Rome Treaties, but by the 1951 Treaty of Paris, which established the European Coal and Steel Community (ECSC) and provided the basic institutional blueprint for the EC and EU Treaties. If the hypotheses about delegation and discretion put forward in Chapter 1 are correct, the historical record of the ECSC's origins should reveal an explicit concern among member governments both to delegate powers to supranational agents and to establish various oversight mechanisms to limit the agency losses arising from such delegation. And indeed, the primary research conducted by Rittberger and others clearly supports the view that problems of delegation and discretion were foremost in the minds of the negotiators of the ECSC Treaty, and largely account for the overall design of the EU's quadripartite institutional structure of Commission, Council, Court, and Parliament.[1]

The ECSC, as is well known, was born in the mind of Jean Monnet, the French Planning Commissioner who first suggested establishing a supranational body to jointly govern the coal and steel industries of France, Germany, and any other European states that might choose to participate. For Monnet, such a Community would have the dual advantage of beginning a gradual process of Franco-German reconciliation and European integration, while at the same time placing the resurgent and militarily sensitive German coal and steel industry under supranational control. As articulated by French Foreign Minister Robert Schuman in the 'Schuman Declaration' of 9 May 1950, the French government was proposing 'that the Franco-German production of coal and steel as a whole be placed under a common High Authority, within the framework of an organization open to the participation of the other countries of Europe'.[2]

Although the general thrust of Monnet's proposals and the concerns underlying them are well known, the most interesting aspect of the proposals for our purposes is the emphasis on the creation of an *independent* and *supranational* High Authority, which would bind France as well as Germany to their joint endeavour and which Monnet saw as the linchpin of his plan. As Monnet wrote to Lord Plowden, his UK counterpart:

The independence of the Authority vis-à-vis Governments and the sectional interests concerned is the precondition for the emergence of a common point of view which could be taken neither by Governments nor by private interests. It is clear that to entrust the Authority to a Committee of Governmental Delegates or to a Council made up of representatives of Governments employers and workers, would amount to returning to our present methods, those very methods which do not enable us to settle our problems. It should be possible to find quite a small number of men of real stature able without necessarily being technicians, and capable of rising above particular or national interests in order to work for the accomplishment of common objectives . . .[3]

In effect, Monnet suggested that only a genuinely independent executive would be able to bind the member governments, and credibly and impartially regulate the coal and steel sector.[4] He therefore hoped to negotiate a broad framework treaty, establishing the High Authority as quickly as possible and with maximum independence, while leaving the technical and institutional details of its mandate for later (Diebold 1959: 49). To some extent, Monnet's vision of the High Authority is reflected in Article 9 of the Treaty of Paris, which provides that:

The High Authority shall consist of nine members appointed for a year and chosen on the grounds of their general competence . . . The members of the High Authority shall, in the general interest of the Community, be completely independent in the performance of their duties. In the performance of these duties, they shall neither seek nor take instructions from any Government or from any other body. They shall refrain from any action incompatible with the supranational nature of their duties.

Nevertheless, although Monnet's logic and his plan for a High Authority were immediately accepted by West German Chancellor Konrad Adenauer, who saw in the Schuman Plan a means of regaining West German influence and sovereignty within a larger European construction,[5] the prospect of unlimited delegation of executive power to the High Authority was far more alarming to the representatives of the Benelux[6] countries. By contrast with the French and German governments—each of which possessed overarching geo-political motivations for the creation of a strong supranational High Authority and considerable independence vis-à-vis their own domestic industries—the Benelux countries were concerned to limit the mandate and the independence of the High Authority to take decisions at variance with national policies crucial to the immediate post-war goal of full employment. Benelux negotiators for the Treaty of Paris therefore insisted on a more restrictive writing of the High Authority's mandate and a far more detailed and constraining set of institutional arrangements than Monnet had suggested.[7] In Rittberger's (2001: 694) words, 'No "blank cheque" would be signed for the High Authority'.

In practice, the demands of the Benelux states translated into the creation of a High Authority whose mandate was written more restrictively than Monnet had proposed[8] and which would be monitored by, and share power with, four other institutional actors: a Council of Ministers, a Court of Justice, a Common Assembly, and a Consultative Committee. Among these four bodies, the intergovernmental Council of Ministers was the highest priority for the Belgian and especially the Dutch delegations, which initially demanded that all High Authority decisions should require a positive endorsement by the Council. Although Monnet refused to restrict the High Authority's power across the board, he did agree to the creation of a Council of Ministers, and subsequent bargaining within the conference focused on identifying the specific issue areas where the High Authority could or could not act without the approval of the Council and the thresholds for overturning its decisions. In the end, the member governments adopted a convoluted scheme in which the relationship of the High Authority to the Council could take any one of seven forms. In many of the core areas of common market for coal and steel, such as the investigation and dissolution of cartels, (1) the High Authority could act alone, independently of the Council. In other, more sensitive areas, however, the High Authority could have to (2) consult the Council, but not require its approval; (3) act only with the agreement of the Council, voting by simple majority; (4) act only with the agreement of the Council, voting by two-thirds majority; (5) act only with the agreement of the Council, voting unanimously; (6) act unless the Council forbad such action, by unanimity; or (7) act only if asked to do so by the states concerned, with the agreement of the Council. Although a complete analysis of the ECSC Treaty provisions is beyond the scope of this brief account,[9] it is clear that the governments negotiating the Treaty of Paris devised the Council primarily as an intergovernmental safeguard against the actions of the High Authority, and tailored its powers with precision depending on the centrality of specific functions to the common market for coal and steel and the sensitivity of those functions for the maintenance of valued national policies.

The creation of the Court of Justice was similarly inspired by Benelux concerns about the High Authority. Early in the negotiations, Monnet proposed that disputes over the acts of the High Authority could be resolved through ad hoc arbitration tribunals, possibly presided over by a judge from the International Court of Justice (Valentine 1954; Duchêne 1994: 210). Later, the member governments agreed to create a new ECSC Court designed specifically to undertake judicial review of the High Authority's actions; yet those same governments were also concerned to limit the activism of the Court itself. As the Dutch government explained to its own parliament during the ratification of the Treaty:

There had to be sought a formula by which, on the one hand, a guarantee was given to the member States and to the enterprises that the Treaty would be followed by the institutions of the Community, while on the other hand the Court was to be prevented from usurping responsibility in the management of affairs.[10]

Put more simply, the Luxembourg government explained during its ratification procedure, the problem was 'to set up a body to control the legality of the acts of the High Authority without lessening that Authority's liberty for action or its responsibility, and to avoid substituting the Court as the central administrative organ'.[11] Furthermore, the Belgian and Dutch governments demanded that legal standing to bring complaints before the Court should be limited to governments of the ECSC's member states—ensuring that the High Authority would remain accountable to member governments but without the potential for uncontrolled litigation from private individuals and firms (Rittberger 2001: 695–7). In the language of principal-agent relations, the member governments consciously and explicitly designed a system of judicial review that would limit their agency losses vis-à-vis the High Authority, without creating additional agency losses vis-à-vis a potentially activist Court and without triggering a flood of private litigation that might conflict with the preferences of the governments themselves.

After extensive negotiations, the member states struck a compromise on both the grounds for judicial review and the standing accorded to public and private actors. Regarding the grounds for annulment of High Authority decisions, the Court was limited to ruling on the legal aspects of High Authority decisions,[12] and was explicitly barred from offering an opinion on the substance of the decision in question. Furthermore, having annulled a High Authority decision, the Court could not substitute a decision of its own, but had to refer the question back to the High Authority, which would be obliged to adopt a new decision. On the question of standing, the treaty provided that any member government or ECSC institution could challenge a decision of the High Authority, and private enterprises could also challenge High Authority decisions applying specifically to them. By contrast, acts of the Council or the Assembly could be challenged only by member governments themselves, thereby limiting the danger that private litigants could use the Court to frustrate the aims of the governments. As with the creation of the Council, therefore, the ECSC Court was designed deliberately to limit agency losses vis-à-vis the High Authority, while at the same time limiting the additional dangers of both judicial activism and private litigation.

The Consultative Assembly, finally, was added to Monnet's initial plan by the French delegation early in the negotiations in response to concerns about the democratic accountability of the High Authority. Monnet's working documents reveal explicitly the motives underlying the creation of the assembly:

Initially we [the French delegation] had not considered such an organ. However, the High Authority is a body that partially fuses states' sovereignty and, from a democratic point of view, its existence cannot therefore be envisaged without the inclusion of a control body. It is for this reason that the French initiators of the plan have thought of a parliamentary control organ comprised of the members of the different national legislatures . . .

This rudimentary assembly is not supposed to have decision-making and executive functions. The High Authority has to be accountable to the assembly. If the assembly is not satisfied with the way the High Authority fulfils its duties, it shall censure the High Authority.[13]

Note that in Monnet's scheme, and in the text of the Treaty of Paris as adopted in April 1951, the Common Assembly would be given no legislative powers at all, but be limited strictly to a control function vis-à-vis the European Parliament. In Duchêne's (1994: 210) words, the Assembly 'was to meet like an annual shareholders meeting once a year, to debate the High Authority's report, and it had only the shareholder's power to throw out the management'. In fact, the German delegation had pressed in the negotiations for a parliament closer to the German Bundesrat, with real legislative powers, but these demands were rejected by the Benelux countries, which would accept the notion of a Common Assembly only if its powers were limited to the supervision and censuring of the High Authority.[14] This point, and the reference to a shareholder-management relationship—one of the classic principal-agent relationships—is worth underlining. While the later European Parliament would acquire budgetary and legislative powers taking it well outside the realm of classical principal-agent relations (see Chapter 4), the Common Assembly began its existence *solely* as a third layer of control over the High Authority, supplementing the intergovernmental Council and the prospect of judicial review through the Court with a weak but explicitly 'democratic' means of control and accountability.

Finally, the member governments also created a quasi-corporatist Consultative Committee composed of coal and steel producers, consumers, and workers, to advise the High Authority; this body, however, was given no power to overturn High Authority decisions or compel its resignation.

Although far from definitive, this brief historical survey demonstrates that questions of delegation and discretion were, in fact, explicit and central to the motivations of member governments in creating the basic institutions of the ECSC and its successors. Indeed, as early as 1958 Ernst Haas noted in *The Uniting of Europe* that 'the other four organs [the Council, the Court, the Common Assembly, and the Consultative Committee] are primarily designed as checks upon the power of the High Authority' (Haas 1958: 43). Later, when the same six member states negotiated the Treaties of Rome establishing the EEC and Euratom, the basic institutional structure of the ECSC was retained, while the powers of the various institutions and their principal-agent relations were adjusted and fine-tuned by the member governments to fit the much broader range of issue areas addressed by those treaties. In the following sections, I turn from this historical sketch of the origins of the ECSC to a more detailed and systematic analysis of the specific patterns of delegation and discretion in the contemporary EC and EU Treaties.

The EC and EU Treaties: General Provisions

Following the Coal and Steel Community, the 1957 EEC Treaty was the founding 'constitutional' document of the European Community, and has since been amended numerous times, most notably in three landmark treaties: the 1986 Single European Act (SEA), the 1992 Maastricht Treaty on European Union, and the 1997 Treaty of Amsterdam. These treaties, incorporated into the *Consolidated Treaties* in 1997, lay out the basic institutional structure of the contemporary European Union, including the delegation of powers to supranational organizations such as the Commission, the Court, and the European Parliament.[15] In legal terms, these treaties constitute the 'primary' or 'constitutional' law of the Union, within which ordinary or 'secondary' legislation is adopted and implemented. Like any constitution, these treaties are characterized by greater stability than secondary legislation, having been amended on only a handful of occasions by unanimous agreement and ratification by all of the member states of the Union. In addition, the EU and the EC treaties contain both general or 'horizontal' provisions outlining the goals and institutional architecture of the Union and issue-specific or 'vertical' provisions specifying the aims of individual policies and the institutional procedures governing the making and implementation of those policies. In this section, I examine the general provisions of the EC and the EU treaties.

The EC Treaty forms the historical core of the Union, dating from the 1957 Treaty of Rome, and today constitutes the first and most active 'pillar' of the EU, alongside a second pillar concerning Common Foreign and Security Policy, and a third pillar on Justice and Home Affairs. In addition to spelling out the objectives of the Community and the policies it pursues, the EC Treaty also lays out the basic objectives, composition, and decision rules governing the activities of supranational agents like the Commission, the Court, and the Parliament. The section of the EC Treaty dealing specifically with the Commission is surprisingly brief, comprising only nine articles (Articles 211–219 EC, ex 155–163) which describe the Commission's tasks and composition. The first of these, Article 211 (ex 155) EC, begins with a non-exhaustive list of the Commission's functions:

In order to ensure the proper functioning and development of the common market, the Commission shall:

—ensure that the provisions of this Treaty and the measures taken by the institutions pursuant thereto are applied;

—formulate recommendations or deliver opinions on matters dealt with in this Treaty, if it expressly so provides or if the Commission considers it necessary;

—have its own power of decision and participate in the shaping of measures taken by the Council and by the European Parliament in the manner provided for in this Treaty;

—exercise the powers conferred on it by the Council for the implementation of the rules laid down by the latter.

Clearly, these provisions, as supplemented by other articles in the treaty, lay out a broad role for the Commission, which is called upon to participate in *setting the agenda* for the EC legislative process; *monitoring and enforcing* primary and secondary EC law, the so-called 'guardian of the treaties' role; and *implementing* policies adopted by the Council. Clearly, these functions correspond closely to the functions spelled out in Chapter 1, including agenda-setting, monitoring, and enforcement, and the adoption of expert and credible regulation. Let us consider each of these functions, very briefly, in turn.

Agenda Setting
Strictly speaking, the power to set the legislative agenda is a legislative rather than an executive function, the possession of which renders the Commission more broadly similar to American Congressional committees—which enjoy significant powers to set the agenda for floor voters in their respective jurisdictional domains—than to regulatory agencies, whose role is limited to implementing rather than proposing legislation. Nevertheless, as Shepsle and others point out, the delegation of agenda-setting power can play an important role in avoiding cyclical majorities and securing principals' commitment to an agreement. In the case of Congressional committees, for example, Shepsle argues that Congressmen commit to logrolling agreements by sharing out jurisdiction among themselves, assigning exclusive agenda-setting powers in various areas to 'preference outliers' in the various committees, and protecting their proposals from being picked apart through more or less constraining amendment rules.

In the EU case, the Commission has been granted the sole right of initiative for nearly all 'first-pillar' or EC legislation, meaning that any legislation adopted by the Council, or by the Council and the Parliament, must proceed on the basis of a proposal from the Commission. This extraordinary delegation of powers to the Commission, Majone (2001) argues, represents a similar act of self-commitment to the project of European integration by member governments, on the plausible assumption that the Commission, like the members of US Congressional committees, is a preference outlier with a strong preference for further integration, and can be expected to use its powers to pursue those aims.

The actual agenda-setting power of the Commission in any given area, however, depends not only on its right of initiative but also on the amendment rule and the voting rules for a given piece of legislation. Within the EC pillar of the Union, the treaties provide that a Commission proposal can be amended only through a unanimous vote of the Council of Ministers—an extraordinarily restrictive amendment rule which, while short of a 'closed rule' requiring a straight up-or-down vote, presents a higher threshold to the adoption of amendments, and hence greater protection for the agenda-setter's proposal, than in most US Congressional legislation.[16] The effect of this amendment rule, in turn, depends upon the voting rule governing the adoption of the legislation. Thus, in cases where unanimous agreement in the Council is required, the Commission's proposal enjoys no special status, in the sense that amendments can be adopted as easily as the Commission's original proposal. However, in those cases where the Council can adopt legislation by qualified majority, the Commission's proposal is much easier to adopt than to amend, and its agenda-setting power is enhanced accordingly.[17]

In a further complication, however, the Commission's agenda-setting powers under qualified majority voting are substantially reduced, if not eliminated, by the co-decision procedure as established in the Maastricht Treaty and amended in the Treaty of Amsterdam. During the early stages of the co-decision procedure, the Commission retains the sole right of initiative, and the Council continues to require a unanimous agreement to amend a Commission proposal. However, in the event of a disagreement between the Council and the European Parliament, representatives of these two bodies form a 'conciliation committee' to iron out their differences and produce a compromise text, which must then be adopted in a straight up-or-down vote in both bodies. During this procedure, the members of the conciliation committee are free to make amendments to their joint text, *without the approval of the Commission*, thereby depriving the latter of its traditional agenda-setting power. Clearly, then, the Commission's agenda-setting power is not uniform but varies according to the dozens of distinct legal bases and voting rules which have been laid down in the treaties and frequently amended in the course of the various intergovernmental conferences of the past two decades.[18]

Guardian of the Treaties: Monitoring and Enforcement Powers
In drafting and amending the treaties, member governments have given considerable attention to the problem of ensuring their own

compliance with the provisions of the treaties, and for this purpose they have delegated extensive powers to both the Commission and the European Court of Justice to monitor and enforce member-state compliance with EC law. The most important treaty provision in this regard is Article 226 (ex 169) EC, in which the Commission is delegated the power to monitor member-state compliance with EC law, provide a warning to the member government in question through the submission of a 'reasoned opinion', and pursue infringement proceedings before the Court of Justice if non-compliance persists. Unlike the ECSC Treaty, the EEC Treaty did not initially include any sanctions to be taken against member states for non-compliance with ECJ rulings.[19] In subsequent treaty revisions, however, the Commission's powers of enforcement have been incrementally increased. In the Single European Act, the Commission was given a new power to bring expedited infringement proceedings before the Court of Justice for certain internal market questions.[20] Six years later in the Maastricht Treaty, the member governments, faced with a sharp increase in non-compliance with ECJ judgments, amended Article 228 (ex 171) EC to give the Commission the power to initiate infringement proceedings against member states for non-compliance with Court decisions, and to propose that the Court issue punitive fines against those member states. The Commission has since initiated such proceedings on a number of occasions, prompting member governments to bring their national laws into compliance rather than face the threat of being fined by the ECJ (Tallberg 1999: 178–81).

The fit between these provisions and the predictions generated by principal-agent analysis is clear enough to require little elaboration here. Clearly, the member governments of the original EEC delegated enforcement powers to the Commission to increase the credibility of their mutual commitment to the aims of the Community, and they have increased the Commission's enforcement powers subsequently for the same reasons. Furthermore, in delegating this power the member governments have also granted the Commission a significant element of discretion both in identifying cases for enforcement and in concluding agreements with member governments in the shadow of an eventual ECJ decision. With regard to the identification of cases, it is clear that the Commission, with a relatively small bureaucracy and limited resources, could not identify and prosecute every instance of national non-compliance with EC law. In practice, therefore, the Commission enjoys some discretion in setting priorities and deciding which cases to bring, in which areas, and against which member states.[21] Similarly, as Jönsson and Tallberg (1998) have pointed out, the Commission does not proceed directly from a reasoned opinion to proceedings before the

ECJ, but typically engages in bilateral negotiations with the offending member government in the hope of reaching a negotiated settlement; and in these negotiations the Commission again enjoys considerable discretion to reach an appropriate political settlement.

The existence of de facto discretion on the part of the Commission illustrates the dilemma encountered by principals when they delegate enforcement powers to an independent agent, referred to as a 'supervisor' in the work of Jonas Tallberg (1999; 2000). On the one hand, in order to act as a credible enforcer, the agent must be seen as independent of the demands and preferences of even the most powerful member governments. This need for insulation and credibility is reflected in the provisions of Article 226, which allow the Commission to initiate infringement proceedings on its own authority without seeking the approval of the Council. By the same token, however, such independence may allow the agent to pursue its own policy agenda by enforcing EC law either more or less vigorously than desired by the member governments, or by initiating proceedings to different degrees across issue areas. In practice, Tallberg (1999) has demonstrated, the Commission has changed its strategies over the past four decades, beginning with a reticent approach that avoided legal proceedings and potential conflicts with member governments during the early years of the EC, and moving gradually to a much more aggressive policy of initiating infringement proceedings regularly against member governments for non-compliance with EC law and with ECJ judgments. Nevertheless, Tallberg (1999: 153–62) concludes cautiously by arguing that the Commission's efforts under Article 226 do *not* represent shirking vis-à-vis the member states, in so far as the move to a more aggressive stance was collectively *supported* by the member governments, which explicitly agreed to an extension of the Commission's enforcement powers in the amendment of Article 95 in the SEA, and Article 228 at Maastricht.

Implementation and Regulation

In addition to its role as a monitor and enforcer of EC law vis-à-vis the member governments, the Commission also plays a more direct role in the *implementation* of EU policies in certain areas. Unlike US executive departments or regulatory agencies, the Commission does not operate a parallel bureaucracy implementing EU policies 'on the ground', a job left to the member governments, albeit under Commission supervision. Nevertheless, the Commission does play an executive role at the European level:

- adopting implementing regulations within the framework of Council and Parliamentary legislation;

- managing EC spending programmes in areas such as agriculture, the Structural Funds, and research and technological development; and
- applying EC laws directly in certain issue areas such competition policy.

Generally speaking, member governments have *not* chosen to delegate sweeping executive powers to the Commission in the body of the treaties. Rather, the treaties specify executive functions in a very few specific issue areas, and provide two more general clauses which empower the Council of Ministers to delegate implementing powers to the Commission in secondary legislation. First, as we have just seen, Article 211 provides that the Commission shall 'exercise the powers conferred on it by the Council for the implementation of the rules laid down by the latter'. Second, the member governments agreed in the Single European Act to add an additional clause to Article 202 (ex 145) EC *requiring* the Council, as a general rule, to 'confer on the Commission, in the acts which the Council adopts, powers for implementation of the rules which the Council lays down'. The delegation of specific implementing powers, however, is left to the discretion of the Council, which 'may impose certain requirements in respect of the exercise of those powers'. In practice, as we shall see below, the Council has created an elaborate system of 'comitology' oversight committees to monitor the Commission in the adoption of implementing regulations. More generally, and in contrast with its agenda-setting and particularly its enforcement functions, the Commission's regulatory powers have only a weak base in the treaties, outside a few key areas such as competition and external trade policies, and the bulk of the Commission's implementing powers therefore derive from secondary legislation, examined in detail below.

Horizontal Control Mechanisms

In sum, the horizontal provisions of the treaty delegate rather extensive and far-reaching powers to the Commission in precisely the areas identified by principal-agent analysis. But how much actual *discretion* accompanies this delegation of powers? More specifically, what are the treaty provisions governing the independence or accountability of the Commission, and what control mechanisms exist to limit the Commission's horizontal powers? At first blush, the language of the treaty suggests, in Article 213 (ex 157) EC, that the Commission is to be entirely independent from its member-state principals:

The Members of the Commission shall, in the general interest of the Community, be entirely independent in the performance of their duties.

In the performance of these duties, they shall neither seek nor take instructions from any government or from any other body. They shall refrain from any action incompatible with their duties. Each Member State undertakes to respect this principle and not to seek to influence the Members of the Commission in the performance of their tasks.

However, the treaty chapter on the Commission, together with other horizontal and issue-specific provisions of the treaties, include a number of administrative procedures and oversight mechanisms that provide member governments with potential influence over individual Commissioners or the entire College of Commissioners as a body. These mechanisms include:

1. *Appointment and dismissal procedures.* The Commission and its President are appointed by the member governments, with a growing role for the European Parliament since the adoption of the Maastricht and Amsterdam Treaties, allowing both sets of actors in principle to influence the initial, or endogenous, preferences of the Commissioners. By contrast, the treaties make only a highly restrictive provision for the removal, or 'compulsory retirement', of individual Commissioners, which may occur only by a decision of the European Court of Justice and only if the Commissioner in question can no longer carry out her duties or has committed serious misconduct. Member governments, moreover, are forbidden to dismiss or even attempt to influence those Commissioners in their duties, although in practice Commissioners are naturally, and usefully, attuned to the political sensitivities of their own member states.

2. *Oversight procedures.* In its agenda-setting role, the Commission is required to place proposals before the member governments in the Council and to secure the requisite—and variable—majority or unanimous vote in favour of its proposals in the Council and, increasingly, the European Parliament. In certain provisions of the treaty, moreover, the Commission is required to consult other institutions and committees, including the Economic and Social Committee, the Committee of the Regions, and various issue-specific committees such as the famous Article 133 Committee which oversees the Commission in international trade negotiations (see Chapter 5). In terms of its implementing powers, by contrast, the treaty itself is vague, allowing only that the Council may set down conditions for the exercise of the Commission's implementing powers. In practice, however, these 'conditions' have developed into an arcane system of hundreds of 'comitology' committees which oversee the Commission in a classic 'police-patrol' fashion.

3. *Administrative law and judicial review.* The EU Treaties themselves are nearly silent on the subject of administrative law, containing

only a few broadly worded provisions such as the requirement in Article 253 (ex 190) EC that the Commission and other EU institutions 'state reasons' for their actions. Nevertheless, the treaties do provide a broad framework for judicial review, most notably in Article 230 (ex 173) EC, which provides for the annulment of EC acts on a variety of grounds; and the European Court of Justice, together with various public and private plaintiffs acting as 'fire-alarm' monitors, has developed these minimal requirements into an increasingly elaborate and constraining system of administrative law.

4. *The budget.* In theory, legislative principals may use the budgetary process to control the staff and the resources available to their agents. Legislators unhappy with the behaviour of a regulatory agency, for example, may reduce the resources available to the agency in response to shirking. However, as noted in Chapter 1, budgetary control is a rather blunt instrument, which may in practice reduce valuable agency outputs unrelated to the observed shirking and costly to the principals as well as the agents. In the EU case, moreover, the use of the budget as a control mechanism is further complicated by the substantial role of the Commission in the adoption of the annual budget, together with the Council of Ministers and the European Parliament (see Chapter 4). Nevertheless, both the Council and the Parliament have on occasion used their partial control of the EU budget to secure leverage on the Commission, either by cutting budgets for the Commission's favoured programmes or, in the case of the Parliament, by withholding the discharge of the annual budget.[22]

5. *Institutional checks.* Finally, the Commission is also subject to additional institutional checks from two Community institutions, each of which has been established as an independent body with a clear mandate to monitor the behaviour of the Commission and other Community institutions. The first of these, the European Court of Auditors, was established in 1975, with a mandate to provide an annual audit of the Community budget, including the actions of the member governments as well as the Commission.[23] In the years since its creation, the Court has issued a series of increasingly critical reports regarding the financial management of both the Commission and the member states. These reports in turn have provided the backdrop for the increasingly strict budgetary supervision of the Commission by the Parliament, culminating in the mass resignation of the Santer Commission in 1999. The second institutional check on the Commission (and other EU institutions) is the Ombudsman, whose office was created by the Maastricht Treaty in response to requests from the European Parliament. According to Article 195 (ex 138e)

EC, the Ombudsman is an independent official, appointed by the Parliament for a renewable five-year term, with a mandate to receive and investigate complaints of maladministration from individual EU citizens, companies, or associations. The first Ombudsman, Jacob Söderman of Finland, was elected in July 1995, and reappointed for a second five-year term in July 2000. In practice, the Ombudsman can receive several thousand complaints a year, of which several hundred may be judged admissible under the Ombudsman's mandate and result in an investigation and report. During 2000, for example, the Ombudsman's office received some 223 admissible complaints, of which 185, or 83 per cent, were lodged against the Commission, most often for lack of transparency, refusal to release documents, late payments to contract-holders, or other avoidable delays.[24] Clearly, the cases investigated by the Ombudsman—like the charges that brought down the Santer Commission in March 1999—concern classic instances of maladministration rather than excessive zeal for unification. Nevertheless, for individual citizens with a grievance against the Commission, the Ombudsman does provide an additional layer of supervision, which often leads to an amicable settlement of the case by the Commission, or the adoption by the Commission of reforms suggested by the Ombudsman.

In sum, the treaties delegate extensive horizontal powers to the Commission in agenda setting, policy implementation, and monitoring compliance with EC law. By the same token, however, the treaties also specify a number of horizontal control mechanisms that place limits on the Commission's discretion. Given their importance as potential sources of member-state influence, I focus in greater detail on three of these control mechanisms in Section II below. Before that, however, we need to look more closely at the executive powers delegated to the Commission on an issue-specific basis in both primary and secondary law.

Patterns of Delegation and Discretion in Issue-Specific Treaty Provisions

In this subsection, I examine issue-specific differences in the extent of delegation and discretion across 35 specific issue areas laid down in the EC and EU treaties. The aim is to map the empirical patterns of delegation across issue areas and to test hypotheses about delegation by examining the relationship between discretion, as the dependent variable, and uncertainty or demand for credible commitments, as independent variables.[25] Once again, as in the previous section,

I examine the provisions of the *Consolidated Treaties* as official acts of delegation, using the distinct headings of the various treaty chapters and titles to define the extent and the boundaries of each issue area (see Appendix A). The primary challenge in this section is to measure in quantitative terms the extent of delegation and Commission discretion across issue areas, including both executive functions—such as regulating economic activities, managing EU funds, or negotiating with third parties—and legislative or agenda-setting functions. In doing so, I draw on existing studies of delegation and discretion in the United States and the European Union, adapting the methods of those studies to the purpose at hand.

The first method involves the construction, for each issue area of the treaties, of a 'delegation ratio', a 'constraint ratio', and finally a 'discretion index' for the Commission across each of the 35 issue areas, following the coding rules laid down by Epstein and O'Halloran (1999*a*), and adapted to the EU with considerable sophistication by Franchino (2001).[26] Put simply, the delegation ratio for a given chapter of the treaties refers to the ratio of treaty provisions delegating powers to the Commission to the total number of provisions in the same chapter.[27] Although this delegation measure is highly sensitive to the total number of provisions in each chapter (that is, the denominator) it provides a good first-cut measure of delegation. Next, for each issue area I calculate a constraint ratio, which is the number of types of control mechanisms which appear in a given chapter, over a denominator consisting of 12 possible control mechanisms listed by Franchino (2001). Third and finally, for each issue area I derive a discretion index, which is defined as the delegation ratio minus the product of the delegation ratio and the constraint ratio.

In the EU treaties, however, much of the issue-specific delegation to the Commission takes the form of agenda-setting powers, that is, the Commission's sole right, in most areas, to propose legislation to the Council of Ministers, rather than the sorts of executive/regulatory functions stressed in the literature on Congressional delegation to regulatory bureaucracies. For this reason, Franchino (2001) suggests that the Commission's legislative functions be omitted from any index of delegation. Like Franchino, I see the value of distinguishing between the executive and the legislative functions delegated to the Commission; at the same time, however, I consider the delegation of agenda-setting powers to be a significant and important act of delegation by member governments, worthy of examination in its own right. In this subsection, therefore, I begin the analysis by constructing an issue-specific index of *executive* delegation in the treaties, and analyse the rather small sample of issue areas in which the treaties delegate binding executive powers to the Commission.

In order to analyse the delegation of executive powers to the Commission across issue areas, I analysed, article by article, the provisions in Part III ('Community Policies') of the EC Treaty, which outlines Community competence, policies, and procedures for each of 32 distinct issue areas, together with one additional issue area ('Citizenship') from Part I of the EC Treaty, and two titles from the EU Treaty, concerning Common Foreign and Security Policy and Justice and Home Affairs, respectively (for details of issue area coding, see Appendix B).

First, with regard to 'delegation,' I have adopted Franchino's (2001: 31) rather conservative rule about the coding of delegation, whereby 'delegation is any major provision that gives . . . the Commission the authority to move the policy away from the status quo'. Such a measure is designed to capture only instances where the Commission acquires genuine executive powers, while excluding those that merely 'associate' the Commission symbolically with a policy or delegate only the right to make non-binding recommendations. The results are shown in the second column of Table 2.1. Using this rather restrictive index, the treaty delegates binding executive powers to the Commission in only ten issue areas, most significantly in the areas of competition policy, where the Commission is delegated significant regulatory powers for the application of EC rules on cartels and concentrations and state aids, in items 1 and 3 respectively; the common commercial policy, in which the Commission serves as the Community's negotiator on trade issues within the sphere of EC competence, item 4; and the European Social Fund, item 2, the relevant provision of which simply notes that 'the Fund shall be administered by the Commission'. Of these four provisions, those dealing with competition and the common commercial policy are the most detailed and delegate the most explicit executive competences. By contrast, Article 147 (ex 124) EC on the European Social Fund is relatively vague, and in practice has required supplementary provisions in secondary legislation to identify the specific powers of the Commission; the relatively high delegation score for the Social Fund should therefore be interpreted with caution. Moving down the list, we see that the chapter on the free movement of workers empowers the Commission to adopt implementing regulations regarding the conditions under which EU nationals may remain in the territory of a member state after having been employed in that state; the chapter on 'approximation of laws', which is the key chapter for legislation under the 1992

TABLE 2.1. *Delegation and discretion of executive powers, Consolidated Treaties*

Issue-area	Delegation (%)	Constraints	Discretion (%)
1. Competition: Undertakings	33.33	0	33.33
2. European Social Fund	33.33	0.0833	30.55
3. Competition: State Aids	28.57	0.0833	26.19
4. Common Commercial Policy	22.22	0.1667	18.52
5. Free Movement of Workers	14.29	0	14.29
6. Approximation of Laws	14.29	0	14.29
7. Transport	15.79	0.25	11.84
8. Agriculture	6.25	0	6.25
9. Social Provisions	4.55	0	4.55
10. EMU: Transitional Provisions	2.5	0.0833	2.4

Note: For methods used in construction of Table, see Appendices B–D. There is no delegation of executive powers in the following categories: Customs Union; Quantitative Restrictions; Right of Establishment; Free Movement of Services; Free Movement of Capital and Payments; Visas, Immigration and Asylum; Tax Provisions; EMU: Economic Policy; EMU: Monetary Policy; EMU: Institutional Provisions; Employment; Customs Cooperation; Education, Vocational Training and Youth; Culture; Public Health; Consumer Protection; Trans-European Networks; Industry; Economic and Social Cohesion; Research and Technological Development; Environment; Development Cooperation; Citizenship; Common Foreign and Security Policy; Justice and Home Affairs.

Source: Consolidated Treaties.

internal market programme, delegates to the Commission the job of accepting or rejecting national provisions adopted on the basis of environment or consumer protection, in so far as such provisions interfere with the free movement of goods and services; and so on.

These functions, which are summarized in Table 2.2, fall largely into two of the aforementioned categories: first, monitoring and enforcing

TABLE 2.2. *Executive powers delegated to the European Commission, Consolidated Treaties*

Issue area	Powers delegated
1. Competition: Undertakings	• Article 85(1) dictates that the Commission 'shall ensure the application of the principles laid down' in the previous articles, and empowers the Commission to investigate cases of suspected infringement, and propose appropriate measures to bring such infringements to an end. • Article 85(2) outlines the procedure whereby the Commission, in response to an infringement, first lays down a 'reasoned decision' and then determines the conditions and details of actions to be taken by member states. • Article 86(3) dictates that the 'Commission shall ensure the application of the provisions of this article and shall, where necessary, address appropriate directives or decisions to Member States'.
2. European Social Fund	Article 147 provides that 'The Fund shall be administered by the Commission'.
3. Competition: State Aids	• Article 88(1) provides that the Commission shall keep under constant review all systems of aids in the member states, and propose 'any appropriate measures' required by the progressive development of the common market. • Article 88(2) provides that, if the Commission finds that state aids are incompatible with the common market, it can order the member state concerned to abolish that aid; and, if the member state does not comply, refer the matter directly to the ECJ. • Article 88(3) requires member states to inform the Commission of new state aids; if the Commission considers these aids incompatible with the common market, it can initiate the procedure in paragraph 2,

TABLE 2.2. *Continued*

Issue area	Powers delegated
	during which member state in question must suspend its proposed measures.
4. Common Commercial Policy	• Article 133(3) delegates to the Commission the power to conduct negotiations with third countries, supervised by a special committee and subject to approval by QMV in the Council (Article 133(4)). • Article 134 delegates to the Commission the power to authorize member states to take any necessary protective measures, and to decide at any time to amend or abolish the measures in question.
5. Free Movement of Workers	Article 39(3d) authorizes the Commission to draw up implementing regulations on the conditions for individuals to remain in the member state where they work.
6. Approximation of Laws	• Article 95(6) delegates to the Commission the power to approve or reject stricter national standards adopted under Article 95(4). • Article 95(9) authorizes the Commission, by derogation from Articles 226 and 227, to take the matter directly to the ECJ if it believes that a member state is making improper use of powers under this article.
7. Transport	• Article 75(4) delegates to the Commission the power to investigate cases of discrimination and to take the necessary measures in accordance with provisions of paragraph 3. • Article 76(1) delegates to the Commission the power to authorize support for particular undertakings or industries which are otherwise prohibited. • Article 76(2) delegates to the Commission the power to examine the rates and conditions referred to in Chapter 1, taking into account a range of factors, and, after consulting member states concerned, take the necessary decisions.

TABLE 2.2. *Continued*

Issue area	Powers delegated
8. Agriculture	Article 38 authorizes Commission broad authority to fix countervailing charges and other measures required when national market organizations distort competition among member states.
9. Social Provisions	Article 138 generally allows the Commission to initiate consultation with the social partners. However, the Commission has no actual executive or agenda-setting power within the social dialogue, except in paragraph 4, where its agreement is required to extend the nine-month deadline.
10. EMU: Transitional Provisions	Article 119(3) allows the Commission to 'authorize the state in difficulty to take protective measures, the conditions and details of which the Commission shall determine'. 'Such authorization', however, 'may be revoked and such conditions and details may be changed by the Council acting by a qualified majority'.

Source: Consolidated Treaties.

compliance with EU competition rules (Articles 35, 75, 85, 86, 88) and/or policing member-state exceptions to such rules (Articles 76, 95, 134); and second, adopting implementing regulations (Article 39, free movement of workers). The exceptions include Article 133, which authorizes the Commission to negotiate on behalf of the Union in international trade negotiations; and Article 147, which was adopted as part of the original Treaty of Rome and is the only treaty article to delegate to the Commission the power to implement a spending programme.

Although these powers are some of the most important executive functions performed by the Commission, it is nevertheless striking that EU member governments have generally chosen to delegate binding executive powers to the Commission in the treaties in only a few issue areas, and that most of these provisions date from the 1957 EEC

Treaty rather than from later amendments. Rather, the issue-specific articles of the treaty tend to delegate either legislative agenda-setting powers (see Chapter 4), or more general, non-binding provisions associating the Commission with the implementation of EU regulations, but without legal authority to take executive decisions. This latter category of 'soft delegation' has expanded with the adoption of the Maastricht and Amsterdam Treaties, where delegation of non-binding powers to the Commission is commonplace. In the Maastricht Treaty, for example, the member governments delegated no binding executive powers, and highly constraining agenda-setting powers, in 'new' issue areas such as culture, public health, industry. However, at the insistence of the United Kingdom and other member governments, each of these chapters features a sort of soft delegation to the Commission, which is authorized 'to take any useful initiative to promote . . . coordination' among member state policies, in the areas of public health, industry, trans-European networks, research and technological development, and international development aid. The extent of 'soft' delegation is even more notable in the Employment Title of the Treaty of Amsterdam, where the Commission plays a central, yet 'soft' role in the so-called 'open method of coordination' (see Conclusions).

An even more striking development is visible in the second and third pillars of the Treaty on European Union, neither of which delegates any binding executive authority to the Commission. As has been well documented elsewhere, member governments explicitly designed these two intergovernmental pillars to exclude supranational influence, and the Amsterdam Treaty went further by delegating executive powers not to the Commission but to the alternative, and presumably more easily controlled, Council Secretariat, which has been charged with preparing actions regarding the Common Foreign and Security Policy (CFSP) and with representing the CFSP as the 'High Representative' of the member states.[28] Similarly, in both the second and third pillars of the treaties the Commission has not been granted its traditional sole right of initiative, but rather shares this right with the member governments, which can, in these two areas, initiate legislation themselves, thereby depriving the Commission of its formal agenda-setting powers. Even in these areas, however, the Commission enjoys the benefit of 'soft delegation', including provisions stating that the Commission 'shall be fully associated' with the work of each pillar, ensuring that the Commission at least has a seat at the table if not binding powers of implementation or legislative initiative.

As for constraints, Franchino (2001) lists twelve potential control mechanisms, above and beyond the horizontal provision for judicial review of Community acts, that member states might adopt to control the Commission, adapted from Epstein and O'Halloran's (1999*a*) list of control mechanisms in the US Congress. Franchino's list of control mechanisms includes the following:

- time limits on delegation;
- spending limits;
- reporting requirements;
- consultation requirements;
- public hearings;
- rule-making requirements;
- appeals procedures;
- exemptions for individuals or classes of individuals;
- a requirement for explicit legislative approval;
- the possibility of legislative overrule;
- a requirement for approval by an executive body; and
- the possibility of overrule by an executive body.

Following Franchino's method, a legislative provision featuring all twelve of these control mechanisms would have a constraint ratio of 1, while one with no control mechanisms would have a score of 0. A quick glance at the figures in the third column of Table 2.1 and the more detailed analysis in the second column of Table 2.3 reveals that the treaties contain relatively few, and a relatively narrow range of, issue-specific control mechanisms. The most common constraint appearing in these articles is the requirement of Commission *consultation* either with a treaty-mandated advisory committee or with specific member governments, as in the cases of the European Social Fund, Common Commercial Policy, and Transport. In addition, the chapter on Transport contains explicit *rule-making requirements*, to the effect that any action under the chapter must take into account the effect of policy on the economic circumstances of carriers; the chapters on State Aids and Economic and Monetary Union (EMU) make *legislative action possible* by allowing the Council to overturn a Commission decision, by unanimity and qualified majority vote (QMV), respectively);[29] and the chapter on Common Commercial Policy makes *legislative action necessary* by requiring a QMV in the Council to ratify the outcome of a Commission negotiation with third parties. These constraints have been clearly and deliberately designed by member governments to limit Commission discretion in these key areas—yet, by contrast with secondary legislation, both the number and the range of control mechanisms included in the treaties is small, reflecting either the broad nature of treaty language in general or a

TABLE 2.3. *Types of constraint in executive delegation, Consolidated Treaties*

Issue area	Type of constraint
1. Competition: Undertakings	None specified
2. European Social Fund	Consultation requirements: advisory committee of member-state, trade-union, and employer's representatives
3. Competition: State Aids	Legislative action possible: Council can overturn Commission decision in Article 88(2) by unanimity
4. Common Commercial Policy	Consultation requirements: Article 133 committee legislative action necessary: final agreements must be approved by Council, by QMV
5. Free Movement of Workers	None specified
6. Approximation of Laws	None specified
7. Transport	Rule-making requirements: measures must take into account the economic circumstances of carriers (Article 74) Consultation Requirements: Commission must consult member state concerned when deciding whether to authorize national regulations that impose differential costs on Community carriers; also, Article 79 establishes advisory committee for transport Exemptions: Article 78 provides explicit exemption for the former East Germany
8. Agriculture	None specified
9. Social Provisions	None specified
10. EMU: Transitional Provisions	Legislative action possible: Council may overrule by QMV Commission decisions to allow member states to take protective measures

Source: Consolidated Treaties.

deliberate effort to allow the Commission wider latitude in these areas than in secondary legislation, or both.

Finally, if we calculate the initial delegation ratio, and then subtract a value which is the product of the delegation and the constraint ratio, we get a *discretion index*, which is reported in the final column of Table 2.1 and roughly measures the total discretion allotted to the Commission in a given issue area. Given the almost uniformly low constraint indices in the treaties, the ranking of issue areas by discretion differs only slightly from the original delegation ranking, with the exception of Transport, which falls two places behind Approximation of Laws and Free Movement of Workers because of the presence of three explicit control mechanisms: exemptions, rule-making and consultation requirements. In sum, then, the treaties explicitly delegate executive powers to the Commission in a relatively small range of issue areas, the most important of which are competition policy and the common commercial policy; and in these areas the Commission is relatively unconstrained by the sorts of control mechanisms discussed in the American literature on regulatory agencies.

Patterns of Delegation and Discretion in Secondary Legislation

At this point, we turn briefly to examine and compare Franchino's (2001) findings regarding the delegation of executive powers to the Commission in a sample of secondary EC legislation. Following an ambitious research design similar to Epstein and O'Halloran's (1999a) sampling procedure, Franchino has created a data-set of 158 pieces of major EC legislation, which he codes for delegation, constraints, and discretion according to rules broadly similar to those adapted for the treaties in the last subsection. Despite some differences in terms of Franchino's coding of issue areas[30] and the differences in length and detail between primary and secondary legislation, his findings not only provide additional data with which to test hypotheses about delegation generally but also allow us to test Majone's (2001) secondary hypothesis that member states delegate broad discretion to the Commission in the treaties in order to ensure credible commitments, while delegating more mundane managerial tasks and less discretion to the Commission in secondary legislation. Franchino's (2001) findings provide at best partial evidence for Majone's hypothesis. Specifically, Franchino's data reveal that member governments have delegated powers much more broadly in secondary legislation, including 71 of 158 pieces of legislation, and in 24 out of Franchino's 41 issue areas, although the average discretion index across all legislation is a modest

4.4 per cent. Clearly, then, member governments have been more willing to delegate executive powers to the Commission, and across a
broader range of issue areas, in secondary legislation than in the
treaties, where the terms of delegation would be more difficult to
change and shirking by the Commission more difficult to correct.

In terms of the issue areas delegated, however, we find no clear, systematic differences in primary and secondary legislation, but a pattern
of partial overlap. Specifically, Franchino (2001: 45) lists ten issue areas
with a discretion ratio of higher than 5 per cent: (1) Competition—
rules for undertakings (20.67 per cent); (2) Monetary compensation amounts (15 per cent); (3) Agriculture—organization of markets
(14.74 per cent); (4) Fishing—organization of markets (10.61 per cent);
(5) Competition—merger control (9.71 per cent); (6) Commercial
policy (7.37 per cent); (7) Agriculture—financial provisions (6.90
per cent); (8) Transport—market conditions (6.51 per cent);
(9) Agriculture—structural policy (6.33 per cent); and (10) Regional
policy (6.21 per cent). As in the case of treaty-based delegation, we
again find competition and commercial policy near the top of the discretion scale, occupying three of the top six places, including the 1989
Merger Regulation. This pattern of delegation suggests that the logic
of credible commitments in these areas operates not only in the treaties
but also in secondary legislation. However, by contrast with the
treaties, and consistent with Majone, we also find significant levels of
discretion for the Commission in the management of EU spending
programmes, including agriculture, fisheries, and regional policy.

Franchino attempts to test two specific hypotheses about the effects
of (1) information intensity and (2) legislative procedure on the discretion allotted to the Commission in any given piece of legislation.[31]
In methodological terms, Franchino uses a combination of indirect
and direct measures for 'information intensity', or what has been
called the complexity or 'inherent uncertainty' associated with a given
piece of legislation. For indirect measures, Franchino follows
Mayhew (1991), Epstein and O'Halloran (1999a) and others in classi-
fying legislation by issue areas, and visually confirming whether
greater discretion is observed in areas that have been considered more
complex. Franchino (2001: 20) also attempts to develop direct measures or 'reasonable proxies for complexity that can be used across
policies and time'; specifically, he measures the number of major provisions in an act that call for 'detailed rules' to be adopted on the
assumption that such provisions reflect the complexity of the legislation to hand and hence the need for the Council to reduce its own
workload.[32] By contrast, Franchino's operationalization of legislative

procedures focuses exclusively on the use of QMV versus unanimous voting in the Council of Ministers, operationalized as a dichotomous or dummy variable; he does not consider the involvement of the EP, which he identifies as a topic for future research.

The results of Franchino's qualitative analysis provide some support for the two hypotheses. First, with regard to information intensity, Franchino notes a significant and positive correlation between the presence of provisions calling for 'detailed rules'—his measure of information intensity—and Commission discretion. However, we run into a common problem of such analyses here, in the sense that a call for 'detailed rules' is at best an imperfect measure of complexity and might indeed be considered by some as a measure of delegation—in which case the correlation between 'detailed rules' and discretion is unsurprising!

Second, with regard to decision rules, Franchino finds that the Council decision-making rule for a given piece of legislation correlates strongly with the extent of Commission discretion, so that a shift from unanimity to QMV increases the discretion index by an average of 2 per cent, which constitutes a substantial effect by comparison with the average discretion index of 4.4 per cent. The causes for this effect, however, are difficult to disentangle. On the one hand, as Franchino and others have pointed out, areas in which unanimity has been retained are presumably among the most sensitive for member governments, which are therefore, not surprisingly, reluctant to delegate powers to the Commission in those areas. In this view, the effect of the decision rule on Commission discretion may be spurious, and both variables may be the effect of a single cause, namely, the sensitivity of the issue area for the member governments. On the other hand, the decision rule may exert, *ceteris paribus*, an independent effect on Commission discretion, in so far as QMV makes it easier for the Council to agree to more extensive delegation and discretion that might otherwise have been blocked by a member-state veto. Franchino provides some anecdotal evidence (2001: 28) that the extension of QMV to new areas has resulted in moderate increases in Commission discretion in subsequent acts, which provides some support for the view that decision rules exert an independent effect on delegation decisions, but more work is needed to establish this point with certainty.

Analysis: Explaining Commission Delegation and Discretion in Primary and Secondary Legislation

To sum up the results of this chapter so far, the member governments of the European Union have delegated significant powers to the

Commission over the past five decades, including extensive horizontal powers of agenda setting, monitoring, and enforcement, and implementation in the treaties; limited issue-specific delegation in the treaties; and a much broader delegation of issue-specific executive powers in secondary legislation. In this subsection, I relate these findings to the hypotheses put forward in Chapter 1 regarding the role of credible commitments and informational intensity, respectively, as determinants of member-state delegation and Commission discretion. I look first at the three broad functions delegated to the Commission in the treaties—monitoring and enforcement, agenda setting, and implementation—before turning to the issue-specific powers of implementation delegated to the Commission in primary and secondary legislation.

If we look first at the functions delegated to the Commission by the treaties, we find some support for Majone's (2001) and Moravcsik's (1998) claim that treaty-based delegation seems to have been designed largely to increase the credibility of member states' commitment to their European obligations rather than to provide expert information in areas of technical complexity and uncertainty. The clearest evidence of this is the Commission's extensive discretion to bring infringement proceedings against member governments for non-compliance with EC law. By contrast with its agenda-setting functions, which invariably require the consent of the Council, and its regulatory functions, where it is subject to active oversight and judicial review, the Commission enjoys extensive powers and broad discretion under Articles 226 and 227, which require neither oversight nor approval from EU member governments. The reasons for this are clear: in order to act as a credible enforcer, the Commission must be seen as independent of the demands and preferences of even the most powerful member governments, and this need for insulation and credibility is reflected in Article 226, which allows the Commission to initiate infringement proceedings on its own authority without seeking the prior approval of the Council.

The Commission's power to set the legislative agenda can be interpreted as motivated either by credible commitments or a by desire to take advantage of the Commission's technocratic expertise. Such an informational motive for agenda setting, however, would not have required the specific provision in the original Article 149 EEC (now Article 250 EC) allowing the Council to amend Commission proposals only by unanimity. The significance of this provision, moreover, was clear to the drafters of the EEC Treaty, according to Pierre Pescatore (1981: 169), a participant in the negotiations. Recent archival research by Tsebelis and Kreppel supports Pescatore's account; they note, for example, that Paul-Henri Spaak, who introduced the unanimity provision in Article 149 as chair of the committee that drafted the treaty, was aware of the power that it conveyed to the Commission. Similarly, Walter Hallstein, a German delegate in the negotiation and later first President of the EEC Commission, noted in 1958: 'proposals made by the Commission can only be amended by a unanimous decision of the Council, here it is interesting to note that the principle of unanimity works out to the advantage of the supranational element' (quoted in Tsebelis and Kreppel 1998: 59). There is, no doubt, a secondary informational component to the Commission's agenda-setting power, as the Commission might be expected to be uniquely aware of and sensitive to the concerns of all 15 member states; nevertheless, the bulk of the available evidence suggests that the original decision to delegate agenda-setting powers to the Commission and to protect its proposals with a formidable amendment rule was motivated by a desire by member governments to commit themselves to their joint supranational exercise by empowering a predictably supranationalist agenda setter. By the same token, however, their failure to do likewise in the second and third pillars suggests that the member governments, while desiring cooperation in the fields of foreign and security policy and justice and home affairs, are unwilling to delegate similar powers in these, more sensitive areas (see Chapter 4).

With regard to implementing and regulatory powers, finally, it is striking that the member governments did not allocate across-the-board regulatory powers to the Commission in the treaties. Instead, the member governments have delegated implementing powers to the Commission selectively by issue area, including both a very few treaty articles—for example, competition and external trade policies—and more extensive delegation in secondary legislation. The patterns of discretion in these areas suggest a mix of motives among member governments. Among the issue areas and functions delegated to the Commission in the Treaties, for example, three of the top four discretion scores are in the areas of competition and external trade policy, both of which are commonly recognized as imposing concentrated costs—typically on producers—in return for diffuse benefits, in the form of competitive markets and consumer choice; in these areas, therefore, delegation of extensive discretion to the Commission fits with Majone's predictions and with the experience of the United States, where competition and trade policies are typically delegated to the executive or to regulatory agencies with significant discretion allocated to each. Among the remaining issue-specific delegations, many of the Commission's powers combine a regulatory function with a monitoring and enforcement function in so far as the Commission is delegated the power to police member-state exemptions to common rules in the areas of the internal market, transport, agriculture, and EMU. Indeed, among the ten issue areas delegating powers in the treaty, only three appear not to fit the credible commitments criteria: the European Social Fund, which is administered by the Commission even though it distributes concentrated benefits to recipients; free movement of workers, where the Commission is authorized to draft implementing regulations on the conditions for individuals to remain in the member state where they work; and social policy, where the Commission has the rather modest power to authorize a nine-month extension in the deadline for negotiations among the social partners. In sum, with minor exceptions, the record of issue-specific delegation in the treaties also supports the claim that member states delegate powers to enhance the credibility of their commitments.

Delegation in secondary legislation, by contrast, displays greater variation in the issue areas delegated and in the apparent motivation of the delegators. With regard to the issue of credible commitments, member states have chosen to delegate extensive discretion to the Commission for commercial and competition policies in secondary as well as primary legislation—suggesting that ensuring the credibility of commitments is an ongoing consideration in secondary legislation as well as in the treaties. By contrast, and consistent with the credible commitments view, member states have refrained from any delegation at all in the vital area of taxation, where benefits as well as costs can be targeted with precision. However, as in Epstein and O'Halloran's study of the United States, the EU case also features extensive delegation to the Commission in other areas—most notably agriculture and fisheries—that are classic pork-barrel policies distributing concentrated benefits to well-mobilized constituencies. In such areas, member governments appear to be motivated primarily by a desire to reduce the workload of the Council and to increase the *speed and efficiency* of implementation, which is vital in the day-to-day management of such markets. Such concerns about the speed of decision-making play at best a minor role in most principal-agent models of decision-making; however, if we consider Epstein and O'Halloran's (1999*a*: 240) argument that the costs and benefits of delegation should be measured 'relative to next best feasible alternative', the concern for speed in the EU context is not a trivial one. As any student of EU policy-making is aware, the European legislative process can be painfully slow, requiring months or even years to reach a qualified majority or unanimous agreement in the Council of Ministers and, in certain issue areas, a majority in the European Parliament (Golub 1999). By contrast, delegation of executive powers to the Commission offers the prospect not only of credible commitment and Brussels-based expertise but also of speedy and efficient decision-making that would otherwise be impossible to achieve through the complex and super-majoritarian legislative procedures in place at the EU level.

II. Keeping a Watchful Eye on the Commission

The Design and Use of EU Control Mechanisms

As we have seen in the previous part of the chapter, member governments have delegated extensive regulatory powers to the Commission over the years, in both primary and especially secondary legislation. As we have also seen, however, such delegation typically comes with constraints attached, in the form of both oversight mechanisms and administrative procedures that limit the Commission's discretion in carrying out its executive powers. In the second part of the chapter, I focus in greater detail on the design of three particular control mechanisms: the appointment and dismissal of the Commission and its members, which has traditionally been the preserve of the member governments, albeit with a growing role for the European Parliament; the 'comitology' system of member-state committees as a method of 'police-patrol' oversight; and, finally, the use of administrative law and judicial review by the European Court of Justice as a means of 'fire-alarm' oversight. As in the first part of the chapter, my primary focus here is on the design of all three mechanisms as deliberate, carefully constructed mechanisms of member-government control over the Commission. As we shall see, member states' choices of control mechanisms have varied systematically both across issue areas—most notably in the widely varying use of different oversight procedures for different issue areas—and over time, as in the growing role of the EP in the nomination of the Commission.

Appointment, Censure, and the 'Parliamentarization' of the Commission

Perhaps the most obvious means by which principals may influence their agents lies in their ability to appoint, remove, and reappoint agency personnel. Simply put, the power of appointment should allow the principals to select agents whose preferences, they believe, will either approximate those of the median voter or produce the outcomes desired by the median voter (Crombez 1997*b*). By contrast, the power of removal and the possibility of reappointment allow the principals to structure the incentives of agents by threatening either removal from or non-reappointment to office. *Ceteris paribus*, principals' control over agents is greatest where principals directly appoint the agent; where terms of office are relatively short; where principals may remove errant agents with relative ease; and where the possibility of reappointment provides agents with an incentive to remain attentive to the preferences of principals. When delegating power to an agent, principals may vary any and all of these parameters in order to insulate the agent from political pressures or to keep the agent closely accountable, or somewhere in between.

In the case of the Commission, EU member governments have granted themselves the central role in the nomination and renomination of the College of Commissioners and its President, who currently serve five-year terms of office; but they have only a highly constrained prospect of removing individual Commissioners for serious misconduct, and are unable directly to dismiss the Commission as a whole from office during its five-year term. At the same time, however, the EU treaties have long provided the European Parliament with the power to dismiss the Commission as a body, and this 'negative' power has been supplemented in recent years by a positive EP role in the nomination of the Commission President and the formal approval of the full College. As a result of these changes, a growing number of analysts argue that the Commission has in effect become 'parliamentarized' through its responsibility to the EP, which can indeed be theorized as a co-principal of the Commission, alongside the member governments. Although the latter claim is certainly an overstatement, the procedures for nomination and removal of the Commission are of vital importance in any principal-agent relationship, and deserve further attention here.

Appointment of the Commission President and College
The EEC Treaty of 1957, like the Coal and Steel Treaty before it, sought to establish an independent, supranational Commission that would pursue the common European interest; hence the strong language discussed above regarding the independence of the Commission and its members. Nevertheless, as in any principal-agent relationship, EU member governments have attempted in the treaties to combine a general respect for the Commission's independence with specific provisions allowing member governments to shape Commission preferences and incentives through the processes of appointment and

reappointment. Under the terms of the EEC Treaty, both the College of Commissioners and its President were appointed for renewable, four-year terms through the unanimous agreement of the member governments (Article 214 EC, ex 158). In practice, this Treaty provision developed into a centralized procedure for the appointment of the President and a decentralized procedure for the appointment of the other members of the College. Typically, the process of nominating a new Commission begins with the nomination and unanimous appointment by the member governments of a candidate for the presidency. The Commission itself holds no agenda-setting power in this decision, which is taken entirely by the member governments and limited by unwritten norms in which the presidency alternates roughly between both large and small member states, and between the centre left and centre right on the European political spectrum. In effect, this procedure means that any candidate for the presidency has to meet with the approval of each and every member government—a demanding criterion, which led, for example, to the United Kingdom's highly publicized veto in 1994 of Jean-Luc Dehaene as the candidate to succeed Jacques Delors and the subsequent nomination of Jacques Santer as a compromise candidate.

Following the collective nomination of the President, individual Commissioners are nominated by the various member governments, with the larger member states—Britain, France, Germany, Italy, and Spain—nominating two Commissioners each, while the smaller member states nominate a single Commissioner each. Although the full Commission thus constituted requires the unanimous, collective approval of the member governments, in practice the nomination of individual Commissioners remains highly decentralized, and member governments generally defer to each other on the nomination of 'their' respective Commissioners. Furthermore, the difficult negotiations about the nomination and composition of the Commission at Amsterdam and later in the negotiation of the Treaty of Nice demonstrate clearly that the member governments value their ability to nominate 'their own' Commissioner, notwithstanding his or her nominal independence. Although member governments have undertaken in the treaties not to attempt to influence their respective Commissioners, it is often argued that Commissioners from individual states bring individual knowledge and expertise about the political conditions in their home countries. In addition, of course, all Commissioners are aware that a possible reappointment lies in the hands of their respective governments, and a substantial majority of all Commissioners are career politicians who may look forward to an eventual return to national political life, which gives them an additional incentive to remain sensitive to their own national—and party-political—settings.[33] As a result, many critics have argued that Commissioners face a tension between their national views and national political ties on the one hand, and their European vocation on the other hand, and might therefore be tempted to vote a 'national line' on sensitive issues.

Since the Maastricht and Amsterdam Treaties, the original nomination procedure has been substantially complicated, in two ways. First, the Treaty of Amsterdam featured a substantial increase in the powers of the Commission President, who had previously served as a 'first among equals' in a collegiate institution in which all decisions were taken by majority vote. In practice, the power of the presidency had grown incrementally over the years, in part through the personal practices of strong leaders such as Roy Jenkins (1977–81) and Jacques Delors (1985–94), and in part through institutional reforms which gave the Commission President a seat at international forums such as the European Council and the Group of Eight (G8) summits. The Treaty of Amsterdam codified the leadership role of the President, specifying that 'The Commission shall work under the political guidance of its President' (Article 219 EC) and that member governments shall henceforth nominate their candidates for the Commission 'by common accord with the nominee for President'. Although the Treaty is vague on the procedure to be followed when a member-state nominee is rejected by the nominee for President, this provision provides in principle a new limitation on the right of member government to name 'their' Commissioners.

Second, and more importantly, the member governments agreed in Maastricht and Amsterdam to include the European Parliament in the procedures for the appointment of the President and of the full Commission, which now serves a five-year term aligned with that the EP. In the first stage of the process, member governments once again nominate a candidate for President, who must then, in a new procedure, be approved by the Parliament.[34] In the second stage, the member governments nominate their individual Commission candidates, and the full body is then subject to an approval vote by the Parliament before taking office. In practice, the European Parliament has exploited these new appointment powers aggressively, amending its internal rules of procedure and holding Senate-style confirmation hearings for individual nominees to the Commission despite the lack of any mention of such hearings in the treaties. In July 1994, during its first use of its Maastricht-based powers, the Parliament only narrowly approved the member-states' nomination of Jacques Santer by a vote of 260 to 238 with 23 abstentions. Subsequently, the relevant Parliamentary committees held extensive and widely publicized hearings with the individual nominees, criticizing five of them publicly on various grounds and winning additional assurances from Santer on several points before eventually approving the new Commission (Jacobs 1999: 7–9).

Some observers have interpreted the Parliament's new role in the appointment of the Commission as the first step toward the parliamentarization of Europe, in which a 'political' Commission would be appointed by and responsible to a majority in the European Parliament. However, as Hix and Gabel (1998) point out, such an interpretation overstates the role of the EP, in two ways. First, by comparison with a national parliamentary system, in which a parliamentary majority can select a prime minister without interference from any other body, at the EU level the Parliament is limited to casting an up-or-down vote on a candidate proposed by the Council of Ministers. Second, Hix and Gabel demonstrate that the voting behaviour of Members of the European Parliament (MEPs) in the Santer investiture vote was significantly influenced, not only by their party group within the EP, but also by members' *national* parties, with a number of MEPs breaking from their party group to vote in favour of Santer under pressure from their own national governments. Nevertheless, although it clearly falls short of a full parliamentary system, the investiture process does provide the EP with power of assent over the choice of the Commission President, and constrains the range of choice for the Council's nomination and hence the endogenous preferences of any incoming Commission.

The European Parliament's Power of Censure

Because the Commission was intended to be independent in its duties, the drafters of the EEC Treaty agreed that the member governments could dismiss neither the Commission nor its President during its term of office. Article 216 (ex 166) EC does allow for the 'compulsory retirement' of individual Commissioners, but only if that Commissioner 'no longer fulfils the conditions required for the conduct of his duties or if he has been guilty of serious misconduct', and only through a decision of the European Court of Justice after an application from the Council or the Commission. In practice, this procedure has been used only once, to remove a Commissioner who had fallen into a coma and was no longer capable of fulfilling his duties.

However, while the member governments have not assigned themselves the right to dismiss the Commission, the original EEC Treaty *did* provide that the European Parliament could, by a two-thirds majority of the votes cast representing an absolute majority of its members, adopt a motion of censure that would require the Commission to resign as a body. Although arguably the Parliament's most important power vis-à-vis the Commission, this provision has never been used, for several reasons. First, the Parliament's power to censure the Commission was traditionally a negative one in that the appointment of a replacement Commission was, until the mid-1990s, left entirely to the member governments, who could have responded by reappointing the same Commission or one further away from the preferences of the Parliament as a whole. In addition, the Parliament and the Commission are often seen as allies in the process of European integration against an intergovernmental Council, and hence the Parliament should normally have little incentive to undermine the Commission through a vote of censure (Hix 1999*a*: 47).

During the 1990s, however, the Parliament became much more aggressive in asserting its powers of censure over the Commission, in part because the new appointment procedures give the EP a role in the nomination of any possible replacement, and in part because the issue of corruption and mismanagement emerged as a salient issue-dimension, cutting across the integration dimension and separating the EP from the Commission. More precisely, the European Parliament repeatedly threatened to censure the Santer Commission during 1998 and 1999, *not* over its activism in the cause of European integration but rather because of mounting evidence of possible mismanagement and corruption within the Commission. The Commission's so-called management deficit—the gap between the Commission's workload and its administrative resources—had long been clear to both practitioners and scholars (Metcalfe 1992; 2000; Laffan 1997*b*). As Metcalfe (2000: 824) points out:

There is a structural bias towards increasing demands on the system without any concomitant increase in management capacities. A combination of factors operating within the EU's institutional framework creates political incentives to take on more tasks while imposing constraints on the acquisition and development of capacities for managing them effectively. In the Council, political decision-makers too readily assume the existence of management capacities and governance structures to implement procedures or dodge the difficult issues about who should provide them. The Commission has been more interested in staking out new territorial claims than insisting on the resources for discharging responsibilities effectively.

In addition to these general concerns about a management deficit, more serious concerns had arisen during the 1990s regarding fraud and mismanagement of Community finances—most notably in the annual reports of the European Court of Auditors, which singled out cases of fraud in the Community's tourism programme as well as lax accounting in the European Community Humanitarian Office (ECHO). These concerns came to a head in early 1999, when several party groups in the European Parliament, in response to increasing reports of fraud and nepotism, scheduled a motion of censure against the Santer Commission. Although the motion failed by a vote of 232 to 293 with 27 abstentions, the Santer Commission was forced to agree to the creation of an ad hoc Committee of Independent Experts (CIE) to investigate claims of mismanagement, fraud, and nepotism in the Commission.[35] Less than two months later, on 15 March, the Committee issued its first report, which did not find any evidence of fraud among the Commissioners themselves, but cited multiple instances of mismanagement in various EU spending programmes as well as a general lack of responsibility among both the services and the Commissioners to whom they were nominally accountable. The details of the Committee's report are beyond the scope of this chapter,[36] but it seemed clear that the Parliament was headed for a vote of censure, and the Santer Commission, after a long and reportedly bitter meeting, offered its collective resignation the next day.

Following the resignation of the Santer Commission, the European Council promptly agreed on 24 March 1999 to nominate Romano Prodi, the former Italian Socialist Prime Minister, as his successor. With a strong European reputation, and having made explicit promises to undertake extensive internal reforms of the Commission and strengthen its links with the EP, Prodi was approved less than two months later on 5 May by a large majority in Parliament, and subsequently took office with his new team of Commissioners in September 1999. In light of the circumstances of his appointment, Prodi has understandably placed great emphasis on reforming the management of the Commission, adopting a new Code of Conduct for Commissioners, supervising the establishment of a new in-house anti-fraud unit (OLAF), and naming returning Commissioner Neil Kinnock as Vice-President for Reform. Since then, the Commission has undertaken a major reform initiative, beginning with the publication of a White Paper titled *Reforming the Commission* in January 2000, and continuing with a process of management and staff reform.[37]

Following the resignation of the Santer Commission, many observers, including most of the EP's leadership, once again claimed that the balance of power between the Commission and the Parliament had shifted decisively, resulting in a 'parliamentarization' of the Commission, which, like a continental European government, now requires a majority vote in order to take office, and serves at the pleasure of a Parliament which can remove it from power at will. However, as Simon Hix (1999*a*: 47) argues, the comparison with national parliamentary systems remains overdrawn:

The Maastricht and Amsterdam Treaties injected an element of parliamentary government by requiring the Commission to have the support of a majority in the EP before taking office; and the right of censure allows the EP to withdraw this support. However, in the process of selecting the Commission president, the member governments are the equivalent of a presidential 'electoral college,' over which the EP can exercise only a veto. The EP cannot propose its own candidate. And, once invested, the Commission does not really require a 'working majority' in the EP. The right of censure is only a 'safety valve,' to be used in the event of serious political or administrative failure by the Commission.

Thus, while the increasing powers of the EP have acted as a growing constraint upon the Commission, the primary principals of the Commission remain the EU member governments, who control the initial delegation of powers to the Commission through the adoption and amendment of treaties, and who continue to play the dominant role in the appointment of the Commission President and 'their' individual Commissioners.

The Politics of Oversight: 'Comitology' as Police-Patrols

In the United States, police-patrol oversight of the bureaucracy is provided primarily by Congressional committees and subcommittees, which receive reports and hold frequent hearings to monitor the behaviour of independent regulatory agencies. In the EU, an equivalent role is played by 'comitology' committees of member-state representatives, which 'assist' or 'supervise' the Commission in its implementation of EC legislation. According to the British House of Lords (1999: para. 2),

'Comitology' is established Community shorthand for the system of procedures involving committees, made up of representatives from Member States and chaired by the Commission, whereby the Member States can exercise some control over the implementing powers delegated to the Commission by the Council.

This definition is clearly consistent with the principal-agent view of comitology as a *control mechanism* designed by member-state principals to supervise their supranational agent—the Commission—in its executive duties. In this view, member government preferences are assumed to be exogenous to the integration process, the aim of comitology is control, and the rules governing a committee *matter* in determining the discretion of the Commission in a given issue area. This approach has been disputed, however, by constructivist and sociological institutionalist scholars such as Joerges and Neyer (1997*a*, *b*), who argue that comitology committees provide a forum in which national and supranational experts meet and *deliberate* in a search for the best or most efficient solutions to common policy problems. In this view, comitology is an arena not for hardball intergovernmental bargaining but rather for a technocratic version of deliberative democracy in which informal norms, deliberation, good arguments, and consensus matter more than formal voting rules, which are rarely invoked. In this section of the chapter, therefore, I review the comitology system as it has evolved over the past four decades, summarize briefly the alternative hypotheses put forward by sociological institutionalists, and present evidence supporting the view that member governments do indeed design and calibrate the choice of comitology committees as a means of control over the Commission.

The Evolution of Comitology, 1962–1999
The origins of comitology can be traced to the early 1960s, when the Council of Ministers, in a 1962 Regulation, delegated to the Commission the power to manage the organization of markets for various agricultural products. According to Christoph Bertram (1967–8: 247–9), the Commission had initially proposed in 1961 that it should manage the market organizations for the various products covered in the regulation, but a majority of the member states 'felt that the powers delegated to the Commission were too extensive and that national administrations would have too little opportunity to influence the decision-making', and the French delegation therefore proposed the creation of mixed bodies of Commission and member-state representatives for the purpose. A compromise was then proposed by the Commission by which the Commission would be obliged to submit all of its decisions under the Regulation to a special committee of member-state representatives, who were authorized to vote on the measure by qualified majority vote. If a qualified majority voted *against* a decision, that decision would then be forwarded for consideration by the Council of Ministers, which could take a different decision by qualified majority; in the absence of such a negative vote, the Commission's decision would stand (Vos 1997: 211). Following the creation of this first 'management committee', the same formula

was repeated in other Council regulations, which delegated implementing powers to the Commission on similar terms.

In 1968, the management committee procedure was followed by a second and more restrictive 'regulatory committee' procedure, in which Commission proposals in areas such as customs cooperation or health and safety would again be scrutinized by committees of member-state representatives; however, by contrast with the management procedure where a qualified majority vote would be required to *reject* the measure and send it to the Council, in regulatory committees a qualified majority in favour of the proposal would be required to *accept* the measure, failing which it would be sent to the Council. Later still, the Council developed a third and less restrictive type of committee, the 'advisory committee', which the Commission was obliged to consult but without any requirement to follow the committee's advice.[38] By 1968, the European Parliament's Legal Affairs Committee had identified the now-familiar classification of advisory, management, and regulatory committees, and in 1970 the European Court of Justice, in its *Köster* ruling, affirmed the legality of Council delegation to the Commission and of the comitology system in general.[39]

During the two decades between the early 1960s and the 1986 signature of the Single European Act, the number and type of 'comitology' committees increased drastically as the Council of Ministers chose to delegate ever-greater implementing powers to the Commission, accompanied in each case by a specific committee of member-state representatives, but without any overarching rules or structure. The adoption of the Single European Act of 1986, and its accompanying plan for the completion of the internal market by the end of 1992, however, forced the issue of the Commission's implementing powers to the fore. Faced with a self-imposed deadline for the completion of the internal market, member governments agreed that the Council of Ministers would henceforth be required to delegate additional implementing powers to the Commission, and that these powers should be regulated by a more systematic set of comitology procedures than those which had grown incrementally over the previous two decades. Accordingly, the member governments agreed to add a new paragraph to Article 202 (ex Art. 145) EC, which called on the Council to:

confer upon the Commission, in the acts which the Council adopts, powers for the implementation of the rules which the Council lays down. The Council may also impose certain requirements in respect of these powers. The Council may also reserve the right, in specific cases, to exercise directly implementing powers itself. The procedures referred to above must be consonant with the principles and rules to be laid down in advance by the Council, acting unanimously on a proposal from the Commission and after obtaining the Opinion of the European Parliament.

The Single European Act, in other words, established the general principle that the member governments in the Council would resort to delegation of implementing powers to the Commission, but it also specified that these powers would be subject to some sort of comitology; that the Council could 'in specific cases' retain implementing powers to itself; and that the Council would agree unanimously—and with only a consultation role for the European Parliament—on a new and systematic framework for comitology committees. In addition, the member governments appended to the Treaty a Declaration (No. 1) to the effect that the Council, 'in the interests of speed and efficiency in the decision-making process', would give 'a predominant place' to the Advisory Committee procedure for internal market legislation, in order to expedite the adoption of the 1992 programme.[40]

The Council Decision of 13 July 1987 provided for the first time for overarching rules concerning the types of comitology committees and the rules governing their operations.[41] In its original proposal, the Commission had proposed a relatively simple scheme in which advisory committees would constitute the most common committee type, with a secondary role for management committees.[42] The European Parliament, in its Opinion, proposed several major changes to the Commission's draft Decision, including the elimination of the most binding regulatory committee procedure and new provisions that would increase the role of the Parliament by requiring the Commission to forward draft implementing measures to the EP as well as to the relevant committee.[43]

The Council, however, rejected the Parliament's amendments in favour of a structure that was more complex and more restrictive than the Commission's original proposal, in three ways. First, the Council's final Decision retained the Commission's three basic committee types—advisory, management, and regulatory—but introduced the so-called 'a' and 'b' variants into both the management and regulatory committee procedures, including the controversial 'safety net' procedure (IIIb) that would allow the Council to overturn a Commission decision by simple majority without putting an alternative policy in its place. Second, the Council Decision introduced two variants of a 'safeguard procedure', which is used in specific cases where the Commission has been allocated powers to adopt temporary safeguard measures (primarily in international trade) and whereby a single member state can call for a Commission decision to be examined by the Council. Third and finally, the final Decision included a provision allowing the Council to retain implementing responsibilities for itself in certain circumstances; such a possibility had been implied by the new Article 145 but left out of the Commission's draft proposal. The resulting committee procedures, and the rules specific to each, are summarized in Table 2.4, adapted from Hix (1999*a*).

TABLE 2.4. *Comitology procedures under the Council Decision of July 1987*

Procedure	Operation of the procedure*
Advisory committees Procedure I	The Commission must take the 'utmost account' of the Committee's opinion, but the Commission is free to enact the measure regardless of that opinion.
Management committees	The Commission can enact the measures unless the Committee opposes the measures by QMV, in which case the matter is referred to the Council, and either:
Procedure IIa	the Commission may enact the measures, but the Council has one month to annul or modify them by QMV; or
Procedure IIb	the Commission must defer enactment of the measures until the Council either rejects or modifies them by QMV, or fails to act within three months.
Regulatory committees	The Commission can enact the measures only if the committee supports the measures by QMV; otherwise, the matter is referred to the Council, and in a set time period either:
Procedure IIIa	'net' or filet procedure: the Council can reject the measures by QMV or modify them by unanimity, but the Commission can enact the measures if the Council approves them by QMV or fails to act; or
Procedure IIIb	'safety-net' or contre-filet procedure: the Council can reject the measures by simple majority or modify them by

Table 2.4. Continued

Procedure	Operation of the procedure*
	unanimity, but the Commission can enact the measures if the Council approves them by simple majority or fails to act.
Safeguard measures	The Commission must notify the Council of the proposed safeguard measures before acting, after which either:
Procedure IVa	the Council may reject or modify the measures by QMV, but the Commission can enact the measures if the Council fails to act in a set time period; or
Procedure IVb	the Council may confirm, amend, or reject the measures by simple majority, and the measures are deemed revoked if the Council fails to act in a set time period.
The Council itself 'Procedure V'	In special cases, the Council reserves the right to exercise direct implementing powers itself.

* In Procedures I–IIIb, the Commission must consult the relevant committee of national experts on the proposed implementation measures; Procedure IV features a Commission proposal directly to the Council; while in Procedure V the Council retains sole responsibility for implementation.

Source: Adapted from Hix (1999*a*: 43).

Between 1987 and 1999, the Comitology Decision structured legislative choices about the delegation of powers to the Commission and the committee structures established to 'assist and support' the Commission in the exercise of its implementing powers. Nevertheless, the comitology system established in the 1987 Decision was not without its detractors, both political and academic, who charged that the 1987 comitology system represented a step backwards from the previous system in that it formally introduced a new procedure (IIIb) that could result in a Council veto and paralysis in the implementation of EC law. Other critics pointed out that comitology committees generally operated behind closed doors and that comitology fared poorly in terms of the normative criteria of transparency, openness, and democratic accountability. In addition, the 1987 Decision provided no guidance on the selection of committee type for a given piece of legislation, which was decided in practice by legislative bargaining among the Commission, the member governments in the Council, and, in so far as it participated in the legislative process, the European Parliament.

Perhaps the most vehement and persistent critic of comitology, however, has been the European Parliament, which has engaged in a long inter-institutional debate with the Council about the design and choice of comitology committees. The EP's objections, as Hix (2000: 70) points out, are twofold. First, the treaties make the Commission formally responsible to the Parliament, which is the only body that can dismiss a Commission in office; comitology committees, however, render the Commission answerable not to the Parliament, which is excluded, but to a committee of member-state representatives, thus weakening democratic control of the implementation process. Parliament has therefore consistently advocated the adoption of the less constraining advisory committee procedure, and argued for the abolition of the regulatory procedure. Second, and more fundamentally, 'the EP should have equal rights with the Council to review, approve and veto proposed implementation measures in those areas where it shares legislative authority with the Council' (Hix 2000: 70). The Parliament has therefore consistently condemned the 1987 Decision, which was adopted under Article 145 as a *Council* Decision and which provided Parliament with no institutional role in the comitology process.

Furthermore, despite being excluded from the actual adoption of the Decision, Parliament has pursued a more or less consistent campaign against comitology, using the legal, budgetary, and political resources at its disposal (Bradley 1997: 230). On the legal front, Parliament attempted in 1988 to challenge the legality of the Decision before the Court of Justice, only to be denied standing by the Court.[44] On the budgetary front, Parliament has frequently used its power to discharge the Union budget to force the Commission to produce information about the number and workings of comitology committees—a strategy that has enjoyed some limited success in terms of transparency but has not produced any change in the fundamental structure of the system (Bradley 1997: 240–3).

The Parliament has therefore joined an ongoing political battle with the other EU institutions, using its legislative powers to press for greater information and greater influence in the comitology process. In 1988, for example, EP President Lord Plumb agreed in an exchange of letters with Commission President Jacques Delors that the Commission would as a matter of practice forward draft implementing measures to the Parliament 'for information' despite the lack of any requirement to do so in the Decision. Even after the Plumb-Delors agreement, however, the Parliament possessed no *rights* within the comitology procedure, and could not influence the final outcome of comitology proceedings.

Finally, the Parliament's displeasure with comitology was amplified further after the entry into force of the Treaty of Maastricht, which made the Parliament a co-legislator with the Council in many issue areas but retained the Council's monopoly on the implementation process through comitology. In 1993, the inter-institutional dispute came to a head when the Parliament used its new powers under the co-decision procedure to veto a draft Directive on the liberalization of telecommunications, primarily because of its dissatisfaction with the comitology provisions. Soon after, the Commission, the Council, and the Parliament signed a new inter-institutional agreement, the so-called *modus vivendi*, which went some way towards satisfying the Parliament's demands. Under this 1994 agreement, the Commission agreed to send draft implementing measures to the European Parliament and inform the Parliament when the comitology commit-tee had given an adverse opinion, and the Commission and Council agreed to take account 'as far as possible' of the Parliament's opinions in such cases. In addition, the Council also agreed that the question of comitology would be referred to the 1996 Intergovernmental Conference, and the Commission accordingly proposed a revision of Article 145 EC. The member governments, however, resisted adopt-ing any Treaty amendments on comitology, and instead annexed Declaration 31 to the Amsterdam Treaty calling on the Commission to submit a new draft Decision by the end of 1999.[45]

Accordingly, the Commission proposed in July 1998 a new draft Decision, which would retain the overall structure of the comitology system—judged to be working satisfactorily by both the Commission and most member states—but make four basic changes to it. The basic thrust of these four reforms were retained by the Council in its June 1999 Decision, but with significant amendments.[46] First, by contrast with the case-by-case selection of committee types under the 1987 Decision, the 1999 Decision included new criteria to guide the choice of implementing procedures, under which the management procedure was to be used for the implementation of the common agricultural and fisheries policies, and more generally for programmes with substan-tial budgetary implications; the regulatory committee procedure was used for measures 'designed to apply essential provisions of basic instruments' particularly in the areas of health and safety; and the advisory committee procedure 'shall be used in any case in which it is considered to be the most appropriate'. Although this provision was intended to provide general guidance in the choice of procedures and minimize the intergovernmental and inter-institutional horse-trading that had previously taken place in comitology choices, the Council nevertheless amended the Commission's proposal to note that 'such criteria are of a non-binding nature', leaving the Council with a continuing margin of discretion in the choice of procedures.[47]

Second, the Commission proposed to simplify the procedures by removing the variants from the management, regulatory, and safeguard procedures, and in particular the *contre-filet* or 'safety-net' variants to which the Commission had long objected. Here again, the Council agreed to the overall thrust of the Commission's proposals, while making substantive as well as stylistic changes to the Commission's draft. With regard to the management committee procedure, the new Decision effectively removes variant IIb, under which the Commission was required to defer application of the measure pending a Council decision, in favour of a single procedure whereby the Commission *may* defer application for up to three months; otherwise, the voting rules in both the committee and the Council remain unchanged from the old management committee procedure.

With regard to the regulatory committee procedure, the Commission presented a simplified single procedure whereby, if the committee failed to support the Commission's proposed measures, the Commission would withdraw the measure and submit a legislative proposal under the relevant treaty article. In negotiations, however, member governments objected to the Commission's proposal, which essentially would force the committee to choose between the Commission's proposal on the one hand and an extended legislative process involving long delays and, in some cases, co-decision with the EP on the other. During the negotiations, therefore, the German Presidency proposed a compromise procedure in which a failure to agree in the committee would result in a reference to the Council of Ministers, which would have three months to either (1) endorse the measures by QMV, after which the measures would be adopted; (2) fail to act, in which case the Commission would adopt the measures; or (3) oppose the measures by QMV, in which case the Commission would re-examine the measures and re-submit them to the committee, with or without amendments, or as a legislative proposal. In this sense, the German Presidency draft was similar to the safety net of the old variant IIIb, except that the Council would need a qualified rather a simple majority vote to block a Commission decision. Precisely for this reason, Denmark, Portugal, and Spain initially refused to approve the compromise, insisting that the Council should be able to block Commission decisions by simple majority in the areas of the environment, social policy, and health. The deadlock was finally broken when the Commission agreed to issue a declaration undertaking in 'particularly sensitive sectors' not to go against 'any predominant position which might emerge within the Council against the appropriateness of an implementing measure'.[48] The new procedures are summarized in Table 2.5.

TABLE 2.5. *Comitology procedures under the Council Decision of June 1999*

Procedure	Operation of the procedure*
Advisory Committees Procedure I	Unchanged.
Management Committees	Variants removed.
Procedure II	The Commission can enact the measures unless the Committee opposes the measures by QMV, in which case the Commission may, but need not, defer the measures for up to three months, during which the Council may take a different decision by QMV
Regulatory Committees	Variants removed.
Procedure III	The Commission can enact the measures only if the committee supports the measures by QMV, otherwise the Commission submits a proposal to the Council, which may act by QMV within a period not to exceed three months. If after three months the Council has not neither adopted nor opposed the proposed implementing act, it shall be adopted by the Commission. However, if the Council indicates by QMV that it opposes the proposal, the Commission may submit an amended proposal to the Council, re-submit its original proposal, or present a legislative proposal on the basis of the Treaty.

TABLE 2.5. *Continued*

Safeguard measures Procedure IV	Variants removed.
	The Commission must notify the Council of the proposed safeguard measures before acting, after which the Council may take a different decision by QMV within a set time period. Alternatively, however, it may be stipulated in the basic instrument that the Council may, by QMV, confirm, amend or revoke the decision, and that, if the Council fails to take a decision, the decision of the Commission 'is deemed to be revoked'.
The Council itself 'Procedure V'	In 'specific and substantiated' cases, the Council reserves the right to exercise direct implementing powers itself.

Source: Council Decision 1999/468/EC of 28 June 1999 laying down the procedures for the exercise of implementing powers conferred upon the Commission.
Official Journal L 184/23–26, 1999.

As a third element in its draft Decision, the Commission proposed
various mechanisms to inform the European Parliament of the activities
of comitology committees, including the transmission of the
Commission's draft decisions, meeting agendas, and other information
to the Parliament, which also received a formal but non-binding right
to express its views within the regulatory committee process and in
cases where it considered that the Commission decision exceeded the
implementing powers provided for in the delegating legislation: the
Commission would then be obliged to re-examine its decision, but need
not follow Parliament's wishes. In essence, the new Decision institutionalized many of the provisions of the 1994 *modus vivendi*, but it fell
short of meeting the Parliament's more radical demands such as those
for the elimination of the regulatory committee procedure and for a
formal right to 'call back' Commission proposals of which it disapproves.
    Fourth, the new Decision contained a number of measures to
increase the transparency of the comitology process for the general
public as well as the Parliament. In addition to the requirement to
transmit certain documents to the EP, Article 7 of the Decision specified that 'the principles and conditions on public access to documents
applicable to the Commission shall apply to the committees'. It also
required the Commission to publish in the *Official Journal*, within

six months of the entry into force of the Decision, a complete list of all comitology committees, to be followed by an annual report on the workings of committees. Finally, references to all the documents forwarded to the Parliament were to be made public in a register to be set up by the Commission in 2001.[49]

In short, the 1999 Council Decision retained the basic structure of the existing comitology system, while providing non-binding criteria for committee selection, reducing the restrictive impact of the 'b' variants of the management and regulatory committees, institutionalizing the consultative role of the European Parliament, and encouraging a limited opening of comitology meetings through new transparency provisions. Nevertheless, the choice of comitology procedures has remained a contentious issue in the adoption of new legislation since the 1999 Decision, and the problems of accountability and transparency have not been resolved to the satisfaction of the system's critics.

Two Images of Comitology

Despite its complexity and obscurity, comitology has attracted increasing attention in recent years from social scientists of all stripes, who have been quick to identify these committees as a distinctive and increasingly important feature of governance in the Union.[50] However, while the various approaches to comitology agree on its general importance in EU governance, they differ starkly in their interpretation of it, with rational choice theorists modelling comitology as a control mechanism used by member states to finely calibrate the extent of Commission autonomy, and sociological institutionalist and constructivist theorists arguing that, far from being a oversight mechanism for control-minded member governments, comitology committees work in practice as a forum for depoliticized, deliberative decision-making in which Commission and member-state representatives work side by side in search of optimal solutions to the challenges of European governance.

The rationalist approach. The rational-choice approach to comitology has already been outlined in Chapter 1, and requires little elaboration here. As we have seen in the previous subsection, the choice of comitology procedures has clear implications for Commission autonomy and member-state control. In a path-breaking set of articles, Steunenberg, Koboldt, and Schmidtchen (1996; 1997) analyse the various procedures established by the 1987 Comitology Decision, demonstrating formally that the Commission enjoys at least some discretion in all variants of comitology, as in each case it can choose its own ideal point from among the set of decisions that will not be reported from the committee to the Council and amended or blocked in the Council. However, the authors also demonstrate that, across a range of assumptions about the preferences of the actors, the Commission enjoys the greatest influence under the advisory committee procedure, in which it is essentially unconstrained; followed by both versions of the management committee, where its decisions can be overturned only by qualified majorities in the committee and the Council; followed in turn by the regulatory (a) procedure, where a blocking minority in the committee can secure a reference to the Council, which can take a different decision by QMV, and finally the regulatory (b) procedure, where the Council need not take a decision by qualified majority but may simply opt to reject the Commission decision and retain the status quo by a simple majority. For this reason, the authors suggest, the Commission should have the following preference ordering:

Advisory committee > management committee > regulatory committee (a) > regulatory committee (b)

This is a testable hypothesis, to which we shall return below.

An additional strand of the rational choice literature has focused on the role of the European Parliament in the comitology process and on the institutional preferences of the Parliament over different types of comitology committees. Once again, Steunenberg, Koboldt, and Schmidtchen (1996; 1997) have modelled various alternative comitology procedures, assessing ways in which the EP might be integrated into existing comitology procedures and the resulting effects of Commission autonomy; while Franchino (2000a, b) has incorporated the Parliament into formal models of institutional choice, deriving the Parliament's preferences over comitology procedures. All else equal, Franchino suggests, the EP should prefer a formal role in the comitology process rather than being left out of comitology as in the 1987 Decision. Franchino also suggests that, to the extent that the EP and the Commission share similar preferences vis-à-vis the Council, the former should be in favour of non-restrictive comitology that leaves the Commission relatively unfettered by the preferences of the member governments. As we shall see, both predictions are strongly supported by EP documents, resolutions, and behaviour over the past several decades.

Sociological institutionalism and constructivism. An alternative image of comitology, derived largely from the sociological institutionalist approach presented in Chapter 1, has been put forward Joerges and Neyer (1997a, b), for whom comitology is not primarily an instrument of member-state control but a forum for a 'deliberative supranationalism', a style of decision-making which they put forward both as a normative ideal by which to judge EU governance and as an empirically accurate description of the workings of comitology in the field of food-stuffs regulation.[51] Comitology has indeed been intentionally designed by member states, Joerges and Neyer argue, and its committees do indeed guarantee that constitutionally designated and nationally legitimate member governments take a seat at the collective suprana-tional table where EC regulations are adopted and implemented.[52]

From this starting point, however, Joerges and Neyer—in common with other constructivist and sociological institutionalist analysts of EU institutions—argue that the actual *working* of comitology departs substantially from the predictions of rational-choice models and of the actors who created them. Indeed, they suggest that rationalist approaches 'lack the conceptual space' for theorizing about the aspect of comitology that they consider to be central, namely, 'the interest of actors involved in finding common solutions to common problems by means of deliberative interaction' (Joerges and Neyer 1997*b*: 618). Specifically, Joerges and Neyer distinguish between two distinct modes of interaction in forums such as comitology, namely, '*strategic bargaining* to maximize particular utilities at the expense of others and *deliberative problem-solving* to maximize collective utilities' (1997*b*: 618, emphasis added). While rational-choice approaches focus only on the first, strategic mode of interaction, Joerges and Neyer (1997*b*: 619) suggest that 'the relative intensity of both modes may vary' and that deliberative problem-solving is most likely under certain conditions, including:

. . . uncertainty about the distributive effects of certain policies, long-term interaction among delegates, as well as their mutual socialization into a com-munity with common problem definitions and collectively shared approaches to dealing them with. Under such conditions governments may be unaware of what their preferences are, or delegates, perceiving themselves as part of a transnational problem-solving community, may be able to change their gov-ernments' perceptions of interests or even simply bypass them.

These conditions, Joerges and Neyer acknowledge, are not always met, and governments often have clear perceptions of their own pref-erences and the distributional consequences of the policies being decided. However, in their study of foodstuffs regulation, they find that the importance of scientific discourse limits the ability of delega-tes to discuss distributional issues—particularly in scientific advisory committees—which in turn focuses debate and deliberation onto sci-entific questions. In addition, the authors point out, delegates not only meet regularly in comitology committees but often have also met as part of advisory committees and working groups involved in the adoption of the legislation in question—an ideal setting for long-term socialization into common European norms. In this way, the authors argue, comitology committees pass from being institutions for the strategic control of the Commission by governmental representatives to being forums for deliberative interaction among experts for whom issues of control and distribution, as well as the carefully contrived institutional rules of their respective committees, recede into the background in favour of a collective search for the technically best solution to a given policy problem.[53]

Joerges and Neyer present a sophisticated and internally consistent picture of comitology based on extensive empirical research including observation of comitology meetings, interviews, and a survey of Commission and member-state representatives in such committees. Some of their findings, moreover, dovetail with other studies of comitology, which also chronicle the extensive participation of individual delegates in multiple committees, the Commission's efforts to achieve broad consensus among delegates, and the rarity of voting and—even more so—sanctioning Commission behaviour. In its 1999 testimony to the British House of Lords, for example, the Commission indicated that only 1 per cent of all implementing regulations were referred from comitology committees to the Council, all under the regulatory procedure; and in most of these cases the reference resulted not from a negative vote but from the failure on the part of the committee to deliver any opinion on the Commission's proposal (House of Lords 1999: para. 44). Falke's (2000: 351) quantitative analysis of comitology in the area of agriculture reveals a similar trend, with only 17 negative opinions out of 59,188 decisions referred by the Commission to comitology committees—a ratio of one in 3,482![54]

Nevertheless, we should be wary of jettisoning the rational-choice account of comitology as a control mechanism too quickly, for three reasons. First, some of the evidence presented in Joerges and Neyer's own study (1997*a*: 280; 1997*b*: 617) suggests that the Commission does indeed play a forceful and consistent role as a corporate actor, bringing issues to a vote where consensus is out of reach and eliciting complaints from many member-state delegations.[55] Indeed, the tabular results of the authors' survey research (1997*a*: 280) reveal that seven of eleven member-state delegations characterize the Commission as acting in its 'own interests' in the Standing Committee on Foodstuffs, whereas only three delegations characterize the Commission as a neutral mediator. Questions to the delegations about the importance of formal rules reveal similarly mixed evidence, with seven delegations responding 'low', while four other delegations, including four of the six largest member states, consider procedural rules to have 'high', 'fairly high', or 'medium' importance. Finally, the miscellaneous-remarks column of their findings shows that three delegations consider the Commission 'too assertive' or 'too dominant', while another suggests that 'only IIIb [the most stringent form of regulatory committee] is acceptable', and another argues for 'No delegation of further competences to the Commission'. Taken as a whole, these findings suggest a comitology system in which deliberation may well take place but also one in which the Commission retains a distinct institutional role, and member governments remain acutely aware of the problem of control.

Second, even if we accept the authors' deliberative supranationalist reading of comitology in the foodstuffs sector, one might argue that this issue area is a most-likely case for deliberative interaction, given the heavy emphasis on science and risk assessment in the foodstuffs sector and the extensive use made not only of implementing committees but also of scientific advisory committees. In other issue areas, such as the implementation of the EU's structural funds, national delegates may have clear preferences over outcomes, feel free to discuss distributive questions, have little need to discuss scientific questions of risk assessment, and therefore focus more extensively on issues of control than Joerges and Neyer's foodstuffs regulators.

Third and perhaps most importantly, we should beware of reading too much into the generally consensual nature of committee decision-making and the infrequency with which committees vote at all, much less to overturn a Commission decision. As we have seen, students of US Congressional oversight committees have often noted the same characteristic feature of the oversight process, which they present as a result of the 'logic of anticipated reactions'. In the case of the EU, this effect is magnified further by the structure of comitology committees, which are invariably chaired by a Commission representative, who might be expected to call a vote only when he or she expected the Commission position to be endorsed by the committee; in this sense, the surprising statistic is not the low number of negative votes but the fact that the committee takes any negative votes at all!

Under these circumstances, how can we study comitology empirically in such a way that would allow us to distinguish and test among these two competing images? More specifically, how might we tell whether comitology committees are designed and used as control mechanisms in which formal rules determine the extent of Commission discretion, as I have hypothesized above, or rather as forums for deliberative supranationalism, as Joerges and Neyer suggest? This question, and my imperfect answer to it, are the subject of the next subsection.

Institutional Choice of Comitology: Empirical Evidence

In response to the problems of rational anticipation discussed above, students of regulatory agencies have pursued two distinct research strategies to test hypotheses about delegation and agency. The first and best established is the use of case studies and process-tracing, which would allow us to understand the respective preferences of actors such the Commission and the member governments, and to examine the process of committee decision-making in practice, in order to determine whether comitology committees are actually employed by member governments as control mechanisms vis-à-vis the Commission. Indeed, this is the approach that I adopt in the second part of this book examining the workings of three different types of committees.[56] As we shall see in Chapters 5 and 6, such case studies allow us to observe the ways in which the Commission attempts to pursue its preferences within the bounds of its statutory discretion and, conversely, the ways in which member governments use comitology committees and other control mechanisms to rein in Commission activism. Even carefully chosen and conducted case studies, however, inevitably capture only a fraction of the universe of cases.

A second approach to the study of comitology, therefore, consists of focusing not on the workings of comitology committees but on the choice of comitology procedures as an institutional choice for member governments and EU institutions. Specifically, and by contrast with sociological approaches, rational-choice approaches suggest that the choice of comitology procedures *matters* in shaping policy outcomes, and that the Commission, the Parliament, and member governments should have systematic preferences over the choice of committee type, which should in turn lead to distinct patterns of institutional choice. With regard to preferences, a rational choice analysis predicts that the Commission should systematically prefer the 'lighter' advisory procedure to the management procedure, and the management procedure to the most stringent regulatory procedure. The Parliament, by contrast, should have a strong preference to be formally included in the comitology procedure, from which it was formally frozen out by the 1987 Decision; the EP should also prefer less constraining regulatory procedures for the Commission if and in so far as its preferences are systematically closer to the Commission's than to the pivotal voter in the Council.

The Council, finally, should generally prefer more restrictive comitology than the Commission or the Parliament, but preferences within the Council should vary across member governments and issue areas as governments attempt to tailor comitology types so as to maximize their expected utility from the delegation decision. More specifically, rationalist approaches predict that member governments will delegate powers and allocate discretion to the Commission with precision, trading off their respective preferences for Commission expertise or credibility against their desire to retain control over Commission actions. By contrast, we would expect to see member governments *not* falling back on agreed-upon norms of what constitutes legitimate institutions in a given issue area, but rather balancing carefully the variable advantages of discretion and control decision by decision, both across and within issue areas.

In order to test these hypotheses about institutional preferences and the choice of comitology committees, I have drawn elsewhere (Pollack 2001) on three bodies of evidence: (1) quantitative data regarding the revealed preferences over comitology of the Commission, the Parliament, and the Council, respectively; (2) qualitative evidence regarding the preferences of the Commission, the EP, and member states drawn from primary sources; and (3) case studies of intergovernmental and inter-institutional negotiations over the choice of comitology, which corroborate the general preferences of the three sets of actors in specific legislative negotiations. I summarize these findings, very briefly, below.

Quantitative Evidence of Comitology Choices

In recent studies, both Rhys Dogan (1997; 2000) and Fabio Franchino (2000*a*) have collected extensive data about the comitology decisions taken by the Council—sometimes in cooperation or co-decision with the EP—across a broad range of issue areas. Dogan's work examines the 'revealed preferences' over comitology of the Commission, the Parliament, and the Council of Ministers, using a data-set of 4,601 pieces of secondary legislation adopted between July 1987 and July 1995, 908 of which (19.7 per cent) include some sort of comitology committee. Specifically, Dogan measures the comitology preferences of the various actors by examining (1) the types of comitology committee proposed by the Commission in its initial legislative proposals, (2) the committee type proposed by the EP in its amendments, and (3) the final decision, which is taken as a measure of Council preferences. Clearly, such measures capture not the sincere preferences of the actors but rather their negotiating positions in an inter-institutional bargaining process.[57] Nevertheless, Dogan's data are valuable for comparing the comitology choices advocated by each of the three actors, which are summarized for 371 pieces of legislation including new comitology procedures in Table 2.6.

Comparing the institutional positions of the three actors across the various comitology types, as well as the absence of committees in column 7, we see that the Commission and the Parliament have systematically proposed delegating the Commission greater discretion than the Council, in its final legislation, has been willing to accept. Thus, for example, the Commission has proposed advisory committees in 48 per cent of the proposals in Dogan's data-set, and the EP has proposed an even higher 52.7 per cent; in its final legislation, however, the Council has frequently tightened the Commission's proposed procedures, opting for advisory committees in only 23.2 per cent of the cases. At the opposite end of the spectrum, the Commission has proposed IIIb, the stricter version of the regulatory procedure, only 1.1 per cent of the time, and the Parliament not at all; yet the Council has opted for this type in 18.1 per cent of all legislation. Overall, Dogan's data on the relative preferences seems to support rational-choice predictions: the Commission generally prefers less constraining comitology measures, with the strong support of the European Parliament, while the Council systematically prefers greater levels of control through more restrictive comitology.

However, as Dogan himself notes, these data present some difficulties for rationalist predictions. The Commission, for example, does generally prefer more permissive comitology, as predicted, but it has also regularly proposed management and even regulatory committees in its 15.7 per cent and 23.6 per cent of its draft proposals, respectively. By contrast, the Parliament has been more likely than the Commission to insist on permissive comitology, proposing the advisory committee procedure more often, and the regulatory committee procedure less

TABLE 2.6. *Institutional comitology preferences: all new procedures*

Institution	I	IIa	IIb	IIIa	IIIb	No Comm.	Misc.	Total
Commission	177 (48.0)	39 (10.6)	19 (5.1)	83 (22.5)	4 (1.1)	45 (12.2)	2 (0.5)	369
EP	194 (52.7)	45 (12.2)	21 (5.7)	43 (11.7)	0	40 (10.9)	25 (6.8)	368
Council	86 (23.2)	48 (12.9)	38 (10.2)	132 (35.6)	67 (18.1)	0	0	371

Note: % figures are given in parentheses.

Source: Adapted from Dogan (2000: 53).

often, than the Commission. This anomaly, however, is troubling only if we take Dogan's data as a measure of sincere preferences by the Commission, the Parliament, and the Council. A Commission legislative proposal is *not* a sincere expression of preferences but rather a stage in a legislative process whereby the Commission frequently hopes to secure the rapid adoption of legislation with as few amendments as possible; this consideration is particularly salient where the Council votes by QMV since the insertion of a sincere comitology choice could endanger what might otherwise be a qualified majority in favour of the Commission's proposed legislation. For this reason, the Commission frequently anticipates the likely comitology choices of the Council, and incorporates these choices into its proposed legislation. Furthermore, such behaviour is decidedly 'rational' if we assume that the Commission's primary goal is the expansion of Community competence through new legislation, with permissive comitology as a secondary goal. Similar considerations apply to the Parliament, particularly in the consultation and cooperation procedures where the EP enjoys the relative luxury of expressing its sincere preferences, since its proposals enjoy no special status—unless endorsed by the Commission—and do not therefore endanger a fragile majority in the Council.

With regard to the final comitology types adopted in secondary legislation, Franchino (2000*a*) undertakes to explain the determinants of comitology choices using a database of 1,372 Directives adopted between 1987 and 1998. Furthermore, unlike Dogan, Franchino explicitly sets out to test rationalist hypotheses about the respective roles of (1) uncertainty, (2) the level of conflict among legislators, and (3) legislative procedure in the choice of comitology procedures. His key findings are threefold:

1. The inherent uncertainty associated with a given policy (measured as the word-count of the Directive in question) is significantly and positively correlated with the existence and stringency of *ex post* comitology controls. As Franchino admits, however, we should be cautious in interpreting this finding, since his use of word-count as a measure of uncertainty is open to question.

2. As predicted, the level of conflict between the Commission and Council (measured as the number of Council amendments to Commission proposals) and between the European Parliament and the Council (measured as the number of EP amendments rejected by the Council) correlates positively with the existence and stringency of *ex post* controls.

3. The legislative procedure—and in particular unanimous voting in the Council—correlates positively and strongly with the presence of more constraining comitology procedures, although the reasons for the correlation are unclear: the relationship between legislative procedure and comitology decisions may be direct in so far as unanimity allows reluctant member states to insist on more constraining comitology procedures, or spurious in so far as both the retention of unanimity and the selection of restrictive comitology procedures reflect the underlying conflict of preferences among member governments.[58]

In sum, Franchino's findings provide at least indirect support for the rational choice claims that comitology rules are drafted deliberately by member governments to constrain the Commission differentially across different pieces of legislation, and that the degree of constraint varies, at least in part, with the types of variables identified by principal-agent analysis. Similarly, Dogan's findings suggest that the Commission, the Parliament, and the Council show systematic differences in revealed preferences over comitology procedures, with the Parliament joining the Commission in its preference for lighter procedures, while the Council regularly, but not invariably, increases the restrictiveness of the procedures proposed by the Commission.

Revealed Preferences over Comitology: Qualitative Evidence

Nevertheless, these quantitative analyses leave some questions unanswered and perhaps some doubts about the quality of the proxies used to measure abstract concepts such as uncertainty and credible commitment. In this subsection, therefore, I draw on primary source documents from the Commission, the Parliament, and member governments, supplemented by interviews with key actors from each body, in order to determine the institutional preferences of all three actors in the comitology triangle, and assess the extent to which they match, and perhaps explain, the behaviour of each actor in Dogan's data-set.

Commission. In the case of the Commission, such a review of the qualitative evidence supports the view, derived both from theory and from the quantitative record of its legislative proposals, that the Commission consistently prefers less rather than more constraining comitology procedures. In the years immediately following the adoption of the 1987 Comitology Decision, the Commission frequently expressed dissatisfaction with the operation of the system, and most notably with the Council's relatively light use of the advisory committee procedure and its extensive use of the IIIb, or safety-net, procedure. In a 1989 report on the working of the Decision, the

Commission considered that 'the situation here is far from satisfactory'. Much of the Commission's ire focused on the use of the IIIb procedure. Specifically, the report argued,

The addition of the safety net (*'contrefilet'*) . . . represents a considerable restriction on the Commission's freedom of action and, consequently, on the scope of delegation. While the regulatory committee procedure (variant IIIa) allows the Commission to exercise its executive powers in the absence of a Council decision, the safety net (*'contrefilet'*) (variant IIIb) allows a simple majority of Member States to block a Commission decision . . . This is why the Commission and Parliament were firmly opposed to this procedure for reasons of institutional balance.

The Commission did admit, however, that 'in practice, the safety net . . . does not appear to have led to deadlock' (CEC 1989: 4). In addition to its concerns about the IIIb procedure, the Commission acidly pointed out that the member governments had manifestly ignored their own commitment, in the declaration attached to the SEA, to give precedence to the advisory committee procedure for internal market legislation adopted under Article 95 (ex 100a). Rather, the member governments had demonstrated a willingness to delegate functions in certain 'sensitive issue areas'—such as research, banking, the veterinary, food, and plant health sectors, and the environment—only if they could retain the safety-net of the IIIb procedure, while in other areas the Council refused to delegate to the Commission at all, preferring to retain implementing powers for itself (CEC 1989: 5–8).

In its day-to-day agenda-setting function, one participant pointed out, the Delors Commission made it a matter of 'dogma' to propose the advisory committee procedure wherever possible, although in areas where the Council had repeatedly adopted the management or regulatory (IIIa) procedures the Commission might anticipate this choice and propose those procedures as well; however, the Commission drew the line at proposing the IIIb procedure, to which it was opposed in principle.[59] This position led to frequent conflicts between the Commission and the Council, most notably when the Commission's refusal to accept a IIIb procedure endangered what would otherwise be a qualified majority in the Council. Faced with such a situation, the Commission would occasionally agree to accept more constraining comitology, including the IIIb procedure, in the second reading of legislation 'where the decision was important and a qualified majority was the only possibility' (CEC 1989: 7).[60] In other words, when the Commission's preference for less restrictive comitology conflicts with its aim of securing the adoption of new legislation by qualified majority, the Commission has demonstrated a willingness to compromise on the former to secure the latter.

By contrast with Delors, the Santer and Prodi Commissions have placed less emphasis on comitology in their inter-institutional relations with the EP and the Council. In its contribution to the 1996 intergovernmental conference, for example, the Santer Commission repeated its principled opposition to the IIIb procedure, but it went on to say that 'With this reservation, the Commission believes that the implementing procedures operate satisfactorily and present no major obstacles to actual implementation', noting that the safety-net procedure had not resulted in a single instance where a decision was not taken. 'Furthermore', the Commission continued, 'these procedures have the definite advantage of more closely involving national government departments; these bear responsibility for applying Community measures in practice' (CEC 1995: paras 51–2). Similarly, in its proposals for the 1999 Decision, the Santer Commission expressed general satisfaction with the working of the comitology system, again a stark rhetorical change from the confrontational approach of the Delors years. However, if we look beyond rhetoric to the substance of the Commission's 1999 proposals, reviewed at length above, we see continuity in the Commission's institutional preferences, including the adoption of guidelines for the choice of procedures designed to avoid the Council's natural tendency to select more restrictive comitology, and the 'simplification' of each procedure in such a way as to increase the discretion available to the Commission by removing the b-variants of the management, regulatory, and safeguard procedures. Similarly, the Commission has generally supported the Parliament's right to be informed about comitology meetings but *not* the Parliamentary demand for a call-back mechanism, which would represent a major loss of discretion for the Commission. In sum, the available evidence suggests that, notwithstanding a change in tone from the Delors to the Santer and Prodi years, Commission preferences for less restrictive comitology have been consistent over the past two decades, in the public and private statements of Commission officials as well as in its behaviour in the legislative process.

European Parliament. The preferences of the European Parliament regarding comitology have already been reviewed extensively above. As was noted there, the Parliament has been active and vocal on the issue of comitology over several decades, with dozens of committee reports and plenary resolutions on the general system of comitology, the adoption of the 1987 and 1999 decisions, and the committee types proposed in specific pieces of legislation. Throughout these documents, reviewed at length by Bradley (1992; 1997) and Hix (2000), Parliament's institutional position has remained remarkably stable, preferring a clear distinction between legislation and implementation, a stronger role for the EP in comitology, and insistence on less restrictive forms of comitology that respect the Commission's right of implementation. In recent years, these principles have been expressed most clearly in the Parliament's report on the Commission's proposals for the 1999 Comitology Decision.[61] The explanatory statement at the beginning of the report summarizes the views of most EP committees, and is worth quoting at length here. Regarding the current system and the Commission's proposed 1998 reforms, the report notes, 'The European Parliament's main criticisms are:

—only Council (or Member State) appointed committees have the right to scrutinise the Commission and refer back its decisions or draft decisions; the European Parliament has no such right;

—a matter is referred back in such a way from the executive to the legislative authority is sent to Council alone, rather than to both branches of the legislative authority (European Parliament and Council);

—the whole system lacks transparency, with several committees of civil servants, the composition of which is not always published and the agendas of which are obscure.[62]

As for the Parliament's preferences for reform, the report specifies four EP priorities: (1) a clear distinction between 'substantial legislation' to be adopted through the legislative process, and 'implementing provisions' to be adopted through comitology; (2) the right to a legislative 'call back'; (3) simplification of the procedures and the elimination of regulatory committees; and (4) greater transparency, with automatic transmission of information from all comitology committees to the EP.[63]

In practice, the EP has operationalized these preferences through various guidelines for its members. For example, the Roumeliotis Report of 1990, adopted several years after the passage of the 1986 Decision, instructs MEPs systematically to delete regulatory committee procedures in favour of management or, in the case of internal market provisions, advisory committees.[64] Needless to say, the views expressed in these reports and guidelines are closely in line with both the predictions of rational-choice theory and the Parliament's behaviour in the legislative process as captured by Dogan's statistical analysis. Nevertheless, despite these guidelines, Parliament, like the Commission, often accepts sub-optimal provisions on comitology in the interest of passing legislation, as Environment Committee Chairman Ken Collins admitted in his opinion for the aforementioned report. In many areas, Collins argues:

Parliament is confronted with an intransigent Council and a Commission whose prime concern is to see the legislation adopted. In the case of non-road mobile machinery, Parliament backed the Commission and re-introduced at second reading the (weaker) management committee procedure the Commission had originally proposed. However, at the stage of conciliation, the Commission' supported Council's choice of a regulatory committee. Parliament itself is not usually willing to sacrifice adoption of legislation or to go to conciliation 'for the sake of comitology'.[65]

For these reasons, and despite the strength of Commission and EP views on comitology, the views of the member governments in the Council are crucial to the choice of comitology procedures in secondary legislation.

The Council and the member governments. By comparison with the Commission and the Parliament, studying the preferences of the Council is considerably more challenging in so far as the Council is composed of 15 member governments with distinct views on comitology generally as well as on the specific type of comitology committee to be adopted in any given piece of legislation. Clearly, we have seen that the Council *collectively* has a preference for more restrictive comitology than either the Commission or the Parliament. Such a preference for greater collective control can be seen in the Council's extensive amendments to the Commission's drafts of both the 1987 and 1999 decisions, in which the Council systematically reinserted greater safeguards, more restrictive procedures, and the possibility of retaining executive powers to itself. Similarly, the Council's systematic tightening of the Commission's and the Parliament's proposed committee types provides evidence of a collective preference to retain the option of monitoring and, if necessary, sanctioning the Commission in its executive functions.

Such a collective preference for greater control, however, masks a more diverse set of preferences both across member governments and across issue areas. The public record of member-state preferences on comitology is generally unrevealing,[66] but interviews with Commission and member-state actors, as well as a careful examination of individual case studies, support the view that member governments do not take consistent positions on comitology choices across the board, nor do comitology preferences track ideological views about European integration with, for example, 'supranationalist' member states supporting light comitology while 'intergovernmentalist' governments support restrictive procedures. Rather, member governments tailor their comitology preferences according to the specific issue area or even the specific piece of legislation to hand, as a function of their substantive interests in a given issue area and their estimation of the Commission's likely behaviour in that area.[67] As one member-state official points out, 'It isn't easy to discern a predictable pattern across the whole spectrum. By subject, however, there is rather more predictability'.[68] Germany, Denmark, and Spain, for example, tend to prefer 'heavier' comitology—that is, regulatory committee procedures or the retention of implementing powers by the Council—in the area of the environment, where they represent the 'leader' and 'laggard' countries, respectively; Germany and Spain are most sensitive to comitology when it comes to spending programmes, where they respectively represent the largest net contributor to and largest net recipient of EU funding; and Germany, Denmark, and Italy tend to prefer more restrictive procedures in the technical adaptation of standards. Similarly, individual member governments may exhibit very different institutional preferences across issue areas, supporting less restrictive comitology for areas of market liberalization such as merger control while demanding more restrictive measures in areas of market regulation, or vice versa. Individual studies of comitology choices support the view that member governments' preferences over the choice of comitology committees are indeed issue-specific, derived from both their substantive preferences and from the coincidence of those preferences with the perceived preferences of the Commission.[69]

More generally, when asked whether the choice of comitology procedures *matters* in the determination of policy outcomes or simply reflects inter-institutional posturing among the Commission, Parliament, and Council, one member-state official replied:

Comitology is certainly *seen* to matter. Much depends on the individuals and the culture of a particular committee, but the Commission can treat advisory and management committees pretty cavalierly, so—if you think that a particular delegated responsibility is politically important—it is not unreasonable to look for a procedure which maximizes your influence. With a regulatory committee, there *is* more pressure on the Commission to work for a consensus or near-consensus solution in the Committee to avoid the delay and hassle of a reference to Council. There *are* still knee-jerk institutional reactions from all sides—and officials in capitals tend to mistrust the Commission or want to hang on to their own prerogatives more than sometimes seems objectively reasonable. But most member states' assessments are based on a fairly hard-headed view of where their national interests lie, which is in turn based on a view of how sympathetic the Commission is likely to be to them.[70]

Although hardly conclusive, such views—supported by the case study presented in the next subsection—suggest both that the choice of comitology rules is perceived by member-state officials to influence policy outcomes in the EU and that member governments do *not* consistently accept legitimate templates in the choice of comitology committees but tailor those choices according to their issue-specific preferences, as predicted by rational-choice theories of institutional design.

Case Study: The Creation of an EU Securities Committee

Finally, in an effort to assess how Commission, EP and member-state preferences interact in the adoption of delegating legislation, I have undertaken three case studies examining the legislative choice of comitology procedures since the 1987 Decision, examining the nature of the disputes, the preferences of the various actors, the arguments put forward in favour of different institutional rules, and the outcomes of such bargaining. Specifically, I selected the three cases which appeared most frequently in a Lexis-Nexis keyword search:[71] (1) the 1995 Open Network Provision Directive on telecommunications, which collapsed in conciliation in 1993 following an inter-institutional dispute between the EP and the Council over comitology; (2) the recent Lamfalussy Committee report on securities regulation, which generated a heated inter-institutional debate between the EP and Council, as well as an intergovernmental debate among the member governments, over the establishment of a new Securities Committee; and (3) the 1999 Eurodac Regulation, in which the Council defied the Commission and the Parliament by retaining implementing powers for itself in certain areas. These three pieces of legislation are, of course, atypical in having generated media coverage of the comitology decision. As we have seen above, however, such inter-institutional conflicts over comitology are not rare but indeed commonplace, and the cases chosen here present the additional benefit of revealing the preferences of the actors and the negotiations among them. Unfortunately, space precludes a discussion of all three cases; I therefore focus on the adoption of the Lamfalussy Report and the creation of a Securities Committee, which illustrates both the inter-institutional and the intergovernmental debates over the choice of comitology committees.

The creation of a new Securities Committee follows from the substantive commitment, made by the Lisbon European Council in

March 2000, to move ahead with the creation of a single market for financial services. Prior to the Lisbon meeting, the Commission had proposed a Financial Services Action Plan for the regulation of European securities markets, including a list of 42 specific measures to be adopted by the Union (CEC 1999). At Lisbon, the member governments committed themselves to the goal of adopting the Commission's action plan as part of the European Council's overall goal of transforming the EU into the world's most competitive economy.[72] Accordingly, the Ecofin Council agreed in July 2000 to create an ad hoc Committee of Wise Men—itself an interesting act of delegation, which was pointedly not entrusted to the Commission itself—led by former Belgian central banker Alexandre Lamfalussy, to report back to the Council on the best means to adopt the Commission's programme and adapt EU regulation to an ever-changing financial marketplace.[73]

The Lamfalussy Committee reportedly considered briefly the idea of creating a single European regulator for the financial sector, modelled on the US Securities and Exchange Commission, but quickly concluded that creating such an agency would require years of intergovernmental negotiation and that such an agency would be hampered by the continuing diversity of national regulations in the area. Nevertheless, the committee insisted on the importance of establishing a genuine internal market for securities and the economic gains that such integration would produce, as well as the need for a speedy and efficient decision-making process in the rapidly changing securities field. To address these issues, the committee proposed a new, four-stage regulatory process, and the creation of two new committees—a Securities Committee of member-state representatives, which would be a regulatory committee under the terms of the 1999 Decision, and an advisory Committee of European Securities Regulators—to advise the Commission on its proposals and coordinate implementation of EU legislation in the member states.

Much of the Lamfalussy Report was premised on the distinction between broad framework legislation and implementing regulations. At the first stage, the Commission would propose legislation after consulting the advisory Committee of National Securities Regulators, and the Council and the Parliament would adopt such framework legislation establishing the broad parameters of EU securities law. In order to facilitate rapid decision-making and flexibility, however, the committee recommended that such framework legislation be limited to the broad outlines of EU policy, leaving the details to implementing regulations adopted at a second stage by the Commission, subject to supervision by the Securities Committee.[74] At the third stage, national securities regulators would coordinate their implementation of EU regulations, while the fourth stage would consist of a vigorous enforcement action by the Commission, which would receive greater resources to instigate legal proceedings against non-compliant member governments.[75]

Although the aims of the Lamfalussy Report were widely supported by the Commission, the Parliament, member governments, and private actors, the committee's suggestions regarding the Securities Committee met predictable resistance from the European Parliament, which objected to the far-reaching legislative power being delegated to the Commission, as supervised by a regulatory Securities Committee, and with only a non-binding supervisory role for the Parliament. Responding to the final version of the report in February 2001, the Parliament approved the goal of the report but revived its earlier demand for a call-back mechanism by which the EP could insist that a Commission measure be dealt with through the normal legislative procedure.[76] Such a call-back mechanism had been explicitly rejected during the negotiation of the 1999 Comitology Decision, and was similarly dismissed by the Committee of Wise Men as being inconsistent with the treaties. Nevertheless, Parliament voted by a majority of 410 to 25 to adopt a resolution calling for a new inter-institutional agreement providing the Parliament with call-back authority, which it suggested could be 'ring-fenced' within the area of securities regulation (Norman 2001*b*). The Commission, however, remained opposed to any Parliamentary call-back, insisting that the proposed Securities Committee was consistent with the treaties and the 1999 Decision, and that any call-back mechanism threatened to slow down the adoption of urgently needed regulations (*European Report* 2001*b*). A large majority of member governments concurred, and rejected Parliament's demands in their agreement at the Stockholm European Council in March.

In addition to Parliamentary concerns, however, the proposed Securities Committee also raised last-minute objections from Germany in the final days before the planned adoption of the report by the Stockholm European Council. Within the Council of Economic and Finance Ministers (or 'Ecofin') that preceded the Stockholm meeting, all of the national delegations agreed that the new Securities Committee should be established as a regulatory committee under the terms of the 1999 Comitology Decision. German Finance Minister Hans Eichel, however, sought additional guarantees that the Commission would not use its newly gained powers under the reformed regulatory committee procedure to push through legislation opposed by a substantial minority of member governments. Eichel's objection was fed in part by a fear that the Commission would push through securities legislation that would favour London over Frankfurt as a centre for securities trading, but also by a previous Commission decision on the financing of the EU programme to erad-icate the BSE epidemic that had been taken over vociferous objections from Germany.[77] As a result, Eichel demanded a commitment from the Commission not to go against the 'predominant views which might emerge in the Council', in effect attempting to reintroduce the old safety-net mechanism whereby a simple majority could block a Commission decision. In response to this demand, Internal Market Commissioner Fritz Bolkestein indicated that such a commitment had already been made by the Commission as part of the 1999 Comitology Decision—but he also noted pointedly that 'the size of a predominant view has never been laid down, not in 1999 by the Commission nor now', and continued to note that 'obviously, it is something less than a qualified majority vote. In other words it is between 50 pct and the qualified majority' (quoted in *AFX European Focus* 2001). This deliberate ambiguity is preserved in the final text prepared for Stockholm, which reads as follows:

The European Council notes that within the framework of the comitology decision of 28 June 1999, the Commission has committed itself, in order to find a balanced solution for those cases of implementing measures in the field of securities markets acknowledged in the light of discussions to be particularly sensitive, to avoid going against predominant views which might emerge in the Council, as to the appropriateness of such measures. This commitment shall not constitute a precedent.[78]

Following that agreement, the European Council approved the Lamfalussy Report at Stockholm, and the Commission formally established the Committee in June of 2001. The question of Parliamentary involvement, however, was not resolved until February 2002, on the basis of a compromise between the Parliament and the Commission, in which Parliament renounced its demand for a call-back mechanism in return for a statement from President Prodi assuring the Parliament that the Securities Committee would operate with 'full transparency vis-à-vis Parliament', which would receive a period of three months to consider draft implementing measures before adoption. In addition, the Commission agreed to accept the inclusion by Parliament of 'sunset clauses' in framework legislation limiting the delegation of implementing powers to a four-year period, after which Parliamentary approval would be required for renewal. This latter provision, an innovation in Parliament's long struggle for greater control over the comitology process, provides the EP with genuine leverage over the implementation process, at least over the medium to long term.[79]

The ultimate significance of these inter-institutional compromises for policy outcomes is, at this writing, unclear. The Stockholm agreement between the Council and the Commission, for example, has been dismissed by Ludlow (2001) as a public-relations event, while other observers, such as the *Financial Times* (2001), expressed the fear that the compromise formula would weaken the Commission in the adoption of future legislation, and possibly grant a de facto veto to big countries. The policy effect of the Stockholm compromise, as well as the Commission's guarantees vis-à-vis Parliament, will emerge only in the coming years when the Commission begins to adopt implementing regulations under the supervision of the Securities Committee. Nevertheless, the case of securities regulation supports the view that member states consciously delegated powers to the Commission so as to benefit from both the *speed* and the *flexibility* of executive decision-making, which, by contrast with the painful slowness of the normal EU legislative process, was seen as vital in order to adopt the Commission's Action Plan before 2005 and adapt it to changing market conditions. However, the inter-institutional and intergovernmental negotiations leading up to the establishment of the Securities Committee also suggest that both the Parliament and member governments remain acutely aware of the problems of control. Indeed, the most striking aspect of the case is that, although all sides had recently adopted a simplified regulatory committee process in the 1999 Decision, they did *not* fall back on that process as a legitimate template, but instead negotiated ad hoc institutional rules with each side seeking explicitly to maximize its own control.

Analysis: Comitology as Police-Patrol Oversight
The empirical findings presented in this subsection clearly support the view that comitology is a mechanism deliberately designed by member governments to control the Commission in the latter's adoption of implementing legislation. As we have seen, all the major institutional actors—the Commission, the Parliament, and the member governments in the Council—are aware of the implications of different committee procedures for member-state control and Commission autonomy, and all three sets of actors display procedural preferences consistent with the predictions of principal-agent analyses. As we have also seen, the Commission consistently prefers less restrictive

comitology procedures, although in practice it has demonstrated a willingness to compromise with the Council on comitology in order to secure the adoption of valued legislation. Furthermore, while the Commission has consistently supported the Parliament's right to information about comitology, it has been equally consistent in its rejection of a Parliamentary call-back mechanism, which would reduce its discretion and create the risk of regulatory delays or paralysis. As for the EP, both the statistical data collected by Dogan and the qualitative analysis presented above support the view that Parliament consistently seeks to maximize its own role in the comitology process—a campaign it has pursued using every legal, financial, and political means at its disposal. In addition to attempting to augment its own powers, the EP has also consistently supported the Commission in its efforts to secure less restrictive comitology, both because its preferences are closer to the Commission than to the Council and because the EP enjoys leverage over the Commission—through the threat of censure—that it does not enjoy over the Council (Jupille 2000: Ch. 2). Within the Council, finally, member governments carefully calculate the likely consequences of different comitology procedures, advocating and bargaining for the committee procedures they consider to be most likely to produce their preferred policy outcomes—*even when the resulting choices clash with the clear and legitimate institutional templates emphasized by sociological institutionalists.*

The findings presented above do *not*, of course, demonstrate that deliberation never takes place in comitology committees. Deliberation, argumentation, persuasion, and collective preference formation may take place in at least some comitology committees, as Joerges and Neyer argue. Indeed, it may be, as many constructivists argue, that institutions established for one purpose (namely, control of the Commission) take on a very different purpose (namely, supranational deliberation) in day-to-day practice. Nevertheless, the evidence presented here *does* demonstrate that the key institutional actors representing the Commission, the Parliament, and member governments—many of whom have extensive experience *within* comitology committees as well—discuss, choose, and calibrate comitology rules *as if* they matter, frequently expending considerable time and energy to secure their preferred committee procedures. Such behaviour seems puzzling to the sociological institutionalist position, but it provides additional support, however indirect, for the view that comitology is indeed an instrument, however imperfect, whereby member-state principals seek to monitor and control the behaviour of the Commission, their supranational agent.

Administrative Law and Judicial Review as Fire-Alarm Oversight

Administrative procedures and law are typically cited in the principal-agent literature on US policy as a means of 'fire-alarm' oversight over regulatory agencies, supplementing police-patrol oversight through Congressional committees. Furthermore, as McCubbins, Noll, and Weingast (1987; 1989) have pointed out, the terms of administrative law and the rules regarding standing before the courts can be used to 'stack the deck' in favour of particular constituencies vis-à-vis the agency in question. In the United States, the most important piece of administrative law is the 1946 Administrative Procedure Act (APA), adopted by Congress after the Second World War in order to specify the basic procedures which US executive agencies must follow in the adoption of implementing regulations. In brief, the APA requires any US regulatory agency to engage in 'notice and comment' rule-making, which includes giving public notice in the *Federal Register* that it is contemplating a rule; allowing individuals to submit comments about the proposed rule; publishing the final rule along with a statement of the rule's 'basis and purpose'; and giving individuals standing to challenge these rules in federal courts, which may strike down rules that are arbitrary, capricious, an abuse of discretion, or in excess of statutory authority.[80] Above and beyond the provisions of the APA, moreover, Congress may and often does write specific and detailed administrative procedures into individual statutes, laying down more or less constraining procedures for agencies in particular areas, requiring specific groups to be consulted as part of the rule-making process, and granting greater or lesser legal standing to individuals and non-governmental organizations to challenge agency decisions in court.

Perhaps most importantly, the administrative rules and procedures laid down in the APA and in specific legislative acts are legally enforceable through judicial review of agency behaviour in federal courts. However, the delegation of judicial review powers to courts raises a second principal-agent problem for legislators in so far as the courts exercising that function might substitute their own procedural or even policy preferences for those of the principals: in effect, agencies would be held to the standards not of the principals themselves but of the judges reviewing their actions. For this reason, Shapiro (1988; 2001*b*) points out, legislative principals may deliberately design not only the agency's mandate but also the judicial review process itself in order to limit the discretion of judges by laying down explicit criteria for judicial review of agency decisions. For example, legislators may establish more or less demanding rules of standing, which in turn encourage or discourage litigation against agencies; more or less demanding standards by which to judge agency behaviour; and broader or narrower remedies to individuals harmed by agency behaviour. In these ways, legislative principals, although never controlling directly the jurisprudence of a court exercising judicial review, can influence the access of various parties to the courts, the standards by which agency behaviour will be judged, and the discretion of judges to substitute their own views for those of the principals.

In the case of the United States, the 1960s and 1970s witnessed a virtual revolution in administrative law as a result of both Congressional and judicial action. During this period, Congress enacted a number of far-reaching laws—such as the National Environmental Protection Act, the Clean Air Act, and the Occupational Safety and Health Act—which extended the reach of social regulation in areas such as the environment, consumer protection, and the protection of health and safety at work. Most of these provisions, moreover, delegated extensive rule-making powers to new and existing agencies such as the Environmental Protection Agency (EPA), the Occupational Health and Safety Administration (OSHA), and the Federal Trade Commission (FTC), while at the same time imposing extensive procedural requirements on them. Perhaps most importantly, many of these new laws extended legal standing to private individuals and non-governmental organizations, acting as 'private attorneys-general' to bring lawsuits against federal agencies for violation of the APA and other administrative rules. In McCubbins, Noll and Weingast's (1987; 1989) terms, Congress sought to 'stack the deck' in favour of a progressive coalition that could press for vigorous regulation by the EPA and OSHA and avoid any possibility that these new agencies would be captured by business interests. The result, which has been well documented by Melnick (1983), Shapiro (1988), and others, was to open the floodgates to litigation from both public-interest groups pressing for more vigorous social regulation and firms seeking to strike down or slow down the imposition of costly new regulations on business. As a result, US regulatory agencies today operate in a political environment characterized by extensive administrative requirements, widespread consultation with all interested parties, and regular challenges to new regulations from all sides in federal courts.

In the European case, the tradition of judicial review of executive action dates back to the Coal and Steel Community, where control of the High Authority was the primary function of the first Court of Justice. Later, in the EEC Treaty of 1957, the powers of the Court were extended considerably to new areas (see Chapter 3), but judicial review of Community acts remained a central responsibility of the both the ECJ and the Court of First Instance (CFI), which was created in 1988 and now has jurisdiction in all judicial review cases brought by private actors. Specifically, the treaties provide two primary bases for judicial review of Community acts:

- Article 230 (ex 173) of the EC Treaty provides that the Court of Justice may review the legality of Community acts adopted by the Commission, as well as by the Council and, in a 1997 amendment in the Treaty of Maastricht, the European Parliament and the European Central Bank. If the Court finds that the act in question has been taken illegally, it has the power under Article 231 (ex 174) EC to declare it void.
- Article 232 (ex 175) EC, by contrast, provides that the Court may examine complaints that the Commission or other EU institutions have *failed* to act where the treaties or other secondary legislation oblige them to do so.

In practice, the action for annulment under Article 230 has proved to be the more important and widely used of the two provisions. During 2000, for example, the ECJ received 38 actions for annulment of Community acts based on Article 230, while the Court of First Instance received 219 such cases, for a total of 257; during the same period, the Court of First Instance received only six cases for failure to act based on Article 232, and the ECJ received none.[81] Article 232 *has* been used successfully on a handful of occasions—most notably in a case brought by the European Parliament against the Council of Ministers for its failure to establish a common transport policy as called for in the treaties— but in practice it has not been widely used as a means to exercise judicial review over the Commission or other EC institutions.[82] For that reason, I concentrate here on the Court's power to review and annul the decisions of the Commission and other Community bodies.[83]

By contrast with the US and other national systems, the criteria for 'standing' to bring a case for annulment under the treaties are relatively restrictive, with a two-tier system of 'privileged' and 'non-privileged' applicants. Member governments, the Council, and the Commission are 'privileged' applicants in that they may bring legal actions against EC institutions at any time, without having to prove a direct interest in the case, while the European Parliament, the Court of Auditors, and the European Central Bank, as 'semi-privileged applicants', may bring actions only for the purpose of protecting their prerogatives. By contrast, a second group of 'non-privileged applicants', consisting of private citizens and firms, have standing only to contest decisions directed to them by name or 'of direct and individual concern' to them. Moreover, the treaties specify that any such proceedings must begin within two months of the publication of the measure in question. As we have already seen, these restrictive provisions on standing were already present in the European Coal and Steel Treaty, where they reflected member governments' concerns about a flood of private litigation whose effects might challenge, rather than uphold, the preferences and prerogatives of the member governments; and similar provisions were inserted in Articles 230 and 232 of the EC Treaty, for similar reasons. By contrast with the US Congressional legislation of the 1960s and 1970s, therefore, the treaties 'stack the deck' in favour of member governments and against private actors when it comes to challenging the acts of the Commission, the Court, and other EC institutions.[84]

Furthermore, in contrast to its expansive or 'teleological' readings of the treaties in other areas (see Chapter 3), the Court has interpreted these restrictive criteria for 'direct and individual concern' strictly, establishing and maintaining an extraordinarily high barrier to the successful lodging of an action for annulment.[85] The Court's jurisprudence in this area has led to claims from critics that the EC courts effectively impose a 'double standard' in which the consistency of *member-state acts* with the treaties is vigorously enforced through individual access to national courts—and thereby to the ECJ under the preliminary reference procedure—while the EU's supranational institutions are effectively shielded from the bulk of potential challenges by the fire-wall of a strict jurisprudence on *locus standi* for Articles 230 and 232.[86]

The Court's motives in maintaining such strict conditions for standing are a matter of debate with the legal community. On the one hand, such an interpretation may simply represent judicial restraint on the part of the Court, which has adhered closely to the intentions of the drafters, who were indeed eager to prevent a flood of private litigation against EC institutions.[87] On the other hand, the Court's restrictive reading of the letter of Article 230 for private litigants stands in stark contrast to its willingness to read the treaty in a more teleological manner elsewhere—including in the landmark *Chernobyl* judgment of 1990, where the Court granted standing to the European Parliament to bring an action for annulment in order to protect its prerogatives vis-à-vis the Commission and the Council, despite the fact that the Parliament was nowhere mentioned in the original, pre-Maastricht text of Article 230. In upholding—or, rather, creating—legal standing for the Parliament in that case, the Court referred to its absence as a 'procedural gap' in the treaty that could not interfere with the Court's duty to maintain the institutional balance of the Community.[88] The Court's activism in that case, granting the Parliament legal standing despite its black-and-white omission from the text of Article 230, stands in clear contrast to its conservatism on individual standing, and has suggested to many critics that the Court is more concerned to protect the prerogatives of the EC institutions than the rights of individuals vis-à-vis those institutions. The effects of this limited standing, finally, are aggravated by the fact that even successful litigants typically face a delay of several years before their cases are actually decided, which in time-sensitive cases like mergers arguably makes effective judicial review impossible.[89]

The limited standing enjoyed by private parties, furthermore, is reinforced by the fact that EC administrative law rests on a very thin basis in the treaties, which contain nothing even remotely comparable to the notice-and-comment requirements of the US Administrative Procedure Act. In the making of both legislation and implementing rules, neither the Commission nor the Council is required by EC administrative law to issue advance notice of rules to the general public—although the Commission often does so, through its various advisory committees and through the issuing of consultative 'Green Papers' and 'White Papers'; nor do the treaties require the kinds of extensive public comment that is now commonplace in American rule-making.[90] This relative weakness of EC administrative law is due in part to the absence of notice-and-comment rules in the *national* governments in many EC member states and in part to the fact that any such expansion of administrative law in the treaties would inevitably be used against the Council—that is, the member governments—as well as the Commission. In any event, despite considerable debate over the desirability of codifying or extending EC administrative law (Harlow 1996), the member governments have repeatedly failed to do so, preferring to rely primarily on the use of police-patrol oversight in the comitology process.

Nevertheless, notwithstanding the weakness of the treaty provisions on administrative law and *locus standi*, an increasing number of actions for annulment have been brought by both governments and private actors in recent years.[91] Furthermore, by contrast with the Court's conservatism on the issue of individual standing, both the ECJ and the CFI have interpreted expansively the very few administrative law provisions of the treaties, which they have applied with increasing rigour to the Commission and other EC institutions. According to Article 230, EC legal acts may be challenged and annulled 'on grounds of lack of competence, infringement of an essential procedural requirement, infringement of this Treaty or of any rule of law relating to its application, or misuse of powers'. This is a fairly broad and abstract list of grounds, which has left the European courts relatively free to develop specific doctrines for judicial review. For example, the Court has interpreted the concept of 'general principles of law' expansively to include principles such as fundamental human rights, proportionality, non-discrimination, and legal certainty—none of which is spelled out in the Treaties but have emerged as part of the Court's own case law. Despite the treaties' silence on these principles, the Court has ruled that failure to conform to any of them renders a Community act subject to annulment.[92]

Similarly, the ECJ and especially the CFI have developed an increasingly extensive jurisprudence on the importance of various *procedural requirements* that are either specified or alluded to in the treaties, most notably the requirement to 'state reasons' specified in Article 253, which forms the bedrock of the Court's decisions in many challenges to Commission actions. In one of the earliest such cases, Germany challenged a Commission decision rejecting Germany's application to import 450,000 hectolitres of wine at a lower rate of duty than the common external tariff. In its decision, the Commission had argued that 'the production of wines of this nature within the Community is amply sufficient' and therefore approved the importation of only 100,000 hectolitres at the reduced rate of duty. In its judgment in *Germany v. Commission*, the Court held that the Commission's statement of reasons was inadequate, vague, and contradictory in that the Commission provided no evidence in support of its claim that Community production of such wines was 'amply sufficient' nor did it explain why, in that case, it was approving the export of 100,000 hectolitres. The Court therefore annulled the Commission decision, noting that:

In imposing upon the Commission the obligation to state reasons for its decision, Article 190 [now Article 253] is not taking mere formal considerations into account but seeks to give an opportunity to the parties of defending their rights, to the Court of exercising its supervisory functions, and to Member states and to all interested nationals of ascertaining the circumstances in which the Commission has applied the Treaty.[93]

In subsequent rulings, the ECJ and the CFI have further developed this line of reasoning with increasing activism over the past decade, engaging not only in procedural review of the stating-reasons requirement (that is, the Commission must state some reasons, no matter how incoherent) but increasingly in substantive review (that is, the stated reasons must be 'well founded'). Furthermore, beyond the requirement to state reasons, the ECJ and the CFI together have established additional procedural requirements—such as the right of access to information, the right of defence, the right to be heard, and the 'duty of care' in public administration—that now bind the Commission in all of its executive acts.[94] On these and other grounds, and in response to complaints from member governments, EC institutions, and increasingly from private individuals and firms, the Court has annulled entirely or in part a growing number of Commission decisions in areas such as the granting of state aids to industry, the imposition of fines on firms found guilty of price-fixing,[95] anti-dumping decisions, and virtually every other type of executive decision taken by the Commission.

In sum, the treaties establish a system of judicial review that is, by American standards, an underdeveloped and highly restrictive means of fire-alarm oversight. By contrast with the detailed provisions of the US Administrative Procedure Act as interpreted and further developed by federal courts and Congress, the treaties feature only a few broad principles of administrative law, although these principles have been interpreted and elaborated by the European courts in increasing detail during the past decade. Similarly, by contrast with the liberal US rules on standing, which can be characterized as a genuine fire-alarm system in which nearly any potential litigant can ring the alarm, EC judicial review is much more selective, 'stacking the deck' against individual litigants and in favour of EC institutions and member governments, which continue to rely more heavily on police-patrol oversight through comitology than on the judicial review provisions of Article 230. For these reasons, the EC judicial review process has been subject to extensive criticism, and even optimistic analysts like Shapiro (2001*a*: 1) concede that European administrative law 'is in its earliest stages of development and is as yet nine-tenths potential and one-tenth reality'. Nevertheless, while the legal standing of individuals to bring cases under Article 230 remains limited, reflecting the common preferences of both member governments and European courts fearing an opening of the floodgates, the principles of administrative law elaborated by the ECJ and the CFI in their case law do provide an additional measure of control over a Commission whose behaviour is now subject to an ever-growing array of court-mandated procedural rules.

III. Conclusions

The findings of this chapter have been elaborated in considerable detail, but can be summarized briefly in four points. First, the member governments of the EU have delegated to the Commission a broad range of functions—including most notably setting the agenda for EU legislation, monitoring member-state compliance with EU law, and implementing such laws through detailed regulations—all of which provide a close fit with the predictions of principal-agent analysis. Put simply, the member governments of the EU delegate to the Commission the same sorts of functions delegated to Congressional committees and regulatory agencies by the US Congress, and for similar reasons.

Second, the member governments have devised an extensive variety of control mechanisms ensuring that the Commission is carefully monitored in its executive functions, although, here again, the examination of the various control mechanisms—appointment and censure, comitology, and judicial review—supports the view that EU institutions are structured carefully to maximize the gains, and minimize the agency losses, of delegation across different issue areas. Thus, in our review of comitology, we have seen how member governments carefully tailor the type of oversight committee to reflect the nature of the Commission's functions and the sensitivity of the issue area in question. Similarly, in terms of judicial review, member governments have deliberately designed and maintained a system of fire-alarm oversight that privileges member governments and other EC institutions over private litigants. Furthermore, as we shall see in Chapters 5 and 6, these control mechanisms are systematically employed by the member governments to exercise effective control over the Commission in its executive functions.

Third, the evidence reviewed above suggests that the primary motivation for treaty-based delegation to the Commission is indeed the demand for credible commitments, as both Moravcsik and Majone suggest. Delegation and discretion in secondary legislation, by contrast, suggests not a single motivation but a mix of motivations, with some areas of high discretion (competition policy, external trade) reflecting a logic of credible commitments, while other areas (agriculture, fisheries) reflect a demand for speedy and efficient decision-making. By contrast, there is little evidence to suggest that the member governments delegate extensive powers or discretion to the Commission in order to secure policy-relevant expertise, which remains primarily in the hands of the member governments and their representatives.

Fourth and finally, the discretion of the Commission varies considerably across both functions and issue areas—and in no function or issue area is member-state control of the Commission complete or perfect. In terms of functions, the Commission enjoys its greatest discretion in the monitoring of member-state compliance with the treaties, while discretion in regulatory and agenda-setting powers varies across issue areas. Across those issue areas, moreover, the member governments subject the Commission to varying degrees of administrative procedure and oversight, ranging from the Commission's broad discretion in competition policy to its more constrained role in the management of EU spending programmes, and the most restricted discretion in sensitive areas of national regulation, taxation, and foreign affairs. This fourth observation, in turn, suggests that the Commission's influence over policy outcomes will vary across issue areas and decision rules—a hypothesis that will be tested, in turn, in Chapters 5 and 6.

CHAPTER 3

The Court of Justice as an Agent: Delegation of Judicial Power in the European Union

In Chapter 2, we examined the patterns of delegation and discretion for the European Commission, noting the remarkably broad array of powers delegated to the Commission in both primary and secondary legislation, the numerous control mechanisms designed to limit the Commission's discretion, and the wide variation in both delegation and discretion across issue areas. In this chapter, devoted to the European Court of Justice, our task is made considerably simpler by the fact that the ECJ has been delegated powers almost exclusively by the treaties, and these powers delegated are almost entirely 'horizontal' rather than 'vertical' or issue-specific, the only exceptions being the second and third pillars of the Maastricht and Amsterdam Treaties, in which ECJ jurisdiction is either excluded or limited in a variety of ways.

In the first part of this chapter, therefore, I focus primarily on the provisions of the Union's constitutive treaties delegating powers to the European Court of Justice, which I argue fit closely the functions of monitoring, enforcement, and incomplete contracting emphasized in the principal-agent literature; and on the relatively small number of provisions providing for explicit member-state control or influence over the Court's behaviour, including the appointment procedure, the prospect of legislative overruling, and the unwritten but nevertheless real prospect of national non-compliance with ECJ decisions. Overall, I suggest, the Court enjoys a remarkable amount of discretion in comparison not only with the Commission but also with national constitutional courts.

Nevertheless, while the Court does appear to enjoy broad discretion in the traditional EC pillar of the Union, in recent years the member governments have shown far greater reluctance to extend similar jurisdiction in the second and third pillars, dealing with Common Foreign and Security Policy and with Justice and Home Affairs, respectively. I therefore analyse the provisions of these treaty chapters in detail to illustrate how member governments, in their 1991 and 1997 revisions of the treaties, dealt with the inherent trade-off between control and the benefits of a 'neutral' interpreter of EU law. Overall, this section of the chapter suggests that member states have indeed delegated broad-ranging powers of interpretation and arbitration to the Court of Justice, granting it significant powers to move the status quo consistently in an integrationist direction, but also that member governments have learned from four decades of activist jurisprudence, to which they have responded with subsequent delegations of power that are more carefully hedged with restrictive treaty language, limited jurisdiction, and other provisions to minimize loss of control to the Court.

Throughout this first part of the chapter, the emphasis is on the Court as the *object* of delegation rather than as a *subject* attempting to make use of its relatively large discretion to pursue its own agenda. While a thorough analysis of the latter point is beyond the scope of this chapter, I nevertheless provide a brief analysis in the second part of the chapter of the Court's most extensive and controversial use of its judicial discretion, namely, the development of the 'preliminary ruling' procedure set down in Article 234 (ex 177) EC. Making full use of this procedure, the Court has proclaimed the doctrines of the direct effect and supremacy of EC law in the member states; created individual rights that are legally enforceable by litigants in national courts; and co-opted national courts and individual litigants as partners in the extension of EC law. More than any other Court activity, this extension of the preliminary ruling procedure has given rise to a great debate between legal and/or neo-functionalist scholars, who see the Court as an independent actor driving an extensive process of legal integration outside the control of member governments, and a neo-rationalist school, which sees the Court as a highly responsive agent of the member governments, carrying out its enforcement functions in conformity with the preferences of the Union's most powerful states. The terms of that debate, and the empirical evidence produced by its participants, lay the essential groundwork for the chapters that follow, and I therefore summarize briefly the state of our empirical knowledge of the ECJ's independence in the application of the preliminary ruling procedure.

As in Chapter 2, I retain a rather narrow focus on the questions of delegation to, and the discretion of, the Court of Justice. I make no effort to summarize the internal organization and workings of the

Court—a project which, as we shall see, is made difficult not only by its complexity but also by the Court's practice of deliberating strictly in secret, thereby rendering it something of a 'black box' to outside observers.[1] Nor do I attempt to describe or explain the preferences or behaviour of individual litigants in bringing cases, or variation in the acceptance of EC legal supremacy and direct effect by national courts. Questions such as these arguably represent the frontier of EU legal research (Mattli and Slaughter 1998), but they lie beyond the focus of the current chapter.

I. Delegation and Discretion

Patterns of Delegation: The Jurisdiction of the ECJ

By contrast with the treaty provisions on the European Commission, which list a variety of delegated functions in Article 211, Article 220 (ex 164) of the EC Treaty specifies the task of the Court of Justice in a single sentence: 'The Court of Justice shall ensure that in the interpretation and application of this Treaty the law is observed.' This basic provision is then elaborated in subsequent articles, which specify in greater detail the Court's 'wide-ranging and multifarious jurisdiction'.[2] Table 3.1 lists all of the areas of jurisdiction granted to the Court by the EC Treaty, including the relevant treaty article, the nature of the Court's jurisdiction, standing of various parties to bring cases, and any explicit limits on the Court's jurisdiction specified in the relevant article.

As Table 3.1 makes clear, the jurisdiction of the Court is concerned overwhelmingly with settling disputes among member governments, EC institutions, and private parties regarding the interpretation of the treaties and other EC law. In the language of rational-choice theory, therefore, most of these functions therefore fit neatly into the functional category of *incomplete contracting*. Like a domestic constitution, the EC Treaty is a broad relational contract, providing only the guiding principles of EC policies as well as procedures for the subsequent adoption of legislation by the various institutions.[3] In practice, however, disputes might be expected to arise—and regularly do arise—among the member governments and institutions regarding the interpretation of the treaty framework and the respective rights and obligations of the various institutions under its provisions. Under these circumstances, the Court plays a fundamental role in filling in the details of the treaty's incomplete contract, ensuring respect for the treaty's procedural requirements, safeguarding the 'institutional balance' among the Council, the Commission, and the Parliament in the

TABLE 3.1. *Jurisdiction of the European Court of Justice in the EC Treaty*

Treaty Article	Nature of jurisdiction	Standing	Limits
226 (ex 169) EC	Enforcement actions against member states	Commission	
227 (ex 170) EC	Enforcement actions against member states	Member governments	
228 (ex 171) EC	Enforcement actions against member states: penalties for non-compliance	Commission	
230 (ex 173) EC	Judicial review of Community acts: action for annulment	EC institutions, member governments, limited standing for private actors	
232 (ex 175) EC	Judicial review: failure to act	EC institutions, member governments, limited standing for private actors	
234 (ex 177) EC	Preliminary references from national courts regarding (1) interpretation of Treaties; (2) validity and interpretation of Community acts; (3) statutes of Community bodies	References from national courts	
235 (ex 178) EC	Non-contractual liability of the	Unspecified	

	Community and its servants for damages		
236 (ex 179) EC	Disputes between Community and its staff	Specified in Staff Regulations	
237 (ex 180) EC	Disputes concerning acts of European Investment Bank, European Central Bank, and national central banks within the European System of Central Banks	Commission, member states, European Investment Bank Board of Directors, Council of the ECB	
238 (ex 181) EC	Judgment pursuant to any arbitration clause in contact concluded by or on behalf of the Community	Unspecified	Requires further action: contract on behalf of Community
239 (ex 182) EC	Disputes between member states relating to treaties, if the dispute is submitted to it under a special agreement between the parties	Member governments	Requires further action: submission of dispute under special agreement

Note: ECJ jurisdiction for visas, immigration, and asylum or for provisions of the Treaty on European Union not included; summarized in Table 3.4.

Source: Consolidated Treaties.

EC legislative process, and interpreting secondary legislation adopted under the treaties. In addition, the Commission and the Court collectively serve a crucial *monitoring* and *enforcement* function vis-à-vis member governments accused of non-compliance with EC law, most notably through direct actions brought by the Commission under Articles 226 (ex 169) EC and indirect actions brought by individual litigants under Article 234.

Among the eleven articles listed in Table 3.1, several require additional action by the member governments (conclusion of contract by or on behalf of the Community, or submission of dispute under a special agreement) in order to confer jurisdiction on the Court; and a number of others concern relatively mundane matters of incomplete contracting, such as the arbitration of disputes between the Community and its civil servants ('staff cases') or the non-contractual liability of the Community for damages vis-à-vis third parties. However, three sets of provisions are clearly more significant, and comprise the vast majority of the ECJ's case load during the past five decades. These are: (1) judicial review of Community acts; (2) enforcement actions against the member states; and (3) preliminary references from national courts and tribunals. Let us consider each of these very briefly in turn.

Judicial Review of Community Acts
The 1957 EEC Treaty featured several provisions, explicitly modelled on those of the earlier ECSC Treaty, allowing the Court to undertake judicial review of the acts of the institutions. As we saw in Chapter 2, these provisions allow EC institutions, member governments, and, in some cases, private parties to bring either actions for annulment of acts for violation of EC law (Article 230) or claims of a 'failure to act' where the treaties clearly require an EC actor to do so (Article 232). Indeed, as we also saw, the primary purpose of the ECSC Court was precisely to exercise judicial review over the actions of the executive High Authority, and the judicial review provisions of the EC Treaty have been similarly used by both public and private actors vis-à-vis the actions of the Commission and other EC institutions.

Nevertheless, unlike many European legal systems, the EC Treaty makes no distinction between judicial review of administrative acts, which is commonplace in most EU member states, and the more far-reaching review of legislative acts, which is less common in the civil-law systems of continental Europe and unknown prior to the EC in the British common-law system. For this reason, the judicial review provisions of Articles 230 and 232 can be and are regularly used by EC institutions and by member governments to challenge the validity of *legislative acts* of the Commission, the Council, and the Parliament on the grounds of lack of competence, infringement of an essential procedural requirement, infringement of the Treaty or of any rule relating to its application, or misuse of powers.

Enforcement Actions Against Member States

Articles 226 and 227 of the EC Treaty provide for either the Commission or the member governments to bring 'direct actions' to the Court in order to enforce the provisions of EC law vis-à-vis non-complying member governments. These two articles, adopted as part of the original 1957 EEC Treaty, were designed as the primary mechanism for monitoring and enforcing member-state compliance with the provisions of the treaties and of secondary legislation. Under Article 226, the Commission was assigned the task of monitoring member-state compliance with EC law, opening infringement proceedings with reasoned opinions against member governments, and, if the government in question failed to comply within a given time-limit, bringing the case before the Court. As we saw in Chapter 2, this enforcement function is one of the Commission's most far-reaching powers under the treaties, and the one for which it enjoys the greatest discretion vis-à-vis member governments. In addition, Article 227 allows member governments to bring suspected cases of non-compliance by other member states before the Court, although in practice the member governments have been hesitant to challenge each other directly before the Court, and prefer to rely on the Commission to bring such cases.

By contrast with the earlier Coal and Steel Community, which allowed the High Authority and the Court to issue fines against member governments as well as private actors, the EC Treaty provided the Court with no explicit sanctions for non-compliance with ECJ rulings, which remained purely declaratory. Specifically, under Article 228 (ex 171) of the original 1957 EEC Treaty, if the Court found that a member state had failed to fulfil an obligation under the treaty, that state would be 'required to take the necessary measures to comply with the judgment of the Court of Justice'. Perhaps as a result, member-state compliance with ECJ decisions has been highly variable cross-nationally, and cases of non-compliance rose alarmingly during the late 1980s and 1990, particularly in the area of the internal market (Tallberg 1999: 131–4). In response to this rising tide of non-compliance with ECJ rulings, the British Conservative government of John Major proposed to the 1991 intergovernmental conference that Article 228 be amended to allow the Commission to propose, and the Court to impose, financial penalties on member governments for non-compliance with ECJ decisions. The origins of this proposal in the Eurosceptic government of John Major, and its unanimous adoption by the member governments in the Maastricht Treaty, underline the importance attached by member governments to monitoring and enforcing compliance as a primary and ongoing incentive for delegation to both the Commission and the Court. In practice, moreover, the Commission has proved willing to propose significant fines for non-compliance by member governments, which have in turn been quick to bring their national legislation into compliance without the need for a formal ECJ ruling against them (Tallberg 1999: 169–72, 178–84). Nevertheless, the revised Article 228 establishes a fairly high threshold for the application of financial penalties, which are not levied automatically upon member governments but require the Commission to open a second, protracted set of infringement proceedings against non-complying member governments. In practice, therefore, this mechanism has proved, in Tallberg's words 'effective when used, but seldom employed' (1999: 178).

Preliminary References

The original Article 177 of the EC Treaty, renumbered Article 234 following the Amsterdam Treaty, creates a 'preliminary reference' procedure whereby national courts and tribunals, when faced with a question or questions of EC law, can request a preliminary ruling from the Court regarding (1) the interpretation of the Treaty, (2) the validity or interpretation of the acts of the Community institutions, and (3) the interpretation of the statutes of bodies created by the Council, where those statutes so provide. The opportunity for, or, in some cases, obligation of national courts to refer such questions of EC law to the ECJ varies depending on the type of national court. According to Article 234, any court or tribunal of a member state *may*, if it considers that a decision on the question is necessary to enable it to give a judgment on the case before it, submit questions of European law for a preliminary ruling from the ECJ. Thus, as we shall see in greater detail below, lower-level courts are not required to request preliminary rulings from the ECJ, but they are entitled to do so, and in practice the bulk of references comes from such lower courts. By contrast, the final paragraph of Article 234 provides that, where a question of EC law is raised before a national court against which there is no possibility of appeal, that court *must* submit the question for a preliminary ruling by the Court of Justice. In either case, the ECJ's preliminary ruling concerns only the interpretation of the relevant provisions of European law, while the application of those provisions to the circumstances of a specific case is left to the relevant national courts. The role of the

ECJ under Article 234, therefore, is not to provide a court of appeal against national court decisions but to ensure that the provisions of EC law are interpreted uniformly throughout the Community.

From a functional perspective, Article 234 appears to play a dual role. First, it provides an additional opportunity for judicial review of *EC acts* by allowing individual litigants the chance to challenge the legality of a Community act in their national courts—the so-called 'plea of illegality'. In this sense, Article 234 serves as a decentralized complement to the centralized judicial review provisions of Articles 230 and 232 analysed above. Second, Article 234 can also serve as a decentralized means of enforcement whereby individuals within the member states can challenge *national laws* for non-compliance with EC law, supplementing the more centralized enforcement procedure of Articles 226–228. Indeed, early analyses of the ECJ by Garrett and others argued that member states' demand for decentralized enforcement of EC law explained both the initial delegation of powers to the Court and their compliance with apparently autonomous Court decisions (Garrett 1992; Garrett and Weingast 1993).

From a theoretical and functional perspective, both roles are consistent with the predictions of principal-agent theory, and in practice Article 234 is indeed used by private litigants to challenge the legality of *both* EC *and* national laws. In historical terms, however, Karen Alter argues persuasively that it is incorrect to assume on the basis of a functional analysis that member governments *intended* the Court to perform this function; in fact, she argues, the negotiators of the EEC Treaty designed the preliminary reference procedure exclusively as a means to challenge Community acts, and the subsequent expansion of the procedure to include challenges to national laws was unintended and unexpected by the framers of the EEC Treaty (Alter 1998; 2000; see also Pescatore 1981). Alter's claim is further supported by a careful reading of the early landmark cases such as the *Van Gend* case establishing the principle of direct effect of EU law in the member states. In that case, the German, Dutch, and Belgian governments argued in briefs before the Court that enforcement cases against a member state could be brought only by the Commission (under Article 226) or the member governments (under Article 227); the Dutch national court's reference was, they argued, therefore inadmissible before the ECJ. Similarly, in the *Costa v. Enel* case establishing the principle of supremacy of EU law, the Italian government argued in its brief that the reference from a Milan court to the ECJ was inadmissible, since under Italian law the lower court was required to give precedence to the more recent national legislation over EC law and 'cannot avail itself of Article 177' (quoted in Stein 1981: 11). Thus, while the member governments may or may not have approved of the subsequent development of the preliminary reference procedure into a means of decentralized enforcement against member states, the bulk of the available evidence supports the view that the drafters of the treaty did *not* design Article 234 for this purpose. In light of the importance of these provisions and the debate over the autonomy of the Court in developing the preliminary ruling procedure, I return to this question in Section II of the chapter, below.

The Court of First Instance

Throughout the first three and a half decades, the jurisdiction conferred by the treaties fell entirely upon a single court, the ECJ. By the mid-1980s, however, the case load of the Court had increased significantly, a substantial backlog of unresolved cases had developed, and the average time to an ECJ decision had increased to as much as two years or longer. In response to the increasing case load of the ECJ and the problems it entailed, the EU's member governments agreed in the 1986 Single European Act to create a new 'Court of First Instance' (CFI) with jurisdiction over staff cases, cases against the Commission under the Coal and Steel Treaty, and competition policy cases brought by private firms. Later, in 1993 and 1994, the Council extended the jurisdiction of the CFI to cover four types of cases:

(1) disputes between the Community and its staff (Article 236 EC, ex 179);
(2) actions for judicial review—including both actions for annulment and for failure to act—brought by private individuals or companies (Articles 230 and 232 EC);
(3) actions for non-contractual liability brought by private individuals or companies (Article 235 EC, ex 178); and
(4) actions in contract brought by private individuals or companies (Article 238 EC, ex 181).[4]

In general, therefore, the CFI now has jurisdiction in actions brought against the Community by private individuals or companies; by contrast, cases brought by member states or Community institutions, as well as all preliminary references, remain within the jurisdiction of the ECJ, which may also receive appeals from the CFI (on points of law only). In practice, more than half of all CFI cases are acts for annulment of EC acts under Article 230, with staff cases against EC institutions representing the second-largest category. Perhaps most interestingly for our purposes, this means that much of the EC's judicial review activity reviewed in Chapter 2—namely, that portion in which private actors contest the validity of Commission and other EC actions—now takes place in the CFI, which has developed a specialization in the area. In terms of the appointment of its judges and its rules of procedure, which might potentially influence its discretion vis-à-vis the member governments, the provisions regarding the CFI closely resemble those of the ECJ.

To summarize this subsection, then, the jurisdiction of the ECJ and the CFI closely fit the predictions of the functionalist theory of delegation in so far as both Courts are delegated the power to enforce member-state compliance with EU law and interpret the incomplete contract of the treaties in disputes among member governments and between member governments and other EU institutions. In addition, Articles 230 and 232 also provide for the possibility of judicial review of the Commission and other EU institutions. Finally, Article 234 gives the Court jurisdiction to respond to preliminary references from national courts, although the warnings of scholars like Alter suggest that Article 234 was not intended to serve as the mechanism for decentralized enforcement against member states into which it later evolved; I shall therefore return to this provision at greater length in Section II below.

Patterns of Discretion: Control Mechanisms and the ECJ

The European Court of Justice, to repeat, has been delegated precisely the kinds of functions predicted by principal-agent analysis and delegated to courts in various domestic contexts. However, the actual *discretion* of the Court to rule autonomously of the preferences of the most powerful member states has not yet been discussed, and it is to this subject that we now turn. In doing so, we can compare the discretion of the Court with two sets of actors. First, and most obviously, we can compare the Court with the analysis of Commission discretion in Chapter 2. Even a brief comparison in this regard reveals that the Court is far less encumbered by either *ex ante* or *ex post* control mechanisms, such as comitology or the threat of censure by the European Parliament, and in this sense the Court clearly enjoys greater discretion in its activities than the Commission. Second, however, we can also compare the Court's discretion, as defined by the treaties, with the discretion allocated to national constitutional courts, which are the ECJ's closest domestic counterparts. Specifically, I examine here three distinct factors that have been hypothesized to influence the discretion of both the ECJ and domestic courts: (1) the provisions regarding the appointment, term of office, reappointment, and removal of European judges; (2) the threat of legislative overruling; and (3) the challenge of legitimacy and concerns about non-compliance with ECJ decisions by national courts and governments.

Appointment, Term of Office, and Removal

The provisions for the appointment, term of office, removal, and reappointment of ECJ judges are set out concisely in Article 223 (ex 167) EC, which provides for ECJ judges and advocates general[5] to be appointed 'by common accord of the member governments for a term of six years' during which they cannot be removed by the member governments individually or collectively.[6] Although the treaty makes no explicit provision requiring the nationality of ECJ judges, in practice member governments have decentralized the selection of ECJ judges, allotting one judge per member state, and national choices are never disputed (R. Dehousse 1999: 7).[7] The treaties, moreover, allow member governments wide latitude in the selection of judges, limited only by the requirement that judges be selected from 'persons whose independence is beyond doubt and who possess the qualifications required for appointment to the highest judicial office in their respective countries'.[8] By contrast with the United States, where judicial nominees face public hearings and difficult confirmation votes before the US Senate, in the European Union neither national legislatures nor the European Parliament plays any role in the nomination or confirmation of ECJ judges, which takes place quietly and largely outside the public eye. Indeed, in some member states the appointment of ECJ judges may be the result of domestic political bargains among parties sharing out key posts such as ambassadorships alongside Commission and Court nominations.[9] Finally, the treaties also provide that retiring judges may be reappointed, in principle by common accord of the member states, but in practice by their 'home' member governments.

In comparative terms, these provisions would seem to provide ECJ judges with less discretion than many of their national counterparts. The appointment of judges, for example, is left entirely to the member governments, with no parliamentary contribution and virtually no public debate, raising the prospect that member governments could select either docile or nationalist judges unlikely to take a strong integrationist view of the treaties. Rather surprisingly, most scholars agree that the member states have made relatively little use of their appointment powers to pack the court with nationalist, or otherwise obedient, judges; whether because they are generally satisfied with the Court's existing jurisprudence, or because internal political logrolling takes precedence over doctrinal matters, or because they anticipate the widely discussed socialization effect on judges to the Court is unclear.[10] Furthermore, it is far from clear that American-style confirmation hearings, which were proposed by the European Parliament in the run-up to the 1996 intergovernmental conference that negotiated the Amsterdam Treaty, would enhance the autonomy or legitimacy of the Court. Rather, as the Court noted in its contribution to the same IGC, such public hearings would be 'unacceptable' since 'prospective appointees would be unable adequately to answer the questions put to them without betraying the discretion incumbent upon persons whose independence must, in the words of the Treaties, be beyond doubt and without prejudging positions they might have to adopt with regard to contentious issues which they would have to decide in the exercise of their judicial function' (ECJ 1995: para. 17).

Perhaps more seriously, their relatively short and renewable terms of office would appear to provide ECJ judges with a strong incentive to remain aware of member-state preferences, or at least the preferences of the member governments that appointed them.[11] Indeed, if we compare the appointment and reappointment procedures and terms of office of the Court of Justice with their closest national counterparts in the constitutional courts of four west European countries and the Supreme Court of the United States (see Table 3.2), we see that the latter invariably receive longer, non-renewable terms, making them less susceptible to influence by those who appoint them.

For this reason, the judges suggested in their contribution to the 1996 intergovernmental conference that 'The Court would not...object to a reform which would involve an extension of the term of office with a concomitant condition that the appointment be non-renewable. Such a reform would provide an even firmer basis for the independence of its members and would strengthen the continuity of its case-law' (ECJ 1995: para. 17). The IGC itself discussed such a reform, but the member governments were not able to agree unanimously on this revision, suggesting that at least some of them prefer the current system and its possibility of exerting some influence, however indirect, on individual judges (R. Dehousse 1999: 15).

Nevertheless, the ECJ combines several features that may compensate, in part, for judges' relatively short and renewable term of office. First, the statute of the ECJ requires that judgments be issued on behalf of the Court as a whole, with no indication of voting and no concurring or dissenting opinions. This provision, which reflects existing practice in the constitutional courts of France and Italy, stands in stark contrast to the United States, where voting records are made

TABLE 3.2. *Appointment and terms of ECJ judges in comparative perspective*

	France	Germany	Italy
Number of members	9	16	15
Recruiting authorities	President (3) Pres. Assembly (3) Pres. Senate (3)	Bundestag (8) Bundesrat (8) by 2/3 majority	National Govt (5) Judiciary (5) Parliament (5) by 2/3 majority of joint session of both chambers
Length of term	9 years	12 years	9 years
Renewable?	No	No	No

	Spain	United States	ECJ
Number of members	12	9	15
Recruiting authorities	National govt (2) Judiciary (2) Congress (4) Senate (4)	President, with advice and consent of Senate	National governments appoint individual judges, confirmed by unanimous Council vote
Length of term	9 years	Life	6 years
Renewable?	No	No	Yes

Source: Adapted from Stone Sweet (2000: 49).

public and both concurring and dissenting opinions are published. In addition, all ECJ judges swear under oath to uphold the secrecy of their deliberations, making it difficult if not impossible for member governments to hold individual judges accountable for their voting record. Hence, as T. C. Hartley (1998: 54) writes, 'it is impossible to accuse a judge of being insufficiently sensitive to national interests or of having "let his government down"; no one outside the Court can ever know whether he vigorously defended the position adopted by his own country or was in the forefront of those advocating a "Community solution" '.[12]

Second, because the appointment process is decentralized among 15 member governments with diverse preferences, it is difficult to conceive of any concerted effort to 'pack' the Court with a particular type of judge. At most, a disgruntled government could select a single judge with nationalist or other ideological views.

Third and finally, while member governments may appoint judicial nominees on the basis of their expected preferences, the knowledge of such preferences is inevitably imperfect, and judges may behave differently on the bench than expected by those who appoint them, as in the case of US Supreme Court Chief Justice Earl Warren, who was nominated to the Court by Republican President Dwight D. Eisenhower but whose Court subsequently issued some of the most important liberal decisions in US judicial history. In the EU case, moreover, the Court is widely held to exert a strong socializing effect upon its members, who are said to have a strong *esprit de corps* and a communitarian outlook (Mancini 1991; Hartley 1998: 54).

Be that as it may, even if the individual judges retain some independence from their national governments, one may nevertheless ask whether the Court as a whole might fear legislative overturning or some other form of punishment by the member governments in response to excessively activist or integrationist rulings; this is the subject of the next subsection.

The Threat of Legislative Overruling

Interpretation of secondary legislation can be overruled with new secondary legislation, and indeed the threat of legislative overruling has been put forward by Cooter and Ginsburg (1996) as the best comparative measure of judicial discretion. This emphasis on legislative overruling has also been incorporated in turn as the central feature of the analyses of the ECJ by Tsebelis and Garrett (2001) and to a lesser extent by Kilroy (1995; 1999), and therefore deserves extended attention here. In Cooter and Ginsburg's game-theoretic analysis, judges have their own policy preferences, which they might be expected to maximize through their power to interpret the law. In doing so, however, judges are constrained by the 'countervailing power of other officials' and in particular by the threat of legislative overrule. 'If judges are constrained by the possibility of legislative repeal of their decisions', they continue,

then the space of judicial discretion expands as overriding the court becomes more difficult. Game theory thus suggests the following prediction: *Courts will become more adventurous in interpreting statutes when the probability decreases of legislative repeal of their decisions.* (Cooter and Ginsburg 1996: 295; emphasis in original)

In operational terms, Cooter and Ginsburg argue, the difficulty of legislative repeal is a function of two variables: (1) the number of effective veto points on new legislation, and (2) the degree of party discipline and number of parties in the governing coalition of the legislature. Regarding the first, the authors identify the number of 'independent vetoes' in terms of institutions, so that a separation-of-powers system like the United States features a relatively demanding three veto points, while a pure parliamentary system would feature only a single veto point: the lower house, for example the British House of Commons. Cooter and Ginsburg do not consider the voting threshold within each of these institutions—which, as we shall see, is vitally important in the EU case—but they do supplement their institutional analysis with an explicitly political analysis focusing on party discipline, measured by the average duration of a given parliamentary coalition, and the number of parties in the governing coalition. In effect, Cooter and Ginsburg predict that courts will enjoy the least discretion in those countries where a lower number of veto points and a small number of disciplined parties make legislative overruling relatively easy, such as the United Kingdom and Japan, while courts in separation-of-power systems with many veto points and weak party discipline will enjoy greater discretion, as for example in the United States.

In empirical terms, the authors measure their dependent variable of judicial discretion using two indicators—a 1–5 scale of expert ratings devised by a small number of comparative law scholars, and the nature and timing of the move to strict liability for consumer product injuries—and they regress these variables against their hypothesized independent variables. Although they concede that their measures of discretion are necessarily imprecise, and that possible control variables have been omitted from the analysis, they nevertheless find empirical support for their claim that judicial discretion does indeed vary systematically with their two variables and most strongly with the number of legislative veto points. It is worth noting, however, that Cooter and Ginsburg's model concerns only judicial interpretation of *statutory legislation*, which can be overruled through the normal legislative process. In cases of *constitutional interpretation*, which can be overturned only though constitutional amendments, the barriers to overruling are typically much higher, featuring super-majorities or additional veto points or both.

Applied to the European Union, Cooter and Ginsburg's model reveals that the barriers to legislative overruling—and hence the effective judicial discretion of the ECJ and the CFI—are significantly higher in the EU than in any individual member state. Traditionally, EC legislation had to clear two veto points: proposal by the European Commission, which may also withdraw legislation at any time in the legislative process, and adoption by the Council of Ministers. In recent years, the European Parliament has become a third veto point where co-decision is required, giving the EU the same effective number of veto points as the United States for all such legislation.

Simply counting the number of veto points, however, overlooks the size of the majorities required for adoption of new legislation within the various institutions. Implicit in Cooter and Ginsburg's analysis is the assumption of simple majority voting in legislatures; by contrast, the Council of Ministers historically took most of its decisions by unanimity, and even QMV—so often, and correctly, presented as a relaxation of EU decision-making rules—still requires a super-majority of more than two-thirds, higher than the thresholds for constitutional amendment in most democratic states. In other words, legislative overruling in the European Union is comparatively difficult in terms of both veto points and the size of the necessary majorities in the Council of Ministers. If we assume, furthermore, that European integration versus national control is an important dimension of political contention in the EU, and that the supranational institutions are generally aligned in favour of 'more Europe', then the importance of the Commission and EP veto points, and the potential discretion of the Court of Justice, are further increased.

Cooter and Ginsburg's political-party variables suggest that the prospects for legislative overrule in the EU are even worse. The Council of Ministers, the EU's primary legislator through most of its history, is composed of national ministers responsible to a rainbow of governments and electorates, with little systematic coordination, much less discipline, among, say, parties of the left and right. Although the situation is more favorable in the European Parliament, where two or three European party groups have long dominated the Parliament and demonstrated remarkable party-group cohesion (Kreppel 1999), the European legislative process remains a far cry from Cooter and Ginsburg's ideal of a single, disciplined, and dominant party that might easily push through overruling legislation in response to judicial activism. In comparative terms, therefore, the barriers to legislative overruling of European courts—in terms of veto points, super-majorities, and political-party variables—are substantially higher than those for any European state, and arguably exceed those of the proverbial home of judicial activism, the United States.

With constitutional interpretation, finally, the barriers to legislative overruling of an ECJ decision rise yet further. In the case of the European Union, a revision of the EU's constitutive treaties can be achieved only through unanimous agreement in an intergovernmental conference among the member governments, followed by ratification in each of the member states. Thus, in its functions as a 'constitutional court' interpreting the treaties, the Court can be overruled only by unanimous agreement among the member states, a higher threshold for overruling than one can observe in any EU member state or the United States, and the 'nuclear option' referred to in Chapter 1. This does not mean that constitutional revision in response to ECJ rulings is impossible—indeed, we shall examine such a revision, the so-called 'Barber Protocol' to the Maastricht Treaty, in Chapter 6—but the number of such revisions is small[13] and the difficulty of securing unanimous agreement in theory lessens the deterrent effect of any such threat.

Nevertheless, while the barriers to legislative overruling in the EU are *comparatively* high for both statutory and constitutional interpretation, *within* the EU system we observe considerable variation in the thresholds for legislative overruling, which in turn have implications for the discretion enjoyed by supranational agents like the ECJ. Tsebelis and Garrett (2001) provide a comprehensive overview of the prospects for legislative overruling of Commission and Court decisions, arguing that these prospects vary both across issue areas and over time, with counter-intuitive implications for supranational discretion. Specifically, Tsebelis and Garrett examine the major changes to EU legislative procedures across three major periods of EU history: the period of the Luxembourg Compromise (1958–87), when the Council legislated by unanimity with only a consultative role for the Parliament; a second period coinciding with the adoption of QMV and the cooperation procedure after the Single European Act; and finally the period since Maastricht, when the Parliament has emerged as an equal co-legislator with the Council.

During the first period, Tsebelis and Garrett argue, the legislative process was largely blocked by the unanimity requirement, which prevented the development of new legislation but also created a large 'core' of Commission and Court acts that were impervious to overruling through new legislation. During the second period, by contrast, the move to QMV in the Council facilitated the adoption of new legislation but by the same token shrank the core of supranational acts impervious to overruling through new legislation. Counter-intuitively, therefore, the period of the Community's 're-launching' effectively *reduced* the discretion of the Commission to implement,

TABLE 3.3. *Thresholds to legislative overruling: the EU in comparative perspective*

	France	Germany	Italy	Spain	United States	EU
Veto points	2	2	2	1	3	2 or 3
Average coalition duration (years)	6.8	6.3	1.3	6	6.9	N/A Composition of Council shifts frequently
Majorities required for new legislation	Simple majority	Simple majority	Simple majority	Simple majority	Simple majority (60% to break legislative filibuster, 2/3 of both houses to override presidential veto)	Qualified majority or unanimity in Council; absolute majority in EP for co-decision votes
Constitutional amendment threshold	3/5 majority in constitutional congress with deputies and senators sitting together	2/3 majority in Bundestag and Bundesrat; fundamental rights provisions inviolable	2/3 majority in upper and lower house; or simple majority in both houses with possibility of national referendum	3/5 majority in Cortes and Senate; higher for rights provisions	2/3 majority of both houses; or by convention 2/3 of all States and ratified by 3/4 of all States	Unanimous agreement and ratification by all member states

Sources: Adapted from Cooter and Ginsburg (1996: 298); Stone Sweet (2000: 59).

and the Court to interpret, secondary legislation. During the post-Maastricht era, finally, a substantial portion of EU legislation is adopted by co-decision, requiring a qualified majority in the Council *and* an absolute majority in the European Parliament. If we assume that these two bodies have diverse preferences—a fairly uncontroversial assumption—then the difficulty of agreeing EU legislation should increase, and the core of Commission and ECJ decisions invulnerable to new legislation should increase once again.[14]

Tsebelis and Garrett's article makes a strong theoretical case for a relationship between legislative procedure and supranational discretion both over time and across issue areas, and generates multiple counter-intuitive hypotheses for future empirical testing. Nevertheless, the parsimony of their 'unified model of the politics of the European Union' makes it at best a starting point for the empirical study of supranational delegation, for several reasons. First, as Tsebelis and Garrett readily concede, their model applies only to the Commission's implementation and Court interpretation of *secondary* legislation, and not to the Court's interpretation of the treaties, amendment of which continues to require the unanimous agreement of the member governments. In fact, however, the Court's 'constitutionalization' of the treaties during the 1960s and 1970s, which Tsebelis and Garrett purport to explain in part through their model, relied overwhelmingly on treaty interpretation, for which the amendment rules remained unchanged both before and after this period.

Second, Tsebelis and Garrett argue that their model explains not only the Court's but also the Commission's discretion, at least in 'the bulk of EU legislation (80 percent for the 1987–95 period) in which comitology is not used' and in the 'roughly 40 percent of the remaining legislation, in which... Council oversight of policy implementation is purely advisory. In both scenarios', they argue, 'passing secondary legislation is the only effective way to rein in Commission implementation activism' (Tsebelis and Garrett 2001: 368–9). As I have shown in Chapter 2, however, restrictive comitology is widely employed by the Council in most legislation where the Commission gains any significant implementing powers; although Garrett and Tsebelis provide no details regarding the nature of the 80 per cent of EU legislation without comitology, it seems likely that much of this legislation does not, in fact, delegate significant powers to the Commission.

Third and finally, Tsebelis and Garrett's analysis disregards the other potential control mechanisms that might be employed by member governments vis-à-vis the Commission and Court, focusing exclusively on legislative overruling as the sole determinant of

Commission and ECJ discretion. As we have just seen, however, the range of possible control mechanisms for these two agents is enormous, and many of these mechanisms can be employed by member governments or third parties more easily and at lower cost than legislative overruling. For all of these reasons, I retain throughout this book Tsebelis and Garrett's fundamental insight about the importance of legislative overruling as a potential determinant of supranational discretion, but I deliberately sacrifice parsimony in order to keep in view the other control mechanisms that provide alternative, and often more credible, mechanisms of member-state control.

Unilateral Non-Compliance and Judicial Legitimacy
Finally, even in the absence direct political influence over court judgments, or indirect influence through the threat of legislative overruling, all courts are constrained by the need to retain *legitimacy* vis-à-vis the legal profession, political authorities, and public opinion. As Mattli and Slaughter (1998: 197) argue:

... courts in countries upholding the rule of law must perceive themselves and be perceived by others as fundamentally non-political actors. They are socialized to understand themselves as agents and servants of the law. Political considerations attach to judicial decisions and may motivate these decisions at the margin. Nevertheless, overt political arguments are illegitimate; actions must be justified with reference to generalizable principles and in a particular technical discourse.[15]

In fact, the authors continue, the demand for judicial legitimacy imposes two distinct constraints on the Court:

First is the constraint of minimum fidelity to the demands of legal discourse: 'the language of reasoned interpretation, logical deduction, systemic and temporal coherence.' Reasoning and results that do not meet these requirements may be challenged as 'unfounded in law' or as indicative that a court is acting *ultra vires*—in excess of its mandate.

As applied to the ECJ, this suggests that the Court is constrained to pursue its institutional or policy preferences within the limits of carefully reasoned legal analysis. Failure to do so is likely to bring forward criticisms not only from EU member governments but also from members of the legal profession[16] and from the national courts that serve as the ECJ's partners applying EC law within the member states.

Second, Mattli and Slaughter (1998: 197) argue that there exists a 'constraint of minimum democratic accountability: the requirement that a court not stray too far from majority political preferences'. This does not, of course, mean that courts should decide cases either implicitly or explicitly with reference to political majorities, since courts are most often consciously designed as non-majoritarian institutions applying the law irrespective of majority demands.

A closer look, however, reveals that judicial decisions that consistently and sharply contradict majority preferences are likely to undermine perceptions of judicial legitimacy and can result in legislative efforts to restrict or even curtail judicial jurisdiction—the scope of judicial power over particular classes of cases. An astute judge will anticipate these reactions and seek to avoid them. (Mattli and Slaughter 1998: 198)

A court's legitimacy, moreover, may be damaged not only by legislative efforts to limit its jurisdiction—an extreme step which, in the case of the ECJ, requires the unanimous agreement of all EU member governments—but also by widespread and persistent non-compliance with its decisions.

As a control mechanism, non-compliance with ECJ decisions can carry high costs for EU member governments. Although the Court has not traditionally had the power to fine member governments for non-compliance with its rulings, such non-compliance may impose five potential costs on member governments. First, a member state with a poor compliance record faces reputational costs vis-à-vis its partners and its own public, particularly in so far as the Commission engages in 'naming and shaming' member states for non-compliance, as it has regularly done since the late 1980s. Second, in cases brought by national courts through the preliminary reference procedure, government non-compliance constitutes defiance not only of the ECJ but also of its own domestic court, whose decision actually applies the ECJ's legal ruling to the case at hand. Third, as we have seen above, the member governments agreed to amend Article 228 at Maastricht, allowing the Commission to propose, and the Court to impose, mandatory fines on member states for non-compliance with ECJ decisions. Although the Article 228 procedure is lengthy and politically sensitive, it does provide member governments with a concrete incentive to comply with ECJ rulings. Fourth, the Court declared in its 1991 *Francovich* decision the principle of 'state liability', whereby member governments may face financial liability for the costs associated with their failure to transpose EC directives into national law.[17] Fifth and finally, while unilateral non-compliance may limit the costs of an ECJ decision, at least in the short term, it cannot actually overturn an ECJ decision, which requires concerted action by all the member governments.

For all of these reasons, existing studies have focused primarily on the difficulty of overturning ECJ decisions through new legislation or treaty revision, and have largely ignored the threat of non-compliance. Nevertheless, despite its associated costs, the threat or act of non-compliance remains a potential constraint on the ECJ, which may come either from national courts reluctant to accept ECJ jurisprudence or from member governments seeking to limit the effects of those judgments on national policy. With regard to the former, a growing number of studies have demonstrated that the ECJ's doctrines of direct effect and supremacy were resisted to a greater or lesser degree by a number of national courts, particularly by higher courts whose position at the top of their legal hierarchy might be threatened by those doctrines (see for example Alter 1996; 1998; 2000; Golub 1996; Slaughter, Weiler, and Stone Sweet 1998). Perhaps the best-known example of such national-court resistance is the ongoing judicial dialogue between the ECJ and the German *Bundesverfassungsgericht* (Federal Constitutional Court) regarding the ECJ's protection of individual rights, as well as its right to interpret authoritatively the Union's legal competence vis-à-vis national constitutional orders. In the 1974 *Internationale Handelsgesellschaft* or *Solange I* case, the German Court indicated that, *so long as* adequate protection of human rights was not guaranteed by EC law, it would reserve to itself the right to scrutinize EC legislation for conformity to principles of fundamental rights enshrined in the German Basic Law.[18] Responding at least in part to the reservations expressed by the *Bundesverfassungsgericht*, the ECJ subsequently developed its own legal doctrine applying the fundamental human rights common to the member states to its judicial review of Community activities.[19] Following the development of this new ECJ jurisprudence, the German Court agreed in a second ruling, the so-called *Solange II*, to accept ECJ decisions on fundamental rights without further review.[20] Finally, in the 1993 *Maastricht* decision, the *Bundesverfassungsgericht* again proclaimed its concerns about ECJ jurisprudence, this time regarding the extent of EC competences, indicating that it reserved the right to review ECJ decisions for conformity to the provisions of the Basic Law.[21]

Refusal to accept ECJ rulings, moreover, is not the only means at the disposal of national courts to resist unwelcome ECJ doctrines. In addition to overt resistance of the type seen in *Solange I* and *Maastricht*, national courts may also avoid unwelcome ECJ decisions by refusing to submit preliminary references to the Court, relying instead on previous ECJ decisions or on their own interpretation of the treaty provisions under the so-called *acte clair* doctrine (Golub 1996; Chalmers 2000). Finally, even where national courts agree to send preliminary references to the ECJ and accept its rulings, the concrete application of those rulings to the case in hand leaves considerable discretion to national courts, which may circumvent the practical effect of ECJ case law in their application of decisions to the case at hand (Conant 2002: Ch. 3). In all of these ways, the ECJ's relationship with national courts, typically depicted as a vital resource for the Court in its conflicts with member governments, serves as a constraint as well, limiting the Court's ability to impose unwelcome judicial doctrines on reluctant national judges.

With regard to national governments, most scholars agree that overt non-compliance with ECJ decisions is costly for member states for the reasons cited above, and therefore relatively rare. However, as Lisa Conant argues, member governments can and frequently do *contain* the effects of ECJ decisions in various ways. Indeed, Conant argues that the national policy responses most often discussed by students of the ECJ—namely, overt non-compliance, legislative overruling, and complete application of new legal rules as policy—are in fact the least common policy responses by member governments. In addition to these three responses, Conant identifies three other possibilities that more accurately capture the individual and collective responses of member governments to ECJ decisions: (1) 'contained compliance', which occurs when member governments interpret ECJ rulings narrowly, 'neglecting the policy implications of judicial decisions while simultaneously respecting individual judgments'; (2) restrictive application, which occurs when member governments place limits and exceptions on judicial principles in domestic or EC legislation; and (3) pre-emption, which occurs when member governments 'carefully construct European or domestic law to avoid *future* judicial interference in particular areas' (Conant 2002: Ch. 2, emphasis added).

The incidence of these various national responses, Conant suggests, is a function of the costs and benefits imposed by a given judicial decision and of the domestic institutional structures that determine the level of public financial support available to litigants to challenge or reinforce the effects of a decision. Thus, for example, if the potential costs of a decision are intense and concentrated, whether on a government or on powerful private actors, governments are most likely to contain its effects through narrow interpretation of the decision to apply only to the case in hand, or they may limit the present or future reach of the decision through new domestic or EC legislation, which Conant argues are the dominant outcomes in the cases she analyses. By contrast, she argues, full compliance with ECJ rulings is comparatively rare, requiring the mobilization of both litigation and political pressure to extend legal principles beyond individual cases and to press governments to apply completely, rather than contain or limit, the legal principles expressed in an ECJ decision. By the same token, however, overt non-compliance and legislative overruling are also rare, reflecting the relatively high costs of both strategies for member governments, although not inconceivable in cases where the costs of a proposed decision are both concentrated and intense and, in the case of legislative overruling, common to most or all member governments.

The specific interest configurations discussed by Conant are beyond the scope of this chapter, as are her detailed case studies. Nevertheless, for our purposes, Conant's analysis underlines the variety of responses available to member governments in response to unwelcome ECJ decisions, and the great variation in responses observed in various national settings and across different issue areas. To be sure, neither contained compliance, nor restrictive application, nor even pre-emption, is capable of overturning ECJ decisions in the narrow sense, and all three have weaknesses as a response to ECJ activism. Both contained compliance and restrictive application are vulnerable to further legal challenges—provided that potential litigants can find the resources to mount such challenges—and to ECJ decisions expanding the application of the original ruling. Similarly, pre-emption through EC legislation requires super-majoritarian or unanimous agreement among the member governments on language sufficiently rigid and precise to preclude future judicial activism. Nevertheless, these responses by national courts and national governments can and do frustrate the Court's efforts to extend EC legal rights to individuals, and result in the uneven application of EC law across issue areas and across member states.

Delegation and Pre-emption in the Treaty on European Union

As it happens, the Treaty on European Union, as adopted at Maastricht and amended at Amsterdam, contains the most notable example of collective member-state pre-emption of future ECJ activism. As we have already seen, the Court's jurisdiction is overwhelmingly horizontal, applying to all provisions of the EC Treaty, with few or no additional powers delegated in issue-specific treaty articles. The 1992 Treaty of Maastricht, however, witnessed the deliberate creation by the member governments of a European Union comprising not only the then-existing Community but also two intergovernmental 'pillars' concerning Common Foreign and Security Policy and Justice and Home Affairs, respectively, as well as several common provisions regarding the approval and amendment of the treaties, the enlargement of the Union, and the provisions for 'closer cooperation'.[22] For the purposes of this chapter, the most important article of the Maastricht Treaty on European Union (TEU) was Article 46 (ex L) EU, which explicitly limited the jurisdiction of the ECJ to (1) the existing EC pillar; (2) conventions adopted under the Justice and Home Affairs pillars, if those conventions so specified; and (3) the final provisions of the Treaty, dealing with the ratification and amendment of the Treaty and the enlargement process. By contrast, ECJ jurisdiction was ruled out for Common Foreign and Security Policy and for Justice and Home Affairs, as well as for other TEU provisions on 'closer cooperation' among sub-groups of EU member states and on the Union's respect for fundamental human rights.[23]

Both at and after the European Council, the pillarized structure of the TEU and the exclusion of supranational actors from the second and third pillars were criticized, most notably by the Commission and the Parliament but also by the more integrationist member governments, which successfully pressed for the inclusion of a provision in the treaty calling for the convening of a pre-scheduled, follow-up IGC just four years later, to reconsider and possibly amend the pillarized structure of the Union and other elements of the TEU. Member-state preferences regarding the pillars, and the jurisdiction of the ECJ in particular, were diverse. On the one hand, a number of member governments including Germany and the Benelux countries were keen to re-examine the pillar structure of the EU and consider the 'communitarization' of Justice and Home Affairs in particular. On the other hand, the French and British governments, which had been among the champions of the pillar structure at Maastricht, were resistant to any change in that structure and to any supranational powers in the second and third pillars. In addition, the Conservative government of UK Prime Minister John Major, under pressure from the Eurosceptic wing of his party, submitted a paper to the 1996 intergovernmental conference attacking the Court for excessive activism and proposing a series of mechanisms that would restrain the Court in the future, including a possible appeals procedure in which the Court could be asked to reconsider its rulings in light of member-state complaints.[24] Although the British government's proposals were comparatively modest and would not have altered the Court's jurisprudence fundamentally, they predictably failed to receive the unanimous support of the other member governments and were quietly dropped during the later stages of the negotiations.

Notwithstanding the failure of the British campaign, the 1997 Amsterdam Treaty itself reflects the tensions among the various member governments and represents a combination of new delegation on the one hand and new instances of pre-emption and new control mechanisms on the other. Specifically, the member governments agreed at Amsterdam to extend the jurisdiction of the Court for various provisions of the TEU, allowing the Court to review the acts of EU institutions for respect of fundamental human rights as well as the procedure for applying the Treaty provisions on 'closer cooperation' among a subset of EU member governments (Article 46). The most important and complex extensions of ECJ jurisprudence, however, concerned the Maastricht third pillar, which was divided at Amsterdam into two sections: (1) a new title on visas, asylum, and immigration, which were 'communitarized' by being brought into the first pillar of the EC Treaty, and (2) police and judicial cooperation, which remained in an amended third pillar of the TEU. In both areas the jurisdiction of the Court was extended by the Amsterdam Treaty—yet, at the insistence of the British and French governments in particular, these new delegated powers were also coupled with unprecedented mechanisms designed to limit the Court's discretion. The post-Amsterdam jurisdiction of the Court in the TEU and in the communitarized third-pillar issues is summarized in Table 3.4.

Within the communitarized issues of visas, asylum, and immigration, the Treaty provides the Court with its traditional powers to interpret the treaty and arbitrate disputes, but with three significant restrictions, spelled out in Article 68 (ex 73p) EC. First, within the new communitarized issues, preliminary rulings may be sought only by national courts against which there is no possibility of appeal, and not by lower courts as in the existing Article 234. This provision was nominally designed to avoid flooding the Court with a wave of immigration and asylum cases, which is a genuine concern in light of the Court's ever-growing case load. Nevertheless, this provision effectively closes off access to the ECJ by lower courts, which have played a vital role in the expansion of EC law over the past four decades; and it limits access to justice for litigants in immigration and asylum cases, many of whom lack the resources to appeal cases to the highest national courts. Second, the Court's jurisdiction explicitly excludes any measures 'relating to the maintenance of law and order and the safeguarding of internal security'. Third and finally, the Council, the Commission, or member states may request the Court to give a ruling on the interpretation of the treaty provisions or of any acts based on these provisions, but the ruling of the Court 'shall not apply to judgements of courts or tribunals of the Member States which have become *res judicata*'. In this way, the treaty guards against functional creep of ECJ jurisprudence from areas of free movement into areas of criminal law and internal security.

In the remaining third-pillar issues of police and judicial cooperation in criminal matters, the Court is given limited jurisprudence to interpret the treaty provisions and subsequent decisions taken under the third

Table 3.4. *Jurisdiction of the European Court of Justice, in the Treaty on European Union*

Treaty Article	Nature of jurisdiction	Standing	Limits
46c–e (ex L) EU	Jurisdiction to interpret TEU articles on closer cooperation, fundamental human rights, amendment of treaties and enlargement of the Union	EC institutions; member governments; private parties where directly and individually concerned; preliminary references	
68 (ex 73p) EC/ 46b (ex L) EU	Extends jurisdiction of Court under TEC to immigration and asylum issues, subject to limitations	EC institutions; member governments; preliminary references from high courts only	No jurisdiction to rule on national measures relating to law and order or internal security; Rulings shall not apply to national court rulings that have become *res judicata*; No standing for private actors; preliminary references limited to high courts
46b (ex L) EU/ 35 (ex K.7) EU	Extends jurisdiction of Court to police and judicial cooperation: interpretation of treaty provisions; judicial review of decisions; and preliminary rulings subject to limits specified in article	Member governments and Commission; no standing for private parties; national courts can request preliminary ruling only if member state signs a declaration to that effect	No jurisdiction regarding behavior of law enforcement authorities; no standing for private actors; no preliminary ruling procedure without explicit declaration from member state

Source: Consolidated Treaties.

pillar; however, the safeguards and limitations on the Court here are even more byzantine, reflecting the sensitive nature of third-pillar issues. Specifically, the Court gains jurisdiction to undertake judicial review of decisions taken under the third pillar, as well as disputes between member states or between the Commission and member states on the interpretation of third-pillar decisions. Put differently, the Court gains the power to interpret the incomplete contract of third-pillar agreements; however, legal standing to bring such cases is restricted solely to the Commission and the member governments, and excludes both the European Parliament and private actors, who do not even enjoy the traditional right to challenge decisions that are of 'direct and individual concern' to them. Second, at the insistence of the UK government, the new Article 35 (ex K.7) EU establishes only a weak, optional version of the preliminary ruling procedure, whereby member states *may* issue a declaration stating that they accept the jurisdiction of the Court, in which case national courts *may*, but need not, request preliminary rulings from the Court in third-pillar areas (Arnull 2000: 118). Finally, in an effort to limit any future activism by the Court, the revised Article 34 (ex K.6) EU pre-emptively provides that framework decisions adopted by the Council 'shall not entail direct effect', thereby forestalling any such extension of individual rights by the Court.[25]

In sum, the provisions of the Treaty on European Union and their evolution from Maastricht to Amsterdam demonstrate both the incentives of member governments to delegate powers to the Court of Justice to monitor compliance and fill in the details of the treaties as an incomplete contract on the one hand, *and* the unwillingness of member governments to risk any repeat of the Court's activism in the EC pillar on the other. This trade-off is visible in the extension of ECJ jurisdiction to the Union's respect for fundamental human rights; in the more grudging extension of jurisdiction in third-pillar issues, with accompanying limits on ECJ discretion; and finally in Common Foreign and Security Policy, where governments used to judicial deference at home have resisted extending any judicial powers at all at the European level.

II. The Expansion of the Preliminary Ruling Procedure: Member Governments, National Courts, and the ECJ

Thus far in the chapter, I have examined the European Court of Justice only as the *object* of delegation in the EU's constituent treaties, making no effort to describe the preferences or behaviour of the Court as a *subject* in EU politics. Nevertheless, as we have just seen, the legal discretion of the Court as an agent is significant, comparing favourably to the Commission as well as to national constitutional courts, and the Court in practice has interpreted its own mandate broadly, adopting an expansive style of treaty interpretation, viewing the treaties as a constitutional text and declaring the supremacy and direct effect of EU law within national legal orders. A complete review of these events is beyond the scope of the current chapter, yet the Court's constitutionalization of the treaties and the resulting scholarly debate about the Court's independence from the member governments constitute a vital backdrop to several of the cases examined in the second part of this book. In this section, therefore, I provide a preliminary exploration of the single most remarkable development in ECJ jurisprudence, namely, the Court's use and expansion of its power to accept preliminary references from national courts. First, I review very briefly the extensive legal and political-science literature suggesting that the Court has effectively 'constitutionalized' the treaties by extending the use of Article 234 beyond the intentions of its framers and beyond the preferences of member governments, turning it into a means through which individual litigants could claim and enforce EC legal rights against their own governments and secure these rights in national courts, which emerged as partners of the ECJ in a new, unified legal order. Second, I review more briefly the criticisms put forward by rational-choice scholars such as Geoffrey Garrett, who have argued that the Court's use of Article 234, far from constituting an independent process of legal integration, in fact followed closely the preferences of the Union's most powerful member governments. Third and finally, I review the existing empirical evidence, both quantitative and qualitative, regarding the relationship between national preferences and the decisions of the ECJ.

The Constitutionalization of the Treaties

The Court's extension of the Article 234 procedure, and its accompanying constitutionalization of the treaties through doctrines such as the direct effect and supremacy of EU law, have been extensively studied by other scholars, and require only a brief summary here. Most such accounts begin with the landmark cases of *Van Gend en Loos* (1963) and *Costa v. ENEL* (1964), in which the ECJ, responding to Article 234 references from lower member-state courts, declared the principles of the direct effect and supremacy of EC law.

The *Van Gend* case began in a Dutch tax tribunal, where a Dutch chemical importer challenged the legality of a customs duty imposed by the Dutch government on chemicals imported from Germany. The plaintiff argued that the Dutch customs duty was in violation of Article 25 (ex 12) of the EEC Treaty, which placed a 'standstill' on the imposition of any new customs duties among the members of the EEC during the transition to the common market. Specifically, the Dutch tribunal asked the Court whether Article 25 'has direct application within the territory of a Member State, in other words, whether nationals of such a State can, on the basis of the Article in question, lay claim to an individual right which the courts must protect'.[26] As we have seen above, the Belgian, Dutch, and German governments argued in briefs before the Court that it lacked jurisdiction in such a case, since an alternative method existed, under Article 226, for the Commission to challenge the Dutch law through infringement proceedings. Had the Court agreed with this position, Article 234 would have remained unavailable to individual litigants seeking to challenge national regulations for lack of conformity to EC law. Siding with the Commission's position, however, the Court instead affirmed its own jurisdiction in the case, on the grounds that observance of the law could be more readily ensured through the vigilance of individuals asserting their rights in national courts.

On the substance of the tribunal's question, the same three governments argued that Article 25 should not be considered to have direct effect, except insofar as Dutch constitutional law conferred that effect. The Court, however, disagreed, taking a broad view of the aims of the treaty and its effects within national legal orders. In perhaps the most cited passage in EC legal history, the Court argued:

The Treaty is more than an agreement which merely creates mutual obligations between the contracting states. This view is confirmed by the preamble to the Treaty which refers not only to governments but to peoples. It is also confirmed more specifically by the establishment of institutions endowed with sovereign rights, the exercise of which affects Member States and their citizens...

In addition the task assigned to the Court of Justice under Article 177, the object of which is to ensure uniform interpretation of the Treaty by national courts and tribunals, confirms that the states have acknowledged that Community law has an authority which can be invoked by their nationals before those courts and tribunals.

The conclusion to be drawn from this is that the Community constitutes a new legal order of international law for the benefit of which states have limited their sovereign rights, albeit within limited fields, and the subjects of which comprise not only the Member States but also their nationals. Independently of the legislation of Member States, Community law therefore not only imposes obligations on individuals, but is also intended to confer upon them rights which become part of their legal heritage...Article 12 must be interpreted as producing direct effects and creating individual rights which national courts must protect.[27]

In later rulings, the Court elaborated on this formulation, establishing that EC Regulations, which require no national implementing legislation in order to take effect, are directly effective both 'vertically' against the state and 'horizontally' against private actors, while Directives, which require national implementing measures in order to take effect, are directly effective only vertically, vis-à-vis the state, and not horizontally.[28]

In 1964, just one year after *Van Gend*, the Court established the second pillar of the EU legal system, namely, the supremacy of EC law over national law. By contrast with the US constitution but like other international agreements, the EEC Treaty contained no 'supremacy clause', in the absence of which the relation between EC law and national law would appear to be governed by the constitutional provisions of the individual member states. The question of supremacy was raised explicitly in *Costa v. ENEL*, in which a shareholder of the Italian utility challenged the Italian law nationalizing the company as being contrary to the provisions of the EEC Treaty. Recognizing a question of European law, the Milan magistrate trying the case sent a preliminary reference to the Court of Justice, asking whether to give priority to the national law or to the provisions of the Treaty. In its intervention before the Court, the Italian government once again contested the Court's jurisdiction in the case, arguing that, under the 'most recent in time' rule of Italian constitutional law, the national provision should take precedence over the EEC Treaty since the former represented the most recent expression of the parliamentary will. Once again, however, the Court accepted jurisdiction in the case, and its decision unequivocally declared the supremacy of EC law over national law:

By contrast with ordinary international treaties [the Court wrote], the EEC Treaty has created its own legal system which, on the entry into force of the Treaty, became an integral part of the legal systems of the Member States and which their courts are bound to apply.

By creating a Community of unlimited duration, having its own institutions, its own personality, [and] its own legal capacity...the Member States have limited their sovereign rights, albeit within limited fields, and have thus created a body of law which binds both their nationals and themselves...It follows from these observations that the law stemming from the Treaty, an independent source of law, could not, because of its special origin and nature, be overridden by domestic legal provisions, however framed, without being deprived of its character as Community law and without the legal basis of the Community itself being called into question.

The transfer by the states from their domestic legal system to the Community legal system of the rights and obligations arising under the Treaty carries with it a permanent limitation of their sovereign rights, against which a subsequent unilateral act incompatible with the concept of the Community cannot prevail.[29]

Taken together, the principles of direct effect and supremacy meant that EC law conferred rights directly on individuals which could be claimed and protected in national courts, even in the face of conflicting national laws. By the end of the 1960s, individual litigants had begun to respond to these new opportunities, bringing cases under EC law which were then referred in increasing numbers to the ECJ by national courts. As a result, the number of Article 234 references grew steadily over the next three decades (see Fig. 3.1), and now constitute by far the largest single category of cases brought before the ECJ.

Nor did the Court's innovative and integrative case law end with the principles of supremacy and direct effect. In subsequent judgments, the Court declared *inter alia* the doctrines of *indirect effect*, according to which national judges are instructed to interpret national law in conformity with EC law;[30] *implied powers*, whereby the Community is empowered to undertake tasks, such as external representation of the member states in the area of fisheries, which are not expressly conferred in the treaties if the exercise of those powers is implied therein;[31]

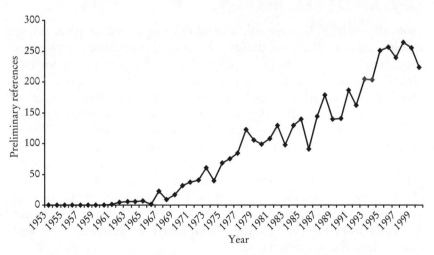

FIG. 3.1. European Court of Justice: preliminary references, 1953–2000
Source: ECJ (2001).

and *state liability*, according to which a national court may hold a member state liable for damages to individuals resulting from improper implementation of an EC Directive.[32] Here again, the preliminary reference procedure was vital, as the Court itself noted in its contribution to the 1996 IGC:

The development of the Community legal order [it wrote] has been to a large extent the fruit of the dialogue which has built up between the national courts and the Court of Justice through the preliminary ruling procedure. It is through such cooperation that the essential characteristics of the Community legal order have been identified, in particular its primacy over the laws of the Member States, the direct effect of a whole series of provisions and the right of individuals to obtain redress when their rights are infringed by a breach of Community law for which a Member State is responsible...

But that is not all. The preliminary ruling system is the veritable cornerstone of the operation of the internal market, since it plays a fundamental role in ensuring that the law established by the Treaties retains its Community character with a view to guaranteeing that the law has the same effect in all circumstances in all the Member States of the European Union. (ECJ 1995: para. 11)

Indeed, moving beyond its 'constitutional decisions', the Court also adopted far-reaching interpretations of specific treaty and secondary law provisions relating to both the liberalization of EC markets and the interpretation of EC social provisions, which are discussed in greater detail below and in Chapters 5 and 6.

The Debate Over ECJ Autonomy

From the early 1980s onward, a number of legal and political-science scholars have interpreted the evolution of the preliminary reference procedure—the creation of directly effective EC legal rights for individuals, the development of a partnership between the ECJ and national courts, and the steady increase in Article 234 references—as the result of autonomous ECJ decision-making, independently or even in defiance of the preferences of the EU member governments. To simplify considerably, such accounts emphasize three key elements that are alleged to have contributed to the Court's extension of the Article 234 procedure and the constitutionalization of the treaties: (1) the activism of the Court of Justice, supported by the Commission; (2) the partnership between the ECJ and national courts within the preliminary reference procedure; and (3) the role of individual litigants in bringing cases before their national courts.[33]

With regard to the first, it is widely agreed by scholars in both law and political science that the European Court of Justice is a sophisticated strategic actor, with 'a clear institutional interest in extending the scope of Community law and its authority to interpret it' (Garrett, Kelemen, and Schulz 1998: 151). Among rational-choice scholars in political science, this assumption is deductive, posited as the premise of a model but not subject to empirical testing. In the legal literature, by contrast, the claim that the Court is pro-integrationist is inductive, based on an extensive reading of the Court's decisions over the past four decades and the off-the-bench writings of judges like Pierre Pescatore, who famously referred to the Court as having *'une certaine idée de l'Europe'*.[34] Trevor C. Hartley (1998: 79) summarizes much of this literature when he writes that:

One of the distinctive characteristics of the European Court is the extent to which its decision-making is based on policy. By policy is meant the values and attitudes of the judges—the objectives they wish to promote. The policies of the European Court are basically the following:

1. strengthening the Community (and especially the federal elements in it);
2. increasing the scope and effectiveness of Community law;
3. enlarging the powers of Community institutions.

These may be summed up in one phrase: the promotion of European integration.

In addition, political scientists and legal commentators agree that the Court's preference for further integration is manifested in a 'teleological' method of interpretation; that is to say, when called to interpret the provisions of the primary or secondary EC law, the Court has repeatedly declined to restrict itself to either the narrow language of the provision in question or the intentions of the framers, but instead interprets those provisions in terms of the broad ends or objectives of the treaties.

An activist Court, however, is insufficient to explain the expansion of the Article 234 procedure and the penetration of national legal systems by EC law, which clearly required the complicity of national courts in referring cases to the ECJ and accepting its jurisprudence. As we have seen, nearly all of the landmark cases in the constitutionalization of the treaties—*Van Gend, Costa v. ENEL, Francovich*, and many others—began as preliminary references from national courts. Furthermore, once the principles of direct effect and supremacy had been established, national courts would continue to play a role by requesting preliminary rulings regarding the compatibility of national laws and regulations with the EC and by their willingness to apply the decisions of the ECJ in specific cases. The acceptance of these doctrines was not, however, immediate or evenly distributed among the courts of the EU member states. As Karen Alter (1996: 462) points out, 'the ECJ was asking national courts for nothing short of a legal revolution' in which the latter would accept the supremacy of the EC Treaty over national laws and even national constitutions, judicial review of national laws for conformity to EC law would challenge long-standing notions of parliamentary sovereignty, and the established hierarchy of higher and lower courts would be disturbed by the addition of the ECJ as the authoritative interpreter of EC law.

In that context, it has been argued, the willingness of national courts to accept ECJ jurisdiction and jurisprudence—and the significant variation in such acceptance both within and across member states—can be explained in terms of the extent to which ECJ rulings 'empowered' national courts within their own domestic political and legal systems (Burley and Mattli 1993; Weiler 1994; Slaughter, Weiler, and Stone Sweet 1998; Mattli and Slaughter 1998: 190–6). ECJ rulings, in this view, could empower national courts in various ways. In the majority of European countries with weak or non-existent traditions of judicial review, ECJ decisions allowed national courts to rule on the compatibility of national laws with the supreme EC law. Alternatively, judges with specific policy preferences would have an incentive to refer cases to the ECJ if and in so far as they expected the resulting decision to be more favourable under EC law than under the provisions of their own national laws (Golub 1996). Finally, Alter (1996; 1998; 2001) argues, the preliminary reference procedure was accepted most readily and used most ambitiously by lower courts, whose judges stood to gain in various ways from a direct relationship with the ECJ. By contrast, national high courts, notwithstanding their legal obligation to refer questions of EC law to the Court of Justice, proved reluctant to do so, resisted accepting the supremacy of EC law over national laws and constitutions, and in some instances even attempted to quash lower-court references to the ECJ. Over time, however, ECJ doctrines filtered into the national legal orders through lower-court decisions, and high courts were reluctantly forced to accept the doctrines and the authority of the Court of Justice.

The complicity or partnership of national courts facilitated EC legal integration even in the face of overt resistance from member governments, in various ways. First, and most obviously, the willingness of national courts to submit references contributed to the growing case load of the Court of Justice, and provided the Court with the opportunity to rule on cases that challenged the core principle of national sovereignty, and that might not have been brought by either the Commission or the member governments as direct enforcement actions.[35] In addition, the integration of national courts into the EC legal order increased the costs of non-compliance for EU member governments. As Weiler and others have pointed out, the Court's decisions under Articles 226 and 227 were, prior to the Maastricht Treaty, purely declaratory, and carried no sanctions in the event of non-compliance by member governments. By contrast, member governments generally face Article 234 judgments coming, not from the ECJ, but from their own national courts, which are left to apply the Court's interpretation of EC law to the case at hand. While it might be comparatively easy to ignore the decisions of an international Court in Luxembourg, member governments find it more difficult to defy the rulings of their own national courts, which may in part explain the surprisingly high rate of compliance by member governments with ECJ decisions under the preliminary ruling procedure (Weiler 1994; Alter 1998; 2001).

Third and finally, both legal and political-science explanations of legal integration have focused increasingly in recent years on the role of individual litigants as 'interlocutors' of the Court of Justice, since it is individual litigants who bring cases before national courts. Drawing on the work of Marc Galanter (1974) and other American students of litigation strategies, such studies make a distinction between 'one-shot' litigants, who may raise EC law issues in the context of a specific legal dispute, and 'repeat players', such as large corporate actors and public interest groups, who may bring cases repeatedly and strategically in order to influence ECJ and national-court jurisprudence and/or attack national legislation for lack of conformity to EC law (Rawlings 1993; Mattli and Slaughter 1998: 186–90; Alter and Vargas 2000; Conant 2002). More generally, these scholars argue that the pattern of Article 234 references can be explained not only by the preferences of national courts but also by the preferences and resources of litigants across member states and across issue areas. For example, Stone Sweet and Brunell (1998) suggest that economic interests are most likely to bring cases and attack national legislation in so far as such legislation creates significant barriers to intra-EC trade; they therefore predict a direct correlation between the level of intra-EC trade and the number of preliminary references. At a lower level of aggregation, Conant and other scholars suggest that patterns of references can be explained by the preferences and the resources available to specific litigants in a given member state, as for example in the case of the United Kingdom, where the presence of a strong Equal Opportunities Commission has played an important role in the bringing of equal pay cases that might otherwise have been beyond the means of individual litigants (see also Alter 2000; Alter and Vargas 2000).

The most forceful exposition of the 'autonomous ECJ' argument can be found in the work of Alec Stone Sweet and his collaborators (Stone Sweet and Caporaso 1998; Stone Sweet and Brunell 1998; Stone Sweet 2000: 153–93), who have argued that the constitutionalization of the treaties was driven, not by the preferences of member governments, but by societal demand, as individual litigants, in reaction to the opportunities presented by European legislation and the ECJ's dispute resolution procedure, challenged national laws and regulations hampering either free trade or other individual rights within the Community. In effect, Stone Sweet and his collaborators argue, 'the constitutionalization process has been driven almost entirely by the relationship among private litigants, national judges, and the ECJ interacting within the framework provided by Article 177' (Stone Sweet and Brunell 1998: 65). More specifically, Stone Sweet and his collaborators argue that the development of intra-EC trade, the gradual increase in EC legislation for the Court to interpret, and the Court's own constitutionalizing decisions have created a virtuous cycle culminating in the development of the new European legal order.

By and large, Stone Sweet and the other scholars mentioned above depict EU member governments as reactive rather than proactive in the process of legal integration, responding and adapting to ECJ decisions which they are unable to influence or overturn. Despite their nominal status as 'masters of the treaty', these scholars argue, EU member governments are unable to control the process of legal integration, for three reasons. First, Burley and Mattli (1993) argue, the Court's language of the law acts both as a 'mask' for the policy implications of the Court's doctrinal interventions and as a 'shield' against political attacks. As Stein (1981) has demonstrated, however, the potential implications of ECJ jurisprudence were in fact clear to the member governments as early as the *Van Gend* and *Costa* cases of the early 1960s, and by the late 1970s and early 1980s the Court's more controversial rulings were coming in for public criticism from heads of state and government like French President Valéry Giscard d'Estaing, German Chancellor Helmut Kohl, and UK Prime Minister John Major. By contrast with the mask and shield argument, Alter (1996; 1998; 2001) and others have argued that the complicity of national courts has increased the costs of non-compliance for member governments, which would have to defy not only an international court but also their own domestic courts in order to avoid complying with ECJ decisions under Article 234. Third and finally, Stone Sweet and Brunell argue, in line with the analysis presented above, that the Court is protected from political interference by the extraordinarily high thresholds to legislative overruling of ECJ decisions, particularly in the Court's interpretation of the treaties, and the high costs of non-compliance with ECJ decisions.

Summarizing their analysis, Stone Sweet and Caporaso (1998: 129) argue that 'the move to supremacy and direct effect must be understood as audacious acts of agency' by the Court. By the same token, however, they argue that:

> ...judicial politics in the EC is not easily captured by P-A imagery. The Court's constitutionalization of the treaty system produced profound structural changes. Among other things, it reconstituted relationships among the ECJ, national judges, and private and public actors at the national and transnational levels. Often enough, the impact of the Court's rule-making is to effectively constrain member-state governments, both individually and collectively. The P-A framework is ill-equipped to capture these dynamics.

The empirical basis for these claims is discussed at some length below; suffice it for the moment to point out that, for Stone Sweet as for the other authors mentioned above, the EU's member governments were peripheral actors in the process of legal integration just described, either unaware of the ECJ's legal revolution thanks to the mask and shield of the law or unable to overturn decisions to which they were averse.

By contrast, Geoffrey Garrett and others have argued that the Court, as an agent of the member governments, is far less independent than either its supporters or its detractors have judged. In his early work on the ECJ, Garrett (1992) presented his most forceful version of the principal-agent account, arguing that the Court, as an agent of the EU's member governments, was bound to follow the wishes of the Union's most powerful member states. Those member states, he argued, had established the ECJ as a means to solve problems of incomplete contracting and monitoring compliance with EU obligations, and they rationally accepted ECJ jurisprudence, even when rulings went against them, because of their longer-term interest in the enforcement of EU law. In such a setting, Garrett and Weingast (1993) suggested, the ECJ might identify 'constructed focal points' among multiple equilibrium outcomes, but it was unlikely to rule against the preferences of powerful EU member states, as Burley and Mattli had suggested.

These early principal-agent analyses, although a welcome corrective to the court-centrism of some earlier works, failed to explore in any detail the precise nature of the principal-agent relationship between the member governments and the Court, and therefore overstated the extent of control exercised by the Union's most powerful member states. In subsequent work, Garrett and others refined these early principal-agent approaches in two distinct ways. First, as we have seen above, Kilroy (1995; 1999) and Tsebelis and Garrett (2001) formulated models based on the threat of, and thresholds to, legislative over-ruling of ECJ decisions, arguing that the Court should be most attent-ive to the preferences of member governments in those cases where its judgments could be most easily overturned—for example, by quali-fied majority in the Council rather than unanimity in Council or treaty amendment.

Second, Garrett, Kelemen, and Schulz (1998) formulated a simple game-theoretical model of ECJ decision-making in which the likeli-hood of an 'adverse decision'—one detrimental to the preferences of EU member governments—is a function of three variables: estab-lished legal precedent, the potential costs of a ruling to the defendant member state, and the likelihood that other member governments will support the defendant and possibly overturn the Court's decision. With regard to the first, Garrett, Kelemen, and Schulz acknowledge earlier criticisms (Mattli and Slaughter 1995) that the Court, as a legal actor, will avoid taking nakedly political or poorly reasoned decisions, and must in fact be concerned with the consistency and legitimacy of those decisions. They therefore hypothesize that 'the greater the clar-ity of the ECJ case law precedent, the lesser the likelihood that the Court will tailor its decisions to the anticipated reactions of the mem-ber governments'. Second, as a straightforward extension of Garrett's earlier reasoning, they argue that 'the greater the domestic costs of an ECJ ruling to a litigant member government', the greater the likeli-hood of national non-compliance, and hence the greater the likelihood that the Court will tailor its judgment to the preferences of the affected member state. Third and finally, they hypothesize that 'the larger the number of member governments adversely affected by [a decision], the greater the likelihood that responses by the litigant governments will move from individual noncompliance to coordinated retaliation', and therefore the greater the likelihood that the Court will be reluctant to offer adverse decisions (Garrett, Kelemen, and Schulz 1998: 150–1).

The ECJ and the Member States: A Review of the Evidence

To some extent, the neo-functionalist and neo-rationalist schools have converged over the course of the past decade, agreeing on some basic assumptions as well as some basic empirical facts (Mattli and Slaughter 1998). For example, the two sides of the debate agree that the Court is a sophisticated strategic actor with a clear preference for further legal integration and a keen awareness of the preferences of the member governments. Furthermore, both sides agree that ECJ decisions adopted since the early 1960s have indeed constitutionalized the treaties, integrating EC and national laws and providing individual litigants with the opportunity to challenge the conformity of national laws with the higher EC law. In this context, the primary remaining disagreement between the two sides concerns the relationship between member-government preferences and the ECJ's Article 234 decisions. To simplify only slightly, Garrett and his co-authors argue that the Court has been and remains highly responsive to the preferences of member governments and should avoid making decisions that run against the interests of powerful member governments, particularly if those decisions are likely to provoke non-compliance or legislative overruling. If these scholars are correct, we should see a strong correlation between the decisions of the Court on the one hand and the preferences of powerful member governments and the ease of legislative overruling on the other hand. By contrast, scholars like Weiler, Burley and Mattli, Alter, and Stone Sweet argue that, because of the complicity of the national courts and the difficulty of sanctioning, the ECJ can rule and regularly has ruled against the explicitly expressed preferences of the member governments, which have lost control of the process of legal integration in favour of individual litigants, national courts, and the ECJ itself. In light of these contradictory hypotheses, what evidence do we have that the decisions of the Court do—or do not—follow the preferences of its member-state principals?

The first study to track systematically the relationship between ECJ jurisprudence and member-state preferences was Eric Stein's 1981 analysis of eleven landmark ECJ decisions on 'constitutional' issues, including the *Van Gend* and *Costa* decisions examined above. For each of these eleven cases, Stein identifies the key constitutional issue in question, namely, direct effect, supremacy, the expansion of direct effect, or the Community's treaty-making power; the positions lodged by member governments and by the Commission in their briefs before the Court; the position of the Advocate-General, who issues a preliminary opinion for the consideration of the Court; and the judges' final ruling. In ten of the eleven cases, Stein notes, at least one member government, and in some cases several governments or the Council as a whole, lodged a brief arguing against the constitutional extension being contemplated, while only a single case featured interventions by member governments in favour. Nevertheless, Stein finds that the Court ruled in favour of an expansive reading of the treaty in all eleven cases and that the Court's ruling was in agreement with the Commission's legal brief in ten of these cases, suggesting that the Court has been led by the Commission in 'the inexorable progression toward more legal integration and more Community power' (Stein 1981: 24).

Stein's findings suggest that the Court retains significant autonomy from member governments, and that the process of legal integration takes place primarily as a result of supranational action by the Commission and Court rather than at the behest of EU member governments. Nevertheless, the generalizability of Stein's findings can be challenged on the grounds that he studies only eleven cases, all of which took place during the early years of the Community between 1963 and 1978, before the Court's rulings became a salient political issue among member governments. Furthermore, all eleven cases were chosen on the dependent variable for an integrative or 'yes' decision, omitting those cases where the Court might have failed to extend, or even retreated from, EC constitutional principles. Finally, as Stein himself notes, the number of member-state briefs in these key cases was generally small, ranging from a single submission in seven cases to a maximum of five in the 1974 *Reyners* case, suggesting either that most member governments were unaware of the significance of these cases, as Burley and Mattli suggest, or that they tacitly approved of the Court's jurisprudence, as Garrett and others have argued. Fortunately, two recent quantitative studies have expanded the set of cases examined and increased our knowledge about the correlation of member-state preferences and Court decisions across a range of issue areas.

The first major quantitative study of Article 234 references was by Stone Sweet and his colleagues, who sought to test the hypothesis, reviewed above, that Article 234 references are correlated strongly with the level of intra-EC trade and the extent of EC-level regulation. Specifically, Stone Sweet his colleagues collected data on Article 234 reference activity from 1961 through mid-1995 for a total of 2,978 references, which were then coded by country of origin, year of referral, national court making the referral, and subject matter. Using this data, the authors examine the relationship among intra-EC trade, European regulation, and Article 234 references both cross-nationally and over time. Comparing the number of preliminary references cross-nationally, they find that 'the linear relationship between intra-EC trade and references is nearly perfect, with countries that trade more with their partners generating higher levels of Article 177 references' (Stone Sweet and Brunell 1998: 67). Over time, they find a similarly strong relationship among intra-EC trade, the production of EC regulations and directives, and the rise of Article 234 references. On the basis of these data, Stone Sweet and Brunell convincingly demonstrate the strong correlation over time among the levels of intra-EC trade, the growth of EC legislation, and the rise of Article 234 references. But what of the member governments? Here, the evidence produced by Stone Sweet *et al.* is less direct, because their primary dependent variable is the frequency of Article 234 references, rather than the outcomes of specific cases. In the area of social policy, however, Stone Sweet and Brunell do examine and code *outcomes* in 91 cases into two categories: 'either the court accepted a national rule or practice as consistent with EC law or declared it to be in violation'. Of these 91 cases, they find, the ECJ declared a violation of EC law in 48, meaning that the Court ruled against member governments in 53 per cent of cases. Among the three largest member states—Britain, France, and Germany, which might be expected to exert greater influence on the Court than smaller members and therefore a higher success rate—the Court ruled violations in 59 per cent of cases. Finally, like Stein, Stone Sweet and Brunell note that the Commission's opinion in a given case is the strongest predictor of the Court's decision, with the ECJ following the Commission in 73 out of 83 cases for a 'success rate' of 88 per cent. They interpret these findings to suggest that EU member governments do not control ECJ rulings, which take place in a context of broad judicial discretion.

Bernadette Kilroy's (1999) study, finally, represents the most direct statistical test of principal-agent hypotheses about the relationship between member-state preferences and ECJ decisions. Specifically, Kilroy models and hypothesizes about two distinct checks on the Court's power: the threat of legislative overrule and the threat of noncompliance. Kilroy's central argument is that 'the threat of noncompliance much more than the threat of overrule constrains the ECJ. This is because noncompliance by even a few member states is of serious concern to the Court of Justice whereas legislative overrule requires action on the part of at least a majority of member states. Consequently, the Court has less room for manoeuvre in the face of noncompliance than in the face of legislative overrule' (Kilroy 1999: 6). In order to test this hypothesis, Kilroy created an original data set of 293 ECJ rulings, including both direct actions and preliminary references, in two issue areas: the free movement of goods and social provisions, which represent the Court's activity in the liberalization and regulation of the European market, respectively.[36] For each case, Kilroy codes the dependent variable, the outcome of the case, as either 'pro-EC' if the Court rules against the legality of a member-state provision or 'pro-member state' if the Court upholds national provisions.[37] As a measure of her hypothesized independent variable, member-state preferences, Kilroy records the submissions of the Commission and the member governments, if any, for each case as the hypothesized independent variable, similarly coding those interventions as pro-EC, pro-member state, or neutral if a member government offered no submissions during written or oral procedure. Using ordered probit analysis, Kilroy then examines the correlation between the preferences of the various member governments, coalitions of member governments, the Commission's position, and the Court of Justice's final decision.

Kilroy's findings, like other ordered probit results, are difficult to interpret, since the results represent not a direct correlation between a dependent and independent variable but the effect of a given independent variable (for example, the position of a given member state) on the probability of a certain value of the dependent variable (for example, a pro-EC decision by the ECJ). Nevertheless, at the risk of oversimplifying Kilroy's analysis, a few key findings can be highlighted here. First, in aggregate terms, Kilroy finds, the Court took a pro-EC position in 160 cases (55 per cent); a pro-member state position in 107 cases (36 per cent); and an intermediate position in 27 cases. Looking first at the effect of individual member government preferences on the probability of particular ECJ rulings, Kilroy finds that, if a member government such as Germany, France, Belgium, the Netherlands, or the UK takes a pro-member state position, the Court is 16 per cent more likely to render a pro-member state ruling than if no member state takes a position; however, contrary to Garrett's (1992) claim that the Court is particularly attentive to the preferences of large member states like France and Germany, Kilroy's findings suggest that the preferences all of the member states, with the notable exception of Italy, have approximately the same impact on the probability of a pro-EC or pro-member state ruling by the ECJ (Kilroy 1999: 400).

Moving from individual member governments to coalitions, Kilroy then tests the hypothesis, derived from the legislative-overrule model, that the Court is sensitive to particular coalitions of member governments constituting the qualified majority or unanimous agreement necessary to overrule ECJ decisions, but not sensitive to smaller coalitions constituting a simple or blocking majority within the Council. In fact, Kilroy finds little support for the legislative overrule position, since the relatively small number of cases—six—in which a qualified majority took a pro-member state position does not allow for generalization.[38] By contrast, Kilroy finds that both simple and even blocking majorities among the member governments have a statistically significant effect on the probability of a particular type of ECJ ruling.

Specifically, she finds that 'the predicted probability of a pro-ms ruling is only 23% when no country or coalition takes a position, while the probability of a pro-EC judgment is 67%. By contrast, when a simple majority takes a pro-ms position, the likelihood of a pro-ms outcome increases 50% to 73%, and the chances of a pro-EC ruling decrease to 18%. Even a blocking minority increase the chances of a pro-ms outcome to 56%' (Kilroy 1999: 405–6).

Kilroy interprets these findings to suggest that the Court is less constrained by the threat of legislative overrule than it is by the threat of non-compliance by a critical mass of member states. However, as Kilroy herself points out, this interpretation can be challenged on the grounds that, rather than responding to the threat of non-compliance, both the Court *and* the member states may be responding to the legal strength or weakness of a case: that is to say, the correlation between member-state interventions and ECJ rulings may represent a common legal assessment by both actors about the merits of the case rather than the political influence of member states over the ECJ. Kilroy attempts to respond to this 'so what?' argument in a later chapter, where she examines a set of seven cases on the equal treatment of part-time workers, demonstrating that the Court issued strongly pro-EC rulings in the first five, while apparently backtracking and issuing pro-member state rulings in the last two. The basis for Kilroy's selection of these cases, however, is not explained, and the case studies themselves make no mention of member-state interventions in each of these cases, pointing only to a 1992 public criticism of the Court by German Chancellor Helmut Kohl as the turning point which apparently led the Court to retreat from its previous jurisprudence. More generally, these cases do not demonstrate in any explicit way that the Court was actually motivated in any of these cases by concerns about member-state non-compliance. Finally, it is worth noting that Kilroy does not test the hypothesis, derived from the work of Garrett and others, that the responsiveness of the Court to member-state preferences should vary with the size of the majority required to overturn the Court's decision through legislative overruling. Although Kilroy does examine the correlation between the size of the member-state coalition taking a position before the Court, her study does not measure, and hence cannot test, the relation between the size of the majority necessary for overruling—that is, QMV, unanimity, or treaty amendment—and the Court's responsiveness to member-government preferences. This latter question remains a promising avenue for future study.

Taken together, the studies surveyed above offer important clues about the relationship between member-state preferences and ECJ rulings, two of which are worth highlighting briefly here. First, the studies by Stein, Stone-Sweet and Brunell, and Kilroy all demonstrate clearly that the Court rules regularly against the publicly expressed preferences of EU member governments—including the largest member governments, which enjoy a success rate before the ECJ that is no better than that of the smaller member governments and worse than that of the Commission. We can, therefore, reject the hypothesis that the Court is particularly responsive to the preferences of large and powerful member states.

Second, however, Kilroy's study demonstrates that the Court is more likely to rule in favour of member-state positions where substantial numbers of member governments express a clear preference for such decisions. Kilroy interprets this finding to suggest that it is the threat of widespread non-compliance rather than the threat of legislative overrule that provides the political context for the Court's decisions; however, in the absence of a clearer picture of the Court's preferences and the causal mechanisms at work, other interpretations remain equally plausible. Given the extreme rarity with which a qualified majority offers negative submissions—only six cases in Kilroy's data-set—it seems likely that the Court relies on less formal means to gauge the likelihood of legislative overrule, which may represent the primary deterrent to integrative ECJ decisions despite the lack of formal submissions by a qualified majority or unanimous group of member states. Alternatively, the submission of multiple member-state submissions in a given case may indeed be a response to the legal merits of a given case, in which case the relationship between member-state submissions and ECJ rulings may be spurious. In order to distinguish among these competing interpretations, we need more qualitative evidence about the mechanisms whereby member governments might influence the ECJ, and the preferences and incentives of the ECJ in issuing its judgments.

III. Conclusions

In the first part of this chapter, I examined the EC and EU Treaties as acts of delegation, attempting to discern patterns in the functions delegated and the discretion allocated to the Court of Justice across issue areas and over time, reaching two primary conclusions. First, in terms of delegated *functions*, the ECJ has been delegated broad-ranging powers to interpret authoritatively EC law, including direct enforcement vis-à-vis member states through Articles 226 and 227, judicial review of Community acts through Articles 230 and 232, and uniform application of EU law in national courts through the preliminary reference procedure of Article 234. These functions, furthermore, clearly fit the standard principal-agent categories of monitoring and enforcing compliance and filling in the details of incomplete contracts first assigned to the Court by Garrett (1992), and they appear to represent a desire to enhance the credibility of member-state commitments— although, in the case of the preliminary reference procedure, the available evidence suggests that the drafters of the EEC Treaty did not intend Article 234 to be used as the decentralized enforcement mechanism into which it later evolved.

Second, the *discretion* assigned to the Court in carrying out these duties is remarkably broad by comparison with both the European Commission and domestic constitutional courts. While the relatively short and renewable terms of office of European judges compares unfavourably with those of their national counterparts, the judges are nevertheless protected from individual pressures by the Court's practice of deliberating in secret and issuing unanimous decisions. Furthermore, as we have just seen, the thresholds to legislative over-ruling and constitutional amendment in the European Union are, in comparative terms, remarkably high, suggesting that the Court has extraordinary discretion to stray from the preferences of its principals without provoking a collective response. These principals may, of course, pre-empt further ECJ activism in new areas, as they did in the creation of the second and third pillars of the European Union; but the Court's *acquis* should prove relatively resistant to member-state reversal. Nevertheless, the Court must also pay attention to the threat of non-compliance by both national courts and national governments, which recent scholarship reveals to be more far-reaching than previous analyses had suggested. For all of these reasons, we should predict that, *ceteris paribus*, the Court will be more successful than the Commission in pursuing its own policy preferences at the expense of the member governments that created it.

In the second part of the Chapter, I turned from the treaties as acts of delegation to consider the Court's constitutionalization of the treaties through the principles of supremacy and direct effect, and the growth of the preliminary reference procedure under Article 234, and I reviewed the various theories offered to explain the Court's jurisprudence and its relationship to both member governments and other interlocutors such as national courts and individual litigants. Here again, I offer two conclusions. First, with regard to theory, Stone Sweet and Brunell are correct in their assertion that a simple principal-agent model of member government-ECJ relations cannot constitute a satis-factory theory of EU legal integration, since the ECJ must necessarily address other actors, including the individual litigants who bring cases as well as the national courts that are responsible for submitting and applying the bulk of all contemporary ECJ decisions. By the same token, however, I would argue that no satisfactory theory of EU legal integration can *omit* the principal-agent relationship between the member governments and the ECJ, since it is this relationship that sets the bounds of ECJ discretion through the adoption and amendment of the treaties and through the threat or use of control mechanisms such as legislative overruling and non-compliance.

Second, with regard to the empirical findings summarized above, it seems clear that the Court does not slavishly follow the dictates of the most powerful EU member states, as a crude neo-realist argument might suggest; nevertheless, Kilroy does demonstrate some correla-tion between member-state preferences and Court decisions. The sig-nificance of this latter finding, however, is unclear in the absence of more qualitative evidence about the relative preferences of, and inter-actions among, the member governments and the Court of Justice. The promise and the difficulties of such analyses are the subject of Chapters 5 and 6 of this book.

CHAPTER 4

The European Parliament as an Outlier: Delegation of Legislative Power in the European Union

Thus far in this study, I have demonstrated that the patterns of delegation and discretion allocated to the European Commission and the Court of Justice fit closely with the predictions of principal-agent analysis. As we have seen, both the Commission and the Court have been delegated functions that are neatly covered under the four categories of monitoring compliance, filling in the details of incomplete contracts, promulgating detailed regulations, and, in the case of the Commission, setting the legislative agenda for the member governments in the Council. In terms of discretion, we have seen that the member governments have, in both primary and secondary legislation, systematically adopted administrative and oversight mechanisms to limit the discretion of both the Commission and the Court. Finally, we have seen that member governments have generally delegated greater discretion to the Court than to the Commission, while calibrating the discretion of the latter across both functions and issue areas.

In this chapter, I extend the analysis beyond the Commission and the Court to the European Parliament. The fundamental argument of the chapter is that, while EU member governments have delegated an ever-expanding set of supervisory, budgetary, and legislative powers to the Parliament though successive treaty amendments, those powers are generally a poor fit with the functions predicted by principal-agent analysis, with the exception of the Parliament's function of overseeing the Commission. Furthermore, the pattern of legislative powers delegated to the Parliament across 35 different issue areas differs starkly from the pattern of agenda-setting powers delegated to the Commission, again suggesting distinct motivations among the member governments vis-à-vis the Commission and the EP. Put simply, the member governments of the Union have delegated to the Parliament a set of powers substantially different from those delegated to the Commission and the Court, and they have allocated discretion to the Parliament in areas that differ systematically from the patterns of discretion observed for the Commission and the Court.

Put even more simply, the European Parliament is an outlier, and delegation to the Parliament seems to be motivated not by functional demands but primarily by an ideological concern on the part of member governments, and their constituents, to enhance the democratic legitimacy of the European Union. Such an ideological motive for delegation is most often stated by the member governments themselves, and even Andrew Moravcsik (1998) in his intergovernmentalist account argues that member governments are guided primarily by ideology in delegating to the EP. Nevertheless, if the EP is not a stereotypical agent, we should not infer from this finding that delegation to the EP takes us into the realm of non-consequential reasoning and a pure 'logic of appropriateness'. Although democratic legitimacy is indeed the primary motivation for those governments—such as the German, the Italian, and the Benelux—that press most emphatically for an increase in EP powers, the specific pattern of member-state preferences, and the specific areas in which EP legislative powers are or are not increased, demonstrate a deliberate effort by member governments to calculate the likely consequences of delegation to the EP and to calibrate their institutional choices to avoid negative consequences of delegation. I therefore argue that, although the Parliament is not a typical agent, rational-choice institutionalist approaches are nevertheless useful for understanding both the decision to delegate powers to the Parliament and the actual influence of Parliament across various legislative procedures.

As in the previous chapters, the focus here is narrowly on the patterns of delegation to, and discretion for, the European Parliament. No attempt is made to discuss the complex internal workings of the Parliament, the nomination and election of its members, the operation of its well-developed committee system, or the cohesion of, and coalitions among, its various party groups, except in so far as these are relevant to the questions of delegation and discretion. Readers interested in these and other aspects of the Parliament and its evolution are advised to consult the definitive textbook by Corbett, Jacobs, and Shackleton (2000) and the concise review of the theoretically oriented literature by Hix (1999a: Ch. 3).

I. Delegation and Discretion

The powers of the European Parliament, like those of the Court of Justice and, to a lesser extent, the Commission, are set out primarily in the EU's *Consolidated Treaties*. By contrast with the relative stability of the Commission's and the Court's powers, however, the powers delegated to Parliament have increased dramatically since the 1957 Treaties of Rome, in which the Parliament played only a minor supervisory role over the Commission and a purely consultative role in EC legislation. Indeed, in a series of treaty amendments over the intervening four decades, the Parliament has gained: (1) supervisory powers over the Commission and other EU institutions, such as the European Central Bank; (2) budgetary powers, which were conferred by two minor treaties in 1970 and 1975 and effectively make the EP a junior partner alongside the Council of Ministers in the EC budgetary authority; and (3) legislative powers, which have gradually increased with the adoption and extension of the consultation, cooperation, assent, and co-decision procedures. These functions and the major treaty reforms that effected them are summarized in Table 4.1.

The first of these three functions fits well with the predictions of the principal-agent model, with the EP serving alongside the Council, the Court of Justice, and other EC institutions as an institutional check on the Commission and other executive agents. The budgetary and legislative powers of the Parliament, however, lie outside the range of functions predicted by standard principal-agent models, suggesting that member governments were motivated by concerns other than a demand for policy expertise or credible commitments when delegating such powers to the Parliament. Let us review each of these powers, very briefly, in turn.

Appointment, Supervision, and Dismissal of the Executive

Supervision and possible censure of the High Authority was the original and only function of the Common Assembly of the European Coal and Steel Community. Later, with the adoption of the EEC Treaty and its various amendments, the Parliament gained legislative and budgetary powers that eclipsed the importance of its supervisory powers over the Commission. Nevertheless, the EP's powers over the Commission—as well as other independent agencies such as the European Investment Bank (EIB) and the European Central Bank (ECB)—have continued to grow over the years, in a variety of areas

TABLE 4.1. *The expansion of the European Parliament's powers, 1957–1997*

Treaty	Supervisory powers	Budgetary powers	Legislative powers
EEC Treaty (1957)	Right to pose questions to and censure Commission.	None	Consultation procedure for 22 Treaty articles.
Luxembourg (1970, 1975)	Right to be consulted on nomination of members of the Court of Auditors.	EP serves, along with Council, as part of 'Budgetary Authority', with power to amend Council's draft budget and to provide discharge of budget.	
Single European Act (1986)			Cooperation procedure established for 10 Treaty articles. Assent procedure for accession and association agreements.
Maastricht (1992)	Right to consultation on nomination of Commission President, ECB members. Right of assent to nomination of full Commission. Standing to bring cases before ECJ to protect its own prerogatives.		Creation of co-decision procedure (I) for 15 Treaty articles. Cooperation procedure extended to total of 16 articles. Assent procedure extended to total of 6 articles. Consultation procedure extended to total of 52 articles. EP excluded from second and third pillars.

	Right to establish temporary committees of inquiry.		Reform of co-decision to make EP an equal partner of Council (removal of third reading).
Amsterdam (1997)	Right of assent in nomination of Commission President.	Second- and third-pillar expenditures to be charged to EC budget (with exception of military or defense expenditures, or if Council decides otherwise by unanimity).	Extension of co-decision to 15 existing and 8 new Treaty articles, for total of 38 articles. Near-elimination of cooperation procedure, except for 4 EMU articles. Extension of assent, total of 13 articles. Consultation extended to total of 66 articles. EP entitled to (amended) consultation or information in second and third pillars. No EP participation for 92 (72 EC and 20 EU) Treaty articles.

Sources: Treaty Establishing the European Economic Community; Treaty of Luxembourg, 1970; Treaty of Luxembourg, 1975; Single European Act; Treaty on European Union; Treaty of Amsterdam; Maurer (2001); Corbett, Jacobs, and Shackleton (2000).

that can be summarized quite briefly here:

- *Right of censure.* The right to censure the executive by a majority of its members was the first and only important power of the ECSC Common Assembly, and was extended to the Commission in the 1957 EEC Treaty. Although this power has never been used, the Parliament has held a number of censure votes over the years, and it was the near-certainty of parliamentary censure that prompted the resignation *en masse* of the Santer Commission in September 1999 (see Chapter 2).

- *Appointment of the Commission.* Unlike most national parliaments in Europe, but like the US Congress and other parliaments in separation-of-powers systems, the European Parliament initially enjoyed no power over the appointment of the Commission or other EU executive agents. However, as we saw in Chapter 2, the Treaty of Maastricht provided that Parliament should be consulted on the choice of the nominee for Commission President and that it should subsequently have the right of assent over the nomination of the entire Commission. In practice, the EP has made full use of these provisions, holding a formal vote on the choice of Jacques Santer as President and holding US Senate-style confirmation hearings for each of the Commission nominees in 1995 (Jacobs 1999). The member states subsequently ratified these practices in the Amsterdam Treaty, formalizing the Parliament's right of assent over the President as well as the full College of Commissioners (Hix 1999*b*).

- *Appointment of other executive actors.* In addition to its growing role in the appointment of the Commission, the EP also enjoys a consultative role in the appointment of the members of the Court of Auditors (a power it acquired in the 1975 budget treaty) and the European Central Bank (Treaty of Maastricht, Article 114 EC). Here again, the Parliament has made aggressive use of its powers, holding public confirmation hearings on the candidates for the President, Vice-President, and Members of the Board of the ECB. In both of these areas, however, the Parliament's vote is only consultative, and in practice the member governments have demonstrated a willingness to ignore negative votes from the Parliament on their proposed candidates. By contrast, Article 195 EC of the Treaty of Maastricht provides Parliament with the sole power of appointment to the office of Ombudsman, and the EP may also name two members to the boards of certain EU administrative agencies such as the European Environment Agency (Corbett, Jacobs, and Shackleton 2000: 233–43).

- *Scrutiny and control of the executive.* Finally, the EP has been granted various powers to monitor and control the executive, including: the right to put written and oral questions to the Commission (Article 197 EC, which appeared in the 1957 EEC Treaty as Article 140); the right to form Committees of Inquiry to investigate alleged cases of maladministration in EU institutions (Article 193 EC, added at Maastricht); control over the discharge of the budget, which has on occasion provided the EP with significant leverage over the Commission (Article 206 EC, added in the 1975 budget treaty); and standing before the Court of Justice for the purpose of protecting its prerogatives vis-à-vis the Commission, the Council, and other EU institutions (Article 230 EC as amended at Maastricht).[1]

The Parliament's steadily growing role in the appointment, supervision, and censure of the Commission and other executive agents falls short of a full 'parliamentarization' of government at the EU level, since Parliament retains only a secondary role in the nomination of the Commission and other EU executive agents. Nevertheless, these powers do provide an additional layer of control over the Commission and other executive agents *and* the potential for democratic legitimization of those bodies that cannot be afforded by comitology, judicial review, or other control mechanisms reviewed in Chapter 2.

Budgetary Powers

During the early, transitional years of the EC, the Community was funded primarily from national contributions, the process of setting the budget was purely intergovernmental, and the EC's major spending policies, such as the Common Agricultural Policy (CAP) and the Structural Funds, had not yet been established. According to the Rome Treaties, this situation was to change at the end of the transitional period, when the Community would take a decision to establish its 'own resources' and a Community budgetary procedure would be established. In 1965, on the eve of this scheduled transition, the Commission of President Walter Hallstein produced ambitious proposals for a Community budgetary system in which the Commission and the Parliament would play a significant role, alongside the Council, in the preparation and adoption of the annual EC budget. The Commission's proposals were broadly supported by five of the then six member governments as the basis for negotiations, but they were rejected by the government of French President Charles de

Gaulle, who was eager to secure guaranteed financing for the CAP—which would disproportionately benefit French farmers—but opposed the supranational elements of Hallstein's proposed system.

Fortunately for de Gaulle, the new own-resources system would have to be adopted under Article 269 (ex 201) EC, which required a unanimous vote from the member governments on the basis of a Commission proposal and after consulting the European Parliament, followed by ratification of the agreement by the parliaments of the various member states. This meant that, although the Council had to act on the basis of a Commission proposal and consult the EP, the French government retained a veto over the adoption of the new system. Furthermore, the Commission's proposals also coincided with the imminent transition from unanimous to qualified majority voting in the Council for many issue areas, which de Gaulle regarded as an unacceptable loss of national sovereignty. In an effort to forestall the scheduled transition to qualified majority voting as well as the Commission's budgetary proposals, de Gaulle famously decided to withdraw French representatives from the Council, resulting in the 'empty chair crisis' of 1965–6. The latter was finally resolved at the end of January 1966 by the so-called Luxembourg Compromise, an ambiguous agreement in which member governments agreed, in effect, to seek unanimous consensus in EC decision-making, even in areas where the treaty allowed qualified majority voting—a development which, as we shall see presently, effectively removed the Commission's formal agenda-setting powers for most EC legislation. On the budgetary question, the member governments agreed on a temporary financing system that would operate until the end of 1969, by which time the Council would again have to consider the establishment of the Community's own resources and a new budgetary system.[2]

In keeping with this deadline, the fundamentals of the present EC budgetary system were negotiated among the member governments in late 1969 and 1970, and formalized as the Treaty of Luxembourg in April 1970. As the first and least-studied delegation of powers to the Parliament since the original Treaties of Rome, these negotiations merit a brief review here, in order to shed light on both the motives of the member governments and the terms of the budgetary process they established.[3] According to the provisions of Article 271 (ex 202) EC, the negotiation of the new budgetary treaty was to take place on the basis of a Commission proposal, which the Commission duly issued in the autumn of 1969. Given the distribution of preferences among the member governments, the Commission proposed a package deal in which the system of 'own resources' and the establishment of definitive funding for the CAP (the primary French demands) would be linked to a strengthening of the budgetary powers of the Parliament (the primary demand of the other five member states).[4] On the subject of the EP's powers, the Commission proposed a system in which Parliament would play a central role by being empowered to amend the draft budget by a simple majority of its members and to increase the total size of the budget subject only to the agreement of the Commission; the Council, by contrast, would enjoy only a single reading of the draft budget, and its amendments could be rejected by an absolute majority, including two-thirds of the votes cast, in Parliament.[5]

Although none of the member governments supported the Commission's 'maximalist' draft, the negotiation of the budgetary treaty once again split the member governments into two camps. On the one side was the French government of de Gaulle's successor Georges Pompidou, who was eager to lock in definitive financing for the CAP by adopting an own-resources system and a new financial regulation for agriculture but resisted any proposals to provide the Parliament with extensive budgetary powers. Ranged against the French were the Commission, the Parliament, and the other five member governments, all of which were determined to ensure a substantial budgetary role for the EP as part of any overall agreement. According to Lindner and Rittberger (2001: 12), this demand by the five was based not on any calculation of the likely consequences but on the norm of democratic legitimacy that acted as a cognitive road map for governments constructing their preferences:

The empirical evidence [they argue] demonstrates that the issue of EP involvement in Community decision-making, though 'logically' linked to the creation of a system of own resources, was at no point during the 1960s linked to the realization of substantive policy goals: none of the archival documents provide a hint that the negotiators projected a certain parliamentary behavior that would produce positive future 'policy streams.' In the negotiations leading to the 1965 disagreement as well as to the Luxembourg Treaty of 1970, the issue of parliamentary involvement was almost exclusively on the basis of competing normative claims of the two major higher level contenders: *Europe as a federation-to-be* and *Europe des états*.

Specifically, the Dutch delegation, under pressure from its national parliament and supported to varying degrees by four other member states and the Commission, made the normative argument that, with the passage of the Community's resources from the national level to the Community level, democratic control of the budget could be restored only by extending budgetary powers to the European

Parliament. By contrast, the French delegation argued the EP should not be granted extensive budgetary powers, such as the right to initiate new budget lines or to increase overall expenditure, that were denied to the French and other national parliaments. Presented at this level of abstraction, the positions of the five and the French do indeed appear as competing higher-level norms, based on a logic of appropriateness rather than a logic of consequences. As Lindner and Rittberger concede, however, the detailed negotiation of the new budgetary provisions not only revealed consequentialist reasoning in the French position but also considerably qualified the pro-Parliamentary positions of the Commission and the other five.

The key issue for France which emerged in the course of the negotiations was the ability of the Parliament to increase the overall size of the budget without the agreement of the Council. Indeed, as Lindner and Rittberger point out, the French government suggested that, rather than attempting to fill a democratic deficit in the Community budgetary procedure, the Commission was 'using the *pretext of democracy* in order to realize its own spending preferences on the assumption that the EP will not be particularly inclined to austerity' (2001: 15). Furthermore, despite its repeated statements of support for the Parliament, Germany, as the largest net contributor to the budget, supported France in its efforts to limit the EP's ability to increase overall spending.[6] According to the terms of the draft 'own resources' agreement, the Community would henceforth have access to up to 1 per cent of the value added tax (VAT) collected by the member governments. According to the calculations of the French government, the revenues from 1 per cent of VAT collections could reach approximately $US 3 billion a year, whereas only a fraction of that sum would be needed to fund the CAP and other existing EC policies. This would leave a huge margin of up to $1.3 billion annually, with which the Parliament could take the initiative to decide on new expenditures in areas such as the staffing and headquarters of EC institutions or the endowment of the Social Fund, or even in areas where the Council had not yet legislated. The French delegation, supported by the Germans, therefore proposed to introduce a distinction between modifications that the Parliament could make to the budget without increasing overall expenditures, by transferring credits from one title to another, and modifications that would increase total expenditures (*Agence Europe* 1970*b*).

Responding to these concerns, the Commission and the Belgian Presidency were asked to work out a compromise, which involved two interrelated changes to the initial Commission draft (*Agence Europe* 1970*c*). First, the Belgian compromise distinguished between expenditures flowing directly from Council legislation, which the Parliament could not amend without the agreement of the Council, and other expenditures, which it could:

It was established that in practice, the fraction of the budget which the Parliament could develop is rather limited, since most expenditures depend automatically on regulations adopted by the Council: if, for example, the intervention price for an agricultural product is fixed at a given level, the resulting expenditures could not be modified by a budgetary decision. The participation of the EP in expenditures of this nature would take place via the normal institutional procedures, that is to say by 'opinion' on the draft regulations and by control of the action of the Commission. There remains nevertheless a considerable margin of actions which do not depend on Council regulations: for example, the number and the level of *fonctionnaires*, buildings, and above all information policy, the conducting of studies and investigations, the endowment of the Social Fund, etc. (*Agence Europe* 1970d; author's translation)

Second, the Presidency proposed that, for the latter category of expenditure, the EP could propose only increases that would not exceed the mean percentage increase of national budgets (*Agence Europe* 1970d). With a few minor adjustments, these two points—the distinction between *compulsory* and *non-compulsory expenditure*, and the notion of a *maximum rate of increase* for the latter—were incorporated into the Luxembourg Treaty, and continue to define the EP's budgetary powers to this day.[7]

The contemporary EC budgetary process is laid out in Article 272 (ex 203) EC, as amended by the Luxembourg Treaties of 1970 and 1975. The annual budget is adopted in five stages, with important roles for the Commission, Council, and EP. Stage one typically begins on 15 June each year, when the Commission submits a 'preliminary draft budget' to the Council.[8] In stage two, the Council has 45 days to examine and amend this proposal and adopt the 'draft budget', which it then forwards to the Parliament. From September to mid-October, Parliament examines the draft budget and makes proposals for changes. Stage four then takes place from mid-October to mid-November, when the Council conducts its second reading of the budget, accepting or rejecting the changes proposed by Parliament. Finally, in stage five, which takes place from mid-November to mid-December, Parliament conducts its second reading, and the final budget is adopted upon receiving the signature of its President.

Despite having the last word in the adoption of the annual budget in stage five, the ability of Parliament to shape the budget is limited by the distinction between compulsory and non-compulsory expenditure. According to the treaty, compulsory expenditure is defined broadly as all expenditure resulting directly from the treaty or from acts adopted in accordance with the treaty, including most notably the Common Agricultural Policy, while non-compulsory expenditure constitutes the balance of Community spending, including the Structural Funds, administrative expenditures, and other internal and external spending policies. This distinction matters, moreover, because the powers of Parliament differ between the two types of expenditure. Specifically, the EP may propose 'modifications' to items of compulsory expenditure, but the decision whether to accept these modifications is made by the Council in its second reading, requiring a qualified majority to *reject* modifications that do not increase total expenditure, but a qualified majority to *accept* any modifications that do increase total expenditure. Parliament, furthermore, is not entitled in its second reading to revive modifications rejected by the Council. Thus, for compulsory expenditure, which remains the largest portion of the EC budget, the EP can increase overall expenditures only with the approval of a qualified majority in the Council, which retains the last word.

By contrast, Parliament's position is stronger with regard to non-compulsory expenditure, where it may propose 'amendments' to the Council's draft budget in its first reading. In this case, the Council may, in its second reading, modify any of the Parliament's amendments by a qualified majority vote; but Parliament is then entitled to reintroduce its amendments in its second reading by an absolute majority of its members and three-fifths of the votes cast. For non-compulsory expenditure, therefore, Parliament enjoys the last word.

Parliament is not, however, free to increase non-compulsory expenditure by as much as it likes. As we have just seen, Germany as well as France supported the establishment of a limit on the EP's ability to increase total expenditures, and the Treaty of Luxembourg therefore introduced a *maximum rate of increase* for non-compulsory expenditure, the formula for which is a variable percentage calculated each year on the basis of growth in Community GDP, national government expenditures, and the rate of inflation. This maximum rate of increase, which was approximately 3 per cent in the 2000 budget, sets a ceiling on the overall growth of non-compulsory spending for both the Council and the Parliament, which can in its second and final reading of the budget introduce amendments equivalent to *one-half* of the maximum rate of increase—Parliament's so-called 'room for manoeuvre'. The combined effect of these two provisions, the compulsory/non-compulsory distinction and the maximum rate of increase, allowed the member governments to pursue their normative goal of increasing the democratic control of the EC budgetary process by allowing the EP to serve alongside the Council in the EC budgetary authority and even adopt the final budget, while at the same time limiting Parliament's ability to tinker with the Common Agricultural Policy, foster new supranational policies, or adopt large increases in overall expenditures.

In practice, the Parliament has behaved much as the French and other member governments predicted it would, using its budgetary powers consistently to increase non-compulsory expenditures within the limits of its room for manoeuvre; allocating additional funds in its second reading to programmes that the Council had 'under-funded' in areas such as cultural policy, education, and trans-European networks; and, most controversially, creating budget lines for new programmes, like the LIFE programme in the environment or the KONVER and URBAN programmes within the Structural Funds, that had no legal basis in Community legislation (Pollack 1994: 115–20; Corbett, Jacobs, and Shackleton 2000: 225–32). In these and other areas, the Parliament has behaved in a sophisticated and strategic manner, concentrating most of its additional spending on small, new programmes in sensitive issue areas where more extensive policies were blocked by resistance among one or more member governments in the Council. Nevertheless, despite the Parliament's careful use of its budgetary powers as well as periodic challenges to the compulsory/non-compulsory distinction, the mechanisms designed by the member governments in April 1970 have operated as they were intended to, limiting the effects of EP activity to the margins of the EC budget.

Since 1988, the traditional budgetary process has been largely supplanted by the European Council's practice of adopting multi-annual 'financial perspectives' defining a ceiling for the EC budget overall and sub-ceilings for broad categories of policies, including the CAP, Structural Funds, other internal policies, external relations, and administration, for each year of a five- to seven-year budget cycle. Following the adoption of each of these financial perspectives in 1988, 1993, and most recently 1999, the Commission, the Council, and the Parliament have adopted inter-institutional agreements establishing the ground rules for the adoption of the annual budget, including the right of Parliament to increase spending in its second reading up to the annual ceilings and sub-ceilings laid down in the perspectives (Corbett, Jacobs, and Shackleton 2000: 228–32; Laffan 1997a). Despite periodic inter-institutional battles, this multi-annual procedure has lent greater predictability to the EC budgetary process while retaining the institutional balance of Article 203, wherein the Council determines the broad lines of the budget, leaving the Parliament to amend and increase spending within a limited margin for manoeuvre. Finally, with the adoption of the Amsterdam Treaty the member states agreed that the administrative and operational expenditures of the second and third pillars should be charged to the EC budget, giving the Parliament some say in these expenditures as well—although here again the member states have built in safeguards, allowing the Council acting unanimously to decide to fund operations through national contributions and exempting all operations with military or defence implications.[9]

In sum, the available evidence supports the view that the primary motivation of most EU member governments in delegating budgetary powers to the EP was *not* to reduce the transaction costs of budgetary decision-making; indeed, the frequency of inter-institutional conflicts in this area has arguably *increased* transaction costs substantially over the past three decades. Rather, as Lindner and Rittberger (2001) demonstrate, both the public and private statements of member-state representatives in the 1969–70 negotiations support the view that the Dutch and other member governments, excepting the French, delegated budgetary powers to Parliament in order to increase the democratic legitimacy of the budgetary process, often at the urging their national parliaments or other constituencies concerned about the non-representative nature of purely intergovernmental decision-making. Nevertheless, as we have also seen, all member governments—including not only the French but also the German and other governments which were in principle in favour of increasing the budgetary powers of Parliament—attempted to calculate the likely consequences of different institutional options, and in the end they selected a model that simultaneously empowered the Parliament as one-half of the Community's 'budgetary diarchy' and limited the Parliament's discretion to produce outcomes unwelcome to the member governments.

Legislative Powers

The original Common Assembly of the Coal and Steel Community was designed solely as a check on the executive High Authority, as we saw in Chapter 2, and played no role whatever in the adoption of secondary legislation under the ECSC Treaty. This omission of the Assembly from the legislative process was to some extent rectified by the Treaties of Rome in 1957, but even these treaties provided only for the non-binding consultation of Parliament for the adoption of legislation under a limited number of treaty articles. During the early years of the European Community, therefore, Parliament remained a minor player in its legislative politics, while the Commission and the

Council played the key legislative roles as agenda-setter and legislator, respectively. The consultation procedure itself, moreover, accounted for only about 30 per cent of the legislative competences granted by the EEC Treaty; in the remaining 70 per cent the Council of Ministers remained the sole legislative authority in the Union, with no obligation even to consult the EP. In subsequent treaty reforms, however, the member governments have adopted and expanded the use of new decision-making procedures—most notably the cooperation, assent, and co-decision procedures—that have increased the legislative powers of the EP vis-à-vis both the Commission and the Council. In the following subsections, I briefly examine these four procedures and the legislative powers they bestow on the Parliament before turning to an analysis of the extension of EP legislative power over time and across issue areas.

No Participation for Parliament

The single most common legislative procedure specified by the Treaties of Rome—and indeed, the most common procedure in the post-Amsterdam *Consolidated Treaties*—features no role whatsoever for the European Parliament. In the original EEC Treaty, more than half of all legal bases providing for the adoption of legislation featured the so-called *avis facultatif* procedure, in which the Commission proposed legislation and the Council disposed, acting as the sole legislative authority for the Community. As we saw in Chapter 2, the Commission's sole right of initiative, together with the unanimity rule for Council amendments to Commission proposals, made the Commission an important part of the legislative process, particularly where the Council could adopt legislation by a qualified or simple majority, making Commission proposals substantially easier to adopt than to amend. In the EEC Treaty, the qualified majority variant of this procedure was used most often in the common commercial policy, where the Council took decisions by qualified majority on the basis of a Commission proposal (Jupille 2000: 34). During much of the EC's history, however, the formal agenda-setting powers of the Commission were limited by the extensive provision for unanimous voting in the Treaty of Rome, where approximately 60 per cent of all legal bases provided for unanimity to adopt legislation in the Council. For the remaining legal bases, moreover, the use of simple and qualified majority voting was restrained for several decades by the Luxembourg Compromise of 1966, which led to the predominance of consensual decision-making in most areas. With the entry into force of the Single European Act (SEA) and subsequent treaty amendments, however, the use of qualified majority has increased dramatically, strengthening the Commission's agenda-setting role. Indeed Jupille (2000: Ch. 2) argues that the simple and qualified majority variants of the *avis facultatif* delegate greater agenda-setting power to the Commission than any other EC legislative procedure adopted since 1957.

Furthermore, it is also worth noting here that, despite the steady and substantial increase in Parliament's legislative power in a growing number of issue areas since the Single European Act, the largest single category of legal bases for legislation in the post-Amsterdam *Consolidated Treaties*—over one-third of all the legal bases in the EC Treaty and more than two-thirds of the legal bases in the EU Treaty—feature no role whatever for the European Parliament, which at best is to be kept informed of events by the Commission or the Council (Maurer 2001). Examples of such Parliamentary non-participation include EC Treaty provisions on state aids; certain provisions on external relations with third countries (free movement of capital and services, setting of customs union duties, and the common commercial policy); recommendations to the member states in certain sensitive areas (employment, culture, education, vocational training, and youth); most articles relating to Economic and Monetary Union; the communitarized treaty provisions relating to visas, immigration, and asylum (for at least the first five years of application of the Amsterdam Treaty); and all of the articles of the Treaty on European Union relating to Common Foreign and Security Policy.

Consultation

The consultation procedure, as laid down in the 22 articles of the EEC Treaty and 11 articles in the Euratom Treaty, provided the Parliament with its first, but non-binding, role in the legislative process. Like the *avis facultatif* procedure, the consultation procedure begins with a proposal from the Commission, which enjoyed the sole right of initiative in the EEC Treaty and continues to enjoy the sole right of initiative in most, but not all, contemporary EC Treaty articles. However, rather than send its proposed legislation to the Council, the Commission first forwards its proposal to the Parliament, which gives its opinion on the proposal, frequently proposing amendments to the Commission draft. The Commission, in turn, may, but need not, modify the proposal to incorporate those EP amendments that it accepts, and sends its proposal to the Council, which may adopt the proposal by simple majority, qualified majority, or unanimity, depending on the legal basis of the legislation in question, but may modify it only by unanimity. Thus, in the issue areas specified by the treaties, and in other areas in which the Commission and the Council have voluntarily agreed to consult Parliament, the EP has a formal opportunity to offer its views on legislation to be adopted by the Council. Nevertheless, both game theorists and practitioners agree that the consultation procedure as laid down in the EEC Treaty provided the EP with no real legislative power. As Corbett, Jacobs, and Shackleton (2000: 178–9) summarize the situation:

These developments gave MEPs the opportunity of being involved in all discussions on Community legislation and policy-making. However, until direct elections and the arrival of full-time MEPs in 1979 [see below], the practical use made of them was limited. In any case, no matter how extensive the possibilities for parliamentary involvement, the bottom line of being able to block proposals or oblige the other institutions to accept changes to them was lacking. The European Parliament could make its opinion known at all stages, but it had no bargaining power if the other institutions failed to respond to its views.

The Parliament's position was improved somewhat in the wake of the 1980 *Isoglucose* ruling, in which the Court of Justice annulled a Community Regulation establishing production quotas for isoglucose on the grounds that the Council did not wait for the Parliament to deliver its opinion as required by the provisions of Article 37 (ex 43) EC. Although the Council, supported by the Commission, argued that the urgent need for the adoption of the Regulation in question justified its failure to wait for an EP opinion, the Court replied with a clear affirmation of the Parliament's procedural rights:

The consultation process provided for in the third subparagraph of Article 43, as in other similar provisions of the Treaty, is the means which allows the Parliament to play an actual part in the legislative process of the Community. Such power represents an essential factor in the institutional balance intended by the Treaty. Although limited, it reflects at Community level that fundamental democratic principle that the peoples should take part in the exercise of power through the intermediary of a representative assembly. Due consultation of the Parliament in the cases provided for by the Treaty therefore constitute an essential formality, disregard of which means that the measure concerned is void.[10]

In addition to annulling the Regulation in question, the *Isoglucose* case established that the Council was obliged to wait for the Parliament to express its opinion and gave the EP a potential power of delay in the consultation procedure. The EP responded to this decision strategically by changing its rules of procedure to allow the EP to delay issuing its opinion until the Commission had taken a position on Parliament's proposed amendments by referring the issue back to committee for further consideration. Although a 1995 Court ruling later placed limits on the Parliament's power of delay, which has to be well-founded and related to the contents of the legislation in question,[11] the *Isoglucose* ruling nevertheless increased the bargaining power of the EP in the consultation procedure in urgent cases where delay might impose costs on the Commission or the Council.

Although the Single European Act and the Maastricht and Amsterdam Treaties introduced new legislative procedures, including the cooperation, co-decision and assent procedures reviewed below, the consultation procedure remains in place for a wide variety of provisions in both the EC and EU Treaties, including some core legislative areas of the internal market—agriculture, competition policy, state aids, indirect taxation, some aspects of environmental policy—as well as certain aspects of EMU, the adoption of anti-discrimination measures, the rules governing voting in local and European elections, the extension of EU citizenship rights, and the adoption of legislation relating to visas, immigration, and asylum.[12] Although the EP itself has consistently campaigned for greater legislative powers in these areas, many of which touch directly upon the rights and concerns of European electorates, in each case one or more member states has refused to consider strengthening the EP role beyond consultation.

Finally, it is worth noting that the Maastricht and Amsterdam Treaties have created two new and more restrictive versions of the consultation procedure. First, in the areas of Economic and Monetary Union and visas, immigration, and asylum, the Parliament enjoys the right to consultation but the Commission shares its right of initiative with the member states or the ECB. In those areas, the Commission's agenda-setting powers are substantially reduced since a member state unhappy with a Commission proposal could in principle introduce its own proposal in place of the Commission draft; this loss of Commission influence, in turn, reduces the Parliament's ability to pressure the Commission to incorporate its amendments into a revised Commission proposal. Second, according to Article 39 (ex K.11) EU, the Council must consult the EP when adopting framework decisions, decisions, and conventions in the areas of police and judicial cooperation in criminal matters; however, by contrast with the traditional consultation procedure, the Council may set down a time limit, which shall not be less than three months, for the EP to deliver its opinion; if the EP fails to act within the prescribed time-limit, the Council can adopt the measure. In effect, Article 39 EU removes the EP's right to delay third-pillar legislation, thus taking away the bargaining leverage that it had acquired for EC legislation after the *Isoglucose* ruling.

Cooperation

The Single European Act of 1986 introduced a new decision-making procedure, known as the cooperation procedure, for some ten articles of the EC Treaty relating to the internal market. In essence, the cooperation procedure adds a second reading for both the European Parliament and the Council of Ministers to the consultation procedure. Thus, in its first reading, the Council, voting by qualified majority, adopts a 'common position' on the basis of a Commission proposal and the Parliament's opinion. This common position is then sent to the Parliament for a second reading, in which the EP may (1) accept the common position, which is then considered to have been adopted; (2) reject the common position, which can then be adopted only by a unanimous vote of the Council in its second reading; or (3) amend the common position by an absolute majority of its members. In the last case, the EP's amended draft is sent back to the Commission, which may, but need not, incorporate the EP's amendments into its own revised draft. If the Commission rejects the EP's amendments, the Council may adopt them in its second reading only by a unanimous vote. However, if the Commission decides to incorporate the amendments into its proposal, the Council requires only a qualified majority to accept that proposal but a unanimous vote to amend. In sum, the cooperation procedure allows the EP to introduce amendments that are easier for the Council to adopt than to amend— but only if and when the Commission accepts those amendments in its revised proposal to the Council.

The implications of the cooperation procedure for the respective powers of the Commission and the Parliament have been explored in a series of articles by George Tsebelis and his critics, who assess EP influence under cooperation differently depending upon their assumptions about issue dimensions, actor preferences, and the precise specification of the Treaty's decision rules. In an influential article, Tsebelis (1994) has argued that the Parliament's right to propose amendments in its second reading provides it with 'conditional agenda-setting power' over the Council. As we have just seen, the Parliament is entitled under the cooperation procedure to propose amendments in its second reading which, if accepted by the Commission, require only a qualified majority in the Council to accept but a unanimous agreement to reject or modify. In Tsebelis's words,

This procedure *may* enable the EP to offer a proposal that makes a qualified majority of the Council better off than any unanimous decision. *If* such a proposal exists, *if* the EP is able to make it, and *if* the Commission adopts it, then the EP has agenda-setting powers. If, however, these conditions are not met, the EP loses agenda-setting power. That is why I characterize the EP's agenda power under the cooperation procedure as *conditional*. (Tsebelis 1994: 131)

By contrast with this conditional agenda-setting power, Tsebelis argues that the EP's conditional veto, which can be overturned only by the unanimous agreement of the Commission and all the member states in the Council, is relatively unimportant since the integrationist EP will nearly always prefer at least some EC legislation to the status quo and hence refrain from using its veto.

Taking issue with Tsebelis' analysis, however, Peter Moser (1996; 1997), Christophe Crombez (2000*b*), and others have suggested that the EP enjoys no greater legislative power under the cooperation procedure than under the consultation procedure, because the Commission retains the key agenda-setting power in both readings and the EP's second-reading amendments enjoy no special status in the Council of Ministers without the agreement of the Commission. Under these circumstances, Moser (1997) suggests, the EP should enjoy agenda-setting powers in the second reading only if it has information unavailable to the Commission, so that the latter's draft can be 'improved' from the Commission's perspective by the adoption of the EP amendment, or if the preferences of the key actors change between the first and second readings, in which case the Commission might accept EP amendments as a means of responding to these shifting preferences. Richard Corbett (2000) offers a similar criticism, suggesting that the conditions for conditional agenda setting are highly restrictive and rarely met since they require both Commission agreement and a willingness in the Council to accept amendments to common positions that are often agreed by consensus and with great difficulty.

In response to such criticisms, Tsebelis (1996) and Tsebelis and Garrett (2000: 31) concede that the agenda-setting powers of the EP depend on a confluence of interests between the EP and the Commission—which was in fact specified as one of Tsebelis' original conditions—but suggest that the Commission might accept EP amendments, for various reasons. The EP may, for example, enjoy leverage over the Commission thanks to its right of censure or by threatening to issue a veto which can be overridden only by unanimous agreement in the Council—although, by Tsebelis' own account, the threat of veto is not likely to be credible as long as the Parliament prefers the proposed legislation to the status quo. Alternatively, Tsebelis and Garrett (2000: 34) suggest, the EP may take advantage of the presence of imperfect information since 'the Commission apparently often overlooks pro-integration items when writing initial proposals. When the Parliament proposes these amendments, it can often significantly change the content of legislation'.

Perhaps most significantly, Tsebelis (1996: 841) points to the empirical records released by the European Parliament, showing that, in the period from 1987 to 1993, the EP proposed 4,572 amendments of which 2,974 were accepted by the Commission and 2,219 were accepted by the Council, giving the EP nearly a 50 per cent rate of success in securing the adoption of its amendments under cooperation. Similarly, a study by Amie Kreppel of the EP's success in securing the adoption of its amendments in the cooperation procedure reveals that the EP enjoyed high rates of Commission and Council acceptance not only for minor amendments but also for substantive, policy-related amendments, which were adopted in roughly 30 per cent of all cases by the Commission and approximately 18 per cent of all cases by the Council. In addition, Kreppel found that, in keeping with the predictions of the conditional agenda-setting model, Commission support for EP amendments was crucial to their ultimate adoption: out of 502 Parliamentary amendments in her data-set, Kreppel finds only three cases in which the Council unanimously adopted an amendment that had been rejected by the Commission; by contrast, the Council accepted more than half (99 out of 189) of all amendments that had been accepted by the Commission, for a success rate of more than 50 per cent (Kreppel 1999). Qualitative studies of the cooperation procedure provide additional support for the view that the EP gained influence under the cooperation procedure, securing the adoption of substantive amendments to legislation in areas such as automobile emissions, health and safety at work, and the marketing and release of genetically modified organisms (Tsebelis 1994; Earnshaw and Judge 1997; Hix 1999*a*: 94; Corbett, Jacobs, and Shackleton 2000: 187–8).

Following its initial adoption in the Single European Act, the scope of application of the cooperation procedure was expanded substantially by the Treaty of Maastricht, which simultaneously created a new co-decision procedure (discussed in the next subsection). Just five years later, however, the Treaty of Amsterdam nearly eliminated the cooperation procedure in favour of a revised co-decision procedure, retaining cooperation only for four treaty articles relating to EMU which the member governments were reluctant to renegotiate. In this sense, the cooperation procedure is of primarily historical interest, as the first treaty reform significantly increasing the legislative powers of Parliament and as a step toward the adoption of the contemporary co-decision procedure.

Co-decision, I and II

The 1993 Maastricht Treaty introduced a new co-decision procedure, which added several steps to the already complex provisions of the cooperation procedure; and this so-called 'co-decision I' procedure was then simplified and extended to additional treaty articles in the 1997 Amsterdam Treaty—'co-decision II'. To summarize as simply as possible, the co-decision procedure is similar to the cooperation procedure through the Council's first reading and adoption of a 'common position', but co-decision features the possibility of a more extensive role for the Parliament and direct Council-EP negotiations in subsequent stages of the procedure. Following the adoption of the Council's common position, the EP undertakes its own second reading in which it may (1) approve the common position, or take no action within three months, in which case the act is deemed to have been adopted; (2) reject the common position, which is then deemed not to have been adopted— the EP thus gains *unconditional veto power* in co-decision;[13] or (3) propose amendments to the common position by an absolute majority of its members. If the EP votes to *amend* the common position, the amended text is once again sent to the Commission, which may incorporate any or all of those amendments into its revised opinion for the Council. The Council in turn may adopt the EP's amendments by qualified majority if those amendments are accepted by the Commission, or by unanimity if the Commission delivers a negative opinion.

By contrast with the cooperation procedure, however, the co-decision procedure concludes with the Council's second reading only if the Council has accepted *all* of the Parliament's proposed second-reading amendments, regardless of whether they have been accepted or rejected by the Commission. If the Council does not approve all the EP's amendments, the President of the Council, in agreement with the President of the Parliament, is required to convene a meeting of the 'conciliation committee', composed of equal numbers of Council and EP representatives, for the purpose of reaching agreement on a joint EP-Council text. According to Article 251 EC, negotiations within the conciliation committee 'shall address the common position on the basis of the amendments proposed by the European Parliament'; agreement shall be reached by a qualified majority vote within the Council delegation and a simple majority of the representatives from the EP; the Commission, by contrast, participates in the conciliation committee and may take 'all necessary initiatives with a few to reconciling the positions of the European Parliament and the Council', but the Commission representative enjoys no vote and no formal powers in the taking of the final decision.

If the conciliation committee is able to hammer out a joint text within six weeks, that text is then sent to both the Council, which may approve the text by qualified majority, and the EP, which may approve by an absolute majority of its members. If both bodies approve the joint text by the required majorities, the legislation is deemed to have been adopted; however, if either the EP or the Council reject the proposed text, the legislation is deemed to have failed.

Finally, under the Maastricht, 'co-decision I', version of the procedure, if the conciliation committee failed to reach agreement on a joint text, the Council was entitled to reaffirm by qualified majority its original common position, which would then become law unless rejected by an absolute majority in the Parliament. However, this provision for a Council 'third reading', which would appear to weaken the position of the EP in negotiations with the Council, was removed in the Amsterdam variant of the procedure ('co-decision II') which explicitly requires the agreement of both houses in order to pass draft legislation into law.

Not surprisingly given its complexity and novelty, the Maastricht version of the co-decision procedure led to lively debate among both rational-choice scholars and EP practitioners about the effects of the co-decision I procedure on the legislative powers of Parliament. In a series of controversial articles, Garrett and Tsebelis argued that, contrary to common perceptions of the co-decision procedure as a step forward for the Parliament, the EP had actually *lost* legislative power in the move from cooperation to co-decision I.[14] To simplify only slightly, Garrett and Tsebelis argued that the Council's option of reaffirming its common position in its third reading shifted the locus of agenda-setting power from the Commission and the Parliament under the cooperation procedure to the Council of Ministers in the Maastricht version of co-decision. Specifically, the co-decision I procedure allowed the Council in its third reading to make a take-it-or-leave-it offer to the Parliament, which was not allowed to propose further amendments but was simply left to choose between the Council's proposal and the status quo. If we assume, moreover, that the preferences of the European Parliament are more integrationist than the pivotal member of the Council of Ministers, then the Parliament was unlikely to veto the Council's common position in favour of the less integrationist status quo, and the Council's bargaining power in the conciliation committee would be strengthened by the prospect that it could reassert its common position if conciliation were to break down. For this reason, Garrett and Tsebelis argued, the transition from cooperation to co-decision I embodied in the Treaty of Maastricht was, in effect, a 'bad deal' for the EP.

Although presented with clarity and rigour, these claims regarding the weakening of the EP in co-decision were disputed by other rational-choice scholars whose models of co-decision employed different assumptions from those in Garrett and Tsebelis's models, as well as by practitioners within the Parliament itself. Among rational-choice scholars, Scully (1997*b*, *c*, *d*), Crombez (1997*a*; 2000*a*), Moser (1997), and Steunenberg (2000) all noted that Tsebelis and Garrett's claims about the reduced legislative powers of the EP were based on a particular modelling of both the cooperation and the co-decision procedures, and that alternative models suggested a more modest agenda-setting role for the EP under cooperation (see above) and/or a stronger position for the EP in co-decision.[15] Furthermore, moving from formal models to empirical evidence, Tsebelis and Garrett's critics noted that, according to the aggregate statistics released by the European Parliament, the EP enjoyed a *greater* rate of success in securing the adoption of its amendments under the Maastricht version of co-decision than under the cooperation procedure—a finding that runs directly counter to the predictions of Garrett and Tsebelis's models.[16]

Among EP practitioners, Richard Corbett has suggested that the European Parliament, faced with Garrett and Tsebelis's prospect of an aggressive Council asserting its right to make a take-it-or-leave-it offer in the third reading, took a long-term rather than myopic view of its own institutional preferences, and adjusted its own internal procedures so as to offset the Council's institutional advantage. As Corbett (2000: 374–5) writes:

Parliament itself was perfectly well aware that the provision of the treaty allowing the Council to reconfirm its position in the absence of agreement in the conciliation committee and challenge Parliament to take it or leave it, had the potential of tipping the scales in Council's favour, and Parliament was determined not to allow this to happen. Rule 78 of Parliament's internal Rules of Procedure was drafted so as to ensure that, should Council attempt such a manoeuvre, Parliament would automatically vote on a rejection motion. Parliament's leadership let it be known that it this would be Parliament's reaction. The first time Council tried it [in the 1995 ONP Directive; see Chapter 2], Parliament overwhelmingly rejected the legislation in question, and Council never tried this manoeuvre again.

Of course, this implied that Parliament would reject particular outcomes which, individually, it would have preferred to the status quo in terms of EU legislation. However, the logic behind it was that this was necessary to establish Parliament's bargaining powers and exert greater influence in the long run.

At the very least, this course of action established a degree of uncertainty in the Council as to what would happen if it did not reach agreement with

Parliament on legislation. It meant that Council treated Parliament as if the Amsterdam Treaty version of co-decision was, in this respect, already in place. Indeed, it paved the way to the Amsterdam Treaty change, which in this respect did no more than entrench reality into the treaty.

Indeed, as Simon Hix (1999*b*) has argued, the member states' decision to remove the third reading from co-decision at Amsterdam should be interpreted *not* as a deliberate extension of the Community's democratic legitimacy through further delegation to the EP but rather as a codification of existing practice which reflected that practice and gave it greater legal certainty.[17]

In any event, with the simplification of the co-decision procedure and the elimination of the third reading, the Amsterdam Treaty has created a more symmetrical 'co-decision II' procedure in which 'the Council and the Parliament are now co-equal legislators and the EU's legislative regime is truly bicameral' (Tsebelis and Garrett 2000: 24). This latter claim is in fact an overstatement of the current situation, since the co-decision procedure even after Amsterdam applies to only about one-quarter of all treaty articles and about one-half of all EC and EU legislation; in the remaining areas, the EP remains the junior partner in the EC legislature. Nevertheless, by contrast with the earlier disputes over the powers of Parliament under co-decision I, there is general agreement among both practitioners and scholars that the revised Amsterdam version of co-decision represents a substantial advance for the Parliament vis-à-vis cooperation and places the EP in a position of formal equality vis-à-vis the Council for a significant portion of EC legislation.

Similarly, there is general agreement among both formal modellers and practitioners that, *ceteris paribus*, the Commission enjoys a weaker position in both versions of the co-decision procedure than under either consultation or cooperation. As Tsebelis (1997) and others have pointed out, the Commission is stripped of its formal agenda-setting power in conciliation since the Council and the EP delegation can jointly agree to amendments according to the respective voting rules in those bodies *without the approval of the Commission*. Recall that, under the cooperation procedure, EP amendments accepted by the Commission could be adopted by qualified majority in the Council, while amendments rejected by the Commission could be adopted only by unanimity; in conciliation, by contrast, the Council can agree to an amended joint text by qualified majority regardless of the position of the Commission. Tsebelis's model, moreover, finds support in the work of substantive scholars such as

Michael Shackleton (2000: 336), who nicely describes the secondary role played by the Commission in the conciliation procedure:

The Commission is present at all trialogues [small meetings of Council, EP, and Commission officials held prior to each conciliation committee] and can play an important part in helping to find compromises. However, its representatives can find themselves in difficulty if they take it upon themselves to express their view on the position of the other two parties too overtly. They are likely to be reminded that the Commission does not enjoy the same rights within conciliation as outside (e.g., the right to withdraw its proposal) and that the Treaty lays down a specific but limited function, namely 'to take all the necessary initiatives with a view to reconciling the positions of the EP and the Council' (Art. 251(4)). The result is that the Commission sometimes feels in a clear position of inferiority, whereas the other two institutions enjoy an increased sense of solidarity which in turn serves to improve the chance of an agreement being found.

Moving beyond such subjective measures, we find that the most extensive quantitative study to date of EP influence under the cooperation and co-decision procedures (Tsebelis *et al.* 1999) provides evidence that (1) the EP enjoyed greater legislative powers under the Maastricht version of co-decision than under cooperation and (2) the Commission played a crucial gatekeeping role for EP amendments under cooperation that was later removed by the adoption of the co-decision procedure. On the basis of an empirical study of the legislative history of some 5,000 EP amendments offered under both the cooperation and the co-decision procedures, Tsebelis and his colleagues produce evidence supporting the European Parliament's claim that, in the aggregate, the EP enjoys greater legislative success in securing the adoption of its amendments under co-decision (I) than under the cooperation procedure. More interestingly for our purposes here, the authors go on to demonstrate that the difference between the cooperation and co-decision procedures is explained almost entirely by the behaviour of the Commission and its variable influence across the two procedures. Specifically, under the cooperation procedure, if the Commission rejects an EP amendment the probability of its acceptance by the Council is a mere 12 per cent, reflecting the substantially greater difficulty of adopting rejected amendments by unanimity in the Council; while under co-decision the probability that an amendment rejected by the Commission will nevertheless be adopted by the Council rises to 33 per cent, illustrating the Commission's reduced influence under co-decision. Put differently, the behaviour of the Commission 'predicts the overall fate of an amendment 85% of the time under cooperation and 70% of the time under codecision' (Tsebelis *et al.* 1999: 34).

Placing these developments in longer-term perspective, Tsebelis and Garrett (2000: 26) argue that the period since the SEA has witnessed a 'secular decline in the Commission's legislative influence since the passage of the SEA' since the Commission's agenda-setting power, which it once held exclusively under the *avis facultatif* and consultation procedures, must be shared increasingly with the European Parliament under cooperation and with the Council and the EP under the Maastricht and Amsterdam versions of the co-decision procedure.[18] As a result of these developments, Tsebelis and Garrett argue, the Commission's primary legislative influence will in the future rely more on 'informal channels—asymmetries of information, persuasion, deal-brokering—than on the formal roles written into the various procedures' (Tsebelis and Garrett 2000: 26).[19] As we saw in Chapter 1 of this book, however, the preconditions for such informal agenda-setting powers are significantly more demanding than those for the Commission's formal agenda-setting powers. Thus, in the future, Commission influence on the legislative process is likely to be highly variable, reflecting both the considerable variation remaining in legislative procedures, which determine the scope for formal agenda setting, and the distribution of information and the clarity of member-state preferences, which determine the prospects for informal agenda setting and political entrepreneurship.

Assent

Finally, the assent procedure provides that, for a small number of treaty articles, the Council may act only after receiving an assenting vote from the Parliament, which is required to take a straight up-or-down vote on the proposed legislation as a whole. In Tsebelis's terms, the assent procedure clearly puts the Council of Ministers in the position of agenda setter since the Council is empowered to make a take-it-or-leave-it offer to the Parliament, which possesses veto power but not the right to offer amendments to the proposed legislation. Originally confined by the Single European Act to the approval of EC association and accession agreements with third countries, the procedure has subsequently been extended to six additional issue areas, including: sanctions in the event of a significant and persistent breach of human rights by a member state (Article 7 EU); special tasks entrusted to the European Central Bank (Article 105 EC); amendments to the protocol of the European System of Central Banks (Article 107 EC); the adoption of the framework regulation for the Structural Funds and the creation of the Cohesion Fund (Article 161 EC); the adoption of a uniform procedure for European elections

(Article 190 EC); and certain categories of international agreements establishing a specific institutional framework, having important budgetary implications, or entailing amendment of an act adopted by co-decision (Article 300 EC). As Corbett, Jacobs, and Shackleton (2000: 204) point out, the member governments have adopted the assent procedure inconsistently across types of legislation:

The assent procedure is a cruder form of co-decision in that there is no scope for Parliament to put forward amendments to the measure in question. This is normal when it comes to international agreements negotiated by the Commission which, as in national parliaments, have to be dealt with on a take-it-or-leave-it basis...It is also understandable for 'constitutional' type measures. However, its continuing application to measures that are typically legislative in character, such as the operational rules for the structural funds, is curious.

Indeed, the assent procedure illustrates the tendency of the member-states to fine-tune the legislative powers of Parliament in unusual ways in order to facilitate, or avoid, specific outcomes. The unwillingness of member governments to allow co-decision for the framework Regulation for the Structural Funds, for example, reflects the extraordinary redistributive potential of the Funds, which have often been a source of contention between Parliament and the Council, and the unwillingness of the Council to allow the Parliament to offer amendments to carefully negotiated intergovernmental bargains.

Similarly, the member governments have manipulated the voting thresholds in the Parliament across the different issue areas, with an absolute majority of members required to approve the accession of new member states, the European electoral system, and penalties for human rights breaches, while only a simple majority of members present is required for the other areas such as the adoption of the Structural Fund Regulations. Furthermore, while the SEA had initially required an absolute majority for approval of association agreements with third countries, this threshold was subsequently lowered to a simple majority at Maastricht in order to facilitate adoption of those agreements despite poor attendance at EP plenary sessions (Bradley 1994).

Finally, it is worth noting that the member states have opted *not* to extend the assent procedure to other international treaties or constitutional provisions, including the approval of international trade agreements (Article 133 EC), other international agreements (Article 300 EC), and revisions to the treaties (Article 49 EU), where the Parliament enjoys at best a consultative role. Here again we see that, rather than following consistent constitutional principles, successive intergovernmental conferences have delegated powers to the EP on a case-by-case basis, anticipating the likely consequences of delegation in different issue areas and responding to the concerns of individual member governments, each of which holds a veto in such delegation decisions.

Summary: The EP's Rise to Co-Legislator

Looking at the development of the European Parliament's legislative powers over time, we see a clear and consistent trend. As we have seen, the Parliament's legislative powers have been increased in each and every treaty revision between 1957 and 1997, and this step-wise increase can be seen graphically in Fig. 4.1, which illustrates the changes in the treaty provisions regarding the various legislative procedures in the EEC Treaty, the Single European Act, the Maastricht Treaty on European Union, and the Treaty of Amsterdam. As Fig. 4.1 makes clear, the Parliament's aggregate legislative powers have increased substantially in each and every treaty reform, with an increasing number of treaty articles providing at least some legislative role for the EP, and increasing use of legislative procedures such as co-decision that provide the EP with greater power to influence policy outcomes.

Understandably, most students of the European Parliament and of EU Treaty reform have emphasized the aggregate and seemingly

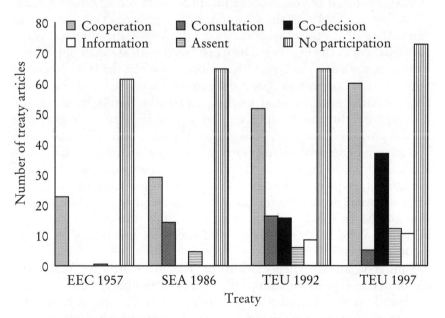

FIG. 4.1. Growth of EU decision-making procedures, 1957–1997
Source: Maurer (1999: 17).

inexorable increase in the legislative powers of Parliament, which has arguably been the biggest 'winner' from recent rounds of treaty reform, especially by comparison with the Commission, which lost agenda-setting powers in the co-decision procedure. In this view, best summarized by Tsebelis and Garrett (2000), the story of the past two decades is the rise of Parliament from consultative assembly to co-equal legislator with the Council in an essentially bicameral legislature.

Although Tsebelis and Garrett (2001) explicitly leave it to others to consider the motivations of member governments in delegating increasing legislative powers to the European Parliament, the evidence of the negotiation of the Single European Act and the Maastricht and Amsterdam Treaties suggests that, as with the supervisory and budgetary powers examined above, the primary motivation of the member governments in delegating legislative powers to the Parliament was to increase the democratic legitimacy of Community legislation through a systematic increase in the powers of Parliament (Moravcsik 1998). In each case, moreover, the Parliament, the Commission, and a number of member governments argued on normative grounds for a systematic, across-the-board increase in the powers of Parliament. In the negotiation of the Single European Act, for instance, the EP, supported by Italy and other member governments, argued for the systematic adoption of the cooperation procedure for all treaty articles providing for QMV in the Council on the grounds that the loss of national vetoes in those areas increased the importance of democratic participation in the legislative process; faced with staunch opposition from Denmark and the United Kingdom, however, the IGC agreed to limit the new cooperation procedure to only ten articles of the treaty, all concerned with internal market legislation. Similarly, all of the member governments except Denmark agreed in principle to grant the EP the power of assent for constitutional issues, but individual member governments placed reservations on most of the relevant treaty articles (for example, France, Britain, and Germany on the revision of the budgetary process; France and Greece on the adoption of a uniform electoral procedure for the EP; France and Ireland on the revision of the treaties) with the result that the power of assent was initially limited to the adoption of association and accession agreements (Corbett 1987: 255–8).

Similarly, in the negotiation of the Amsterdam Treaty the Commission argued for a simplification of Community decision making based on broad normative principles rather than the sort of case-by-case extensions of EP legislative power that had taken place in the SEA and Maastricht Treaties. Specifically, the Commission proposed a system with only three legislative procedures: co-decision would be used for the adoption of all legislation, which according to the Commission's definition 'should be binding and general in scope and should determine essential elements of Community action'; the assent procedure would be used for 'constitutional' reforms and international agreements; and the consultation procedure would apply for all other areas, including specific measures implementing broader framework legislation.[20] This approach, moreover, was accepted as the basis for negotiations by a majority of member governments and by the Irish Presidency of the Union, which incorporated a similar provision into the text of its December 1996 draft treaty.[21]

However, in the final negotiation of the Amsterdam Treaty—as in the SEA and Maastricht—member governments made little pretence of respecting the Commission's proposed scheme, opting instead for a case-by-case approach to the extension of co-decision as well as other legislative procedures, taking into account the anticipated consequences of delegation in specific issue areas and the sensitivities of each of the Union's 15 member governments. Hence, while the EP's aggregate legislative influence has increased in each successive round of treaty amendment, this aggregate increase should not obscure the equally important cross-issue variations that remain in the respective legislative powers of the Commission and the Parliament after Amsterdam.

In order to capture and analyse these issue-specific variations in the legislative powers of the Commission and the EP, I return to the 35 issue areas examined in Chapter 2, re-coding each of these areas in terms the delegation of legislative rather than executive powers. In doing so, I follow Jupille (2000) who derives 'procedural preference rankings' for the Commission and the European Parliament across nine distinct legislative procedures. Jupille's ranking system is based on the primary assumption that the Commission and the Parliament seek to maximize their own influence in the legislative process in order to influence policy outputs. On the basis of assumptions similar to those summarized in the discussion of the various legislative procedures discussed above, Jupille derives procedural preference rankings for the Commission and Parliament across nine of the most common legislative procedures in the EC Treaty, illustrated in Table 4.2.

Following Jupille, the various EC legislative procedures—including the simple majority, qualified majority, and unanimity variants of the *avis facultatif*, consultation, cooperation, co-decision, and assent procedures—can be ranked for each supranational organization on an ordinal scale ranging from 1 (most preferred) to 9 (least preferred).

TABLE 4.2. *Procedural preference rankings, Commission and European Parliament*

Procedure	Commission	EP
AVFS	1	7
AVFQ	2	8
CNSQ	3	5
SYNQ	4	2
CODQ	5	1
AVFU	6	9
CNSU	7	6
AVCU	8	4
CODU	9	3
Intergovernmental decision-making; shared right of initiative	10	10

Explanation of rules. Avis facultatif: Commission tables a proposal that the Council can amend (by unanimity) and adopt (by one of three available voting rules: unanimity, QMV, or simple majority). No role for EP. Three variants: AVFU: unanimity in Council; AVFQ: QMV in Council; AVFS: simple majority in Council (when none specified in Treaty).
Consultation procedure: Commission proposes, Council disposes, but EP must be consulted. EP has power only to delay. CNSQ: QMV in Council; CNSU: unanimity in Council.
Assent (or avis conforme): Council decides by unanimity, and EP can accept or reject by voting up or down. AVCU: Assent with unanimity in Council.
Cooperation: Commission proposes, Council disposes; EP can suggest amendments which, if accepted by Commission, can be adopted by QMV but changed only by unanimous vote in Council. SYNQ: Cooperation with QMV in Council. SYNY: Cooperation with unanimity in Council.
Co-decision: Commission proposes, legislation co-decided by Council and EP. CODQ: Co-decision with QMV in Council; CODU: Co-decision with unanimity in Council.
Note on other procedures with a shared right of initiative or purely intergovernmental decision-making: Decision-making procedures in which the Commission possesses no agenda-setting power, or in which the Commission enjoys only agenda setting-power shared with other actors—for example, member governments or the European Central Bank—are coded as 10 for the Commission. In the case of the Parliament, purely intergovernmental voting procedures are also coded as 10, as are articles with a shared right of initiative and exclusion of the Parliament. Finally, in a few articles, the EP retains a right to consultation despite a shared right of initiative. In these cases, the Parliament enjoys a non-binding right of consultation but no ability to influence the content of legislation through its indirect influence on the Commission; these articles are therefore also assigned a score of 10.
Source: Adapted from Jupille (2000: 57).

As Jupille points out, this table provides only a rough ordinal ranking of the Commission's and Parliament's procedural preferences, and does not indicate the cardinal distances between adjacent choices—for example, the extent to which the Commission prefers AVFQ over CNSQ, or the EP prefers CODQ to SYNQ; nevertheless, Jupille finds that both the Commission and the Parliament adopt positions in inter-institutional procedural disputes that are overwhelmingly consistent with the preferences predicted in Table 4.2, strengthening our confidence that his ranking captures real differences in the legislative power of each institution across procedures. By contrast with Jupille's study, however, the coding of various new procedures in the Maastricht and Amsterdam Treaties requires the addition of a tenth, residual category of purely intergovernmental decision-making, or of decision-making procedures in which the Commission is forced to share its right of initiative with the member governments or other institutional actors, such as the European Central Bank, thereby removing the formal agenda-setting powers of the Commission and the indirect influence of the European Parliament. For this reason, such procedures—which apply in the areas of Economic and Monetary Union; visas, immigration, and asylum; Justice and Home Affairs; and Common Foreign and Security policy— are collectively assigned a ranking of 10 for both the Commission and the Parliament.

Jupille's ranking system provides the additional benefit of pointing out that there exists no single 'supranational' procedural ranking as a counterpoint to 'intergovernmental' decision making but rather a distinct set of rankings for the Commission and the Parliament, which are differentially empowered by the various procedures. Thus, for example, while both the Commission and the Parliament can both be expected to prefer co-decision with qualified majority in the Council (CODQ, ranked as 5 for the Commission and 1 for the EP) to co-decision with unanimous voting (CODU, ranked as 9 and 3, respectively) or to purely intergovernmental decision making (ranked as 10 for both actors), the procedural powers and preferences of the two institutions are not identical. For example, consistent with empirical findings presented above, the European Parliament prefers the qualified majority variant of the co-decision procedure to the cooperation procedure (ranking of 1 for CODQ versus 2 for SYNQ) or indeed to any other procedure at all; while the Commission, because of its loss of agenda-setting powers in the co-decision procedures, 'loses' in the transition from cooperation to co-decision, with a score of 5 for CODQ and 4 for SYNQ. By contrast, the Commission enjoys its greatest agenda-setting

powers in the simple- and qualified-majority variants of the *avis facultatif* procedure and in the qualified majority variant of the consultation procedure, each of which ranks relatively far down the
Parliament's procedural reference rankings, with scores of 7, 8, and 5,
respectively.

For our purposes, Jupille's categories and rankings, as adapted
above, provide us with a means to classify and rank the issue-specific
delegation of legislative powers to the Commission and the
Parliament in the *Consolidated Treaties*. By contrast with the analysis
of executive delegation in Chapter 2, however, the Treaties often feature more than one legislative procedure per issue area, requiring us
to disaggregate many issue areas into distinct legal bases for legislation, each with its own associated legislative procedure. In the EC
Treaty's chapter on tax provisions, for example, two distinct legal
bases are provided: Article 93 (ex 99) EC, which allows for harmonization of national provisions by unanimous agreement of the Council
with consultation of the EP (CNSU); and Article 92 (ex 98) EC, by
which the Council may agree by qualified majority on a proposal
from the Commission (AVFQ) to authorize a member state's adoption of certain charges on imports and exports for a limited period.
A more extreme case is the chapter on the economic policy aspects
of EMU, which specifies 14 legal bases with five distinct legislative
procedures (AVFQ, SYNQ, CNSQ, AVFU, and CNSU) for various
phases of the 'excessive deficit' procedure. Other issue areas feature
even greater variation, including not only a combination of Jupille's
nine basic procedures but also a shared right of legislative initiative for
certain Treaty articles (for example, EMU-Monetary Policy, Justice
and Home Affairs) or provisions allowing for the temporary use of
certain procedures, followed by a possible shift to more supranational
procedures after a five-year transitional period (for example, visas,
immigration, and asylum).

Disaggregating issue areas by legal bases as indicated in the previous paragraph yields a total of 117 distinct legal bases across 35 issue
areas. The results are shown in Table 4.3, in which the various legal
bases are listed in order of the Parliament's procedural preference
rankings, beginning with the qualified majority variant of co-decision
and proceeding through the various other procedures to purely intergovernmental decision-making at the end of the table. Although not a
complete listing of all the legal bases for EU legislative action—it
omits notably institutional questions and some international agreements—Table 4.3 conveys the extraordinary diversity of legislative

TABLE 4.3. *Legislative powers of the European Parliament*

Issue area	Treaty Article	Legislative procedure	Commission score	EP score	Comments/restrictions on Commission/EP
Free Movement of Workers: General	TEC Art. 40	CODQ	5	1	
Right of Establishment: General	TEC Art. 44(1)	CODQ	5	1	
Right of Establishment: Coordination of laws for foreign nationals	TEC Art. 46(2)	CODQ	5	1	Directives only
Right of Establishment: Mutual recognition of diplomas	TEC Art. 47(1)	CODQ	5	1	Directives only
Right of Establishment: Self-employed persons	TEC Art. 47(2)	CODQ	5	1	
Visas, Immigration and Asylum: Visas, list of third countries and uniform format, after five years	TEC Art. 67(4)	CODQ	5	1	
Transport: General provisions	TEC Art. 71(1)	CODQ	5	1	
Transport: Provisions for sea and air transport	TEC Art. 80(2)	CODQ	5	1	
Approximation of Laws: Adoption of measures for internal market	TEC Art. 95	CODQ	5	1	Rule-making priorities, exclusions

TABLE 4.3. *Continued*

Issue area	Treaty Article	Legislative procedure	Commission score	EP score	Comments/restrictions on Commission/EP
Employment: Incentive measures	TEC Art. 129	CODQ	5	1	No harmonization
Social Provisions: Adoption of Directives	TEC Art. 137(2)	CODQ	5	1	Exclusions for certain issue areas
Social Provisions: Adoption of measures to ensure equal opportunities between men and women	TEC Art. 141(3)	CODQ	5	1	
European Social Fund: Adoption of implementing provisions	TEC Art. 148	CODQ	5	1	
Education, Vocational Training and Youth: Incentive measures for education	TEC Art. 149(4)	CODQ	5	1	No harmonization
Education, Vocational Training and Youth: Adoption of measures	TEC Art. 150(4)	CODQ	5	1	No harmonization
Consumer Protection: Adoption of measures to support, supplement, and monitor member-state (MS) policies	TEC Art. 153(4)	CODQ	5	1	
Trans-European Networks: Adoption of guidelines and measures	TEC Art. 156	CODQ	5	1	Special QMV: requires approval of MS concerned

Economic and Social Cohesion: Adoption of European Regional Development Fund Regulation	TEC Art. 162	CODQ	5	1	
Research and Technological Development: Adoption of Framework Programme	TEC Art. 166(1)	CODQ	5	1	
Research and Technological Development: Adoption of rules on participation and dissemination	TEC Art. 167	CODQ	5	1	
Research and Technological Development: Adoption of supplementary programmes	TEC Art. 168	CODQ	5	1	Special QMV: requires approval of MS concerned
Research and Technological Development: Participation in programmes by several MS	TEC Art. 169	CODQ	5	1	
Environment: Adoption of measures to achieve objectives of Art. 174	TEC Art. 175(1)	CODQ	5	1	
Environment: Adoption of action programmes	TEC Art. 175(3)	CODQ	5	1	
Development Cooperation: Adoption of multi-annual programmes and other measures	TEC Art. 179(1)	CODQ	5	1	
EMU: Economic Policy, Adoption of rules for multilateral surveillance procedure	TEC Art. 100(1)	SYNQ	4	2	

TABLE 4.3. *Continued*

Issue area	Treaty Article	Legislative procedure	Commission score	EP score	Comments/restrictions on Commission/EP
EMU: Economic Policy, Prohibition of privileged access to financial institutions	TEC Art. 102(2)	SYNQ	4	2	
EMU: Economic Policy, Definitions for application of prohibition of government bail-outs	TEC Art. 103(3)	SYNQ	4	2	
EMU: Monetary Policy, Harmonization of denominations and specifications for coins	TEC Art. 106(2)	SYNQ	4	2	
Free Movement of Workers: Social security	TEC Art. 42	CODU	9	3	
Right of Establishment: Self-employed persons, requiring change to national laws	TEC Art. 47(2)	CODU	9	3	
Culture: Incentive measures	TEC Art. 151(5)	CODU	9	3	No harmonization
Citizenship: Adoption of provisions to facilitate exercise of EU citizenship rights	TEC Art. 18(2)	CODU	9	3	
EMU: Monetary Policy, Delegation of special tasks (banking supervision) to ECB	TEC Art. 105(6)	AVCU	8	4	

Description	Article	Procedure			Notes
Economic and Social Cohesion: Adoption of Structural and Cohesion Fund Regulations	TEC Art. 161	AVCU	8	4	
Agriculture: General	TEC Art. 37(2)	CNSQ	3	5	Rule-making ('shall take account')
Agriculture: Replacement of National Market Orgs.	TEC Art. 37(3)	CNSQ	3	5	
Services: Liberalization Directives	TEC Art. 52	CNSQ	3	5	Rule-making priorities, Directives only
Visas, Immigration and Asylum: Provisional measures	TEC Art. 64	CNSQ	3	5	
Visas, Immigration and Asylum: Visas, list of third countries and uniform format, first 5 years	TEC Art. 67(3)	CNSQ	3	5	
Competition: Rules applying to undertakings	TEC Art. 83(1)	CNSQ	3	5	
Competition: State Aids, adoption of regulations	TEC Art. 89	CNSQ	3	5	
EMU: Economic Policy, Detailed rules for application of Protocol on excessive deficit procedure	TEC Art. 104(14)	CNSQ	3	5	
EMU: Transitional Provisions, Consultation of EMI on draft legislation	TEC Art. 117(6)	CNSQ	3	5	
EMU: Transitional Provisions, Abrogation of derogations	TEC Art. 122(2)	CNSQ	3	5	

Table 4.3. *Continued*

Issue area	Treaty Article	Legislative procedure	Commission score	EP score	Comments/restrictions on Commission/EP
Employment: Adoption of annual guidelines	TEC Art. 128(1)	CNSQ	3	5	
Research and Technological Development: Adoption of specific programmes	TEC Art. 166(4)	CNSQ	3	5	
Research and Technological Development: Creation of joint undertakings and other structures	TEC Art. 171	CNSQ	3	5	
Visas, Immigration and Asylum: Visas, after 5 years	TEC Art. 62	CNSU	7	6	
Visas, Immigration and Asylum: Asylum and immigration measures, after 5 years	TEC Art. 63	CNSU	7	6	
Visas, Immigration, and Asylum: Judicial cooperation in civil matters, after 5 years	TEC Art. 65	CNSU	7	6	
Visas, Immigration, and Asylum: Measures for intergovernmental cooperation, after 5 years	TEC Art. 66	CNSU	7	6	
Transport: Derogation for provisions with serious effects on employment, transport facilities	TEC Art. 71(2)	CNSU	7	6	

Tax Provisions: Harmonization of legislation	TEC Art. 93	CNSU	7	6	
Approximation of Laws: Adoption of Directives for common market	TEC Art. 94	CNSU	7	6	Directives only
EMU: Economic Policy, Replacement of Protocol on excessive deficit procedure	TEC Art. 104(14)	CNSU	7	6	
EMU: Transitional Provisions, Delegation of third-stage tasks to EMI	TEC Art. 117(7)	CNSU	7	6	
Common Commercial Policy: Extension to services and intellectual property	TEC Art. 133(5)	CNSU	7	6	
Social Provisions: Adoption of certain Directives concerning for example social security	TEC Art. 137(3)	CNSU	7	6	
Industry: Adoption of specific actions to support action taken in member states	TEC Art. 157(3)	CNSU	7	6	Rule-making requirement: no distortion of competition
Economic and Social Cohesion: Specific action outside the Funds	TEC Art. 159	CNSU	7	6	
Environment: Adoption of measures of fiscal nature or relating to energy or land-use planning	TEC Art. 175(2)	CNSU	7	6	

TABLE 4.3. *Continued*

Issue area	Treaty Article	Legislative procedure	Commission score	EP score	Comments/restrictions on Commission/EP
Environment: Option to move some decision-making to QMV	TEC Art. 175(2)	CNSU	7	6	
Citizenship: Adoption of provisions for EU nationals to vote in local elections	TEC Art. 19(1)	CNSU	7	6	
Citizenship: Adoption of provisions for EU nationals to vote in EP elections	TEC Art. 19(2)	CNSU	7	6	
Citizenship: Adoption of provisions to add to citizenship rights specified in Treaty	TEC Art. 22	CNSU	7	6	Requires ratification by national parliaments
Customs Union: Setting common customs tariff duties	TEC Art. 26	AVFQ	2	8	
Right of Establishment: Exemptions for certain activities	TEC Art. 45	AVFQ	2	8	
Services: Extending provisions to third-country nationals	TEC Art. 49	AVFQ	2	8	
Capital: Free movement to or from third countries	TEC Art. 57(2)	AVFQ	2	8	

Capital: Temporary safeguard measures	TEC Art. 59	AVFQ	2	∞	Time limit of six months
Capital: Economic sanctions against third countries	TEC Art. 60(1)	AVFQ	2	∞	
Capital: Revocation of sanctions by member states	TEC Art. 60(3)	AVFQ	2	∞	
Transport: Prohibition of discrimination by carriers	TEC Art. 75(3)	AVFQ	2	∞	
Competition: State Aids, designation of categories of aid compatible with common market	TEC Art. 87(3)e	AVFQ	2	∞	
Tax Provisions: Authorization of national charges on imports and exports	TEC Art. 92	AVFQ	2	∞	
Approximation of Laws: Adoption of Directives to remove distortions to internal market	TEC Art. 96	AVFQ	2	∞	
EMU: Economic Policy, Adoption of economic policy guidelines	TEC Art. 99(2)	AVFQ	2	∞	Commission 'recommendation'; EP 'informed'
EMU: Economic Policy, Recommendations to member states on economic policy	TEC Art. 99(4)	AVFQ	2	∞	Commission 'recommendation'; EP 'informed'
EMU: Economic Policy, EC financial assistance to member state after natural disaster	TEC Art. 100(2)	AVFQ	2	∞	EP informed

TABLE 4.3. *Continued*

Issue area	Treaty Article	Legislative procedure	Commission score	EP score	Comments/restrictions on Commission/EP
EMU: Economic Policy, Determination of excessive deficit in member state	TEC Art. 104(6)	AVFQ	2	8	Commission 'recommendation'; special QMV
EMU: Economic Policy, Recommendation to member state with excessive deficit	TEC Art. 104(7)	AVFQ	2	8	Commission role unclear; special QMV
EMU: Economic Policy, Making recommendations public	TEC Art. 104(8)	AVFQ	2	8	Commission role unclear; special QMV
EMU: Economic Policy, Council gives notice to member state to take deficit-reduction measures	TEC Art. 104(9)	AVFQ	2	8	Commission role unclear; special QMV
EMU: Economic Policy, Council measures against member state with excessive deficit	TEC Art. 104(11)	AVFQ	2	8	Commission role unclear; special QMV; EP informed
EMU: Economic Policy, Abrogation of measures after correction of excessive deficit	TEC Art. 104(12)	AVFQ	2	8	Commission role unclear; special QMV
EMU: Monetary Policy, Arrangements for international exchange-rate agreements	TEC Art. 111(3)	AVFQ	2	8	

Policy area	Treaty article	Procedure			Notes
EMU: Monetary Policy, Formulation of EU negotiating position in EMU-related int'l negotiations	TEC Art. 111(4)	AVFQ	2	8	
EMU: Institutional Provisions, Composition of Economic and Financial Committee	TEC Art. 114(3)	AVFQ	2	8	EP informed
EMU: Transitional Provisions, Assessment of member-state preparation for EMU	TEC Art. 121(2)	AVFQ	2	8	Commission 'recommendation'
EMU: Transitional Provisions, Granting of derogation to member states	TEC Art. 122(1)	AVFQ	2	8	Commission 'recommendation'
Employment: Council recommendations to member states	TEC Art. 128(4)	AVFQ	2	8	
Common Commercial Policy: Directives harmonizing grants on exports to third countries	TEC Art. 132	AVFQ	2	8	
Education, Vocational Training and Youth: Recommendations	TEC Art. 149(4)	AVFQ	2	8	Recommendations only
Capital: Free movement to or from third countries constituting step back from liberalization	TEC Art. 57(2)	AVFU	6	9	
EMU: Economic Policy, EC financial assistance to member state	TEC Art. 100(2)	AVFU	6	9	EP informed

TABLE 4.3. *Continued*

Issue area	Treaty Article	Legislative procedure	Commission score	EP score	Comments/restrictions on Commission/EP
EMU: Monetary Policy, Representation of EU in EMU-related international negotiations	TEC Art. 111(4)	AVFU	6	9	
EMU: Transitional Provisions, Adoption of fixed conversion rates for EMU currencies	TEC Art. 123(4)	AVFU	6	9	
EMU: Transitional Provisions, Adoption of conversion rates for late joiners	TEC Art. 123(5)	AVFU	6	9	
Culture: Recommendations	TEC Art. 151(5)	AVFU	6	9	Recommendations only
EMU: Monetary Policy, Amendment of certain articles of ECB Statute	TEC Art. 107(5)	AVCU-shared	10	10	Choice of two procedures: AVCU on proposal from CEC or AVCQ on proposal from ECB; Commission therefore shares right of initiative

EMU: Monetary Policy, Adoption of provisions in ECB Statute	TEC Art. 107(6)	CNSQ-shared	10	10	Choice of two procedures: traditional CNSQ or CNSQ on basis of ECB recommendation
EMU: Monetary Policy, Conclusion of exchange-rate agreements with third parties	TEC Art. 111(1)	CNSU-shared	10	10	Shared right of initiative with ECB
Visas, Immigration and Asylum: Visas, first 5 years	TEC Art. 62	CNSU-shared	10	10	Shared right of initiative
Visas, Immigration and Asylum: Asylum and immigration measures, first 5 years	TEC Art. 63	CNSU-shared	10	10	Shared right of initiative
Visas, Immigration and Asylum: Judicial cooperation in civil matters, first 5 years	TEC Art. 65	CNSU-shared	10	10	Shared right of initiative
Visas, Immigration and Asylum: Measures for intergovernmental cooperation, first 5 years	TEC Art. 66	CNSU-shared	10	10	Shared right of initiative
Visas, Immigration and Asylum: Switch to CODQ, change in powers of ECJ for Title IV	TEC Art. 67(2)	CNSU-shared	10	10	Shared right of initiative
EMU: Transitional Provisions, Mutual assistance of member states in difficulty	TEC Art. 119(2)	AVFQ-shared	10	10	Shared right of initiative

TABLE 4.3. *Continued*

Issue area	Treaty Article	Legislative procedure	Commission score	EP score	Comments/restrictions on Commission/EP
CFSP: Adoption of general guidelines	TEU Art. 13(1)	AVFU-shared	10	10	Shared right of init.; EP informed generally in pillar 2; QMV by derogation, but single MS can block vote
CFSP: Adoption of common strategies	TEU Art. 13(2)	AVFU-shared	10	10	Shared right of init.; EP informed generally in pillar 2; QMV by derogation, but single MS can block vote
CFSP: Adoption of joint actions	TEU Art. 14(1)	AVFU-shared	10	10	Shared right of init.; EP informed generally in pillar 2; QMV by derogation, but single MS can block vote
CFSP: Adoption of common positions	TEU Art. 15	AVFU-shared	10	10	Shared right of init.; EP informed generally in pillar 2; QMV by derogation, but single MS can block vote

CFSP: Authorization and ratification of international negotiations	TEU Art. 24	AVFU-shared	10	Shared right of init.; EP informed generally in pillar 2; QMV by derogation, but single MS can block vote
Justice and Home Affairs: Adoption of common positions, framework decisions, conventions, etc.	TEU Art. 34	AVFU-shared	10	Shared right of init.; EP informed generally in pillar 3; QMV by derogation, but single MS can block vote
Justice and Home Affairs: Authorization of closer cooperation	TEU Art. 40	AVFQ-shared	10	Shared right of init.; EP informed generally in pillar 3; QMV by derogation, but single MS can block vote
EMU: Monetary Policy, Adjustment rates within an exchange-rate system	TEC Art. 111(1)	AVFQ-shared	10	Shared right of initiative of with ECB; EP informed

procedures in the post-Amsterdam European Union and the extent to which the Commission's guidelines were discarded in practice by the member governments. With regard to the use of co-decision, it remains the case, as the Commission wrote in 1996, that 'the distribution of areas under co-decision is...fragmentary and arbitrary'.[22] Thus, while many of the most important legislative areas for the internal market and its flanking policies have been transferred to co-decision with qualified majority, legislative acts in other areas continue to be adopted, at the insistence of one or more member governments, under other procedures including: co-decision with unanimity voting in the Council (CODU: includes culture, free movement of workers with regard to social security, and citizenship rights); assent (AVCU: adoption of Structural and Cohesion Fund Regulations); and consultation (CNSQ and CNSU: agriculture, services, visas, and harmonization of tax provisions).

The scope of application of the assent and consultation procedures is similarly haphazard. As we have seen, the assent procedure does apply to some quasi-constitutional issues like the adoption of a uniform electoral procedure or the delegation of tasks to the ECB, and to some international agreements, namely, association and accession agreements and those with financial implications which impinge on the EP's budgetary powers. By contrast, however, member states have deliberately withheld the right of assent for international agreements in the area of trade, where the Council ratifies agreements with no Parliamentary role, and for constitutional issues including the revision of the treaties, where the EP has repeatedly requested the power of assent only to be rebuffed by the member governments. Finally, as Table 4.3 makes clear, the member states have opted not to extend the consultation procedure to all other legal bases, as the Commission has proposed. Rather, the post-Amsterdam Treaties retain a large number of issue areas in which the Council acts, either by qualified majority or by unanimity, solely on the basis of a Commission proposal. In the second and third pillars, finally, the EP receives only a right to be kept informed (second pillar) or an amended version of consultation that limits the EP's power of delay (third pillar). In sum, while EU member governments have repeatedly delegated ever greater powers to the EP in response to concerns about the democratic legitimacy of EU decision making, the willingness of individual member governments to delegate legislative powers in specific areas has varied substantially as a function of each member government's substantive interests and its calculation of the likely consequence of increased EP powers—a point to which I shall return below.

Patterns of Discretion: Member Governments and Members of the European Parliament

We have already noted above that, from the point of view of principal-agent analysis, the Parliament is an outlier in terms of the functions delegated to it by the member states in successive treaty revisions. What of the *discretion* of the EP and its members? Having delegated extensive legislative and other powers to the EP, to what extent have member governments retained the power, individually or collectively, to control the preferences and the behavior of MEPs? Here again we find that the EP is something of an outlier when compared with both the Commission and the Court. On the one hand, by contrast with the Commission and the Court, whose statutory independence is affirmed in Articles 213 and 223 EC, the relevant provisions of the *Consolidated Treaties* make no such reference to the independence of the EP; nor do the member states undertake not to attempt to influence its members, as they do for the Commission. Put differently, the Treaties declare the Commission and the Court to be politically insulated, non-majoritarian bodies, while the EP is explicitly designed to be a politically engaged and majoritarian assembly. On the other hand, moving from the declaratory level to the presence or absence of actual control mechanisms, we see that the EP and its members are subject to relatively *few* control mechanisms comparable to those that constrain the Commission and, to a lesser extent, the Court. Specifically, member governments can neither appoint nor remove the members of the EP, who are selected by national parties and elected by national electorates; nor is the EP subject to active member-state oversight or extensive provisions of administrative law similar to those that apply to the Commission in its executive capacity. Hence, just as the functions delegated to the EP differ from those of the Commission and the Court, so the control mechanisms associated with traditional principal-agent relations seem to be largely absent in the member states' relations with the European Parliament.

Nevertheless, the EP and its members do not operate in complete isolation from member-state constraints and pressures. Like all EC institutions, the EP is required to operate within the procedural rules established by the treaties, and its actions are subject to judicial review under certain conditions. In addition, member governments individually retain some ability to influence MEPs through their influence on the national parties responsible for MEP selection, while collectively they retain the ability through treaty amendment to increase or decrease the powers of the Parliament, providing an incentive for the EP to behave in a 'responsible' fashion.

First, with regard to the selection and election of candidates for the European Parliament, the original EEC Treaty did not provide for direct election of MEPs, who until 1979 were appointed by the respective national parliaments of the member states. According to Article 138 (now 190) of the original EEC Treaty, the Parliament itself was to 'draw up proposals for elections by direct universal suffrage in accordance with a uniform electoral procedure in all Member States'. Such proposals, however, would require the unanimous agreement of all the member governments, followed by ratification in each member state in accordance with its own constitutional requirements. Although the Parliament reacted quickly to its mandate, producing detailed proposals in 1961, 1963, 1969, and 1973, the Council repeatedly failed to agree either to direct elections or to a uniform electoral procedure, largely because of opposition from successive French Gaullist governments wedded to intergovernmentalist rather than supranational institutional arrangements for the Community. In 1974, however, the Paris summit of heads of state and government negotiated a compromise in which the French government of President Georges Pompidou agreed in principle to the direct election of the Parliament in return for the institutionalization of the intergovernmental European Council. The Parliament, in turn, produced new proposals in 1976 for the direct election of its members, and this proposal was adopted, with amendments, by the Council later that year (Corbett, Jacobs, and Shackleton 2000: 11). The first direct elections were then held in June 1979, and four additional rounds of elections have since been held, most recently in June 1999. Despite this success, the member governments have yet to agree to a uniform electoral procedure, and the EP party groups remain federations of national parties rather than coherent and centralized European parties (Hix and Lord 1997). Candidates for the Parliament are therefore selected by their individual *national* parties and elected by national electorates on the basis of electoral systems that continue to vary from one member state to another.

In theory, MEPs are responsible not to EU member governments but to their regional or national electorates, who are their electoral 'principals'. However, as Simon Hix and others have demonstrated, the relationship between MEPs and their electorates is in practice mediated by several factors which make MEPs accountable primarily to their national political parties rather than directly to their electorates. First, because of the low visibility of the EP and its activities in the member states, as well as the relatively low salience of European issues, EP elections tend to be 'second-order' elections, waged largely by national parties on national issues and with outcomes reflecting the relative popularity of political parties in their respective member states (Bowler and Farrell 1993). Second, most EU member states employ proportional representation electoral systems in which national party leaderships determine the content and the ranking of candidates on party lists. 'Consequently, for most MEPs, the chance of standing as a candidate and being *reselected* is not determined by his or her party group in the EP, but by his or her national party leadership' (Hix 1999*a*: 75). In practice, then, the current system of candidate selection and election encourages MEPs to cultivate relations with national as well as European party leaderships, and provides national parties and, indirectly, national governments with a potential source of leverage over MEPs who share a party affiliation with those governments.[23]

Second, in addition to their role in the selection of MEP candidates through national political parties, member governments collectively may exert indirect pressure on the Parliament through their exclusive right to amend the EU's constitutive treaties and hence to increase—or reduce—the legislative powers of Parliament. As we have seen, the threat, or promise, of treaty revision is at best a blunt instrument of control because of the difficulty and infrequency of such revisions in the EU; nevertheless, in so far as MEPs seek greater legislative, budgetary, and supervisory powers in the future, they are entirely reliant upon the willingness of the member governments to delegate such powers in treaty reforms, and this reliance may in theory generate pressure on the EP to avoid repeated and persistent clashes with the member governments in the Council of Ministers. There is indeed some evidence of such an effect from various leaders of the Parliament, who after each successive treaty reform have called upon MEPs to be 'responsible' in the use of their newly acquired powers.[24] Further indirect evidence of such an effect may be derived from the critical political reactions and press coverage of the EP as a whole that has followed in the few instances when the EP has vetoed important legislation under the co-decision procedure.[25] Nevertheless, the importance of such considerations should not be overstated. Unlike the Commission and the Court of Justice, MEPs can and do claim democratic backing for their positions as well as a set of powers that are entrenched in the treaties, and with only minor, indirect sources of member-state leverage over their activities. For all of these reasons, the Parliament has demonstrated a clear and repeated willingness to confront the Council of Ministers in an adversarial fashion over the negotiation and adoption of the annual budget, legislation, and inter-institutional agreements.[26]

II. Conclusion: A Logic of Appropriateness?

> The collective will of the EU governments in the past decade has manifestly been geared to democratizing decision making by empowering the Parliament.
>
> Tsebelis and Garrett (2000: 32).

The relentless increase of EP powers over the past four decades constitutes one of the most striking examples of delegation in the history of the European Union or any other international organization. As the constitutive principals and 'masters of the treaties', EU member governments have repeatedly and unanimously chosen to delegate important supervisory, budgetary, and legislative powers to the Parliament and to make that Parliament directly accountable to national electorates. Nevertheless, as we have seen over and over again in this chapter, the functions delegated to the European Parliament fit poorly with the predictions of the transaction-cost approach regarding the motives of delegating principals and the functions delegated by them to supranational agents. Specifically, and by contrast with the Commission and the Court of Justice, the functions of the European Parliament do *not* generally include monitoring compliance, filling in the details of an incomplete contract, adopting implementing regulation, or even setting the legislative agenda, since the Parliament's legislative powers lie primarily at the decisional rather than the agenda-setting stage. Of the three major EP functions described in this chapter, only the EP's power to supervise the Commission, the EIB, and the ECB is understandable in principal-agent terms as a check on the power of the latter organizations; the Parliament's budgetary and legislative functions, by contrast, fit poorly or not at all into the functions predicted by principal-agent models.

How, then, might we explain the repeated delegation of ever greater supervisory, budgetary, and legislative powers to the European Parliament? Is it possible, as suggested at several points in this chapter, that delegation to the EP can be explained in terms of pure democratic ideology or a logic of appropriateness, as suggested by the sociological institutionalist approach in Chapter 1, rather by than a rationalist logic of consequences? At first glance, delegation of budgetary powers to the EP does indeed seem to derive entirely from normative considerations, or a 'logic of appropriateness', in which the EU's member governments delegate powers not in order to reduce transactions costs or indeed to maximize any stream of benefits calculated to result from such delegation, but rather because the empowerment of a directly elected European Parliament is normatively desirable and democratically *legitimate*. Even Andrew Moravcsik, whose theory of intergovernmental bargaining models delegation as a means to ensure credible commitments and plays down the role of supranational ideology as a motivation driving the process of European integration, concedes the primary role of ideology in delegation to the EP:

Ideology best explains, as even the credible commitments view concedes it should, variation in the willingness of countries to promote and accept institutional delegation in areas where the consequences were highly uncertain and relatively minor—notably, increased powers for the European Parliament. Here the geopolitical ideology of chief executives, parliamentary parties, and publics appears to have been decisive. Pressures for greater EP powers came from countries with a tradition of European federalism and with strong domestic parliamentary systems: Germany, Italy, and the Benelux countries. Opposition came from countries, such as Britain, France, and Denmark, with a tradition of skepticism about European federalism or strong executives. (Moravcsik 1998: 376)

Lindner and Rittberger (2001) likewise argue that in the absence of clear distributive consequences, negotiators are likely to draw on norms, such as parliamentary democracy, as focal points or road maps in the choice of EU institutions, while Renaud Dehousse (1998: 599) has suggested that the supervisory, budgetary, and legislative powers of Parliament represent an attempt by the member governments 'to inject ever greater doses of parliamentarism into the European institutional system'. The evidence presented above tends to support the dominant view that the delegation of powers to the EP appears to have been motivated largely by concerns about the democratic (or undemocratic) character of EU decision making among the leaders of the member governments or among their constituents (for example, the German Federal Constitutional Court or the strongly federalist parliamentary parties in countries like Italy, Belgium, and the Netherlands) rather than by the functionalist motivations highlighted in principal-agent models.

Nevertheless, to suggest that member governments were motivated by concerns about the democratic deficit in delegating to Parliament is *not* to suggest that those member governments were motivated solely by a logic of appropriateness nor that they ceased to pay attention to the likely consequences of delegation to the EP in specific issue areas. Rather, the historic and functional pattern of delegation to the EP supports the view that the influence of democratic or federalist ideology is greatest where the distributional implications of delegation are either unclear or unimportant. In many areas, however, member governments clearly *were* able to anticipate the likely consequences of delegating specific powers to the EP, and in such areas even the champions of a strengthened EP have agreed to structure the supervisory, budgetary, and legislative powers of Parliament to limit agency losses.

With regard to the nomination of the Commission, for example, the member governments had available a clear institutional template—the parliamentary system of government—for appointment of the executive. Such a model, regularly invoked by participants in the various intergovernmental conferences, suggested that the Parliament should not simply approve but also nominate the President and members of the Commission. Nevertheless, there is little evidence that the member governments seriously considered renouncing their collective right to appoint the Commission President or their individual right to 'their own' Commissioners—a right defended not only by the traditionally intergovernmentalist British and French but also, and most vociferously, by the traditionally supranationalist Benelux countries, eager to maintain a voice with the Commission through their right of appointment.[27]

Similarly, as we have seen, the negotiation of the EC budgetary system in 1969 and 1970 revealed not only a normative contest between a *Europe as a federation-to-be* and *Europe des états* but also a careful analysis by all member governments of the likely consequences of different institutional arrangements and a final design that incorporated Parliament into the EC budgetary authority while minimizing agency losses.

Finally, a similar concern for the likely consequences of delegation is apparent in member-state choices about the delegation of *legislative* power to the EP. As we have seen above, the Commission, the Parliament, and a number of member states have argued in favour of a consistent, systematic incorporation of Parliament in the legislative process, with the co-decision procedure used consistently for legislative acts while the assent procedure would be used for 'constitutional' decisions and international agreements, and the consultation procedure would be employed for other, essentially regulatory acts. In practice, however, even the Parliament's advocates among the member governments have not been willing to support such a consistent, across-the-board strengthening of the EP's legislative powers. For this reason, the delegation of legislative powers has proceeded on a case-by-case basis, reflecting the anticipated consequences of delegation in specific issue areas and the specific sensitivities of individual member governments.

In short, in delegating powers to the European Parliament, EU member governments have been guided largely by a normative concern for the democratic legitimacy of the Union and its policies rather than by a concern to reduce the transaction costs of EU policy-making. In this regard, the Parliament is an outlier with regard both to the predictions of principal-agent analysis and to the empirical cases of the Commission and the Court of Justice, which strongly support the principal-agent, transaction-cost view of delegation in the EU. Nevertheless, although the norm of parliamentary democracy has indeed been the overarching motivation for delegation to the EP, that norm has not been translated directly into the institutional structure of the Union, for two reasons. First, as constructivist theorists point out, norms are frequently contested, and in the EU case the norm of a European parliamentary democracy has been disputed by governments (most notably the French) and other actors who have suggested that the proper repositories of democratic legitimacy are national parliaments and national governments rather than a supranational assembly like the EP.[28] Second, and more importantly for our purposes here, norms of democratic legitimacy and a logic of appropriateness have in practice been trumped repeatedly by a careful calculation of consequences, among the champions as well as the critics of the European Parliament, if and in so far as the consequences of delegation to the EP were clear, and clearly undesirable, from the point of view of one or more of the Union's member governments.

Part II
AGENCY AND AGENDA SETTING

CHAPTER 5

———

Liberalizing Europe: The Commission, the Court, and the Creation of a European Market

So far, we have seen how the member governments of the European Union have systematically delegated specific functions to the Commission, the European Court of Justice, and the European Parliament, and tailored the discretion of these actors through the use of more or less constraining control mechanisms. More specifically, we have seen that the record of delegation to the Commission and the Court of Justice strongly supports the hypotheses that member-state principals delegate specific functions to their agents in order to reduce the transaction costs of EU policy-making, and that the discretion of each agent reflects issue-specific demands by member governments for credible commitments and for speedy and efficient decision-making. In this chapter and the next, we turn from our initial focus on delegation to a focus on agency, testing two further hypotheses about (1) the *preferences* of supranational agents such as the Commission and the Court and (2) the *conditions* under which these agents might be able to influence policy outcomes through their executive, judicial, and agenda-setting powers. Regarding the preferences of supranational actors, I hypothesized in Chapter 1 that supranational agents are characterized by a common preference for greater competences for themselves and for the European Union as a whole, including both the liberalization of the European internal market and the reimposition of social regulations from the European level, and that these organizations represent their preferences consistently vis-à-vis other actors despite the presence of internal conflicts within each organization. Regarding the conditions under which supranational actors may exert an independent causal influence on policy outcomes, the hypotheses put forward in Chapter 1 suggest that the discretion of an agent—more specifically, the ability to pursue an integrationist agenda and move policy outcomes beyond what member governments would collectively have decided—is a function of the *ex ante* and *ex post* control mechanisms established by member governments to control supranational agency in a given issue area.

As we also saw in Chapter 1, however, direct studies of Commission behaviour invariably encounter the problem of anticipated reactions whereby supranational agents such as the Commission may rationally anticipate the reactions of their principals as well as the probability of sanctions, and adjust their behaviour in advance to avoid costly sanctions. If this is so, then agency behaviour which at first glance seems autonomous may in fact be subtly influenced by the preferences of the principals, even in the absence of any overt sanctions. Furthermore, as Huber and Shipan (2000) correctly point out, single case studies are poorly suited for testing hypotheses since they seldom allow us to observe the effects of variation across the hypothesized independent variable. For this reason, Chapters 5 and 6 employ a *comparative* case-study approach, examining six case studies selected for variation across the hypothesized independent variable—that is, member-state control mechanisms—and incorporating within-case process-tracing in order to multiply the observable implications of theory and observe hypothesized causal mechanisms at work.

In this chapter, I begin by examining three cases of *market liberalization* representing a variety of member-state control mechanisms ranging from formal agenda-setting (the Commission's negotiating power in external trade policy) through executive action with member-state oversight (in the case of competition policy) and finally the Court's power of constitutional interpretation (in the case of the free movement of goods within the Union). The first case study examines the Commission's powers as the Union's chief negotiator in the area of external trade, where it enjoys the power to set the EU agenda by negotiating agreements with third countries that can subsequently be accepted by a qualified majority among the member governments. The case focuses specifically on the Commission's controversial 'Blair House' agreement on agricultural policy with the United States, and traces the member-state reaction to this agreement and the subsequent debate over the extension of the Commission's trade powers to the 'new areas' of services and intellectual property. The second case study examines the area of competition policy, with a special focus on the negotiation of the 1989 Merger Control Regulation, which delegated to the Commission the power to review European-wide mergers, as well as the Commission's subsequent decision to reject the proposed merger between the Canadian aircraft manufacturer de Havilland and the Franco-Italian consortium ATR, and the resulting controversy regarding the renewal and extension of the Commission's powers in the area of merger control. The third case study examines the role of the European Court of Justice in the interpretation of the treaty provisions on the free movement of goods within the EU, with a special focus on the Court's 1979 ruling in *Cassis de Dijon*, which established the principle of 'mutual recognition' of national regulations within the European Union, and the 1991 *Keck and Mithouard* decision in which the Court retreated from the more far-reaching implications of *Cassis*.

I. The Commission as Negotiator and Agenda Setter in the Uruguay Round

The Commission's delegated authority in the area of external trade policy constitutes, alongside competition policy, some of its oldest and most important powers, specified directly in the body of the 1957 EEC Treaty. Under the original Article 113 EEC, now slightly amended as Article 133 EC, the Community possesses exclusive competence in the area of commercial policy, and the Commission is designated as the sole and exclusive negotiator for the Community for all international trade negotiations.[1] The Commission, however, is not given a free hand to negotiate whatever agreements it likes at the international level. Rather, the Commission begins the process by proposing a negotiating mandate to the member governments, which may amend and adopt the Commission's mandate within the so-called 'Article 133 Committee', a committee of senior national officials who approve, by a qualified majority, the Commission's negotiating mandate. The Article 133 Committee also monitors the Commission's conduct of the negotiations, and may, in response to a request from the Commission, amend the Commission's negotiating mandate, again by qualified majority. Furthermore, all international trade agreements negotiated by the Commission must be ratified in a final qualified majority vote in the Council of Ministers, imposing a final check on the Commission's negotiating authority.[2]

In theoretical terms, the Commission's role in external trade policy is closely analogous to the position of chief negotiator in Putnam's two-level games model (Putnam 1988; Evans, Jacobson, and Putnam 1993). In Putnam's model, all international negotiations take place simultaneously at two levels: At the international level, or Level 1, chief negotiators bargain with their foreign counterparts in an effort to reach a mutually beneficial agreement. At the domestic level, or Level 2, the same chief negotiator engages in bargaining with her domestic constituencies, which must ultimately ratify the contents of any agreement struck at Level 1.

For each state, Putnam specifies a 'win-set', which is the set of international agreements at Level 1 that are likely to be ratified in a straight up-or-down vote at Level 2. States with small win-sets, he argues, are likely to enjoy greater bargaining power in international negotiations since they can credibly claim to be able to ratify only a narrow range of agreements, although these states also run the risk of failing to reach any agreement or of 'involuntary defection', that is, failure to secure domestic ratification of agreements concluded at Level 1. Each state's win-set, in turn, is determined by three factors. The first, and most obvious, of these is the preferences and power of domestic actors at Level 2, who must ratify any agreement reached at Level 1. The second is the political institutions at Level 2, which establish the ratification procedures specific to any given state; the more demanding the ratification procedure, Putnam argues, the smaller the win-set and the greater the likelihood of involuntary defection. The third factor determining the size of the win-set is the preferences and the bargaining strategies of the chief negotiators, who can direct side-payments or sanctions to their own or their counterparts' domestic constituencies in order to manipulate the size and shape of their respective win-sets.

Perhaps most importantly for our purposes, Putnam also highlights the pivotal role of the chief negotiator, whose preferences, like those of any agent, may diverge from those of her domestic principals and who may be able to influence the substance of an agreement by virtue of her dual role at both the international and the domestic bargaining tables. At the international level, for example, a chief negotiator may adopt strategies to strengthen her own Level 1 bargaining position by manipulating or misrepresenting the nature of her own win-set at Level 2 or by manipulating the win-set of her adversaries through the selective application of side-payments or sanctions to key domestic actors in other states.

Conversely, a chief negotiator may employ international pressures and her own strategic position at both tables to manipulate her own domestic constituencies. A chief negotiator may, for example, be eager to effect some domestic policies or reforms but be unable to do so because of resistance from a coalition of domestic interests. In a two-level negotiation, however, the chief negotiator may plausibly argue to her own domestic constituents that her preferred policies are in fact necessary in order to reach agreement at the international level and must therefore be accepted in order to enjoy the benefits of the over-all agreement. The chief negotiator's domestic position may be further strengthened if, as in the case of the United States' 'fast track' author-ity, the resulting international agreement must be ratified in a straight up-or-down vote, thus providing the chief negotiator with formal agenda-setting power and increasing the likelihood of ratification at the domestic level (Putnam 1998: 448). In sum, the chief negotiator's central position at both the international and the domestic tables may strengthen her bargaining leverage at both tables simultaneously.

In his liberal intergovernmentalism model, Andrew Moravcsik has adapted Putnam's two-level games approach to the study of the European Community, in which EC member governments act as chief negotiators between their domestic polities and parliaments on the one hand and their fellow member governments on the other hand. According to Moravcsik, this privileged position has allowed member governments to increase their own autonomy vis-à-vis their domestic constituencies by concentrating resources—initiative, informa- tion, institutions, and ideas—in the hands of the member governments negotiating in Brussels. In Moravcsik's model, national parlia-ments and other domestic constituencies are simply left to rubber-stamp the decisions taken by member governments in Council, and the net effect of the Community's two-level game has been to strengthen rather than weaken the member governments of the EC (Moravcsik 1994).

Applying Putnam's model to the external relations of the Com-munity, however, reveals that EC trade negotiations are not a two-level but a three-level game: At Level 1, the Commission negoti-ates with representatives of the United States and other trading part-ners in order to reach international trade agreements. These agreements must then be ratified at Level 2, representing the inter-governmental Article 133 Committee and the Council of Ministers. Finally, at Level 3, national governments seek domestic ratification of decisions taken at Community level.[3]

In this three-level game, the Commission should theoretically enjoy many of the advantages of Putnam's chief negotiator, manipu-lating and misrepresenting its own win-set to increase its bargaining leverage at the international level and using external pressures to increase its 'domestic' bargaining leverage vis-à-vis both the member governments at Level 2 and national interest groups at Level 3. If we accept with Sophie Meunier and most other students of EC external trade policy that 'the Commission can generally be characterized as

more liberal than the majority of the member states', we should therefore expect the Commission to seek to negotiate agreements that are
as liberal in terms of trade liberalization as a qualified majority among
the member governments will accept (Meunier 2000: 112). The possibilities of the Commission's role as chief negotiator in external trade
policy, and its limits, are well illustrated by the negotiation of the
Uruguay Round and its most contentious element, agriculture.

The Uruguay Round, the Common Agricultural Policy, and the Commission

Convened in 1986 in the Uruguayan capital of Punta del Este, the
Uruguay Round of the General Agreement on Tariffs and Trade
(GATT) was to address a number of new issues in the area of international trade, including most notably trade in services, trade-related
intellectual property issues (TRIPs), trade-related investment issues
(TRIMs), and the creation of a new World Trade Organization to
encompass the existing GATT. In each of these areas, the Uruguay
Round attempted to establish rules for issues which had previously
been outside the domain of multilateral international trade negotiations. Indeed, both services and TRIPs involved areas of so-called
'mixed competence' for which the member states agreed to negotiate
with one voice and appointed the Commission as their sole negotiator,
but without prejudice to the ultimate distribution of competences
between the member states and the Community.[4]

Undoubtedly the most difficult issue, however, and one in which
the Community had clear and exclusive competence as a result of the
Common Agricultural Policy, was agriculture.[5] Agriculture had been
included in previous rounds of the GATT but various exemptions to
GATT rules meant that states were in effect free to adopt national, or
Community, systems for subsidizing and protecting national production and for export subsidies as well. By the late 1980s, however, the
United States was determined to secure a substantial reduction in agricultural subsidies, especially in the EC, where both subsidies and
exports had grown rapidly in the course of the previous decade.
Indeed, it was largely American concerns about agricultural subsidies
which led the Reagan Administration to press in 1985 for the opening
of the Uruguay Round.

Not surprisingly, the initial US and EC negotiating positions on
agriculture were poles apart. For its part, the Reagan Administration
put forward a radical proposal, often called the 'zero option', calling
for the complete elimination of agricultural subsidies by the year 2000.

To the Commission and the member governments of the Community, on the other hand, such an approach was anathema as it would threaten the fundamental principles of the Common Agricultural Policy. Put simply, the CAP is based on a series of guaranteed, Community-wide prices for the various agricultural products. Within the Community, the CAP establishes a so-called 'intervention price' for each commodity, beneath which the Community will automatically buy in any excess production. In addition, the CAP establishes a 'threshold price' for each item, which in most cases is considerably higher than the world market price. The Community then imposes a variable import levy, equal to the difference between the Community threshold price and the world price, on all imports into the EC, while at the same time granting export subsidies equal to the difference between the Community's internal market price and the world price. The result of this system, to simplify only a bit, was high and stable agricultural prices for EC farmers, coupled with chronic overproduction of certain products—the legendary lakes of wine and mountains of butter—and increasing levels of EC agricultural exports at the expense of the United States and other agricultural producers.[6]

The Uruguay Round therefore presented the Commission with both challenges and opportunities. As chief negotiator for the Community, the Commission would face the challenge of reconciling the far-reaching demands of the United States and other states at the international level with the entrenched resistance to any reform of the CAP among EC farmers and among their representatives in the Council of Agriculture Ministers and the Article 133 Committee. The nature of this challenge is well illustrated by the abortive Brussels meeting of the GATT in December 1990, which was intended to conclude the Uruguay Round in time for the pre-established deadline of 31 December 1990. For this 'final' round of negotiations, the Commission would require a revised negotiating mandate by 15 October, but the Council of Ministers was deadlocked for months in approving the Commission's proposals largely because of German and French reluctance to make any agricultural concessions on the eve of the first all-German elections and the intergovernmental conference (IGC) that would lead in 1992 to the Maastricht Treaty. Finally, in mid-November 1990 the 'Jumbo' Council of foreign and agriculture ministers approved a new mandate for the Commission, but this mandate was narrow and inflexible, leaving the Commission little room to make concessions and leading US negotiators to observe that 'the Commission would not negotiate until it had a mandate from the Council and could not negotiate once it had been given one'.[7]

At the Brussels meeting in December, the United States modified its earlier 'zero option' proposal on agriculture, calling instead for a 75 per cent reduction in internal subsidies and a 90 per cent reduction in export subsidies over a ten-year period beginning in 1990. By contrast, the Community's opening position in the negotiations called for only a 30 per cent cut in internal supports from 1986 levels (approximately half of which had already been achieved within the EC) and no firm commitments on export subsidies (a position rejected by most of the major parties to the negotiations, including not only the United States but also the Cairns group of agricultural producers led by Australia). In response to these demands and to a possible breakdown of the Brussels meeting over agriculture, the Commission indicated that it might be willing to be more flexible and undertake more specific commitments on export subsidies in return for concessions from the United States and others on issues such as market access, services, and intellectual property. The Commission's proposal, however, had not been cleared with the EC's national trade and agriculture ministers, who did not take part in the actual negotiations but nevertheless attended the Brussels meeting to monitor the Commission's behaviour. Upon hearing about the Commission's offer, French Agriculture Minister Louis Mermaz argued that the Commission had exceeded its mandate, and the Commission was publicly rebuked by the Council, leading to a collapse of both the Commission's credibility and the Brussels meeting, which broke up amid nearly universal condemnation of the Community by the other delegations. Put simply, the Brussels meeting demonstrated that the Commission, despite its key role as chief negotiator, could not press too far ahead of the member governments in its proposals without risking a backlash and a correction by recalcitrant member states.

On the other hand, as Putnam points out, the Commission's presence at both negotiating tables—the EC and the international—also provided it with the possibility of using external pressure to strengthen its negotiating position internally, and vice versa. The Commission, and in particular President Jacques Delors and Agriculture Commissioner Ray MacSharry, therefore established a dual strategy with two central goals. First, Delors and MacSharry would design and steer through the Council a far-reaching reform of the bankrupted CAP, designed to make the CAP sustainable through the long term and avoiding any possible bankruptcy or renationalization of the system, while at the same time making the CAP compatible with the minimum demands of the Community's trading partners. Second, and equally importantly, the Commission would present the newly reformed CAP to its trading partners as the Community's bottom-line offer, beyond which the Commission could argue that its hands were tied. Ross, although eschewing the language of two-level games, nevertheless sums up the Commission strategy perfectly in his account of the actions of Delors *cabinet* official, Jean-Luc Lamarty:

Once on the table, Jean-Luc thought, the reform would almost certainly grant the Commission more maneuvering room on the Uruguay Round front, both internally and externally. The fact that CAP reform was in progress would set limits on external pressures while the need for CAP reform to succeed in the Uruguay Round would work internally.[8]

This is indeed what took place, but the process was to take several years, leading to open conflicts between the Commission and the United States, between the Commission and the EC member states, and within the Commission itself.

Internal Bargaining: The 1992 CAP Reform

The debacle at the December 1990 meeting of the GATT had made clear, at least to the Commission, the need for substantial agricultural reform in order to unblock the GATT negotiations, providing the Commission with a strong external incentive to press for CAP reform. In addition, however, the CAP in the early 1990s faced an internal crisis, with rising agricultural surpluses and a spiralling budget which, according to Commission estimates, was expected to increase by some 30 per cent in 1991. Such expenditures would, if left unchecked, lead to the breaching of the Community's agricultural guidelines established by the European Council in 1988, and could well create pressures for the renationalization of agricultural policy in the Community. Fearing the collapse and possible renationalization of the CAP, Directorate-General VI (Agriculture) began work in late 1990 on a series of proposals for a radical reform of the CAP designed to bring spending under control and reduce the need for export subsidies to bring the CAP into line with the demands of the Uruguay Round negotiations.[9] In February 1991, after an extended 'seminar' and debate, the full Commission approved a general communication to the Council on the need for reform, followed in August by a detailed reform plan, often referred to as the MacSharry reforms.[10]

MacSharry's message to the Council about the state of the CAP and the need for reform was unequivocal:

It appears in these conditions that the Community's agricultural policy cannot avoid a succession of increasingly serious crises unless its mechanisms are fundamentally reviewed so as to adapt them to a situation different from that of the sixties...

The Commission wishes to emphasize that the status quo is the one option that it considers not to be viable. If the present policy is not changed rapidly, the situation on the markets and, as early as the current year the budget position, will become untenable.[11]

In response to this crisis, MacSharry proposed a sweeping set of reforms, the heart of which consisted of a shift from price support to direct payments to farmers. More specifically, the prices of a number of agricultural products would be cut severely, most notably for wheat, which would be cut by some 35 per cent to a target price of 100 European currency units (ecus) per ton, near world-market levels.[12] Farmers would then be compensated for their loss of income through a system of direct payments linked to the total acreage of each farm. Finally, compensation would be 'modulated' so that small farmers would receive greater compensation than large farms, and in all cases compensation would be linked to a commitment to set aside acreage to avoid overproduction in the future. Although the Commission plan would not save money in the short term, and indeed might lead to a slight increase in agricultural spending to finance direct payments to farmers, in the long term the plan would reduce the CAP's incentive to overproduce and hence its persistent pressures on the EC budget.[13] A final consideration, unspoken but implicit in the Commission's proposals, was that the proposed reforms would bring EC agricultural prices closer into line with world prices and thereby reduce the trade-distorting effects of the CAP and the need for export subsidies that were the most sensitive issue in the GATT negotiations. In short, MacSharry's proposed reforms would increase the size of the Community's win-set, and hence the Commission's negotiating mandate, while at the same time drawing a clear and conspicuous bottom line beyond which the Community could refuse to compromise with the US.

In Kingdon's (1984) terms, the stalled Uruguay Round negotiations and the budgetary pressures in early 1991 provided the Commission an important 'window of opportunity' to press for a far-reaching reform of the CAP, which had been rejected or watered down by a coalition of farm lobbies and agriculture ministers in previous years. Nevertheless, MacSharry's proposals faced unanimous opposition among both the agriculture ministers and EC farm groups when he introduced them to Council in February 1991, and passage was by no means assured. Some member states, such as Great Britain, Denmark, and the Netherlands, supported MacSharry's case for CAP reform but opposed his plans for modulated payments, which they argued would benefit inefficient small farmers at the expense of the larger and more efficient British, Danish, and Dutch farmers. At the other extreme, France initially resisted the move from price support to direct payments, while Germany fought for price cuts considerably less draconian than the 35 per cent cut in wheat prices sought by MacSharry. Community farm groups, finally, joined the agriculture ministers in their hostility to MacSharry's proposals, which they argued would decrease farm incomes and were being proposed only in response to bullying from the United States.

The twin pressures of the Uruguay Round and the budget, however, eventually led the member governments to support the broad lines of MacSharry's proposals, although several specific provisions of the plan were altered in Council bargaining during the first half of 1992. More specifically, in order to reach agreement the Portuguese Presidency of the Council proposed a series of compromises on the Commission proposal, including the abandonment of the Commission's proposed modulation scheme to benefit small and medium-sized farmers, which MacSharry reluctantly accepted. More contentious, however, was the Presidency's proposed compromise on the cuts in the price of wheat, which were the linchpin of MacSharry's reform proposals. Whereas MacSharry had proposed a 35 per cent cut in the price of wheat, from 155 ecus per ton to 100 ecus, Portuguese Agriculture Minister Arlindo Cunha in April proposed a compromise cut of 27 per cent, or 112 ecus per ton, largely to appeal to Germany, a high-cost producer. MacSharry, however, reportedly dug in his heels and refused to agree to such a cut, which would lead to continuing overproduction and sabotage the Commission's negotiating position within the GATT. Instead, he persuaded Cunha to propose a new price of 110 ecus, 'a 29 per cent cut close to the 30 per cent the Commission had always set out to achieve, with a 1 per cent psychological sweetener to enable Germany to feel it was in the "20s"' (Gardner 1992a). The Germans accepted the proposal and the Council, after a last-minute snag on the question of Italian milk quotas, adopted the most radical reform of the CAP since the policy's inception in the 1960s. The Commission had compromised on modulation and on wheat prices, but the central, radical element of the Commission's reform—the shift from price support to direct payments—remained intact in the final Council bargain, leading one of the Commissioner's aides to label the reforms 'son of MacSharry, definitely' (quoted in Gardner 1992b). Remarkably, the member governments had adopted in its essentials a reform plan which they, together with the EC's farmers, had been unanimous in rejecting only 18 months earlier.

External Bargaining: Negotiating Blair House

Having secured the passage of CAP reform, MacSharry and the Commission returned to the agriculture negotiations with the United States, armed with the MacSharry reforms as the Community's new bottom-line negotiating position. The GATT negotiations had dragged on during 1991 and early 1992, including a desperate attempt to broker agreement by GATT director-general Arthur Dunkel, but the negotiations had once again been deadlocked over agriculture as the French and the Irish objected to the agricultural provisions of Dunkel's Draft Final Act. The talks were further delayed in the summer of 1992, moreover, by Mitterrand's reluctance to alienate French farmers on the eve of the French referendum on the Maastricht Treaty, which was ratified by only a narrow margin on 20 September. Finally, in late September 1992 US-EC negotiations on agriculture resumed.

The Uruguay Round negotiations were further complicated, however, by the emergence of a new agricultural dispute between the EC and the United States, involving EC subsidies to Community oilseeds producers. Under a 1962 GATT agreement, the EC had agreed to grant US oilseeds duty-free status, yet beginning in the 1970s the Community offered subsidies to European oilseeds processing, contributing to a significant decline in the US share in the European oilseeds market. The US government accordingly took the oilseeds dispute to a GATT arbitration panel, which ruled in 1990 and again in 1992 that the EC subsidies were illegal, and in April 1992 the US announced its intention to impose punitive tariffs on $1 billion of EC agricultural imports. While technically distinct from the Uruguay Round talks, the oilseeds dispute thus became linked for bargaining purposes with the outcome of the Uruguay Round and led to hard bargaining between American and EC negotiators in October and November of 1992.

These negotiations led to conflict *within* the Commission when, on the eve of the US Presidential elections in early November, MacSharry and Trade Commissioner Frans Andriessen travelled to Chicago, along with British Agriculture Minister John Gummer as president-in-office of the Council, for last-minute talks with US Trade Representative Carla Hills and Agriculture Secretary Edward Madigan. In Chicago, MacSharry and Andriessen came close to reaching a global agreement with Hills and Madigan on the oilseeds dispute as well as the outstanding Uruguay Round issues of internal supports and export subsidies, when Commission President Jacques Delors again raised the issue of the Commission's negotiating mandate.

As Ross (1995: 211–12) tells the story,

Delors, with the French at his back...telephoned MacSharry to warn him that the proposed deal went beyond CAP reform and the Commission's negotiating mandate. Delors also announced that he would oppose the deal in the Commission and was confident of winning, and that were the deal to go forward, it would be vetoed by at least two member states. MacSharry promptly resigned from his role as oilseeds negotiator and, with Andriessen, went back to Brussels to confront the Commission President, with whom neither was on cordial terms...Delors was outvoted in the Commission on the issue of the negotiating mandate.

On 10 November, five days after handing in his resignation, MacSharry therefore returned as the Commission's chief negotiator on agricultural issues and resumed the agricultural negotiations with the lame-duck but activist team of Hills and Madigan, who increased the pressure on the EC by announcing the imposition of $300 million in retaliatory tariffs aimed at European agricultural products. The EC, in turn, considered counter-retaliatory tariffs, which were blocked only by the opposition of the British and the Germans. For the first time in years of negotiation, the United States and the European Community seemed to be on the brink of a trade war.

On 20 November, however, the Commission and the Americans, meeting at Blair House in Washington, DC, signed the so-called Blair House 'Pre-Agreement', resolving both the oilseeds dispute and the Uruguay Round agricultural issues. On oilseeds, the Community agreed to curtail domestic production by 10–15 per cent in terms of acreage, responding to a key US demand. The Uruguay Round portion of the deal contained agreements on internal supports, specifying which types of support would be eligible for inclusion in the 'green box' of non-trade-distorting supports allowed by the GATT, as well as on export subsidies, where the volume of exports receiving subsidies would be cut by 21 per cent rather than the 24 per cent demanded by the US or the 18 per cent offered by the EC. The Commission, finally, also obtained a so-called 'peace clause' under which the United States agreed not to challenge EC agricultural subsidies for a period of six years.[14]

Reneging, Renegotiating, and Wrapping Up: From Blair House to Marrakesh

At Blair House, the Commission had reached the long-sought-after agreement on agricultural issues with Washington, thereby clearing the way for the conclusion of the Uruguay Round, which would follow roughly a year later in December 1993. It had done so, however, by agreeing to a package that had not been explicitly agreed to by the member states, raising the problem of ratification by the Council. As Woolcock and Hodges (1996: 318) note in their excellent analysis:

Blair House...illustrates the risks inherent in a strategy in which the Commission 'gets out ahead' of a consensus among the member states. Such a strategy may make for flexibility, but when major member states are not 'implicated' in the deal they are free to attack it and thus undermine EC credibility.

In particular, the Blair House agreement came under persistent attack from France, where farmers burned US flags in the streets of Paris and Agriculture Minister Jean-Pierre Soisson argued that the Commission had exceeded its mandate by negotiating an agreement with the United States which went beyond the CAP reforms agreed to in May. The French Socialist government, moreover, was worried about the upcoming French legislative elections, which the Gaullist majority was heavily favoured to win, and resisted taking any action that might alienate the powerful farm vote (Buchan 1992*b*).

The British and Danish Presidencies avoided putting the Blair House agreement to an immediate vote in the Council, where such a vote could in theory be taken by QMV over French objections, while successive French governments carried on a year-long assault against the agreement. In early March of 1993, just prior to the elections, France announced in the Council that it would oppose approval of the Blair House agreement 'by all means' including the invocation of its right of veto under the Luxembourg Compromise. The new Gaullist Balladur government, which took over after March of 1993, took a more cautious approach, calling for a renegotiation of the Blair House agreement without forcing the collapse of the overall Uruguay Round, from which France as a major exporter stood to benefit. On 8 June Balladur agreed to ratify the oilseeds part of the Blair House agreement, which was the basis for the threatened white wine tariffs against French farmers, but he continued to demand a renegotiation of the Uruguay Round side of the agreement. Such a renegotiation was resisted, however, by the new Trade Commissioner, Sir Leon Brittan, and by a majority of the member states, which were concerned about reopening the difficult and delicate package agreed to at Blair House.

The French position, however, was strengthened by two factors. First, the member governments agreed in the autumn of 1993 to ratify the final Uruguay Round package by consensus, and not by QMV as specified in Article 133, thus giving France a potential veto over the results of the Round. Second, and more importantly, Balladur prevailed on German Chancellor Helmut Kohl at their 28 August summit meeting to support the French position in the interest of the wider Franco-German relationship. This German change of position was crucial, and in September the Council of Ministers instructed Brittan to ask for 'amplifications or additions' to the Blair House agreement with Washington (Preeg 1995: 163–4).

Against this European background, the Clinton Administration, eager to reach agreement before the expiry of the US 'fast-track' authority, agreed to a series of 'clarifications' of the Blair House agreement at a meeting in Brussels on 1–3 December 1993, which went a considerable way toward responding to French demands. As Preeg (1995: 166–7) writes,

…the Americans made very significant concessions that altered the Blair House concessions to the advantage of European—especially French—farmers. The 21 percent reduction in subsidized exports was spread evenly over the six-year implementation period and, more importantly, the base period from which to measure the reduction was moved up from 1986–90 to 1991–92, thus allowing a higher level of subsidized exports throughout. The French wheat farmers gained in the order of 8 million tons over six years. A formula was also included for the EU to dispose on world markets its 25 million tons of grain stocks. Another US concession extended from six to eight years the period of the so-called peace clause…In sum, the French had achieved a significant watering down of the agreement made by the EC negotiators a year earlier, while the basic framework for reversing the upward trend of subsidized exports and cutting them back by about a fifth over six years was maintained.

With the agricultural issue out of the way, the contracting parties of the GATT completed the final package of the Uruguay Round negotiations on 15 December 1993 and, in a complex intergovernmental bargain involving side-payments to France and Portugal, the Council of Ministers unanimously approved the outcome of the negotiations on the following day.[15] Formal signature of the Final Act took place on 15 April 1994 in Marrakesh.

Analysis: The Commission as Chief Negotiator and Agenda Setter in the Uruguay Round

The case of the Uruguay Round agriculture negotiations, in sum, presents a mixed picture of the Commission's autonomy and influence as negotiator and agenda setter for the Community in the area of external trade policy. On the one hand, we have seen how the Commission purposefully and successfully harnessed external US pressures and internal budgetary pressures to produce and steer through the Council a far-reaching reform of the CAP designed to put the policy on secure financial footing, as well as making it compatible with the demands of the Uruguay Round. The Commission's success in this regard is particularly striking in light of the entrenched opposition to fundamental reforms among the member governments in the Agriculture Council, where at the beginning of 1991 not a single government had proposed, or supported, the shift from price supports to direct payments that constituted the core of MacSharry's reforms. Nevertheless, as several analysts have pointed out, it is difficult to argue counter-factually that CAP reform would not have been adopted in the absence of an entrepreneurial Commission, since the external pressures of the GATT and the internal budgetary pressures on the CAP in the early 1990s both made such a reform imperative (Paarlberg 1997; Patterson 1997). In that context, the Commission played a key role in shaping the content of the 1992 reform and shepherding it through a reluctant Council of Ministers, but it did so in a context where some type of reform was likely even in the absence of such entrepreneurial action.

Moving from the MacSharry reforms to the Commission's negotiation of the Blair House agreement, however, we find that the Commission, having negotiated what it believed to be a successful trade-liberalizing agreement at Blair House, was forced into an embarrassing involuntary defection when the Council of Ministers refused to ratify the agreement and instead ordered its renegotiation. This limit on the Commission's influence in external trade policy in turn reflects two fundamental factors.

First, in line with the analysis put forward in Chapter 1, the Commission's ability to get 'out in front' of the member governments is limited by the administrative and oversight procedures formally established by the treaties and most notably by the Article 133 Committee. Although in principle the chief negotiator on behalf of the European Union, and therefore subject to all the informational and institutional advantages of such a position, the Commission is in practice limited by the negotiating mandate granted to it by this committee of member-state representatives (Johnson 1998). The Article 133 committee also performs a crucial monitoring function, shadowing Commission negotiators 'in the field' and thereby minimizing the Commission's informational advantages and facilitating sanctioning in the event that the Commission's position goes beyond the collective position of the member governments, as in the 1990 Brussels meeting. Finally, the requirement of Council ratification of any Commission agreement by qualified majority places a clear limit on the EC's 'win-set' and therefore on the range of agreements that the Commission can negotiate with third parties on behalf of the Community. In the language of Kalypso Nicolaidis's (1999) analysis, the Article 133 Committee, together with the requirement of ratification by the Council, allow the member governments to limit the *flexibility* of the Commission's negotiating mandate, the *autonomy* of the Commission in negotiations, and the *authority* of the Commission in terms of its ability to secure ratification of the resulting agreement.

Second, however, in addition to these formal, treaty-based *ex ante* and *ex post* control mechanisms we must consider the member governments' informal norm, within both the Article 133 Committee and the Council of Ministers, of approving the Commission's mandate and ratifying international agreements by consensus rather than the QMV that is technically allowed according to the letter of the treaties. In so far as it is actually employed in the Council, this informal norm of consensus voting—widely noted by students of both EC trade policy and the Council of Ministers[16] and explicable in terms of 'diffuse reciprocity' among the member governments[17]—effectively imposes a unanimity voting rule among them. While such a rule has been shown to maximize the bargaining leverage of the Community and its most conservative member governments vis-à-vis third countries—hence the French insistence on consensus in the ratification of the Blair House agreement—it also has the effect of decreasing drastically the formal agenda-setting powers of the Commission, as well as the likelihood of a reaching agreement.[18] In the Uruguay Round case, the Commission would in all likelihood have succeeded in securing the ratification of the Blair House agreement had the Council proved willing to ratify the agreement by qualified majority; in practice, however, Germany and the other member governments proved unwilling to isolate France, which thus managed to block the adoption of the agreement. In so far as the informal norm of consensual voting extends to other cases and other issue areas—a question subject to empirical investigation—the Commission's formal agenda-setting powers may in fact be systematically weaker than formal models of agenda setting under qualified majority suggest. I shall return to this point in Chapter 6 and again in the Conclusion.

Finally, although it takes us beyond the specifics of the Blair House agreement, it is important to note that, following the conclusion of the Uruguay Round, a major dispute arose between the Commission and the member governments regarding the competence of the EC and the Commission in the negotiation and ratification of agreements on 'new issues' such as trade in services and intellectual property, which touch not only on tariffs and duties but also on 'behind-the-border' issues such as culture and audiovisual policy. During the Uruguay Round, the member governments had agreed to allow the Commission to act as the exclusive EC negotiator for these new issues as well as for the traditional issues of trade in goods, but without prejudice to the final distribution of competence between the two levels. As ratification approached, however, a majority of the member governments insisted on the right to ratify individually the sections of the Round dealing with new trade issues such as services and intellectual property, while the Commission argued that the entire agreement should be ratified by the Community under Article 133 of the Treaty. Concerned about the considerable difficulties that such individual ratifications might pose for its authority in future trade negotiations, the Commission appealed the question of competence to the European Court of Justice, which in November 1994 handed down a decision which largely supported the position of the member states.[19] While the Community did indeed possess exclusive competence to negotiate on trade in goods as well as on non-tariff barriers to such trade, the Court held that in the areas of services and intellectual property rights the Community and the member states were jointly competent to negotiate agreements with third parties, and instructed the Commission and the Council to work together to mitigate the results of this mixed competence. Three years later, within the intergovernmental conference that culminated in the Amsterdam Treaty, the Commission attempted to secure the adoption of an amendment to Article 133 giving it exclusive competence to negotiate in these two areas; given the implacable opposition of France and the United Kingdom, among others, however, the IGC was able to agree only to a provision allowing the member states to decide, by a unanimous vote and on a case-by-base basis, whether to delegate to the Community exclusive competence in these two areas.

Throughout these debates, the Commission behaved predictably in favouring a broad interpretation of Article 133 and, after its loss in the ECJ, proposing an amendment of that article to delegate negotiating powers for services and intellectual property issues to itself. However, as Meunier and Nicolaidis (1999) have argued, the post-Uruguay Round debate challenges the assumptions of principal-agent models of delegation, in two ways. First, the authors point out that, despite its substantive interest in international trade liberalization, the United Kingdom, like Denmark and several other member governments, was opposed to the delegation of authority to the Commission in this area, suggesting that Britain's ideological views about the desirability of further integration trumped its economic interests, which should have favoured delegation to the Commission on the grounds that 'policy stream' resulting from such delegation would have been closer to the UK's own liberal preferences on trade. The conclusion to be drawn from this observation, they argue, is that member-government positions regarding the delegation of power to the Commission reflect both issue-specific preferences and general ideological positions on the desirability of European integration, with the relative weight of each varying across member states and over time. By and large, the delegation decisions examined in the first half of this book suggest that issue-specific considerations typically dominate broader ideological views about integration in the delegation decisions of member governments, at least where the consequences of such delegation can be predicted with a reasonable degree of certainty. Nevertheless, Meunier and Nicolaidis's study raises an important question regarding the relative weight of these two considerations, which should be the subject of further empirical research.

Second and finally, research by Meunier and Nicolaidis, like the earlier study by Jónsson (1998), suggest that the Court's surprising ruling against the Commission may reflect political pressures on the Court given the strongly expressed preferences of several member governments, the controversy over the Court's earlier *Barber* judgment (see Chapter 6), and the reluctance of member governments to delegate additional powers to the ECJ in Maastricht (see Chapter 3). In fact, it is difficult to demonstrate definitively whether the Court was, or was not, subject to political pressure in a single case, for reasons discussed in Section III of this chapter. Nevertheless, the Court's negative opinion in this case, and its impact on the Commission's thus-far unsuccessful campaign to expand its negotiating competence to services and intellectual property issues, point to the close interrelationship between the Commission and the ECJ and the frequent reliance of the former on the latter in its disputes with the member governments, as we shall see in several other case studies below.

II. The Commission as Regulator: The 1989 Merger Control Regulation and the De Havilland Case

In the area of competition policy, a number of analysts have correctly identified the Commission's powers on antitrust and state aids issues as 'the first supranational policy' in the EC.[20] Influenced by pressure from the United States and the West German government, and guided in part by the parallel provisions of the ECSC Treaty, the drafters of the EEC Treaty incorporated strong competition policy provisions in the treaty and empowered the Commission to enforce those rules. The rules themselves fall into two broad groups: the first, laid down primarily in Articles 81 and 82 (ex 85 and 86) EC and elaborated in Regulation 17 of 1962, concern anti-competitive practices by firms, such as cartels and abuse of dominant positions, while the second, laid down in Articles 90–92 (ex 92–94) EC, concern the compatibility of state aids with the common market. As we saw in Chapter 2, the powers and the discretion of the Commission in these two areas constitute, together with external trade policy, the most important areas of treaty-based delegation to the Commission, featuring the delegation of extensive powers and relatively few control mechanisms that might allow member governments to influence the Commission in the exercise of those powers. In each of these areas, moreover, the Commission has acted as the Community's primary competition authority, using its powers with increasing boldness from the 1980s onwards to promote the liberalization of EU markets in various sectors.

Articles 81 and 82 form the core of EU antitrust policy as directed against private actors. Under the provisions of Article 81, inter-firm agreements and concerted practices which might affect inter-state trade or distort competition within the common market—for example, market sharing, price fixing, and cartels—are generally forbidden, while Article 82 concerns the abuse of a dominant position by firms which use their market power to distort competition and affect EC trade by imposing unfair prices, limiting production, or discriminating among consumers. These provisions, strengthened by the adoption of an important implementing regulation (Regulation 17/1962), provided the legal basis for the Commission's increasingly strict enforcement of EU antitrust rules, particularly those on cartels and concentrations, as well as for the Commission's initial efforts to extend the scope of its activities to include merger control in the 1960s and 1970s (see below).

The structure of the treaty provisions on state aids are similar to those regarding cartels and anti-competitive agreements, except that they are addressed to the member states. Thus, under Article 87 (ex 92) EC, state aids to industry which serve to distort competition within the Community are generally considered to be incompatible with the treaty and forbidden. Articles 92(2) and 92(3), however, then list certain categories of aid which either are, or may be considered to be, compatible with the common market and are thus allowed under the treaty. Although the Commission's formal powers in the area of state aids mirror those under Articles 81 and 82, the political difficulties of challenging member states directly regarding the provision of aid to troubled national industries have been greater than the enforcement of antitrust laws against private actors; perhaps for this reason, the Commission has traditionally applied EC state aid rules 'with a light touch', approving the majority of proposed state aids to industry (F. McGowan 2000: 129).

During the 1970s, a period of both economic crisis and a sclerotic integration process, the Commission's enforcement of its competition powers is widely considered to have been lax as the Commission tolerated cartels in sectors such as sugar, steel, and shipbuilding, and routinely approved sizeable state aids to declining industries. In the 1980s, however, under Competition Commissioners Peter Sutherland and Sir Leon Brittan, the Commission took advantage of the neo-liberal preferences of the member governments and the completion of the internal market to make greater use of the Commission's existing powers, cracking down on both cartels and anti-competitive practices, imposing larger fines on firms found to be have violated EC rules, and specifying conditions for state aids to industry.[21] We should be cautious, however, about attributing causal significance to Sutherland's and Brittan's activism in this area. While both Commissioners were indeed determined to apply Community competition rules with renewed vigour, their efforts also coincided with the liberal turn toward the market among member-state governments, making the causal roles of the member states and the Commission exceedingly difficult to disentangle.

In this context, the case of merger control offers a promising case for the study of member-state delegation to the Commission and the latter's use of its powers to pursue its own integrationist agenda. For although the original EEC Treaty did not delegate to the Commission the power to regulate European mergers, the Commission actively sought such powers in a 16-year campaign from the early 1970s onwards, culminating in the delegation of official merger control powers in the 1989 Merger Control Regulation (MCR). In this section, I first examine the legislative history of the 1989 Regulation, looking at the efforts of the Commission—aided indirectly but importantly by the Court of Justice—to acquire powers in this area, and the motivations and concerns of the member governments in the adoption of the Regulation. In the second part of the section, I examine the Commission's implementation of the Merger Control Regulation, with a special focus on the most famous and controversial decision in the history of EU merger control, namely, the Commission's first rejection of a proposed merger (ATR/De Havilland) in 1991, examining the pressure exerted on the Commission by member governments, the resulting controversy about the scope of Commission powers, the subsequent reform of the Merger Control Regulation in 1997, and its application since then.

The Road to the 1989 Merger Control Regulation

In the contemporary European Union, the Commission's merger control policies are among its most well-known and important, yet the EEC Treaty was completely silent on the Commission's competence to regulate mergers, which was confirmed only with the adoption of the 1989 Merger Control Regulation after a long campaign by the Commission itself.[22] In order to understand the nature of the Commission's victory in this area, it is important to note that the Commission's competition powers under the Treaty of Rome, although far-reaching, did not include the power to vet mergers and acquisitions, even under Article 82 on the abuse of a dominant position. As Goyder (1993: 386) writes:

...there seems little doubt that those responsible for the drafting of Article 86 [ex 82] did not intend that it should give control over mergers to the Commission. Neither the actual wording of the Article nor the evidence of those who participated in the negotiations leading up to the Treaty or in its early administration support any contrary argument.

Nevertheless, Goyder continues, the absence of any direct control over mergers and acquisitions was seen as a great weakness by the Commission and its Directorate-General IV in charge of competition, and so the Commission decided in the early 1970s to apply Article 82 to prevent a merger which would strengthen the pre-existing dominance of a firm within a particular market.

In its 1972 decision, the Commission prohibited the Continental Can group from acquiring a Dutch packaging company, TDV, arguing that such a merger would increase Continental Can's already large market share in the Benelux countries and in Germany, and thus constitute an abuse of the company's dominant position. Continental Can, however, appealed the Commission decision to the European Court of Justice, whose landmark 1973 ruling overturned the Commission's decision on the facts of the case while supporting the Commission's interpretation of Article 82. More specifically, the Court ruled that the Commission had not demonstrated that the merged Continental Can/TDV group would indeed acquire a dominant position within the markets specified by the Commission, and therefore allowed the merger to go ahead. The Court also ruled, however, that the Commission was correct in arguing that it could use Article 82 to prevent a firm which already enjoyed a dominant position within a given market from further expanding its market share through mergers and acquisitions.[23]

Continental Can was a landmark ruling in terms of its expansive reading of the Commission's powers under the EEC Treaty, but from the Commission's perspective it was not a satisfactory legal basis for exercising control over mergers within the EC since the impact of the Court's decision was limited to mergers and acquisitions by firms which *already* enjoyed a dominant position and not to mergers which would *create* such a dominant position. The Court's decision, moreover, would give the Commission only *post hoc* jurisdiction over mergers, not the prior notification and control of mergers which it sought. In 1973, the Commission therefore proposed to the Council a draft Merger Control Regulation that would give the Commission the power to review Community mergers and acquisitions in all cases where the joint turnover of the undertakings concerned exceeded a threshold of one billion ecus. In its draft Regulation, the Commission suggested that all proposed mergers above this threshold should be subject to prior notification to the Commission, which would then take a decision within twelve months subject to judicial review by the ECJ. Unfortunately for the Commission, which attempted periodically to revive the proposal throughout the 1980s, its draft regulation remained deadlocked in the Council of Ministers for 16 years, stymied by fundamental member-state opposition to any increase in the Commission's supranational powers in competition policy.

A major step forward was taken, however, with the 1987 *Philip Morris* ruling of the European Court of Justice. In the *Philip Morris* case, the Court of Justice ruled that Article 81, which deals with cartels and other anti-competitive practices, could apply to agreements between two or more companies that allowed one of the companies to obtain legal or de facto control over the other.[24] The practical effect of the Court's decision was to provide the Commission with a backdoor means of reviewing mergers and acquisitions, and the Commission responded by successfully applying Article 81 to a number of high-profile mergers, imposing conditions on the takeover by British Airways of British Caledonian and blocking the acquisition of Irish Distillers by GC and C Brands. As a result, the European business community was left uncertain as to its legal responsibilities, which would emerge only in the incremental case law of the Court of Justice, and began lobbying for an EC Merger Control Regulation that would spell out clearly the powers of the Commission and the responsibilities of business. As Allen (1996: 171) writes:

From the Commission's perspective the great advantage of this merger regime, using Article 85 [now 81], was the uncertainty it generated. This served to put pressure on the doubting member states to settle for a better worked-out and potentially more limited merger regulation. By a combination of luck and skill the Commission had managed to create a problem which the Council felt could be eased only by passing the legislation it had previously refused to consider.[25]

Furthermore, as Cini and McGowan (1998: 118) point out, the Court's ruling in *Philip Morris* also coincided with a dramatic increase in cross-border European mergers and acquisitions in the late 1980s, with numbers rising from 115 in 1982–3 to 208 in 1984–5, 492 in 1988–9, and 622 in 1989–90. This rise in cross-border merger activity, together with the legal uncertainty generated by the *Philip Morris* decision, provided a new impetus and increased business support for the Commission's effort to acquire formal merger review powers.

In March 1988, therefore, at the urging of then Competition Commissioner Peter Sutherland, the Commission introduced a new, amended version of its 1973 proposal for an EC Merger Control Regulation. Under the terms of the Commission's draft Regulation, the Commission would be delegated exclusive competence to under-take advance reviews of all proposed mergers or takeovers—'concen-trations', in the words of the Regulation—'with a European dimension' that could 'give rise to a dominant position' in the EC mar-ket. Like earlier versions of the draft Regulation, the Commission's 1988 draft would not apply to all mergers undertaken within the EC but only to mergers above a dual threshold, whereby (1) the combined annual turnover of the two companies must exceed Ecu 1 billion, while (2) the turnover of the smaller of the two companies must exceed Ecu 50 million. In addition, the draft included an exception for groups with more than three-quarters of their combined sales in a single member state, which would remain within the competence of national competition regulators. With regard to procedure, the draft Regulation would require advance notification of any proposed merger falling within the proposed thresholds, after which the Commission's Merger Task Force (MTF) would undertake a two-month preliminary investigation—the so-called phase 1, later short-ened to one month by the Council—at the end of which the Commission could either clear the merger or announce its intention to undertake a more detailed, phase-2 investigation during which it would collect additional information, including through a formal hearing open to the firms in question as well as member governments and third parties. At the end of this second phase, which could last at most four months, the Commission could accept the merger, reject it outright, or agree with the companies on the adoption of 'remedies' such as the divestiture of specific assets in order to address the competition concerns raised in the Commission's review (CEC 1988; see also Dawkins 1988*a*).

In terms of the analysis offered in Chapter 1, the Commission enjoyed at best modest agenda-setting powers vis-à-vis the member governments in the adoption of the MCR, since unanimity would be required for the adoption of the Regulation and each member state could insist on its preferred amendments to the Commission proposal as a precondition for the adoption of the Regulation. Nevertheless, the Court's ruling in *Philip Morris*, together with the rising number of cross-border takeovers and mergers in the years following the adoption of the Single European Act, had drastically increased the demand by firms for legal certainty, with multinational corporations in particular clamouring for a 'one-stop shop' for the vetting of European-scale mergers.[26] Indeed, after the *Philip Morris* ruling an increasing number of firms began voluntarily submitting their proposed mergers to Brussels as well as to individual member-state regulators as a guarantee of legal certainty.[27] Under the circumstances, *The Economist* pointed out, the Commission could effectively practise 'blackmail', continuing to regulate cross-border mergers and acquisitions 'using its current, clumsy powers until the member states adopt the regulation'. Under the circumstances, Sutherland pointed out, 'The issue is not whether Europe has a merger policy but what type it has' (quoted in *The Economist* 1988: 73).

As an act of delegation, the Merger Control Regulation posed a series of important questions for the member governments as principals, including (1) the thresholds above which the Commission would acquire merger-control authority; (2) the relationship between national regulatory authorities and the Commission; (3) the criteria laid down in the Regulation according to which the Commission would assess the merger; (4) the possibility of direct member-state oversight through the use of comitology committees; and (5) the question of administrative law and the prospect of judicial review of Commission decisions. Agreement on these points required nearly two years of negotiation in the Council, resulting in a Regulation that defined the scope of Commission power more narrowly than the Commission's original proposal (points 1 and 2) but nevertheless allocated significant discretion to the Commission in its implementation of the Regulation (points 3, 4, and 5). The pattern of member-government preferences over delegation, moreover, reveals striking differences across the five points, reflecting the substantive issue-specific preferences of the various governments. Let us consider each, very briefly, in turn.

First, with regard to the thresholds—which would define the nature of a 'European' merger and hence the scope of the Commission's powers—the Commission proposed that EC jurisdiction apply in all cases in which the combined world turnover of the undertakings involved was at least 1 billion ecus, with a Community turnover of at least 50 million ecus for each of the undertakings within the Community. These thresholds were resisted, however, by Britain, France, and Germany, all of which proposed a threshold of 10 billion ecus in joint world turnover, leaving smaller mergers to be assessed by their own established national regulators. By contrast, the Netherlands, Italy, and other smaller countries, many of which had no national competition regulators at the time, sought lower thresholds on the order of 2 billion ecus, which would allow them to make use of Commission competence and expertise for a far larger number of mergers (Dawkins 1988*b*). In early 1989, the Commission proposed a compromise proposal, specifying thresholds of five billion ecus in world turnover for the proposed concentration, and 250 million ecus in Community turnover for each company; these thresholds, however, would be subject to later review and amendment by QMV in the Council of Ministers. The United Kingdom government initially insisted that any revision of the thresholds be subject to unanimous approval but later compromised on this point, leading to the adoption of the dual threshold of 5 billion and 250 million ecus, which was incorporated in the 1989 Regulation, with a scheduled review by the Council in 1993 (Kellaway 1989; *European Report* 1990).[28]

A second and related issue concerned the relationship between the Commission and national regulatory authorities, which split the member states into two camps and led to the insertion of three special clauses into the final text of the Regulation. On one side, Germany with its powerful *Bundeskartellamt* (Federal Cartel Office) wanted national regulators to retain authority to prohibit mergers affecting competition in specific national markets, even where the merger in question had been approved by the Commission. This proposal was resisted by much of the business community, which feared that the German proposal would expose merging firms to 'double jeopardy' and remove the benefits of a one-stop shop for European merger control (Hampton 1989). In a compromise, the German government agreed to a provision that would allow national regulators to request the Commission to refer a proposed merger for review by national competition authorities; the decision whether to make such a reference, however, would be left to the discretion of the Commission.[29] By contrast with this 'German clause', the Netherlands and other small member states pressed for and received a provision, the so-called 'Dutch clause', allowing individual member states to ask the Commission to review a proposed merger which fell short of the thresholds mentioned above if the resulting concentration threatened to create or strengthen a dominant position within their national market.[30] Finally, Article 21(3) of the Regulation allowed member states to apply national legislation designed to 'protect legitimate national interests' in the fields of public security, plurality of the media, and prudential rules, provided that the latter were compatible with the general principles and other provisions of EC law. Although the latter provision would seem to provide the member governments with an escape clause against unwelcome Commission decisions, this provision was invoked only three times during the first decade of the MCR, and in each case the Commission insisted on being kept informed of any measures proposed by a member state in accordance with Article 21(3) (Faull and Nikpay 1999: 235).

The third contentious issue among the member states concerned the balancing of competition and other criteria which the Commission would be required to apply in taking merger control decisions. Here again the member states were split into two camps according to their substantive preferences. The first camp, led by Germany and Great Britain, as well as Competition Commissioner Leon Brittan, argued for the criteria to be strictly limited to competition issues—namely, the possibility for firms to acquire or strengthen a dominant position as a result of a proposed merger—in line with the language of Article 82 as well as their own approach to mergers and acquisitions; while the second group, led by France, wanted to include social and industrial policy considerations among the criteria which the Commission could apply in assessing proposed mergers.[31] The Council's final version represented a compromise, closer to the German and British position with its emphasis on the strict application of competition rules but with a brief reference, in Article 2(1), allowing the Commission to consider in its decisions 'development of technical and economic progress provided that it is to consumers' advantage and does not form an obstacle to competition' (Goyder 1993: 398). A classic intergovernmental compromise, papering over substantive differences with vague compromise language, this provision would allow the Commission considerable discretion in deciding on the extent to which social and industrial policy considerations would or would not inform individual merger decisions.

The fourth and fifth important aspects of the Merger Control Regulation from a principal-agent perspective concerned the various control mechanisms, including both oversight and administrative procedures, that would bind the Commission in its day-to-day decision-making. With regard to oversight, there was general agreement among the member states that the advisory committee procedure—already in operation in other areas of competition policy, including the *post hoc* merger decisions already being taken by the Commission under Article 81 after the *Philip Morris* decision—would be replicated in Article 19 of the MCR, which requires the Commission to submit draft decisions resulting from stage-two investigations to an Advisory Committee on Concentrations.[32] As with other advisory committees in the competition and other sectors, the Commission is obliged to take 'utmost account' of the Committee's decision and 'inform the Committee of the manner in which its opinion has been taken into account', but the Commission is not required to follow the Committee's opinion, which is not legally binding (see Chapter 2). Like other areas of competition policy, therefore, the MCR provides at best a weak instrument for member-state influence through comitology.

Nevertheless, despite the relatively unconstraining comitology procedures of the MCR, critics of the Regulation argued that the Commission remained exposed to political pressures through the member-state-appointed College of Commissioners. Under the terms of the Regulation, final decision on all phase-2 merger decisions require approval of the full College, in theory allowing for the introduction of social or industrial policy considerations and presenting the prospect that decisions of the Merger Task Force might be overturned in the College as a result of lobbying by national governments or private interests. This danger of 'politicization' should not be overstated, as Damro (2001: 22) points out, in so far as phase-1 merger approvals, which account for about 95 per cent of all EC merger decisions, require the approval only of the Commissioner for Competition rather than the full College. For the remaining 5 per cent of merger decisions taken in phase 2, moreover, member governments seeking to influence a merger decision would face the difficult task of convincing a simple majority of Commissioners to overturn the draft decision of the Merger Task Force, the contents of which are typically public knowledge by the time they reach the full College.[33] Nevertheless, the College would indeed prove to be an obstacle to the Commission's first rejection of a proposed merger, as we shall see below.

With regard to administrative law, finally, all decisions of the Commission would, as in other issue areas, be reviewable by the

Court of Justice, and later by the Court of First Instance, to assess their conformity with the provisions of the Regulation and of the Treaties.[34] Nevertheless, as we saw in Chapter 2, the requirements of standing to challenge a Commission decision remain demanding under Article 230 EC. Furthermore, the time-sensitive nature of merger and takeover decisions, coupled with lengthy nature of proceedings before the ECJ and the CFI, mean that, in practice, 'an appeal to the CFI is actually an unrealistic option for the merging firms. In fact, it is highly unlikely that firms will appeal conditions set by the [Merger Task Force] unless there is a significant point of principle that may affect future, long-term business considerations. As competition authorities are aware, firms essentially have to take what they get' (Damro 2001: 32–3). These difficulties of timely effective judicial review of merger decisions has not escaped critics of the Commission in the private sector, who have complained that the Commission was effectively 'jury, judge and executioner' in merger decisions.[35] These concerns, finally, have been magnified in practice by the Commission's de facto process of engaging in negotiations about divestitures and other remedies with the parties to a proposed merger—a process which is relatively opaque to outsiders and grants the Commission significant power to influence the terms under which individual mergers are, or are not, authorized in the EU.[36]

In sum, after 15 years of active Commission advocacy coupled with stalemate in the Council of Ministers, the period 1988–9 witnessed the relatively rapid adoption of a Merger Control Regulation which granted the Commission the sole authority and wide discretion to assess mergers of a European scale.[37] During this period, the *Philip Morris* decision had effectively given the Commission a crude form of merger control authority, without, however, generating legal certainty or a 'one-stop shop' for the increasing number of cross-border European mergers and acquisitions. In the 1989 Merger Control Regulation, the member governments responded to business demands and to the largely unexpected and unwelcome consequences of the *Philip Morris* decision by delegating explicit powers and wide discretion to the Commission, mirroring its already extensive discretion in other areas of competition policy but raising substantially the Commission's proposed thresholds and hence limiting the scope of the Commission's powers. However, the ability of the Commission to make use of these provisions, to establish its credibility as a European merger authority, and to secure the subsequent extension of its competences by the member states, remained to be seen.

Implementing the Merger Control Regulation:
The De Havilland Merger and Beyond

The difficulties faced by the Commission as a regulator, its relation-ship to the member states, and the danger of 'politicization' were all illustrated vividly by the Commission's decision to block the acquisi-tion of the Canadian aircraft manufacturer De Havilland by ATR, the Franco-Italian consortium of state-controlled Aerospatiale of France and the Italian company Alenia. In the proposed deal, ATR, the number-one producer of turbo-prop passenger places in the world, was to purchase De Havilland, the number-two manufacturer best known for its Dash 8 range of 30–50 seat turboprop aircraft, from US-based Boeing. However, the proposal, which was notified to the Commission in May 1991, immediately raised competition concerns in the Merger Task Force and among competing manufacturers like British Aerospace, Fokker of the Netherlands, and Deutsche Aerospace (Dasa) because of the potential establishment of a domin-ant position for the merged company in the global market for turbo-prop passenger planes.

After a complete, two-stage investigation, the Merger Task Force recommended in September 1991 that the De Havilland merger be rejected on the grounds that it would create a dominant position for the combined firm in the relevant market, which the Task Force defined as global market for commuter (turboprop) planes with between 20 and 70 seats. The proposed merger, it pointed out, would give ATR/De Havilland a 50 per cent share of the world market and 67 per cent of the EC market for commuter planes of this size. Within specific size-ranges—20–39 seats, 40–59 seats, and above 60 seats—moreover, the combined firm would have an even greater dominant position, taking as much as 76 per cent of the EU market and 75 per cent of the global market for planes with around 70 seats. Such a dom-inant position, it suggested, would probably force existing competitors out of the market, while potential entrants would likely be discouraged from entering it. 'In due course', the review concluded, 'the dominant position would be likely to lead to a quasi-monopoly'.[38]

Within the College of Commissioners, which would be called on to take the final decision on the De Havilland merger, Competition Commissioner Leon Brittan took a hard line, writing to Commission President Jacques Delors that 'we must *not* allow this merger to pro-ceed' and planning to make the De Havilland merger a test case, as the Commission had already approved all 52 mergers, five with condi-tions, submitted to it during the first year of operation of the MCR (Ross 1995: 178; Brittan 2000: 98). Brittan was opposed, however, by

Delors, by the other French and Italian Commissioners, and by Industrial Policy Commissioner Martin Bangemann, who argued that the merger would give European aircraft manufacturers the economies of scale they needed to compete on world markets and criticized the definition of the relevant market put forward by the Merger Task Force.[39] Finally, after days of lobbying within the Commission by Brittan and his *cabinet*, the Commission voted narrowly, by nine votes to seven, to block the De Havilland merger. Ross's (1995: 178) discussion of the vote is particularly telling, and is worth quoting in full:

Beyond the other Commission liberals (Andriessen, Schmidhuber, and Christophersen), Cardoso, MacSharry, Dondelinger, Millan, and Marin all voted with Brittan. For each of these commissioners Brittan's hard politicking had been central. Most said simply that they were giving way to the 'commissioner in charge,' although others, including Millan (a British Labourite with whom Brittan almost never saw eye to eye) and Dondelinger, indicated that they disagreed with Brittan even though 'giving way.' Manuel Marin, the swing vote, gave an utterly incomprehensible argument to explain himself, but seemed to have traded his vote for help from Brittan on a pending project to reorganize the European fishing fleet, an essential Spanish dossier. When it became clear that he would lose, Delors, as was his usual practice, abstained.[40]

The result was presented by Brittan as a victory in which the Commission had 'demonstrated its determination to apply fully and fairly the new Regulation and to protect companies and consumers against the damaging effects that would follow the creation of such a dominant market position'.[41] Similarly, the *Financial Times* and other observers speculated that the De Havilland decision would strengthen the credibility of the Commission as an independent, impartial regulator, which had resisted political pressure to apply pure competition criteria on the basis of the MTF recommendation (Gardner, Simon, and Leadbetter 1991).

Nevertheless, the immediate result of the decision was a political backlash against Brittan, not only by the firms affected but also by the Italian and especially the French governments. In France, Prime Minister Edith Cresson announced the government's 'disapproval' of the rejection and reserved France's right to appeal the decision to the ECJ, while Transport Minister Paul Quiles called in the October meeting of the Transport Council for a review of the Merger Control Regulation following the Commission decision (*European Report* 1991*b*). Foreign Minister Roland Dumas also denounced the decision, arguing to his fellow foreign ministers that the aim of EC competition policy should be 'to strengthen, not hinder, the competitiveness of

European industry' (quoted in Buchan 1991) and noting that France reserved the right to resort to political action in the Council of Ministers as well as judicial appeal to the ECJ. 'To the extent that the Commission exceeds its competence', Dumas announced to journalists, 'use must be made of control mechanisms' (*Agence France Presse* 1991*b*). In the end, however, the control mechanisms available to France and Italy were relatively weak, and Brittan, backed this time by Delors, remained defiant, telling the European Parliament that 'No responsible competition authority would have taken a different view' and noting that nobody wanted a system that only served the interests of 'the countries which shout loudest' (Hill 1991*b*).[42]

By contrast with the irritation of the French and Italian governments, which criticized the Commission for the strictness of its decision in the De Havilland case, the government of Germany, the *Bundeskartellamt*, and other critics of EC merger control attacked the Commission for its alleged laxity in merger control and particularly for the potential politicization of the process illustrated by the close vote in the College of Commissioners, and called for the establishment of a free-standing and independent European Cartel Office (Cini and McGowan 1998: 126–31).

As Wilks and McGowan (1995) point out, the criticisms were threefold. First, it was argued, the Commission's implementation of the Regulation lacked transparency, with the Commission frequently striking up informal agreements with the companies they were regulating. Second, the Commission was accused, particularly by German observers, of violating the principle of subsidiarity by refusing to refer competition cases to national competition authorities which requested the right, under Article 9 of the MCR, to assess the competitive effects of a merger in a specific national market.[43] Third and finally, critics argued that the Commission's enforcement of the Merger Control Regulation was excessively lax and 'politicized', with the Commission approving mergers which should have been blocked and improperly applying social and industrial policy criteria to merger decisions (Wilks and McGowan 1995).

In light of these concerns, the *Bundeskartellamt*, supported by the German Economics Ministry, pressed for the creation of a European Cartel Office (ECO) independent of the Commission, which would decide merger cases on the basis of narrowly defined competition criteria, thus insulating the decision-making process from potential politicization in the college of Commissioners. The creation of such a new agency, however, would require an amendment to the treaties and hence a unanimous agreement from member governments with starkly conflicting preferences about the nature of such a fundamental reform.[44] Indeed, the German government pressed its case for an ECO within the 1996 intergovernmental conference but was unable to attract the support of other member states, such as France, which have traditionally been more sympathetic to social and industrial policy concerns (Buckley 1996). In this sense, the status-quo default condition of the Merger Control Regulation, together with the difficulty of amending the treaties, has favoured the Commission, whose powers in the area of merger regulation have remained relatively secure despite multiple attacks from the various member governments.

By the same token, however, the climate of pervasive criticism following the Commission's decision in De Havilland and other merger cases provided infertile soil for any extension of the Commission's powers in the scheduled review of the MCR in 1993. In keeping with its original proposals in the negotiation of the Regulation, the Commission had hoped to propose that the Council lower the thresholds from 5 billion ecus for joint worldwide turnover and 250 million ecus for individual company turnover within the Community to 2 billion and 100 million, respectively. According to the rules laid down in the Regulation, the Commission would require only a qualified majority vote in the Council to approve the new thresholds, an easier target than the unanimous vote required to adopt the initial Merger Control Regulation. Furthermore, the Commission's proposal was broadly backed by European business, including the peak employers' association UNICE, which was eager to expand the 'one-stop shop' provided by the Regulation for European-level mergers (*European Report* 1993*b*). An initial survey of member state positions, however, revealed fundamental opposition to the Commission's proposal from Germany and the United Kingdom, which found the Commission's enforcement too lax and were therefore reluctant to lower the thresholds, and from France, which found it too strict and proposed raising the thresholds on several occasions (Hill and Barber 1993). In July 1993, therefore, incoming Commission Commissioner Karel Van Miert withdrew the Commission's proposal, bluntly asking 'what is the point of proposing something if you know it won't be accepted?'[45] Instead, Van Miert proposed to continue with the existing thresholds for three more years and to suggest new thresholds in the light of experience in 1996.

In January 1996, the Commission duly issued a consultative 'Green Paper' on the review of the MCR, renewing its case for lowering the thresholds to 2 billion and 100 million ecus for combined world turnover and individual company turnover, respectively (CEC 1996*a*). After extensive consultation with member governments and industry revealed widespread support from industry but continuing opposition from the British, French, and German governments to lowering the thresholds, the Commission issued a compromise proposal to the Council. In its draft amending Regulation, the Commission first proposed to lower the thresholds to Ecu 3 billion and Ecu 150 million, respectively, a compromise proposal aimed at securing member-state support. In addition, or failing agreement on a general reduction of the thresholds, the Commission proposed a parallel and lower set of thresholds—Ecu 2 billion and 100 million, respectively—for proposed mergers that would otherwise have to be notified in at least three member states. During the course of the 1990s, the Commission pointed out, such multiple notifications falling under the Ecu 5 billion threshold had increased in line with the continuing rise in cross-border mergers and acquisitions, threatening to deprive business of the one-stop shop which the MCR had been designed to provide (CEC 1996*b*).[46]

Despite widespread support for a lowering of thresholds in the business community, the Commission's proposal continued to face entrenched resistance from Germany and other member governments as well as from the British and German competition authorities. In November 1996, the Industry Council held a vote on a generalized reduction of the thresholds to the Ecu 3 billion and Ecu 150 million proposed by the Commission, but the proposal garnered the support of only seven member governments, most from small states with less developed competition authorities: Austria, Belgium, Finland, Greece, Portugal, Italy, and the Netherlands. Another seven member states, representing Germany, the UK, France, and other member states with well-developed systems of merger control—Spain, Denmark, Sweden, and Ireland—voted against the Commission's proposal, while Luxembourg abstained, effectively killing off any possibility of a generalized reduction in the thresholds (Tucker 1996; *European Report* 1996). Following the November meeting, negotiations focused on Van Miert's fall-back position, which would provide for lower thresholds for mergers that would otherwise require multiple notifications.

After much debate, the Council finally agreed in 1997 to an amending Regulation providing for two alternative sets of thresholds, namely, the original 1989 thresholds, which remained unchanged, and a complex formula for an extended Commission competence in the event of multiple notifications. Specifically, the new Article 1(3) of the Regulation provides that the Commission's competence would be extended to mergers meeting the following criteria: a combined aggregate world turnover of Ecu 2.5 billion or more; a combined aggregate turnover of Ecu 100 million or more in each of at least three member states; aggregate turnover of Ecu 25 million or more for at least two of the firms concerned within each of the three member states; aggregate Community-wide turnover of Ecu 100 million or more for at least two of the firms concerned; and no more than two-thirds of the aggregate turnover of each firm within a single member state.[47] The amending Regulation was welcomed as a modest step forward by Van Miert, and it does indeed provide a modest increase in the Commission's competence to regulate merger activity. Nevertheless, it is striking that the member governments remained unwilling to support a generalized lowering of the thresholds despite widespread support from the business community and a relatively weak QMV requirement, and the 1997 Regulation serves as a useful illustration of the Commission's difficulty in securing additional powers in an area, like merger regulation, in which its decisions inevitably cause controversy and anger from at least some member governments, national regulators, firms, and other critics.

Analysis: An Independent Regulator?

The case of the merger control regulation—its adoption, application, and subsequent amendment in 1997—illustrates both the possibilities for the Commission to use its existing powers strategically to extend the range of its competences and the limits to such efforts imposed by the Commission's statutory discretion, limited agenda-setting powers, and the strong preferences of the EU member governments. If we examine first the adoption of the Merger Control Regulation, we see that the Commission had long favoured an extension of its own powers to include advance review of European-scale mergers but that its efforts had been blocked by the weakness of its agenda-setting powers under unanimous voting in the Council. Nevertheless, as we have also seen, the Commission's persistent application of existing treaty provisions to merger control, supported by the Court in *Continental Can* and *Philip Morris*, effectively changed the *status quo*, granting the Commission partial competence at a time of rising cross-border mergers and acquisitions and increasing demand for legal certainty by the European business community. Once again, the Commission's agenda-setting powers in this area were limited by the unanimity voting rule in the Council, which extensively amended the Commission's proposals in the final MCR; nevertheless, under pressure from firms eager to replace the uncertainty that followed the *Philip Morris* decision with a clear legal basis for European merger control, the Council's 1989 Regulation represented the first extensive delegation of new competition powers to the Commission since the adoption of the EEC Treaty and Regulation 17 in the late 1950s and early 1960s. Although considerations of credibility and efficiency clearly played a part in the Council's decisions, as predicted by transaction-cost theories of delegation, the prior actions of the Commission and the Court of Justice provided a crucial impetus for the timing and content of the MRC. Put differently, the actions of the Commission and the Court prior to 1989 effectively shaped the incentives of the member governments by altering the status quo so that, while the Council took the ultimate decision, it did so in the shadow of the actions of the Commission and the Court.

Moving from the adoption to the implementation of the Regulation, and in particular the De Havilland case examined above, we find that the balance sheet is again mixed. Intended as a test case by Commissioner Leon Brittan, the De Havilland decision demonstrated publicly the potential for politicization of merger decisions in the College of Commissioners and the imperfect insulation of the Commission from political pressures. By the same token, however, Brittan's success in securing the rejection of the merger also increased the credibility of the Commission as a competition regulator and established a precedent whereby the College generally accepts and endorses the analyses of its Merger Task Force, which has since demonstrated its willingness and ability to reject or demand extensive conditions for the approval of proposed mergers even in the face of very public recriminations from the affected firms and member governments. Indeed, Mario Monti, the current Commissioner for Competition at this writing, has been described as an 'unabashed activist', blocking a record eight mergers and courting controversy vis-à-vis the United States government, with his 2001 rejection of the proposed G.E.-Honeywell merger, as well as EU member governments and private industry (Guerrera and de Jonquières 2001). In sum, the Commission's wide discretion under the MCR has allowed it to apply EC merger law with considerable independence from member governments, thereby promoting its aim of a single, competitive, internal market.

Turning from implementation to member-state response and subsequent delegation, finally, we have seen how the controversy prompted by the Commission's decisions made the EU's largest member governments reluctant, albeit for diverse reasons, to condone anything more than a modest extension of the Commission's powers in their subsequent reviews of the Regulation. By the same token, however, the member governments collectively have not been able to agree on any *weakening* of the Commission's power and discretion in the area of merger control, which now seems well entrenched in law and in practice. Indeed, a survey of the Commission's merger policy decisions over the past decade, although far beyond the scope of this chapter, would suggest that, notwithstanding the occasional controversy courted by the Commission in its individual decisions, the Merger Control Regulation is operating largely as intended by the member governments and largely to the satisfaction of European industry as well.[48] For this reason, the next revision of the Merger Control Regulation—the process for which began in late 2001 with the publication of another Commission Green Paper—is likely to fine-tune the criteria for merger assessment, the negotiation of remedies, and the possibilities for judicial review without imposing any major changes in the overall regulatory competence of the Commission in the field of merger control (CEC 2001).[49]

III. The Court of Justice and Free Movement of Goods: From Cassis de Dijon to Keck and Mithouard

The free movement of goods is, and has been since its inception in the 1957 EEC Treaty, the 'core business' of the European Community and the most important element of its market-making agenda. Indeed, in economic terms a common market such as the EC is defined as an area in which goods, services, capital, and labour circulate freely without duties and in which the member states adopt a common level of duty on goods entering the market from without (Swann 1992: 11). In principle, the free movement of goods within the European common market is made possible by (1) the establishment of the customs union and the corresponding abolition of all tariffs on goods traded among the member states, which was completed in July of 1968, and (2) the elimination of quantitative restrictions on trade *and measures having equivalent effect*. The basic rule regarding the latter is set out in Article 28 (ex 30) EC, which provides that:

Quantitative restrictions on imports and all measures having equivalent effect shall, without prejudice to the following provisions, be prohibited between Member States.[50]

A classic example of 'negative integration', Article 28 was a sweeping prohibition of member-state efforts to restrict imports from other EU member states; yet, in keeping with the EEC Treaty's nature as a framework agreement or incomplete contract, the precise nature of the prohibition, and in particular the concept of 'all measures having equivalent effect', was left strikingly vague, subject only to the exceptions spelled out in Article 30 (ex 36) EC, which provides that:

The provisions of Articles 30 to 34 shall not preclude prohibitions or restrictions on imports, exports or goods in transit justified on grounds of public morality, public policy or public security; the protection of health and life of humans, animals or plants; the protection of national treasures possessing artistic, historic or archaeological value; or the protection of industrial and commercial property. Such prohibitions or restrictions shall not, however, constitute a means of arbitrary discrimination or a disguised restriction on trade between Member States.

In practice, the interpretation of these treaty provisions, and hence of the legality or illegality of member-state laws restricting intra-Community trade in goods, has fallen to the European Court of Justice, whose role in the creation of an internal market for goods is the focus of the final case study in this chapter. As we saw in Chapter 3, the interpretation of the treaties in theory provides the ECJ with extraordinary discretion vis-à-vis EU member governments, since the latter have relatively few means to influence the Court in its decisions beyond the relatively costly resort to either treaty amendment, requiring unanimous agreement and ratification by all member states, or unilateral non-compliance, with its attached political and reputational costs. By comparison with the two previous case studies of Commission behavior, therefore, we should expect to see the Court relatively unconstrained in its interpretation of the treaties and free to pursue its traditionally expansive interpretation of the objectives and the detailed provisions of the treaties.

In studying the preferences of the Court and its relation to the member governments, however, we encounter methodological obstacles not present in the previous studies of Commission activity. From the perspective of the outside observer, the internal deliberations—and hence the sincere preferences—of the Court are a 'black box' thanks to the judges' rule of deliberating in secret and issuing a single collective opinion. We can, of course, examine the text of the decision and its relation to the opinion of the Advocate-General and the various arguments put forward in the hearing of the case for clues regarding the preferences and the reasoning of the Court, but the decision itself cannot be taken as a measure of the Court's sincere preferences since in any given decision the Court may be expected rationally to anticipate the reactions of the member governments and other interlocutors, subject to uncertainty, and to incorporate their preferences and concerns into its ruling. Furthermore, unlike the cases examined above, in which the Commission proposed an executive action to which the member governments were called upon formally to reply, the Court issues only a single decision in each case to which there is no appeal, eliminating the prospect of multiple principal-agent interactions within a single case.

Nevertheless, as Garrett, Kelemen, and Schulz (1998) point out, the difficulties of studying the Court can be offset by a careful research design; specifically, they advocate two strategies for the study of ECJ-member-state interactions. First, like Pollack (1998) and the case studies in this book, Garrett, Kelemen, and Schulz concentrate on cases that generate controversy between the Court and EU member states on the grounds that 'there is little to be gained from analyzing the vast body of ECJ case law that has not generated controversy between the Court and national governments' (Garrett, Kelemen, and Schulz 1998: 151). Second, however, they look beyond individual cases to examine 'broad streams of controversial case law where the Court repeatedly confronts similar legal principles but in different contexts' (Garrett, Kelemen, and Schulz 1998: 151). Using this method, they seek to test their hypotheses that the Court is *most likely* to defer to anticipated member-state reactions (1) where the precedent is relatively unclear, leaving the Court free to accommodate member states without reversing precedents, (2) where the costs of compliance to individual member states are high, increasing the likelihood of non-compliance, and (3) where large numbers of member states are adversely affected, increasing the likelihood of legislative overruling.

In light of these considerations, in order to examine the preferences of the ECJ and its autonomy vis-à-vis the member governments, I focus here on the ECJ's case law interpreting the scope of Article 28, with special attention to what is arguably the most famous, controversial, and well-documented judgment in the Court's history: the 1979 *Cassis de Dijon* ruling in which the Court first enunciated the principle of mutual recognition of national standards. The *Cassis* case generated extraordinary controversy among EU member governments, particularly in the months and years following the judgment when the Commission seized on it as a platform from which to launch a new strategy of regulatory harmonization, thus providing another important test case regarding the relationship between the Court, the Commission, and the member governments.

In addition, the *Cassis* judgment has generated extraordinary controversy within the academic community, where three distinct interpretations of the Court's judicial and political role have been put forward. The first interpretation, put forward by various legal and political science scholars, sees the *Cassis* ruling as an audacious act of agency by the Court, which defied the stated preferences of the member states and instituted a revolutionary principle for the realization of the internal market (e.g. Weiler 1991; 1994; Burley and Mattli 1993; Stone Sweet and Brunell 1998). By contrast, rational-choice theorists have put forward a preliminary principal-agent analysis of the ruling, suggesting that the Court's ruling in *Cassis* was either in keeping with the preferences of the most powerful member governments, in particular Britain and France (Garrett 1992), or else served as a focal point among multiple equilibria for member governments that were broadly in favour of trade liberalization but could not agree on a specific mechanism, such as mutual recognition, to realize that objective (Garrett and Weingast 1993). Rather than defying EU member governments, these authors suggested, the Court was influential precisely because its ruling anticipated and conformed to their preferences. As we saw in Chapter 3, however, these early principal-agent analyses did not model the specific control mechanisms, or lack thereof, which might allow the member governments to influence the Court, and thus overestimated the latter's responsiveness to the former. A third and final interpretation, put forward by Karen Alter and Sophie Meunier-Aitsahalia (1994), focuses primarily on the *effects* of the ruling, suggesting that the Court's real importance in *Cassis* was as a *provocateur* prompting the Commission to produce a politically controversial harmonization strategy which in turn mobilized interest groups within the member states, leading in time to the adoption of the internal market programme.

The case study presented here draws extensively on primary sources, and on the various works mentioned above, to examine the Court's powers of interpretation in the area of the free movement of goods, the nature of the case-law precedent for *Cassis*, the preferences of the member states in the case, and the reception of the decision by the Commission, the member governments, and private interests. Going beyond *Cassis* itself, however, I examine the subsequent line of cases in which the Court progressively extended its already broad interpretation of Article 28 only to surprise the legal community by once again restricting its reach in the 1993 *Keck v. Mithouard* decision, which exempted national legislation on what the Court called 'selling arrangements' from the scope of Article 28. As a major—indeed, the only—reversal of the Court's case-law precedent on the free movement of goods, *Keck* presents a particularly important test case. In the review that follows below, therefore, I examine the case-law precedent, the position of the member governments, and the Court's legal reasoning in *Keck* in an effort to explain the Court's apparent retreat from its earlier expansive reading of Article 28, and the extent to which this retreat can be attributed to pressure from EU member governments individually or collectively. I begin, however, by examining the *Cassis* decision, its precedents, and its consequences.

The ECJ and Article 28, from Dassonville to Cassis

In the context of the principal-agent approach laid out in Chapters 1 and 3, the member governments of the EEC adopted a framework agreement, or incomplete contract, for the creation of a European customs union, and delegated to the Commission and the Court of Justice the power to fill in the details of that incomplete contract. With regard to Article 28, moreover, those details were not self-evident; indeed, as Anthony Arnull (2000: 229) points out, there was a lively debate during the early years of the Community regarding the definition of 'measures having equivalent effect' (MEEs) and hence the scope of Article 28 vis-à-vis national laws and regulations. In the most restrictive view, only national measures that discriminated directly against imports—so-called 'distinctly applicable' measures—would be considered as measures having equivalent effect to quantitative restrictions, and hence falling within the discipline of Article 28. By contrast, a second and more expansive reading of Article 28 held that any national measure that restricted inter-state trade among EEC members would be considered a measure having equivalent effect, and therefore banned under Article 28 unless it could be justified by reference to public health, public safety, or the other considerations laid down in Article 30.

Under the terms of the EEC Treaty, the power to fill in the details of this incomplete contract was delegated in the short term to the Commission, which had the power, under Article 33(7) EEC (now repealed) to 'issue directives establishing the procedure and timetable in accordance with which Member States shall abolish, as between themselves, any measures in existence when this Treaty enters into force which have an effect equivalent to quotas'. Although this delegation of powers was limited to those national measures already in existence when the treaty entered into force and was to last only until the end of the transitional period—that is, the end of 1969—the Commission nevertheless adopted Directive 70/50, which provided the first Community-level interpretation of Article 28. In the Directive, the Commission dealt with both 'distinctly applicable measures', which discriminated explicitly against imported goods and were clearly outlawed by Article 28, and what have since come to be known as 'indistinctly applicable measures', that is, national laws and regulations that do not distinguish explicitly between domestic and foreign goods, but which—in laying out requirements for the marketing of products in terms of shape, size, weight, composition, presentation, or identification—could nevertheless exert a restrictive effect on the free movement of goods within the Community. Such indistinctly applicable measures, the Commission held, would be caught by Article 28 in so far as 'the restrictive effects on the free movement of goods are out of proportion with their purpose' and 'the same objective can be attained by other means which are less of a hindrance to trade' (quoted in Arnull 2000: 230). Although limited in its effect and later superseded by the case law of the ECJ, the Commission Directive embodied a broad reading of Article 28 to encompass both distinctly and indistinctly applicable measures, and applied a test of proportionality to the latter—both points which would later be taken up by the Court.

Outside the limited scope of Directive 70/50, the power to interpret the scope of Article 28 after the transitional period lay with the Court of Justice, which first examined the issue in the 1974 *Dassonville* case. Mr Dassonville was an importer who had legally purchased a consignment of Scotch whisky in France for sale in Belgium. Having done so, however, he found himself subject to criminal proceedings in Belgian courts since he had failed to produce a certificate of origin issued by the British customs authorities. In his defence Dassonville argued that the Belgian requirement constituted a measure having equivalent effect to quantitative restrictions, since it restricted the free movement of goods (in this case, whisky) within the common market (in this case, from France to Belgium). The Court agreed, holding that such a requirement would constitute a measure having equivalent effect and offering for the first time a definitive definition of that concept:

All trading rules enacted by Member States which are capable of hindering, directly or indirectly, actually or potentially, intra-Community trade are to be considered as measures having equivalent effect to quantitative restrictions.[51]

Like the Commission's, the Court's interpretation of MEEs was a broad one, encompassing not only measures that discriminated directly against exports but also non-discriminatory or indistinctly applicable measures that were nevertheless capable of hindering intra-Community trade. The far-reaching implications of the *Dassonville* formula were elaborated and made explicit some five years later in the 1979 ruling in *Rewe-Zentral AG v. Bundesmonopolverwaltung für Branntwein*—the so-called *Cassis de Dijon* case.

Like *Dassonville*, *Cassis* began as a dispute between a German importer (Rewe-Zentral AG, based in Cologne) and a national regulator (the German Federal Monopoly Administration for Spirits) over the trade-restrictive effects of a national regulation. As is well known, the plaintiff in the case had applied for permission to import into Germany a consignment of Cassis de Dijon, a liqueur legally manufactured and marketed in France. German authorities denied permission to import the product, however, since under German law fruit liqueurs could be marketed only if they had a minimum alcohol content of 25 per cent, whereas Cassis typically has an alcohol content of between 15 and 20 per cent. In its plea before the Hessian tribunal trying the case, the plaintiff argued that the German regulation constituted a measure having equivalent effect to quantitative restrictions and was therefore in conflict with Article 28; the tribunal suspended the proceedings in order to send a request for a preliminary ruling to the Court of Justice, asking whether a national regulation such as the one in question would fall within the scope of Article 28.[52]

In analysing the Court's options in such cases, Garrett, Kelemen, and Schulz suggest that we should examine (1) the Court's legal precedents, (2) the costs of an adverse opinion to the member state in question (here, Germany), and (3) the number of member states likely to be affected by that opinion. In terms of precedent, the broad interpretation of MEEs in *Dassonville* certainly suggested that the Court would interpret the German regulation on the alcohol content of fruit liqueurs as a measure 'capable of hindering, directly or indirectly, actually or potentially, intra-Community trade' and therefore falling under the general prohibition in Article 28. In terms of the likely reaction of EU member governments, the Court was made aware of the position of the German government, which intervened with its own brief in the proceedings and made two key arguments in favour of the national regulation. First, Germany argued that the primary purpose of the law was to protect public health since, in its view, alcoholic beverages with a low alcohol content may more easily induce a tolerance towards alcohol than more highly alcoholic beverages. Second, the government claimed that the regulation was designed to protect consumers against unfair practices by producers and distributors of alcohol products, who might otherwise attempt to deceive consumers expecting a certain alcohol content in their beverages. By contrast, the Commission intervened in the case in favour of the plaintiff, supporting the view that the regulation in question should be prohibited as a violation of Article 28. No other member government intervened in the case, whose far-reaching conclusion was not yet known.

Given the clarity of the *Dassonville* precedent, the relatively small economic importance of the sector (that is, fruit-based liqueurs), the lack of intervention from other member governments, and the supportive nature of the brief from the Commission—which as we saw in Chapter 3 is the single best predictor of ECJ decisions—we might expect the Court once again to adopt a broad interpretation of Article 28 and hence rule against the German regulation as a measure having equivalent effect to quantitative restrictions. And, indeed, the Court so ruled, rejecting both of the German government's arguments. With regard to the first claim regarding the protection of public health, the Court noted that 'such considerations are not decisive since the consumer can obtain on the market an extremely wide range of weakly or moderately alcoholic products and furthermore a large proportion of alcoholic beverages with a high alcohol content freely sold on the German market is generally consumed in diluted form'.[53] With regard to the second claim, about the protection of consumers, the Court suggested that the German regulation prohibiting the marketing of weaker liqueurs was disproportionate to its stated aim 'since it is a simple matter to ensure that suitable information is conveyed to the purchaser by requiring the display of an indication of origin and of the alcohol content on the packing of products'.[54] In light of these considerations, the Court went on to rule against the German government as to the compatibility of the German law with the provisions of Article 28:

It is clear from the foregoing that the requirements relating to the minimum alcohol content of alcoholic beverages do not serve a purpose which is in the general interest and such as to take precedence over the requirements of the free movement of goods, which constitutes one of the fundamental rules of the Community.

In practice, the principal effect of requirements of this nature is to promote alcoholic beverages having a high alcohol content by excluding from the national market products of other member states which do not answer that description.

It therefore appears that the unilateral requirement imposed by the rules of a member state of a minimum alcohol content for the purposes of the sale of alcoholic beverages constitutes an obstacle to trade which is incompatible with the provisions of Article 30 [now 28] of the Treaty.[55]

In other words, on the substance of the case, the Court ruled, against the wishes of the German government, that such a regulation was an MEE within the meaning of Article 28 and therefore prohibited by the Treaty.

The Court, however, did not stop with a straightforward application of the *Dassonville* formula to the German regulation but extended its previous jurisprudence, in two ways. First, immediately following the previous paragraph, the Court added perhaps the most well-known passage from the *Cassis* decision, to the effect that:

There is therefore no valid reason why, provided that they have been lawfully produced and marketed in one of the member states, alcoholic beverages should not be introduced into any other member state.[56]

Although ostensibly a simple extension of the *Dassonville* formula, the implications of this passage went far beyond the case at hand, suggesting that member states would be required, as a general rule, to allow the importation and marketing of goods from other member states provided only that those goods met the production and marketing requirements in their country of origin. This principle, later referred to as the 'mutual recognition' of standards, was qualified, however, by a second principle, the 'rule of reason', whereby national regulations would be considered consistent with the treaty provided that they met certain requirements and were proportional to their stated aims. In the words of the Court:

In the absence of common rules relating to the production and marketing of alcohol...it is for the Member States to regulate all matters relating to the production and marketing of alcohol and alcoholic beverages on their own territory.

Obstacles to movement within the Community resulting from disparities between the national laws relating to the products in question must be accepted in so far as those provisions may be recognized as being necessary in order to satisfy mandatory requirements relating in particular to the effectiveness of fiscal supervision, the protection of public health, the fairness of commercial transactions and the defence of the consumer.[57]

This list of 'mandatory requirements', the Court would later explain, was indicative rather than exhaustive, and the Court would later specify additional mandatory requirements that might justify national regulations that hindered intra-Community trade in goods. Nevertheless, while the Court's judgment acknowledged that there were considerations that might justify exceptions to the principle of free movement, it also insisted that it was for the Court alone to identify and define those mandatory requirements. Furthermore, even where a national regulation satisfied one of these requirements in its aims, such a regulation would also be subjected to a proportionality test in order to determine whether the regulation in question was proportional and necessary to achieve its stated aim. In sum, the 'rule of reason' promised to subject national regulations to careful scrutiny, with a wide interpretation being given to the concept of 'measures having equivalent effect' and a relatively narrow interpretation given to the mandatory requirements and the exceptions to the principle of free movement.

Responding to Cassis

The Court's judgment in *Cassis* took both the Commission and the member states by surprise. In Alter and Meunier-Aitsahalia's (1994: 550) words, 'Even the German government had expected the Court to rule against its regulation, but no one had anticipated that the Court would draw such wide conclusions from the case, as the phrase at the end of its judgment seemed to imply'. As the same authors point out, it was the Commission's entrepreneurial interpretation of the decision as much as the decision itself that contributed to the later political and scholarly controversy over the ruling. During the 1970s and into the 1980s, the Commission had campaigned for the completion of the internal market, repeatedly warning the member states about the proliferation of non-tariff barriers to intra-Community trade in the form of national regulations restricting the free movement of goods. In that context, the Commission had produced a succession of reports and legislative initiatives designed to tackle non-tariff barriers and complete the internal market, only to be rebuffed repeatedly by the member governments in the Council. From the Commission perspective, the decision of the Court in *Cassis* provided the seeds of a new approach to the completion of the internal market as well as the legitimacy conferred by a definitive ECJ interpretation of the treaty. Accordingly, the Commission issued a special communication in March 1980, laying out its interpretation of the consequences of the ECJ decision. First, in light of the Court's broad reading of Article 28, the Commission indicated its intention to initiate infringement proceedings against a wide range of national regulations:

The Commission will…have to tackle a whole body of commercial rules which lay down that products manufactured and marketed in one Member State must fulfil technical or qualitative conditions in order to be admitted to the market of another and specifically in all cases where the trade barriers occasioned by such rules are inadmissible according to the very strict criteria set out by the Court. The Commission is referring in particular to rules covering the composition, designation, presentation and packaging of products as well as rules requiring compliance with certain technical standards. (CEC 1980)

Second, the Commission indicated that it would focus its harmonization efforts on those national regulations that could be justified according to the ECJ's rule of reason:

The Commission's work of harmonization will henceforth have to be directed mainly at national laws having an impact on the functioning of the common market where barriers to trade to be removed arise from national provisions which are admissible under the criteria set by the Court... The Commission will be concentrating on sectors deserving priority because of their economic relevance to the creation of a single internal market. (CEC 1980)

In outline form, the Commission's interpretation of *Cassis* served as the kernel for its 'new approach' to harmonization and in turn for the internal market programme approved by the member states in 1985 and incorporated into the 1986 Single European Act. For this reason, Garrett and Weingast (1993) have argued that the ECJ decision in *Cassis* represented a 'constructed focal point' around which member-states' collective preference for a policy of mutual recognition converged.

However, as Alter and Meunier-Aitsahalia have convincingly demonstrated, the immediate response of the member governments to the Court's decision—and even more to the Commission's communication—was far from supportive. Contrary to Garrett's (1992) original claims, the concept of mutual recognition was not welcomed but raised concerns, most notably among the French, German, and Italian governments, that the Commission's approach would lead to an erosion of existing national standards. In Alter and Meunier-Aitsahalia's (1994: 550) words:

There are grave empirical problems with the focal point argument in terms of its application to the *Cassis* case. Not only was there no consensus for mutual recognition before the *Cassis* verdict, there was also no consensus after the verdict. Interviews with the German government and the Commission revealed that mutual recognition was not, and is still not today, the preferred policy for the majority of member states. In addition, contrary to Garrett's assertions, Germany and France have been the strongest opponents of mutual recognition because, as high-standard countries, they have the most to lose.

In short, they conclude, 'the Court's verdict went well beyond what was being debated with respect to harmonization policy in 1978', and hence it cannot be assumed that the Court's ruling simply reflected the collective preferences of the member states.

Nevertheless, while they attribute considerable autonomy to the Court in reaching its unexpectedly broad conclusions in the case, Alter and Meunier-Aitsahalia also point to the dangers of assuming that the Court's new doctrine, once proclaimed in *Cassis*, would automatically produce policy results within the member states, since a purely judicial application of mutual recognition and the rule of reason could occur only on a case-by-case basis, as individual member-state regulations were challenged either before national courts or by the Commission in infringement proceedings against the member states. For this reason, they do not examine the line of case law that followed from *Cassis* but instead focus on the reception of the decision in the political arena, arguing that the Court's primary political importance in *Cassis* was as a *provocateur*, providing the stimulus for a public debate which was subsequently taken up by the Commission, by the member governments, and ultimately by private interests throughout the EU. Although the Court and the Commission both contributed to this debate,[58] they argue, neither actor was able to force its preferred policy on the member governments, whose ultimate decisions in the Single European Act were based on a compromise reflecting the concerns of mobilized interests and the various member states (Alter and Meunier-Aitsahalia 1994: 553).

Alter and Meunier-Aitsahalia are correct to suggest that ECJ decisions do not lead automatically to policy results in the member states, and to draw our attention to the political debate generated by the *Cassis* decision; nevertheless, for our purposes in understanding the Court's discretion vis-à-vis the member governments, it is worthwhile to remain within the judicial realm and to examine at least briefly the growing number of both preliminary references and Commission infringement proceedings provoked by *Cassis* decision, and the Court's subsequent interpretation of Article 28.

Elaborating on Cassis: From German Beer to Keck and Mithouard

In absolute terms, the number of ECJ cases relating to the free movement of goods has increased steadily in the years since the *Cassis* ruling, in terms of both preliminary references and Commission infringement proceedings, providing the Court with a steady stream of cases in which to refine and extend the principle of mutual recognition and the rule of reason. While a thorough chronological examination of the case law is beyond the scope of this case study,[59] three major developments are worth highlighting.

First, in terms of evidence for deference to member-state preferences, it may be noted that the Court continued to expand upon the indicative, but not exhaustive, list of mandatory requirements in the *Cassis* decision. In the famous 1988 *Danish Bottle* case, for example, the Court expanded the list of mandatory requirements to include protection of the environment, thus allowing Denmark to retain a national prohibition on the importation of beer in cans which the Commission had sought to invalidate as an infringement of Article 28.[60] Later rulings expanded the list still further, to the protection of press diversity and the financial balance of social security systems (Arnull 2000: 265). In Kilroy's (1995; 1999) terminology, these decisions represent 'pro-member state rulings' in that they expand the list of requirements on which member states can rely to defend national regulations against the discipline of Article 28; by the same token, however, these mandatory requirements have generally been strictly interpreted by the Court in specific cases. Moreover, even in those cases where a national measure is found to be justifiable in terms of one of the Court's mandatory requirements, the measure remains subject to a proportionality test to determine whether the restrictive effects on intra-Community trade are necessary to achieve the aim of the legislation. In many cases—including the *Cassis* case itself, as well as many of those reviewed below—national measures are found to satisfy the mandatory requirements, only to be invalidated because the aims of those measures can be achieved through less trade-restrictive means such as mandatory labelling.

Second, in applying the *Dassonville* definition of MEEs in specific cases, the Court demonstrated a repeated willingness to rule against the interests of large member states in cases with large political as well as economic stakes, such as the German beer and the Italian pasta cases of the mid-1980s. In the former case, the Commission brought infringement proceedings against Germany, whose sixteenth-century beer-purity law, the *Reinheitsgebot*, prohibited the marketing in Germany of beer with additives. Although the law was staunchly defended by the German government, Bavarian politicians, German brewers, and public opinion, the Court upheld the Commission's argument that the law constituted an MEE within the *Dassonville* definition. Applying the *Cassis* test, the Court held that the stated aim of the law, consumer protection, satisfied the mandatory requirements stated in *Cassis*, but that this aim could be met through mandatory labelling of ingredients and could not justify the exclusion from the German market of beers legally produced and marketed in other member states.[61]

In the Italian pasta case, a German exporter of pasta challenged an Italian law requiring the use of hard or durum wheat in the manufacture of pasta. In this case, Italy argued that the law served the aim of consumer protection and health, and received support for this view in the opinion of the Advocate-General in the case, Federico Mancini. Once again, however, the Court ruled that the Italian law acted as a measure having equivalent effect under Article 28, and that the aims of the law could be met through a labelling requirement that would not have the effect of hindering intra-EC trade in goods.[62] Although decisions such as these could not in themselves create a single market for beverages or food, when taken together with the findings reported by Stone Sweet and Brunell (1998; see also Chapter 3), the evidence from these cases nevertheless supports the view that the Court is not cowed by pressure from individual member states, ruling regularly against large as well as small member states, on politically charged and economically important questions, in its application of Article 28.

Third, the Court's jurisprudence throughout the 1980s and early 1990s continued to expand, even beyond the *Dassonville* and *Cassis* decisions, the scope of Article 28 as applied to national laws and regulations. In a series of cases starting in the early 1980s, the Court ruled that the scope of Article 28 was broad enough to include as MEEs a number of national laws regulating not only the characteristics of imported or domestic products but also various marketing methods in so far as these might be expected to exert an effect on intra-EC trade. Specifically, the Court held that the concept of 'measures having equivalent effect' was broad enough to include a Dutch law restricting the ability of businesses to offer customers free gifts as a sales-promotion device;[63] a French law prohibiting door-to-door sales of educational materials;[64] a Luxembourg law restricting the use of advertising practices that were legal and commonly used in neighbouring Belgium;[65] and a French law forbidding the marketing of films on videocassettes until twelve months after their release in theatres.[66] The latter case, *Cinéthèque*, was particularly noteworthy as it generated an explicit dialogue regarding the scope of Article 28 between the Court and its Advocate-General in the case, Lord Slynn. In his preliminary opinion for the Court, Slynn argued that a law such as the one in question should be held to be outside the scope of Article 28:

[I]n an area in which there are no common Community standards or rules, where a national measure is not specifically directed at imports, does not discriminate against imports, does not make it any more difficult for an importer to sell his products than it is for a domestic producer, and gives no protection to domestic producers, then in my view, *prima facie*, the measure does not fall within Article 30 [now 28] even if it does in fact lead to a restriction or reduction of imports. (Quoted in Arnull 2000: 278)

The Court, however, was 'in an expansive mood' (Rawlings 1993: 314) and refused to accept Slynn's proposed restriction on the scope of Article 28, ruling instead that the French law was indeed a measure

having equivalent effect, albeit justified by the mandatory requirements laid down in *Cassis*.

The dangers of such an expansive interpretation of Article 28 were
revealed, however, in a series of cases in the late 1980s and early 1990s,
including most notably the famous 'Sunday trading' cases and the
aforementioned *Keck and Mithouard* decision. The former cases,
which have been analysed in detail by Richard Rawlings (1993) and
others, concerned the compatibility with Article 28 of a British law
prohibiting retail stores from marketing products on Sundays. As
Rawlings demonstrates with microscopic attention to local as well as
European detail, the Sunday-trading cases can be traced to the efforts
of English and Welsh local governments to enforce the Shops Act of
1950, which prohibited retail sales on Sundays, against department
stores which had long defied the law. In *Torfaen BC v. B & Q plc*, the
first of three major cases to reach the Court, a local authority brought
criminal proceedings against B & Q, a department store, for violation
of the Shops Act. In its defence, B & Q pointed out that the British
law, by requiring shops to remain closed on Sundays, had the effect of
reducing substantially the sales of imported, as well as domestic, products, and suggested that the law was therefore contrary to Article 28. The
local magistrate, in turn, directed a request for a preliminary
ruling to the ECJ, asking whether such a law should be considered
as an MEE within the meaning of Article 28 and, if so, whether it
satisfied the Court's mandatory requirements and the principle of
proportionality.

In *Torfaen*, as in *Cinéthèque*, the Court was being asked to extend
the scope of Article 28 to a national law which was at best indirectly
connected with the free movement of goods within the Community.
Indeed, as Rawlings (1993) points out, the primary aim of the defendants in the case was not to facilitate the marketing of foreign goods but
rather to use Article 28 as an instrument of domestic deregulation,
striking down by European judicial fiat an act which they had failed
to repeal through the domestic legislative process. Under the circumstances, Advocate-General Van Gerven, like Slynn in the *Cinéthèque*
case, urged the Court to take a more restrictive view of Article 28,
which should be declared applicable only to national rules which had
the effect of screening or partitioning the common market. A
'mechanical application' of the *Dassonville* principle, Van Gerven suggested, would force the Court to 'decide in an increasing number of
cases on the reasonableness of policy decisions of member states taken
in innumerable spheres where there is no question of direct or indirect, factual or legal discrimination against, or detriment to, imported

products' (quoted in Rawlings 1993: 316). Once again, however, the Court elected to reassert its precedent in *Cinéthèque*, suggesting that the law in question fell within the scope of Article 28 and that its aim was consistent with the mandatory requirements of *Cassis*, but leaving it for national courts to determine whether the restrictive effect of the law was proportional to its aims.[67]

In the event, however, the Court's brief and somewhat Delphic ruling in *Torfaen* caused confusion in the legal community and in British courts, which variously upheld or struck down the enforcement of the Shops Act depending on their interpretation of the aims of the law and the proportionality test. The ensuing confusion resulted in the submission of a second request from a British court for a preliminary ruling, the case of *Stoke-on-Trent and Another v. B & Q*, in which the Court was asked to clarify the basis on which national courts were to establish whether national rules exerted an excessively restrictive effect on intra-Community trade. In that decision, the Court indicated that, in assessing the restrictive effects of a national regulation, 'it must be considered whether the effects are direct, indirect, or purely speculative and whether those effects do or do not impede the marketing of imported products more than the marketing of national products'.[68] On that basis, but without explicitly breaking from the traditional application of *Dassonville* and *Cassis*, the Court ruled clearly that Article 28 did not apply to national laws restricting Sunday trading.

Throughout the Sunday-trading saga, a number of legal scholars, including Eric White, who had represented the Commission in *Torfaen* and other Article 28 cases, had criticized the Court's ever widening interpretation of Article 28 and its lack of clarity about the scope and limits of the article (White 1989; Mortelmans 1991; Steiner 1992). To simplify a complex set of arguments, the Court's critics pointed to four primary difficulties in the Court's previous case law. First, as we have seen above, the Court's case-by-case approach and lack of clarity on the scope of Article 28 and the nature of the *Cassis* proportionality test had produced considerable legal uncertainty, and in the *Torfaen* case had led to the uneven application of the law within Britain. Second, even the defenders of a traditionally broad interpretation of Article 28 admitted that such an interpretation could encourage challenges to national laws that had little if any relation to the free movement of goods in the Community, and therefore invited abuse by private litigants. Third, the predictable flood of such cases would likely force the Court to accept a growing case load of more and more difficult decisions balancing national legislative aims against the Community goal of free movement. Fourth and finally, an excessively wide reading of Article 28 posed the risk that 'national courts will be driven to defiance in the face of challenge to national measures, often controversial, and enacted after due debate, which do not appear to them to jeopardize the proper functioning of the single market' (Steiner 1992: 751). For all of these reasons, legal scholars presented a range of proposals, the most well known of which was White's (1989) suggestion that a distinction be drawn between national measures relating to the *characteristics of products*, such as alcohol content, which would fall within the scope of Article 28, and those measures which merely regulated the *circumstances* under which they may be marketed in a given member state, the latter category falling outside the scope of the article. In the event, the Court was eventually to adopt a standard close to White's suggestion in the landmark 1993 decision in *Keck and Mithouard*.

Like *Cassis* and the Sunday trading cases, the *Keck* decision began as an Article 234 reference from a national court. In this case, the Tribunal de Grande Instance in Strasbourg sought a clarification of the scope of Article 28 in the context of criminal proceedings brought against Mr Keck and Mr Mithouard, the owners of two supermarkets charged with reselling products in an unaltered state at prices lower than their actual purchase price, which was illegal under a French regulation prohibiting sale at a loss. In their defence, Keck and Mithouard contended that the French regulation was incompatible with Article 28, and the French tribunal sought the Court's opinion on this question.

The issues raised by this case were complex, reflecting the inconsistent rulings of the Court in previous cases regarding the scope of Article 28. As Advocate-General Van Gerven noted in two extensive opinions, some of the Court's previous jurisprudence suggested that rules concerning the marketing of a product, such as the question of Sunday trading or sale at a loss, fell within the definition of MEEs within the meaning of Article 28. Nevertheless, in reviewing the Court's case law as well as the interventions of the French government, the Commission, and the plaintiffs in the case, Van Gerven also pointed to the difficulties of defining the scope of Article 28 in this case. According to the previous case law of the Court, in assessing the consistency of national regulations under Article 28 'it must be considered whether [their] effects are direct, indirect, or purely speculative and whether those effects do or do not impede the marketing of imported products more than the marketing of national products'.[69] As Van Gerven pointed out, the parties to the case answered that question differently, with the French government claiming that the effects on intra-Community trade were purely speculative, while the Counsel for Mr Mithouard claimed that the effects on imports were restrictive; the Commission took a middle position, considering that the effects were either indirect or speculative and conceding that 'there is no evidence to suggest that the regulation of resale at a loss has a direct effect on intra-Community trade'.[70] In the Opinion, Van Gerven recalled his previous opinion in the first Sunday-trading case, noting that his proposal for a more limited application of Article 28 had been rejected by the Court in that decision. In light of the Court's previous rulings, Van Gerven continued,

I will thus assume from now on that the broad *Dassonville* formula still remains the cornerstone of the Court's case-law concerning the sphere of application of Article 30 [now 28] of the EEC Treaty. In order to avoid any confusion, I think that the Court owes a duty to the national courts to make this quite clear.[71]

Applying the *Dassonville* formula in this present case, Van Gerven concluded that the French regulation did indeed constitute a measure having equivalent effect and was therefore subject to the rule of reason from *Cassis de Dijon*. Applying this rule, Van Gerven concluded that the French unconditional prohibition on resale at a loss was motivated by an aim consistent with the mandatory requirements laid down in *Cassis* but went farther than necessary to achieve that end, since it caught not only predatory practices by distributors but also legitimate sales-promotion techniques. For this reason, he argued, France would 'do well to amend its legislation to bring it more into conformity with European law'. Nevertheless, he continued, the application of the French law to the specific cases of Mr Keck and Mr Mithouard created 'no more than a purely hypothetical effect on trade between Member States and certainly no more than an hypothetical hindering of trade flows'. For this reason, the Advocate-General concluded by proposing that the Court should respond to the national court that 'In a situation such as that with which the main proceedings are concerned, Article 30 [now 28] of the EEC Treaty does not preclude a statutory prohibition of resale at a loss'.[72]

The Opinion of the Advocate-General in this case is worth citing at length in large part because it indicates more openly than the Court's final decision the complexity of the case, the confused nature of the precedent on this issue, the pressure on the Court to clarify its position, and the arguments of the various parties—that is, the French government, the Greek government, and the Commission—which submitted observations in the case. Furthermore, as we have just seen, the Advocate-General's second opinion would clearly have allowed the Court to reaffirm the *Dassonville* precedent while at the same time ruling *in favour of France* on the substance of the case. Put differently, the Court faced little member-state pressure to overturn its line of precedent in *Keck*, given the weak interest generated by other member governments besides France and Greece and the ease with which the Court could have ruled in favour of France on the substance of the case without conceding any point of law.

Nevertheless, in its judgment of 24 November 1993, the Court dramatically and famously qualified its previously expansive reading of Article 28. The Court did not overturn the general principles of *Dassonville* and *Cassis*, which were reaffirmed in paragraph 15 of the opinion:

It is established by the case law beginning with 'Cassis de Dijon'... that, in the absence of harmonization of legislation, obstacles to free movement of goods which are the consequence of applying, to goods coming from other Member States where they are lawfully manufactured and marketed, rules that lay down requirements to be met by such goods (such as those relating to designation, form, size, weight, composition, presentation, labelling, packaging) constitute measures with equivalent effect prohibited by Article 30 [now 28]. This is so even if those rules apply without distinction to all products unless their application can be justified by a public-interest objective taking precedence over the free movement of goods.[73]

At this point, had it sought only to rule that the French law was compatible with the provisions of Article 28, the Court could easily have decided that, despite its potential to restrict intra-Community trade in goods, the aims of the French law were consistent with the 'rule of reason' laid down in *Cassis*. Nevertheless, the Court took the opportunity of the *Keck* decision to revisit its previous case law on this issue, deciding in the next paragraph that:

By contrast, *contrary to what has previously been decided*, the application to products from other Member States of national provisions prohibiting certain selling arrangements is not such as to hinder directly or indirectly, actually or potentially, trade between Member States within the meaning of the Dassonville judgment (Case 8/74 [1974] ECR 837), so long as those provisions apply to all relevant traders operating within the national territory and so long as they affect in the same manner, in law and in fact, the marketing of domestic products and of those from other Member States.

Provided that those conditions are fulfilled, the application of such rules to the sale of products from another Member State meeting the requirements laid down by that State is not by nature such as to prevent their access to the market or to impede their access to the market or to impede access any more than it impedes the access of domestic products. *Such rules therefore fall outside the scope of Article 30 [now 28] of the Treaty.*[74]

The Court's ruling in *Keck* did not overturn either the *Dassonville* or *Cassis* decision, but it did overturn or at least 'clarify' other previous rulings and explicitly restricted the scope of application of Article 28 vis-à-vis national regulations on 'selling arrangements'—a point confirmed by the Court in subsequent decisions (Weatherill 1996; Eeckhout 1998). *Keck* therefore provides an extraordinary and thus far unique example of a U-turn in the Court's application of the treaty provisions on the free movement of goods.

The important question for our purposes here is: why did they do it? In terms of Garrett, Kelemen, and Schulz's hypotheses, the Court's decision in *Keck* is puzzling because it explicitly overturns an—admittedly confused—line of precedent as well as the opinion of the Advocate-General in the case. Furthermore, we find little or no empirical evidence in favour of the authors' other two hypotheses, focusing respectively on the costs of a decision to the member-state in question (which might provoke an act of non-compliance) and on the number of member states likely to be adversely affected by the decision (which might provoke legislative overruling). In the *Keck* case, there is little or no evidence that France was contemplating non-compliance with the Court's eventual ruling. Furthermore, had it been concerned about French non-compliance, the Court could easily have ruled with France on the substance of the case while reaffirming its traditionally broad reading of Article 28. In any event, as we have seen above, the Court had repeatedly proved willing to rule against large member states on politically charged issues, and there is little reason to believe that the Court would hesitate in the face of French opposition in this case given its rulings in the German beer and Italian pasta cases.

Finally, with regard to Garrett, Kelemen, and Schulz's third hypothesis, there is no evidence to suggest that a precedent-reaffirming decision in *Keck* would have been met with widespread opposition among the member governments. As we have seen, aside from France, only one other member state, Greece, intervened in the case, which otherwise received little public attention until the Court's surprising ruling was revealed. More generally, despite the Court's higher political profile in the 1990s as a result of its decisions in cases like *Barber, Kalanke*, and the Irish abortion case—all of which led to member-state attacks on the Court and to specific member-state responses in the Maastricht and Amsterdam Treaties—none of the Court's Article 28 decisions of the early 1990s, including the Sunday-trading cases, had resulted in widespread political controversy or member-state declarations against the Court that might have raised the prospect of a political backlash or the threat of a legislative overrule by the member governments. Finally, as Miguel Poiares Maduro (1999: 99–101) has argued, the Court's ruling in Keck has been followed not by across-the-board retrenchment in free-movement rulings, but rather by a series of bold rulings in which the Court interpreted broadly the treaty provisions regarding the free movement of both labour and of services—in which case the *Keck* decision represents not a retreat from activism but rather the court shifting 'the focus of its activism from the free movement of goods to the other freedoms'. In sum, there is little or no evidence pointing to pressure from the member-state principals as the primary cause of the Court's about-face in *Keck*.

Why, then, might the Court have reversed itself? As noted earlier, any answer to this question should be regarded as tentative since the internal deliberations of the Court are closed to outside observers and the Court's very brief opinion in *Keck* cannot itself be read as a sincere expression of the Court's preferences and motives in the case. Nevertheless, the Court's decision, together with the two Opinions submitted by Advocate-General Van Gerven, suggest that the Court was motivated, at least in part, by repeated calls for clarification of previous case law by national courts and by members of the legal profession in light of the confusion and controversy generated by the Sunday-trading cases. The Court's specific decision to declare selling arrangements as falling outside the scope of Article 28, in turn, appears to reflect the judges' frustration at private litigants' use of Article 28 to challenge national laws for reasons that had little or nothing to do with the free movement of goods within the Community, and concerns about the Court's own workload if the stream of such cases were not cut off by a definitive ruling on the application of Article 28.[75]

More generally, the Court's ruling in *Keck*—and the broad sweep of its Article 28 jurisprudence since *Dassonville*—provides support for the view, expressed by Stone Sweet and Brunell, that the Court does indeed enjoy extraordinary discretion vis-à-vis the member governments in its interpretation of EC Treaty provisions and that, in their words, 'the constitutionalization process has been driven almost entirely by the relationship among private litigants, national judges, and the ECJ interacting within the framework provided by Article 177' (Stone Sweet and Brunell 1998: 65). More specifically, the evidence reviewed above suggests that the Court's ruling in *Keck* came, *not* as a result of political pressure from the member governments, but primarily in response to arguments and pressure from the Court's

other interlocutors: private litigants, national courts, and the legal profession (Weiler 1994). We cannot, of course, conclude on the basis of
the evidence presented above that the Court is *never* influenced by
member-state pressure—a conclusion that would require a careful
examination of more than the two cases examined above if not,
indeed, access to the internal deliberations of the Court. Indeed, as we
shall see in Chapter 6, the ECJ jurisprudence has in other cases been
explicitly limited by EU member governments in the form of a treaty
revision, providing an illustration of the very real limits to the Court's
discretion. Within those limits, however, the Court has exercised its
authority to expand upon, and then contract, its interpretation
of Article 28, with greater apparent regard for the views of the legal
community than for those of its member-state principals.

IV. Conclusions

In this chapter, I have examined in detail three case studies of supranational decision-making, seeking to test hypotheses about (1) the
'pro-European' or competence-maximizing preferences of supranational agents and (2) the conditions under which those agents might
be able to influence policy outcomes independent of the preferences
of their principals. Regarding the first, I hypothesized at the outset
that the Commission and the Court would share a common preference for deeper European integration and employ their statutory discretion to move policy outcomes in that direction. Regarding the
second, I hypothesized that, *ceteris paribus*, the ability of the
Commission and the Court to influence policy outcomes would be a
function of the administrative and oversight mechanisms established
by the member governments for each organization in a given issue
area. Across all three cases, this second hypothesis suggested that the
autonomy and influence of supranational actors was expected to
increase as we moved from Commission agenda-setting (external
trade) to Commission executive action (merger control) and finally to
the Court's interpretation of the treaties (free movement of goods).
Within each case, moreover, the second hypothesis suggested that, in
the event of a conflict between the Commission or the Court and the
member governments, dissatisfied governments would employ available control mechanisms such as comitology or legislative overrule in
an effort to limit agency losses to their supranational agents.

By and large, the evidence reviewed in this chapter supports both
hypotheses. With regard to the preferences of the various actors, the

Commission behaved as a competence-maximizer across all three cases, seeking to increase the Community's and its own policy competences and to use those competences to create a single internal market free from internal trade barriers and distortions to competition, and to liberalize EC trade with third countries. Similarly, in its jurisprudence on the free movement of goods and in its judgments on the Commission's use of Article 81 and 82 in the field of merger control, the Court has embraced an expansive interpretation of the treaties, maximizing the power of EU institutions and their reach into national legal systems in order to remove intra-EC trade barriers and distortions to competition. As we also saw, however, the Court did issue one unexpected and restrictive ruling, Opinion 1/94, interpreting narrowly the scope of the Community's and the Commission's trade competence under Article 133. Although not studied in detail in this chapter, the surprising ruling in Opinion 1/94 and its restrictive impact on the Commission's thus-far-unsuccessful campaign to acquire unconditional competence to negotiate agreements on trade in services and intellectual property underlines the importance of the Commission-Court tandem in all three of the cases, and provides tentative evidence that the Court may have been influenced by member-state pressures in issuing its opinion in that case.

With regard to the influence of supranational institutions on policy outcomes, a comparison across the three cases reviewed in this chapter supports the hypothesis that, all else being equal, supranational influence increases as we progress from agenda-setting (external trade) to executive action (merger control) to ECJ constitutional interpretation (free movement). Just as importantly, however, within-case analysis reveals additional details about the ways in which the Commission and the Court seek to make use of their statutory discretion, and the ways in which member governments seek to reassert control in the event of supranational activism. In the Uruguay Round case, for example, we found that the Commission does indeed enjoy a privileged position as chief negotiator on behalf of the Community, and sought to use this position to promote both CAP reform internally and a relatively liberal agreement on agricultural trade vis-à-vis the United States. By the same token, however, we also found that the member governments successfully constrained the Commission's autonomy through the use of the Article 133 committee, which was repeatedly and explicitly employed as an effective control mechanism by dissatisfied member governments. Furthermore, and in contrast with agenda-setting models that assume minimum-winning coalitions in a Council that votes strictly by qualified majority, we found that in practice the Commission's potential agenda-setting power was limited by the Council's de facto use of consensus decision-making, which in the case of the Blair House agreement negated what would otherwise have been a 'winning' proposal under qualified majority.

Moving to the merger control case, we found that the Commission, using its treaty-based powers and with the support of the ECJ, was able to establish a regulatory presence in the field of merger control, which in turn led to the adoption of the 1989 Merger Control Regulation delegating significant powers and discretion to the Commission to regulate European-level mergers. Since the adoption of the MCR, moreover, the Commission has demonstrated its willingness and ability to reject and impose conditions on mergers even in the face of heavy lobbying from the affected firms and from member governments, which attempted to lobby individual Commissioners and sought, unsuccessfully, to reconsider the mandate of the Commission following the 1991 rejection of the De Havilland merger. Given the strong statutory basis for Commission discretion in the area of merger control, such attempts to retrench Commission powers have invariably failed, yet the dissatisfaction of various member governments has also prevented any major increase in Commission competences, which have increased only marginally since 1989.

Finally, examining the Court's jurisprudence on Article 28 from *Cassis* to *Keck*, we saw the ECJ acting with considerable autonomy vis-à-vis the member governments, and expanding its interpretation of Article 28 in *Cassis* and other cases in spite of the opposition of powerful member governments, and then restricting the reach of Article 28 in *Keck* primarily in response to pressure from national courts, individual litigants, and the legal community rather than from the member governments. Nevertheless, in other areas of law the Court has encountered more intense governmental pressure and the limits of its own discretion, as we shall see in the next chapter.

CHAPTER 6

Regulating Europe: The Commission, the Court, and the Regulation of the European Market

In the previous chapter we saw how, across three different issue areas, the Commission and the Court of Justice have used their discretion to press for the creation of a single European market. Although both supranational agents have encountered limits to their discretion—as in the Council's rejection of Blair House, or the difficulty encountered by the Commission in rejecting politically sensitive mergers and increasing its authority in this area—the Commission and Court have, on balance, played an independent causal role in the construction of Europe's internal market.

In this chapter, the analytical focus is once again on the agenda-setting, executive, and judicial powers of the Commission and the Court, but this time focusing on the re-regulation of the European market and the adoption, implementation, and interpretation of social policies at the European level. As in the previous chapter, the analysis is organized in terms of three case studies, progressing from relatively modest Commission agenda-setting powers under QMV in the area of worker health and safety, through the Commission's executive powers in the area of the Structural Funds, supervised variously by advisory or management committees, and finally examining the Court of Justice's controversial interpretation of the principle of equal pay for equal work in the 1991 *Barber* decision. As in the previous chapter, I seek to test two hypotheses. First, I hypothesize that the Commission and the Court will behave as competence-maximizers, seeking to develop social policies as well as market liberalization at the EU level. Second, I hypothesize that the discretion of the Commission and the Court, and their ability to force the pace of EU social integration, is a function of the control mechanisms established by member governments, and that these proceed from relatively constraining demands of agenda setting in the working time case, through the less restrictive comitology procedures that obtain in the Structural Funds, and finally to the least constraining demands of Treaty interpretation in the Court's *Barber* decision. As in the previous chapter, however, I examine not only the variation in final outcomes across cases but the nature of the principal-agent interactions *within* each case, including the preferences of the actors, and the use of various control mechanisms to limit the discretion of the Commission and the Court in their efforts to regulate the European market.

I. The Commission as Agenda Setter:
The Working Time Directive

The adoption of European social regulations represents one of the core elements of the 'regulated capitalism' model of European integration reviewed in Chapter 1. Precisely because of the sensitivity of social regulation, however, delegation of significant executive powers to the Commission in this area is rare. The treaties, for example, delegate no regulatory powers to the Commission in the area of social policy; and Franchino (2001) similarly finds no delegation of powers to the Commission in his data-set in the area of social policy, and only a modest (2.61 per cent) level of delegation in the related area of health and safety in the workplace. However, the treaties and secondary legislation in the EU do provide an executive role for the Commission in the administration of the Social Fund and other Structural Funds, subject variously to an advisory or management committee procedure roughly comparable to the merger control case in the previous chapter, and the Structural Funds case is accordingly examined at length in the second section of this chapter.

In addition to its role as an administrator of EU funds, the member governments have delegated significant agenda-setting power to the Commission in Article 118a EC of the Single European Act, now incorporated into a substantially revised Article 137 EC after Amsterdam, which provided for the adoption of minimum EC standards in the area of health and safety in the workplace by qualified majority in the Council and in cooperation with the European Parliament. Although not identical to the structure of delegation in the case of external trade policy, where the Commission acts as chief negotiator as well as agenda setter, the Commission's powers in workplace health and safety are analytically similar to those of the Uruguay

Round case in that both areas require a positive endorsement by a qualified majority in the Council of Ministers in order to ratify Commission initiatives. Furthermore, as in the case of external trade policy, the regulation of workplace health and safety has produced considerable friction between the Commission and the member governments, providing a promising area in which to examine the extent to which and the ways in which the Commission attempts to use its agenda-setting powers to advance European social integration, and the responses of the member governments to these attempts. Specifically, this section examines one of the first and certainly the most controversial of the Directives adopted under the workplace health and safety provisions of the SEA: the Working Time Directive of 1993.[1]

The issue of working time has long been one of the central issues of social policy within each of the member states, including questions such as the length of the working day, the length of the working week, rights to breaks, daily and weekly rest periods, and various provisions regarding night work. At the time of the adoption of the 1993 Directive, all of the member governments of the EU had adopted at least some statutory provisions on working time with the exception of the United Kingdom, which had no statutory restrictions on the length of the working day or week, daily or weekly rest periods, breaks, or night work (Lewis 1998*a*: 373; Gray 1997). Among the other member states, moreover, individual regulations and practices varied in terms of both the contents of statutory regulations and the respective roles allocated to government regulations and collective bargaining in the setting of working-time standards. This diversity of member-state practice, together with the cost and sensitivity of working time as an area of social policy, meant that the European Community faced significant obstacles in establishing any binding regulations on the subject. Indeed, prior to the 1980s, the issue of working time had been subject to only one non-binding Council recommendation, adopted in 1975, on the principle of the 40-hour work week.[2]

Despite these obstacles, the expansion of EU competence to include the issue of working time had been a long-standing goal of the Commission, which in the early 1980s launched a major initiative to address the problem of working time in the context of a common EC approach to the problem of rising unemployment. During this period, the new Socialist government of François Mitterrand in France, as well as governments in Belgium, the Netherlands, and Italy, had begun to experiment with initiatives to increase employment by reducing the length of the working week, either by statute, as in the case of France, which introduced a 39-hour week in 1982, or through collective bargaining agreements between the representatives of labour and industry, which accepted shorter hours in return for greater worker flexibility. Seeking to capitalize on what the Commission perceived to be an emerging consensus among the member states, Social Affairs Commissioner Ivor Richards introduced a 'Draft Council Recommendation on the Reduction and Reorganization of Working Time' in 1983. In its Communication, the Commission presented 'the case for a positive policy on working time as part of the strategy to combat unemployment', arguing that both the Community and its member governments should support the reorganization and reduction of working time as an instrument of employment policy designed to increase employment through measures such as work sharing. However, recognizing the sensitive nature of the policy and opposition to the proposal among EU employer associations and in the Conservative government of British Prime Minister Margaret Thatcher, the Commission opted for a 'soft law' document rather than binding legislation, proposing only a draft Recommendation on the subject and noting that 'what is required at the political level is not the imposition of binding and inflexible obligations—and it is for this reason that the Commission has decided not to propose a binding instrument in this field—but rather the establishment of political objectives and guidelines which state clearly the need for solidarity and the readiness of governments to provide the necessary support' (CEC n.d.; see also *Financial Times* 1983; Cheeseright 1983). The Commission often uses such non-binding or 'soft-law' instruments as a means of establishing a legal presence in sensitive issue areas (Cram 1997: 107–11), but in this case the Commission's proposals were consistently rejected by the United Kingdom, which blocked the necessary unanimous agreement in the Council of Ministers (see for example Gottlieb 1983; Groom 1984).

Negotiating the Working Time Directive

The 1987 Single European Act, however, offered the Commission a new opportunity to propose and secure the adoption of not only a recommendation but binding legislation on working time by way of the new EC Treaty provisions on health and safety in the workplace. At the 1985 IGC, the Commission, the Danish government, and several other national delegations had put forward proposals for extending EC competence in social policy, including a Danish proposal for a new article allowing the Community to establish *minimum standards* in the area of health and safety in the workplace, explicitly leaving individual member states free to adopt stricter standards. Most of the proposed social policy provisions in the IGC met with considerable resistance from the United Kingdom, which again blocked most of the proposed changes. In the area of worker health and safety, however, the United Kingdom agreed to a provision for the adoption of minimum standards in worker health and safety, by QMV, although it did insist upon the addition of a paragraph stipulating that the Community would not place any unnecessary burdens on small and medium-sized firms (Corbett 1987: 251). The resulting Article 118a, incorporated at Amsterdam into an extensively revised Article 137 EC, provided as follows:

1. Member States shall pay particular attention to encouraging improvements, especially in the working environment, as regards the health and safety of workers, and shall set as their objective the harmonization of conditions in this area, while maintaining the improvements made.
2. In order to help achieve the objective laid down in the first paragraph, the Council, acting according to the procedure referred to in Article 189c [the cooperation procedure] and after consulting the Economic and Social Committee, shall adopt by means of Directives minimum requirements for gradual implementation, having regard to the conditions and technical rules obtaining in each of the Member States.
    Such Directives shall avoid imposing administrative, financial and legal constraints in a way which would hold back the creation and development of small and medium-sized undertakings.
3. The provisions adopted pursuant to this article shall not prevent any Member State from maintaining or introducing more stringent measures for the protection of working conditions compatible with this Treaty.

At the time of its adoption by the 1985 intergovernmental conference, Article 118a was interpreted narrowly as a 'flanking area' for the internal market rather than the legal basis for a full-fledged EU social policy which had been explicitly rejected by Thatcher. The Delors Commission, however, saw the adoption of the internal market programme as the first stage in a larger effort to create a 'social Europe', and chose to interpret Article 118a more broadly to incorporate the question of working time, which the Commission had previously approached primarily as an employment issue. More broadly, the Commission was playing what Martin Rhodes (1995) has called the 'legal base game' and what Joseph Jupille (2000) refers to as 'procedural politics', in which each institutional actor seeks the adoption of legislation under the legal basis most likely to secure its preferred outcome. In the social policy areas like working time or the rights of pregnant workers, the use of Article 118a meant that Directives could be adopted on the basis of QMV in the Council, with the cooperation procedure for the European Parliament, thereby allowing the Commission to outflank potential opposition or vetoes by individual member states.

In September 1990, therefore, the Commission issued a 'Proposal for a Council Directive Concerning Certain Aspects of the Organization of Working Time' including an extensive analysis of the status quo in each of the member states and a 15-article draft Directive for consideration by the Council and the European Parliament (CEC 1990). After a review of the situation in the Community and a defence of the use of Article 118a for the adoption of the Directive, the Commission made specific proposals regarding the minimum daily rest period (eleven hours); a minimum weekly rest period (24 hours, in addition to the daily rest period of eleven hours, for a total of 35 hours); and various provisions on shift work and night work, the most important of which was an eight-hour daily limit for night-workers, including overtime. The Commission also mentioned, but provided no specific proposals for, the maximum length of the working week, the right to rest breaks during the working day, and the right to an annual paid vacation. Finally, the Commission proposal included the possibility of a limited number of derogations in cases of an actual or imminent accident, seasonal work, or collective agreements, provided that compensatory rest periods were granted to the employees.

As Gray (1997) and others have pointed out, the Commission's proposed Directive was not radical, in the sense that most member states already had similar or more stringent legislation in force in all of these areas; nevertheless, adoption of the Directive would establish the precedent of EC competence for the regulation of working time, and conformity with its minimum standards would require minor changes in the legal provisions of most member states and substantial changes in Ireland and the UK.

Under the cooperation procedure, the first reading of the Commission proposal took place in the European Parliament, which proposed 40 declaratory and substantive amendments relating primarily to weekly rest periods, working time reduction (without loss of pay) and flexibility, overtime, control and monitoring, and improvement of workers' health and safety. The Commission incorporated twelve of the EP's amendments, in whole or in part, in its revised proposal to the Council, the most significant of which involved raising the minimum

daily rest period from eleven to twelve hours and introducing a provision for a minimum annual paid leave of four weeks, which had been
left to the discretion of member states in the original draft.[3] However,
as the Commission pointed out in its explanatory memorandum:

A number of amendments were not accepted by the Commission. Many of
these went beyond purely health and safety considerations and were therefore
not considered to be within the scope of the Directive based on Article 118A
of the EEC Treaty. Others were considered to impose unjustifiable burdens
on employers, especially SMEs, or to allow insufficient flexibility, given the
variety of circumstances in which the Directive will need to be applied in the
different Member States. (CEC 1991*b*: 2)

Put simply, while the Commission was sympathetic to some of the
more progressive amendments put forward by the EP, it rejected those
amendments which it considered would endanger the potential qualified majority in the Council or the validity of the legal basis of Article
118a.

   Within the Council of Ministers, the Commission's proposal for a
Directive on Working Time met with reservations from several member governments, including most notably Denmark, which relied
heavily on collective agreements rather than national legislation in the
area of working time; Ireland, which would have to change certain
aspects of national laws to comply with the terms of the draft
Directive; and France, which sought a binding maximum length for
the working week below the eventual limit of 48 hours. The draft met
with more fundamental resistance, however, from the Conservative
government of John Major in the United Kingdom. In part, this opposition reflected the specific features of working time, where the
United Kingdom in the early 1990s possessed no statutory entitle-
ments regarding the length of the working week, daily and weekly rest
periods, or mandatory breaks during the working day. In practice,
moreover, some 15.5 per cent of all UK employees worked more than
48 hours per week; 6.1 per cent usually worked seven days a week; and
26.6 per cent were entitled to less than four weeks paid holiday a year
in the terms of their employment contracts (Gray 1997: 324).
Implementation of the Commission's draft Directive, therefore,
would require substantial changes to UK law and practice, and the
British government came under heavy pressure from domestic business to reject the Directive, which the Confederation of British
Industry later estimated would cost UK businesses over £5 billion a
year to implement (Jones 1991).[4] More generally, the Conservative
governments of Margaret Thatcher and John Major had long resisted

any creeping role for the EC in the area of social regulation, which would require fundamental changes to the Thatcherite social policies of those governments. For this reason, and despite having agreed to the text of Article 118a in the Single European Act, Thatcher's government had subsequently opted out of the non-binding 1989 Charter of Fundamental Social Rights, which was explicitly cited in support of the Commission's working-time initiative, and Major famously did the same vis-à-vis the Social Protocol adopted as part of the 1992 Maastricht Treaty.

Thus, in response to the Commission's 1990 proposal for a Directive on working time, Major's government criticized the choice of Article 118a as the legal basis, arguing that the Commission had provided no scientific evidence linking the health and safety of workers to the much more general provisions of the draft Directive, which the British argued should be adopted either on the basis of Article 308 (ex 235) EC, which would require unanimity in the Council and thus be vulnerable to a British veto, or, later, on the basis of the Maastricht Social Protocol, from which Britain enjoyed an opt-out. Under the provisions of Article 149 EC, however, such a decision to change the Commission's proposed legal base would require a unanimous vote in the Council, which was impossible given the general support for the draft Directive among the other member governments.

Under the circumstances, the British government pursued a two-track bargaining strategy vis-à-vis the Commission and the other member governments. Initially, British Employment Secretary Michael Howard and other British officials took a hard line, repeatedly noting the estimated costs of complying with a 48-hour week in the United Kingdom, challenging the use of Article 118a as the legal basis for the Directive, and threatening to vote against the Directive and to challenge its legality before the European Court of Justice. By early 1992, however, in the shadow of a possible vote and an uncertain legal case before the ECJ, British officials took a more conciliatory approach, noting that the United Kingdom might be able to live with the proposed Directive provided that its concerns, including voluntary opt-outs from the 48-hour week, excluded sectors, and other derogations, were addressed (Lewis 1998a: 390).[5]

This second, more conciliatory approach, coupled with the preference for consensual decision-making within the Council, was successful in securing a number of concessions to the British position. Indeed, it is a striking feature of the negotiations that, although the United Kingdom was effectively isolated in its position on both the legal basis and many, though not all, of the substantive provisions of the Commission's draft, the other member governments did not move quickly to a vote over UK objections, as indeed they were entitled to do under the provisions of the treaties.[6] Instead, as Jeffrey Lewis points out, successive presidencies of the Council made extraordinary efforts to reach a consensus among the member governments, repeatedly delaying a vote on the draft Directive[7] and attempting to bring the United Kingdom 'on board' by offering the UK government significant concessions in a number of areas, including extensive exemptions and derogations from the terms of the Directive. The result of this effort to achieve consensus was a significant delay in the adoption of the Council's 'common position' issued in June 1993, nearly three years after the original Commission proposal, and the ultimate adoption of a Directive that, in the words of one critic, was 'riddled with holes' (Chair of the European Trade Union Confederation, quoted in Lewis 1998*a*: 368).

The original Commission proposal, for example, explicitly extended to all Community workers, although it allowed limited derogations for certain sectors. In the extended negotiations, however, the British delegation successfully pressed for the exclusion of a number of sectors from the Directive, including air, rail, road and sea transport, sea fishing and other work at sea, and 'junior doctors' or doctors-in-training, who generally work long hours in the United Kingdom (Lewis 1998*a*: 385). In addition to these blanket exclusions, the Council also agreed to allow member states to derogate from the provisions on the Directive in the case of management executives; family workers; religious workers; hospital workers; dock or airport workers; gas, water, and electricity production; press, radio, television, and film production; and in tourism, agriculture, and postal services.[8]

With regard to the most contentious element of the Directive, the maximum 48-hour ceiling on the length of the working week, the British pressed for an extended 'reference period' over which the average working week of 48 hours would be enforced. In its proposed amendments, the European Parliament had proposed a reference period of 14 days, meaning that the maximum working time of 48 hours could be averaged out over at most two weeks. Within the Council, France pressed for a somewhat less demanding reference period of two months, while Germany, supported by the United Kingdom, sought a six-month period. In the end, the Council members split the difference, settling on a four-month reference period which could, however, be extended through a derogation to as much as six months or up to a year through collective bargaining. More importantly, the British also secured a derogation whereby 'a Member

State shall have the option not to apply Article 6' provided that no worker is required to work more than 48 hours over a seven-day period without the worker's agreement, and that no worker is subjected to any detriment because of unwillingness to perform such work. This derogation would be valid for at least seven years following the entry into force of the Directive, after which the Council would, on the basis of a Commission proposal, re-examine the derogation and 'decide on what action to take'.[9] A similar derogation regarding paid vacations provides member states with a three-year transition period during which employers may be required to offer three rather than four weeks' paid vacation. Yet another amendment specified that the minimum weekly rest period could 'in principle' include a Sunday, as Germany and other countries preferred, but the decision on this question would be left to member governments to decide on the basis of 'the diversity of cultural, ethnic, religious, and other factors in the Member States'.

On the basis of this compromise proposal, the Danish Presidency of the Council finally scheduled a vote in the Council on a 'common position' on 1 June 1993. Although other member governments had hoped to secure a positive vote from Britain, the UK government abstained from the vote to signal its disagreement without being outvoted, and the incoming British Employment Secretary David Hunt publicly announced in his press conference that 'Even though we have won all of our key points, the directive is still an abuse of Treaty powers to try to regulate the working time of people on phoney health and safety grounds'. He went on, 'I can now announce that we shall be taking our fight to the European Court of Justice when there is a final agreement on this directive' (quoted in Lewis, 1998a: 398; see also *Press Association* 1993). Almost without exception, participants and observers of the negotiations agreed that the Commission's initial draft Directive had been substantially weakened, with Hunt commenting that 'we have drawn most of the teeth from this Directive' (quoted in Gardner and Taylor 1993). Nevertheless, Social Policy Commissioner Padraig Flynn defended the results, claiming that the Directive 'will send an important signal to the workers of Europe that the Community does care about workers' rights and is not just a "capitalist club" as some suggest'. More candidly, Flynn admitted that:

There are of course those who argue that the Commission's original approach was weak and that the text agreed today was weaker still. With regard to both these points I would point out that politics is the art of the possible. The Commission's proposal did break new ground and has succeeded where a proposal for a recommendation on working time failed a few years ago. Secondly, while the Commission is not happy with some of the changes made, in particular the exclusion of a number of sectors from the scope of the directive, the introduction of a maximum working week of 48 hours is a considerable strengthening. So taken as a whole I believe it is a good package and I will be recommending it to the European Parliament, when it goes there for a second reading.[10]

The Parliament, in its second reading of the Directive, introduced or reintroduced 18 amendments,[11] of which six, all relatively minor, were accepted entirely or in part by the both the Commission (CEC 1993)[12] and by the Council in its final Directive.[13] The final Council Directive of 23 November 1993, therefore, looked substantially similar to the Council's common position five months earlier.

The UK's Legal Challenge to the Directive

On 8 March 1994, as promised, the government of the United Kingdom brought an Article 230 action for annulment, Case C-84/94, *United Kingdom v. Council*, before the European Court of Justice. In its action, the UK Government called for the Directive to be annulled, fully or in part, on four distinct grounds: (1) a defective legal basis, namely the use of Article 118a; (2) breach of the principle of proportionality, a 'general principle' of EC law; (3) misuse of powers; and (4) infringement of an essential procedural requirement.[14]

In deciding on this case, as Derek Beach (2001: 155–67) has argued persuasively, the Court had little to fear in terms of legislative overruling since the Council had voted overwhelmingly in favour of the Directive; yet the defiant mood of John Major's government, and the significant financial and political costs likely to be imposed by an adverse ECJ ruling, posed a non-trivial risk of overt non-compliance by the UK. This possibility of non-compliance was highlighted, moreover, by the British government's reaction to the preliminary opinion of Philippe Léger, the Advocate-General in the case, on 12 March 1996. In his opinion, which was not binding on the Court but was considered likely to form the basis of its arguments, Léger dismissed the UK's objection to the use of Article 118a as the legal basis of the Directive, suggesting that the concept of worker health and safety, and in particular the Danish-inspired concept of the 'working environment', should be interpreted broadly and therefore that the Council had acted correctly in accepting the Commission's proposal of Article 118a as the legal basis for the Directive.[15]

Although not definitive, the opinion of the Advocate-General prompted a wave of political debate both within and outside the

UK government, which was under particular political pressure vis-à-vis European issues in the spring of 1996. Earlier that year, in response to revelations about the link between bovine spongiform encephalopathy (BSE) in British cattle and the human illness Creuzfeld-Jacob disease, the Commission had imposed a global ban on the export of British beef, imposing painful costs on British farmers. In response to the Commission decision, which was supported by all the other member governments in the Council, Major's government implemented a policy of 'non-cooperation' in the Council of Ministers, systematically blocking the adoption of all EU legislation for which unanimous votes were required. At the same time, Major's government also came under increasing pressure from below, including a razor-thin political majority in the House of Commons, a potential Eurosceptic rebellion from within the ranks of his own party, and the certainty of elections which would have to be held by mid-1997.

Not surprisingly, therefore, the Advocate-General's decision was greeted with derision and defiance by the UK government and its backbench Conservative supporters. Eurosceptic MP Bill Cash, for example, suggested that the adoption of the Directive through the QMV provisions of Article 118a was 'typical of the way the Court and Commission operate—using underhand, backdoor methods to bypass sensible working practices'. Indeed, Major himself condemned both the Directive and the Advocate-General's ruling, telling the House of Commons that 'It is precisely because of legislation like this and stupidities like this that the EU is becoming uncompetitive and losing jobs to other parts of the world'.[16] Meeting in early May after the Advocate-General's opinion, the cabinet committee on defence and overseas policy reportedly considered three options in response to a likely ECJ ruling against the UK. First, the ministers 'could bite their collective lip and prepare the necessary legislation' to transpose the Directive into national law, particularly in light of the fact that the Commission's draft proposals had been weakened in response to UK concerns. Second, the government could simply delay the preparation of the implementing legislation pending the next election in mid-1997, one year hence. It was, however, the third and most extreme position that received the most support at the meeting, namely, unilateral non-compliance with the decision, possibly extending the government's 'non-cooperation' strategy beyond the BSE issue to insist upon the overturning of the ECJ ruling at the 1996 intergovernmental conference, due to begin in June.[17]

In short, as Beach (2001: 159–60) points out, the Working Time case raised the prospect of the first overt act of member-state defiance of an ECJ ruling since 1979, when the French government had defied an ECJ ruling on the marketing of sheep meat. As it happened, however, the June meeting of the European Council in Florence witnessed the resolution of the BSE issue and hence an end to the UK's primary grievance against the Union. Perhaps more importantly, the British government's legal advisers indicated to the government that any act of non-compliance would likely be challenged, successfully, in national courts, and that both the government and individual ministers could be held liable under the 'state liability' principle of the *Francovich* decision for losses incurred by individuals as a result of British non-compliance. As a result, the cabinet reversed its earlier position, retreating from its discussion of non-compliance and arguing instead for the (unlikely) aim of seeking to reverse the judgment in the coming intergovernmental conference.[18] Hence, by the eve of the Court's final ruling in November 1996, the probability of overt UK non-compliance had decreased from the 'spring of discontent' described by Beach (2001: 155), and the most likely scenario was one of delay in which the government would begin the process of consultation and drafting implementing legislation but postpone its adoption until after the next election. Nevertheless, the displeasure of the UK government with the Court as a result of the working-time decision and other rulings was evident, and would later lead it to propose a scaling-back of the Court's powers within the intergovernmental conference (see Chapter 3).

We cannot know whether and how the judges of the ECJ considered the prospect of UK defiance of its decision, since its deliberations are secret. In the event, however, the judgment betrays little willingness to accommodate the British position, except on a single, minor, point. On the primary plea raised in the UK action for annulment, namely, the inadequacy of Article 118a as a legal basis for the adoption of working-time regulations, the Court dismissed most of the arguments marshalled by the British government. In response to the UK government's argument that the legal basis of the Directive was defective, the Court prefaced its specific discussion of the Working Time Directive with an extraordinarily broad general interpretation of the scope of Article 118a:

There is nothing [the Court argued] in the wording of Article 118a to indicate that the concepts of 'working environment,' 'safety' and 'health' as used in the provisions should, in the absence of other indications, be interpreted restrictively, and not as embracing all factors, physical or otherwise, capable of affecting the health and safety of the worker in his working environment, including in particular certain aspects of the organization of working time.

On the contrary, the words 'especially in the working environment' militate in favour of a broad interpretation of the powers which Article 118a confers upon the Council for the protection of the health and safety of workers. Moreover, such an interpretation of the words 'safety' and 'health' derives support from the preamble to the Constitution of the World Health Organization to which all Member States belong. Health is there defined as a state of complete physical, mental and social well-being that does not consist only in the absence of illness or infirmity.[19]

Moving from this general reading of Article 118a to the particulars of the case, the Court held that, although the Directive might serve the secondary purpose of facilitating a decline in unemployment, its primary aim as expressed in the text was to protect the health and safety of workers, while the contents of the Directive were similarly geared to the protection of worker health and safety, broadly conceived. The Court similarly dismissed the UK arguments about the alleged breach of the principle of proportionality, the misuse of powers, and the failure to state reasons on the part of the Council. Nevertheless, while the Court declined to annul the Directive in its entirety, it did single out the second sentence of Article 5, which specified that the weekly rest period mandated by the Directive should 'in principle' include a Sunday. Although the Court noted that the question of whether to include Sunday in the weekly rest period was ultimately left to the member states, 'the fact remains that the Council has failed to explain why Sunday, as a weekly rest day, is more closely connected with the health and safety of workers than any other day of the week'. The Court accordingly ruled that the second sentence of Article 5, 'which is severable from the other provisions of the directive, must be annulled'.[20] In sum, the ECJ's ruling vindicated the Commission's broad interpretation of Article 118a, and opened the way for the further innovative use of the workplace health and safety work provisions of the treaty, which have since been used to adopt a wide range of progressive legislation at the Community level.[21] As one Commission official told the *Financial Times* of 13 November 1996 following the decision, 'The Court has endorsed the Commission's decision to stray beyond the traditional definition of health and safety as something to do with hard hats. It has given us a good, broad interpretation of what is meant in the Treaty'. Similarly, Commissioner Flynn, in his press conference following the announcement of the decision, announced that it was 'a good day for Social Europe' and, more concretely, that the Commission would be guided by the Court's broad reading of Article 118a when drafting future proposals (CEC 1996c). By contrast, John Major's government remained defiant, agreeing to begin the process of consultation to implement the Directive in UK law, but simultaneously announcing its intention to reverse the effects of the Directive, reintroduce unanimous voting in health and safety regulation, and reconsider the Court's jurisdiction in the 1996 intergovernmental conference.[22] In addition, Major sent a formal letter to then Commission President Jacques Santer, urging Santer not to propose new legislation under Article 118a until the dispute had been definitively addressed by the forthcoming IGC; Santer, however, replied that 'the Commission retains its right of initiative as provided for by the Treaty, and this also applied to Article 118a' (quoted in *European Report* 1996*b*).

In the event, the Major government found little support for overturning either the Working Time Directive or Article 118a; furthermore, before the conclusion of the conference in June 1997, the new Labour government of Prime Minister Tony Blair reversed Major's position on this issue, agreeing to retain the provisions of Article 118a in the new Article 137 EC and accept the integration into the treaty of the Maastricht Social Protocol, which would henceforth become binding on the UK.[23] For its part, the Commission responded to the decision by issuing a consultative White Paper on the extension of the Directive to the excluded sectors in 1997 (CEC 1997) and later introduced a proposal for an amending Directive for this purpose (CEC 1998), which was adopted by the Council in June 2000 and extends the provisions of the Directive, in modified form and with derogations, to mobile workers, fishermen, offshore workers, and doctors-in-training as of 1 August 2003.[24] As for the original 1993 Directive, the Commission suggests in a recent report 'the compliance of the national measures taken with the Directive is relatively good' with the UK and other member states transposing at least the minimum standards of the Directive, while other member states have retained or established stricter standards (CEC 2000*c*).

Finally, it is worth noting that the Commission's preference for, and strategic use of, legal bases providing for QMV in the Council is not limited to the case of the Working Time Directive. As Joseph Jupille has demonstrated, the Commission and the European Parliament both argue consistently for legal bases that will increase their respective influence on the content of European legislation. Indeed, in examining the subset of 34 procedural disputes that ended before the European Court of Justice, Jupille finds that his hypothesized procedural preference rankings, summarized in Chapter 4, correctly predict 100 per cent of the interventions from both the Commission and the Parliament (Jupille 2000: 145). Looking at the substance of the ECJ's decisions in such cases, moreover, Jupille finds a striking and consistent pattern in which 'the ECJ strongly favors the European Commission, appears generally indifferent to the EP, and strongly disfavors member states and the Council of Ministers'. Specifically, Jupille calculates for each actor the rank difference between the ECJ's choice of legal base and the alternative rule proposed by each actor, once again on a scale from 1 to 9, finding that on average ECJ rulings improve Commission influence by 2.5 rank steps, leave EP influence basically unchanged, and reduce Council influence by 2.6 rank steps (Jupille 2000: 147). Although these findings clearly call for additional study regarding the substance of the various disputes, in the aggregate they suggest that the Commission, like the Parliament and the Council, consistently seeks to increase its legislative powers through the strategic choice of legal bases and that, unlike the Parliament or the Council, it consistently succeeds in doing so before the Court of Justice.

Analysis: A Limited Success for Commission Agenda Setting

To summarize this case study, the role of the Commission, as well as the Court and Parliament, in the adoption of the Working Time Directive once again yields a complex and mixed picture. At one level, the adoption of the Directive under Article 118a despite the staunch resistance of the United Kingdom represents a victory for the agenda-setting powers of the Commission, supported by the Court of Justice in its traditionally broad reading of the treaties. As we have seen, the Commission, with the support of the European Parliament, had repeatedly sought during the 1980s to secure some EC role in the regulation of working time, if only through the soft-law mechanism of a recommendation, but was unable to do so, reflecting its weak agenda-setting powers prior to the adoption of Single European Act. After the entry into force of the SEA, however, the Delors Commission, with its strong vision of a social Europe, moved aggressively to take full advantage of its agenda-setting powers under Article 118a, playing the 'legal base game' and maximizing the impact of the new article in the adoption of legislation like the Working Time and Pregnancy Directives. In this endeavour, moreover, it could count on the support of the European Parliament, which proposed a series of strengthening amendments to the Commission's proposals, and of the European Court of Justice, which upheld Article 118a as the proper legal base for the Directive. Furthermore, as we have seen, the successful adoption of the Working Time Directive and the defeat of the UK legal challenge opened the way for the subsequent adoption of new and progressive Directives under Article 118a and the extension of the Working Time Directive to new sectors following the election of a Labour government in the UK in May 1997.

However, the case of the Working Time Directive also demonstrates the limits of the Commission's agenda-setting powers, limits that arise not only from the formal requirement of a qualified majority in favour of its proposal, which existed already in 1991, but also from the informal practice among the member governments of striving for consensus within the Council. In Lewis' (1998*a*) account, the Working Time Directive constitutes a failure of the 'Community method' since the member governments failed to reach a consensus and the United Kingdom abstained from the final decision, which it then challenged before the ECJ. Nevertheless, as Lewis also points out, the member governments made repeated efforts to achieve such consensus, postponing votes repeatedly and making concessions to the British in an attempt to bring them 'on board' despite their formal ability to outvote the UK on the basis of the Commission's original proposal. Indeed, for our purposes, the Working Time Directive illustrates once again the limits on the Commission's agenda-setting powers imposed by the Council's informal norms of consensus and diffuse reciprocity. In the case of the Blair House agreement analysed in Chapter 5, the Commission failed to secure a qualified majority of the vote primarily because Germany was reluctant to allow France to be outvoted on such a politically charged question, and thus refused to support the Commission. Similarly in the case of the Working Time Directive, the Commission's proposals of 1990 and 1991 would almost certainly have commanded a qualified majority among the member governments in substantive terms, yet the member governments, bound by a norm of diffuse reciprocity and hoping to reach a consensus including the United Kingdom, agreed repeatedly, and unanimously, to amend the Commission's proposals to address the UK's concerns. In the case of the Working Time Directive, the effect was to delay the adoption of the Directive by several years while negotiations continued, and to weaken the Directive that was eventually adopted through the dilution of standards and the insertion of exemptions and derogations. More generally, the Working Time case and the Blair House case together suggest that, in so far as the member governments in the Council conform to norms of consensus and diffuse reciprocity, the ability of the Commission to exploit conflicting preferences and secure the adoption of its preferred legislation by a minimum-winning coalition of member governments—that is, a qualified majority—is substantially weakened. I shall return to this point in the conclusion of the book.

II. The Commission as Executive: The Case of the Structural Funds

In EC parlance, 'structural policy' refers to the administration of the Community's Structural Funds—the European Regional Development Fund, the Social Fund, and the Guidance Section of the European Agricultural Guidance and Guarantee Fund—created primarily to reduce regional disparities in the Community.[25] In the 1970s and the early 1980s, these Funds were essentially a redistributive share-out, agreed as side payments in larger intergovernmental bargains, and the Commission's executive role in implementing the Structural Funds was a minor one. By the mid-1980s, however, the largest contributing member states had become concerned with the efficient expenditure of the increasingly large Structural Funds, especially in the new southern member states of Greece, Spain, and Portugal, and they began pressing for greater control over, and monitoring of, the use of EC funds. For these contributing member states, delegation of powers to the Commission would essentially solve a compliance problem in the efficient expenditure of EU funds in all of the member states, but with an obvious emphasis on the net recipients. The decisions by the member states to incorporate the Structural Funds into the treaties in the Single European Act in 1987 and to double the funds available to them in 1988 further increased the importance of sound financial management in the disbursement and expenditure of the Funds.

In Kingdon's (1984) terms, these calls for greater control created a 'window of opportunity' for a new and more ambitious structural policy, with a greater role for the Commission. And it was in this context that an entrepreneurial Delors Commission again seized the initiative, proposing a series of Structural Fund Regulations that simultaneously increased Community monitoring of Fund expenditures to include 'value for money' while substantially increasing the Commission's role in both the planning and implementation of the Funds, which would henceforth take on a genuine Community dimension. The Commission's proposed reforms, which were adopted with very few amendments by the Council of Ministers, were based on four principles: (1) *concentration* of the Funds' resources in the neediest areas; (2) *partnership* among the Commission, the member governments, and regional authorities in the planning and implementation of the Funds; (3) *programming*, whereby member states would be required to submit comprehensive development programmes for each region rather than individual development projects as in the past; and (4) *additionality*, the principle that any Community funds should be additional to, rather than replace, national development funds in a given area.[26]

Under the 1988 reforms, roughly 90 per cent of the Structural Fund budget went to finance measures proposed by the member states under the Community Support Frameworks (CSFs) devised in partnership by the member governments, the Commission, and the regional authorities designated by member governments. The remaining 10 per cent of the Funds were allocated to 'Community Initiatives' (CIs), EC-wide programmes designed by the Commission to focus on a particular socio-economic problem or a particular type of region. It was these Community Initiatives that provided the Commission with its most important source of power vis-à-vis both national and regional governments. Put simply, with Community Initiatives the Commission were able, with or without the cooperation of regional governments, to present member governments with a given sum of Community funding, for a given purpose and on a take-it-or-leave-it basis.[27] In 1989, for example, the Commission created the Envireg programme, which directed 500 million ecus at Objective 1 regions for environmental protection measures 'which had not always received sufficient consideration within the development plans of some Member States'.[28] In terms of the theory sketched out in Chapter 1, Marc Smyrl (1998) has argued convincingly that the Delors Commission's entrepreneurial proposals for the 1988 Structural Fund reforms qualify as a successful case of informal agenda setting, with the member governments agreeing to an extensive restructuring of the existing Funds and a significant delegation of power to the Commission, whose ambitious use of these powers the member governments had not foreseen.

Commission Activism and Member-State Response:
The RECHAR Controversy

Between 1988 and 1993, the Commission exercised its new powers vigorously, building strong networks to sub-national regions, launching Community Initiatives that reflected the policy agendas of the Commission rather than the member states, and insisting that all member states satisfy the additionality principle. Indeed, in the most famous case of conflict under the 1988 reforms, the Commission's insistence on additionality in the granting of aid brought it into direct conflict with the British government of Prime Minister John Major. In that case, the Commission designed a Community Initiative programme, dubbed RECHAR, the benefits of which would accrue largely to coal-mining regions in Scotland. In order to secure these benefits, however, the UK government would have to satisfy the Commission regarding the proper application of the principle of additionality as laid down in Article 9 of the 1988 framework Regulation for the Structural Funds. When the UK government refused to do so, Commissioner Bruce Millan froze the UK funds, creating a political confrontation between the Commission and Major's government. Finally, in response to pressure from the Commission above and regional governments below, and with a general election looming, Major's government backed down and agreed to the Commission's demands in return for its share of RECHAR funding. For many analysts, this RECHAR incident became emblematic of the Commission's renewed power and influence vis-à-vis even the most powerful member states (McAleavey 1993; Marks 1993). In the RECHAR case, as with Envireg and other Community Initiatives, member governments complained that the Commission was either interfering in internal affairs or duplicating efforts already under way within the CSFs; but, faced with the possible loss of EC funding, member governments typically gave in and participated in these programmes on the Commission's terms.

Despite the Commission's initial victory in the RECHAR controversy, its position vis-à-vis the member governments was fundamentally weakened by the fact that the 1988 Fund Regulations, and hence its own executive powers, were set to expire at the end of 1993 and required a unanimous vote from the member governments for re-authorization—the EU equivalent of a US 'sunset provision'. In Scharpf's (1988) terms, the default condition for the Commission's powers was not the status quo but expiration, meaning that a positive decision would be required to re-authorize the Commission's powers through a new framework Regulation to be adopted by 31 December 1993. Under the rules of the Single European Act, moreover, the unanimous agreement of the Council would be required for the adoption of the framework Regulation establishing the priorities and procedures to be employed in all three Funds. These decision rules considerably strengthened the position of member governments— including, but not solely, the British government—seeking to clip the Commission's wings by demanding substantial changes in the Fund Regulations. And indeed, the various EU member governments, as well as the Court of Auditors and the European Parliament, had in the interim expressed a number of complaints about the implementation of the 1988 reforms. These included, *inter alia*, at least four major issues.[29]

First, a number of member governments complained, and the Commission itself acknowledged, that the three-stage planning system laid down in the 1988 Regulations—namely, the drawing up of national development plans by member states, the adoption of CSFs by the Commission in cooperation with the member states and regions, and the submission and approval of Operational Programmes (OPs)—had created unnecessary bureaucracy for member governments and should be simplified.

Second, many national policy-makers complained about the system for designating the regions eligible for assistance under Objectives 2 and 5b, whereby the Commission identified the eligible regions under the conditions specified in the Fund Regulations. It was argued that area coverage was fragmented and that lack of coordination between DG XVI (regional policy) and DG IV (competition) led to discrepancies between regions designated as eligible for EC Structural Funds and those regarded as eligible for national state aids under EC competition policy. The member states therefore recommended greater coordination within the Commission as well as a greater role for member governments in the designation of Objective 2 and 5b regions within their respective territories (Yuill *et al.* 1993: 74).

Third, in keeping with their ongoing concerns with 'value for money', northern member states, led by the UK, continued to demand more effective *ex ante* assessment and *ex post* monitoring and evaluation of programmes. In this specific area, and notwithstanding the RECHAR controversy, the United Kingdom in particular remained an advocate of delegating significant implementing powers to the Commission.

Fourth, and rather predictably, there was widespread irritation among the member states, not simply the UK, with the Community Initiatives. Most member states, for example, argued that there were too many CIs and that each of these individual CIs spread a small amount of EC funding across a wide area, decreasing their effectiveness. The bureaucratic requirements for these initiatives, moreover, remained equally onerous for the member states regardless of the size of the programmes, with the result that a large proportion of these funds were spent on administration. Most importantly, however,

...policy-makers believe strongly that there is too little consultation with Member States regarding the introduction of CIs. Indeed, the negotiation process has been described as a 'complete sham' with the predominance of self-interest. Member States say that they are often taken completely by surprise when new CIs are launched. However, Member States and regions have a vested interest in receiving as much EC finance as possible, and it is difficult for them to object constructively to Commission proposals without harming their changes of obtaining funding. Policy-makers are frequently under political pressure, especially at regional levels, to apply for and use CI funds regardless of whether the money is limited and the measures are inappropriate or undesirable. (Yuill *et al.* 1993: 77)

Thus, by 1993, the member governments had a clear incentive to reassert control over this least predictable and controllable aspect of the 1988 reforms—and would indeed do so, as we shall see.

Negotiating the 1993 Structural Fund Reforms

In early 1993, following the adoption of the Delors II budgetary perspectives for 1993–9 at the Edinburgh European Council, the Commission submitted proposals for the new Fund Regulations, which were described by the Commission as largely a continuation of the principles of the 1988 reforms, with several administrative changes to improve the efficiency of the Funds.[30]

Put simply, the Commission proposed to retain the four basic principles of the 1988 reforms while making slight changes to each. Briefly, these principles, and the proposed changes, are as follows:

1. *Concentration* of the Funds' resources on the neediest areas. Here, in keeping with the agreement of the Edinburgh European Council, the four poorest EU member states were promised a doubling of their receipts from the Structural and Cohesion Funds combined; within the Structural Funds themselves, the share of the Funds directed to Objective 1 regions would rise from 63 per cent to 70 per cent by 1999.
2. *Partnership.* Here the provisions would be altered only slightly by specifying that the social partners, that is, representatives of industry and trade unions as chosen by the member governments, could take part in the design and implementation of the Funds, in partnership with the Commission, the regions, and the member states.
3. *Programming.* Largely in response to member-state complaints, the Commission proposed a simplification of the planning procedure, reducing the existing three-stage plan to two stages, by allowing member governments to submit their national development plans and their applications for Operational Programmes in a single document.
4. *Additionality.* The wording of the additionality provisions, as laid down in Article 9 of the draft Coordination Regulation, would,

unlike the 1988 Regulation, specify the criterion for meeting the additionality requirement and the obligations of the Member States in this regard. Thus, for each Objective, 'the Commission and Member State concerned shall ensure that the Member State maintains, in the whole of the territory concerned, its public structural or comparable assistance at least at the same level as in the previous programming period taking into account, however, the macroeconomic circumstances in which the funding takes place including the implementation of convergence programmes [for EMU]'.

Finally, with regard to the Community Initiatives, the Commission had proposed in its initial communications that 15 per cent of the Funds' resources go to the CIs. In December 1992, however, the Edinburgh European Council indicated that the CIs should comprise between 5 per cent and 10 per cent of the Funds, and the Commission, predictably, proposed the high end of this range, 10 per cent for the CIs from 1994 to 1999. With regard to the working of CIs, the Commission suggested that these would be fewer in number and organized around a specific set of priorities. The Commission also proposed some minor administrative changes which would allow a small portion of the funds to be spent outside the traditional Objectives 1, 2, and 5b areas and allow two or more member states to file a single application for cross-border initiatives such as INTERREG.

Many of these proposals were intended to address the concerns of various member governments about the operation of the 1988 Fund Regulations, expressed both informally and in the conclusions of the Maastricht Treaty and the Edinburgh European Council. In the event, however, these Commission proposals did not go far enough to address the concerns of the member governments,[31] which proceeded to change the substance of the Commission's proposals in several non-trivial ways so as to respond to concerns about the distribution of funds, efficiency, and above all member-state control of the Funds' operation. Five specific changes, of varying importance, deserve particular attention here.

First, largely at the insistence of the UK, the wording of the provisions for monitoring and assessment were strengthened, with more detailed monitoring procedures and more explicit requirements for both prior appraisal and *ex post* evaluation. With regard to prior appraisal, the Council draft, unlike the Commission version, specifies that 'Assistance will be allocated where appraisal shows medium-term economic and social benefits commensurate with the resources deployed'. Furthermore, in an interesting twist, whereas the Commission draft had specified that 'Assessment shall primarily be the responsibility of the member states', the Council changed the wording of the relevant Article to associate the Commission with the process of appraisal and evaluation. These changes clearly reflected the concerns of the contributing member states to ensure rigorous evaluation, and Commission supervision, of expenditures in all the member states in order to ensure 'value for money'. Once again, in this single regard, the 1993 framework Regulation actually *strengthened* Commission powers above and beyond those of the 1988 Regulations.

Second, at the insistence of the UK, France, and Germany, member states were given a greater role in the designation of Objective 2 and 5b regions. Thus, whereas Article 9 of the Commission's proposed Framework Regulation simply had the Commission draw up a list of Objective 2 regions, the final version of Article 9 as adopted by the Council has each member state proposing to the Commission a list of Objective 2 areas, on the basis of which, 'in close consultation with the member state concerned', the Commission then adopts the final list of Objective 2 areas. A similar system was established for Objective 5b areas.

Third, the wording of the Commission's provisions on additionality was altered. The definition of additionality in terms of expenditure during the previous programming period was retained from the Commission's proposal, but whereas the Commission proposal specified that this definition should take into account macroeconomic circumstances and convergence policy, the Council's final draft added: 'as well as a number of specific economic circumstances, namely privatizations, an unusual level of public structural expenditure undertaken in the previous programming period and business cycles in the national economy.' The effect of this new definition was to leave member governments more room than the Commission's original draft to decrease structural expenditure without violating the additionality provisions, in keeping with the strong preferences of the UK and other member governments.

Fourth, the section of the Regulation dealing with partnership—often identified along with the additionality provisions as the most radical elements of the 1988 Regulations since they allowed the Commission to build direct, multi-level links with subnational regions—was amended to strengthen the 'gatekeeper' role of the member governments, noting explicitly that the designation of appropriate sub-national partners within each member state would remain the responsibility of the member governments rather than the Commission or the sub-national regions themselves.

Fifth and finally, the Council amended the Commission's provisions regarding the Community Initiatives. Thus, for example, the amount to be devoted to the CIs was reduced from 10 per cent to 9 per cent of the total Structural Fund budget. More importantly, the Council created *de novo*, in a new Article 29a of the Coordination Regulation, a Management Committee for the Community Initiatives. Under the Management Committee procedure, the Commission would adopt Community Initiatives which would apply immediately, but these initiatives would have to be submitted to the Management Committee, which could approve or reject them by a qualified majority; if the committee rejected the Commission's proposals, the Council could, acting within a month of the committee vote, take a different decision by QMV. Predictably, therefore, the Commission openly 'deplored' the creation of the new Management Committee.[32] In the event, the new Management Committee approved the Commission's proposals for new CIs, but the existence of such a committee meant that the Commission could stray only so far from the wishes of the member governments without risking having its decision overturned by the Council of Ministers.[33]

Put simply, the 1993 Fund Regulations decreased Commission discretion in two ways, by imposing new administrative procedures limiting the scope of the Commission's mandate and by tightening oversight procedures through more restrictive comitology. As a result of these changes, and by contrast with the Commission's forcefulness in during the 1988–93 period, the Community Initiatives adopted for the period 1994–9 under the new Fund Regulations were subject to an extended consultation with the member governments, the EP, and other interested actors such as regional and local authorities and the social partners. By contrast with the striking independence of the Commission in the selection of the early CIs, the Commission in June of 1993 published a consultative 'Green Paper' on the future of the Community Initiatives, which proposed a trimmed-down series of initiatives concentrated in five priority areas: cross-border and inter-regional cooperation, rural development, outermost regions, employment and vocational training, and adaptation to industrial change. This initial list of objectives and programmes was then modified, however, after consultation with the member states and the EP, to include new initiatives on fishing (PESCA) and urban problems (URBAN), and, in response to the intergovernmental bargain struck over GATT ratification in December 1993, on a 400 million-ecus aid programme for the Portuguese textiles industry (CEC 1994a). These revised proposals, for 13 initiatives spread over seven priority areas, were then approved by the new Management Committee and formally adopted by the Commission in June 1994 (CEC 1993*b*).

Similarly, and notwithstanding the more far-reaching claims that the 1988 fund reforms signalled the development of a multi-level 'Europe of the Regions', a growing number of empirical studies have demonstrated that, far from outflanking the member governments, the inclusion of sub-national governments in the Structural Funds has very much mirrored the priorities and the prior experiences of the individual member governments. Thus, for example, as Hooghe (1996) and her collaborators have demonstrated, inclusion of sub-national regions in the planning and implementation of the Funds has been most advanced in federal Germany and Belgium, where regional governments have indeed established direct contacts with the Commission and offices in Brussels, and least advanced in unitary states like Greece and the United Kingdom, where national governments retain their key positions as a gatekeepers between the Commission and sub-national governments.[34]

Analysis: Delegation, Activism, and Discipline

To sum up the Structural Funds case, the Commission was able in 1988 to capitalize on widespread member-state concerns about 'value for money' to receive significant new powers to draw up Community Initiatives, to play a central role in drawing up CSFs with the member governments and the regions concerned, and to police the expenditure and the additionality of EC funds. During the five-year lifespan of the 1988 Fund Regulations, Millan and the Commission used these delegated powers aggressively, funding Community Initiatives in line with the Commission's own policy agenda and coming into direct conflict with the United Kingdom over the issue of additionality. Given the significant planning and policing powers of the Commission and the requirement of unanimity to alter such powers, the Commission was able effectively to put its own stamp on the previously intergovernmental Structural Funds. In 1993, however, the Commission's delegated powers for structural policy were scheduled to expire, and the unanimity voting rule favoured reformers like the UK, which successfully insisted on changes to the 1993 Fund Regulations in line with their own preferences.

Finally, it is worth noting that the subsequent reform of the Structural Fund Regulations in 1999 continued this process of partial 'renationalization'. Like the previous Fund Regulations, the 1999 reforms were adopted after the European Council's adoption of a seven-year financial perspective for the period from 2000 to 2006, during which Structural Fund expenditures are to be maintained at a rate of 0.46 per cent of the Union's collective GDP, which constitutes a consolidation of the 1999 funding level. Like the previous Fund reforms, the 1999 Regulations are designed to simplify existing procedures, most notably by reducing the total number of priority objectives from six to three and the total number of Community Initiatives from 13 to four; and to guarantee value for money with the creation of a so-called 'performance reserve' constituting 4 per cent of each member state's total funding which will be held back by the Commission until the halfway point in the current funding cycle and allocated to the most efficient programmes within the respective member states. In addition to these Commission-proposed reforms, however, the member governments once again amended the Commission's draft proposals, adopting additional reforms guaranteeing them greater control over the designation of eligible regions, the selection of sub-national partners, the principle of additionality, and the size and content of the Community Initiatives. With regard to additionality, the new Regulations continued to identify additionality as a core principle of the Funds, but the flexible language of the 1993 Regulation was again retained, and the member governments explicitly removed the Commission's reference to additionality as one of the criteria for the allocation of the new performance reserve. Most strikingly, the member governments reduced the funds available for Community Initiatives from 9 per cent to only 6 per cent of the budget, and earmarked nearly half of this amount for a single initiative, INTERREG, thereby drastically reducing the Commission's discretion in the allocation of the Funds.[35]

In sum, the Commission's initial success in securing the adoption of the 1988 Structural Fund reforms and in aggressively implementing its own priorities during the period from 1988 to 1993 met with a member-state backlash and partial legislative overrule in the 1993 and 1999 Fund reforms, largely because the default condition in this case—expiration of the Fund Regulations—strengthened the hand of member governments unhappy with the previous activism of the Commission. Nevertheless, as Sutcliffe (2000) points out, neither the 1993 nor the 1999 Regulations have entirely renationalized the Funds. Notwithstanding the partial rewriting of the Commission's mandate and the narrowing of its discretion between 1988 and 1999, the Commission retains considerable powers and discretion in the implementation of the Structural Funds and indeed gained some limited additional powers in both reforms relating to the proper expenditure of EU funds by member governments. We may therefore expect that the Commission will continue to pursue its own, 'European' preferences in the implementation of the Structural Funds, albeit within a zone of discretion narrower than that of the 1988–93 period.

III. *The Court of Justice and Equal Pay:*
The Barber *Decision*

The 1957 EEC Treaty did not provide for a Community policy on equal opportunities between men and women, nor did it establish a specific legal basis for the adoption of Community rules in this area. Indeed, although the original EEC Treaty did contain a chapter on social policy, these provisions in the original Articles 117 and 118 EEC, now the heavily amended Articles 136 and 137 EC, were essentially a non-binding expression of social aspirations rather than a set of commitments that were legally binding on the member governments. Nevertheless, in spite of the general weakness of the social provisions in the Treaties of Rome, equal pay for men and women emerged as an important point in the negotiations among the framers of the EEC Treaty and as one of the few legally binding social commitments in the form of Article 119 EEC, now Article 141 EC, as amended, whose interpretation was left to the Court of Justice in one of its most active and contested lines of jurisprudence. In this final case study, I analyse the origins of Article 141 (ex 119) EC in the negotiations among the founding member states and the Court's broad interpretation of the meaning of that article in its initial case law, before focusing on the Court's controversial decision in the 1991 *Barber* case, the member-state response, and the Court's subsequent case law. As we shall see, the Court's interactions with its member-state principals have been more openly conflictual, and the limits of its discretion more evident, than in the free-movement cases analysed in Chapter 5.

Article 141 (ex 119) and the ECJ

The origins of Article 119 EEC lay not in the generalized commitment of the member governments in 1957 to women's rights—indeed, no such commitment existed at the time—but primarily in French concerns that different national standards regarding equal pay for men and women could serve to distort economic competition among the member states. Specifically, the French government feared that France's domestic requirement of equal pay for men and women would disadvantage French firms vis-à-vis firms in other member states, especially Italy, where no equal pay laws existed and the costs of female labour were correspondingly lower. Within the inter-governmental conference negotiating the Rome Treaties, therefore, and notwithstanding the German opposition in the IGC to any inter-ference in the area of wages and prices, France successfully pressed for a legally binding commitment among the member states to equal pay for men and women, which appeared in the treaty as Article 119 EEC and required that 'Each Member State shall during the first stage [that is, by 1 January 1962] ensure and subsequently maintain the applica-tion of the principle that men and women should receive equal pay for equal work'. As Catherine Barnard (1996: 327) summarizes the his-torical record, 'Article 119 was included in the Treaty for economic purposes; any social benefits were merely an advantageous con-sequence of the desire to avoid distortions of competition'.

Furthermore, Article 119 itself lay dormant for much of the first two decades of the Community's history, regarded by most analysts as an aspiration rather a firm legal obligation upon member govern-ments which might in turn confer directly effective rights upon indi-viduals in the member states. Thus, although the Treaty established a deadline of 1 January 1962 by which the principle of equal pay was to have been fully implemented in the member states, in practice the implementation of that principle continued to vary significantly across member states after the deadline, and the Commission, despite threats to initiate infringement proceedings against the member states, took no such action during the 1960s or 1970s.

However, as Evelyn Ellis (1998) and others[36] have recounted in great detail, Article 141 was in effect 'activated' by a series of preliminary ref-erences brought before the ECJ by national courts seeking to clarify its legal status and effect within the member states. The landmark case, by all accounts, was the second *Defrenne* judgment, handed down by the Court in 1976.[37] The case concerned a Belgian flight attendant, Ms Defrenne, who had been paid a lower wage by her employer, Sabena Airlines, than male 'cabin stewards' doing the same work. In her case, Ms Defrenne claimed that this unequal pay for men and women con-stituted a violation of Article 141, which was to have been legally bind-ing throughout the Community from 1962. In this case, as in two other cases brought by or on behalf of Ms Defrenne, the Belgian tribunal hearing the case sent a request for a preliminary ruling to the Court of Justice, asking whether the Article 141 was directly effective and con-ferred rights on individuals within the national legal orders, notwith-standing the absence of national implementing legislation, and if so from what date. Intervening in the case, the governments of the United Kingdom and Ireland both argued forcefully that Article 119 was not intended to be directly effective but required implementing legislation within the member states. Furthermore, both governments pointed out, a retroactive application of the principle of equal pay within the member states would be economically devastating for employers, driving many into bankruptcy and exerting a negative impact of the economies of the member states. Nevertheless, the Court ruled in *Defrenne II* that Article 141 pursued both an economic aim of removing economic distortions to competition and a social aim of improving the living and working standards of EC citizens; as such, the Court continued, 'the principle of equal pay forms part of the foundations of the Community' and should therefore be interpreted broadly rather than restrictively. Furthermore, in conferring a clear and unequivocal obligation upon the member governments, Article 141 also conveyed legal rights upon individual women and men, and as such was directly effective in national legal orders, both horizontally against individual employers and vertically against member governments. In so ruling, however, the Court conceded that the direct effect of Article 141 might not have been clear to employers before the date of the decision, and the Commission's failure to initiate infringement proceedings 'was likely to consolidate the incorrect impression as to the effects of Article 119'.[38] Given this previous lack of clarity and the potentially adverse economic effects of a retroactive application of the article as pointed out by the UK and Ireland, the Court decided to limit the retroactive effect of the decision, which could therefore be relied on only in respect of periods of pay after the date of the decision, on 8 April 1976, except in regard to individuals who had initiated legal proceedings before that date.

Notwithstanding the Court's limitation on the retroactive effects of the decision, *Defrenne II* was a landmark decision in its declaration that Article 141 was directly effective within the national legal orders of the member states and thereby conferred not only legal obligations upon the member states but legal rights upon individual women and men. In the years following *Defrenne*, a growing number of individual litigants sought to assert their right to equal pay under Article 141, resulting in a steady stream of far-reaching ECJ decisions which interpreted the meaning of terms such as 'pay', 'equal work', and 'discrimination' in Article 141. Despite the broad language of the original Article 119, which defined pay as 'the ordinary basis or minimum wage or salary and any other consideration, whether in cash or kind, which the worker receives, directly or indirectly, in respect of his employment from his employer', the Court had begun in the first (1971) *Defrenne* decision with a conservative step, declaring that national government-sponsored social security systems fell outside the concept of pay as defined by Article 141. Such 'social security schemes or benefits, in particular pensions, directly governed by legislation without any element of agreement with the undertaking or the occupational branch concerned, which are obligatorily applicable to general categories of workers' did not fall within the concept of pay in Article 141, being determined 'less by the employment relationship between the employer and the worker than by considerations of social policy'.[39] In effect, the Court was acknowledging the right of member governments to pay unequal pensions and other benefits to men and women on social-policy grounds, and restricting the concept of pay to those benefits resulting directly from the employment relationship between a worker—or a group of workers, in the case of collective bargaining—and her or his employer. With this significant exception, however, the Court went on in later decisions to adopt a broad interpretation of the concept of pay, which was not confined to basic pay but included overtime pay, special bonus payments, health and insurance benefits, travel expenses, expatriation allowances, company cars, and any other 'consideration' that an employee receives 'in respect of his employment' (Ellis 1998: 64–9). Perhaps most importantly for our purposes, the Court ruled in the 1984 *Bilka* decision that, notwithstanding the previous exclusion of national social security schemes from the concept of pay, employer-funded supplementary pension schemes, which provide benefits above and beyond those offered by state schemes, *do* constitute pay within the meaning of Article 141, and women must therefore be granted equal access to such schemes on the same terms as their male counterparts.

In addition to the gradual expansion of the definition of pay in Article 141, the Court's rulings expanded the effect of the article in other ways, most obviously by interpreting broadly the concept of discrimination to include not only direct discrimination but also indirect discrimination against women, for example by systematically paying full-time and part-time workers differently, if and in so far as women represent the vast majority of part-time workers and men the majority of full-time workers.[40]

Counterfactually, it its highly unlikely that EC member governments would have adopted legislation implementing the direct effect of the original Article 119, the expansion of the concept of pay, and the expansion of the concept of discrimination to include indirect as well as direct discrimination, in the absence of these crucial ECJ decisions.

In this sense, most analysts agree, the Court's expansive interpretation of the article almost certainly exerted an independent causal effect on the integration process and on political outcomes within the member states, where private litigants have moved, albeit at an uneven pace across member states, to enforce their rights through national courts (Ellis 1998; Cichowski 1998; Stone Sweet and Caporaso 1998). Nevertheless, while the Court's decisions appeared to run ahead of the Community legislator—the Council—in decisions like *Defrenne II*, analysts dubious of the Court's independence and causal impact have pointed to the contemporary legislative activism of the Council, which from the mid-1970s onwards adopted a number of Directives not only on equal pay but also on equal treatment in the workplace, which in some instances went beyond the Article 141 decisions of the Court and indicate a willingness of the member governments to legislate progressive sex equality Directives during this period. At the very least, it is fair to say that, despite their far-reaching nature, the Court's rulings in the *Defrenne II* and other cases did not prompt a backlash from the member governments, which made few if any political attacks on the Court and no attempts to overturn the effects of ECJ decisions through amendment of Article 141, during the 1970s and 1980s.[41] By contrast, the Court's progressive ruling in the 1991 *Barber* decision, extending the scope of equal pay in Article 141 to occupational social security schemes, did occasion such controversy; the rest of this section is therefore devoted to a detailed analysis of the Court's decision in *Barber*, the member-state response with the adoption of the so-called 'Barber Protocol' to the Maastricht Treaty, and the subsequent rulings of the ECJ, to elucidate the preferences of the various actors and the extent of ECJ responsiveness to member-state demands.

The Barber *Decision and Protocol*

Douglas Harvey Barber v. Guardian Royal Exchange Assurance Group, like *Defrenne* and many other equal-pay cases, was brought by an individual litigant—in this case, a man—before a national court, which in turn referred a set of five questions of EC law for interpretation by the Court of Justice. Mr Barber was a long-time employee of the Guardian Royal Exchange Assurance Group, a UK insurance firm, when he was compulsorily retired in 1980 at the age of 52. As an employee, Barber was also a member of Guardian's occupational pension scheme, an employer-funded scheme which was 'contracted-out' from the UK social security system and provided more generous benefits than the state scheme. Upon his forced retirement, Barber was offered a one-time redundancy payment, but not an immediate pension, which was deferred, in keeping with company rules, until the age of 62. Under the national social security system, the normal pensionable age for men (65) was higher than that for women (60), a difference reproduced in the Guardian pension scheme which featured a retirement age of 62 for men but only 57 for women, with the result that, under company rules regarding compulsory retirement, a 52-year-old woman in his situation would have been entitled to an immediate pension while Barber himself was forced to wait ten years to begin receiving his pension. Barber therefore considered that he had fallen victim to discrimination on the basis of sex, and instituted proceedings against Guardian for breach of the UK Sex Discrimination Act. Despite losing his initial case and a first appeal before an employment tribunal, Barber and later his widow pursued another appeal to the British Court of Appeal, which asked the ECJ to give a preliminary ruling on five questions of EC law, the most important of which asked whether the definition of 'pay' under Article 141 extended to contracted-out occupational pension schemes.[42]

The question whether occupational pension schemes should be considered as 'pay' within the meaning of Article 141 was not a new one for the Court. In the first *Defrenne* decision in 1975, the Court had considered whether employer contributions to statutory social security schemes established by the member governments constituted 'pay' within the meaning of Article 141. Although such social security benefits are not 'in principle alien' to the concept of pay, the Court decided, employer contributions to state social security schemes benefiting general categories of workers are determined primarily by national social policies rather than by the employment relationship, and therefore do not constitute 'a direct or indirect payment to the worker'.[43] Later, however, in the 1984 *Bilka* decision, the Court ruled that supplementary pension schemes funded by an employer and incorporated into the contract between the employer and employee do indeed constitute pay within the meaning of Article 141, and are therefore subject to the equal-pay provisions of the latter.[44] The question to be decided in *Barber* concerned the possible extension of the concept of pay to include not only private, contractual pension schemes but also contracted-out schemes designed not to supplement to a state social security scheme but as a substitute for part of it. This question had been put to the Court in the 1981 *Worringham* case, with Advocate-General Warner suggesting that, as a substitute for a state social-security scheme, contracted-out schemes such as the one in question should not be considered to constitute pay within the meaning of Article 141.

In its final decision, however, the ECJ decided the case on different grounds, thereby avoiding the issue of the status of contacted-out pension schemes as pay.[45] Precedent for the Court's decision in *Barber* was, therefore, unclear, although Advocate-General Van Gerven for his part suggested that Article 141 should be interpreted to extend to contracted-out pension schemes and to pensionable ages in so far as such schemes were specific to the employees of a particular company and their terms established access to an important part of the employee's overall payment package.[46]

Article 141 and the resulting case law, however, did not constitute the only precedent in this area, for the Council of Ministers, acting as the Community legislator, had adopted two Directives—a 1979 Directive on equal treatment in social security[47] and a more specific 1986 Directive on equal treatment in occupational social security schemes[48]—with explicit provisions regarding the equalization of pensionable ages. During the negotiation of these Directives, the member governments had been unable to agree on provisions regarding the equalization of pensionable ages for men and women. Both Directives therefore provide explicit derogations from the principle of equal treatment for the 'determination of pensionable age for the purpose of granting old-age or retirement pensions, and the possible implications for other benefits' (Hervey 1994: 329). Indeed, in its defence, Guardian pointed to the exemption in Article 9 as justification for its—and the UK government's—practice of applying different retirement ages to men and women. Thus, an ECJ ruling that occupational social security schemes constitute pay within the meaning of Article 141, and therefore that unequal pension benefits or retirement ages are inconsistent with the treaties, would constitute an explicit repudiation of the long-standing derogations in these two Directives.

In addition to the question of precedent,[49] Garrett, Kelemen, and Schulz (1998) and other principal-agent analyses also direct our attention to the preferences of EU member governments, which might act as a deterrent to an integrationist decision by the Court if either unilateral non-compliance by a member state or collective overturning of a decision by the member-states appears likely. As it happened, the British government did intervene before the Court in the *Barber* case, insisting that the derogation in the 1986 Directive provided legal justification for the differential treatment of men and women regarding pensionable ages and emphasizing strongly the potentially disastrous financial consequences of the Court's ruling for private pension schemes in the United Kingdom. Although no other member governments took the opportunity to intervene in the *Barber* proceedings, the potential financial consequences of an expansive ruling in *Barber* were also highlighted by private firms and pension funds, which calculated that UK pension funds alone could face an immediate bill of up to £30 billion, with an additional bill of £2 billion a year thereafter, if the Court required the equalization of pension benefits and pensionable ages in its decision. The Court's decision was therefore anticipated with widespread anxiety both by governments and by the politically powerful pensions lobby in the various member states, and the financial as well as political consequences of a far-reaching decision should therefore have been clear to the Court in its deliberations.[50]

Despite this clear expression of preferences by the UK and private interests, the Court ruled in *Barber* that contracted-out occupational pension schemes constituted pay within the meaning of Article 141, and that discrimination between men and women within such schemes was therefore contrary to the treaties. In addition, the Court made explicit for the first time that the setting of different retirement ages for men and women constituted discrimination and was therefore forbidden by Article 141, which as primary law overrode the derogations contained in the secondary-law provisions of the 1979 and 1986 Directives.[51] In effect, the Court continued and built upon its previous, expansive interpretation of Article 141, and decided with the plaintiff and the Commission against the defendant and, indirectly, the UK government. However, in a now-infamous provision, the Court opted to impose a temporal limitation on the effects of its judgment. In the decision, the Court pointed explicitly to the derogations contained in the 1979 and 1986 Directives, noting that 'In the light of those provisions, the Member States and the parties concerned were reasonably entitled to consider that Article 119 did not apply to pensions paid under contracted-out schemes and that derogations from the principle of equality between men and women were still permitted in that sphere'.[52] Under the circumstances, the Court continued, 'overriding considerations of legal certainty preclude legal situations which have exhausted all their effects in the past from being called into question where that might upset retroactively the financial balance of many contracted-out schemes'.[53] The Court therefore opted to follow its earlier example in *Defrenne II*, as well as the advice of the Commission in its intervention, limiting the retroactive effect of the decision as follows:

It must therefore be held that the direct effect of Article 119 [now 141] of the Treaty may not be relied upon in order to claim entitlement to a pension with effect from a date prior to that of this judgement, except in the case of workers or those claiming under them who have before that date initiated legal proceedings or raised an equivalent claim under the applicable national law.[54]

The Court's reasoning in this paragraph has been much criticized in both the legal literature and in political discourse for being vague and open to multiple interpretations, with potentially enormous financial implications for pension schemes throughout the EU. As Advocate-General Van Gerven would point out in a later opinion, the Court's decision in *Barber* could be interpreted in any of four distinct ways. The first and most conservative interpretation would apply the principle of equal treatment only to workers who became members of an occupational pension scheme as from 17 May 1990, depriving the *Barber* ruling of almost all retroactive effect. A second interpretation would have the principle of equal treatment applied to payments payable in respect of periods of service after 17 May 1990 for all workers, regardless of the date of their membership. In a third interpretation, the principle of equal treatment would be applied to all pensions payable for the first time after 17 May 1990; while the fourth and most far-reaching interpretation would apply the principle of equal treatment to all pension payments made after that date.[55] Clearly, the range of possible interpretations of the *Barber* ruling was wide, with enormous legal and financial consequences for workers and pension funds depending on the interpretation ultimately selected by the Court in later, clarifying cases.

The reasons for the Court's vagueness on this point have been the subject of much speculation, with some authors suggesting that it reflected an oversight on the part of the Court (Arnull 2000: 473), while others have suggested that the Court deliberately made a vague ruling in order to determine the reaction of the member governments before specifying the implications of the ruling in greater detail (Garrett, Kelemen, and Schulz 1998). In any event, the UK and other member governments did not wait for the Court to elaborate upon its ruling in *Barber*, as it was expected to do in a series of cases referred by national courts in the UK, the Netherlands, and Germany in the course of 1991, but moved to limit the effects of the judgment through a dramatic and unprecedented revision of the treaty as part of the 1991 intergovernmental conference culminating in the Maastricht Treaty. Specifically, on the eve of the Maastricht summit in December 1991, the Dutch government—which held the rotating Presidency of the Community, as well as facing a potentially enormous financial cost to its large and influential private pension industry—introduced a draft text for a protocol limiting the effects of the *Barber* decision to benefits earned in respect of employment after 17 May 1990. Although strongly supported by the UK and German governments, the Dutch protocol was initially rejected by the Italian, Belgian, French, and

Danish governments, whose pensions funds were already subject to equal pensionable ages under national law.[56] In effect, the negotiating positions of the member governments lined up predictably in accordance with the interests of their respective pension industries and with little or no regard for the overall intergovernmentalist or supranational complexion of the various governments. Nevertheless, the latter governments later dropped their opposition in the final bargaining session of the Maastricht summit, and the six-line provision was adopted as the 'Protocol Concerning Article 119 of the Treaty Establishing the European Community' and attached to the Treaty of Maastricht. The protocol reads, in its entirety, as follows:

For the purposes of Article 119 [now 141] of this Treaty, benefits under occupational social security schemes shall not be considered as remuneration if and in so far as they are attributable to periods of employment prior to 17 May 1990, except in the case of workers or those claiming under them who have before that date initiated legal proceedings under the applicable national law.

In effect, the member governments had chosen the second of the four interpretations outlined above, thereby clarifying and limiting the potential liabilities of pension funds throughout the EU. Although greeted with relief and enthusiasm by private pension funds in the UK and elsewhere (Cohen and Hill 1991; Cowie 1991; Dobie 1991), the adoption of the Protocol was controversial in the legal and women's rights communities (Hervey 1994; Hunter 1991), and its immediate and long-term effects remained unclear. Some critics, like Tamara Hervey (1994: 330) have suggested that the Protocol 'effectively restor[ed] the political compromise found in the provisions of the [1979 and 1986] Directives' since the principle of equal pay would be enforced only for benefits dating from May of 1990, and the full effect of the decision would be felt only after 40 years, that is, a pensionable lifetime of work following the *Barber* decision. In fact, full equality with regard to occupational pensions will indeed take decades to achieve, but the Protocol does not restore the *status quo ante* under which both member governments and private actors had enjoyed an *indefinite* derogation from the principle of equal pay for occupational pensions.

In addition, Hervey and others pointed out, the legal status of the Protocol posed a more far-reaching series of questions about the constitutional status of the Court and its relation to the member states. Was the Protocol an amendment to Article 141, as some analysts suggested, or were the member governments engaging in an unconstitutional usurpation of the Court's powers as the definitive interpreter of the treaties? How would, or should, the Court respond to the

Protocol in its subsequent decisions? Most broadly, did the unprecedented nature of the Barber Protocol represent a political backlash
against the Court, possibly prompting the Court to retreat from the
judicial activism of its past, as several distinguished scholars and jurists
(Mancini and Keeling 1995; Renaud Dehousse 1999) suggested?
Although the last of these questions, analysing the broad scope of ECJ
jurisprudence following the Maastricht Treaty, is beyond the scope of
the present chapter,[57] we can nevertheless examine the Court's post-
Maastricht rulings applying Article 141 to contracted-out occupational
pension schemes, to determine whether these rulings constituted a
continuation of, or a retreat from, the Court's previous positions.

The Court's Subsequent Article 141 Decisions: Retreat or Advance?

As noted above, the lack of clarity of the *Barber* ruling prompted an
immediate wave of new Article 141 cases from national courts, asking
the ECJ to clarify (1) the nature of the temporal limitation imposed in
Barber and interpreted by the member states in the Protocol, as well
as other outstanding issues including: (2) whether the temporal limitation on the payment of benefits in Barber also extended to the right
to *join* a pension fund; (3) the scope of Article 141 vis-à-vis other
types of occupational pensions besides those analysed in *Barber*;
(4) the ways in which member governments and pension funds should
go about equalizing pensionable ages in light of *Barber*; and (5) the
legality of using sex-based actuarial tables in the calculation of pension
benefits. In each of these cases, the Court faced a choice: whether to
proceed with its previous, and generally expansive, interpretation of
Article 141 or to retreat to a more restrictive reading of that provision
in light of the political backlash from the member governments.
Although space prohibits an extensive analysis of each and every subsequent Article 141 case brought before the Court,[58] a brief analysis
of the Court's post-*Barber* case-law reveals a mixed record, with the
Court's jurisprudence continuing its expansive reading of Article 141
on some questions, but retreating—possibly in the face of member-
state pressures—in others.

Clarification of the Temporal Limitation in Barber

In terms of both the substantive impact of the *Barber* decision and the
Court's principal-agent relationship with the member governments,
the first and most important task was to clarify the meaning of the
temporal limitation in *Barber*, particularly in light of the member governments' collective intervention in the Protocol to the Maastricht

Treaty. That question was posed in a series of cases referred by national courts in 1991 and analysed by Advocate-General Van Gerven in a joint opinion on four interrelated cases (*Ten Oever, Moroni, Neath*, and *Coloroll*) dealing with unresolved issues from *Barber*. Although not binding on the Court and reflecting only the view of the Advocate-General in a particular case, such opinions are nearly always more detailed, and often more frank, in their analysis than the collective decisions of the Court itself and provide valuable clues about the positions of the key actors and the reasoning behind the Court's decisions. As Van Gerven noted, the interpretation of the temporal limitation in *Barber* had 'enormous' financial implications for pension funds in various member states, and the question had brought forward interventions from the Commission, five member governments (Denmark, Germany, Ireland, the Netherlands, and the United Kingdom), and pension funds and trustees, in addition to the plaintiffs and defendants in the various cases. Of these parties, all the member states, the Commission (in its *Coloroll* intervention) and all the intervening pension funds and trustees opted for the second interpretation—that the principle of equal opportunity applied to all benefits earned in relation to service after the date of the *Barber* decision, but not before—which was also the collective interpretation of the member governments in the Barber Protocol. By contrast, Van Gerven noted, no parties supported the first and most conservative interpretation, which 'would deprive the *Barber* judgment of almost all retroactive effect'.[59] At the other extreme, the fourth interpretation, according to which the principle of equal opportunity would apply to all pension benefits payable after 17 May 1990, was supported only by the defendants in the *Coloroll* case. Such an interpretation, in Van Gerven's view, 'goes too far', showing 'no regard at all for the financial balance of occupational pension schemes, as established in good faith on the basis of calculation factors based on different pensionable ages for men and women', and its adoption 'would mean that the temporal limitation of the judgment decided on by the Court would have almost no significance and that the useful effect of the limitation imposed by the Court would largely vanish'.[60] The third interpretation, that the principal of equal pay should apply to all pensions payable for the first time after 17 May 1990, had been supported by the Commission in its written interventions in the *Ten Oever, Moroni*, and *Neath* cases, but it was later abandoned in *Coloroll* and in the oral hearing in favour of the second interpretation, and Van Gerven himself rejected such an interpretation both because of its failure to respect the principle of legal certainty and because of the arbitrary discrimination it would establish between workers whose pensions were payable for the first time before 17 May 1990 and those who would receive their first payments after that date. Under the circumstances, Van Gerven argued strongly for the second interpretation, which fitted most easily with the Court's argument in *Barber* that both employers and pension funds had assumed in good faith that the derogation from the principle of equal pay for the question of pensionable ages remained valid. Specifically, Van Gerven argued:

The fact that the good faith of the parties concerned, in particular of employers and occupational pension funds, is to be taken into account means that, before *Barber*, those parties, in the belief that Article 119 was not applicable, could promise pensions and make payments based on a different pensionable age for men and women. The financial balance of the pension schemes concerned could therefore be maintained on that basis before the judgment. Only in respect of the periods of service after *Barber* did employers know that in administering occupational pension schemes and calculating the contributions to be made to them account had to be taken of a pensionable age which was the same for men and women. All these factors argue in favour of not allowing obligations entered into and payments made before the date of the *Barber* judgment to be affected.[61]

This interpretation, Van Gerven noted, 'largely coincides' with that adopted in the Barber Protocol, whereas if the Court came to a different conclusion 'its decision would be entirely superseded as soon as the Treaty on European Union enters into force'.[62]

In the event, the Court did follow both the reasoning of the Advocate-General and the collective preference of the member states in the Barber Protocol in its October 1993 judgment in *Ten Oever*. In a brief decision which, unlike Van Gerven's opinion, made no reference to the Protocol, the Court recalled the reasons underlying its decision to limit the retroactive effect of the decision in *Barber*, and continued that

...it must be made clear that equality of treatment in the matter of occupational pensions may be claimed only in relation to benefits payable in respect of periods of employment subsequent to 17 May 1990, the date of the *Barber* judgment, subject to the exception in favour of workers or those claiming under them who have, before that date, initiated legal proceedings or raised an equivalent claim under the applicable national law.[63]

In effect, Garrett, Kelemen, and Schultz (1998: 167) suggest, the Court's ruling said: 'this is what we meant all along: The member governments did not overrule us; they simply helped us clarify a point'.[64] Nevertheless, the Court's rather terse reasoning and the more detailed analysis by Van Gerven should not be too readily dismissed as a smokescreen for the Court's capitulation to overwhelming political pressure. Clearly, the Court *did* face pressure to adopt the interpretation offered by the Barber Protocol rather than some other interpretation that would probably have been overturned when the Maastricht Treaty entered into force, as well as opening a debate about the legal status of the protocol itself. On the other hand, Van Gerven and other legal scholars convincingly argue that the interpretation offered in *Ten Oever* really *was* in all likelihood that intended by the Court in *Barber*, since the first interpretation was exceedingly conservative and the third and fourth appeared to violate the principle of legal certainty underlying the adoption of the temporal limitation in the first place. In sum, the Court's decision in *Ten Oever* was almost certainly overdetermined by precedent, legal reasoning, and political pressure. Elsewhere in *Ten Oever* and in other decisions, however, the Court would confront a series of additional questions that would provide the opportunity to build upon or retreat from the precedent set down in *Barber*.

Temporal Limitation on Right of Access to Occupational Pension Schemes

Having accepted the Protocol's interpretation of the temporal limitation in *Barber*, and having extended that limitation to all occupational pension schemes and to survivors' pensions (see below), the Court nevertheless demonstrated, in the 1994 *Vroege* and *Fisscher* decisions, its willingness to interpret the Barber Protocol restrictively to apply only to the calculation of benefits rather than the right to join a pension scheme. In the first case, Ms Vroege worked for a company whose pension fund was open only to men and unmarried women who worked at least 80 per cent of a full day. In 1991 the rules were changed, providing that any worker above the age of 25 who worked 25 per cent of a full day or more could join the scheme, allowing Ms Vroege to join the scheme from that date; but Ms Vroege argued that such a limitation was incompatible with Article 141 and she claimed to be eligible for membership from 8 April 1976, the date of the decision in *Defrenne II* which established the direct effect of that Article. In effect, the *Vroege* case, and a similar set of questions posed in the *Fisscher* case involving a married woman who had been excluded from membership in a pension fund open only to unmarried women and to married and unmarried men, invited the Court to decide whether the right to join a pension scheme fell within the scope of Article 141 and, if so, whether the temporal limitation laid down in *Barber* applied also to the right to join occupational pension schemes. In addition, the

Dutch tribunal asked the Court specifically whether the Barber Protocol, which had entered into force with the Maastricht Treaty in November 1993, affected the outcome of the case, providing the Court with its first opportunity to comment directly upon the status and effects of the Protocol.

In its decision, the Court pointed out that the temporal limitation in *Barber*, as in other similar cases, was invoked on the basis of two criteria, namely, that the decision in question must pose (1) a 'risk of serious difficulties' (2) with regard to past legal relations 'established in good faith'.[65] In the *Barber* case, both of these criteria were met since the financial effects of the decision on British and other pension funds would be enormous, and the setting of different retirement ages for men and women 'could reasonably have considered to be permissible' in good faith by employers and pension funds under the derogations in the 1979 and 1986 Directives. By contrast, however, the *Vroege* case, like *Fisscher*, did not involve the question of pensionable ages or the benefits resulting therefrom but simply the right to join an occupational pension scheme. On this point, the Court noted that it had made clear as early as the 1984 *Bilka* decision that Article 141 covered the right to join occupational pension schemes, access to which must be offered without direct or indirect discrimination on the basis of sex; the *Bilka* decision, moreover, included no temporal limitation comparable to those in *Defrenne II* or *Barber*. For this reason—and despite the arguments of the Belgian and UK governments, as well as the defendants, all of whom intervened to suggest that the temporal limitation in *Barber* should extend to this case as well[66]—the Court concluded that the temporal limitation in *Barber* did *not* extend to the right to join an occupational pension scheme, which could therefore be relied upon from 8 April 1976, the date of the judgment in *Defrenne*.[67] Although greeted with anger in the United Kingdom (Moore 1995: 167), the Court's decision was, in Ellis's (1998: 81) words, 'a perceptive ruling on the part of a Court which did not wish its earlier decision in *Bilka* to be effectively restricted by later legislation'.

Finally, by contrast with earlier cases in which the relationship of ECJ judgments to the Protocol had been left implicit, the Court was asked specifically whether Protocol No. 2 affected the judgment in *Vroege* and *Fisscher*. According to the Court, 'the crucial point is whether Protocol No. 2 is intended only to clarify the limitation of the effects in time of the *Barber* decision, as set out above, or whether it has wider scope'. On this point, the interveners were split, with the UK government pointing to the broad wording of the Protocol to suggest that 'it applies to every kind of discrimination based on sex

which may exist in occupational pension schemes, including discrimination concerning the right to join such schemes' while the
Commission and the German government agreed that the Protocol
should be read narrowly in conjunction with the *Barber* judgment.
Siding with the latter view, the Court acknowledged that the Protocol
was stated in general terms and was therefore applicable to all benefits paid under an occupational pensions schemes and not simply
contracted-out schemes, but went on to note that the Protocol did
not, 'any more than the *Barber* judgment, deal with, or make any provision for, the conditions of membership of such occupational
schemes'. For this reason, the Court concluded, 'Protocol No. 2 does
not affect the right to join an occupational pension scheme, which
continues to be governed by the *Bilka* judgment'.[68]

The ruling in *Vroege*, largely reiterated in *Fisscher*, represents a clear
attempt by the Court to restrict the scope of the Barber Protocol.
Nevertheless, in the *Fisscher* case, the Court did place an important practical limitation on the ability of women to join pension schemes retroactively by requiring that a right of membership also entailed an
obligation by the employee to pay retroactively any matching contributions required by the scheme in question. In her observations, Ms
Fisscher had argued that retroactive payment of contributions would
constitute a substantial financial obstacle to women seeking to claim
their rights under Article 141, a view that met with considerable sym-
pathy among feminist critics of the ruling. On this point, however, the
Commission, the United Kingdom, and Advocate-General Van Gerven
were in agreement that 'it would be incompatible with Article 119 to
require employers or pension funds to pay contributions for female
employees when male employees have had to pay their contributions
themselves since this would create fresh discrimination',[69] and the Court
followed this position in its judgment, ruling that a worker's right to join
an occupational pension scheme retroactively did not allow the worker
to avoid paying contributions to the fund for the period in question.[70]
In practice, it is no doubt correct to argue, as Ms Fisscher did, that the
employee's requirement to make retroactive contributions constitutes a
practical hindrance to an individual's ability to take advantage of her
rights under Article 141. In so deciding, however, the Court was not
simply caving in to pressure from the member states but ruling in line
with its own legal precedent and with the advice of the Commission and
its Advocate-General, as well as the member governments; furthermore,
in such cases where employees are able and willing to make retroactive
contributions to contributory pension schemes, employers throughout
the Union are now under a legal obligation to do the same.

The Scope of Article 141 vis-à-vis Other Types of Pension Schemes

A third important question raised by several post-*Barber* references concerned the extension of the scope of Article 141 beyond contracted-out pension schemes to all occupational pensions and to other types of pensions as well. On both questions, the Court took a broad view of the scope of Article 141 and of its decision in *Barber*. First, as we have seen, the Court held explicitly in *Ten Oever* and in subsequent decisions (*Moroni, Coloroll*) that the analysis of contracted-out occupational pension schemes in *Barber*, including both the prohibition of discrimination on the basis of sex and the temporal limitation on the decision, necessarily applied to both supplementary and contracted-out occupational pension schemes, and without regard to the contributory or non-contributory nature of the scheme in question, thus extending substantially the reach of the decision.[71]

Second, again in *Ten Oever*, the Court confronted a similar question with regard to survivor's pensions, which in this case were paid to widows of male employees but not widowers of female employees, leading Mr Ten Oever, a widower, to allege a violation of the right to equal pay in Article 141. On this question, the interveners were split, with the plaintiff, the Commission, and the UK government arguing that the concept of 'pay' in Article 141 should be taken to encompass survivors' pensions, while the defendants and the governments of Netherlands and Germany argued that it should not.[72] Reiterating its previous rulings that 'the concept of pay, within the meaning of the second paragraph of Article 119, comprises any consideration, whether in cash or in kind, whether immediate or future, provided that the worker receives it, albeit indirectly, in respect of his employment from his employer', the Court ruled that a survivor's pension fell within this definition of pay, since the obligation arose clearly from the employment relationship and was paid to the survivor 'by reason of the spouse's employment'.[73] Although the Court went on to rule—in line with the stated preferences of the UK, the Netherlands, and the German governments—that such survivor's pensions were subject to the temporal limitation laid down in *Barber*, its further extension of the definition of 'pay' in these cases represents a continuing expansion of the scope of Article 141.

Equalizing Pensionable Ages

In light of the previous decisions, it was clear that, for the period from 17 May 1990, pension funds throughout the EU would henceforth be required to equalize the pensionable ages of men and women. However, this requirement left one major question unclear: would pension funds be required to harmonize *upwards*, generally by lowering men's retirement ages to the lower level prevailing among women, or would they be allowed to harmonize *downwards*, raising women's retirement ages to the higher level currently reserved for men? This question, alongside many others, was raised in three cases (*Coloroll, Avdel Systems*, and *van den Akker*) decided on the same day in 1994.[74] In each case, the defendants pointed to the Court's precedent in the second *Defrenne* decision, which required the pay of disadvantaged employees (typically, but not always, women) to be raised to the level of the advantaged employees. However, as Van Gerven pointed out in his opinion in the *Coloroll* case, the precedent in *Defrenne II* and related cases applied to discrimination *in the past*, the rectification of which would require employers to raise the pay of disadvantaged employees to that of their advantaged counterparts rather than retroactively decreasing the pay of the advantaged employees. As applied to the effects of the *Barber* decision on the equalization of pension fund benefits,

This means that, pending new adjusted rules, the rule applicable under the existing scheme provisions to members of the more favored sex must also be applied to members of the less favored sex. As regards the past, or, more precisely, as regards pension benefits which relate to periods of service performed in the past, the principle of equal treatment therefore requires that the benefits of the disadvantaged sex be brought up to the level of those of the advantaged sex.[75]

By contrast, he suggested, the precedent in *Defrenne II* did not require pension funds to harmonize upwards with response to future benefits:

However, in the case of benefits based on new rules adapted to the principle of equal treatment which govern periods of service in the future, the situation is different. Like the Commission, I take the view that Community law does not preclude a reduction of such benefits, so long as those benefits are set at a level which is the same for men and women. To take any other view would entail undesirable Community interference in a policy area which, in the present state of Community law, belongs to the sphere of competence of the Member States, which, as the Court has repeatedly emphasized, enjoy a reasonable margin of discretion as regards both the nature of the protective measures and the detailed arrangements for their implementation.[76]

In its decision in *Coloroll*, the Court echoed the Advocate-General on both points, albeit more tersely:

Once the Court has found that discrimination in relation to pay exists and so long as measures for bringing about equal treatment have not been adopted by the scheme, the only proper way of complying with Article 119 [now 141] is to grant to the disadvantaged workers the same advantages as those enjoyed by the other workers.

However, as regards periods of service subsequent to entry into force of rules designed to eliminate discrimination, Article 119 [now 141] does not preclude achievement of equal treatment by reducing the advantages of the favoured persons since it merely requires that men and women should receive the same pay for the same work without imposing any specific level of pay.[77]

In this decision, the Court exercises judicial restraint, refusing to lay down by judicial fiat a uniform retirement age with enormous financial consequences throughout the Union in the absence of a decision by the Council (Arnull 2000: 480). As such, the Court's ruling in *Coloroll* has been criticized as a retreat from previous case law in the face of member-state pressure and one which may potentially *worsen* the situation of women workers, who stand to see their pensionable ages raised from 60 to 65 in many cases as a result of the Court's unwillingness to apply the *Defrenne II* standard in this case (Ellis 1998: 82). Similar criticisms have been directed at the Court's decision, in *Avdel*, to prohibit transitional arrangements designed to phase in the equalization of men's and women's pensionable ages. Although such transitional arrangements were clearly designed to benefit women, the Court ruled that 'achievement of equality cannot be made progressive on a basis that still maintains discrimination, even if only temporarily'.[78] It is unclear from the legal record whether the Court's rulings in these cases were driven by pressure from member governments or by a formalistic reading of Article 141 which does not, indeed, appear to provide the legal basis for a decision as far-reaching as the establishment of a uniform pensionable age. It is clear, however, that the Court's decisions in these cases constitute a retreat from, or at least a limitation upon, the legal principles laid down in *Defrenne II*, and constitute *prima facie* evidence of a retreat from the judicial activism of the earlier case.

The Use of Sex-Based Actuarial Tables

In a final set of questions, raised in the *Neath* and *Coloroll* cases, the Court was asked whether it was compatible with Article 141 for the payments made under a pension scheme to be calculated on the basis of actuarial calculations, 'in particular actuarial assumptions about the different life expectancy of men and women, which lead to different results for men and women'. On this question, a number of pension funds and several member states intervened to defend the practice of using sex-based actuarial calculations to evaluate a fund's financial liabilities since, all else equal, women live on average longer than men and might therefore be expected to collect their pension for a longer period after retirement. On the basis of these actuarial calculations, however, pension fund members who opt to take a one-time capital sum rather than a periodic pension might be paid different amounts, with men generally receiving a lower amount than women. This practice was challenged by Mr Neath, who received a smaller lump-sum payment than a woman with his employment record would have received. Although defended by pension funds and member governments, the practice of making unequal capital sum payments to men and women on the basis of sex-based actuarial calculations was criticized by the Commission and by Advocate-General Van Gerven in his opinion, on the grounds that the principle of equal pay should be applied individually and not on a category basis: 'The fact that women generally live longer than men has no significance at all for the life expectancy of a specific individual and it is not acceptable for an individual to be penalized on account of assumptions which are not certain to be true in his specific case.'[79] After reviewing various justifications for sex-based actuarial calculations put forward by the governments of the Netherlands, UK, and Denmark, Van Gerven therefore concluded that, while Article 141 did not preclude the use of sex-based actual calculations in the management of a pension fund and the calculation of its liabilities, it did require that the determination of employee contributions and benefits should take place on the basis of the same criteria for women and men.

On this question, however, the Court unusually departed from the advice of the Commission and its Advocate-General, ruling in favour of the position defended by the various member governments. In its decision, the Court made a distinction between (1) periodic pension payments such as the monthly cheques received by most pensioners following their retirement, which clearly fell within the scope of Article 141 and its requirement of equality between men and women; and (2) 'the funding arrangements chosen to secure the periodic payment of the pension', including the use of sex-based actuarial factors affecting differently the overall size of lump-sum payments to men and women, which 'remain outside the scope of Article 119'.[80] By contrast to the previous set of cases regarding the equalization of pensionable ages, in *Neath* and *Coloroll* the beneficiaries of the Court's judgment are women employees who may continue to receive larger lump-sum retirement settlements on the basis of sex-based actuarial calculations. Nevertheless, here as in the previous cases, the Court has been criticized for its relatively narrow reading of Article 141 and for its tolerance of unequal payments to men and women that had been rejected by Van Gerven and the Commission.[81]

Analysis: Barber *and the Limits of* European Judicial Discretion

What are we to make of the Court's ruling in *Barber*, the member-state response with the Barber Protocol, and the subsequent line of cases? In a previous study of ECJ equal opportunities decisions, Garrett, Kelemen, and Schulz (1998: 168) argue that the *Barber* decision itself represents a miscalculation on the part of the Court which 'did not anticipate the strength of government opposition' to its decision. Given the financial implications of the decision and the fact that the member governments found it unacceptable, they continue, those governments did not passively abide the decision but collectively restrained the Court through the Barber Protocol. Finally, the authors argue that, although the Court had initially been willing to circumvent the intentions of the member governments in its decisions up to and including *Barber*, 'Once the governments had clearly signaled their resolve through a treaty revision...the Court retreated'.

Garrett, Kelemen, and Schulz are surely correct to suggest that the *Barber* decision and the member-state response to it illustrate the limits to the Court's discretion, even in constitutional interpretation, and its receptiveness to the strongly expressed collective preferences of the member governments. By contrast to the Court's record in the interpretation of Article 28 (ex 30) EC, where it drastically expanded and later, in *Keck*, restricted its reading of the treaty with little apparent regard for member-state preferences, in *Barber* and later cases the Court came up vividly against member-state preferences and the limits of its discretion. Nevertheless, a careful reading of the evidence in this case, as well as subsequent developments not examined in Garrett, Kelemen, and Schulz's 1998 article, suggest a slightly more nuanced reading of the developments reviewed above, in three ways. First, it should be pointed out, *Barber* was unusual, if not unique, in the history of ECJ jurisprudence in several senses, including the enormous financial implications of the decision for powerful interests in most member states, the wave of follow-up cases in light of the legal uncertainty generated by the *Barber* ruling, and the coincidence of these cases with the conclusion of an ongoing intergovernmental conference which allowed the member governments to amend the treaty and pre-empt the Court's subsequent jurisprudence at relatively low cost.[82] Thus, while the Barber Protocol does exemplify the possible resort to treaty reform as the ultimate sanction against ECJ activism, the case is unusual in terms of both the controversy it generated and the member-state response it provoked. By contrast, the vast majority of ECJ decisions, including many of the most far-reaching in terms of constitutional interpretation and European integration, involve more modest financial costs, greater diversity of member-state response, and hence a far lower likelihood of collective response through treaty revision of the sort undertaken following *Barber*. Having been exercised following *Barber* and on several other occasions, the threat of treaty revision may no longer be the 'nuclear option', but it remains relevant only to the small number of cases in which an ECJ decision raises an overwhelming outcry among the member governments.

Second, the post-*Barber* Article 141 case law of the ECJ provides only partial support for Garrett, Kelemen, and Schulz's claim that the Court has 'retreated' following the Barber Protocol. On the one hand, the Court did appear, in the *Ten Oever* case, to roll over to the preferences of the member governments, accepting in its entirety the interpretation of the *Barber* decision offered in Protocol No. 2. Similarly, the Court has been criticized for conservatism in some of its post-Maastricht decisions, including the possibility for pension funds to harmonize pensionable ages downwards (*Coloroll, Avdel, van den Akker*) and the Court's decision to allow the use of actuarial tables in making differential one-time pension payments to men and women (*Neath*). In other cases, however, the Court has followed and extended its more progressive precedents, clarifying and extending the reach of Article 141 to all occupational pensions and to survivors' pensions (*Ten Oever, Moroni,* and *Coloroll*); requiring pension funds to harmonize upwards pending reform of pension schemes (*Coloroll, Smith v Avdel, van Akker*); and interpreting the temporal limitation in *Barber* restrictively to exclude the right to join a pension scheme (*Vroege* and *Fisscher*), which remains valid back to the date of the *Defrenne II* judgment. Indeed, one might argue that the Court's post-*Barber* jurisprudence, rather than constituting a generalized retreat, represents a return to the pre-*Barber* pattern in which the Court generally, but not always, opts for a broad interpretation of Article 141, most often over the objections of one or more, but not all, member governments.

Third and finally, while the effect of the Court's *Barber* decision was limited by its adoption of a temporal limitation, and *may* have been limited by Protocol No. 2 (assuming that the latter did not simply express the intent of the Court in the former) it is nevertheless indisputable that the Court's decision in *Barber*, together with later decisions in the same direction, have substantially changed and expanded the meaning and application of Article 141, which is now held to apply to all occupational and survivors' pensions and to the question of retirement ages for men and women, albeit with a temporal limitation, and to the right to join occupational pension schemes, without a temporal limitation. Counter-factually, it is highly unlikely that the member governments would have adopted such decisions themselves in the absence of an activist ECJ, since any such decisions would have required a unanimous agreement among the member governments.[83] Nevertheless, when the Commission in 1995 proposed a technical amendment of the 1986 Directive to bring it into line with the Court's rulings in *Barber* and subsequent decisions, 'on the grounds of legal certainty',[84] effectively asking the Council to accept and ratify all the ways in which the Court had altered or overridden the terms of that Directive, the member governments agreed to such an amendment with little debate and with only minor amendments to its draft proposal.[85] Thus, while its discretion is not without limit, even in constitutional interpretation, the Court clearly 'mattered' in extending the scope of Article 141, and with it the right to equal pay among European women and men.

IV. Conclusions

In this chapter, I once again set out to determine whether the European Commission and the Court of Justice have sought to use their delegated powers to advance the process of European integration through the adoption of EU social regulations, and, if so, whether their ability to do so varied, as hypothesized, as a function of the varying administrative and oversight procedures established by member governments to control each agent across various issue areas. Once again, as Chapter 5, both hypotheses are strongly supported. With regard to the preferences of supranational agents, we have seen that in all three cases reviewed in this chapter—the Working Time Directive, the Structural Funds, and the *Barber* decision—the Commission and the Court have both pressed consistently for the adoption, implementation, and enforcement of binding EU social standards.

With regard to the autonomy and influence of these agents, a cross-issue comparison again supports the hypotheses put forward in Chapter 1, with Commission and Court influence generally increasing as we progress from the agenda-setting powers of the Commission in the Working Time Directive, through its executive action in the implementation of the Structural Funds, to the Court's interpretation of the principle of equal pay for men and women in its Article 141 jurisprudence. Once again, moreover, process-tracing within each case illuminates the specific ways in which the Commission and the Court attempt to exploit their statutory discretion and the ways in which dissatisfied member governments attempt, with varying degrees of success, to rein in their efforts. In the case of the Working Time Directive, we find the Commission strategically using its sole right of initiative to propose a draft Directive that might garner the support of a qualified majority in the Council of Ministers, despite bitter UK opposition, and we find the Court, in a supporting role, enthusiastically endorsing the Commission's broad reading of the health and safety provisions of Article 118a. Nevertheless, as in the external-trade case of the Blair House agreement, we find that a dissatisfied member government (in this case, the UK) was able to capitalize on the Council's informal norm of consensus, extracting concessions from the other member governments and substantially weakening the Commission's initial draft before eventually abstaining from the adoption of the Directive.

In the implementation of the Structural Funds, we find a case in which the Council of Ministers delegated extensive executive powers and discretion to the Commission in the 1988 Structural Fund Regulations, only to find that the Commission then used these powers to press in the RECHAR case and elsewhere a European agenda that ran strongly counter to the preferences of one or more member governments. In this case, however, the expiration of the Commission's mandate in 1993 provided the United Kingdom and other member governments with a chance to amend the original act of delegation, restricting the Commission's future discretion through the use of strengthened administrative and oversight procedures.

In the Court's interpretation of the principle of equal pay in Article 141, finally, we witness the Court's remarkable discretion vis-à-vis the member governments, whose individual and collective preferences (for example, in the 1979 and 1986 Directives on equal pay in social security schemes) were consistently overruled by ECJ jurisprudence; yet we also witness the *limits* to ECJ discretion, with the relatively rare imposition by the member governments of a treaty amendment (the Barber Protocol) designed to limit the effects of an ECJ judgment. The details of the three cases reviewed in this chapter, however, differ in telling ways from the comparable cases of agenda setting, executive action, and constitutional interpretation reviewed in Chapter 5, in ways that both challenge classical principal-agent models and suggest additional hypotheses for future testing. I return to these differences, and their implications for principal-agent models of delegation, in the concluding chapter.

CONCLUSIONS

CONCLUSIONS

Conclusions: A Europe of Agents, A World of Agents

The delegation of executive, judicial, and legislative (agenda-setting) functions to political agents, and the principal-agent problems that invariably result from such acts of delegation, are a generic feature of both domestic and international political life. Although first explored systematically by political scientists in the study of American regulatory agencies and Congressional committees, the phenomenon of delegation is also inherent in the domestic politics of other countries, including the parliamentary systems of Europe which can be theorized as 'chains of delegation' leading from mass electorates to parliamentarians to government ministers and thence to the civil servants who actually implement policies in the name of the people, their ultimate principals. In recent years, moreover, the explicit delegation of political power in many domestic polities has accelerated, as a growing number of developed and developing countries experiment with the creation of independent regulatory agencies and central banks.[1] Delegation is not, however, limited to domestic politics but plays an important role in international politics as well, with the increasing delegation of power by states to an ever-growing number of international executives, secretariats, development banks, dispute-resolution bodies, and tribunals and courts in the European Union and beyond.

In this book, I have drawn on theories of delegation, agency, and agenda setting in American politics to develop and test hypotheses about the delegation of powers by member-state principals to supranational organizations and about the effects of such delegation in terms of supranational agency and agenda setting in the European Union. Simplifying only slightly, I have argued that EU member governments delegate to the European Commission and the European Court of Justice—but not to the European Parliament—for essentially the same transaction-cost reasons that motivate national legislators to delegate powers to Congressional and parliamentary committees, independent regulatory agencies, and courts. Like domestic legislators, EU member states delegate powers and discretion to their supranational agents deliberately and with care, delegating a set of core functions that serve to secure their commitment to mutual cooperation and allow for speedy and efficient decision-making, while at the same time designing administrative and oversight mechanisms to tailor supranational discretion across different types of functions and different issue areas. Like domestic legislators, however, EU member governments have discovered that delegation, despite its benefits, necessarily entails some agency costs, as agents pursue their own preferences within the discretion allocated to them by the invariably imperfect control mechanisms employed in any principal-agent relationship. Indeed, the effort by the European Commission and Court of Justice to employ their statutory discretion to advance the process of European integration, and their variable success in doing so across issue areas and over time, has been the subject of much of this book.

In this concluding chapter, I summarize the book's empirical findings; lay out an agenda for the further study of delegation, agency, and agenda setting in European and international politics; and assess the normative implications of a Europe, and a world, of agents.

I. Summary of Empirical Findings

Delegation and Discretion

In the first half of the book, I set out to test two principal-agent hypotheses about (1) the *functions* delegated to the Commission, the Court, and the Parliament, and (2) the *discretion* allocated to these agents through the variable use of administrative and oversight procedures across agents and issue areas. With regard to the first question, transaction-cost models of delegation have identified four specific functions that are likely to be delegated to supranational agents in order to provide either policy-relevant information or credible commitments: monitoring compliance, filling in the details of incomplete contracts, adopting credible and expert implementing regulations, and setting the formal agenda for the legislative process. With regard to the second question, about the discretion of supranational agents, transaction-cost theorists have predicted that legislative principals will not adopt a one-size-fits-all approach but will tailor their use of administrative and oversight mechanisms as a function of the demand for either policy-relevant information or credible commitments, or both. To simplify only slightly, these hypotheses have been strongly supported for both the Commission and the Court of Justice but not for the European Parliament. Let us examine each, very briefly, in turn.

The European Commission

With regard to the Commission, the extensive survey of its powers and discretion in Chapter 2 suggests five fundamental points in response to the hypotheses specified above. First, we have seen that the *functions* delegated to the Commission fit closely with those predicted by transaction-cost models. Almost without exception, the Commission's delegated powers fall into three of the four categories specified in existing principal-agent models, namely: *monitoring member-state compliance* with EC law, by bringing infringement proceedings against member governments before the ECJ; *setting the agenda* for Council decision-making, through the Commission's sole right of initiative in the first pillar and its shared right of initiative in the second and third pillars; and *adopting implementing regulations* for a wide range of Community policies. If we compare the EU to comparable institutions in the United States, therefore, we see that the Commission plays multiple but familiar roles in the politics of the EU, combining many of the functions performed in the US by both Congressional committees, which play the role of legislative agenda setters, and independent regulatory agencies.

Second, if we turn from the functions delegated to the *discretion* enjoyed by the Commission, we see that, from the very beginnings of European integration in the European Coal and Steel Community, the member governments have deliberately created and periodically modified a variety of control mechanisms to limit agency losses to the Commission; indeed, the present-day Council of Ministers, Court of Justice, and European Parliament were initially designed primarily as checks on the ECSC's High Authority. Since then, the repertoire of member-state control mechanisms has increased impressively to include, *inter alia*, procedures for the appointment, reappointment, and censure of the College of Commissioners; a system of 'comitology' oversight committees through which member governments monitor and, if necessary, sanction Commission behaviour; a system of administrative law and judicial review by the European Court of Justice; budgetary control by both the Council of Ministers and the European Parliament; and institutional checks by bodies such as the Court of Auditors and the European Ombudsman.

Third, however, the control mechanisms established by the member governments to limit the discretion of the Commission are not 'one size fits all' but have been carefully tailored across different types of functions and different issue areas. Across functions, we have seen how member governments have allocated extensive discretion to the Commission in its monitoring-and-enforcement function, where, like the Court of Justice, it is subject to relatively few control mechanisms, while the Commission generally enjoys less discretion in its regulatory and agenda-setting functions. Within the latter two functions, moreover, the Commission enjoys highly variable levels of discretion across issue areas, with extensive powers in the areas of competition policy and external trade, somewhat less discretion in the management of policies such as agriculture and fisheries, and the most restricted discretion in other areas such as national health and safety regulations, taxation, and foreign affairs. This fine-tuning of Commission discretion by EU member governments is most evident in the choice of comitology committees, but extends to the adoption of administrative law and other control mechanisms as well.

Fourth, with regard to the determinants of Commission discretion, the evidence examined in Chapter 2 suggests that EU member governments are motivated by a variety of transaction-cost-related concerns in delegating powers and discretion to the Commission, with a concern for credible commitments emerging alongside a concern for speed and efficiency as the primary motives for delegation. Within the treaties, EU member governments have allocated the Commission its most extensive discretion in the monitoring and enforcement of EC law, followed closely by a careful delegation of regulatory powers in specific issue areas like competition and external trade policy, and finally the setting of the Council's legislative agenda. As we have seen, this pattern of delegation across both functions and issue areas supports Moravcsik's (1998) and Majone's (2001) view that the delegation decisions of EU member governments have been motivated primarily by a desire to ensure the credibility of their common commitment to the integration process, as well as the credibility of their common policies and regulations vis-à-vis market actors. By contrast, the cross-issue pattern of delegation provides relatively little support for the informational rationale for delegation of the Commission's executive and agenda-setting powers, which are not generally concentrated in the most scientifically and technically complex areas and in which the Commission in any event enjoys significantly less policy-relevant expertise than all but the smallest member governments. Nevertheless, while the informational rationale is largely unsupported by the empirical evidence examined here, a third transaction-cost-related motivation for delegation to the Commission has emerged largely inductively from this study, namely, the demand for 'speedy and efficient decision-making'. As we have seen throughout this book, the sometimes agonizing slowness of the EU legislative process imposes significant transaction costs in policy areas that require constant management, like agriculture or fisheries policies, or rapid decision making, as with the 1992 internal market programme and the 1999 Financial Services Action Plan, and the member governments have responded in these areas by delegating significant powers and discretion to the Commission, albeit under member-state supervision.

Fifth and finally, however, it should be noted that the member governments have collectively opted *not* to delegate powers in several areas—such as environmental policy, consumer protection, and food safety, among others—in which one might expect that the Commission would be able to lower transaction costs by adopting credible regulation, centralizing policy expertise, and facilitating speedy and efficient decision-making. The member governments' failure to delegate in these areas may be attributed to a number of factors, including the diversity of existing national rules and preferences, mistrust of the Commission as a result of previous policy failures—for example, the 1996 BSE scandal—and above all the super-majoritarian or unanimity requirement for EU delegation decisions, which results in a lowest-common-denominator pattern of supranational delegation in which the concerns of a single member government can prevent indefinitely the delegation of powers seen as 'functional' by the rest of the governments.

The European Court of Justice

The pattern of delegation to the Court of Justice provides similar support for both hypotheses. First, in terms of delegated functions, the scope of the ECJ's treaty-based jurisdiction—most notably, its powers of direct enforcement vis-à-vis member states through Articles 226 and 227, judicial review of Community acts through Articles 230 and 232, and uniform application of EU law in national courts through the preliminary reference procedure of Article 234—clearly fit the standard principal-agent categories of monitoring and enforcing compliance and filling in the details of incomplete contracts. In terms of the motives for delegation, both a functional analysis and the historical record appear to support the view that EU member governments have been motivated primarily by a concern for credible commitments in their delegation of extensive jurisdiction to the ECJ, although, in the case of the preliminary reference procedure, the available evidence suggests that the drafters of the EEC Treaty did not intend Article 234 to be used as the decentralized enforcement mechanism into which it was later developed by the ECJ in cooperation with national courts.

Moving from delegation to discretion, we have seen that the discretion allocated to the Court in carrying out its duties is remarkably broad by comparison with both the Commission and domestic constitutional courts. While the relatively short and renewable terms of office of European judges compare unfavourably with those of their national counterparts, ECJ judges are nevertheless protected from individual pressures by the Court's practice of deliberating in secret and issuing unanimous decisions. Furthermore, the thresholds to legislative overruling and constitutional amendment in the European Union are, in comparative terms, remarkably high, suggesting that the Court has extraordinary discretion to stray from the preferences of its principals without provoking a collective response. The member governments of the Union may pre-empt further ECJ activism in new areas, as they did in the creation of the second and third pillars of the European Union, but the Court's *acquis* has proved remarkably resistant to member-state reversal in either treaty reform or secondary legislation. The threat of non-compliance by national courts and national governments, finally, remains a real one which has been highlighted by recent scholarship by Conant (2002) and others, but there is little evidence in this or other studies to suggest that opposition from a single member government, whether large or small, is sufficient to influence the Court in its interpretation of the treaties. In sum, the Court's extensive statutory discretion and the weakness of the various control mechanisms available to member governments explain the extraordinary independence of the ECJ in its interpretation of EU law, as demonstrated in the second half of this book.

European Parliament

By contrast with the Commission and the Court, the historical and functional pattern of delegation to the European Parliament provides little support for the transaction-cost, principal-agent hypotheses laid out in Chapter 1 of this book. On the one hand, as we have seen, the EU's member governments have repeatedly and unanimously chosen to delegate important supervisory, budgetary, and legislative powers to the Parliament, increasing those powers in each and every revision of the treaties between 1957 and 1997. On the other hand, however, the functions delegated to the European Parliament in the treaties are a poor fit with the predictions of principal-agent models. Specifically, and by contrast with the Commission and the Court of Justice, the functions of the European Parliament functions do *not* generally include monitoring compliance, filling in the details of an incomplete contract, adopting implementing regulation, or even setting the legislative agenda (since the Parliament's legislative powers under co-decision lie at the decisional rather than the agenda-setting stage). Of the three major functions delegated to the EP, only the power to supervise the Commission, the EIB, and the ECB is understandable in principal-agent terms as a check on the power of these organizations; the Parliament's budgetary and legislative functions, by contrast, fit poorly or not at all into the functions predicted by principal-agent models.

The reason for this poor fit, I suggested in Chapter 4, is that EU member governments have delegated increasing powers to the European Parliament, not because such delegation is likely to reduce the transaction costs of EU policy making—indeed, these costs have arguably *increased* as a result of parliamentary participation—but rather because the empowerment of a directly elected European Parliament is seen by member governments and their constituents as normatively desirable and democratically *legitimate*. Indeed, one might argue that the increase in the powers of Parliament represents not a logic of consequences but a logic of appropriateness, in which a legitimate institutional form—parliamentary democracy—has been transposed from national settings to the European Union. In this view, delegation of powers to the EP might be considered as a case of 'institutional isomorphism' in which particular institutions are adopted and spread not as a result of functional analysis but rather because these institutions come to be seen as legitimate or appropriate in public discourse. Nevertheless, while norms of democratic legitimacy have clearly been an important motivation for member governments in their decisions to delegate powers to the European Parliament, those decisions have *not* been guided purely by a logic of appropriateness or with a blind eye to the potential consequences of such delegation. Rather, the historic and functional pattern of delegation to the EP supports the view that the influence of democratic ideology is greatest where the distributional implications of delegation are either unclear or unimportant. By contrast, in the many areas where member governments *were* able to anticipate the likely consequences of delegating specific powers to the EP, even the champions of a strengthened EP have agreed to structure the supervisory, budgetary, and legislative powers of Parliament to limit agency losses. As a result of this pattern of delegation—motivated by member-state concerns about democratic legitimacy but limited by concerns about potentially adverse consequences—the contemporary European Union represents a hybrid system, with a powerful Parliament enjoying full co-legislator status in a growing number of areas while simultaneously being excluded from legislation in other issue areas, as well as from important budgetary decisions, Commission nomination, ratification of international trade agreements, and other functions which the EU's member governments have decided, at least for the moment, to retain for themselves.

Agency and Agenda Setting

In the second part of the book, I tested two additional sets of hypotheses, about the preferences of supranational actors such as the Commission and the Court, and about the conditions under which these agents might be able to influence policy outcomes through their executive, judicial, and legislative (agenda-setting) powers. Regarding *preferences*, I hypothesized that supranational agents are characterized by a common preference for greater competences for the European Union as a whole and a specific preference for greater competences for themselves, with regard to both the liberalization of the European market and its re-regulation at European level. Regarding the *conditions* under which supranational agents might exert an independent causal influence on policy outcomes, I hypothesized that the ability of an agent to pursue an integrationist agenda and move policy outcomes beyond what member governments would collectively have decided is a function of the control mechanisms established by member governments to limit supranational discretion in a given issue area.

An overview of the six cases examined in Chapters 5 and 6 strongly supports the principal-agent view of supranational organizations seeking strategically to exploit their discretion to promote *une certaine idée de l'Europe*, while member governments behave equally strategically in their use of various control mechanisms to limit agency losses from delegation. By the same token, however, careful within-case process-tracing, together with an explicit comparison of the paired cases of agenda setting, executive action, and constitutional interpretation, reveal some unexpected findings and several hypotheses for future testing.

First, with regard to the preferences of supranational organizations, we find in nearly every case that the Commission and the Court, often supported by the European Parliament, do indeed behave as competence-maximizers, almost invariably advocating a broad interpretation of the objectives and powers of the European Union as laid down in the treaties, including the creation as well as the regulation of the Single European Market. Furthermore, despite the regular differences of opinion among its Commissioners and Directorates-General, the

Commission, like the Court and the Parliament, has generally behaved coherently and predictably vis-à-vis EU member governments according to a shared organizational preference for greater European integration. For this reason, and despite the obvious multiplicity of actors and preferences within each organization, the unitary rational-actor assumption of supranational agents as competence-maximizers has proved to be a useful simplifying assumption for the purpose of this study.

Nevertheless, despite their general and common preference for greater integration, the preferences of the Commission, the Court, and the Parliament are *not* identical. As competence-maximizers, the three organizations share a similarly broad vision of the powers of the Community and the Union as such, but the specific preferences of the Commission, the Court, or the Parliament in any case also reflect the differences in their institutional positions vis-à-vis the member governments and each other. Many of the EU's inter-institutional struggles over comitology (Chapter 2) and legal-base disputes (Chapters 4 and 6), for example, pit the Commission against the European Parliament, which has sought consistently and against Commission opposition to increase its influence through an increased role in the making and implementation of EC legislation. Largely for this reason, Westlake (1994) has aptly described the Commission and the Parliament as both 'partners and rivals' in the policy process. Needless to say, the EP's subsequent role in the 1999 resignation of the Santer Commission has since underlined the rivalrous aspect of the relationship.

Relations between the Court and the Commission reveal similar tensions. As we have seen, the Commission and Court often work in close tandem, with the Commission emerging as the strongest predictor of ECJ decisions, while the Court frequently supports the Commission in legal disputes with the Council or individual member governments. Indeed, four of the six cases reviewed in this book— merger control, free movement of goods, working time, and equal pay—found the Commission and the ECJ acting in tandem to press for both the liberalization of the European market and the adoption of EU-level social regulations. Once again, however, the Court's preferences and incentives are not identical to those of the Commission. As the 'guardian of the Treaties' and in particular as the administrative Court of the Community, the ECJ—as well as, increasingly the CFI—also serves as an institutional check on the Commission, and in that context has ruled against Commission initiatives on a number of occasions, as we saw in Chapter 2. Indeed, the importance of the Commission-Court tandem was revealed most spectacularly in the case of external trade, where the Court of Justice, possibly under pressure from member governments with intense preferences, ruled against the Commission's proposed interpretation of Article 133, dealing a major blow to the latter's effort to expand its own and the Community's trade competence.

To move from the preferences to the autonomy and influence of the Commission and the Court, the case studies presented in the second part of the book provide general support for the predicted pattern of increasing influence of the Commission and Court as we move across the three categories of (1) formal Commission agenda-setting (the Blair House agreement and the Working-Time Directive); (2) executive powers with member-state oversight and administrative law (merger control and administration of the Structural Funds); and (3) the Court's powers of constitutional interpretation (free movement of goods, equal pay). In the first set of cases, the Commission has been constrained to propose either negotiated agreements or legislative drafts that can secure the approval of at least a qualified majority of member governments. In the second set of cases of executive action, by contrast, the Commission has enjoyed greater discretion to advance the cause of European integration through its implementation of the Merger Control Regulation and the Structural Funds, subject to the more-or-less constraining control mechanisms prescribed by their respective regulations. In the third and final set of cases, the Court has employed its extraordinary discretion in constitutional interpretation to expand considerably the scope of the Treaty provisions regarding both the free movement of goods and equal pay for men and women.

We should, of course, be cautious in reaching conclusions based on patterns of variation across a relatively small number of cases, particularly where those cases do not constitute a representative sample and therefore do not allow us to hold all possible control variables constant. Fortunately, the use of within-case analysis and process-tracing allows us to identify the hypothesized causal mechanisms at work, while the pair-wise comparison of 'like' cases of agenda setting, executive action, and constitutional interpretation allows us to identify secondary sources of variation in supranational influence and autonomy. Once again, such within-case analysis and pair-wise comparison generally support the picture of principal-agent relationships outlined in Chapter 1 of this book, while also revealing a few unexpected elements and generating additional hypotheses for future testing. Let us consider each pair of cases, very briefly, in turn.

Commission Agenda Setting: The Blair House
Agreement and the Working Time Directive

Looking first at the two cases of formal agenda setting by the Commission, we see that in each case the Commission attempted to make strategic use of its power of initiative to secure its preferred outcomes, namely, a successful trade agreement and the liberalization of the CAP in the first case, and the adoption of binding working-time legislation in the second. Significantly, however, in both cases the formal agenda-setting powers of the Commission were weakened by the Council's informal norm of consensual decision-making. According to a purely formal analysis in which member governments vote sincerely on the basis of issue-specific preferences, the Commission in each case could rationally have expected to secure the adoption by QMV of its proposals, with few or no amendments adopted by unanimous vote in the Council. Such a formal reading of the treaty rules, however, ignores the informal norm of diffuse reciprocity in Council decision-making, as a consequence of which member governments in the majority were reluctant to outvote isolated member governments—France in the Blair House case, the UK in the Working Time case—whose preferences could otherwise have been disregarded. In practice, this reluctance to outvote isolated member governments led the Council to require renegotiation of the first Blair House agreement in the first case, and to accept far-reaching amendments to mollify the United Kingdom in the second.

This informal norm of consensus decision-making should *not* lead us to assume that the formal decision rule of qualified majority is meaningless, and the de facto rule for Council voting is unanimity. In the working-time case, for example, the Council's informal norm of consensual decision making led the other member governments to make far-reaching concessions to the UK government, but ultimately the Danish Presidency of the Council, for which working time was a particular priority, proved willing to put the issue to a vote. Evidence from other studies similarly suggests that the Council does indeed vote in a substantial minority of cases, and that in other cases Council bargaining takes place 'in the shadow of the vote', making consensus among the member governments easier to reach (Golub 1999; Galloway 2001: 95). Nevertheless, the informal norm of consensual decision making does suggest that formal models of Commission's agenda setting based on the assumption of minimum winning coalitions may overstate the Commission's real agenda-setting powers. This question, together with the effect of the co-decision procedure on the Commission's agenda-setting powers, discussed in Chapter 4, provide promising areas for further study.

The Commission as Executive: Merger Control and the Structural Funds

The second set of cases are similar, and provide similar levels of support for the principal-agent approach of this book, in that they each demonstrate a Commission determined to expand the scope of its own and the Community's powers in the creation and regulation of a unified European market, and using its executive discretion to do so. In the merger control case, the Commission, supported by the ECJ, first used its executive powers under the original EEC Treaty to secure a foothold in the field of merger control, leading ultimately to the adoption of a Merger Control Regulation delegating explicit powers and significant discretion in this area. Since the adoption of the MCR, moreover, the Commission has proved willing to apply EC merger rules forcefully and in the face of opposition from powerful firms and member governments. Similarly in the case of the Structural Funds, the Delors Commission successfully proposed and secured the adoption in 1988 of a Structural Fund Regulation delegating significant powers and discretion to the Commission, which immediately used its powers to implement the Funds in ways that clashed directly with the preferences of the UK and other member governments. In both cases, therefore, EU member governments agreed to delegate extensive executive powers and equally extensive discretion—exemplified by the use of advisory committees in both Regulations—to the Commission, which the latter then used to pursue its European agenda in the face of member-state opposition.

From this common point, however, the stories of merger control and the Structural Funds diverge. In the merger control case, as in other areas of competition policy, the Council of Ministers adopted a Regulation of indefinite duration; in Scharpf's (1988) terms, therefore, the 'default condition' for merger control was the continuation of the Commission's existing powers until such time as the Council agreed to amend or repeal the original Regulation. As predicted by Scharpf, the effect of this default condition has been that, in the absence of unanimous agreement among the member governments, the Commission's powers and discretion under the MCR have proved resistant to either reduction, despite the efforts of several member governments, or further delegation, as with the very modest expansion of the Commission's jurisdiction to multiple-notification cases in the 1997 amending Regulation. In the Structural Funds case, by contrast, the Commission enjoyed broad discretion under the 1988

Regulations, but the default condition in that case was the expiration of those Regulations, and hence the Commission's powers, on 31 December 1993. As we have seen, the resulting requirement for the Council to adopt a new Regulation by unanimous agreement empowered the UK and other dissatisfied member governments to insist on significant limits to the Commission's statutory discretion, which was reduced in both the 1993 and 1999 Structural Fund Regulations. The comparison of the two cases therefore suggests that, in addition to variations in administrative law and comitology, variation in the default condition of the act delegating powers to an agent plays a vital role in determining the discretion of that agent vis-à-vis its principals over the long term.

The ECJ and Constitutional Interpretation: Free Movement of Goods and Equal Pay

In the third set of cases, finally, we find evidence of both the remarkable extent and the ultimate limits of ECJ discretion. The extent of ECJ discretion is most evident in the free movement cases, where the Court adopted a remarkably expansive reading of Article 28 and its prohibition on 'measures having equivalent effect'. Starting with *Dassonville* and *Cassis* and continuing with a string of landmark cases in the 1980s and 1990s, the Court proved willing to subject member-state regulations to the strict '*Cassis* test', in the process striking down many politically sensitive national measures that restricted intra-Community trade. While the Court later retreated from some of the more far-reaching implications of these rulings in the 1993 *Keck* decision, moreover, the available evidence suggests that the Court's U-turn was inspired primarily by pressures from national courts, litigants, and the legal community, rather than from EU member governments. Similarly in the area of equal pay, the Court proved willing on repeated occasions to adopt a broad interpretation of the concepts of equal pay and discrimination in Article 141 EC, in several cases overruling the collective preferences of the member governments as expressed in submissions to the Court and in secondary legislation. Nevertheless, the Court's ruling in *Barber* finally led the member governments to respond with an amendment to the treaties limiting the retroactive effect of that ruling, after which the Court appears to have beaten a partial retreat in its subsequent equal-pay decisions. The *Barber* decision is unusual, I have argued, in terms of its enormous financial implications for a large number of member states, which prompted the adoption of the so-called Barber Protocol at Maastricht; nevertheless, it provides a vivid illustration of the fact that the Court's discretion is limited, even in the area of constitutional interpretation.

The Engines of Integration?

Finally, we return to the questions raised in the introduction to this book: do the Commission, the Court, and the Parliament *matter*—do they deserve the status of an independent causal variable—in the politics of the European Union? Are the EU's supranational organizations indeed 'the engines of integration', that is, the motivating force behind the major integrative developments of the past five decades? The answer to the first question, on the basis of the evidence examined in this book, is an unequivocal 'yes'. To be sure, the Commission, the Court, and the Parliament are all constrained by the limited powers delegated to them and by the administrative and oversight mechanisms established by member governments to limit their discretion, and the influence of each actor over policy outcomes varies across issue areas primarily as a function of these various control mechanisms. However, in each of the cases examined in this book— all of which were selected as 'hard cases' for supranational influence given the presence of clear member-state preferences and open conflict among principals and agents—the Commission and the Court have been able to exert at least some influence over policy outcomes, which counter-factually would not have been adopted by the member governments in the absence of supranational action. In sum, on the basis of the Commission and ECJ cases examined reviewed in this book, together with similar studies of the Parliament's influence in the legislative process,[2] it seems clear that, despite their limited and variable discretion across issue areas and over time, the EU's supranational agents do indeed 'matter'.

Turning to the second question, however—whether the Commission, the Court, and the Parliament are '*the* engines of integration'— our answer must be more qualified. On the one hand, we have seen that the Commission, Court, and Parliament have indeed served repeatedly as 'engines of integration' within their limits of their statutory discretion, exerting an independent causal impact on EU policy outcomes and pushing forward both the creation and the regulation of the Single European Market. In this sense, the supranationalist vision of leaders such as Jean Monnet and Walter Hallstein, as well as the neo-functionalist integration theories of Ernst Haas and others, have been largely vindicated. On the other hand, the principal-agent analysis and the empirical evidence presented in this book suggest that the ability of the EU's supranational agents to push forward the integrationist project is circumscribed, to a greater or lesser extent and in predictable ways, by the preferences and the acts of delegation adopted by their member-government principals. Furthermore, as

Moravcsik (1998; 1999) has pointed out in his review of the EU's periodic intergovernmental conferences, the member governments have repeatedly proven their ability to act as their own 'engines of integration', putting forward proposals and negotiating far-reaching integrative agreements among themselves with little or no supranational input. The Commission, the Parliament, and the Court have, of course, made serious and valuable contributions to the various intergovernmental conferences held in recent years, most notably with regard to the Single European Act; yet the absence of Commission proposals and brokering did not prevent member-state officials from negotiating the landmark treaties establishing the European Coal and Steel Community in 1951 or the EEC in 1957. Since the Single European Act, moreover, there has been a generally noted secular decline in supranational influence within the various intergovernmental conferences, as member governments have participated with increasing preparation and increasingly clear preferences, and with key mediating and brokering roles being played by the Council Presidency and its secretariat rather than by the Commission. In sum, the Commission, the Court of Justice, and the European Parliament are causally important actors in the processes of European integration, but they are actors in an intergovernmental play written, and periodically rewritten, by the EU's member governments.

II. Empirical Implications: A Europe of Agents, a World of Agents

Throughout this book, the empirical focus has been on the delegation of powers to, and the agency and agenda-setting activities of, three supranational agents, namely, the Commission, the Court of Justice, and the Parliament. The implications of the principal-agent approach outlined in this book, however, extend far beyond these three supranational organizations to include the European Central Bank and the welter of 'independent' European agencies established by the EU member states over the past decade, as well as to other international executives, secretariats, development banks, dispute-resolution bodies, tribunals, and courts established by other regional and global institutions. Although a thorough analysis of these developments is far beyond the scope of this concluding chapter, a brief review of these EU and other international developments will serve to illustrate the generalizibility of the theory laid out in this book, and lay out a broad research agenda for the study of delegation, agency, and agenda setting in European and international politics.

A Europe of Agents?

Delegation to supranational agents began, but by no means ended, with the Commission, the Court, and the Parliament. Over the past decade, EU member governments have supplemented these bodies with a powerful European Central Bank and with a proliferation of 'independent' agencies with a dizzying array of functions and institutional structures. While creating and empowering these new supranational agencies, however, the member governments have also developed new, 'post-regulatory' modes of governance in which supranational agents play a secondary, and largely unstudied, role. In addition to these developments, moreover, the EU's member governments agreed in December 2000 to the Treaty of Nice, designed to prepare the Union for its imminent enlargement, and subsequently opened a wide-ranging public debate on the future of Europe which is to culminate in yet another intergovernmental conference and possibly a 'European constitution' in 2004. While a full discussion of these developments is beyond the scope of this concluding chapter, each development presents important questions for the future study of delegation, agency, and agenda-setting in the contemporary European Union, and merits at least a brief examination here.

The European Central Bank

The European Central Bank, created by the Treaty of Maastricht and now fully functioning as the collective central bank of the twelve member states of the Euro-zone, is without doubt the most spectacular example of supranational delegation in the European Union since the EEC Treaty of 1957. The basic institutional blueprint of the ECB was first proposed by the 1991 Delors Committee, composed primarily of European central bankers, and finalized in the negotiation of the Maastricht Treaty, where the German government successfully pressed for an independent central bank on the model of its own Bundesbank, with a mandate to pursue price stability as its sole objective.[3] To this end, the Maastricht Treaty delegates the management of European monetary policy to the ECB's 18-member Governing Council, including the six members of the Executive Board—a President, a Vice President, and four additional members, all appointed by common accord of the member governments after consulting the EP—and the twelve governors of the national central banks participating in the Euro.

In the language of principal-agent analysis, the ECB has been referred to as the most independent central bank in the world, and indeed its statutory independence is remarkable by comparison with other EC institutions as well as national central banks. The members of the ECB's Executive Board serve the longest terms of any EC civil servants, at eight years, and these terms are non-renewable, providing its members with little individual incentive to cater to the preferences of the member governments that appointed them; similarly, the treaty provides that the national central banks of the Euro-zone must enjoy statutory independence from their national governments, further insulating the bank from political pressures. Like the Court of Justice, moreover, but unlike many other central banks, the ECB deliberates in secret, making it impossible for member governments to identify the views or voting patterns of any individual member. The treaty does include a requirement that the Bank issue an annual report, and the members of its Executive Board have in practice agreed to testify regularly before the European Parliament, but in general the ECB is less transparent than other central banks like the Federal Reserve Bank of the United States or the Bank of England, where voting records and transcripts of meetings are generally made public, either immediately or after a short delay. In terms of the Bank's mandate, the Maastricht Treaty is unequivocal in identifying price stability as the ECB's sole objective, but the Bank enjoys complete discretion in defining its own monetary target and setting interest rates to achieve this objective. Finally, by contrast with the Federal Reserve, whose statute can be amended at any time by a majority decision in the Congress, the key articles of the Statute of the ECB can be amended only with the unanimous agreement of all the member states, setting an extraordinarily high threshold to legislative overruling of the ECB's decisions or mandate.

The delegation of these far-reaching monetary powers and discretion to the ECB has led to both scholarly and political debates about both the motives of the delegating member governments and the normative desirability and positive effects of the Bank's extraordinary independence. Regarding the former, Moravcsik (1998), Majone (2000), and others have pointed to the ECB as a classic case of delegation to increase the credibility of member-state commitment to their common aim of a stable, non-inflationary monetary policy. By contrast, however, Kathleen McNamara (2002) has argued that the economic case for delegating significant powers and independence to central banks is less compelling than functional theories of delegation suggest, and that the spread of independent central banks, including the ECB, can be explained as a process of institutional isomorphism whereby organizational forms considered to be successful and legitimate in one setting diffuse and are copied in other settings 'even if

these rules are materially inappropriate to their needs'. Such delegation, McNamara suggests, 'is rational and instrumental as the
principal-agent framework suggests, but only when placed within a
particular cultural and historical context that legitimizes delegation—
specifically, the culture of neoliberalism and price stability'
(McNamara 2002: 4). Delegation to independent central banks like the
ECB, she concludes, is driven less by the 'functional requirements of
economic management' than by ideational factors and by the power
of certain groups in society who can expect to gain disproportionately
from central banks' emphasis on price stability. There is a tension in
this last aspect of McNamara's argument, in which ideas appear alternately as independent causal factors and as a legitimizing ideology for
delegation decisions with clear redistributive consequences within
states. Nevertheless, McNamara's provocative analysis suggests closer
attention to both norms of legitimacy *and* the domestic distributive
implications of delegation to supranational actors like the ECB.

Finally, in a second major strain of the literature, critics and defenders of independent central banks have debated whether the ECB's
statutory independence is necessary and sufficient for the Bank to
establish its credibility in international currency markets, or whether,
conversely, the Bank has been granted too much independence, at the
expense of transparency and democratic accountability. Critics of
ECB independence typically point to the secrecy of the Bank's deliberations, the lack of accountability to either the member governments
or the European Parliament, and the 'constitutional' status of its
Statute, all of which make the ECB less transparent and less accountable than even the most independent national central banks.[4] Political
actors within the European Parliament and in the member states have
raised similar concerns, calling for greater accountability of the ECB
to Parliament and possibly the creation of a European 'economic government' to counterbalance to the ECB and perhaps set monetary targets for it.[5] Defenders of the ECB's independence, by contrast, note
that the decision not to make Governing Council votes public, like the
other aspects of its mandate, was taken by the member governments
for the same reason that the ECJ deliberates in secrecy, namely, to protect its members against political pressures from their respective member governments (Issing 1998; Chote 1998). The central bankers
themselves, moreover, have been fiercely protective of their independence, with ECB President Wim Duisenberg famously noting
that, while it is normal for politicians to offer their opinions on monetary policy, 'it would be very abnormal for the suggestions to be
listened to'.[6] Regardless of one's normative views of central bank

independence, the relationship of the ECB to its political principals promises to be one of the most important, and most difficult, research questions facing students of the EU in the coming years.

European Agencies

The ECB, although the most spectacular example of delegation to a new EU institution, is not the only quasi-independent agency created by the Union in recent years. In addition to the European Court of Auditors and the Office of the Ombudsman reviewed in Chapter 2, the EU has created a dozen independent agencies over the past three decades, which in themselves present an intriguing field of study regarding the institutional design of supranational delegation. By and large, the powers delegated to these agencies have been modest, in part because of resistance from member governments voting by unanimity in the Council, and in part because the ECJ's *Meroni* doctrine, dating back to the 1950s, appears to rule out large-scale delegation to bodies not mentioned in the Union's founding Treaties, for fear of disturbing the Union's institutional balance.[7] During the 1970s, the Council of Ministers created several so-called 'first-generation' agencies, like the European Center for the Development of Vocational Training and the European Foundation for the Improvement of Living and Working Conditions, but these remained marginal actors at best, with no regulatory powers and small budgets devoted primarily to the collection and dissemination of research in their respective areas. During the 1990s, however, the Council of Ministers created no fewer than ten 'second-generation' agencies with a variety of functions and an equally large array of administrative and oversight mechanisms giving varying roles to member governments, the Commission, the European Parliament, the 'social partners', and other actors.[8] Although a full survey of these agencies is once again beyond the scope of this chapter, the dozen existing European agencies provide a laboratory for the delegation of powers by the member governments as well as the means by which those governments seek to keep their agencies accountable.

In terms of functions, the Commission's classification scheme groups existing agencies into four categories according to the nature of their activities (CEC 2001*b*). The first group, 'agencies facilitating the operation of the internal market', includes the three agencies that have been delegated genuine regulatory powers, namely, the Office for Harmonization in the Internal Market, the Community Plant Variety Office, and the European Agency for the Evaluation of Medicinal Products (EMEA). These agencies, in cooperation with the Commission and national counterparts, play important regulatory roles in registering trade marks, protecting industrial property rights, and approving pharmaceuticals for marketing in the EU, respectively. By contrast, the agencies in the second group (European Environment Agency, European Center for Drugs and Drug Addition, European Monitoring Center on Racism and Xenophobia) enjoy no independent regulatory powers but simply collect and disseminate information in their respective areas, leaving the adoption of binding regulations to member states and Community institutions. A third group of agencies again enjoys 'soft' powers to promote the European social dialogue (European Center for Vocational Training, European Foundation for Improvement of Living and Working Conditions, European Agency for Health and Safety at Work) and the fourth group performs specific executive functions (European Training Foundation, Translation Center for the Bodies of the European Union, European Agency for Reconstruction).

Perhaps most interestingly for our purposes here, the EU's member governments have not created a one-size-fits-all institutional structure for these agencies but have, rather, designed specific administrative procedures as well as distinct patterns of membership and voting rights for each agency's management board. Everson *et al.* (2001) have collected useful data on the funding mechanisms, administrative procedures, and the membership of each agency's management board, demonstrating the variety of administrative and oversight mechanisms adopted. Administrative law provisions vary wildly across agencies, with the strictest procedural requirements and the most constraining administrative and judicial review provisions predictably reserved for the three regulatory agencies, although these enjoy greater budgetary autonomy from the Council given their ability to charge fees for their services. Oversight procedures are equally varied. In some cases, like the EMEA, appointment of the agency's director is the sole prerogative of the Council, and the member states also dominate the agency's management board and the regulatory committees overseeing its activities, while for other agencies the Commission, the European Parliament, and representatives of industry and trade unions play an important role alongside member-state representatives in the agencies' management boards and the nomination of their directors. Such a diversified pattern of delegation and discretion provides *prima facie* support for the rational-choice prediction that member-state principals will tailor the discretion of their respective agents depending on their concerns about information, credible commitments, and speedy and efficient decision-making, but the systematic study of both delegation to European agencies and the operation of these agencies is in its infancy, and represents another important topic for future research.

The 'Open Method of Coordination' and 'Soft Delegation'

At the same time as EU member states have been moving to create new administrative agencies in some issue areas, in other areas they have adopted 'new governance' procedures, including the so-called 'open method of coordination' (OMC) in which binding supranational regulations are eschewed in favour of a non-binding or 'soft' process of intergovernmental coordination.[9] The open method of coordination is often described as a 'post-regulatory' process of governance, in contrast to the Community's traditional command-and-control style of regulation, and provides for coordination rather than harmonization of member-state policies. Based on previous EU experience in areas like employment policy and codified by the Portuguese Presidency of the Union at the March 2000 Lisbon European Council, the open method of cooperation is typically characterized as an intergovernmental and legally non-binding form of policy coordination based on the collective establishment of policy guidelines, targets, and benchmarks, coupled with a system of periodic 'peer review' in which member governments present their national programmes for consideration and comment by their EU counterparts. By and large, the OMC has been used not as a replacement for but as a complement to the traditional 'Community method' in areas where member governments have been reluctant to adopt binding regulations, as in the area of employment policy.

The open method of coordination remains controversial both politically and in the academic community, with some considering it a flexible means to address common policy issues and foster mutual learning among the member governments without encroaching on sensitive areas of national sovereignty, while others suggest that the essentially intergovernmental and non-binding nature of the process allows the member governments to pay symbolic attention to key issues without undertaking any real, binding policy action.[10] For our purposes, however, the most interesting question about the OMC concerns the role, if any, of the EU's supranational actors in the process. If we take as an example the employment title of the Amsterdam Treaty, which is typically put forward as the best exemplar of the OMC, we find that the Commission is granted no binding executive powers, and indeed the so-called European Employment Strategy is itself entirely non-binding, relying entirely on peer review, public pressure, and mutual learning to produce changes—if any—in national policies. Largely for this reason, the Commission's 2001 White Paper on Governance argues that the OMC 'should not be used when legislative action under the Community method is possible' and that 'the Commission should be closely involved and play a coordinating role' (CEC 2001c: 22).

Indeed, as the Commission suggests, the European Employment Strategy is *not* exclusively intergovernmental but features both a *de jure* and *de facto* agenda-setting role for the Commission, which is given responsibility for drafting both the annual Employment Guidelines (adopted by qualified majority in the Council after consultation of the EP) and recommendations for member states (adopted by qualified majority with no role for the EP). Although the Council can amend the Commission's proposals by unanimity, and has regularly done so, the Commission nevertheless enjoys its traditional agenda-setting powers in this area, and can therefore shape the guidelines and benchmarks against which member-state policies are evaluated. Preliminary case-study evidence from the early years of the Employment Strategy suggests that the Commission does indeed play an important role in defining the broad lines of the Employment Guidelines, although member governments regularly agree by unanimity to remove or water down the Commission's numerical targets, and that the public nature of the Commission's annual report and draft recommendations allow it to shape the process of 'peer review' among the member governments.[11] While only suggestive, such studies point to the role of the Commission in the ostensibly 'intergovernmental' OMC as another promising area for future research.

The Treaty of Nice and Beyond
Throughout this book, I have extensively analysed the provisions of the *Consolidated Treaties*, namely, the EC and EU Treaties as amended by all subsequent revisions up to and including the 1997 Amsterdam Treaty. Amsterdam was not, however, the final amendment of the treaties, not least because that treaty failed to agree upon three fundamental reforms—the expansion of QMV, the re-weighting of votes in the Council of Ministers, and the number and distribution of Commissioners—that were seen to be crucial to the successful enlargement of the Union from its current 15 members to a future membership envisaged at 27 or more. Disappointed at the failure to reach agreement on these three issues, several member governments successfully pressed for the convening of yet another intergovernmental conference which would focus narrowly on these 'leftovers' from Amsterdam and on any other changes that might be necessary to allow the Union to operate efficiently with a substantially enlarged membership. A new IGC was duly convened in early 2000, and a draft treaty was signed at a tumultuous European Council meeting in Nice that December. Despite a cascade of critical commentary from the press about the late-night wrangling at the summit and the untidy

compromises reached there, the Nice Treaty does address the fundamental issues posed by enlargement, including the adaptation of the Union's institutions to function with an enlarged membership of 27 member states.[12]

The Treaty of Nice is not yet in force at this writing, having been ratified by only seven member states as of January 2002, and having been explicitly rejected in a referendum in Ireland on 29 March 2001 with a follow-up referendum still pending at this writing. Because the treaty was not in force at the time of writing, and because of the possibility that the treaty may in fact not enter into force as currently written, the amendments introduced there have not been integrated into the analysis presented in this book. In the event, however, the Treaty of Nice makes very few changes in the powers and discretion of the Commission, the Court, and the Parliament, for the simple reason that member governments deliberately restricted the scope of the IGC and the treaty to those amendments necessary to prepare for enlargement, and sought deliberately not to alter 'institutional balance' of the Union in doing so. The result is a treaty that alters slightly the composition of the Commission, the Court, and the Parliament in the context of an enlarged Europe, and delegates slightly greater powers and discretion to the Commission and the EP, without fundamentally altering the nature of the principal-agent relationship between each organization and its member-state principals.

As Table C.1 makes clear, the primary changes to the Commission relate to its membership. Under the terms of the treaty and its accompanying annexes, the future European Commission will include one Commissioner per member state up to a maximum size of 27, at which point the size of the Commission will be reduced and member states will take turns nominating Commissioners according to a predetermined system of rotation. Although revolutionary in so far as the larger member governments have agreed to the appointment of only a single Commissioner each, in return for greater voting weight in the Council, this outcome again demonstrates the importance that member governments attach to having 'their own' Commissioner and does not fundamentally influence the discretion of the Commission vis-à-vis the member governments collectively. In other ways, however, the Nice Treaty will benefit the Commission, which in the future will be appointed by a qualified majority rather than a unanimous vote among the member governments, thereby removing the ability of member governments with extreme preferences to veto potential candidates, as the United Kingdom vetoed the nomination of Jean-Luc Dehaene to the Presidency in 1994. In addition, the Commission

TABLE C.1. *The Treaty of Nice: Summary of provisions relating to the powers and discretion of the Commission, the Court of Justice, the European Parliament, and the Council of Ministers*

Commission

- *Size and composition.* Future Commissions will be composed of one Commissioner per member state, up to a maximum of 27. Beyond that number, the Commission will be composed of fewer Commissioners than member states (exact size to be decided by Council), with member states nominating candidates by a system of rotation on a strictly equal basis. (NB: bargaining linkage to redistribution of voting weights in Council.)
- *Nomination procedures.* President and Commission to be appointed by qualified majority of member states, rather than unanimity as at present.
- *Powers of President* strengthened.
- *Agenda-setting power* enhanced through modest expansion of QMV.
- *External trade policy.* EC competence extended to services and intellectual property, but with exceptions and retaining unanimity for certain areas.

Court of Justice/Court of First Instance

- *Size and composition.* Court will continue to be composed of one judge per member state. No change in length or renewability of mandate.
- *Jurisdiction.* No extension of ECJ jurisdiction, but restructuring of respective jurisdictions of ECJ and CFI, and possibility of creating 'judicial panels' below the CFI to deal with minor cases, such as staff cases.
- *Justice and Home Affairs/Police and Judicial Cooperation.* Limitations on ECJ jurisdiction unchanged.

European Parliament

- *Size and composition.* Maximum size increased from 700 to 732, allocation of seats adjusted to increase weight of larger member states.
- *Legislative powers.* Co-decision procedure modestly extended to 15 existing legal bases; procedure itself left unchanged. Assent extended to two additional legal bases (breach of fundamental rights; enhanced cooperation in areas subject to co-decision). No change to consultation, cooperation procedures.

TABLE C.1. *Continued*

- *Standing before the Court of Justice*. EP granted standing to bring cases for annulment (Art. 230 EC) and ask for ECJ opinions on international agreements (Article 300 EC) on same terms as member states.

Council of Ministers

- *Voting weights* altered to increase weight of larger states (NB: bargaining linkage to size of Commission).
- *Qualified majority voting threshold* may increase from current 71.5% to as high as 73.4% in a Union of 26.
- *Qualified majority voting extended* to 37 existing legal bases immediately, eight additional legal bases in the future.

Sources: Treaty of Nice; Galloway (2001).

gains a moderate increase in its trade competence under the revised Article 133, and some additional agenda-setting powers with the transfer of a number of legislative provisions from unanimity to QMV. In a similar fashion, the size of the European Parliament and the allocation of seats among member states were adjusted for a Union of 27 members, and the EP gained some additional legislative powers with the modest extension of the co-decision and assent procedures, as well as enhanced legal standing before the Court of Justice. As for the ECJ and the CFI, finally, the collective jurisdiction and discretion of the EC courts was left fundamentally unchanged at Nice. However, in response to the prospect of a 27-member Court, as well as the growing backlog of cases afflicting both courts, the member governments agreed to the creation of additional chambers within the ECJ to try cases without convening a full plenary, as well as the shift of certain types of cases to the CFI and the possible creation of 'judicial panels' to deal with minor cases (staff cases as the first and most obvious example). In short, the Treaty of Nice, when and if it eventually enters into force, will modestly increase the powers and discretion of the Commission and the Parliament, while possibly reducing the case load on the ECJ but otherwise leaving its jurisdiction unchanged.

Finally, however, it is worth noting that, before the Treaty of Nice has even been ratified, the member governments have collectively agreed to yet another intergovernmental conference in 2004, which will be broader than the Nice IGC, addressing fundamental constitutional questions about the distribution of powers between the member states and the European Union, the democracy and transparency of the EU policy process, the appointment of the Commission, the legislative powers of Parliament, and the possible adoption of a formal 'constitution' for the Union. The December 2001 meeting of the Brussels European Council formally launched this constitutional debate with the issuing of an open-ended 'Declaration on the Future of the European Union' and the creation of a 'Convention on the Future of Europe', composed of representatives of the member governments, the Commission, the European Parliament, and national parliaments, to draft the agenda for the 2004 intergovernmental conference.[13] Although it is too early to speculate on the outcome of either the Convention or the subsequent intergovernmental conference, it is clear that they will stimulate the most far-reaching debate about the role of the EU's supranational institutions in the history of the Union, raising both analytical and normative questions to which I return in the final section of this chapter.

A World of Agents

As we have seen throughout this book, both the phenomenon of delegation to supranational agencies and the scholarly literature on such delegation are most developed in the European Union, which has been and remains the most heavily institutionalized and 'supranational' international organization. Nevertheless, the delegation of powers to supranational executives, secretariats, development banks, dispute-resolution bodies, tribunals, and courts is a broader phenomenon. Examples of long-standing international organizations with substantial expertise, staff, and other resources include most notably the Bretton Woods institutions (the World Bank and the International Monetary Fund) as well as the various UN institutions (the United Nations Development Programme, UNESCO, UNICEF, the Secretariat, and others) created under US leadership after the Second World War. A second wave of delegation followed in the 1990s with the establishment of new executive and judicial bodies such as the European Bank for Reconstruction and Development (EBRD), the Dispute Settlement Body of the World Trade Organization (WTO), the arbitration panels of the North American Free Trade Agreement (NAFTA), the Hague Tribunal established to try suspected war criminals from the former Yugoslavia, and the International Criminal Court established (albeit without US participation) in 2002.

Like the literature on European integration, the international relations theory literature has until recently neglected questions of delegation to, and agency and agenda setting by, international organizations. Like intergovernmentalists in the study of European integration, realist and neo-realist theorists in international relations have generally assumed that international organizations are created by and respond to the preferences of the most powerful states in the international system (see for example Waltz 1979; Mearsheimer 1995). By contrast, constructivist scholars have in recent years highlighted the potential autonomy of international organizations, their internal organizational cultures, and their potential roles as propagators or teachers of norms in international politics (Finnemore 1996; Barnett and Finnemore 1999);[14] yet with the exception of Barnett and Finnemore (1999), these scholars focused almost exclusively on the ways in which international organizations might influence states, paying less attention to the possibility that states might in turn influence the endogenous preferences and the behaviour of international organizations through the types of control mechanisms identified by the principal-agent literature.

Fortunately, this neglect of delegation and agency questions in the study of international organizations appears to be ending, with several recent studies applying principal-agent analyses to non-European international organizations asking about the conditions under which states might delegate more or less extensive power and discretion to international organizations and the autonomy of those organizations from their principals.[15] As in the European Union, the study of international organizations using principal-agent approaches raises three important sets of questions, about delegation, agency, and agenda setting, respectively.

The first set of questions concerns the act of delegation itself, and the conditions under which states are likely to allocate more or less discretion to their agents. This set of questions, includes, among many others, the following:

1. In delegating powers to international organizations, are states motivated primarily by transaction-cost considerations, such as a demand for credible commitments, policy-relevant information, or speedy and efficient decision-making, as I have suggested in the case of the EU? Do states generally delegate the functions predicted by principal-agent models of delegation—monitoring compliance, solving problems of incomplete contracting, adopting regulations, and setting the legislative agenda—as in the case of the EU? Or do states base their delegation decisions on a logic of appropriateness, adopting

institutional designs based on their perceived legitimacy in the light of generally accepted international norms?

2. How do states structure the act of delegation in non-EU contexts in order to limit the discretion of their agents? Do states delegate different degrees of discretion across issue areas or grant greater discretion to certain types of agents, for example courts, while keeping executive agents more closely accountable to their member-state principals? And what kind of control mechanisms do states design in non-EU contexts in order to influence the preferences and behaviour of their agents? Preliminary studies of the IMF, the World Bank, and other international development organizations suggest that the United States and other countries have deliberately crafted a multiplicity of control mechanisms vis-à-vis those bodies, including procedures for the nomination and removal of their leaders; more or less constraining mandates; variable levels of funding and staff; and direct oversight through boards of governors representing the member states themselves (Martin 2000; Nielson and Tierney 2001*a*, *b*). Systematic attempts to map variation in the use of control mechanisms across international organizations, however, remain in their infancy, as do attempts to explain such variation.

3. To what extent does the decision to delegate functions to international organizations reflect the views of the most powerful state or states in the international system? Once again, existing work on the Bretton Woods institutions suggests that the structure of delegation to those institutions was determined in large part by a hegemonic United States, but the delegation of powers to more recently created organizations, such as the World Trade Organization, was undertaken in many instances with great reluctance by the United States, which in several cases has refused to subject itself to the authority of new international organizations and tribunals, such as the International Criminal Court.

4. More generally, to what extent and how are power differentials among states 'built in' to the structure of delegation to international organizations? Here again, a preliminary demonstrates variation across organizations, with the Bretton Woods institutions adopting both formal and informal procedures, such as weighted voting systems or the right of certain powerful actors to nominate the leaders of specific organizations, which explicitly give greater weight to more powerful states, while other international organizations, such as UNESCO, reflect the principle of sovereign equality among the members. Once again, mapping and explaining such variation in the differential influence accorded to multiple member-state principals remains a promising and, as yet, unexplored avenue of study.

5. How can we explain the preferences of states regarding the desirability of delegating powers and discretion to international

organizations? Are states' delegation decisions based on issue-specific calculations of the 'policy streams' likely to result from specific acts of delegation, as suggested by principal-agent analysis? Or do states formulate their preferences about delegation on the basis of broad ideological positions, with 'liberal internationalists' favouring and 'isolationists' opposing delegation across the board? To what extent do delegation decisions create distributive conflicts *within* states, whether between executives and legislatures or among groups or classes in society, and how are the resulting preferences over international delegation aggregated into a single, 'national' position?

6. Finally, have other states, regional organizations, or global organizations learned from the experience of delegation in the European Union? Throughout this book, we have seen how EU member governments regularly adjust the mandate of the Commission in response to perceived shirking by the latter, and how those same governments have undertaken treaty reforms to pre-empt future activism by the ECJ. Preliminary evidence from the negotiation and design of other regional organizations, such as North American Free Trade Area Agreement (NAFTA), Mercosur, and the recently created African Union, suggest that non-European actors have similarly learned from the EU experience, delegating powers to supranational secretariats and tribunals in some areas while deliberately steering away from the EU model in other areas, but more comparative research is needed to assess the extent to which the EU experience has been used as a policy model—or as a negative model of what to avoid—in other regional contexts. Indeed, all of the aforementioned questions, as basic and fundamental as they may seem, have only begun to be addressed explicitly in the empirical study of international organizations, and the answers will require extensive historical analysis of delegation decisions as well as qualitative and quantitative comparisons of the functions and discretion of the wide variety of regional and global international organizations.

A second set of questions concerns the agency and autonomy of international organizations vis-à-vis the states that created them. Here again, despite several decades of neo-liberal institutionalist work on the causal importance of international institutions, there have until recently been few if any explicit attempts to theorize and empirically test hypotheses about the conditions under which international organizations might be able to act on their own preferences and exert an independent causal influence on international policy outcomes. In several recent studies, however, Nielson and Tierney (2001*a, b*) formulate and test explicit hypotheses about the conditions under which member-state principals might influence the lending behaviour of international development institutions like the World Bank. Citing the constructivist and other literature depicting the Bank as a 'runaway bureaucracy' with a large staff, considerable expertise, access to privileged information, and a central place in the epistemic community of development economics, Nielson and Tierney (2001*a*) adopt the World Bank as a 'hard case' for member-state control and seek to show that despite its accumulated expertise the Bank remains responsive to its member-state principals and in particular to its largest single donor, the United States. Following a research design similar to Weingast and Moran (1983), Nielsen and Tierney examine the interaction of the Bank with its principals over the controversial issue of environmental lending, where the Bank's staff initially resisted any major changes in its lending practices in response to US and global pressure. Using case-study analysis, the authors convincingly illustrate the use of budgetary and other control mechanisms brought to bear by the US Congress and other member-state principals, and trace the subsequent introduction of institutional reforms to increase the incentives for staff to engage in environmental lending, which subsequently increased during the course of the 1990s. They conclude by arguing that the Bank, as an agent of the member governments and in particular of its largest shareholder, the United States, adopted environmental lending reforms *not* in response to pressure from global civil society, as constructivists would argue, but rather in response to the more immediate and consequential threats brought to bear by its immediate principals. In a second study (Nielson and Tierney 2001*b*), the authors engage in an explicit comparison of three international development banks, demonstrating a correlation between the environmental preferences and voting power of member-state principals and the environmental-lending behaviour of the organizations. Although still the exception, Nielson and Tierney's studies represent an important step forward in the theoretically informed and empirically rigorous study of principal-agent relationships among member states and international organizations, and serve as models for future studies. Similarly, Barnett and Finnemore's (1999) critique of principal-agent models directs our attention toward factors that have thus far remained under-theorized in principal-agent approaches, including the organizational culture of international agents, which may explain the preferences, and possibly pathologies, of those agents, and the full range of power resources, such as moral authority, that might be utilized by international agents in their interactions with member-state principals.

Third and finally, there is a need for greater work on the conditions under which international organizations are able to set the formal and informal agenda for their member-state principals. With regard to formal agenda setting, we find few if any examples of formal agenda-setting powers for any international organization comparable to the Commission's first-pillar powers, which combine a sole right of initiative with the possibility of qualified majority voting and a restrictive (unanimity) amendment rule. By and large, governments in other international organizations have opted not to delegate formal agenda-setting powers to international organizations but rather retain such powers themselves, either collectively or on a rotating basis. Nevertheless, as Lisa Martin (2000) points out, informal equivalents to such powers may exist in various organizations such as the International Monetary Fund, where lending decisions are taken by the IMF executive board on the basis of a proposal from the organization's staff, and with an informal rule that such lending decisions are voted up or down without amendments.

With regard to informal agenda setting, finally, an increasing number of studies have suggested that international organizations, as well as transnational coalitions and social movements, are capable of 'setting the agenda' for international agreements by strategically framing issues for consideration by states and other international and domestic actors.[16] This book, like Moravcsik (1998; 1999) and other studies of supranational entrepreneurship in the EU, suggests caution about attributing causal influence to such informal agenda setters in the absence of careful process tracing and counter-factual analysis. Nevertheless, for many international organizations and office holders—including, for example, the UN Secretary-General and 2001 Nobel Peace Prize-winner Kofi Annan—such informal agenda-setting power constitutes the primary if not the only source of influence vis-à-vis their member-state principals and the international community. For this reason, rigorous and carefully designed studies of informal agenda setting by international organizations will be crucial in establishing the full causal importance of these actors, for good or ill, in international politics.

III. Normative Implications: Delegation, Discretion, and Democracy

Throughout this book, I have taken a positive rather than a normative approach to questions of delegation and discretion, asking what kinds of functions are delegated to supranational organizations, under which conditions member-state principals grant discretion to their agents, and how supranational agents like the Commission exploit their discretion to advance the process of European integration. All of these questions, however, have strong normative implications for the governance of Europe, and it is with a brief discussion of these implications that I conclude.

In much of the literature on the Commission, as well as on the Court and the Parliament, the stated or unstated assumption is that autonomous or even activist behaviour by European agents is normatively desirable. From the early days of Monnet, Haas, and Hallstein, most scholars of European integration have been explicitly or implicitly in favour of further integration. In that context, they have generally, and correctly, assumed that the Commission and other EU agents are in favour of 'more Europe' and have therefore assigned a positive normative assessment to autonomous Commission behaviour, which is most often presented in terms of 'entrepreneurship' or 'leadership'.[17] And indeed, the case studies presented in this book support the view that the Commission, the Court, and the Parliament are pro-European in their preferences and often use their discretion to carry integration to a higher level in terms of market liberalization, social regulation, and institutional development.

Nevertheless, an increasing number of scholars have pointed in recent years to the inherent tension between the delegation of powers from the national to the supranational level on the one hand and the normative value of democratic control on the other hand. The case that the EU is characterized by a 'democratic deficit' is typically made in two stages. First, it is argued, the EU is eroding national legislation and regulations, both directly and indirectly, thereby thwarting the democratically expressed preferences of national citizens and their legislatures. The most direct routes whereby the EU erodes national regulations are of course through the legislative process, when EU regulations replace or constrain national laws, and through the judicial process, when the European Court of Justice declares national regulations incompatible with the treaties as in the free-movement cases examined in Chapter 5. Moreover, even where EU legislation and ECJ jurisprudence leave national regulations untouched, it is often argued that the free movement of capital mandated by the Union may set in train a process of regulatory competition in which national governments face pressures to adjust national regulations in an effort to make them more attractive to mobile capital. At the extreme, this process of regulatory competition may lead to a 'race to the bottom' in which national governments competitively deregulate national environmental and social regulations (Streeck 1996: 85–6). In recent years, Vogel and others have argued that regulatory competition need not result in a race into the bottom, and can even lead states to ratchet standards upward (Vogel 1995; Sun and Pelkmans 1995); nevertheless, from the perspective of democratic theory, the expressed preferences of national electorates are sacrificed to the purported economic goods of the common market. In the words of Claus Offe (2000: 73–4), the *acquis communautaire*—the body of legislation accumulated by the European Union and devoted primarily to market liberalization—now threatens the West European *acquis nationale* of strong liberal democracy and well-developed welfare states.

This raises a second question: whether a race to the bottom might be averted, and democracy regained, at the EU level. On this score, many contributors to the debate are pessimistic, pointing to the distant and opaque nature of EU decision-making; the strong role of indirectly elected politicians in the Council of Ministers and unelected officials in the Commission and the Court; the weakness of the European Parliament and the second-order nature of its elections; and the bias of the treaties in favour of market liberalization over social regulation (Williams 1991; Greven 2000: 37). Furthermore, even if these institutional flaws in the EU Treaties were addressed, Joseph Weiler and others have suggested that Europe lacks a *demos*, a group of people united by a sense of community or 'we-feeling' that could provide the constituent basis for democracy and for the extension of the civil, political, and social rights to all of its members (Weiler 1995; Greven 2000: 44). The European Union has arguably attempted to establish such a political space, with extensive consultation of civil-society groups and periodic election of representatives to the European Parliament, but in practice the European political sphere remains limited to a relatively few Brussels insiders, stunted in its development by the diversity of languages and political cultures throughout the Union. For both of these reasons, Edgar Grande (2000: 120) argues, the EU's democratic deficit is as much structural as institutional and is therefore unlikely to be overcome in the short term through EU institutional reforms.

From this perspective, delegation of powers to non-majoritarian EU bodies such as the Commission and the Court of Justice is likely to exacerbate the EU's democratic deficit, since decisions previously taken by elected representatives are now diverted to the more distant, unelected, and imperfectly accountable Eurocrats in Brussels and judges in Luxembourg. Furthermore, some of the 'solutions' devised by member governments to Commission agency are themselves suspect from the perspective of democratic legitimacy. Comitology, for example, offers member governments a reliable and carefully calibrated mechanism for oversight of the Commission in its various executive functions; by the same token, however, comitology committees have also been criticized for their opacity, for their exclusion of members of the European Parliament and civil society groups, and for taking legislative decisions that should properly be adopted by a democratically accountable legislature.

Such criticisms of the EU's democratic credentials should not be accepted without question. As Andrew Moravcsik (2001: 120) points out,

...the few areas of genuinely independent EU activity—such as constitutional adjudication, central banking, multilateral trade negotiations, and antitrust enforcement—are precisely those excluded from direct democratic control in most national polities, to allow the smooth and fair functioning of government.

Indeed, one might go as far as to argue that, in each of these areas, delegation to the EU's supranational agents serves to replace the increasingly ineffective and fragmented efforts of unelected national bureaucrats, judges, and central bankers with the more effective and coherent policies and judgments of their European counterparts—which is why member governments have agreed to delegate such powers in the first place.

Nevertheless, the normative critique of EU democracy sketched out above does raise a final question for this book: how might the delegation of powers to the Commission, the Court, and the Parliament be structured to ensure not only an acceptable degree of control for EU member governments but also an acceptable degree of democratic legitimacy vis-à-vis the peoples of Europe? In this context, and simplifying considerably, we can identify three primary options for institutional design and reform: parliamentarization, deliberation, and constitutionalization.

The first of these options, parliamentarization, involves the strengthening of the EU's parliamentary and majoritarian elements, most notably by strengthening the European Parliament. In this view, the Parliament should be given full powers of co-legislation with the Council of Ministers, except perhaps in 'constitutional' issues involving the surrender of national sovereignty; a role in the periodic negotiation and approval of changes to the Union's constitutive treaties; and an enhanced role in the supervision of the Commission, which could at the extreme be drawn from and answerable to the EP on the model of national parliamentary systems. Such reforms, it is argued, together with the adoption of a single electoral system for all MEPs and the development of a strong European party system that would make MEPs less beholden to national parties and national governments, could in time enhance the democratic credentials of the Union and contribute to the creation of a genuine European public sphere.

The parliamentary approach has the dual advantage of drawing upon a model familiar to nearly all Europeans and building upon the incremental increases in the powers of the European Parliament over the past four decades. Nevertheless, such an approach is not without drawbacks. While it is true, for example, that EU member governments have been willing on repeated occasions to delegate legislative, budgetary, and supervisory powers to the Parliament, they have also demonstrated a repeated reluctance to increase the powers of Parliament where such delegation could lead to adverse policy consequences. The further parliamentarization of the EU, therefore, is likely to take place on an incremental, case-by-case basis rather than through the more systematic transformation advocated by adherents of the parliamentary model.

More fundamentally, other critics argue that, even if member governments were able to agree to such delegation, the Union's structural democratic deficit—the lack of a European demos or public sphere—would be resistant to a quick institutional fix. Direct elections of MEPs might, in the fullness of time, foster the development of a European identity or the creation a genuine transnational public sphere, but the time lag for such developments is likely to be measured in generations, and in the meantime the 'so-called European parliament' (Greven 2000: 50) would remain a second-order legislature, distant from the EU's citizens and largely unaccountable to them.

Perhaps most importantly for our purposes, one of the core elements of the parliamentary model, the subjection of the Commission to parliamentary control, poses a potential threat to the credibility of the Commission as a regulator and enforcer of EU law. As have seen in this book, EU member governments have deliberately and repeatedly allocated the Commission and the Court considerable discretion in the setting of the legislative agenda, the enforcement of EU law, the implementation of selected EU policies, and the negotiation of external trade agreements, in the belief that insulating these bodies from majoritarian political pressures would lead to more credible and efficient legislation, regulation, and law enforcement. In that context, Majone (2000) has argued, increasing the accountability of the Commission to the Parliament could have the perverse and presumably undesired effect of 'politicizing' the Commission and thereby reducing the credibility of EU legislation, regulation, and law enforcement across a wide range of issue areas. In this sense, the parliamentarization of the EU may undermine its effectiveness, or 'output' legitimacy, without substantially improving its democratic accountability, or 'input' legitimacy.

In light of these difficulties, a number of authors have suggested that the appropriate model for the EU is not majoritarian democracy, with its unrealistic assumptions of a European demos and its danger of creating 'structural minorities' in the absence of such a demos, but deliberative democracy, in which citizens, or at least their representatives, collectively deliberate in search of the best solution to common problems (Joerges and Neyer 1997*a*, *b*; Risse 2000; Zürn 2000; Joerges 2001). As we saw in Chapter 2, this ideal of 'deliberative supranationalism' has been put forward most forcefully and convincingly by Joerges and Neyer, who see in contemporary comitology committees a promising forum for deliberative problem-solving among both supranational and national officials who are constrained to present arguments and evidence in favour of their proposals. Although such a vision has been criticized by various scholars as technocracy by any other name, Joerges has recently argued that the concept of deliberative supranationalism as practised in comitology committees is in fact a *corrective* to technocratic decision making by American-style regulatory agencies. 'The much maligned comitology', Joerges argues, 'has the advantage over agencies of the American pattern in that it structures risk policy pluralistically, that national bureaucracies have to face up to the positions of their neighbor states, and that interests and concerns in the Member States cannot be filtered out' (Joerges 2001: 9). On a pragmatic note, moreover, Joerges argues that, rather than proposing ideal-typical models of European governance based on either domestic European or American experiences, 'it may be quite reasonable to start from institutional innovations which have already come about in the course of European market integration, ask whether they can already count as tried and tested, and discuss their normative merits' (Joerges 2001: 2).

Notwithstanding the potential benefits of deliberative decision making, critics continue to express both empirical and normative doubts about the deliberative-supranationalism model as a corrective for the democratic deficit in EU decision making. As an empirical matter, we simply do not know how often, and under what conditions, Commission and member-state officials deliberate, as opposed to bargaining from fixed national positions, in large part because comitology meetings continue to take place behind closed doors. The most recent reform of comitology in 1999 has resulted in a greater degree of transparency in so far as the composition and agendas of committee meetings are now part of the public record, but comitology meetings generally remain closed to the public, making it difficult to ascertain whether the interests and concerns of particular societal groups are being adequately represented.[18] Indeed, some critics have suggested that the model of deliberation among a small group of public officials meeting *in camera* makes it a questionable substitute for open parliamentary decision making. As Arthur Benz has argued, 'Deliberative negotiations and cooperation improve the effectiveness of state activities, but they are at the same time linked with unequal chances of participation and an infringement of the principle of public accessibility' (quoted in Zürn 2000: 98).

For these and other reasons, an increasing number of scholars have recently advocated a third option, namely, the 'constitutionalization' of procedural controls that would ensure minimum levels of transparency and public participation in regulatory policy making by the Commission and other EU institutions. To some extent, the Commission itself has opened the debate, publishing a White Paper on Governance in July 2001 and calling for various reforms including the online publication of information on preparation of policy through all stages of decision-making, minimum standards and a code of conduct for consultation with civil-society groups, and the establishment of a systematic dialogue with local and regional governments in the various member states (CEC 2001*c*).

Laudable as such reforms may be, however, they fall far short of the guarantees offered to citizens by administrative law in the United States and other national polities. Advocates of constitutionalization, therefore, suggest the adoption of more far-reaching and binding reforms, including most notably a European version of the American Administrative Procedure Act.[19] As we saw in Chapter 2, the APA provides the broad administrative-law framework for federal regulatory policy making in the United States, including the basic requirement of 'notice-and-comment' rule-making as well as extensive standing for individuals to challenge executive decisions in federal courts. The APA and the American regulatory process are not without their critics, who point to the judicialization of policy making and the resulting gridlock that can afflict American regulatory agencies subject to legal challenges on every conceivable front. As one Swedish parliamentarian remarked upon hearing a presentation about the APA, 'If that is the regulatory process in America, then God bless Europe'.[20] Nevertheless, as Francesca Bignami (1999) has convincingly demonstrated, a modified version of notice-and-comment rule-making could provide the European Union with a model for a more open and accountable regulatory process while limiting the threat of judicial overload by allowing challenges to rules only after their enforcement and making more extensive use of national courts and the preliminary ruling procedure for challenges to EU rules.

On a final note, and returning to positive analysis, the diversity of member-state preferences and the unanimity requirement for treaty reforms means that, in practice, the Union is unlikely to opt in the short or medium term for any one of the three models discussed above. Instead, the most likely outcome is a conceptually untidy combination of the three, namely: a modest and incremental increase in the legislative powers of the European Parliament, stopping short of full parliamentarization; the continuation of the highly uneven and quasi-public experiment in deliberation through committees, but with greater transparency; and a piecemeal strengthening of EU administrative law and its enforcement by the European and national courts. Europeans could do worse.

APPENDIX A

Selected Articles, *Consolidated Treaties*

I. *The European Commission*

Article 202 (ex 145) EC

To ensure that the objectives set out in this Treaty are attained the Council shall, in accordance with the provisions of this Treaty . . .

—confer upon the Commission, in the acts which the Council adopts, powers for the implementation of the rules which the Council lays down. The Council may impose certain requirements in respect of the exercise of these powers. The Council may also reserve the right, in specific cases, to exercise directly implementing powers itself. The procedures referred to above must be consonant with principles and rules to be laid down in advance by the Council, acting unanimously on a proposal from the Commission and after obtaining the Opinion of the European Parliament.

Article 211 (ex 155) EC

In order to ensure the proper functioning and development of the common market, the Commission shall:

—ensure that the provisions of this Treaty and the measures taken by the institutions pursuant thereto are applied;
—formulate recommendations or deliver opinions on matters dealt with in this Treaty, if it expressly so provides or if the Commission considers it necessary;
—have its own power of decision and participate in the shaping of measures taken by the Council and by the European Parliament in the manner provided for in this Treaty;
—exercise the powers conferred on it by the Council for the implementation of the rules laid down by the latter.

Article 213 (ex 157) EC

1. The Commission shall consist of 20 Members, who shall be chosen on the grounds of their general competence and whose independence is beyond doubt.

The number of Members of the Commission may be altered by the Council, acting unanimously . . .

The Commission must include at least one national of each of the Member States, but may not include more than two Members having the nationality of the same State.

2. The Members of the Commission shall, in the general interest of the Community, be completely independent in the performance of their duties.

In the performance of these duties, they shall neither seek nor take instructions from any government or from any other body. They shall refrain from any action incompatible with their duties. Each Member State undertakes to respect this principle and not to seek to influence the Members of the Commission in the performance of their tasks.

The Members of the Commission may not, during their term of office, engage in any other occupation, whether gainful or not. When entering upon their duties they shall give a solemn undertaking that, both during and after their term of office, they will respect the obligations arising therefrom and in particular their duty to behave with integrity and discretion as regards the acceptance, after they have ceased to hold office, of certain appointments or benefits. In the event of any breach of these obligations, the Court of Justice may, on application by the Council or the Commission, rule that the Member State concerned be, according to the circumstances, either compulsorily retired in accordance with Article 216 or deprived of his right to a pension or other benefits in its stead.

Article 214 (ex 158) EC

The Members of the Commission shall be appointed, in accordance with the procedure referred to in paragraph 2, for a period of five years, subject, if need be, to Article 201.

II. The European Court of Justice

Article 220 (ex 164) EC

The Court of Justice shall ensure that in the interpretation and application of this Treaty the law is observed.

Article 221 (ex 165) EC

The Court of Justice shall consist of 15 Judges...

Should the Court of Justice so request, the Council may, acting unanimously, increase the number of Judges...

Article 223 (ex 167) EC

The Judges and Advocates-General shall be chosen from persons whose independence is beyond doubt and who possess the qualifications required for appointment to the highest judicial office in their respective countries or who are jurisconsults of recognized competence; they shall be appointed by common accord of the member governments for a term of six years...

Retiring Judges and Advocates-General shall be eligible for reappointment...

Article 226 (ex 169) EC

If the Commission considers that a Member State has failed to fulfil an obligation under this Treaty, it shall deliver a reasoned opinion on the matter after giving the state concerned the opportunity to submit its observations.

If the State concerned does not comply with the opinion within the period laid down by the Commission, the latter may bring the matter before the Court of Justice.

Article 227 (ex 170) EC

A Member State which considers that another Member State has failed to fulfil an obligation under this Treaty may bring the matter before the Court of Justice.

Before a Member State brings an action against another Member State for an alleged infringement of an obligation under this Treaty, it shall bring the matter before the Commission.

The Commission shall deliver a reasoned opinion after each of the States concerned has been given the opportunity to submit its own case and its observations of the other party's case both orally and in writing.

If the Commission has not delivered an opinion within three months of the date on which the matter was brought before it, the absence of such an opinion shall not prevent the matter from being brought before the Court of Justice.

Article 228 (ex 171) EC

1. If the Court of Justice finds that a Member State has failed to fulfil an obligation under this Treaty, the State shall be required to take the necessary measures to comply with the judgment of the Court of Justice.

2. If the Commission considers that the Member State concerned has not taken such measures it shall, after giving the State the opportunity to submit its observations, issue a reasoned opinion specifying the points on which the Member State concerned has not complied with the judgment of the Court of Justice.

If the Member State concerned fails to take the necessary measures to comply with the Court's judgment within the time-limit laid down by the Commission, the latter may bring the case before the Court of Justice. In doing so it shall specify the amount of the lump sum or penalty payment to be paid by the Member State concerned which it considers appropriate in the circumstances.

If the Court of Justice finds that the Member State concerned has not complied with its judgment it may impose a lump sum or penalty payment on it.

This procedure shall be without prejudice to Article 227.

Article 230 (ex 173) EC

The Court of Justice shall review the legality of acts adopted jointly by the European Parliament and the Council, of acts of the Council, of the Commission and of the ECB, other than recommendations and opinions, and of acts of the European Parliament intended to produce legal effects vis-à-vis third parties.

It shall for this purpose have jurisdiction in actions brought by a Member State, the Council or the Commission on grounds of lack of competence, infringement of an essential procedural requirement, infringement of this Treaty or of any rule of law relating to its application, or misuse of powers.

The Court of Justice shall have jurisdiction under the same conditions in actions brought by the European Parliament, by the Court of Auditors and by the ECB for the purpose of protecting their prerogatives.

Any natural or legal person may, under the same conditions, institute proceedings against a decision addressed to that person or against a decision which, although in the form of a regulation or a decision addressed to another person, is of direct and individual concern to the former.

The proceedings provided for in this Article shall be instituted within two months of the publication of the measure, or of its notification to the plaintiff, or, in the absence thereof, of the day on which it came to the knowledge of the latter, as the case may be.

Article 231 (ex 174) EC

If the action is well founded, the Court of Justice shall declare the act concerned to be void.

In the case of a regulation, however, the Court of Justice shall, if it considers this necessary, state which of the effects of the regulation which it has declared void shall be considered as definitive.

Article 232 (ex 175) EC

Should the European Parliament, the Council or the Commission, in infringement of this Treaty, fail to act, the Member States and the other institutions of the Community may bring an action before the Court of Justice to have the infringement established.

The action shall be admissible only if the institution concerned has first been called upon to act. If, within two months of being so called upon, the institution concerned has not defined its position, the action may be brought within a further period of two months.

Any natural or legal person may, under the conditions laid down in the preceding paragraphs, complain to the Court of Justice that an institution of the Community has failed to address to that person any act other than a recommendation or an opinion.

The Court of Justice shall have jurisdiction, under the same conditions, in actions or proceedings brought by the ECB in areas falling within the latter's field of competence and in actions or proceedings brought against the latter.

Article 234 (ex 177) EC

The Court of Justice shall have jurisdiction to give preliminary rulings concerning:

(a) the interpretation of this Treaty;
(b) the validity and interpretation of acts of the institutions of the Community and of the ECB;
(c) the interpretation of the statutes of bodies established by an act of the Council, where those statutes so provide.

Where such a question is raised before any court or tribunal of a Member State, that court or tribunal may, if it considers that a decision on the question is necessary to enable it to give judgment, request the Court to give a ruling thereon.

Where any such question is raised in a case pending before a court or tribunal of a Member State against whose decisions there is no judicial remedy under national law, that court or tribunal shall bring the matter before the Court of Justice.

Article 245 (ex 188) EC

The Statute of the Court of Justice is laid down in a separate Protocol.

The Council may, acting unanimously at the request of the Court of Justice and after consulting the Commission and the European Parliament, amend the provisions of Title III of the Statute.

The Court of Justice shall establish its Rules of Procedure. These shall require the unanimous approval of the Council.

Article 68 (ex 73p) EC

1. Article 234 shall apply to this Title under the following circumstances and conditions: where a question on the interpretation of this Title or on the validity or interpretation of acts of the institutions of the Community based on this Title is raised in a case pending before a court or tribunal of a Member State against whose decisions there is no judicial remedy under national law, that court or tribunal shall, if it considers that a decision on the question is necessary to enable it to give judgment, request the Court of Justice to give a ruling thereon.

2. In any event, the Court of Justice shall not have jurisdiction to rule on any measure or decision taken pursuant to Article 62(1) relating to the maintenance of law and order and the safeguarding of internal security.

3. The Council, Commission or a Member State may request the Court of Justice to give a ruling on a question of interpretation of this Title or acts of the institutions of the Community based on this Title. The ruling given by the Court of Justice in response to such a request shall not apply to judgments of courts or tribunals of the Member States which have become res judicata.

Article 35 (ex K.7) EU

1. The Court of Justice of the European Communities shall have jurisdiction, subject to the conditions laid down in this Article, to give preliminary rulings on the validity and interpretation of framework decisions and decisions, on the interpretation of conventions established under this Title and on the validity and interpretation of the measures implementing them.

2. By a declaration made at the time of the signature of the Treaty of Amsterdam or at any time thereafter, any Member State shall be able to accept the jurisdiction of the Court of Justice to give preliminary rulings as specified in paragraph 1.

3. A Member State making a declaration pursuant to paragraph 2 shall specify that either:

(a) any court or tribunal of that State against which there is no judicial remedy under national law may request the Court of Justice to give a preliminary ruling on a question raised in a case pending before it and concerning the validity or interpretation of an act referred to in paragraph 1 if that court or tribunal considers that a decision on the question is necessary to enable it to give judgment, or

(b) any court or tribunal of that State may request the Court of Justice to give a preliminary ruling on a question raised in a case pending before it and concerning the validity or interpretation of an act referred to in paragraph 1 if that court or tribunal considers that a decision on the question is necessary to enable it to give judgment.

4. Any Member State, whether or not it has made a decision pursuant to paragraph 2, shall be entitled to submit statements of case or written observations to the Court in cases which arise under paragraph 1.

5. The Court of Justice shall have no jurisdiction to review the validity or proportionality of operations carried out by the police or other law enforcement services of a Member State or the exercise of the responsibilities incumbent upon Member States with regard to the maintenance of law and order and the safeguarding of internal security.

6. The Court of Justice shall have jurisdiction to review the legality of framework decisions and decisions in actions brought by a Member State or the Commission on grounds of lack of competence, infringement of an essential procedural requirement, infringement of this Treaty or of any rule of law relating to its application, or misuse of powers. The proceedings provided for in this paragraph shall be instituted within two months of the publication of the measure.

7. The Court of Justice shall have jurisdiction to rule on any dispute between Member States regarding the interpretation or the application of acts adopted under Article 34(2) whenever such dispute cannot be settled by the Council within six months of its being referred to the Council by one of its members. The Court shall also have jurisdiction to rule on any dispute between Member States and the Commission regarding the interpretation or the application of conventions established under Article 34(2)(d).

Article 46 (ex L) EU

The provisions of the Treaty establishing the European Community, the Treaty establishing the European Coal and Steel Community and the Treaty establishing the European Atomic Energy Community concerning the powers of the Court of Justice of the European Communities and the exercise of those powers shall apply only to the following provisions of this Treaty:

(a) provisions amending the Treaty establishing the European Economic Community with a view to establishing the European Community, the Treaty establishing the European Coal and Steel Community and the Treaty establishing the European Atomic Energy Community;

(b) provisions of Title VI, under the conditions provided for by Article 35;

(c) provisions of Title VII, under the provisions provided for by Article 11 of the Treaty establishing the European Community and Article 40 of this Treaty;

(d) Article 6(2) with regard to the action of the institutions, insofar as the Court has jurisdiction under the Treaties establishing the European Communities and under this Treaty;

(e) Articles 46 to 53.

III. The European Parliament

Article 189 (ex 137) EC

The European Parliament, which shall consist of the representatives of the peoples of the States brought together in the Community, shall exercise the powers conferred upon it by this Treaty.

The number of Members of the European Parliament shall not exceed seven hundred.

Article 190 (ex 138) EC

1. The representatives in the European Parliament of the peoples of the States brought together in the Community shall be elected by direct universal suffrage.

2. The number of representatives elected in each Member State shall be as follows...

In the event of amendment to this paragraph, the number of representatives elected in each member state must ensure appropriate representation to the peoples of the States brought together in the Community.

3. Representatives shall be elected to a term of five years.

4. The European Parliament shall draw up a proposal for elections by direct universal suffrage in accordance with a uniform procedure in all Member States or in accordance with principles common to all Member States.

The Council shall, acting unanimously after obtaining the assent of the European Parliament, which shall act by a majority of its component members, lay down the appropriate provisions, which it shall recommend to Member States for adoption in accordance with their respective constitutional requirements.

5. The European Parliament shall, after seeking an opinion from the Commission and with the approval of the Council acting unanimously, lay down the regulations and general conditions governing the performance of the duties of its Members.

Article 191 (ex Article 138a)

Political parties at European level are important as a factor for integration within the Union. They contribute to forming a European awareness and to expressing the political will of the citizens of the Union.

Article 192 (ex 138b) EC

Insofar as provided in this Treaty, the European Parliament shall participate in the process leading up to the adoption of Community acts by exercising its powers under the procedures laid down in Articles 251 and 252 and by giving its assent or delivering advisory opinions.

The European Parliament may, acting by a majority of its members, request the Commission to submit any appropriate proposal on matters on which it considers that a Community act is required for the purpose of implementing this Treaty.

Article 197 (ex 140) EC

The European Parliament shall elect its President and its officers from among its Members.

Members of the Commission may attend all meetings and shall, at their request, be heard on behalf of the Commission.

The Commission shall reply orally or in writing to questions put to it by the European Parliament or by its Members.

The Council shall be heard by the European Parliament in accordance with the conditions laid down by the Council in its Rules of Procedure.

Article 198 (ex Article 141) EC

Save as otherwise provided in this Treaty, the European Parliament shall act by an absolute majority of the votes cast.

The Rules of Procedure shall determine the quorum.

Article 201 (ex 144) EC

If a motion of censure on the activities of the Commission is tabled before it, the European Parliament shall not vote thereon until at least three days after the motion has been tabled and only by open vote.

If the motion of censure is carried by a two-thirds majority of the votes cast, representing a majority of the Members of the European Parliament, the Members of the Commission shall resign as a body. They shall continue to deal with current business until they are replaced in accordance with Article 214. In this case, the term of office of the Members of the Commission appointed to replace them shall expire on the date on which the term of office of the Members of the Commission obliged to resign as a body would have expired.

IV. Budgetary Provisions

Article 272 (ex 203) EC

1. The Financial Year shall run from 1 January to 31 December.

2. Each institution of the Community shall, before 1 July, draw up estimates of its expenditure. The Commission shall consolidate these estimates in a preliminary draft budget. It shall attach thereto an opinion which may contain different estimates.

The preliminary draft budget shall contain an estimate of revenue and an estimate of expenditure.

3. The Commission shall place the preliminary draft budget before the Council not later than 1 September of the year preceding that in which the budget is to be implemented.

The Council shall consult the Commission and, where appropriate, the other institutions concerned whenever it intends to depart from the preliminary draft budget.

The Council, acting by a qualified majority, shall establish the draft budget and forward it to the European Parliament.

4. The draft budget shall be placed before the European Parliament not later than 5 October of the year preceding that in which the budget is to be implemented.

The European Parliament shall have the right to amend the draft budget, acting by a majority of its Members, and to propose to the Council, acting by an absolute majority of the votes cast, modifications to the draft budget relating to expenditure necessarily resulting from this Treaty or from acts adopted in accordance therewith.

If, within 45 days of the draft budget being placed before it, the European Parliament has given its approval, the budget shall stand as finally adopted. If within this period the European Parliament has not amended the draft budget nor proposed any modifications thereto, the budget shall be deemed to be finally adopted.

If within this period the European Parliament has adopted amendments or proposed modifications, the draft budget, together with the amendments or proposed amendments or proposed modifications shall be forwarded to the Council.

After discussing the draft budget with the Commission and, where appropriate, with the other institutions concerned, the Council shall act under the following conditions:

(a) the Council may, acting by a qualified majority, modify any of the amendments adopted by the European Parliament;

(b) with regard to the proposed modifications:

—where a modification proposed by the European Parliament does not have the effect of increasing the total amount of expenditure of an institution, owing in particular to the fact that the increase in expenditure which it would involve would be expressly compensated by one or more proposed modifications correspondingly reducing expenditure, the Council may, acting by qualified majority, reject the proposed modification. In the absence of a decision to reject it, the proposed modification shall stand as accepted;

—where a modification proposed by the European Parliament has the effect of increasing the total amount of expenditure of an institution, the Council may, acting by a qualified majority, accept this proposed modification. In the absence of a decision to accept it, the proposed modification shall stand as rejected;

—where, in pursuance of one of the two preceding subparagraphs, the Council has rejected a proposed modification, it may, acting by a qualified majority, either retain the amount show in the draft budget or fix another amount.

The draft budget shall be modified on the basis of the proposed modifications accepted by the Council.

If, within 15 days of the budget being placed before it, the Council has not modified any of the amendments adopted by the European Parliament and if the modifications proposed by the latter have been accepted, the budget shall be deemed to be finally adopted. The Council shall inform the European Parliament that it has not modified any of the amendments and that the proposed modifications have been accepted.

If within this period the Council has modified one or more of the amendments adopted by the European Parliament or if the modifications proposed by the latter have been rejected or modified, the modified draft budget shall again be forwarded to the European Parliament. The Council shall inform the European Parliament of the results of its deliberations.

6. Within 15 days of the draft budget being placed before it, the European Parliament, which shall have been notified of the action taken on its proposed modifications, may, acting by a majority of its Members and three-fifths of the votes case, amend or reject the modifications to its amendments made by the Council and shall adopt the budget accordingly. If within this period the European Parliament has not acted, the budget shall be deemed to be finally adopted.

7. When the procedure provided for in this Article has been completed, the President of the European Parliament shall declare that the budget has been finally adopted.

8. However, the European Parliament, acting by a majority of its Members and two-thirds of the votes cast, may, if there are important reasons, reject the draft budget and ask for a new draft to be submitted to it.

9. A maximum rate of increase in relation to the expenditure of the same type to be incurred during the current year shall be fixed annually for the total expenditure other than that necessarily resulting from this Treaty or from acts adopted in accordance therewith.

The Commission shall, after consulting the Economic Policy Committee, declare what this maximum rate is as it results from:

—the trend, in terms of volume, of the gross national product within the Community;

—the average variation in the budgets of the Member States; and

—the trend of the cost of living during the preceding financial year.

The maximum rate shall be communicated, before 1 May, to all the institutions of the Community. The latter shall be required to conform to this during the budgetary procedure, subject to the provisions of the fourth and fifth subparagraphs of this paragraph.

If, in respect of expenditure other than that necessarily resulting from this Treaty or from acts adopted in accordance therewith, the actual rate of increase in the draft budget established by the Council is over half the maximum rate, the European Parliament may, exercising its right of amendment, further increase the total amount of that expenditure to a limit not exceeding half the maximum rate.

Where the European Parliament, the Council or the Commission consider that the activities of the Communities require that the rate determined according to the procedure laid down in this paragraph should be exceeded, another rate may be fixed by an agreement between the Council, acting by a qualified majority, and the European Parliament, acting by a majority of its Members and three-fifths of the votes cast.

10. Each institution shall exercise the powers conferred upon it by this Article, with due regard for the provisions of the Treaty and for acts adopted in accordance therewith, in particular those relating to the Community's own resources and to the balance between revenue and expenditure.

V. *Legislative Provisions*

Article 250 (ex 189a) EC

Where, in pursuance of this Treaty, the Council acts on a proposal from the Commission, unanimity shall be required for an act constituting an amendment to that proposal, subject to Article 251(4) and (5).

As long as the Council has not acted, the Commission may alter its proposal at any time during the procedures leading to the adoption of a Community act.

Article 251 (ex 189b) EC

1. Where reference is made in this Treaty to this Article for the adoption of an Act, the following procedure will apply.

2. The Commission shall submit a proposal to the European Parliament and the Council.

The Council, acting by a qualified majority after obtaining the opinion of the European Parliament,

—if it approves all the amendments contained in the European Parliament's opinion, may adopt the proposed act as amended;
—if the European Parliament does not propose any amendments, may adopt the proposed act;
—shall otherwise adopt a common position and communicate it to the European Parliament. The Council shall inform the European Parliament fully of the reasons which led it to adopt its common position. The Commission shall inform the European Parliament fully of its position.

If, within three months of such a communication, the European Parliament:

(a) approves the common position or has not taken a position, the act in question shall be deemed to have been adopted in accordance with that common position;

(b) rejects, by an absolute majority of its component members, the common position, the proposed act shall be deemed not to have been adopted;

(c) proposes amendments to the common position by an absolute majority of its component members, the amended text shall be forward to the Council and the Commission, which shall deliver an opinion on those amendments.

3. If, within three months of the matter being referred to it, the Council, acting by a qualified majority, approves all the amendments of the European Parliament, the act in question shall be deemed to have been adopted in the form of the common position thus amended; however, the Council shall act unanimously on the amendments on which the Commission has delivered a negative opinion. If the Council does not approve all the amendments, the President of the Council, in agreement with the President of the European Parliament, shall within six weeks convene a meeting of the Conciliation Committee.

4. The Conciliation Committee, which shall be composed of the members of the Council or their representatives and an equal number of representatives of the European Parliament, shall have the task of reaching agreement on a joint text, by a qualified majority of the members of the Council or their representatives and by a majority of the representatives of the European Parliament. The Commission shall take part in the Conciliation Committee's proceedings and shall take all the necessary initiatives with a view to reconciling the positions of the European Parliament and the Council. In fulfilling this task, the Conciliation Committee shall address the common position on the basis of the amendments proposed by the European Parliament.

5. If, within six weeks of its being convened, the Conciliation Committee approves a joint text, the European Parliament, acting by an absolute majority of the votes cast, and the Council, acting by a qualified majority, shall each have a period of six weeks from that approval in which to adopt the act in question in accordance with the joint text. If either of the two institutions fails to approve the proposed act within that period, it shall be deemed not to have been adopted.

6. Where the Conciliation Committee does not approve a joint text, the proposed act shall be deemed not to have been adopted.

7. The periods of three months and six weeks referred to in this Article shall be extended by a maximum of one month and two weeks respectively at the initiative of the European Parliament or the Council.

Article 252 (ex 189c) EC

Where reference is made in this Treaty to this Article for the adoption of an act, the following procedure shall apply:

(a) The Council, acting by a qualified majority on a proposal from the Commission and after obtaining the opinion of the European Parliament, shall adopt a common position.

(b) The Council's common position shall be communicated to the European Parliament. The Council and the Commission shall inform the European Parliament fully of the reasons which led the Council to adopt is common position and also of the Commission's position.

   If, within three months of such communication, the European Parliament approves this common position or has not taken a decision within that period, the Council shall definitively adopt the act in question in accordance with the common position.

(c) The European Parliament may, within the period of three months referred to in point (b), by an absolute majority of its component Members, propose amendments to the Council's common position. The European Parliament may also, by the same majority, reject the Council's common position. The result of the proceedings shall be transmitted to the Council and the Commission.

If the European Council has rejected the Council's common position, unanimity shall be required for the Council to act on a second reading.

(d) The Commission shall, within a period of one month, re-examine the proposal on the basis of which the Council adopted its common position, by taking into account the amendments proposed by the European Parliament.

The Commission shall forward to the Council, at the same time as its re-examined proposal, the amendments of the European Parliament which it has not accepted, and shall express its opinion on them. The Council may adopt these amendments unanimously.

(e) The Council, acting by qualified majority, shall adopt the proposal as re-examined by the Commission.

Unanimity shall be required for the Council to amend the proposal as re-examined by the Commission.

(f) In the cases referred to in points (c), (d) and (e), the Council shall be required to act within a period of three months. If no decision is taken within this period, the Commission proposal shall be deemed not to have been adopted.

(g) The periods referred to in points (b) and (f) may be extended by a maximum of one month by common accord between the Council and the European Parliament.

Article 253 (ex 190) EC

Regulations, directives and decisions adopted jointly by the European Parliament and the Council, and such acts adopted by the Council or the Commission, shall state the reasons on which they are based and shall refer to any proposals or opinions which were required to be obtained pursuant to this Treaty.

APPENDIX B

Issue-Area Categories
for Tables 2.1–2.3

Issue-area categories are drawn, with a few exceptions noted below, from the bold-faced title and chapter headings laid down in the 'Consolidated Version of the Treaty Establishing the European Community' (hereinafter the EC Treaty, or TEC) and the 'Consolidated Version of the Treaty on European Union' (hereinafter the EU Treaty, or TEU). Specifically, categories 1–32 are drawn from Part Three of the EC Treaty, entitled 'Community Policies'; category 33 is drawn from elsewhere in the EC Treaty; categories 34–35 represent the second and third pillars of the EU Treaty. A complete list of issue areas follows (with Treaty article numbers in parentheses):

1. The Customs Union (TEC Articles 25–27)
2. Prohibition of Quantitative Restrictions Between Member States (TEC 28–31)
3. Agriculture (TEC 33–38)
4. Free Movement of Workers (TEC 39–42)
5. Right of Establishment (TEC 43–48)
6. Free Movement of Services (TEC 49–55)
7. Free Movement of Capital and Payments (TEC 56–60)
8. Visas, Asylum, Immigration and Other Policies Relating to the Free Movement of Persons (TEC 61–69)
9. Transport (TEC 70–80)
10. Rules on Competition Applying to Undertakings (TEC 81–86)
11. Rules on Competition: Aids Granted by States (TEC 87–89)
12. Tax Provisions (TEC 90–93)
13. Approximation of Laws (TEC 94–97)
14. EMU: Economic Policy (TEC 98–104)
15. EMU: Monetary Policy (TEC 105–111)
16. EMU: Institutional Provisions (TEC 112–115)
17. EMU: Transitional Provisions (TEC 116–124)
18. Employment (TEC 125–130)
19. Common Commercial Policy (TEC 131–134)
20. Customs Cooperation (TEC 135)
21. Social Provisions (TEC 136–145)
22. European Social Fund (TEC 146–148)
23. Education, Vocational Training and Youth (TEC 139–150)
24. Culture (TEC 151)
25. Public Health (TEC 152)
26. Consumer Protection (TEC 153)

APPENDIX C

Coding Rules for Executive
Delegation and Discretion,
Tables 2.1–2.3

The coding rules for Tables 2.1–2.3, follow the guidelines laid down in Appendix D of Epstein and O'Halloran (1999a), as amended for the EU by Franchino (2001).

Counting Major Provisions

The number of major provisions in a section of the Treaty is counted following these rules:

- Articles and numbered paragraphs count as separate provisions.
- Sub-paragraphs and indents do not count if they merely elaborate on the previous paragraph, but they do count if they include new substantive authority.
- Unnumbered paragraphs count as separate provisions only if they are substantively distinct.
- If a paragraph is followed by a colon and a list of elements, even if numbered, and if the elements of the lists merely elaborate on the main point of the paragraph, then the paragraph and accompanying list count as one provision.

Counting Major Provisions Delegating Powers

According to Franchino (2001: 18), an act of delegation is 'any major provision that gives...the Commission the authority to move the policy away from the status quo'. As noted in the text, this is a relatively narrow operationalization of delegation, which excludes the delegation of advisory, non-binding, or 'soft' powers. More specifically, Franchino (2001: 36) provides an indicative list of examples of delegation to the Commission:

- The right to issue implementing regulations or to take decisions with some discretion.
- Imposition of fines and penalties.
- Carrying out negotiations with third countries.
- Extension of discretionary authority to new issues or economic sectors.
- Carrying out inspections or conducting investigations or inquiries—only if they complement other powers such as those to take decisions or to impose penalties.
- Request of information—only if it complements powers to take decisions, to carry out investigations, to tax, or to impose penalties.

- The authorization of the right to take measures that may alter the policy.
- The right to grant derogations and exemptions.

By contrast, the following (Franchino 2002: 32) are examples of what delegation to the Commission is *not*:

- Examination of member states' measures by the Commission but without the power to alter them or with only the facility to issue recommendations or opinions.
- Design and issuance of certificates, forms, and documents.
- Diffusing or exchanging information, setting rules for information exchange, notifying measures, ensuring professional secrecy.
- General calls to implement provisions.
- Calls for the Commission to issue reports, unless the latter are used as the basis for legally binding legislation.
- Membership of committees... without the power to adopt legally binding legislation.
- General calls to the Commission to 'take any useful initiative to support... coordination' among the member states, since such provisions (in the articles on industry and public health) do not specify the nature of the power conferred.

Finally, note that Franchino (2001: 32) explicitly excludes from the scope of delegation any agenda-setting powers, which he regards as a legislative rather than an executive power (see Chapter 2 for a discussion on this point).

Like Franchino, I have found that determining whether a provision delegates policy authority has been 'rather straightforward'; in cases of doubt, I have followed Franchino's call to code 'conservatively' so that the scores for certain titles—employment, EMU, industry, and public health—are lower than they might be if agenda-setting powers or other 'soft' powers were counted as delegation.

Categories of Procedural Constraints

In this section, I adopt unchanged Franchino's (2001: 33–7) list of twelve procedural constraints on Commission delegation.

1. Time Limits
2. Spending Limits
3. Reporting Requirements
4. Consultation Requirements
5. Public Hearings
6. Rule-Making Requirements
7. Appeals Procedures
8. Exemptions
9. Legislative Action Required
10. Legislative Action Possible
11. Executive Action Required
12. Executive Action Possible

Rules for Calculating Delegation Ratio, Constraint Ratio, and Discretion Index

Delegation ratio: Dc (provisions delegating to Commission)/T (total provisions)
Constraint ratio: Cc (constraints on Commission)/TC (total constraints, or 12)
Discretion index: Dc/T – [(Cc/TC)*(Di/T)]

APPENDIX D

Sample Coding Sheet for
Tables 2.1–2.3

Title: Transport (Arts 70–80)

I. Delegation and Discretion, Including Agenda Setting

Delegation? Yes

1. Number of provisions: 19
2. Number of provisions with delegation to Commission: 3
   - Article 75(4) delegates to the Commission the power to investigate cases of discrimination and take the necessary measures in accordance with provisions of paragraph 3.
   - Article 76(1) delegates to the Commission the power to authorize support for particular undertakings or industries, which are otherwise prohibited.
   - Article 76(2) delegates to the Commission the power to examine the rates and conditions referred to in Chapter 1, taking into account a range of factors, and, after consulting member state concerned, take the necessary decisions.
   - NB: Article 77 allows the Commission to make recommendations to member states; non-binding, therefore not coded as 'delegation'.

Delegation ratio: Dc (provisions delegating to Commission)/T (total provisions) = 3/19 = 0.1579

II. Procedural Constraints

1. Time Limits
2. Spending Limits
3. Reporting Requirements
4. Consultation Requirements: Yes, Articles 76(2) and 79
5. Public Hearings
6. Rule-Making Requirements: Yes, Article 76(2)
7. Appeals Procedures
8. Exemptions: Yes, Article 78 on former East Germany
9. Legislative Action Required
10. Legislative Action Possible
11. Executive Action Required
12. Executive Action Possible

Constraint ratio: Cc (constraints on Commission)/TC (total constraints, or 12)
3/12 = 0.25

III. Discretion Index

Discretion index: Dc/T − [(Cc/TC)*(Di/T)]
.1579 − [.1579 * .25] = 0.1184

NOTES

Introduction

1. For representative works and commentaries on the neo-functionalist/intergovernmentalist debate, see Haas (1958); Hoffmann (1966); Lindberg and Scheingold (1970); Pentland (1973); Haas (1976); and Taylor (1983).
2. For an excellent presentation of the EU from a comparative politics perspective, see Hix (1999*a*).
3. See the conclusion of this book for an extended discussion of the democratic deficit literature in the European Union.
4. See for example Moe (1984); Kiewiet and McCubbins (1991); Epstein and O'Halloran (1999*a*).
5. See for example Shepsle (1979; 1986; 1989); Riker (1980); Tsebelis (1990); Krasner (1988).
6. See for example Shepsle and Weingast (1984; 1987*a*); Riker (1986); Ordeshook and Schwartz (1987); Tsebelis (1994).
7. See for example Krehbeil (1989; 1991).
8. See for example Weingast and Moran (1983); McCubbins and Schwartz (1987); Moe (1987); McCubbins, Noll, and Weingast (1987; 1989). For good reviews of the principal-agent literature, see Moe (1984); Shepsle and Weingast (1995); Epstein and O'Halloran (1999*a*: Ch. 2).
9. The transaction-cost rubric actually encompasses many of the previously cited literatures, many of which emphasized the various costs associated with the making of public policy or with the control of the bureaucracy. For good overviews of the transaction cost approach, see Epstein and O'Halloran (1999*a*); Huber and Shipan (2000).

Chapter 1

1. The informational rationale for delegation is summarized most succinctly by Epstein and O'Halloran (1999*b*: 379), who argue that 'Executive agencies are created by Congress to make policy in areas where legislators have neither the time nor the expertise to do so themselves.' For good general accounts of the transaction-cost approach to institutional design, with an emphasis on informational problems, see Epstein and O'Halloran (1999*a*); Huber and Shipan (2000).
2. On the importance of credible commitments, see Gatsios and Seabright (1989); Moravcsik (1998); Shipan and Huber (2000: 30–2); Majone 2000; and section I of this chapter.
3. For an excellent review of the literature, see Martin and Simmons (2001).
4. The example of the medieval merchant is drawn from Milgrom, North, and Weingast (1990). The literatures on both Congressional delegation and international organizations are large and varied. On the former, see for example Weingast and Marshall (1988). On delegation to international organizations, see Keohane and Martin (1994); Pollack (1997); Moravcsik (1998).
5. A related argument is put forward by Fiorina (1982), who explains such delegation as an effort to 'shift the responsibility'—and the blame—for painful regulations

from political principals to an agent. In this view, regulatory bureaucracies absorb the blame for unpopular policies and allow legislators to step in and reap the credit for solving any problems that may arise (see also Epstein and O'Halloran 1999a: 30–2).

6. The essentials of Epstein and O'Halloran's argument, which includes both *ex ante* administrative procedures and *ex post* oversight in the definition of discretion, is set out in an article (1999b: 37) which outlines their position as follows: 'Our approach begins with the fact that the limits of agency discretion are set explicitly by *Congress*. When agencies are first established, their scope of operations, details of procedures, and exemptions from agency control are enumerated in the implementing legislation. If Congress wishes to grant agencies wide latitude, it may state only that they regulate "in the public interest"; otherwise, it may establish more detailed criteria concerning agency findings and subsequent actions. In contrast to those who define discretion as whatever an agency can get away with, we argue that often Congress prefers to set ex ante limits on agency discretion *more stringent* than those implied by their ex post power to overturn agency decisions.'

7. After an exhaustive review, Epstein and O'Halloran identify a list of 14 possible constraints: appointment power limits, time limits, spending limits, legislative action required, executive action required, legislative veto, reporting requirements, consultation requirements, public hearings, appeals procedures, rulemaking requirements, exemptions, compensations, and direct oversight. For details of the definition and operationalization of their 'discretion ratio', see Epstein and O'Halloran (1999a: 86–109).

8. According to Krehbiel (1991), legislators create Congressional committees precisely to provide their members with an incentive to acquire such policy-relevant information; yet, as Epstein and O'Halloran (1999a) explain, the Congressional committee system itself imposes transaction costs, particularly when the members of such committees are 'outliers' with preferences distinct from the median floor voter, who use their agenda-setting powers to pursue their own interests at the expense of non-members.

9. The specific prediction in Epstein and O'Halloran (1999a: 197) is that 'all else being equal, policy areas shrouded in uncertainty will tend to be delegated at higher rates'.

10. For good discussions, see Gatsios and Seabright (1989); Horn (1995); Majone (1996); Epstein and O'Halloran (1999a: 1–4).

11. Specifically, 'Governments are likely to accept…delegation as a means to assure that other governments will accept agreed legislation and enforcement, to signal their own credibility, or to lock in future decisions against domestic opposition' (Moravcsik 1998: 73).

12. Similarly, Huber (2000) suggests that 'granting substantial autonomy to civil servants will have the greatest payoff to ministers when conflict of interest between ministers and civil servants is low. As conflict increases, the benefits of granting autonomy decrease'. Specifically, Huber hypothesizes that the likelihood of such conflicts increases in the presence of politicized bureaucracies, coalition governments, and portfolio volatility, and that legislators and governments should therefore delegate less authority and discretion to civil servants under such conditions.

13. In an earlier study (Epstein and O'Halloran 1996), the same authors examined changes in the degree of discretion allowed to American presidents in US trade laws during the twentieth century, and similarly concluded that Congress is most likely to increase executive discretion during times of unified government and most likely to decrease discretion—or leave it unchanged—during times of divided government.

14. See for example Majone (1996); Cram (1994; 1997); Pollack (1994; 1998); Ross (1995); Tsebelis (1994); Garrett (1995*a*); Hartley (1998); Rasmussen (1998); Tallberg (1999); and Tsebelis and Garrett (2001). Interestingly, a similar set of assumptions also guided the work of earlier scholars in both the neo-functionalist and the intergovernmentalist traditions. Neo-functionalists, much influenced by the empirical cases of Jean Monnet's High Authority and Walter Hallstein's activist Commission, placed the Commission at the centre of their analysis, assuming more or less explicitly that the Commission was in favour of integration and would act as a catalyst for the gradual centralization of authority at the supranational level. Later, intergovernmentalist scholars argued that member governments remained the central actors and the gatekeepers of the integration process; however, by and large these scholars did not question the integrationist preferences of the Commission and other supranational organizations but simply the ability of these organizations to realize their preferences over the objections of the member governments.

15. For good discussions of the Commission's internal diversity, and the policy networks formed among the Commission and other public and private actors, see Cram (1994); Ross (1995); Cini (1996); Peterson and Bomberg (1999); Hooghe (1999*a*, *b*).

16. In fact, as Tsebelis (1995) points out, the European Parliament in some instances votes by an absolute majority of its members, which imposes a higher threshold than simple majority voting. Nevertheless, Tsebelis demonstrates that his fundamental findings hold even where the EP diverges from simple majority voting, and the rational-choice literature on the EU is uniform in its treatment of the Commission, the Court, and the Parliament as unitary actors.

17. For bibliographic reviews of the runaway-bureaucracy literature, see Kiewiet and McCubbins (1991: Ch. 1); Weingast and Moran (1983: notes 1 and 3); and McCubbins and Schwartz (1987: 435).

18. For an extended discussion of the APA and US administrative law more generally, see Chapter 2.

19. See for example Kilroy (1995); Garrett, Kelemen, and Schulz (1998); Tsebelis and Garrett (2001); for an extended discussion of this literature, see Chapter 3.

20. For a complete discussion of the Commission's agenda-setting powers vis-à-vis the Council and the European Parliament, see Chapter 4.

21. Studies claiming an informal or entrepreneurial role for the European Commission include Zysman and Sandholtz (1989); Peterson (1991); Sandholtz (1992); Marks (1993); and many of the essays in Nugent (1997). For a good review of these works and their underlying assumptions, see Moravcsik (1999).

22. For a good discussion of informal agenda setting among private actors, see Cowles (1995).

23. Among these studies are Peterson (1991); Sandholtz (1992); Zysman and Sandholtz (1989); Cowles (1995); and Moravcsik (1998; 1999), who argues that the Commission's influence in the negotiation of the Single European Act can be attributed, not to its informational advantage over member states or its unique ability to mediate and broker agreements, but rather to its successful attempt to mobilize a latent transnational coalition of export-oriented multinational corporations.

24. For good statements of the former view, see Zysman and Sandholtz (1989) and Sandholtz (1992). For the latter view, see Moravcsik (1998; 1999).

25. Interviews with Commission and European Parliament officials, July 1997, October 1998, and February 1999; Franklin Dehousse (1999); McDonagh (1998). For an extended discussion of the Commission's agenda-setting role at Amsterdam, see Pollack (1999).

26. For seminal statements of such an approach, see March and Olsen (1984; 1989); Hall (1986: 21); Thelen and Steinmo (1992); Wendt (1999); Risse (2000).

27. For explicit arguments about informal agenda setting by the European Commission, see for example Sandholtz (1992); Lord and Winn (1998); and Friis (1998).
28. See for example Dogan (1997); Franchino (1999; 2001). For an extended discussion of such studies, see Chapter 2.
29. These policies, moreover, dovetail closely with Epstein and O'Halloran's (1999*a*: 206–11) classification of the most complex issue-areas based on committee hearings data.
30. Interview, Commission official, London, March 1995.
31. Similarly in their study of the delegation stage, Epstein and O'Halloran (1999*a*) have used divided government in the United States as a proxy for policy conflict between legislators and agents, on the assumption that Congress will hesitate to delegate extensive discretion to an agency whose chief is appointed by the President.
32. Examples of American studies relying heavily on roll-call voting include Bawn (1997); Epstein and O'Halloran (1999*a*).
33. Random selection of cases, it is worth noting, is an unpromising approach in such a study because it is unlikely to provide sufficient variation across the hypothesized independent variables. Similarly, as Garrett, Kelemen, and Schulz (1998: 151) write, 'there is little to be gained from analyzing the vast body of ECJ case law [or of Commission regulation] that has not generated controversy between the Court [or the Commission] and national governments'.
34. For studies adopting similar approaches, see Pollack (1998); Garrett, Kelemen, and Schulz (1998); Tallberg (1999).

Chapter 2

1. This section draws largely on Rittberger's excellent and theoretically informed primary research, as well as on Valentine (1954); Haas (1958); Diebold (1959: 47–77); Milward (1992: 46–83); Monnet (1978); Duchêne (1994: 181–225); Küsters (1988); Dumoulin (1988); Kersten (1988); and more generally the essays in Schwabe (1988). In keeping with Moravcsik's (1998: 80) dictum, however, I rely as heavily as possible on the primary sources cited in these studies, taking care not to mistake secondary interpretations of the authors for primary evidence. For a good collection of primary documents relating to the negotiation of the ECSC Treaty, including the reservations of the Belgian and Dutch delegations and their industries, see the Schuman Plan Collection of the Leiden University Historical Institute at www.let.leidenuniv.nl/history/rtg/res1/schumanplan.html
2. Robert Schuman, 'Declaration of 9 May 1950', reproduced in Weigall and Stirk (1992: 58–9).
3. Jean Monnet, 'Letter from Jean Monnet to E. Plowden, 25 May 1950', reproduced in Weigall and Stirk (1992: 59).
4. In the words of Monnet's biographer François Duchêne (1994: 202), 'a common authority with true powers was vital—in order to be effective and impartial and to take the first step to a European federation...Accepting the principle of a High Authority with independent powers was the entry ticket to the Schuman talks'. Largely for this reason, the British government took the decision not to participate in the talks. For a good discussion, see Diebold (1959: 49–53).
5. Duchêne (1994: 207) notes that, in their first meeting after the declaration of the Schuman Plan, 'Adenauer endorsed two points: a High Authority with its own powers; and negotiations solely to set it up—meaning that political institutions came first and material issues could be worked out later'.

6. Belgium, the Netherlands, and Luxembourg.

7. Rittberger (2001: 697) cites the American ambassador to Belgium, who summarized the demands of the Benelux countries: 'First, a more flexible and limited jurisdiction for the High Authority—on an issue-by-issue basis—than contemplated by the French shall be put in place. Second, the High Authority should share its decision-making powers with an intergovernmental/ministerial organ.' On the concerns of the Benelux countries, see also Diebold (1959: 61–77; Duchêne (1994: 209–10); Milward (1992: 46–83); and especially Dumoulin (1988) and Kersten (1988).

8. Thus, for example, the setting of wages was explicitly ruled outside the competence of the High Authority, while High Authority action in other areas was made contingent on the approval of the Council of Ministers.

9. For a detailed discussion of the High Authority's jurisdiction within the original Treaty of Paris, see Haas (1958: 52–5).

10. *Memorie van Toelichting*, no. 2228, no. 3, 1950–1951, p. 33, col. 2, as translated and quoted in Valentine (1954: 8).

11. *Compte Rendu*, 1950–1951, p. 127, quoted in Valentine (1954: 8).

12. Specifically, the treaty provided that actions of the High Authority could be challenged if it exceeded its powers under the treaty (*ultra vires*); if it violated an essential procedural requirement; if it violated the treaty or any rule of law pertaining to its application; in case of 'misapplication of power'; or if it failed to act where the treaty clearly called for such action. See ECSC Treaty Articles 31–35; Haas (1958: 56–7); and Valentine (1954: *passim*). These grounds for annulment were later copied and modified in the EEC and Euratom Treaties, as we shall see later in this chapter.

13. Quoted in Rittberger (2001: 698).

14. As Rittberger (2001: 699) points out, 'A strong Parliament with legislative powers, as preferred by Germany, was ... absolutely unacceptable for the Benelux countries as this would have created another actor with substantial decision-making powers whose decisions could produce detrimental effects with regard to domestic policy objectives'. See also Kersten (1988: 295).

15. In addition to these three landmark treaties, the original Rome Treaties have also been amended *inter alia* by the 1967 Merger Treaty, consolidating the executive, court, and parliaments of the ECSC, EEC, and Euratom; by the 1970 and 1975 budgetary treaties, discussed in Chapter 4; and by the Treaty of Nice, which has not yet been ratified at this writing and is therefore not included in the analysis in this book.

16. Article 250 EC (ex 189a) reflects in turn the wording of the original Article 149 EEC, which initially established the unanimity amendment rule for EC legislation.

17. As we shall see in Chapter 4, however, the protection against amendment provided by this article does not extend to the conciliation committee within the co-decision procedure, wherein a joint committee of Council and EP representatives may agree to amendments without the agreement of the Commission. For a detailed discussion, see Chapter 4.

18. For a thorough discussion of the Commission's agenda-setting powers, and an issue-by-issue comparison with the legislative powers of the European Parliament, see Chapter 4.

19. In addition to the Article 226 procedure, a second procedure is outlined in Article 227 (ex Art. 170), whereby non-compliance by one member state can be raised before the Court by another member state. In practice, however, member governments have generally been reluctant to challenge each other directly in Court, and the Article 227 procedure has been used only rarely in the Community's history.

20. Specifically, Article 95(4) (ex Art. 100a(4)) allows member states to adopt stricter national standards than Community standards in areas such as the environment and consumer protection, but only if the Commission certifies that these standards are not a disguised barrier to trade. Under this provision, if the Commission determines that the standards in question are a disguised form of protectionism it may, by derogation from Article 226, bring the matter directly to the ECJ.

21. This Commission discretion, moreover, has been explicitly recognized by the European Court of Justice, which has allowed the Commission wide latitude in its decision whether to initiative infringement proceedings. For a good discussion, see Weatherill and Beaumont (1999: 308).

22. In 1996, for example, the European Parliament delayed the discharge of the budget to demonstrate its displeasure at the Commission's record of financial control. Similarly, the EP has regularly used its budgetary powers to force the Commission to divulge information regarding the comitology process. For good discussions, see Hix (2000); Corbett, Jacobs, and Shackleton (2000: 252–5).

23. The provisions regarding the Court's members are similar to those of the Court of Justice, with the 15 members of the Court appointed by the member governments for six-year, renewable terms, and with members taking an oath to be independent in their actions. See Articles 246–248 EC (ex Arts. 188a–188c). For a detailed, up-to-date discussion of the Court of Auditors and its relationship to the Commission, see Laffan (1999).

24. For details of the Ombudsman's 2000 case load, see the European Ombudsman (2001).

25. In addition, the systematic mapping of the extent of delegation to the Commission across these issue areas will later allow an explicit comparison with patterns of delegation to the Court of Justice and the EP, which are examined in Chapters 3 and 4, respectively.

26. For details of the methods followed in the collection of the data presented in this Chapter, see Appendices B–D.

27. Both Epstein and O'Halloran (1999*a*) and Franchino (2001) examine delegation in secondary legislation, and limit their analysis to 'major provisions', that is, the substantive provisions of legislation excluding preambles and other non-binding provisions. The issue-specific provisions of the treaties, however, generally lack such prefatory material, and I therefore include *all* provisions from the relevant chapters or titles in the denominator of the delegation ratio.

28. For good accounts of the negotiation of the Maastricht Treaty, see for example Laursen and Vanhoonacker (1992); Cloos *et al.* (1993); Corbett (1994); Ross (1995); Moravcsik (1998); and Dyson and Featherstone (1999).

29. The potential of these provisions has recently been illustrated by two instances in which Commission state-aids decisions—on agriculture and road transport—have been overturned by a unanimous Council, prompting protestations and a legal challenge from the Commission. For good discussions, see, for example, Dombey and Guerrera (2002); *European Report* (2002*a*); and Dombey (2002*a*, *b*).

30. Franchino deliberately eschews Treaty-based definitions of issue areas in favour of more narrowly defined issue areas of his own design.

31. Franchino also examines and analyses the discretion allowed to member governments in their implementation of EU law. However, given the focus on delegation to the Commission in this chapter, I do not discuss those findings here.

32. In addition to this 'detailed rules' measure, Franchino examines two other measures of information intensity: the establishment of an 'action plan' in a given issue area, such as the various action programmes on social policy and the environment adopted by the Council since the 1970s; and the establishment of advisory committees. Franchino hypothesizes that both action plans and advisory committees

reflect the complexity of an issue area and efforts by the Council to maximize the provision of policy-relevant information. It is worth noting, however, that such action programmes and advisory committees may also be a measure of the political sensitivity of an issue area in so far as the Commission is known to propose action programmes as 'soft-law' precedents in areas where member states resist binding legislation, and member states respond by establishing advisory committees to maximize their own input in such areas. In any event, Franchino does not attempt to test either of these factors on Commission discretion, focusing exclusively on their relation to member-state discretion in implementing Community law.

33. On the other hand, as Page and Wouters (1994: 454–6) demonstrate, the average age of a Commissioner upon leaving office is a relatively advanced 58 years, and only about one-third of all retiring Commissioners gain any sort of elective office after their stint in Brussels.

34. Article 214 (ex Art. 158) TEC. The Maastricht Treaty provided for the EP to be consulted on the choice of President, leaving it unclear whether the EP actually enjoyed a veto. During the selection of Jacques Santer as President in 1994, however, the German Presidency of the Council indicated that, in the event of a negative vote in the Parliament, it would propose a new candidate to the Council. The treaty was subsequently amended at Amsterdam to make clear that the EP does indeed have the power of assent over the selection of the Commission President. See Jacobs (1999: 4–5).

35. For details, including the text of the EP resolution establishing the CIE, see *European Report* (1999).

36. For details, see Committee of Independent Experts (1999*a, b*) as well as the excellent analysis in Craig (2000).

37. For the text of the White Paper, see CEC (2000*b*). On the subsequent process of Commission reform, see Spence (2000). Also *European Report* (2001*a, c*); *The Economist* (2001*a*); and the Commission's reform website at http://europa.eu.int/comm/reform/index_en.htm.

38. For more on the historical development of the comitology system, see for example Vos (1997: 212); Bertram (1967–8); Haibach (2000).

39. For discussion of *Köster* and other ECJ rulings on delegation and comitology, see Bradley (1992: 697–9); Lenaerts and Verhoeven (2000: 650–8).

40. Tellingly, a House of Lords report (1986) noted that 'Many organisations expressed concern about the lack of Commission accountability under the Advisory Committee procedures. It is undoubtedly true that the Advisory Committee procedure would expedite the opening-up of the internal market, but such a procedure offers no safeguards to the interests of particular national governments or industries' (para 18). Such an explicit trade-off, between rapid adoption of regulations on the one hand and accountability on the other would later be made in other cases, most recently in the proposals of the Lamfalussy Committee on the liberalization of securities markets, discussed below.

41. Decision 87/373/EEC. *Official Journal* L 197/33.

42. COM(83)35 final.

43. *Official Journal*, No. C297 of 24 November 1986, p. 94.

44. Case 302/87, *European Parliament v. Council*, [1988] ECR 5616. Since 1988, the Maastricht Treaty granted the Parliament explicit standing to bring cases for annulment under Article 230 (ex. Art. 173) of the EC Treaty. For a good review of the 1988 Decision and the subsequent case law, see Bradley (1997: 243–50).

45. For detailed analyses of the Parliament's views on comitology, and its inter-institutional battle with the Council, see for example Bradley (1992; 1997); Steunenberg, Koboldt, and Schmidtchen (1997); and Hix (2000).

46. For the text of the Commission's proposal, see *Official Journal* C 279/5, 1998; for analyses of the proposal, see House of Lords (1999) and Turk (2000). For the text of the Council Decision, see *Official Journal* L 184/23–26, 1999, analysed in detail by Lenearts and Verhoeven (2000).

47. According to Lenaerts and Verhoeven (2000: 669), the decision to insert the 'non-binding' language was designed to address member states' fear that the introduction of criteria could provide the basis for litigation, as well as to maintain a margin of choice for the Council.

48. For details of the negotiation and the Commission Declaration, see *Agence Europe* (1999); see also Lenaerts and Verhoeven (2000: 677).

49. In addition to these basic provisions, the 1999 Decision also provided for the repeal of the 1987 Decision and the gradual replacement of existing committees with the new committee procedures specified in the Decision. For a discussion of this and other minor changes, see Lenaerts and Verhoeven (2000).

50. The theoretically informed literature on comitology is large and growing. See *inter alia* Pedlar and Schaefer (1996); Steunenberg, Koboldt, and Schmidtchen (1996; 1997; 1999); Vos (1997; 1999); Joerges and Neyer (1997*a*, *b*); Dogan (1997); Wessels (1998); Franchino (1998; 1999; 2000*a*, *b*); Christiansen and Kirchner (2000); and Andenas and Türk (2000).

51. The relation between Joerges and Neyer's normative and empirical arguments is complex, and is worth citing verbatim to avoid misrepresenting of their argument: 'The following account of the comitology system in the foodstuffs sector', they write, 'is not meant to prove the empirical validity of our general normative claims. We merely intend to show that regulatory practices in the foodstuffs sector already reflect a kind of normative reasoning that is in agreement with our general normative argument' (Joerges and Neyer 1997*b*: 613).

52. In their discussion of the 1987 Comitology Decision, for example, Joerges and Neyer (1997*b*: 614) point out that 'member states were not willing to loosen their intergovernmental grip on the implementation process'. Indeed, they argue, 'this simultaneous concern for the risks of delegation and the costs of control goes a long way in explaining the institutional complexity of comitology. The different procedures foreseen by the comitology decision represent specific combinations of autonomy of the Commission and control by member states' (1997*b*: 616).

53. 'Comitology is indicative of a reorientation of European regulation away from hierarchical policy formulation. The new emphasis is on the development of coordination capacities between the Commission and member state administrations with the aim of establishing a culture of inter-administrative partnership which relies on persuasion, argument and discursive processes rather than on command, control and strategic interaction' (Joerges and Neyer (1997*b*: 620).

54. This consensual nature of comitology, moreover, is not a recent development. In his early study of management committees, for example, Bertram noted that, of the 762 decisions taken by the Commission during the first five years of the management committee procedure, only four resulted in a negative vote from the relevant committee, and of these only one decision was modified by the Council of Ministers (Bertram (1967–8: 250–3). In addition, Bertram's portrayal of agricultural management committees in the 1960s conveys a similar sense of technocratic cooperation: '[D]iscussions held in committee...are marked by the endeavour on the part of all those concerned to reach agreement rapidly. The chairman gives delegations ample opportunity to discuss the draft, ask questions, and make suggestions. Committees, by the tasks put to them as well as their composition, are in fact panels of experts whose only concern is to come to a working arrangement as swiftly as possible. This explains the efforts made by all participants to avoid if possible a negative opinion, as this may lead to appeal to the Council. They are

not particularly "supranationally"-minded, but prefer that the Commission decide finally instead of the decision going to the Council for appeal, because it goes through more quickly and duplication of business is avoided' Bertram (1967–8: 251).

55. Joerges and Neyer's text is worth quoting at length: 'The overloaded agendas and the pressure of the Commission to proceed according to tight schedules', they point out, 'are central concerns of most of the delegations. The period of time in which national delegations have to respond to the Commission's proposals and formulate their own positions is sometimes only a few weeks which often leaves no time for domestic consultations with all interested parties. Furthermore, *the Commission does not hesitate to take a vote on proposals* if consensus is out of reach and voting is the only way to succeed within such time constraints. Consequently, *almost all delegates express concerns about the Commission being too assertive in pushing for results or for using its competencies too expansively*. Some even argue that the whole process of negotiation is not only heavily influenced but also dominated by the Commission' Joerges and Neyer (1997*b*: 617).

56. These three committees are, respectively, the Article 133 committee for the common commercial policy, the advisory committee for EU merger control, and the advisory committee—later changed to a management committee—for the Structural Funds. See Chapters 5 and 6.

57. The use of the final decision is, in fact, an imperfect proxy for the Council's preferences, since the legislation adopted may have been influenced by the agenda-setting powers of the Commission—where the Council votes by qualified majority—or the legislative powers of Parliament, especially under the cooperation and co-decision procedures. Given that both the Commission and the Parliament show a revealed preference for 'lighter' comitology, Dogan's measures probably *understate* the Council's collective preference for more restrictive committee procedures.

58. For an extended discussion of Franchino's methods and findings, see Franchino (2000*a*: 74–88).

59. Interview, former Commission official, May 2001.

60. The Commission's willingness to compromise on comitology for particularly important legislation was also mentioned by a former senior Commissions official, interviewed May 2001.

61. European Parliament, *Report on the Proposal for a Council Decision laying down the procedures for the exercise of implementing powers conferred upon the Commission (COM(98)0380)*, Committee on Institutional Affairs, Rapporteur: Maria Adelaide Aglietta, EP Document A4-0169/99. Drafted by Maria Adelaide Aglietta for the Committee on Institutional Affairs, the Report includes detailed opinions from 15 Parliamentary committees, which collectively provide both an overall picture of the EP's view as well as the specific grievances and demands of committees dealing with specific issue areas. Among the opinions in the report, those by the committees on budgets, budgetary control, and foreign, security, and defence policy are particularly interesting for highlighting the problems distinctive to those areas. The reports by the Committees on Environment, Public Health and Consumer Protection (rapporteur: Ken Collins) and Rules of Procedure, Verification of Credentials and Immunities (rapporteur: Richard Corbett) are also useful for their lucid analyses of the workings of the 1987 Decision and the 1994 *modus vivendi*.

62. EP Document A4-0169/99, 13.

63. EP Document A4-0169/99, 14.

64. EP Document A3-310/90, quoted in Hix (2000: 71).

65. EP Document A4-0169/99, 81.

66. In the 1996 intergovernmental conference negotiations, for example, most member governments issued ritualistic statements on comitology, generally expressing support for the simplification of the 1987 Decision, but with little detail regarding the workings of comitology or specific preferences about the choice and reform of comitology procedures. For good surveys, see 'Intergovernmental Conference: Briefing No. 21 (First update: 17 March 1997): COMITOLOGY', accessed from the European Parliament website on 28 May 1998, at www.europarl.eu.int/dg7/fiches/en/fiche21.htm; and 'La Commission: Comitologie', accessed from the Europa website on 7 July 1996, at www.cec.lu/en/agenda/igc-home/general/fiches/1-24.htm.

67. Interview, member state official, 7 August 2001.

68. Correspondence, member state official, 12 November 2001.

69. See, for example, the cases of the ONP/Voice Telephony Directive and the establishment of the Securities Committee, reviewed in Pollack (2001), and the evolution of British comitology preferences in the area of the Structural Funds, examined at length in Chapter 6 of this book.

70. Correspondence, member state official, 12 November 2001.

71. A Lexis-Nexis Academic Universe search on 21 May 2001, using 'European' as a primary and 'comitology' as a secondary search term produced 213 articles, spanning the period from December 1986 to May 2001. Of these 213 articles, 18 concerned the ONP Directive; 9 concerned the Lamfalussy Report and its follow-up, another 9 looked at the negotiation of the 1999 Comitology Decision, and 3 dealt with the Eurodac Regulation. In addition, 4 articles related to various national stabilization programmes under the Stability Pact for EMU; 4 dealt with Commission decisions about the approval and marketing of genetically modified organisms; and six others related to the adoption of various research and development programmes.

72. For more on the Lisbon European Council, see Rhodes, Goetschy, and Mosher (2000).

73. The initiative to establish such a committee was taken by French Finance Minister Laurent Fabius, who reportedly hoped that the committee would recommend a European securities regulator to be based in Paris. By contrast, the UK government was reportedly opposed to the establishment of such a committee, and insisted on the participation of British Treasury official Sir Nigel Wicks as a condition for its establishment. See *The Economist* (2001*b*).

74. In fact, although very few observers took note of this fact, the Commission itself had explicitly called for the creation of such a Securities Committee, which would be constituted as a regulatory committee, in its 1999 Financial Services Action Plan. See CEC (1999: 15, 30).

75. Committee of Wise Men (2001).

76. Christopher Huhne, a Liberal Democratic MEP on Parliament's Economic and Monetary Committee, pointed out the trade-off for the Parliament. 'We are supporting the securities committee as an absolutely crucial way of moving with developments in the markets. But we believe such a powerful body needs a long-stop, and it will be very difficult to get a parliamentary majority unless there is an appeals procedure.' Quoted in Peter Norman (2001*a*).

77. Norman and Barber (2001) and Ludlow (2001: 7. The Commission's action in the BSE case has since been the subject of a legal challenge by the German Finance Ministry; see Hulverscheidt, Williamson, and Koch (2001).

78. Stockholm European Council: Presidency Conclusions. Press Release: Stockholm (24-0302001) – Nr: 100/10, Annex I: Resolution of the European Council on More Effective Securities Market Regulation in the European Union, Stockholm, 23 March 2001.

79. For good discussions of the Commission/Parliament compromise, see: Norman (2001*c*; 2002); *European Report* (2002*b*). The text of Prodi's statement can be found in CEC (2002).

80. For good discussions of notice-and-comment rulemaking, see Shapiro (1988: 43–4) and Bignami (1999). On the political origins of the APA, see McNollgast (1999), who argue that the APA was adopted deliberately by a Democratic Congressional majority seeking to 'hard-wire' the policies of the New Deal against tampering or lax implementation by future Republican Presidents.

81. Statistics on the judicial activities of the Court of Justice and the Court of First Instance are taken from the 2000 *Annual Report (extracts)* of the ECJ, available on the Court's website at http://curia.eu.int/en/pei/rapan.htm.

82. For a good discussion of the case-law on Article 232 (ex Art. 175), see Weatherill and Beaumont (1999: 306–13).

83. The actions for annulment and failure to act are not the only possible means though which an EU institution, member state, or private actor can challenge a Community act. In addition to these two provisions, Articles 238 (ex Art. 178) and 288 (ex. 215) give the Court jurisdiction regarding the contractual and non-contractual liability of EU institutions vis-à-vis third parties, which effectively allows those parties to sue EC institutions for damages. In addition, Article 239 (ex Art. 179) gives the Court jurisdiction over disputes between the community and its servants. Since the early 1990s, these types of cases are dealt with exclusively by the Court of First Instance.

84. For a good discussion of the framers' intent in these articles, see Rasmussen (1998: 186).

85. The literature on *locus standi* under Article 230 is extensive, and dominates the literature on European judicial review more generally. A thorough discussion of this literature is beyond the scope of this chapter. For good, and generally critical, surveys of the ECJ jurisprudence on *locus standi* for individual plaintiffs in actions for annulment, see Arnull (2000) Albors-Llorens (1996); Rasmussen (1998: 169–202); and Ward (2000).

86. For particularly forceful statements of this 'double-standard' argument, see Rasmussen (1998: 198–202); Ward (2000: 9–13 et seq.).

87. Similarly, the Court itself has shown a concern about opening the floodgates to public-interest litigation against Community actions, most notably in its ruling in *Greenpeace v. Commission*, where the Court explicitly denied standing to Greenpeace and other environmental groups on the grounds that the organization did not demonstrate direct and individual concern in challenging an EC environmental decision. The Advocate General's report provided an unusually clear and revealing statement of the 'floodgates' argument, noting that 'If the Court were ultimately to follow the proposal of the appellant associations, in future every measure of a Community institution concerning the environment or having an impact on it could be expected, on each occasion, to form the subject-matter of proceedings brought by a plethora of environmental associations'. Quoted in Brown and Kennedy (2000: 158–9).

88. Case C-70/88, *Parliament v. Council*, [1990] ECR I-2041. The member governments, it is worth noting, confirmed the Court's jurisprudence in the Treaty of Maastricht, which explicitly extended standing to the EP for the purpose of extending its prerogatives. For a good discussion, see Arnull (2000: 34–40).

89. A particularly vivid example of this problem concerned the Commission's controversial decision in July 2001 to reject the proposed merger of the US firms General Electric and Honeywell. During the dispute, critics complained that the Commission was effectively 'jury, judge, and executioner', deciding on both the legality of the merger and on any required remedies, while any appeal of a

negative Commission decision was likely to take at least two years—by which time the merger would surely have been abandoned. See for example Glackin (2001); Hirst (2001).

90. For an excellent comparison of EC administrative law with the procedures of the APA, see Bignami (1999: Sections V and VI).

91. The study of EC administrative law is young but burgeoning. For good discussions, see *inter alia*, Schwarze (1992); Harlow (1996); Shapiro (1996); Weatherill and Beaumont (1999: 244–313); Albors-Llorens (1996); Nehl (1999); Bignami (1999); Ward (2000: 202–60); and Shapiro (2001*a*).

92. In the 1978 *Atalanta* judgment, for example, a Commission Regulation was challenged and annulled on the grounds that its penalties, requiring private actors to forfeit the entirety of their security if obligations imposed by a contract were not fulfilled, were disproportionate to the seriousness of the offence. Case 240/78, *Atalanta v. Produktschap voor Vee en Vlees*, [1979] ECR 2137.

93. Case 24/62, *Germany v. Commission*, [1963] ECR 63.

94. For excellent reviews of recent case law on procedural requirements in Commission decisions, see Nehl (1999) and Shapiro (2001*a*).

95. See for example the 1993 *Wood Pulp* judgement, in which the Court annulled a 1984 Commission Decision imposing fines of up to 500,000 ecus on 42 wood pulp producers allegedly engaged in price fixing. The Court ruled that the Commission's charges against the firms had not been set out sufficiently clearly in the Commission's statement of objections, thereby violating the firms' right of defence. Joined cases C-89/95, C-104/85, C-114/85, C-116/85, C-117/85, and C-125/85, *Ahlström Oskaheyhtiö v. Commission*, [1993] ECR I-1317.

Chapter 3

1. There are, nevertheless, a number of sources that characterize the internal workings of the Court of Justice and the Court of First Instance without revealing the details of their deliberations. See in particular Brown and Kennedy (2000); Arnull (2000); and Edward (1995).

2. Brown and Kennedy (2000: 5). In addition to the text of the treaties, the Court's powers and constraints are detailed in the Statute of the ECJ, which is appended to the treaty in the form of a protocol and can be amended, at the request of the Court and after consulting the Commission and the EP, by a unanimous vote of the Council. By contrast, the Court adopts its own Rules of Procedure, but these must also be approved unanimously by the Council of Ministers (Article 245 EC, ex 188).

3. For good discussions of the EC Treaty as an incomplete contract or framework agreement, see, *inter alia*, Garrett (1992); Garrett and Weingast (1993); Garrett (1995*a*); Pollack (1997); Stone Sweet and Brunell (1998).

4. Note that only the relevant EC Treaty articles are cited here and subsequently in this chapter. For the corresponding articles of the ECSC and Euratom Treaties, and details regarding the Council Decisions laying down the jurisdiction of the CFI, see Hartley (1998: 62); Arnull (2000: 14–18).

5. In addition to the 15 judges on the Court, there are an additional eight advocates-general who undertake any necessary legal research on pending cases and make 'reasoned submissions' to the judges, who may, but need not, be guided by the advocate-general's opinion. The advocates-general therefore play a key role in the life of the Court; however, since the Treaty and Statute provisions regarding the appointment and terms of office of the advocates-general are basically identical to those of the judges (Hartley 1998: 54), the discussion here focuses exclusively on the judges.

6. The member states cannot compel the resignation of ECJ judges, who can be dismissed only by the unanimous agreement of the other judges and advocates-general that the judge in question 'no longer fulfils the requisite conditions or meets the obligations arising from his office'. Article 6 of the Statute of the Court of Justice, quoted in Hartley (1998: 53).

7. The de facto rule of one judge per member state is reflected in Article 221 (ex 165) EC, which originally provided for six judges, and now calls for 15 judges on the ECJ, with the possibility of changing the number of judges by a unanimous vote of the Council of Ministers.

8. This provision, while seemingly innocuous, was absent from the 1951 Treaty of Paris creating the Court of Justice of the European Coal and Steel Community, and was deliberately inserted by the drafters of the Treaties of Rome (Pescatore 1981: 172–3).

9. Similar provisions regarding the appointment, term of office, and reappointment of CFI judges are laid out in Article 225 (ex 168a).

10. For good discussions, see R. Dehousse (1999: 15); Beach (2001: 79).

11. The implications of these provisions, moreover, were clear to the drafters and contemporary critics of the ECSC Treaty where they first appeared, as Valentine (1954: 12–14) has demonstrated in his review of the ratification debates.

12. Here again, Valentine demonstrates that the importance of deliberating in secrecy for judicial independence was understood by at least some contemporary actors. See Valentine (1954: 13) for details.

13. Examples, besides the Barber Protocol, include a similar Protocol to the Maastricht Treaty limiting the effect of an ECJ decision on the rights of abortion service providers; and the 1997 revision to Article 141 (ex 119) which reaffirmed the right of member governments to pursue positive discrimination, also known as affirmative action, on behalf of women.

14. For formal proofs of these arguments, see Tsebelis and Garrett (2001: 376–83).

15. For extended discussions of judicial legitimacy and the ECJ, see also Mattli and Slaughter (1995); Gibson and Caldeira (1995).

16. For prominent examples, see Rasmussen (1986) and Hartley (1998), both of whom criticize the legal activism of the Court not primarily because of its pro-integration effects but because of the perceived weakness of the legal reasoning used by the Court to support such integrationist decisions.

17. Joined Cases C-6/1990 and 9/1990, *Francovich and Bonifaci v. Italy*, [1991] ECR I-5357. For a brief discussion of *Francovich* and the principle of state liability, see Section II of this chapter.

18. *Internationale Handelsgesellschaft*, [1974] 2 CMLR 549.

19. For good overviews of the Court's fundamental rights jurisprudence, see Craig and de Burca (1998: 296–348); Alston, Bustelo, and Heenan (1999).

20. *Wunsche Handelsgesellschaft*, [1987] 3 CMLR 225.

21. *Brunner*, [1994] 1 CMLR 57. For a good discussion of the case and its implications, see Herdegen (1994).

22. For good historical discussions of the negotiation of the TEU and its three-pillared structure, see Cloos, Reinisch, Vignes, and Weyland (1993); Corbett (1994); Ross (1995); Moravcsik (1998); Dyson and Featherstone (1999).

23. With the notable exception of the Barber Protocol, discussed above and in Chapter 6, the Court's jurisdiction within the EC pillar was not a major topic of discussion at Maastricht, which actually *increased* the powers of the Court through the new provision allowing the Court to levy fines for non-compliance under Article 228. In addition, the Maastricht Treaty made several other modest changes to the Court's procedures and jurisdiction, most notably by expanding the Council's ability to transfer certain categories of cases unanimously from the ECJ to the CFI,

and expanding its judicial review function to include the acts of the European Central Bank (ECB) and standing for Parliament and the ECB to bring cases to protect their prerogatives. For a good discussion, see Robinson (1994).

24. For the text of the UK's complaints against the ECJ, see Davis (1995). For excellent accounts of the UK's campaign against the ECJ, see Alter (1998); Tallberg (1999: 232–8).

25. In addition to these new Justice and Home Affairs provisions, Anthony Arnull (1999: 109–11) points out, the Amsterdam Treaty also features multiple efforts by the member governments to pre-empt future ECJ activism through detailed and explicit legal phrasing that contrasts sharply with the vague framework language of the early treaties. The most striking of these is the language of the revised Article 141(4), which was intended to contain, if not reverse, the Court's earlier ruling regarding the legality of a 'positive discrimination', or affirmative action, scheme in Bremen. See Case C-450/93, *Kalanke v. Bremen*, [1995] ECR I-3105.

26. Case 26/62, *Van Gend en Loos*, [1963] ECR 1, quoted in Stein (1981: 4).

27. Ibid.

28. For a good review of the Court's jurisprudence on the direct effect of EC law, see Craig and de Burca (1998: 163–212).

29. Case 6/64, *Flaminio Costa v. ENEL*, [1964] ECR 585.

30. Case 14/83, *Von Colson and Kamann v. Land Nordrein Westfalen*, [1984] ECR 1891.

31. Case 22/70, *Commission v. Council [ERTA]*, [1971] ECR 263.

32. Joined Cases 6/90 and 9/90, *Francovich and Bonifaci v. Italy*, [1991] ECR I-5357.

33. Seminal texts describing and interpreting the constitutionalization of the treaties include: Stein (1981); Weiler (1981; 1991; 1994); Burley and Mattli (1993); Mattli and Slaughter (1995; 1998); Alter (1996; 1998; 2001); Golub (1996); Stone Sweet and Caporaso (1998); Stone Sweet and Brunell (1998); Slaughter, Weiler, and Stone Sweet (1998).

34. Quoted in Mancini and Keeling (1995: 403). On the Court's integrationist preferences, see *inter alia* Stein (1981); Rasmussen (1986; 1998); Mancini (1991); Burley and Mattli (1993); Weiler (1991; 1994); Stone Sweet and Brunell (1998); Hartley (1998).

35. In support of this claim, Alter (1996: 485, n. 32) notes that a number of the landmark decisions in ECJ history, including the 1979 *Cassis de Dijon* case discussed in Chapter 5 and the 1975 *Defrenne* case examined in Chapter 6, were taken in response to preliminary references after the Commission had decided not to pursue infringement proceedings against the member states in question.

36. Stone Sweet and Brunell (1998), it should be noted, also examine the Court's case law in these two issue areas, and I similarly examine cases regarding the free movement of goods and equal pay for men and women in Chapters 5 and 6, respectively.

37. In cases where multiple questions were put to the Court, Kilroy (1999: 387–90) coded each of these questions separately, averaging the scores for all of the questions in order to obtain a coding for the Court's decision.

38. It is, however, worth noting that the Court issued a pro-member state ruling in all six of these cases, which are not discussed in any qualitative detail (Kilroy 1999: 403–4).

Chapter 4

1. For an extensive discussion of the EP's power of scrutiny and control over the executive, see Corbett, Jacobs, and Shackleton (2000: 246–69).

2. For details on the Empty Chair Crisis and its aftermath, see Pattison de Menil (1978); Newhouse (1967).
3. For extended accounts of the 1969–70 negotiation of the CAP and the Luxembourg Treaty, see Pollack (1995a: Ch. 3); Moravcsik (1998: Ch. 3); and Lindner and Rittberger (2001).
4. *Bulletin of the European Communities [Bull EC]* (1969a: 13–16; 1969b: 15–16); and *Agence Europe* (1969).
5. *Bull EC* (1969b: 15–16).
6. In addition to its concerns about allowing the EP to increase EC *expenditures*, the German delegation also opposed a modification, put forward by the Commission and the European Parliament, that would have allowed the Community to increase its own *resources* without the need for national ratification, as in the existing Article 201 EEC. Like other member governments, Germany opposed any change to the own-resources provisions of the treaty and formulated a constitutional reserve on the issue, arguing that the German Basic Law would not permit the allocation of new resources to the Community without national parliamentary ratification. Despite Commission and Parliamentary pressure, therefore, the proposal was quietly dropped during the negotiations. For good discussions, see *Agence Europe* (1970a, e).
7. For the text of the Council's February agreement on these questions, see *Bull EC* (1970).
8. Dates listed here correspond to contemporary practice in which the budgetary process begins several months earlier than the deadline dates listed in Article 272.
9. Article 28 (ex J.18) EU and Article 41 (ex K.13) EU.
10. Case 138/1979, *SA Roquette Frères v. Council of the European Communities* (Isoglucose Production quotas), [1980] ECR 3333, para. 33.
11. Case C-65/93, *European Parliament v. Council*, [1995] ECR I-643.
12. For a complete list of legal bases covered by consultation in the *Consolidated Treaties*, see Corbett, Jacobs, and Shackleton (2000: 184).
13. In the original Maastricht version of the procedure, co-decision I, the EP could signal to the Council its intention to reject the common position, triggering a preliminary Council-EP meeting in which the former could explain its position to the latter. This provision, which was seen to complicate the procedure without producing any real change in the balance of power between the Council and the EP, was eliminated in the Amsterdam, co-decision II, version of the procedure.
14. This paragraph draws from the arguments presented in Tsebelis (1997); Garrett (1995b); and Tsebelis and Garrett (2000).
15. A thorough survey of the theoretical debate is beyond the scope of this chapter. Key points of the debate concern, *inter alia*, the assumptions about EP and member-state preferences, which in turn influence the likelihood of an EP veto of the Council's common position and hence the equilibrium outcome of the procedure (Crombez 1997a); the scope of the Council's ability to alter the substance of the EP's amendments in its third reading, which is unclear from the text of Article 251 EC and affects the nature of the Council's 'take-it-or-leave-it' offer to the EP (Moser 1996); and the significance of the Parliament's repeatedly revealed preference for co-decision over cooperation (Scully 1997b; Steunenberg 2000). For useful surveys of the debate, see Hix (1999a: 88–94); Steunenberg (2000).
16. Once again, a complete review of this literature is beyond the scope of the current chapter. For a good review of the empirical evidence of EP influence under the cooperation and co-decision (I) procedures, see Hix (1999a: 94–6); and Tsebelis *et al.* (1999), discussed briefly below.
17. In this author's view, Hix thus provides a compelling explanation for the decision by the 1996 intergovernmental conference to simplify the co-decision

procedure and to codify the EP's existing practice of voting on the nomination of the full Commission as well as its President. Both instances can indeed be seen, in Hix's words, as 'constitutional agenda-setting through rule interpretation'. Hix's argument cannot, however, be generalized to all acts of delegation to the Parliament since most such acts, including, *inter alia*, the extension of co-decision to new areas in the Amsterdam Treaty, do not simply codify existing practices but delegate new powers to the Parliament.

18. 'The power of the Commission as a legislator', Tsebelis and Garrett (2000: 26) argue, 'has been eroded in each one of the revisions of the Rome treaty. In the EU's founding treaty, the Commission alone had agenda setting power (in the consultation procedure). The Commission had to share its agenda-setting role with the Parliament under cooperation. Codecision I effectively shifted agenda setting to the Council; the Council and the Parliament share effective agenda-setting under codecision II. Moreover, the lessening of the Commission's legislative influence will only be exacerbated in the future if, as seems likely, more issue areas will be brought under the reformed codecision'. To this list of developments, moreover, we might add the growing list of issue areas, including issues of justice and home affairs, common foreign and security policy, and Economic and Monetary Union, in which the Commission is required to share its right of initiative with the member states and/or other EC institutions.

19. Despite his differences with Tsebelis and Garrett over the interpretation of EP power under co-decision, Crombez (2000*b*: 367) makes a similar point: 'Any legislative influence the Commission may have under codecision II results from informational advantages, informal powers, and its role in the implementation of EU policies.'

20. *Commission Report on the Scope of the Codecision Procedure*, reproduced in the *Bulletin of the European Union* (1996), accessed on the Europa website on 14 October 2001 at http://europa.eu.int/abc/doc/off/bull/en/9607/p203001.htm. In addition, the Commission noted, 'it is customary for instruments in all areas of activity to "delegate" powers to take implementing measures, which the codecision procedure is not used for'.

21. *Conference of the Representatives of the Governments of the Member States, The European Union Today and Tomorrow: Adapting the European Union for the Benefit of its Peoples and Preparing it for the Future. A General Outline for a Draft Revision of the Treaties*, Brussels, 5 December 1996, Conf 500/96 LIMITE. For summaries of the positions of the Commission, EP, and member governments on the codecision procedure in the 1996 intergovernmental conference, see *Intergovernmental Conference Briefing Number 9 (First Update: 14 March 1996): CODECISION PROCEDURE*, accessed on the Europarl website on 19 August 1998 at www.europarl.eu.int/dg7/fiches/en/fiche8.htm, and *Commission Report on the Scope of the Codecision Procedure*, which quotes the conclusions of the 1995 'Reflection Group' that prepared the agenda for the 1996 IGC. According to that report, with regard to codecision, 'a large majority is in favour of extending it. Most would extend it to all legislation adopted by the Council by qualified majority. Another view would focus attention on matters currently dealt with by the cooperation procedure, whereas others suggest a case-by-case approach. One member, in principle, opposes any extension'.

22. *Commission Report on the Scope of the Codecision Procedure*, Section I, part 2.

23. Preliminary evidence for such leverage is provided by Hix and Lord's (1995) study of the 1995 investiture vote for incoming Commission President Jacques Santer, in which many Socialist MEPs broke from their party group to support Santer's candidacy, apparently under pressure from their own—socialist— national governments.

24. Throughout its history, the activism and the chronic absenteeism of MEPs have tainted that body with the charge of irresponsibility, leading to demands by politicians and analysts that the EP demonstrate its responsibility before acquiring additional powers; during the negotiation of the Maastricht Treaty, for example, the editors of *The Economist* argued that, rather than a 'big bang' increase in EP powers, it would be 'better to let the parliament advance in small steps, and to let it prove at each stage that it is worthy of further reward'; see *The Economist* (1991). Reflecting these concerns, EP leaders have urged such responsibility on their members, particularly following the passage and entry into force of the Maastricht and Amsterdam Treaties; see for example the comments of EP President Egon Klepsch following the agreement of the Maastricht Treaty in David Buchan (1992*a*).

25. See for example the bitter criticism of the Parliament from Financial Affairs Commissioner Fritz Bolkestein and other observers following the EP's July 2001 decision to reject the Commission's proposed Takeovers Directive after 13 years of negotiations (Osborne and Milner 2001); and the similar criticisms of the EP following its rejection of a Directive on the regulation of biotechnology in 1995 (Barber 1995*a, b*).

26. See for example Corbett, Jacobs, and Shackleton (2000).

27. The questions of the number of Commissioners and the individual right of member governments to nominate Commissioners were left unresolved at the Treaty of Amsterdam. The Treaty of Nice, agreed in December 2000 and currently awaiting ratification by the member governments following its rejection by referendum in Ireland, provides for the member governments to nominate one Commissioner each until the number of Commissioners reaches 27, at which point a system of rotating appointments will be established on the principle of strict equality among member governments. See Conclusions for a discussion of the terms of the Treaty of Nice.

28. For a discussion of the debate on the democratic deficit, and the desirability of the EP versus national parliaments as the repositories of democratic legitimacy, see Conclusions.

Chapter 5

1. According to Meunier and Nicolaidis (1999: 479–80), this initial delegation of power reflected the view of the framers that the delegation of powers to the EC level would serve to 'insulate the policy-making process from domestic pressures, thus promoting a more liberal international trade order' while at the same time facilitating the conclusion of trade agreements with third countries, thereby increasing the EC's external influence.

2. For good summaries of the EC trade-policy process, see Paemen and Bensch (1995); Woolcock and Hodges (1996); Johnson (1998); Meunier and Nicolaidis (1999); Meunier (2000); and Woolcock (2000).

3. For good discussions of EC trade negotiations as a three-level game, see Dusek (1995); Pan (1996); Paarlberg (1997); and Patterson (1997).

4. For a good discussion of mixed competence in the Uruguay Round, see Woolcock and Hodges (1996: 302).

5. The account of the Uruguay Round negotiations and the 1992 CAP reform presented here is necessarily brief, focusing primarily on the role of the Commission. For more complete discussions, see Stewart (1993); Ross (1995);

Paemen and Bensch (1995); Preeg (1995); Pan (1996); Woolcock and Hodges (1996); and Webber (1998).

6. For a brief, clear discussion of the pre-1992 CAP, see Stewart (1993: 145–9).

7. Quoted in Woolcock and Hodges (1996: 314). For excellent discussions of the Brussels meeting and the intra-EC bargaining which preceded it, see Woolcock and Hodges (1996: 314–15) and Preeg (1995: 116–22).

8. Quoted in Ross (1995: 113).

9. On the early discussions within DG VI during 1990, see *Agra Europe* (1991).

10. For good discussions of the initial debates on CAP reform within the Commission, see Ross (1995: 109–14).

11. For the text of the Commission Communication, see *Europe Documents*, No. 1689, 8 February 1991.

12. The ecu, or European currency unit, was used as the budgetary unit of account for the European Community budget and other legislation prior to the adoption of the Euro.

13. For details of the Commission's proposals, see Swinbank (1993).

14. For a good discussion see Preeg (1995: 144–7).

15. For an excellent discussion of the final agreement, emphasizing the complex intergovernmental bargaining required for Community ratification of the Uruguay Round, see Devuyst (1995).

16. On the Council's informal rule of consensus decision-making, see for example Hayes-Renshaw and Wallace (1995) and Lewis (1998*a*, *b*). For good discussions of consensus decision-making in external trade policy, see Meunier and Nicolaidis (1999) and Meunier (2000).

17. On the principle of diffuse reciprocity, see Keohane (1986).

18. For a rigorous discussion of the effects of different voting rules and varying levels of Commission discretion on the bargaining power of the Community vis-à-vis third countries, see Meunier (2000).

19. Opinion 1/94, 15 November 1994, ECR I-123.

20. For good general discussions of EC competition policy, including merger control, see Allen (1983; 1996); Montagnon (1990); Goyder (1993); Neven, Nutall, and Seabright (1993); McGowan and Wilks (1995); Cini and McGowan (1998); Faull and Nikpay (1999); F. McGowan (2000); and Damro (2001).

21. For good discussions see Montagnon (1990); Allen (1996); Cini and McGowan (1998); F. McGowan (2000).

22. The discussion in this section draws in part on Hölzer (1990); Neven, Nutall, and Seabright (1993); Goyder (1993: 387–407); Bulmer (1994); Allen (1996: 169–75); Damro (2001); on the primary sources cited below, and on interviews with two former senior Commission officials. For the text of the Regulation, see 'Council Regulation (EEC) No. 4064/89 of 21 December 1989 on the Control of Concentrations Between Undertakings', *Official Journal* L395/1 of 21 December 1989.

23. Case 6/72, *Europemballage Corporation and Continental Can Company Inc. v. Commission of the European Communities*, [1973] ECR 215.

24. Joined cases 142 and 156/1984, *British-American Tobacco Company Ltd and R. J. Reynolds Industries Inc. v. Commission of the European Communities*, [1987] ECR 4487.

25. Regarding the financial uncertainty generated by the *Philip Morris* decision, and the subsequent rise in business support for the MCR, see also Bulmer (1994).

26. On business support for the MCR and its demand for legal certainty and a one-stop shop for European mergers following the *Philip Morris* ruling, see also Donkin (1988); Hampton (1988). As Hampton points out, the *Philip Morris*

decision 'threw everyone into a state of confusion. If the Commission was to have the very real powers afforded by the Treaty over anti-competitive conduct extended to mergers and takeovers, it would make some sense for the Commission to be able to pass a merger in advance and then desist from enforcing the Treaty later'. See also the evidence of UK business support for the MCR contained in House of Lords, Select Committee on the European Communities (1996).

27. Indeed, William Dawkins (1989*a*) suggested, 'it can hardly be worth the bother' for the Commission to press for the formal adoption of the MCR 'when companies are already flocking to Brussels authorities by the score to get their cross-frontier merger and takeover plans vetted under existing EC competition rules'. In practice, Dawkins pointed out, the number of Commission merger decisions increased from 15 in 1987 to 25 in 1988, with a further 36 provisional written clearances.

28. In addition to raising the Commission's proposed thresholds, the Council further reduced the scope of the Commission's powers by reducing from three-quarters to two-thirds the percentage of combined sales in a single member state which would allow national regulators to retain jurisdiction over the case.

29. Such Article 9 references, Damro (2001: 20) notes, are relatively rare, constituting at most 3–4 per cent of all EC merger decisions.

30. This provision was intended for use by smaller member states without the means to assess specific cases, but in practice has been used only twice to refer proposed mergers that were subsequently blocked by the Commission. For good discussions, see Faull and Nikpay (1999: 234); and Cini and McGowan (1998: 120–1).

31. Similarly, Spain and Italy sought to have regional development considerations taken into account (Dawkins 1989*b*).

32. The same article also stipulates that 'the Commission shall carry out the procedures set out in this Regulation in close and constant liaison with the competent authorities of the Member States, which may express their views upon those procedures'.

33. Indeed, as Damro (2001: 23) points out, during the first eleven years of the Merger Control Regulation the College has challenged only a single draft decision of the Merger Task Force, which the latter was able to redraft within the timelines specified in the Decision.

34. Article 21(1) of the Regulation is explicit on this point: 'Subject to review by the European Court of Justice, the Commission shall have sole jurisdiction to take the decisions provided for in this Regulation.'

35. See for example Glackin (2001) and Hirst (2001).

36. Notwithstanding these difficulties, in June 2002 the Court of First Instance for the first time annulled a merger decision by the Commission, ruling that the Commission's rejection of the merger of two British travel firms had been 'vitiated by errors' in its economic analysis as well as procedure. Despite coming some three years after the Commission's initial decision, the Court's ruling establishes a heightened standard of review for future merger decisions, and may lead to future procedural and substantive changes within the Merger Task Force. For good discussions, see Guerrera (2002); Kay (2002); Buck and Guerrera (2002).

37. As Damro (2001: 24) summarizes, the MCR provides the member governments with multiple avenues of influence, yet 'significant obstacles stand in the way of each avenue for Member State influence', including the non-binding nature of the advisory committee opinions, the difficulties of lobbying the Commission, and the relative weakness of judicial review.

38. For the text of the final Commission decision, see CEC (1991*a*).

39. Commissioners Bangemann and Van Miert were reported to have argued that, had the market been defined in terms of commuter aircraft up to 90 seats, the

ATR-De Havilland merger would have been shown to have a far smaller market share (*European Report* 1991*a*).

40. For accounts of the internal Commission debate on the De Havilland merger, see also Brittan (2000: 98–9); Donovan (1991); *Agence France Presse* (1991*a*); Hill (1991*a*); European Report (1991*a*).

41. Quoted in 'Commission Prohibits Acquisition by Aerospatiale/Alenia of De Havilland', RAPID Press Release—IP; 896 of 2 October 1991.

42. Within the Commission, meanwhile, Bangemann and other Commissioners called for a change to the Commission's internal procedures which allowed the Commissioner in charge of competition to take decisions in the first stage of a merger review without consulting the full College. Here again, Brittan received the support of a majority of the Commissioners, although he did agree to inform other Commissioners before opening a second-stage investigation into a proposed merger. See for example *European Report* (1991*c*); Wolf (1991; 1992); *Transport Europe* (1992).

43. See also *The Economist* (1992).

44. For a strong rebuttal to the European Cartel Office proposal, and a defence of the Commission's performance under the MRC, see Ehlermann (1995).

45. Quoted in *International Securities Regulation Report* (1993). See also Hill (1993); *Agence Europe* (1993*c*).

46. For a good review of the proposal, see House of Lords, Select Committee on the European Communities (1996).

47. 'Council Regulation (EC) No 1310/1997 of 30 June 1997 Amending Regulation (EEC) No 4064/1989 on the Control of Concentrations between Undertakings', *Official Journal* L 180 of 9 July 1997, pp. 1–6. In addition to the new thresholds for multiple notifications, the amending Regulation also includes technical changes to the application of the Regulation to the banking sector and full-function joint ventures. For good discussions of the final negotiations and the 1997 amending Regulation, see Emma Tucker (1997); *European Report* (1997); Leone (1997); Faull and Nikpay (1999: 205–74).

48. For good, up-to-date reviews of EU competition policy, see Cini and McGowan (1998: 116–34); Damro (2001); and the Commission's most recent annual report (CEC 2000*a*).

49. For good discussions, see Guerrera and de Jonquières (2001); Burnside (2001).

50. Article 29 (ex 34) includes similar ban on quantitative restrictions on exports, and all measures having equivalent effect, between member states.

51. Case 8/74, *Procureur du Roi v. Benoît and Gustave Dassonville*, [1974] ECR 852.

52. Specifically, the referring court asked, 'Must the concept of measures having an effect equivalent to quantitative restrictions on imports contained in Article 30 of the EEC Treaty be understood as meaning that the fixing of a minimum wine-spirit content for potable spirits laid down in the German *Branntweingesetz*, the result of which is that traditional products of other Member States whose wine-spirit content is below the fixed limit cannot be put into circulation in the Federal Republic of Germany, also comes within this concept?' The Court also put a second question regarding the consistency of the German law with Article 37 EC, now repealed, dealing with state monopolies of a commercial character, which the Court held to be inapplicable in the case. Case 128/78, *Rewe-Zentral v. Bundesmonopolverwaltung für Branntwein*, [1979] ECR 649, para. 5.

53. *Rewe*, para. 11.

54. *Rewe*, para 13.

55. *Rewe*, para 14.

56. *Rewe*, para 14.

57. *Rewe*, para. 8.
58. Indeed, Alter and Meunier-Aitsahalia (1994: 552) argue that 'Both the decision itself and the Commission's response were necessary to produce the new harmonization policy'.
59. But see White (1989); Craig and de Burca (1998: 580); Maduro (1999); and Arnull (2000: 227–97) for excellent reviews of the Court's Article 28 jurisprudence following *Cassis*.
60. Case 302/86, *Commission v. Denmark*, [1988] ECR 4607.
61. Case 178/1984, *Commission v. Germany*, [1987] ECR 1227. On the political controversy generated by the case, see Peel (1986; 1987); Tuohy (1986). For a critical reading of the decision, with its risk of backlash among German public opinion, see Hermann (1987).
62. Case 407/1985, 3 *Glocken GmbH and Gertraud Kritzinger v. USL Centro-Sud and Provincia autonoma di Bolzano*, [1988] ECR 4233. See also Dickson (1988*a,b*).
63. Case 286/81, *Oosthoek's Uitgeversmaatschappij*, [1982] ECR 4575.
64. Case 282/87, *Buet and Another v. Ministère Public*, [1989] ECR 1235.
65. Case C-362/88, *GB-INNO-BM*, [1990] ECR I-667.
66. Joined Cases 60 and 61/84, *Cinéthèque v. Fédération Nationale des Cinémas Français*, [1985] ECR 2605.
67. Case 145/88, *Torfaen BC v. B & Q plc*, [1990] CMLR 337.
68. Case C-169/91, *Council of the City of Stoke-on-Trent and Norwich City Council v. B&Q*, [1992] ECR I-6635, para. 15.
69. *Stoke-on-Trent*, para. 15.
70. Opinion of Mr Advocate-General Van Gerven delivered on 28 April 1993, Criminal Proceedings against Bernard Keck and Daniel Mithouard, Joined Cases C-267/1991 and C-268/1991, [1993] ECR I-6097, para. 6.
71. Opinion of Mr Advocate-General Van Gerven, para. 8.
72. Opinion of Mr Advocate-General Van Gerven, paras 14–15.
73. Joined Cases C-267/1991 and C-268/1991, *Keck and Mithouard*, [1993] ECR I-6097, para. 15.
74. *Keck*, para. 16; emphasis added.
75. In Weatherill's (1996: 885) words, '*Keck* was doubtless intended to empower national courts to dismiss far-fetched attempts to deploy internal market law which were clogging up the Community judicial system with the minutiae of purely local affairs'.

Chapter 6

1. In addition to the primary sources cited below, I have also benefited from the careful analyses of the negotiation of the Working Time Directive by Jeffrey Lewis (1998*a*) and the analyses of the 1996 ECJ decision in *United Kingdom v. Council* by Margaret Gray (1997) and Derek Beach (2001: 155–67).
2. 'Council Recommendation 75/457/EEC of 22 July 1975 on the Principle of the 40-Hour Work Week and the Four Weeks' Annual Paid Holiday', *Official Journal* L 199/1 of 30 July 1975.
3. For a detailed analysis of the amendments offered by the EP in its first and second readings of the Working Time Directive, and the acceptance or rejection of those amendments by the Commission and Council, see the database collected by George Tsebelis and his collaborators at www.polisci.ucla.edu/tsebelis/ The author is grateful to Amie Kreppel for bringing this resource to my attention.
4. In a later speech, Sir Brian Corby, the President of the Confederation of British Industry, again challenged both the cost and the legal basis of the proposed

Directive: 'It is presented as a health and safety measure, although no evidence as yet has been produced to demonstrate how health and safety will be improved... The directive runs completely counter to the principle of subsidiarity agreed at Maastricht, which expresses the reality that these matters cannot be regulated effectively at Community level. In short, it is a thoroughly bad piece of draft legislation, a misguided piece of Euro-nonsense which can only damage competitiveness and cost jobs.' Quoted in *PR Newswire European* (1992).

5. Although Lewis (1998*a*) attributes the UK Government's conciliatory approach largely to Shepherd, such a position seems to have emerged first in late 1991; see Hill (1991*c*).

6. Despite its agenda-setting powers under Article 118a, the Commission did not have the power to call a vote within the Council of Ministers, a right reserved to the member state occupying the presidency of the Council.

7. Lewis (1998*a*: 390) notes that, while Germany favoured the adoption of the Directive, its officials 'preferred consensus' and made it clear that Germany would not vote on the issue in early 1992, advocating further negotiations to bring the British on board. See also *European Report* (1992).

8. For the specific provisions of the Directive, see 'Council Directive 93/104/EC of 23 November 1993 Concerning Certain Aspects of the Organization of Working Time', *Official Journal* L 307/18 of 13 December 1993.

9. The text, moreover, is unclear whether the derogation would expire or remain in place in the absence of a clear Council decision (Ramsey 1994). In either event, the derogation represents a significant victory for the UK and, in the words of an Irish diplomat interviewed by Lewis (1998*a*: 394)—a 'masterpiece of draftsmanship' which is essentially 'as far away as one can get from a derogation, or time limited exception, towards an opt-out, without actually arriving'.

10. *Comments by Commissioner Flynn During the Post-Council Press Conference— Directive on the Organisation of Working Time*, RAPID Press Release, IP: 93-417.

11. 'Decision on the Common Position Established by the Council with a View to the Adoption of a Directive Concerning Certain Aspects of the Organization of Working Time' (C3-0241/93–SYN 295), *Official Journal* C 315/125 of 22 November 1993.

12. See also the data collected by Tsebelis *et al.* at www.polisci.ucla.edu/tsebelis/

13. 'Council Directive 93/104/EC of 23 November 1993 Concerning Certain Aspects of the Organisation of Working Time', *Official Journal* L 307/18 of 13 December 1993. For good analyses of the terms of the Directive, see Gray (1997) and Ramsey (1994).

14. Case C-84/1994, *United Kingdom v. Council*, [1996] ECR I-5755. For good legal and political-science analyses of the Court's ruling, see respectively Gray (1997: 344–54) and Beach (2001: 155–69).

15. Opinion of Advocate-General Léger, Case C-84/94 *United Kingdom v. Council*, ECR I-5755.

16. Cash and Major both quoted in Wolf and Milne (1996).

17. For a good discussion, see Stephens (1996).

18. Good accounts of the government's deliberations are provided in Stephens (1996); Wastell and Kirkbride (1996); Bevins (1996).

19. Case C-84/1994, *United Kingdom v. Council*, [1996] ECR I-5755, para. 15.

20. Para. 37.

21. For an excellent discussion of the EU Directives on workplace health and safety, emphasizing the innovative and progressive elements of European legislation, see Eichener (1997).

22. See for example Southey and Prestion (1996); *European Report* (1996*b*); Rice (1996). On the UK's 1996 campaign to rein-in the ECJ, see also Chapter 3 of this book.

23. In this sense, the specifics of Article 118a and the dispute over the legal basis of the Working Time Directive is now of largely historical interest; yet the persistence of overlapping legal bases for EU legislation, featuring different Council voting rules and different levels of Parliamentary participation, provide a continuing source of 'procedural politics' among EU member states and institutions, and legal base cases to be resolved by the ECJ. For an excellent discussion, see Jupille (2000).

24. 'Directive 2000/34/EC of the European Parliament and of the Council of 22 June 2000 Amending Council Directive 1993/104/EC Concerning Certain Aspects of the Organisation of Working Time to Cover Sectors and Activities Excluded from that Directive', *Official Journal* L 195 of 1 August 2000. However, the Commission did not include 'seafarers' in its Directive, out of concern that 'overly strict legislation is liable to weaken the competitiveness of ships sailing under the flag of a Member State'; it therefore encouraged a collective agreement between two sides of the industry, based on the voluntary standards of the International Labor Organization, and extended the same standards to all ships using Community ports through a separate Directive. For details, see 'Council Directive 1999/63/EC of 21 June 1999 Concerning the Agreement on the Organization of Working Time of Seafarers Concluded by the European Community Shipowners' Association (ECSA) and the Federation of European Transport Workers' Unions in the European Union (FST)', *Official Journal* L 167 of 2 July 1999; and 'Directive 1999/95/EC of the European Parliament and of the Council of 13 December 1999 Concerning the Enforcement of the Provisions in Respect of Seafarers' Hours of Work on Board Ships Calling at Community Ports', *Official Journal* L 14 of 20 January 2000. A separate proposal for a Directive on the organization of working time for road-transport workers and self-employed drivers is pending at this writing.

25. This section draws largely on Pollack (1995*a, b*; 1998), which contain more extensive primary references for the 1988 and 1993 Structural Fund reforms.

26. For the text and explanatory note of the Commission's 1987 proposals for Structural Fund reform, see CEC (1987; 1988*b*). For the text of the Framework Regulation as adopted by the Council, see 'Council Regulation (EEC) No. 2052/88 of 24 June 1988 on the Tasks of the Structural Funds and their Effectiveness and on Coordination of their Activities between Themselves and with the Operations of the European Investment Bank and the Other Existing Financial Instruments', *Official Journal* L 185 of 15 July, pp. 9–19. Specific implementing regulations for each of the individual structural funds can be found in the same issue of the *Official Journal*.

27. For background on the Community Initiatives adopted under the 1988 Regulations, see CEC (1993*b*).

28. CEC (1993*b*), sheet on Envireg.

29. For an excellent and thorough discussion of member-state concerns about the 1988 reforms, see Yuill *et al.* (1993: 63–8).

30. The Commission's initial ideas for the Fund reforms were expressed in its mid-term evaluation, CEC (1992). For the Commissions' formal proposals, see CEC (1993*c, d*).

31. For member-state responses to the Commission's proposals, see, for example, House of Commons (1993*a, b*); Assemblée Nationale (1993); Sénat (1993); Agence Europe (1993*a*).

32. *European Report* (1993*a*); *Agence Europe* (1993*b*).

33. In addition to these Council-induced changes, it is also worth noting that the Commission also took aboard a number of Parliamentary amendments, the most notable of which was that the Commission should also notify the Parliament

before the final adoption of Community Initiatives, as well as providing the Parliament with regular information about national development plans, the CSFs, and implementation of the Funds.

34. For an excellent attempt to explain the patterns of variation in the inclusion of regional governments in the Structural Funds, see Marks (1996). For an early study of the role of the regions in the post-1988 Structural Funds, see Anderson (1990).

35. The text of the 1999 Regulations is reproduced in CEC (2000*d*). For an excellent analysis of the negotiation of the Regulations, see Sutcliffe (2000) and the analyses by Bache (1998), Peterson and Bomberg (1999: 146–72), and Allen (2000).

36. For good discussions of the Court's equal-pay jurisprudence, and EU equal opportunities policy more generally, see for example Mazey (1995); Hoskyns (1996); Cichowski (1998); Ellis (1998); Arnull (2000); and Pollack and Hafner-Burton (2000).

37. Case 43/75, *Defrenne v. SABENA [Defrenne II]*, [1976] ECR 455.

38. Para. 73.

39. Case 80/70 *Defrenne v. Sabena [Defrenne I]*, [1971] ECR 445, paras 7–8, quoted in Arnull (2000: 471).

40. Case 96/80, *Jenkins v. Kingsgate*, [1981] ECR 911. For a good discussion of direct and indirect discrimination in the Court's case law, see Ellis (1998: 109–24).

41. The Council did, however, respond to the 1984 *Bilka* decision with the 1986 Directive on equal treatment in occupational social security schemes, inserting several derogations to the principle of equal pay, which were in turn later overturned by the Court in *Barber* (see below).

42. The other questions concerned, *inter alia*, the status of redundancy payments as 'pay' under Article 141, whether Article 141 would be infringed in a case such as Barber's, and the direct effect of Article 141 in such cases. For details, see Case C-262/88, *Barber v. Guardian Royal Exchange*, [1990] ECR 1889.

43. Case 43/75, *Defrenne v. Sabena* (Defrenne I), [1976] ECR 455, paras 7–9.

44. Case 170/84, *Bilka-Kaufhaus GmbH v. Karin Weber von Hartz*, [1986] ECR 1607.

45. Case 69/180, *Susan Jane Worringham and Margaret Humphreys v. Lloyds Bank Limited*, [1981] ECR 767.

46. Opinion of Mr Advocate-General Van Gerven delivered on 30 January 1990, *Barber v. Guardian Royal Exchange*, [1990] ECR 1889.

47. 'Directive 79/7/EEC on the Progressive Implementation of the Principle of Equal Treatment for Men and Women in Matters of Social Security', *Official Journal* L 1979 L6/24 of 10 January 1979.

48. 'Directive 86/378/EEC on the Implementation of the Principle of Equal Treatment for Men and Women in Occupational Social Security Schemes', *Official Journal* L 1986 L225/40 of 12 August 1986.

49. In an unusual opinion, Van Gerven anticipated that the Court might not agree with his assessment that Article 141 extended to contracted-out occupational pension schemes, and therefore prepared parallel opinions alternately applying Article 141 or the 1976 Equal Treatment Directive to the case to hand.

50. See for example Short (1990); Dyer (1990); Raif (1990).

51. Case C-262/88, *Barber v. Guardian Royal Exchange*, [1990] ECR 1889, esp. paras 21–30.

52. Para. 43.

53. Para. 44.

54. Para. 45.

55. Joined Opinions of Mr Advocate-General Van Gerven Delivered on 28 April 1993 [*Ten Oever, Moroni, Neath, Coloroll*], [1993] ECR I-4879, para. 10.

56. On the negotiation of the Protocol, see for example Cohen (1991); Cohen and Hill (1993); *Financial Times* (1991).
57. But see Beach (2001) for an overview suggesting that, *pace* the 'retreat' analysis, the Court has continued to adopt a broad interpretation of the Treaties and secondary legislation after Maastricht.
58. But see Moore (1995), Eylenbosch and Verreth (1996), Whiteford (1996), and Arnull (2000: 472–81) for excellent reviews of the post-*Barber* case law in this area.
59. Joined Opinions of Mr Advocate-General Van Gerven Delivered on 28 April 1993 [*Ten Oever, Moroni, Neath, Coloroll*], [1993] ECR I-4879, para. 10.
60. Paras 19, 22.
61. Para. 21.
62. Para. 23.
63. Case C-109/1991, *Ten Oever v. Stichting Bedrijfspensioenfonds*, [1993] ECR I-4879, para. 19.
64. In fact, the Court itself would not refer to the Protocol explicitly until the later *Vroege* and *Fisscher* cases, when the effect of the Protocol was the subject of explicit questions from a Dutch tribunal; see below for a discussion of both cases.
65. Case C-57/1993, *Vroege*, [1994] ECR I-4541, para. 20.
66. For a good discussion, and a forceful rebuttal, of the arguments put forward by the British and Belgian governments, see Joined Opinions of Mr Advocate-General Van Gerven Delivered on 7 June 1994 [*Vroege, Fisscher*], [1994] ECR I-4541, paras 13–17.
67. Case C-57/1993, *Vroege*, [1994] ECR I-4541, paras 19–32.
68. Paras 33–43.
69. Joined Opinions of Mr Advocate-General Van Gerven Delivered on 7 June 1994 [*Vroege, Fisscher*], [1994] ECR I-4541, paras 29–30.
70. Case C-128/1993, *Fisscher*, [1994] ECR I-4583.
71. Case C-110/1991, *Moroni*, [1993] ECR I-6591; and Case C-200/1991, *Coloroll*, [1994] ECR I-4389, esp. paras 63–71.
72. Joined Opinions of Mr Advocate-General Van Gerven Delivered on 28 April 1993 [*Ten Oever, Moroni, Neath, Coloroll*], [1993] ECR I-4879, paras 44–51.
73. Case C-109/1991, *Ten Oever v. Stichting Bedrijfspensioenfonds*, [1993] ECR I-4879, para. 13.
74. Case C-200/1991, *Coloroll*, [1994] ECR I-4389; Case C-408/1992, *Avdel Systems*, [1994] ECR I-4435; and Case C-28/1993, *van den Akker*, [1994] ECR I-4527.
75. Joined Opinions of Mr Advocate-General Van Gerven Delivered on 28 April 1993 [*Ten Oever, Moroni, Neath, Coloroll*], [1993] ECR I-4879, para. 60.
76. Ibid.
77. Case C-200/1991, *Coloroll*, [1994] ECR I-4389, summary, para. 3.
78. Case C-408/1992, *Avdel Systems*, [1994] ECR I-4435; and Case C-28/1993, para. 26, quoted in Arnull (2000: 477).
79. Joined Opinions of Mr Advocate-General Van Gerven Delivered on 28 April 1993 [*Ten Oever, Moroni, Neath, Coloroll*], [1993] ECR I-4879, para. 28.
80. Case C-152/1991, *Neath v. Steeper*, [1993] ECR I-6935.
81. See for example Eylenbosch and Verreth (1996: 138); Ellis (1998: 86); Arnull (2000: 481).
82. Interview, ECJ judge, Florence, November 2001.
83. The relevant treaty provision for the adoption of the Directive is Article 94 (ex 100) EC, which requires unanimity voting in the Council and consultation of the European Parliament.
84. Commission of the European Communities, 'Proposal for a Council Directive Amending Directive 86/378/EEC on the Implementation of the Principle of Equal Treatment for Men and Women in Occupational Social Security

Schemes', *Official Journal*, C 218 of 23 August 1995, p. 5. See also *European Report* (1995).

85. 'Council Directive 96/97/EC of 20 December 1996 Amending Directive 86/378/EEC on the Implementation of the Principle of Equal Treatment for Men and Women in Occupational Social Security Schemes', *Official Journal* L 046 of 17 February 1997, pp. 20–4. See also *European Report* (1996c, d). For its part, the European Parliament, and in particular its Committee on Women's Rights, criticized the Commission for simply implementing rather than further developing the Court's jurisprudence, and proposed a number of progressive amendments which would have gone farther than the ECJ, but these were dismissed by the Council, where a unanimous agreement on such far-reaching decisions was unattainable. See Marques (1996).

Conclusions

1. For comparative discussions of delegation in domestic politics looking beyond the US case, see for example Huber (1998; 2000); Bergman, Müller, and Strøm (2000); Huber and Lupia (2001); Huber, Shipan, and Pfahler (2001); Thatcher and Stone Sweet (2002); Pollack (2002); and the essays in Bergman, Müller, and Strøm (2000) and Thatcher and Stone Sweet (2002).
2. See references in Chapter 4.
3. For good discussions of the negotiation of the Maastricht Treaty provisions on EMU, see for example Moravcsik (1998); Dyson and Featherstone (1999).
4. See for example Berman and McNamara (1999); Verdun (1998); Mackie (1997); de Grauwe (1998).
5. See for example *European Report* (1998); Barber (2000).
6. The Commission has also defended the independence of the ECB, warning that respect for such independence was 'crucial...to the credibility of monetary policy' in the Euro-zone; quoted in Munchau and Buckley (1998).
7. Cases 9/56 and 10/56, *Meroni v. High Authority*, [1958] ECR 1148.
8. For detailed analyses of the European agencies, see Everson (1995); R. Dehousse (1997); Kreher (1997); Majone (1997); Shapiro (1997); Everson *et al.* (2001); Kelemen (2001); and CEC (2001b).
9. For good discussions of the OMC, see Rhodes, Goetschy, and Mosher (2000); Wallace (2000); Trubek and Mosher (2001); Héritier (2001); Hodson and Maher (2001).
10. For a good overview of the debate, see Mosher's essay in Rhodes, Goestchy, and Mosher (2000).
11. For a preliminary analysis of the Commission's role in the adoption and implementation of the 'gender mainstreaming' provisions of the Employment Strategy, see Pollack and Hafner-Burton (2000: 441–5).
12. The text of the Treaty of Nice, together with an exhaustive 'IGC 2000 archive', can be found on the Europa web site at http://europa.eu.int/comm/nice_treaty/index_en.htm. For valuable commentaries on the IGC and the Treaty, see for example Dinan (2000–2001); Galloway (2001); Ludlow *et al.* (2001).
13. 'Laeken Declaration on the Future of Europe', Annex 1 to the Presidency Conclusions of the Laeken European Council, 14–15 December 2001, available on-line at: http://www.europa.eu.int/council/off/conclu/index.htm.
14. For an excellent review of this literature, see Nielsen and Tierney (2001b).
15. See, in addition to the EU literature cited above, Keohane and Martin (1994); Barnett and Finnemore (1999); Martin (2000); Pollack *et al.* (2000); Nielson and

Tierney (2001*a*, *b*). See also Goldstein *et al.* (2000), Keohane, Moravcsik, and Slaughter (2000), and the rest of the essays in the special issue on 'Legalization and World Politics' in *International Organization*, 54/3, which features a number of useful discussions of delegation of judicial authority in international politics. Finally, in May 2002, as this book was going to press, Brigham Young University hosted a conference on the subject of 'Delegation to International Organizations', which explored a number of the questions raised in this section from multiple theoretical perspectives and with empirical reference to both EU and non-EU cases. Unfortunately, time considerations preclude a thorough discussion of the papers presented at the workshop, which collectively promise to push forward our conceptualization as well as our empirical knowledge of delegation in international politics; interested readers may, however, consult the papers on the conference website, consulted on 16 June at: http://faculty.wm.edu/mjtier/.

16. See for example Finnemore (1996); Wapner (1996); Keck and Sikkink (1998); Price (1998); Barnett and Finnemore (1999).

17. See for example Nugent (1995; 2000: Chapter 9); Cini (1996); Endo (1999); and Drake (2000).

18. See, however, Case T-188/97, *Rothmans v. Commission*, [1999] ECR II-2463, in which the Court of First Instance annulled the Commission's refusal to release the minutes of a comitology meeting. The Commission had refused access to the minutes on the grounds that the committee, and not the Commission itself, was the true author, but this argument was rejected by the CFI.

19. For good discussions, see Bignami (1999) and Schmitter, Majone, and Moravcsik (2000).

20. Interview, Swedish parliamentarian, Florence, December 2001.

REFERENCES

Aberbach, Joel D. (1990). *Keeping a Watchful Eye: The Politics of Congressional Oversight*. Washington, DC: Brookings Institution.

AFX European Focus (2001). 'EU summit: Securities Text Will Make Decision-making More Flexible—Bolkstein'. 22 March.

Agence Europe (1969). 16 September.

—— (1970*a*). 16 January.

—— (1970*b*). 19 January.

—— (1970*c*). 20 January.

—— (1970*d*). 21 January.

—— (1970*e*). 3 February.

—— (1993*a*). 7–8 June.

—— (1993*b*). 15 July.

—— (1993*c*). 'Commission Decides to Leave Mergers Regulation Unchanged'. 29 July.

—— (1999). 'Coreper Resumes Talks on Reform of Commission's Powers of Execution in the Framework of Co-decision—Agreement in Sight'. 7 June.

Agence France Presse (1991*a*). 'EC Leans Towards Green Light for De Havilland Takeover'. 1 October.

—— (1991*b*). 'France to Use Powers for Reversal of EC's De Havilland Veto'. 4 October.

Agra Europe (1991). 'Continuing Confusion on Commission's CAP Reform Plans'. 15 February.

Albors-Llorens, Albertina (1996). *Private Parties in European Community Law: Challenging Community Measures*. New York: Oxford University Press.

Allen, David (1983). 'Managing the Common Market: The Community Competition Policy', in H. Wallace, W. Wallace, and C. Webb (eds), *Policy-making in the European Community* (2nd edn). London: John Wiley and Sons.

—— (1996). 'Competition Policy: Policing the Single Market', in Helen Wallace and William Wallace (eds), *Policy-making in the European Union* (3rd edn). Oxford: Oxford University Press.

—— (2000). 'Cohesion and the Structural Funds: Transfers and Trade-Offs', in Helen Wallace and William Wallace (eds), *Policy-making in the European Union* (4th edn). New York: Oxford University Press.

Alter, Karen J. (1996). 'The European Court's Political Power: The Emergence of an Authoritative International Court in the European Union'. *West European Politics*, 19: 458–87.

—— (1998). 'Who are the Masters of the Treaty? European Governments and the European Court of Justice'. *International Organization*, 52: 125–52.

—— (2000). 'The European Union's Legal System and Domestic Policy: Spillover or Backlash?' *International Organization*, 53: 489–518.

—— (2001). *Establishing the Supremacy of European Law: The Making of an International Rule of Law in Europe*. New York: Oxford University Press.

—— and Meunier-Aitsahalia, Sophie (1994). 'Judicial Politics in the European Community: European Integration and the Path-Breaking *Cassis de Dijon* Decision'. *Comparative Political Studies*, 26: 535–61.

Alter, Karen J. and Vargas, Jeannette (2000). 'Explaining Variation in the Use of European Litigation Strategies: European Community Law and British Gender Equality Policy'. *Comparative Political Studies*, 33: 452–82.

Alston, Philip, Bustelo, Mara R., and Heenan, James (eds) (1999). *The EU and Human Rights*. New York: Oxford University Press.

Andenas, Mads and Türk, Alexander (eds) (2000). *Delegated Legislation and the Role of Committees in the EC*. Boston: Kluwer Law International.

Anderson, Jeffrey (1990). 'Skeptical Reflections on a Europe of Regions: Britain, Germany and the ERDF'. *Journal of Public Policy*, 10: 417–47.

Arnull, Anthony (1999). 'Taming the Beast? The Treaty of Amsterdam and the Court of Justice', in David O'Keefe and Patrick Twomey (eds), *Legal Issues of the Amsterdam Treaty*. Oxford: Hart Publishing.

—— (2000). *The European Union and Its Court of Justice*. New York: Oxford University Press.

Aspinwall, Mark D. and Schneider, Gerald (2000). 'Same Menu, Separate Tables: The Institutionalist Turn in Political Science and the Study of European Integration'. *European Journal of Political Research*, 38: 1–36.

Assemblée Nationale (1993). *Rapport d'information déposé par la délégation de l'Assemblée Nationale pour les Communautés Européennes*, No. 221. Paris: Assemblée Nationale.

Bache, Ian (1998). *The Politics of European Union Regional Policy: Multi-Level Governance or Flexible Gatekeeping?* Sheffield: Sheffield Academic Press.

Barber, Lionel (1995). 'Vote Underlines MEP's Volatility'. *Financial Times*, 3 March.

Barber, Tony (2000). 'Bundesbank Chief Slaps Down Fabius: Welteke's Riposte Highlights ECB's Sensitivity to Political Involvement'. *Financial Times*, 18 July.

Barnard, Catherine (1996). 'The Economic Objectives of Article 119', in Tamara K. Hervey and David O'Keeffe (eds), *Sex Equality Law in the European Union*. New York: John Wiley & Sons.

Barnett, Michael N. and Finnemore, Martha (1999). 'The Politics, Power, and Pathologies of International Organizations'. *International Organization*, 54: 699–732.

Bawn, Kathleen (1995). 'Political Control versus Expertise: Congressional Choice About Administrative Procedures'. *American Political Science Review*, 89: 62–73.

—— (1997). 'Choosing Strategies to Control the Bureaucracy: Statutory Constraints, Oversight, and the Committee System'. *Journal of Law, Economics and Organization*, 13: 101–26.

Beach, Derek (2001). *Between Law and Politics: The Relationship Between the European Court of Justice and EU Member States*. Copenhagen: DJOF Publishing.

Bergman, Torbjörn, Müller, Wolfgang C., and Strøm, Kaare (2000). 'Parliamentary Democracy and the Chain of Delegation'. *European Journal of Political Research*, 37: 255–60.

—— —— (eds), (2000). 'Parliamentary Democracy and the Chain of Delegation'. Special issue of *European Journal of Political Research*, 37/3.

Berman, Sheri and McNamara, Kathleen R. (1999). 'Bank on Democracy: Why Central Banks Need Public Oversight'. *Foreign Affairs*, 78: 2–8.

Bertram, Christoph (1967–1968). 'Decision-Making in the EEC: The Management Committee Procedure'. *Common Market Law Review*, 5: 246–64.

Bevins, Anthony (1996). 'Defiance on Working Time Evaporates'. *Independent*, 8 November.

Bignami, Francesca (1999). 'The Administrative State in a Separation of Powers Constitution: Lessors for European Community Rulemaking from the United States' (Harvard Jean Monnet Working Paper). Available on-line at www.jeanmonnetprogram.org/papers/99/990502.html.

Bowler, S. and Farrell, D. (1993). 'Legislator Shirking and Voter Monitoring: Impact of European Parliament Electoral Systems upon Legislator-Voter Relationships'. *Journal of Common Market Studies*, 31: 45–69.

—— —— (1995). 'The Organization of the European Parliament: Committees, Specialization and Coordination'. *British Journal of Political Science*, 25: 219–43.

Bradley, Kieran St Clair (1992). 'Comitology and the Law: Through a Glass, Darkly'. *Common Market Law Review*, 29: 693–721.

—— (1994). '"Better Rusty Than Missin"? Institutional Reforms of the Maastricht Treaty and the European Parliament', in David O'Keeffe and Patrick Twomey (eds), *Legal Issues of the Maastricht Treaty*. London: Chancery Law Publishing.

—— (1997). 'The European Parliament and Comitology: On the Road to Nowhere?' *European Law Journal*, 3: 230–54.

Brittan, Leon (2000). *A Diet of Brussels: The Changing Face of Europe*. London: Little, Brown and Company.

Brown, Lionel Neville and Kennedy, Tom (2000). *The Court of Justice of the European Communities*. London: Sweet and Maxwell.

Buchan, D. (1991). 'Delors Attacks French Critics of De Havilland Decision'. *Financial Times*, 7 October.

—— (1992*a*). 'Master Fixer'. *Financial Times*, 22 January.

—— (1992*b*). 'French Government Faces Fury at Home'. *Financial Times*, 21 November.

Buck, Tobias and Guerrera, Francesco (2002). 'Brussels U-Turn on Carnival Merger May Signal Policy Shift'. *Financial Times*, 17 July.

Buckley, Neil (1996). 'Brussels Seeks More Power on Mergers'. *Financial Times*, 10 July.

Bulletin of the European Communities [Bull EC] (1969*a*). September–October.

—— (1969*b*). December.

—— (1970). March.

Bulletin of the European Union (1996). July–August; http://europa.eu.int/abc/doc/off/bull/en/9607/p203001.htm.

Bulmer, S. (1994). 'Institutions and Policy Change in the European Communities: The Case of Merger Control'. *Public Administration*, 72: 423–44.

Burley, Anne-Marie and Mattli, Walter (1993). 'Europe Before the Court: A Political Theory of Legal Integration'. *International Organization*, 47: 41–76.

Burnside, Alec (2001). 'A Fairer Deal for Europe'. *Financial Times*, 12 December.

Calvert, Randall, Moran, Mark, and Weingast, Barry (1987). 'Congressional Influence Over Policymaking: The Case of the FTC', in Mathew McCubbins and Terry Sullivan (eds), *Theories of Congress: The New Institutionalism*. Cambridge: Cambridge University Press.

CEC (Commission of the European Communities) (1980). 'Communication from the Commission Concerning the Consequences of the Judgment Given by the Court of Justice on 20 February 1979 in case 120/78 ('Cassis de Dijon')'. *Official Journal* C 256 of 3 October, p. 2.

—— (1987). *Reform of the Structural Funds*, COM(87)376 final of 24 August.

—— (1988*a*). 'Amended Proposal for a Council Regulation (EEC) on the Control of Concentrations between Undertakings', *Official Journal* C 130 of 19 May, p. 4.

—— (1988*b*). *Amended Proposal for a Council Regulation (EEC) on the tasks of the Structural Funds and on coordination of their activities between themselves and with the operations of the European Investment Bank and other existing financial instruments*, COM(88)144 final of 23 March.

—— (1989). *Delegation of Executive Powers to the Commission*, SEC(89)1591 final of 28 September.

CEC (Commission of the European Communities) (1990). *Proposal for a Council Directive Concerning Certain Aspects of the Organization of Working Time*, COM (90) 317 final – SYN 295, Brussels 20 September.

—— (1991*a*). 'Commission Decision 1991/619/EEC of 2 October 1991 Declaring the Incompatibility of a Concentration (Case No. IV/M.053 – Aerospatiale–Alenia/de Havilland)'. *Official Journal* L 334 of 5 December, pp. 42–61.

—— (1991*b*). *Amendment to the Proposal for a Council Directive Concerning Certain Aspects of the Organization of Working Time*, COM (91) 130 – SYN 295, Brussels, 23 April.

—— (1992). *Community Structural Policies: Assessment and Outlook*, COM(92)84.

—— (1993*a*). 'Re-examined Proposal for a Council Directive Concerning Certain Aspects of the Organization of Working Time'. COM(93)578 final of 16 November.

—— (1993*b*). *Community Initiatives*. Luxembourg: Office for Official Publications of the European Communities.

—— (1993*c*). 'Proposal for a Council Regulation (EEC) Amending Council Regulation (EEC) No 2052/88 on the Tasks of the Structural Funds and Their Effectiveness and on Coordination of Their Activities between Themselves and with the Operations of the European Investment Bank and the Other Existing Community Financial Interests', COM(93)67 final of 12 March.

—— (1994*a*). *The Future of the Community Initiatives Under the Structural Funds*, COM(94)46.

—— (1994*b*). *Guide to the Community Initiatives* (1st edn). Luxembourg: Office for Official Publications of the European Communities.

—— (1994*c*). 'The Operation of the Community Structural Funds 1994–1999', COM (93)124 final of 7 April 1993.

—— (1995). *Commission Report for the Reflection Group*. Luxembourg: Office for Official Publications of the European Communities.

—— (1996*a*). *Green Paper on the Review of the Merger Regulation*, COM(96)19 of 31 January.

—— (1996*b*). 'Communication from the Commission to the Council and to the European Parliament Regarding the Revision of the Merger Regulation'. COM (1996)313 of 12 September.

—— (1996c). 'Statement by Padraig Flynn, European Commissioner with responsibility for employment and social affairs on the European Court of Justice ruling on the UK Challenge to the "Working Time Directive"'. RAPID Press Release, IP: 96–1011.

—— (1997). *White Paper: Sectors and Activities Excluded from the Working Time Directive*, COM(97)334 final of 15 July.

—— (1998). *Communication on the Organisation of Working Time in the Sectors and Activities Excluded from Directive 93/104/EC of 23 November 1993*, COM(98)662 final of 18 November.

—— (1999). *Financial Services: Implementing the Framework for Financial Markets: Action Plan*, COM (1999)232 of 11 May.

—— (2000*a*). *European Community Competition Policy: XXXth Report on Competition Policy*. Luxembourg: Office for Official Publications of the European Community.

—— (2000*b*). *White Paper: Reforming the Commission*, COM(20)2000 of 1 March.

—— (2000*c*). *Report from the Commission: State of Implementation of Council Directive 93/104/EC of 23 November 1993 Concerning Certain Aspects of the Organisation of Working Time ('Working Time Directive')*, COM (2000) 787 final of 1 December.

464   References

CEC (Commission of the European Communities) (2000d). *Structural Actions 2000–2006: Commentary and Regulations*. Luxembourg: Office for Official Publications of the European Communities.

—— (2001a). *Green Paper on the Review of Council Regulation (EEC) No 4064/89*, COM(2001)745/6 of 11 December, available on the *Europa* web site at http://europa.eu.int/comm/competition/mergers/review/#green_paper.

—— (2001b). *Administrative Agencies*; www.europa.eu.int/agencies/_docs/resume_en.pdf

—— (2001c). 'European Governance: A White Paper'. COM (2001) 428 final of 25 July.

—— (n.d.). *Draft Council Recommendation on the Reduction and Reorganisation of Working Time*. COM(83)543 final.

Chalmers, Damien (2000). *The Much Ado about Judicial Politics in the United Kingdom: A Statistical Analysis of Reported Decisions of United Kingdom Courts Invoking EU Law 1973–1998* (Harvard Jean Monnet Working Paper 200/1); www.jeanmonnetprogram.org/papers/00/000101.html.

Cheeseright, Paul (1983). 'EEC Urged to Encourage Worksharing'. *Financial Times*, 21 September.

Chote, Robert (1998). 'Secret Voting Would Put ECB Independence at Risk'. *Financial Times*, 24 September.

Christiansen, Thomas, Jorgensen, Knud Erik, and Wiener, Antje (1999). 'The Social Construction of Europe'. *Journal of European Public Policy*, 6: 528–44.

Christiansen, Thomas and Kirchner, Emil (eds) (2000). *Committee Governance in the European Union*. New York: St Martin's Press.

Cichowscki, Rachel (1998). 'Empowerment through Supranational Venues: Women's Activism, the European Court and the Evolution of Sex Equality Policy in the EU'. Paper prepared for delivery at the Annual Meeting of the American Political Science Association, Boston, 3–6 September.

Cini, Michelle (1996). *The European Commission: Leadership, Organisation, and Culture in the EU Administration*. New York: Manchester University Press.

—— and Lee McGowan (1998). *Competition Policy in the European Union*. New York: St Martin's Press.

Cloos, J., Reinisch, G., Vignes, D., and Weyland, J. (1993). *Le Traité de Maastricht: Genèse, analyse, commentaires*. Brussels: Bruylant.

Coen, David (1997). 'The Evolution of the Large Firm as a Political Actor in the European Union'. *Journal of European Public Policy*, 4: 91–108.

Cohen, Norma (1991). 'Diplomatic End to Pensions Saga'. *Financial Times*, 14 December.

—— and Hill, Andrew (1991). 'Pension Pact Could Save Industry up to Pounds 50bn'. *Financial Times*, 12 December.

Committee of Independent Experts (1999a). *First Report on Allegations Regarding Fraud, Mismanagement and Nepotism in the European Commission*, consulted on-line at www.europarl.eu.int/experts/report1_en.htm on 24 May 2002.

—— (1999b). *Second Report on Reform of the Commission: Analysis of Current Practice and Proposals for Tackling Mismanagement, Irregularities and Fraud*, consulted on-line at www.europarl.eu.int/experts/default_en.htm on 24 May 2002.

Committee of Wise Men (2001). *Final Report of the Committee of Wise Men on the Regulation of Securities Markets*. Brussels, 15 February. Consulted on-line at http://europa.eu.int/comm/internal_market/en/finances/general/lamfalussyen.pdf on 24 May 2002.

Conant, Lisa (2002). *Justice Contained: Law and Politics in the European Union*. Ithaca, NY: Cornell University Press.

Cooter, Robert D. and Ginsburg, Tom (1996). 'Comparative Judicial Discretion'. *International Review of Law and Economics*, 16: 295–313.

Corbett, Richard (1987). 'The 1985 Intergovernmental Conference and the Single European Act', in Roy Pryce (ed.), *The Dynamics of European Union*. New York: Croom Helm.

——(1994). *The Treaty of Maastricht*. Harlow: Longman Current Affairs.

——(2000). 'Academic Modelling of the Codecision Procedure: A Practitioner's Puzzled Reaction'. *European Union Politics*, 1: 373–8.

——, Jacobs, Francis, and Shackleton, Michael (2000). *The European Parliament* (4th edn). London: Catermill.

Cowie, Ian (1991). 'Maastricht Cuts Pounds 50bn off Equal Pensions Cost'. *Daily Telegraph*, 12 December.

Cowles, Maria Green (1995). 'Setting the Agenda for a New Europe: The ERT and EC 1992'. *Journal of Common Market Studies*, 33: 501–26.

Cox, Gary W. and McCubbins, Matthew D. (1993). *Legislative Leviathan: Party Government in the House*. Berkeley: University of California Press.

Cram, Laura (1994). 'The European Commission as a Multi-organisation: Social Policy and IT Policy in the EU'. *Journal of European Public Policy*, 1: 195–217.

——(1997). *Policy-making in the EU: Conceptual Lenses and the Integration Process*. London: Routledge.

——(1999). 'The Commission', in Laura Cram, Desmond Dinan, and Neill Nugent (eds), *Developments in the European Union*. Basingstoke: Macmillan.

Craig, Paul (2000). 'The Fall and Renewal of the Commission: Accountability, Contract and Administrative Organization'. *European Law Journal*, 6/2: 98–116.

——and de Búrca, Graínne (1998). *EU Law: Cases, Text and Materials*. Oxford: Oxford University Press.

Crombez, Christophe (1996). 'Legislative Procedures in the European Community'. *British Journal of Political Science*, 26: 199–228.

——(1997a). 'The Co-Decision Procedure in the European Union'. *Legislative Studies Quarterly*, 22: 97–119.

——(1997b). 'Policy Making and Commission Appointment in the European Union'. *Aussenwirtschaft*, 52: 63–82.

——(2000a). 'The Treaty of Amsterdam and the Codecision Procedure', in Mark D. Aspinwall and Gerald Schneider (eds), *The Rules of Integration*. Manchester: Manchester University Press.

——(2000b). 'Codecision: Towards a Bicameral European Union'. *European Union Politics*, 1: 363–8.

Damro, Chad (2001). 'Capture and Control: The Institutional Dynamics of EU Regulatory Independence'. Paper prepared for the European Community Studies Association Seventh Biennial International Conference, Madison, Wisconsin, US, 31 May–2 June.

David, David (1995). '1996 Intergovernmental Conference: European Court of Justice' (letter to Carlos Westendorp), 25 September.

Dawkins, William (1988a). 'EC Merger–Vetting Plans Revised'. *Financial Times*, 2 March.

——(1988b). 'EC Merger Plans Make Marginal Progress'. *Financial Times*, 22 December.

——(1989a). 'EC Merger Controls Take Shape'. *Financial Times*, 6 February.

——(1989b). 'French Coax EC States Towards Entente on Merger Controls'. *Financial Times*, 31 July.

de Grauwe, Paul (1998). 'Law unto Itself'. *Financial Times*, 12 November.

Dehousse, Franklin (1999). *Amsterdam: The Making of a Treaty*. London: Kogan Page.

Dehousse, Renaud (1997). 'Regulation by Networks in the European Community: The Role of European Agencies'. *Journal of European Public Policy*, 4: 246–61.

——(1998). 'Institutional Architecture After Amsterdam, Parliamentary System or Regulatory Structure?' *Common Market Law Review*, 35: 595–627.

——(1999). *The European Court of Justice: The Politics of Judicial Integration*. New York: St Martin's Press.

Devuyst, Youri (1995). 'The European Community and the Conclusion of the Uruguay Round', in C. Rhodes and S. Mazey (eds), *The State of the European Union, 3: Building a European Polity?* Boulder, CO: Lynne Rienner.

Dickson, Tim (1988a). 'Court Blow to Italian Pasta Curbs'. *Financial Times*, 15 July.

——(1988b). 'Legal Ruling on Pasta Gives EC Food for Thought'. *Financial Times*, 20 July.

Diebold, William (1959). *The Schuman Plan: A Study in Economic Cooperation (1950–1959)*. New York: Frederick A. Praeger.

Dinan, Desmond (2000–2001). 'IGC Watch 2000: Parts 1–4'. Originally published in the *ECSA Review*, 13/2–4, and 14/1. Available on-line at www.eustudies.org/IGCWatchSeries.html.

Dobie, Claire (1991). 'EC Pension Ruling Lifts Threat to Industry'. *Independent*, 13 December.

Docksey, Christopher and Williams, Karen (1994). 'The Commission and the Execution of Community Policy', in Geoffrey Edwards and David Spence (eds), *The European Commission*. Harlow: Longman Current Affairs.

Dogan, Rhys (1997). 'Comitology: Little Procedures with Big Implications'. *West European Politics*, 20: 31–60.

——(2000). 'A Cross-Sectoral View of Comitology: Incidence, Issues, and Implications', in Thomas Christiansen and Emil Kirchner (eds), *Europe in Change: Committee Governance in the European Union*. Manchester: Manchester University Press.

Dombey, Daniel (2002a). 'Collision Course'. *Financial Times*, 3 May.

——(2002b). 'Defeat for Brussels over Haulier Tax'. *Financial Times*, 4 May.

——and Guerrera, Francesco (2002). 'Little-Noticed Treaty Clause May Curb Monti's Power'. *Financial Times*, 18 February.

Donkin, Richard (1988). 'CBI Chief Repeats Call for European Takeover Rules'. *Financial Times*, 14 July.

Donovan, Patrick (1991). 'EC May Block Air Takeover'. *Guardian*, 24 September.

Dowding, Keith (2000). 'Institutionalist Research on the European Union: A Critical Review'. *European Union Politics*, 1: 125–44.

Drake, Helen (2000). *Jacques Delors: A Political Biography*. New York: Routledge.

Duchêne, François (1994). *Jean Monnet: The First Statesman of Interdependence*. New York: W.W. Norton and Company.

Dumoulin, Michel (1988). 'La Belgique et les débuts du Plan Schuman', in Klaus Schwabe (ed.), *The Beginnings of the Schuman Plan*. Baden-Baden: Nomos.

Dusek, Daniel (1995). 'The Negotiation of the Czech-EC Association Agreement' (unpublished undergraduate senior thesis). Cambridge, MA: Harvard University.

Dyer, Claire (1990). 'Law: A Cat Among the Pensions'. *Guardian*, 16 May.

Dyson, Kenneth and Featherstone, Kevin (1999). *The Road to Maastricht: Negotiating Economic and Monetary Union*. New York: Oxford University Press.

Earnshaw, David and Judge, David (1995a). *Prelude to Codecision: A Qualitative Assessment of the Cooperation Procedure in the 1989–94 European Parliament*. Luxembourg: European Parliament Directorate-General for Research, Project IV/93/54.

————(1995b). 'From Cooperation to Codecision: The European Parliament's Path to Legislative Power', in J. J. Richardson (ed.), *Policy Making in the European Union*. London: Routledge.

Earnshaw, David and Judge, David (1995c). 'Early Days: The European Parliament, Co-Decision and the European Union Legislative Process Post-Maastricht'. *Journal of European Public Policy*, 2: 624–49.

——— (1997). 'The Life and Times of the European Union's Cooperation Procedure'. *Journal of Common Market Studies*, 35: 543–54.

The Economist (1988). 'Wanted: A New Referee for European Fair Play', 5 November.

——— (1991). 'The Road from Strasbourg'. 13 April.

——— (1992). 'The EC's Competition Policy: Pleasing Nobody'. 14 March.

——— (2001a). 'Neil Kinnock, Europe's Anglo-Saxon Reformer'. 3 March.

——— (2000b). 'A Ragbag of Reform'. 3 March.

ECJ (European Court of Justice) (1995). *Report of the Court of Justice on Certain Aspects of the Application of the Treaty on European Union*. Luxembourg, May. Consulted on-line on 1 September 1996 at www.cec.lu/en/agenda/igc-hom/eu-doc/justice/cj_rep/html.

——— (2000). 'Statistical Information of the Court of Justice (2000)', Consulted on-line on 17 December 2001 at http://curia.eu.int/en/stat/index.htm.

Eeckhout, Piet (1998). 'Recent Case-law on Free Movement of Goods: Refining Keck and Mithouard'. *European Business Law Review*, 9/7–8: 269–72.

Edward, David (1995). 'How the Court of Justice Works'. *European Law Review*, 20: 539–58.

Edwards, Geoffrey and Spence, David (eds) (1995). *The European Commission*. Harlow: Longman Current Affairs.

Ehlermann, Claus-Dieter (1995). 'Case for a Cartel Body'. *Financial Times*, 7 March.

Eichener, Volker (1997). 'Effective European Problem-Solving: Lessons from the Regulation of Occupational Safety and Environmental Protection'. *Journal of European Public Policy*, 4: 591–608.

Ellis, Evelyn (1998). *European Community Sex Equality Law* (2nd edn). Oxford: Clarendon Press.

Endo, Ken (1999). *The Presidency of the European Commission Under Jacques Delors: The Politics of Shared Leadership*. New York: St Martin's Press.

Epstein, David and O'Halloran, Sharyn (1994). 'Administrative Procedures, Information, and Agency Discretion'. *American Journal of Political Science*, 38: 697–722.

——— (1996). 'Divided Government and the Design of Administrative Procedures: A Formal Model and Empirical Test'. *Journal of Politics*, 58: 373–97.

——— (1999a). *Delegating Powers: A Transaction Cost Politics Approach to Policy Making under Separate Powers*. New York: Cambridge University Press.

——— (1999b). 'Asymmetric Information, Delegation, and the Structure of Policy-Making'. *Journal of Theoretical Politics*, 11: 37–56.

European Ombudsman (2001). *Annual Report 2000*. Luxembourg: Office for Official Publications of the European Communities. All the annual reports of the Ombudsman, and other documentation, are available on the Ombudsman's web-site at www.euro–ombudsman.eu.int.

European Report (1990). 'Competition: Council Adopts Merger Control Regulation', 7 January.

——— (1991a). 'Competition: Commission Split over De Havilland Decision', 2 October.

——— (1991b). 'Competition: A Political Crisis Over De Havilland Veto?' 9 October.

——— (1991c). 'Competition: Merger Probe Procedure Questioned after De Havilland', 16 October.

——— (1992). 'Social Affairs Council: Working Time and Pregnant Women Top of June 24 Agenda', 24 June.

European Report (1993*a*). No. 1876, 17 July.

—— (1993*b*). 'Council Looks at Commission Merger Regulation Report'. 29 September.

—— (1995). 'Equal Opportunities: Commission Adapts Directive to Barber Ruling', 20 May.

—— (1996*a*). 'Merger Control: Council Seals the Death of the Threshold Reduction Debate', 16 November.

—— (1996*b*). 'UK Urges IGC to Revise EU Treaty's Social Provisions', 16 November.

—— (1996*c*). 'Equal Opportunities: Directive on Professional Pension Schemes to be Amended', 24 July.

—— (1996*d*). 'Social Affairs Council: Broad Agreement on Burden of Proof Directive', 4 December.

—— (1997). 'Merger Control: Council Streamlines Procedures for Cross-Border Mergers'. 26 April.

—— (1998). 'ECB: European Parliament Calls for Tighter Democratic Control', 4 April.

—— (1999). 'European Union: MEPs Put Commission Team on Probation', 16 January.

—— (2001*a*). 'Administrative Reform: Commission Hopes to Implement New Policy in 2003', 3 March.

—— (2001*b*). 'Finance Council: Ministers Welcome Lamfalussy Report, Directives on Investments and Banks', 14 March.

—— (2001*c*). 'Commission Reform: Kinnock Runs into Conflict with Council Caution and Parliamentary Reservations', 4 July.

—— (2002*a*). 'Agriculture: Commission Takes Council to Court over Portuguese Aid Decision', 2 March.

—— (2002*b*). 'Financial Services: Vote Raises Hopes of Progress on Securities Market Reform', 26 January.

Evans, Andrew (1999). *The EU Structural Funds*. New York: Oxford University Press.

Evans, Peter B., Jacobson, Harold K., and Putnam, Robert D. (eds) (1993). *Double-Edged Diplomacy: International Bargaining and Domestic Politics*. Berkeley: University of California Press.

Everson, Michelle (1995). 'European Agencies: Hierarchy Beaters?' *European Law Journal*, 1: 180–204.

—— Majone, Giandomenico, Metcalfe, Les, and Schout, Adrian (2001). *The Role of Specialized Agencies in Decentralising EU Governance*. Report Presented to the Commission Working Group on Governance; www.europa.eu.int/comm/governance/areas/group6/contribution_en.pdf.

Eylenbosch, Ann and Verreth, Kathleen (1996). 'Equal Treatment for Men and Women in Complementary Pensions: Answers or Unsolved Questions?' *Journal of European Social Policy*, 6/2: 123–46.

Falke, Josef (2000). 'Comitology: From Small Councils to Complex Networks', in Mads Andenas and Alexander Türk (eds), *Delegated Legislation and the Role of Committees in the EC*. Boston: Kluwer Law International.

Faull, Jonathan and Nikpay, Ali (1999). *The EC Law of Competition*. Oxford: Oxford University Press.

Ferejohn, J. and Weingast, Barry (1992). A Positive Theory of Statutory Interpretation'. *International Journal of Law and Economics*, 12: 263–79.

Ferejohn, John A. and Shipan, Charles R. (1989). 'Congressional Influence on Administrative Agencies: A Case Study of Telecommunications Policy', in Larry Dodd and Bruce Oppenheimer (eds), *Congress Reconsidered* (4th edn). Washington, DC: Congressional Quarterly Press.

Financial Times (1983). 'Work-Hour Cuts Left to Member Governments', 15 September.

—— (1991). 'Unisex in Pensions', 16 December.

—— (1995). 'Patent Folly', 2 March.

Financial Times (2001). 'Editorial Comment: Lamfalussy Lite', 28 March.

Finnemore, Martha (1996). *National Interests in International Society*. Ithaca, NY: Cornell University Press.

Fiorina, Morris P. (1982). 'Legislative Choice of Regulatory Forms: Legal Process or Administrative Process?' *Public Choice*, 39: 33–71.

Franchino, Fabio (1998). 'Institutionalism and the Commission's Executive Discretion: An Empirical Analysis'. *European Integration online Papers*, 2/6, http://eiop.or.at/eiop/texte/1998–006.htm.

—— (1999). 'The Determinants of Control of Commission's Executive Functions'. *European Integration online Papers*, 3/2, http://eiop.or.at/eiop/texte/1999–0002a.htm.

—— (2000*a*). 'Control of the Commission's Executive Functions: Uncertainty, Conflict and Decision Rules'. *European Union Politics*, 1: 63–92.

—— (2000*b*). 'Commission's Executive Discretion, Information, and Comitology'. *Journal of Theoretical Politics*, 12: 155–81.

—— (2001). 'Delegating Powers in the European Union'. Paper presented at the Seventh Biennial International Conference of the European Community Studies Association, Madison, Wisconsin, 31 May–2 June.

Friis, Lykke (1998). '"The End of the Beginning" of Eastern Enlargement: Luxembourg Summit and Agenda Setting'. *European Integration online Papers*, 2/7, http://eiop.or.at/eiop/texte/1998–007a.htm.

Fuchs, Gerhard (1994). 'Policy-making in a System of Multi-level Governance: The Commission of the European Community and the Restructuring of the Telecommunications Sector'. *Journal of European Public Policy*, 1: 177–94.

Galanter, Marc (1974). 'Why the "Haves" Come Out Ahead: Speculations on the Limits of Legal Change'. *Law and Society Review*, 9: 95–160.

Galloway, David (2001). *The Treaty of Nice and Beyond: Realities and Illusions of Power in the EU*. Sheffield: Sheffield Academic Press.

Gardner, David (1992*a*). 'Basis of a Deal on Radical CAP Reform in Sight'. *Financial Times*, 21 May.

—— (1992*b*). 'Reforms with a Grain of Sense: The EC's Agricultural Package, Brokered by Ray MacSharry, Will Cut Output and Food Prices'. *Financial Times*, 22 May.

——, Simon, Bernard, and Leadbeater, Charles (1991). 'Brussels Blocks De Havilland Takeover: Move May Boost Credibility of Commission as an Impartial Competition Watchdog'. *Financial Times*, 3 October.

—— and Taylor, Robert (1993). 'UK to Challenge EC's 48-Hour Working Week'. *Financial Times*, 2 June.

Garrett, Geoffrey (1992). 'International Cooperation and Institutional Choice: The European Community's Internal Market'. *International Organization*, 46: 533–60.

—— (1995*a*). 'The Politics of Legal Integration in the European Union'. *International Organization*, 49: 171–81.

—— (1995*b*). 'From the Luxembourg Compromise to Codecision: Decision-Making in the European Union'. *Electoral Studies*, 14: 289–308.

——, Kelemen, R. Daniel, and Schulz, Heiner (1998). 'The European Court of Justice, National Governments, and Legal Integration in the European Union'. *International Organization*, 52: 149–76.

—— and Tsebelis, George (1996). 'An Institutional Critique of Intergovernmentalism'. *International Organization*, 50: 269–99.

—— and Weingast, Barry (1993). 'Ideas, Interests, and Institutions: Constructing the European Community's Internal Market', in Judith Goldstein and Robert O. Keohane (eds), *Ideas and Foreign Policy*. Ithaca, NY: Cornell University Press.

Gatsios, Konstantine and Seabright, Paul (1989). 'Regulation in the European Community'. *Oxford Review of Economic Policy*, 5: 37–60.

Gerus, Victoria (1991). 'Comitology within the European Community's Policy-Making Process: A Mechanism of Political Control in the Inter-Institutional Relations of the Council of Ministers and the Commission' (unpublished manuscript). Cambridge, MA: Harvard University.

Gibson, James L. and Caldeira, Gregory A. (1995). 'The Legitimacy of Transnational Legal Institutions: Compliance, Support, and the European Court of Justice'. *American Journal of Political Science*, 39: 459–89.

Glackin, Michael (2001). 'GE to Appeal Against EC Deal Decision'. *Scotsman*, 4 July: 3.

Goldstein, Judith, Kahler, Miles, Keohane, Robert O., and Slaughter, Anne-Marie (2000). 'Introduction: Legalization and World Politics', *International Organization*, 54: 385–99.

Golub, Jonathan (1996). 'The Politics of Judicial Discretion: Rethinking the Interaction between National Courts and the European Court of Justice'. *West European Politics*, 19: 360–85.

——(1999). 'Decision Making Efficiency in the European Community'. *International Organization*, 53: 733–64.

Gormley, Laurence (1994). 'Reasoning Renounced? The Remarkable Judgment in Keck and Mithouard'. *European Business Law Review*, March: 63–7.

Gottlieb, Henry (1983). 'Europe Considers Shortening the 40-Hour Week'. *Associated Press*, 23 November.

Goyder, D. G. (1993). *EC Competition Law* (2nd edn). Oxford: Clarendon Press.

Grande, Edgar (2000). 'Post-National Democracy in Europe', in Michael Greven and Louis Pauly (eds), *Democracy Beyond the State? The European Dilemma and the Emerging World Order*. New York: Rowman and Littlefield Publishers.

Grant, Charles (1994). *Delors: Inside the House that Jacques Built*. London: Nicholas Brealey.

Gray, Margaret (1997). 'A Recalcitrant Partner: The UK Reaction to the Working Time Directive' in Ami Barav and Derek Wyatt (eds), *Yearbook of European Law* (Oxford: Clarendon Press), 17: 323–62.

Green, Donald P. and Shapiro, Ian (1994). *Pathologies of Rational Choice Theory*. New Haven, CT: Yale University Press.

Greven, Michael Th. (2000). 'Can the European Union Finally Become a Democracy?', in Michael Greven and Louis Pauly (eds), *Democracy Beyond the State? The European Dilemma and the Emerging World Order*. New York: Rowman and Littlefield.

——and Pauly, Louis W. (eds) (2000). *Democracy Beyond the State? The European Dilemma and the Emerging World Order*. New York: Rowman and Littlefield Publishers.

Groom, Brian (1984). 'EEC to Push on Working Time'. *Financial Times*, 30 June.

Guerrera, Francesco (2002). 'Ruling on Airtours Will Affect EU Competition Policy: Commission Overruled by Court of First Instance'. *Financial Times*, 7 June.

——and de Jonquières, Guy (2001). 'Unfair Competition'. *Financial Times*, 11 December.

Haas, Ernst B. (1958). *The Uniting of Europe*. Stanford: Stanford University Press.

——(1976). 'Turbulent Fields and the Theory of Regional Integration', *International Organization*, 30: 173–212.

Haibach, George (2000). 'The History of Comitology', in Mads Andenas and Alexander Türk (eds), *Delegated Legislation and the Role of Committees in the EC*. Boston: Kluwer Law International.

Hall, Peter A. (1986). *Governing the Economy: The Politics of State Intervention in Britain and France*. New York: Oxford University Press.

Hampton, Celia (1988). 'A Word of Caution on EC Merger Control'. *Financial Times*, 29 September.

—— (1989). 'Merger Rule Draft Upsets Industry'. *Financial Times*, 23 November.

Harlow, Carol (1996). 'Codification of EC Administrative Procedures? Fitting the Foot to the Shoe or the Shoe to the Foot'. *European Law Journal*, 2: 3–25.

—— (1999). 'European Administrative Law and the Global Challenge', in Paul Craig and Graínne de Búrca (eds), *The Evolution of EU Law*. New York: Oxford University Press.

Hartley, Trevor C. (1998). *The Foundations of European Community Law*. New York: Oxford University Press.

Hayes-Renshaw, Fiona and Wallace, Helen (1995). *The Council of Ministers*. New York: St Martin's Press.

Herdegen, Matthias J. (1994). 'Maastricht and the German Constitutional Court: Constitutional Restraints for an "Ever Closer Europe"'. *Common Market Law Review*, 31: 235–49.

Héritier, Adrienne (2001). 'New Modes of Governance in Europe: Policy Making without Legislating?' Paper presented at the European University Institute, Florence.

Hermann, A. H. (1987). 'Beer and an EC Legal Hangover'. *Financial Times*, 19 March.

Hervey, Tamara (1994). 'Legal Issues Concerning the *Barber* Protocol', in David O'Keeffe and Patrick M. Twomey (eds), *Legal Issues of the Maastricht Treaty*. London: Chancery Law Publishing.

Hill, Andrew (1991*a*). 'Brussels Split on De Havilland Sale'. *Financial Times*, 1 October.

—— (1991*b*). 'Brittan Defiant Over De Havilland'. *Financial Times*, 9 October.

—— (1991*c*). 'Countdown to Maastricht: EC Working Time Directive Shelved: Dutch Presidency Rules Out Vote Before End of Year on 48-Hour Week and Sunday Day of Rest'. *Financial Times*, 4 December.

—— (1993). 'Brussels Scales Down Ambitions on Mergers: Commission Forced to Abandon Plans to Vet More Cross-Border Mergers'. *Financial Times*, 9 July.

—— and Barber, Lionel (1993). 'Opposition Mounts to Widening Brussels' Merger Role'. *Financial Times*, 1 March.

Hirst, Clayton (2001). 'The Lowdown: Bush Hates Him, Brown Hates Him, and EMI Hates Him? So What's Mr. Monti Doing Right?' *Independent on Sunday*, 24 June: 5.

Hix, Simon (1994). 'The Study of the European Community: The Challenge to Comparative Politics', *West European Politics*, 17: 1–30.

—— (1998). 'Dimensions and Alignments in European Union Politics: Cognitive Constraints and Partisan Responses'. *European Journal of Political Research*, 35: 69–106.

—— (1999*a*). *The Political System of the European Union*. New York: St Martin's Press.

—— (1999*b*). 'Constitutional Agenda-Setting through Discretion in Rule Interpretation: Why the European Parliament Won at Amsterdam'. Paper prepared for delivery at the 1999 Annual Meeting of the American Political Science Association, Atlanta, 2–5 September.

—— (2000). 'Parliamentary Oversight of Executive Power: What Role for the European Parliament in Comitology', in Thomas Christiansen and Emil Kirchner (eds), *Committee Governance in the European Union*. New York: St Martin's Press.

—— and Gabel, Matthew (1998). 'The Ties that Bind: Partisanship and the Investiture Procedure for the EU Commission President.' Working Paper, London School of Economics.

Hix, Simon and Lord, Christopher (1995). 'The Making of a President: The European Parliament and the Confirmation of Jacques Santer as President of the Commission'. *Government and Opposition*, 31: 62–76.

—— (1997). *Political Parties in the European Union*. New York: St Martin's Press.

Hodson, Dermott and Maher, Imelda (2001). 'The Open Method as a New Mode of Governance: The Case of Soft Economic Policy Co-ordination'. *Journal of Common Market Studies*, 39: 719–46.

Hoffmann, Stanley (1966). 'Obstinate or Obsolete? The Fate of the Nation-State and the Case of Western Europe'. *Daedalus*, 95: 862–915.

Hölzer, H. (1990). 'Merger Control', in P. Montagnon (ed.), *European Competition Policy*. London: Royal Institute for International Affairs.

Hooghe, Liesbet (ed.) (1996). *Cohesion Policy and European Integration*. New York: Oxford University Press.

—— (1999a). 'Images of Europe: Orientations to European Integration among Senior Officials of the Commission'. *British Journal of Political Science*, 29: 345–67.

—— (1999b). 'Supranational Activists or Intergovernmental Agents? Explaining the Orientations of Senior Commission Officials Toward European Integration'. *Comparative Political Studies*, 32: 435–63.

—— and Marks, Gary (1997). 'The Making of a Polity: The Struggle over European Integration'. *European Integration online Papers*, 1/4, http://eiop.or.at/eiop/texte/1997–004a.htm.

Horn, Murray J. (1995). *The Political Economy of Public Administration*. New York: Cambridge University Press.

Hoskyns, Catherine (1996). *Integrating Gender: Women, Law and Politics in the European Union*. London: Verso.

House of Commons (1993a). 'Structural Funds 1994–99', in *Twenty-Sixth Report from the Select Committee on European Legislation*. London: HMSO.

—— (1993b). 'Structural Funds', in *Thirty-Eighth Report from the Select Committee on European Legislation*. London: HMSO.

House of Lords, Select Committee on the European Communities (1986). *Delegation of Powers to the Commission (Final Report)*. London: HMSO.

—— (1996). *Review of the EC Merger Regulation, with Evidence*. London: HMSO.

—— (1999). *Delegation of Powers to the European Commission: Reforming Comitology*. London: HMSO.

Huber, John D. (1998). 'How Does Cabinet Instability Affect Political Performance: Credible Commitment, Information, and Health Care Cost Containment in Parliamentary Politics'. *American Political Science Review*, 92: 577–92.

—— (2000). 'Delegation to Civil Servants in Parliamentary Democracies'. *European Journal of Political Research*, 37: 397–413.

—— and Lupia, Arthur (2001). 'Cabinet Instability and Delegation in Parliamentary Democracies'. *American Journal of Political Science*, 45: 18–33.

—— and Shipan, Charles R. (2000). 'The Costs of Control: Legislators, Agencies, and Transaction Costs'. *Legislative Studies Quarterly*, 25: 25–52.

——, ——, and Pfahler, Madelaine (2001). 'Legislatures and Statutory Control of Bureaucracy'. *American Journal of Political Science*, 45: 330–45.

Hulverscheidt, Claus, Williamson, Hugh, and Koch, Rainer (2001). 'Germany to Sue over BSE Crisis'. *Financial Times*, 5 June.

Hunter, Teresa (1991). 'Pensions Struggle Goes on Despite Equality Setback'. *Guardian*, 14 December.

International Securities Regulation Report (1993). 'Commission Backs Off Decision to Enhance Merger Review Powers', 10 August.

Issing, Otmar (1998). 'Open for Business: Criticisms of the European Central Bank for Not Being Accountable are Misplaced'. *Financial Times*, 22 September.

Jacobs, Francis B. (1999). 'Nominations and Appointments: An Evolving EU Model'. Unpublished ms, May.

——, Corbett, Richard, and Shackleton, Michael (1995). *The European Parliament* (3rd edn). New York: Longman.

Joerges, Christian (2001). '"Deliberative Surpanationalism"—A Defense'. *European Integration online Papers*, 5/8, http://eiop.or.at.eiop/texte/2001–0008a.htm.

—— and Neyer, Jürgen (1997*a*). 'From Intergovernmental Bargaining to Deliberative Political Process: The Constitutionalization of Comitology'. *European Law Journal*, 3: 273–99.

———— (1997*b*). 'Transforming Strategic Interaction into Deliberative Problem-Solving: European Comitology in the Foodstuffs Sector'. *Journal of European Public Policy*, 4: 609–25.

Johnson, Michael (1998). *European Community Trade Policy and the Article 113 Committee*. London: Royal Institute for International Affairs.

Jones, George (1991). 'Clash with Brussels on 48-hour Week Euro-Directive Would Add £5 billion to Industry's Costs and Cut Overtime Pay, Cabinet is Told'. *Daily Telegraph*, 25 October.

Jönsson, Christer and Tallberg, Jonas (1998). 'Compliance and Post-Agreement Bargaining'. *European Journal of International Relations*, 4: 371–408; www.frankcass.com/jnls/wep.htm.

Jónsson, Óli Jón (1998). 'Master or Servant? The European Court of Justice and the Member States of the European Union: A Case Study'. Master's thesis, Department of Political Science, University of Lund.

Judge, David, Earnshaw, David, and Cowan, Ngaire (1994). 'Ripples or Waves: The European Parliament in the Community Policy Process'. *Journal of European Public Policy*, 1: 27–52.

Jupille, Joseph (2000). 'Procedural Politics: Issue, Interests, and Institutional Choice in the European Union'. Unpublished dissertation, University of Washington.

—— and Caporaso, James A. (1999). 'Institutionalism and the European Union: Beyond International Relations and Comparative Politics'. *Annual Review of Political Science*, 2: 429–44.

Kay, John (2002). 'A Missing Element: The Airtours Case Showed How EU Merger Proceedings Fail to Give Consumers a Voice'. *Financial Times*, 18 June.

Keck, Margaret and Sikkink Kathryn (1998). *Activists Beyond Borders*. Ithaca, NY: Cornell University Press.

Kelemen, R. Daniel (2001). 'The Politics of "Eurocratic" Structure and the New European Agencies'. Unpublished ms.

Kellaway, Lucy (1989). 'EC Ministers Hand Brussels the Power to Vet Large Mergers'. *Financial Times*, 22 December.

Keohane, Robert O. (1984). *After Hegemony*. Princeton: Princeton University Press.

—— (1986). 'Reciprocity in International Relations'. *International Organization*, 40: 1–28.

—— and Martin, Lisa L. (1994). 'Delegation to International Institutions'. Paper prepared for a conference on 'What is Institutionalism Now?', University of Maryland, 14–15 October.

——, Moravcsik, Andrew, and Slaughter, Anne-Marie (2000). 'Legalized Dispute Resolution: Interstate and Transnational'. *International Organization*, 54: 457–88.

Kersten, Albert (1988). 'A Welcome Surprise? The Netherlands and the Schuman Plan Negotiations', in Klaus Schwabe (ed.), *The Beginnings of the Schuman Plan*. Baden-Baden: Nomos.

Kiewiet, D. Roderick and McCubbins, Matthew D. (1991). *The Logic of Delegation: Congressional Parties and the Appropriation Process*. Chicago: University of Chicago Press.

Kilroy, Bernadette (1995). 'Member State Control or Judicial Independence: The Integrative Role of the Court of Justice'. Paper delivered at the 1995 Annual Meeting of the American Political Science Association, Chicago, 31 August–3 September.

—— (1999). 'Integration Through Law: ECJ and Governments in the EU'. Ph.D. dissertation, UCLA.

King, Gary, Keohane, Robert O., and Verba, Sidney (1994). *Designing Social Inquiry: Scientific Inference in Qualitative Research.* Princeton: Princeton University Press.

Kingdon, John W. (1984). *Agendas, Alternatives, and Public Policies.* Boston: Little, Brown.

Krasner, Stephen D. (1988). 'Sovereignty: An Institutional Perspective,' *Comparative Political Studies* 21: 66–94.

Krehbiel, Keith (1987). 'Why Are Congressional Committees Powerful?' *American Political Science Review*, 81: 929–35.

—— (1991). *Information and Legislative Organization.* Ann Arbor: University of Michigan Press.

—— (1998). *Pivotal Politics.* Chicago: University of Chicago Press.

Kreher, Alexander (1997). 'Agencies in the European Community: A Step Towards Administrative Integration in Europe'. *Journal of European Public Policy*, 4: 225–45.

Kreppel, Amie (1999). 'What Effects the European Parliament's Legislative Influence? An Analysis of the Success of EP Amendments'. *Journal of Common Market Studies*, 37: 521–38.

—— and Tsebelis, George (1999). 'Coalition Formation in the European Parliament'. *Comparative Political Studies*, 32: 933–66.

Küsters, Hanns Jürgen (1988). 'Die Verhandlungen über das institutionelle System sur Gründung der Europäischen Gemeinschaft für Kohle und Stahl', in Klaus Schwabe (ed.), *The Beginnings of the Schuman Plan.* Baden-Baden: Nomos.

Laffan, Brigid (1997a). *The Finances of the European Union.* Basingstoke: Macmillan.

—— (1997b). 'From Policy Entrepreneur to Policy Manager: The Challenge Facing the European Commission'. *Journal of European Public Policy*, 4: 422–38.

—— (1999). 'Becoming a "Living Institution": The Evolution of the European Court of Auditors'. *Journal of Common Market Studies*, 37: 251–68.

Laursen, Finn and Vanhoonacker, Sophie (eds) (1992). *The Intergovernmental Conference on Political Union.* Maastricht: European Institute of Public Administration.

Laver, Michael (1997). 'Government Formation in the European Parliament'. *Aussenwirtschaft*, 52: 223–48.

Lenaerts, Koen and Verhoeven, Amaryllis (2000). 'Towards a Legal Framework for Executive Rule-Making in the EU? The Contribution of the New Comitology Decision'. *Common Market Law Review*, 37: 645–86.

Leone, Velia M. (1997). 'Commission to Get More Power under the EC Merger Regulation'. *Euro Watch*, 9/9, 27 June.

Levy, R. (1997). 'Managing the Managers: The Commission's Role in the Implementation of Spending Programmes', in Neill Nugent (ed.), *At the Heart of the Union: Studies of the European Commission.* Houndmills: Macmillan.

Lewis, Jeffrey (1998a). 'Constructing Interests: The Committee of Permanent Representatives and Decision-Making in the European Union'. Unpublished dissertation, University of Wisconsin.

—— (1998b). 'Is the "Hard Bargaining" Image of the Council Misleading? The Committee of Permanent Representatives and the Local Elections Directive'. *Journal of Common Market Studies*, 36: 479–504.

Lindberg, Leon N. and Scheingold, Stuart A. (1970). *Europe's Would-be Polity.* Englewood Cliffs, NJ: Prentice-Hall.

Lindner, Johannes and Rittberger, Berthold (2001). 'The Creation, Interpretation and Contestation of Institutions Taking Historical Institutionalism Seriously'. Paper prepared for presentation at the fourth Pan-European IR Conference of the European Consortium for Political Research (ECPR), Canterbury, 8–10 September.

Lohmann, Susanne and O'Halloran, Sharyn (1994). 'Divided Government and US Trade Policy: Theory and Evidence'. *International Organization*, 48: 595–632.

Lord, Christopher and Winn, Neil (1998). 'Garbage Cans or Rational Decision? Member Governments, Supranational Actors and the Shaping of the Agenda for the IGC'. Unpublished ms.

Loth, W. (1998). 'Hallstein and de Gaulle: The Disastrous Confrontation', in W. Loth, W. Wallace, and W. Wessels (eds), *Walter Hallstein: The Forgotten European?* Basingstoke: Macmillan.

Ludlow, Peter (1991). 'The European Commission', in Robert O. Keohane and Stanley Hoffmann (eds), *The New European Community*. Boulder, CO: Westview.

—— (2001). 'The European Council at Stockholm and the Governance of Europe'. *A View from Brussels: A Commentary on the EU*, No. 11 (April). Brussels: Center for European Policy Studies.

——, Ross, George, Philippart, Eric, Meunier, Sophie, Nicolaidis, Kalypso, de Búrca, Gráinne, and de Witte, Bruno (2001). 'Analyzing the Treaty of Nice'. *ECSA Review*, 14/2: 1, 3–11; www.eustudies.org/NiceTreatyForum.html.

Lupia, Arthur and McCubbins, Mathew (1994). 'Learning from Oversight: Fire Alarms and Police Patrols Reconsidered'. *Journal of Law, Economics and Organization*, 10: 96–125.

Lustick, Ian S. (1996). 'History, Historiography, and Political Science: Multiple Historical Records and the Problem of Selection Bias'. *American Political Science Review*, 90: 605–18.

McAleavey, Paul (1993). 'The Politics of European Regional Development Policy: Additionality in the Scottish Coal Fields'. *Regional Politics and Policy*, 3: 88–107.

McCubbins, Mathew, Noll, Roger, and Weingast, Barry (1987). 'Administrative Procedures as Instruments of Political Control'. *Journal of Law, Economics, and Organization*, 3: 243–77.

—————— (1989). 'Structure and Process, Policy and Politics: Administrative Arrangements and the Political Control of Agencies'. *Virginia Law Review*, 75: 431–82.

—— and Page, Talbot (1987). 'A Theory of Congressional Delegation', in Mathew McCubbins and Terry Sullivan (eds), *Congress: Structure and Policy*. New York: Cambridge University Press.

—— and Schwartz, Thomas (1987). 'Congressional Oversight Overlooked: Police Patrols versus Fire Alarms', in Mathew McCubbins and Terry Sullivan (eds), *Congress: Structure and Policy*, 426–40. New York: Cambridge University Press.

McDonagh, Bobby (1998). *Original Sin in a Brave New World: The Paradox of Europe: An Account of the Negotiation of the Treaty of Amsterdam*. Dublin: Institute of European Affairs.

McGowan, Francis (2000). 'Competition Policy: The Limits of the European Regulatory State', in Helen Wallace and William Wallace (eds), *Policy-Making in the European Union* (4th edn). New York: Oxford University Press.

McGowan, Lee (1997). 'Safeguarding the Economic Constitution: The Commission and Competition Policy', in Neill Nugent (ed.), *At the Heart of the Union: Studies of the European Commission*. Houndmills: Macmillan Press.

—— and Wilks, Stephen (1995). 'The First Supranational Policy in the European Union: Competition Policy'. *European Journal of Political Research*, 28: 141–69.

McKelvey, Richard (1976). 'Intransitivities in Multidimensional Voting Models and Some Implications for Agenda Control'. *Journal of Economic Theory*, 12: 472–82.

Mackie, David (1997). 'Beyond Independence'. *Financial Times*, 8 August.

MacMullen, Andrew (1996). 'Evaluating Integration Theory: The Appointment of European Commissioners'. *Diplomacy and Statecraft*, 7: 221–43.

——(1997). 'European Commissioners 1952–1995: National Routes to a European Elite', in Neill Nugent (ed.), *At the Heart of the Union: Studies of the European Commission*. Houndmills: Macmillan Press.

——(1999). 'Political Responsibility for the Administration of Europe: The Commission's Resignation March 1999'. *Parliamentary Affairs*, 52: 703–18.

McNamara, Kathleen R. (2002). 'Rational Fictions: Central Bank Independence and the Social Logic of Integration'. *West European Politics*, 25: 47–76.

McNollgast (1999). 'The Political Origins of the Administrative Procedure Act'. *Journal of Law, Economics and Organization*, 15: 180–217.

Maduro, Miguel Poiares (1999). *We the Court: The European Court of Justice and the European Economic Constitution*. Oxford: Hart Publishing.

Majone, Giandomenico (1994). 'The Rise of the Regulatory State in Europe'. *West European Politics*, 17: 77–101.

——(1996). *Regulating Europe*. New York: Routledge.

——(1997). 'The New European Agencies: Regulation by Information'. *Journal of European Public Policy*, 4: 262–75.

——(2000). 'The Credibility Crisis of Community Regulation'. *Journal of Common Market Studies*, 38: 273–302.

——(2001). 'Two Logics of Delegation: Agency and Fiduciary Relations in EU Governance'. *European Union Politics*, 2: 103–21.

Mancini, G. Federico (1991). 'The Making of a Constitution for Europe', in Robert O. Keohane and Stanley Hoffmann (eds), *The New European Community*. Boulder, CO: Westview Press.

——and Keeling, David T. (1995). 'Language, Culture and Politics in the Life of the European Court of Justice'. *The Columbia Journal of European Law*, 1: 397–413.

March, James, G., and Olson, Johan P. (1984). 'The New Institutionalism: Organizational Factors in Political Life'. *American Political Science Review*, 78: 734–49.

——(1989). *Rediscovering Institutions: The Organizational Basis of Politics*. New York: Free Press.

Marks, Gary (1993). 'Structural Policy and Multilevel Governance in the EC', in Alan Cafruny and Glenda Rosenthal (eds), *The State of the European Community, 2: The Maastricht Debates and Beyond*. Boulder, CO: Lynne Rienner.

——(1996). 'Decision-Making in Cohesion Policy: Charting and Explaining Variations', in Liesbet Hooghe (ed.), *Cohesion Policy and European Integration*. New York: Oxford University Press.

Marques, Helena Torres (Rapporteur) (1996). 'Report on the Commission Proposal for a Council Directive Amending Directive 86/378/EEC on the Implementation of the Principle of Equal Treatment for Men and Women in Occupational Social Security Schemes' (COM(95)0186 – C4–0422/95 – 95/0117(CNS)), European Parliament document A4–0356/96 of 25 July.

Martin, Lisa L. (2000). 'Agency and Delegation in IMF Conditionality'. Unpublished ms, Harvard University.

——and Simmons, Beth A. (eds) (2001). *International Institutions: An International Organization Reader*. Cambridge, MA: MIT Press.

Mattli, Walter and Slaughter, Anne-Marie (1995). 'Law and Politics in the European Union: A Reply to Garrett'. *International Organization*, 49: 183–90.

Mattli, Walter and Slaughter, Anne-Marie (1998). 'Revisiting the European Court of Justice'. *International Organization*, 52: 177–209.

Maurer, Andreas (1999). *What Next for the European Parliament?* London: The Federal Trust.

——(2001). 'Democratic Governance in the European Union—The Institutional Terrain after Amsterdam', in Jörg Monar and Wolfgang Wessels (eds), *The European Union after the Treaty of Amsterdam*. London: Continuum.

——Wessels, Wolfgang, and Mittag, Jürgen (2000). 'Europeanisation in and of the EU System: Trends, Offers and Constraints'. Paper for the DFG-workshop 'Linking EU and National Governance'. Mannheim, 1–3 June.

Mayhew, David (1991). *Divided We Govern: Party Control, Lawmaking, and Investigations 1946–1990*. New Haven, CT: Yale University Press.

Mazey, Sonia (1995). 'The Development of EU Equality Policies: Bureaucratic Expansion on Behalf of Women'. *Public Administration*, 73: 591–609.

Melnick, R. Shep (1983). *Regulation and the Courts: The Case of the Clean Air Act*. Washington, DC: Brookings Institution.

Metcalfe, Les (1992). 'After 1992: Can the Commission Manage Europe?' *Australian Journal of Public Administration*, 51: 117–30.

——(2000). 'Reforming the Commission: Will Organizational Efficiency Produce Effective Governance?' *Journal of Common Market Studies*, 38: 817–41.

Meunier, Sophie (2000). 'What Single Voice? European Institutions and EU-U.S. Trade Negotiations'. *International Organization*, 54: 103–35.

——and Nicolaidis, Kalypso (1999). 'Who Speaks for Europe?' The Delegation of Trade Authority in the EU'. *Journal of Common Market Studies*, 37: 477–501.

Milgrom, Paul, North, Douglass, and Weingast, Barry (1990). 'The Role of Institutions in the Revival of Trade: The Law Merchant, Private Judges and the Champagne Fairs'. *Economics and Politics*, 3: 1–23.

——and Roberts, John (1990). 'Bargaining Costs, Influence Costs, and the Organization of Economic Activity', in James Alt and Kenneth Shepsle (eds), *Perspectives on Positive Political Economy*. New York: Cambridge University Press.

Mearsheimer, John (1995). 'The False Promise of International Institutions'. *International Security*, 19: 5–49.

Milward, Alan (1992). *The European Rescue of the Nation-State*. Los Angeles: University of California Press.

Moe, Terry M. (1984). 'The New Economics of Organization'. *American Journal of Political Science*, 28: 739–77.

——(1987). 'An Assessment of the Positive Theory of Congressional Dominance'. *Legislative Studies Quarterly*, 12: 475–520.

——(1990). 'The Politics of Structural Choice: Toward a Theory of Public Bureaucracy', in Oliver E. Williamson (ed.), *Organization Theory: From Chester Barnard to the Present and Beyond* (New York: Oxford University Press).

Monnet, Jean (1978). *Memoires*. London: Collins.

Montagnon, P. (ed.) (1990). *European Competition Policy*. London: Royal Institute for International Affairs.

Moore, Sarah (1995). '"Justice Doesn't Mean a Free Lunch": The Application of the Principle of Equal Pay to Occupational Pension Schemes'. *European Law Review*, 20/2: 159–77.

Moravscik, Andrew (1991). 'Negotiating the Single European Act', in Robert O. Keohane and Stanley Hoffmann (eds), *The New European Community*. Boulder, CO: Westview Press.

——(1993). 'Preferences and Power in the European Community: A Liberal Intergovernmentalist Approach'. *Journal of Common Market Studies*, 31: 473–524.

Moravscik, Andrew (1994). 'Why the European Community Strengthens the State: International Cooperation and Domestic Politics' (Center for European Studies Working Paper Series No. 52). Cambridge, MA: Harvard University.

—— (1995). 'Liberal Intergovernmentalism and Integration: A Rejoinder'. *Journal of Common Market Studies*, 33: 611–28.

—— (1998). *The Choice for Europe: Social Purpose and State Power from Messina to Maastricht*. Ithaca, NY: Cornell University Press.

—— (1999). 'A New Statecraft? Supranational Entrepreneurs and International Cooperation'. *International Organization*, 53: 267–306.

—— (2001). 'Despotism in Brussels? Misreading the European Union'. *Foreign Affairs*, 80: 114–22.

—— and Nicolaidis, Kalypso (1998). 'Explaining the Treaty of Amsterdam: Interests, Influence, Institutions'. *Journal of Common Market Studies*, 37: 59–85.

Mortelmans, Kamiel (1991). 'Article 30 of the EEC Treaty and Legislation Relating to Market Circumstances: Time to Consider a New Definition?' *Common Market Law Review*, 28: 115–27.

Moser, Peter (1996). 'The European Parliament as an Agenda-Setter: What are the Conditions? A Critique of Tsebelis'. *American Political Science Review*, 90: 834–8.

—— (1997). 'The Benefits of the Conciliation Procedure for the European Parliament: Comment to George Tsebelis'. *Aussenwirtschaft*, 52: 57–62.

Munchau, Wolfgang and Buckley, Neil (1998). 'ECB Chief Rejects Political Influence on Monetary Policy'. *Financial Times*, 4 November.

Nehl, Hanns Peter (1999). *Principles of Administrative Procedure in EC Law*. Oxford: Hart Publishing.

Neven, Damien, Nuttall, Robin, and Seabright, Paul (1993). *Merger in Daylight: The Economics and Politics of European Merger Control*. London: Centre for Economic Policy Research.

Newhouse, John (1967). *Collision in Brussels*. New York: Norton.

Nicolaidis, Kalypso (1999). 'Minimizing Agency Costs in Two-Level Games: Lessons from the Trade Authority Controversies in the United States and the European Union', in Robert Mnookin, Larry Susskind, and Pacey Foster (eds), *Negotiating on Behalf of Others*. Thousand Oaks, CA: Sage.

Nicoll, Sir William (1994). 'The European Parliament's Post-Maastricht Rules of Procedure'. *Journal of Common Market Studies*, 32: 403–10.

Nielson, Daniel and Tierney, Michael (2001*a*). 'Principals and Interests: Agency Theory and Multilateral Development Bank Lending'. Unpublished ms.

—— —— (2001*b*). 'Principles or Principals? Agency Theory, International Organizations and World Bank Lending'. Unpublished ms.

Norman, Peter (2001*a*). 'Lamfalussy Set for Battle on Securities Market Regulation: EU states, Commission and Parliament Are at Odds'. *Financial Times*, 15 February: 8.

—— (2001*b*). 'MEPs Demand Say on Securities'. *Financial Times*, 16 March.

—— (2001*c*). 'Hopes Reviving for EU Securities Reform'. *Financial Times*, 21 December.

—— (2002). 'Reform of EU Securities Rules Moves a Step Closer'. *Financial Times*, 23 January.

—— and Barber, Lionel (2001). 'Berlin Objects to Lamfalussy'. *Financial Times*, 22 March.

North, Douglass C. (1990). *Institutions, Institutional Change and Economic Performance*. New York: Cambridge University Press.

Nugent, Neill (1994). *The Government and Politics of the European Union*. Durham: Duke University Press.

—— (1995). 'The Leadership Capacity of the European Commission'. *Journal of European Public Policy*, 2: 603–23.

Nugent, Neill (ed.) (1997). *At the Heart of the Union: Studies of the European Commission*. Houndmills: Macmillan.

—— (2000). *The European Commission*. New York: St Martin's Press.

Offe, Claus (2000). 'The Democratic Welfare State in an Integrating Europe', in Michael Greven and Louis Pauly (eds), *Democracy Beyond the State? The European Dilemma and the Emerging World Order*. New York: Rowman and Littlefield Publishers.

Ordeshook, Peter C. and Schwartz, Thomas (1987). 'Agenda and the Control of Political Outcomes'. *American Political Science Review*, 81: 179–200.

Osborne, Andrew and Milner, Mark (2001). 'Tied Vote Scuppers European Single Financial Market'. *Guardian*, 5 July.

Ostner, Ilona and Lewis, Jane (1995). 'Gender and the Evolution of European Social Policies', in Stephan Leibfried and Paul Pierson (eds), *European Social Policy: Between Fragmentation and Integration*. Washington, DC: Brookings Institution.

Paarlberg, Robert (1997). 'Agricultural Policy Reform and the Uruguay Round: Synergistic Linkage in a Two-Level Game?' *International Organization*, 51: 413–44.

Paemen, Hugo and Bensch, A. (1995). *From the GATT to the WTO: The European Community in the Uruguay Round*. Leuven: Leuven University Press.

Page, Edward (1997). *People Who Run Europe*. Oxford: Oxford University Press.

—— and Wouters, Linda (1994). 'Bureaucratic Politics and Political Leadership in Brussels'. *Public Administration*, 72: 445–59.

Pan, Eric (1996). *Europe and the World: External Relations, Internal Dynamics*. Proceedings of the Thirteenth Annual Graduate Student Conference, Institute on Western Europe, Columbia University, New York, 28–30 March.

Patterson, Lee Ann (1997). 'Agricultural Policy Reform in the European Community: A Three-Level Game Analysis'. *International Organization*, 51: 135–65.

Pattison de Menil, Lois (1978). *Who Speaks for Europe? The Vision of Charles de Gaulle*. New York: St Martin's Press.

Pedlar, Robin H. and Schaefer, Guenther F. (eds) (1996). *Shaping European Law and Policy: The Role of Committees and Comitology in the Political Process*. Maastricht: European Institute of Public Administration.

Peel, Quentin (1986). 'Bonn Battles for Pure Brew'. *Financial Times*, 14 May.

—— (1987). 'W. German Beer Law Overruled'. *Financial Times*, 13 March.

Pentland, Charles (1976). *International Theory and European Integration*. London: Macmillan.

Pescatore, Pierre (1981). 'Les Travaux du "Groupe Juridique" dans la Négociation des Traités de Rome'. *Studia Diplomatica*, 34: 159–92.

Peters, B. Guy (1992). 'Bureaucratic Politics and the Institutions of the Community', in Alberta Sbragia (ed.), *Europolitics: Institutions and Policymaking in the "New" European Community*. Washington, DC: Brookings Institution.

Peterson, John (1991). 'Technology Policy in Europe: Explaining the Framework Programme and Esprit in Theory and Practice'. *Journal of Common Market Studies*, 29: 281–308.

—— (1997). 'The Santer Commission: The European Commission in Normative, Historical and Theoretical Perspective'. *Journal of European Public Policy*, 6: 46–65.

—— and Bomberg, Elizabeth (1999). *Decision Making in the European Union*. New York: St Martin's Press.

Petite, Michel (1998). 'The Treaty of Amsterdam'. Harvard Jean Monnet Chair Working Papers Series 2/98; www.law.harvard.edu/Programs/JeanMonnet/papers/98/98-2-.html.

Pierson, Paul (1996). 'The Path to European Integration: A Historical Institutionalist Analysis'. *Comparative Political Studies*, 29: 123–63.

Pollack, Mark A. (1994). 'Creeping Competence: The Expanding Agenda of the European Community'. *Journal of Public Policy*, 14/2: 95–145.

——(1995*a*). *Creeping Competence: The Expanding Agenda of the European Community*. Unpublished Ph.D. dissertation, Harvard University.

——(1995*b*). 'Regional Actors in an Intergovernmental Play: The Making and Implementation of EC Structural Policy', in Sonia Mazey and Carolyn Rhodes (eds), *The State of the European Union, 3: Building a European Polity*. Boulder, CO: Lynne Rienner.

——(1997). 'Delegation, Agency and Agenda Setting in the European Community'. *International Organization*, 51: 99–135.

——(1998). 'The Engines of Integration? Supranational Autonomy and Influence in the European Union', in Wayne Sandholtz and Alec Stone Sweet (eds), *European Integration and Supranational Governance*. New York: Oxford University Press.

——(1999). 'Delegation, Agency and Agenda Setting in the Treaty of Amsterdam'. *European Integration online Papers*, 3/6, http://eiop.or.at/eiop/texte/1999–006a.htm.

——(2001). 'Control Mechanism or Deliberative Democracy? Two Images of Comitology'. Paper presented at the workshop on European Union institutions, University of Washington, Seattle, 4–5 May.

——(2002). 'Learning from the Americanists (Again): Theory and Method in the Study of Delegation'. *West European Politics*, 25: 200–19.

——and Hafner-Burton, Emilie (2000). 'Mainstreaming Gender in the European Union'. *Journal of European Public Policy*, 7: 432–56.

——, Shapiro, Martin, Alter, Karen J., and Helfer, Laurence R. (2000). 'Do the Lessons of EU Legal Integration "Travel"?' *ECSA Review*, 13/1: 2–6; www.eustudies.org/win_2000.html.

Preeg, E. H. (1995). *Traders in a Brave New World: The Uruguay Round and the Future of the International Trading System*. Chicago: University of Chicago Press.

Press Association (1993). '"Ruse" Jibe at Working Week Court Challenge', 2 June.

Price, Richard (1998). 'Transnational Civil Society Targets Landmines'. *International Organization*, 52: 613–44.

PR Newswire European (1992). 'CBI Calls for Rejection of Working Time Directive', 29 April.

Putnam, Robert D. (1988). 'Diplomacy and Domestic Politics: The Logic of Two-Level Games', *International Organization*, 42: 427–60.

Raif, Shenai (1990). 'Insurance Industry Braced for Pensions Upheaval'. *Press Association Newsfile*, 17 May.

Ramsey, L. E. (1994). 'The Working Time Directive'. *European Law Review*, 19: 528–35.

Rasmussen, Hjalte (1986). *On Law and Policy in the European Court of Justice: A Comparative Study in Judicial Policymaking*. Boston: Martinus Nijhoff.

——(1998). *The European Court of Justice*. Copenhagen: GadJura Publishing.

Raunio, Tapio (1997). *The European Perspective: Transnational Party Groups in the 1989–1994 European Parliament*. Aldershot: Ashgate.

Rawlings, Richard (1993). 'The Eurolaw Game: Some Deductions from a Saga'. *Journal of Law and Society*, 20: 309–40.

Raworth, Philip (1994). 'A Timid Step Forwards: Maastricht and the Democratisation of the European Community'. *European Law Review*, 19: 16–33.

Reich, Norbert (1994). 'The "November Revolution" of the European Court of Justice: Keck, Meng and Audi Revisited'. *Common Market Law Review*, 31: 459–92.

Rhodes, Martin (1995). 'A Regulatory Conundrum: Industrial Relations and the "Social Dimension" ', in Stefan Leibfried and Paul Pierson (eds), *Fragmented Social Policy: The European Union's Social Dimension in Comparative Perspective*. Washington, DC: Brookings Institution.

——, Goetschy, Janine, and Mosher, Jim (2000) 'The Lisbon European Council and the Future of European Governance'. *ECSA Review*, 13/3: 2–7; www.eustudies.org/lisbonforum.html.

Rice, Robert (1996). 'Guns Lock on Old Target'. *Financial Times*, 26 November.

Riker, William (1980). 'Implications from the Dis-equilibrium of Majority Rule for the Study of Institutions'. *American Political Science Review*, 74: 432–47.

——(1986). *The Art of Political Manipulation*. New Haven, CT: Yale University Press.

Ringquist, Evan J. (1995). 'Political Control and Policy Impact in EPA's Office of Water Quality'. *American Journal of Political Science*, 39: 336–63.

Risse, Thomas (1996). 'Exploring the Nature of the Beast: International Relations Theory and Comparative Policy Analysis Meet the European Union'. *Journal of Common Market Studies*, 34: 53–80.

——(2000). 'Let's Argue! Communicative Action in World Politics'. *International Organization*, 54: 1–39.

Rittberger, Berthold (2001). 'Which Institutions for Europe? Explaining the Institutional Design of Europe's First Community'. *Journal of European Public Policy*, 8: 673–708.

Robinson, William (1994). 'The Court of Justice after Maastricht', in David O'Keeffe and Patrick M. Twomey (eds), *Legal Issues of the Maastricht Treaty*. London: Chancery Law Publishing.

Ross, George (1995). *Jacques Delors and European Integration*. New York: Oxford University Press.

Sandholtz, Wayne (1992). 'ESPRIT and the Politics of International Collective Action'. *Journal of Common Market Studies*, 30: 1–22.

——(1993). 'Choosing Union: Monetary Politics and Maastricht'. *International Organization*, 47: 1–40.

——(1996). 'Membership Matters: Limits of the Functional Approach to European Institutions'. *Journal of Common Market Studies*, 34: 403–29.

Sasse, Christophe, Poullet, Edouard, Coombes, David, and Deprez, Gerard (1977). *Decision Making in the European Community*. New York: Praeger Publishers.

Scharpf, Fritz W. (1988). 'The Joint-Decision Trap: Lessons from German Federalism and European Integration'. *Public Administration*, 66: 239–78.

——(1999). *Governing in Europe: Effective and Democratic?* New York: Oxford University Press.

Schmidt, Susanne K. (1997). 'Sterile Debates and Dubious Generalizations: European Integration Theory Tested by Telecommunications and Electricity'. *Journal of Public Policy*, 16: 233–71.

——(2000). 'Only an Agenda Setter? The European Commission's Power over the Council of Ministers'. *European Union Politics*, 1: 37–61.

Schmitter, Philippe C., Majone, Giandomenico, and Moravcsik, Andrew (2000). 'Democracy and Constitutionalism in the European Union'. *ECSA Review*, 13/2: 2–7; www.eustudies.org/DemocracyForum/htm.

Schwabe, Klaus (ed.) (1988). *The Beginnings of the Schuman Plan*. Baden-Baden: Nomos.

Schwarze, Jürgen (1992). *European Administrative Law*. London: Sweet and Maxwell.

Scully, Roger M. (1997a). 'Policy Influence and Participation in the European Parliament'. *Legislative Studies Quarterly*, 22: 233–52.

Scully, Roger M. (1997*b*). 'The EP and the Co-Decision Procedure: A Reassessment'. *Journal of Legislative Studies*, 3: 57–73.

——(1997*c*). 'The EP and Co-Decision: A Rejoinder to Tsebelis and Garrett'. *Journal of Legislative Studies*, 3: 93–103.

——(1997*d*). 'Positively My Last Words on Co-Decision'. *Journal of Legislative Studies*, 3: 144–6.

Sénat (1993). Rapport d'information fait au nom de la délégation du Sénat pour les Communautés européennes sure la réforme relative aux missions et à la coordination des fonds structurels, No. 325. Paris: Sénat.

Shackleton, Michael (2000). 'The Politics of Codecision'. *Journal of Common Market Studies*, 38: 325–42.

Shapiro, Martin (1988). *Who Guards the Guardians?* Athens: University of Georgia Press.

——(1996). 'Codification of Administrative Law: The US and the Union'. *European Law Journal*, 2: 26–47.

——(1997). 'The Problem of Independent Agencies in the United States and the European Union'. *Journal of European Public Policy*, 4: 276–7.

——(2001*a*). 'The Institutionalization of European Administrative Space'. Unpublished ms.

——(2001*b*). 'Judicial Delegation Doctrines: U.S., U.K. and France'. Paper presented at the Workshop on 'The Politics of Delegation to Non-Majoritarian Institutions in Europe'. European University Institute, San Domenico di Fiesole, Italy, 9–10 March.

Shepsle, Kenneth A. (1979). 'Institutional Arrangements and Equilibrium in Multidimensional Voting Models'. *American Journal of Political Science*, 23: 27–60.

——(1986). 'Institutional Equilibrium and Equilibrium Institutions', in Herbert Weisberg (ed.), *Political Science: The Science of Politics*. New York: Agathon.

——(1989). 'Studying Institutions: Some Lessons from the Rational Choice Approach'. *Journal of Theoretical Politics*, 1: 131–47.

——and Weingast, Barry R. (1984). 'Uncovered Sets and Sophisticated Voting Outcomes with Implications for Agenda Control'. *American Journal of Political Science*, 28: 49–74.

————(1987*a*). 'The Institutional Foundations of Committee Power'. *American Political Science Review*, 81: 85–104.

————(1987*b*). 'Why Are Congressional Committees Powerful?' *American Political Science Review*, 81: 935–45.

————(1994). 'Positive Theories of Congressional Institutions'. *Legislative Studies Quarterly*, 19: 145–79.

————(eds) (1995). *Positive Theories of Congressional Institutions*. Ann Arbor: University of Michigan Press.

Short, Eric (1990). 'Ruling on Pensions Could Cost Businesses Pounds 30bn'. *Financial Times*, 19 February.

Slaughter, Anne–Marie, Weiler, Joseph, and Stone Sweet, Alec (eds) (1998). *The European Court and National Courts-Doctrine and Jurisprudence: Legal Change in Its Social Context*. Oxford: Hart Publishing.

Smyrl, Marc E. (1998). 'When (and How) Do the Commission's Preferences Matter?' *Journal of Common Market Studies*, 36: 79–100.

Southey, Caroline and Prestion, Robert (1996). 'Major Threatens Showdown over EU Social Policy: Frosty Response after European Court Defeat on Working Hours'. *Financial Times*, 13 November.

Spence, David (2000). 'Plus ca change, plus c'est la même chose? Attempting to Reform the European Commission'. *Journal of European Public Policy*, 7: 1–25.

Stein, Eric (1981). 'Lawyers, Judges, and the Making of a Transnational Constitution'. *American Journal of International Law*, 75: 1–27.

Steiner, Josephine (1992). 'Drawing the Line: Uses and Abuses of Article 30 EEC'. *Common Market Law Review*, 29: 749–74.

Stephens, Philip (1996). 'Reluctant Step Back from the Brink'. *Financial Times*, 27 June.

Steunenberg, Bernard (1996). 'Agency Discretion, Regulatory Policymaking, and Different Institutional Arrangements'. *Public Choice*, 86: 309–39.

Steunenberg, Bernard (2000). 'Seeing What You Want to See: The Limits of Current Modelling on the European Union'. *European Union Politics*, 1: 368–73.

——, Koboldt, Christian, and Schmidtchen, Dieter (1996). 'Policymaking, Comitology, and the Balance of Power in the European Union'. *International Review of Law and Economics*, 16: 329–44.

———— (1997). 'Beyond Comitology: A Comparative Analysis of Implementation Procedures with Parliamentary Involvement'. *Aussenwirtschaft*, 52: 87–112.

———— (1999). 'Strategic Power in the European Union: Evaluating the Distribution of Power in Policy Games'. *Journal of Theoretical Politics*, 11: 343–70.

Stevens, Anne, and Stevens, Handley (2001). *Brussels Bureaucrats? The Administration of the European Union*. New York: Palgrave.

Stewart, T. (ed.) (1993). *The GATT Uruguay Round: A Negotiating History. Vol. 1: Commentary*. Deventer: Kluwer Law.

Stone Sweet, Alec (2000). *Governing with Judges: Constitutional Politics in Europe*. New York: Oxford University Press.

—— and Brunell, T. L. (1998). 'Constructing a Supranational Constitution: Dispute Resolution and Governance in the European Community'. *American Political Science Review*, 92: 63–81.

—— and Caporaso, James A. (1998). 'From Free Trade to Supranational Polity: The European Court and Integration', in Wayne Sandholtz and Alec Stone Sweet (eds), *European Integration and Supranational Governance*. New York: Oxford University Press.

—— and Thatcher, Mark (eds) (2002). 'The Politics of Delegation'. Special issue of *West European Politics*, 25/1.

Streeck, Wolfgang (1996). 'Neo-Voluntarism: A New Social Policy Regime?' in Gary Marks, Fritz W. Scharpf, Philippe C. Schmitter, and Wolfgang Streek, *Governance in the European Union*. Thousand Oaks, CA and London: Sage.

Sun, Jeanne-Mey and Pelkmans, Jacques (1995). 'Regulatory Competition in the Single Market'. *Journal of Common Market Studies*, 33: 67–89.

Sutcliffe, John B. (2000). 'The 1999 Reform of the Structural Funds Regulations: Multi-Level Governance or Renationalization?' *Journal of European Public Policy*, 7: 290–309.

Swann, Dennis (1992). *The Economics of the Common Market*. Harmondsworth: Penguin.

Swinbank, A. (1993). 'CAP reform 1992'. *Journal of Common Market Studies*, 31: 359–72.

Tallberg, Jonas (1999). *Making States Comply: The European Commission, the European Court of Justice and the Enforcement of the Internal Market*. Lund, Sweden: Lund Political Studies 09, Department of Political Science, Lund University.

—— (2000). 'The Anatomy of Autonomy: An Institutional Account of Variation in Supranational Influence'. *Journal of Common Market Studies*, 38: 843–64.

Taylor, Paul (1983). *The Limits of European Integration*. New York: Columbia University Press.

Tetlock, Philip E. and Belkin, Aaron (eds) (1996). *Counterfactual Thought Experiments in World Politics: Logical, Methodological, and Psychological Perspectives*. Princeton, NJ: Princeton University Press.

Thatcher, Mark and Stone Sweet, Alec (2002). 'Theory and Practice of Delegation to Non-Majoritarian Institutions'. *West European Politics*, 25/1: 1–22.

Thelen, Kathleen, and Steinmo, Sven (1992). 'Historical Institutionalism in Comparative Politics', in Sven Steinmo, Kathleen Thelen, and Frank Longstreth (eds), *Structuring Politics: Historical Institutionalism in Comparative Analysis*. New York: Cambridge University Press.

Transport Europe (1992). 'Competition: Merger Control Compromise Awaits Test of Another De Havilland', 27 February.

Trubek, David M. and Mosher, James (2001). 'EU Governance, Employment Policy, and the European Social Model'. Paper presented at the conference on 'Reconfiguring Work and Welfare in the New Economy', Madison, Wisconsin, 10–12 May.

Tsebelis, George (1990). *Nested Games: Rational Choice in Comparative Politics*. Berkeley: University of California Press.

——(1994). 'The Power of the European Parliament as a Conditional Agenda Setter'. *American Political Science Review*, 88: 129–42.

——(1995). 'Conditional Agenda Setting and Decision-Making *Inside* the European Parliament'. *Journal of Legislative Studies*, 1: 65–93.

——(1996). 'More on the European Parliament as a Conditional Agenda-Setter: Response to Moser'. *American Political Science Review*, 90: 839–44.

——(1997). 'Maastricht and the Democratic Deficit'. *Aussenwirtschaft*, 52: 29–56.

——and Geoffrey Garrett (1997*a*). 'Agenda Setting, Vetoes, and the European Union's Co-Decision Procedure'. *Journal of Legislative Studies*, 3: 74–92.

————(1997*b*). 'More on the Co-Decision Endgame'. *Journal of Legislative Studies*, 3: 139–43.

————(2000). 'Legislative Politics in the European Union'. *European Union Politics*, 1: 9–36.

————(2001). 'The Institutional Foundations of Intergovernmentalism and Supranationalism in the European Union'. *International Organization*, 55: 357–90.

——and Kalandrakis, Anastassios (1999). 'European Parliament and Environmental Legislation: The Case of Chemicals'. *European Journal of Political Research*, 36: 119–54.

——and Kreppel, Amie (1998). 'The History of Conditional Agenda Setting in European Institutions'. *European Journal of Political Research*, 33: 41–71.

——, Jensen, Christian B., Kalandrakis, Anastassios, and Kreppel, Amie (1999). 'Legislative Procedures in the European Union'. Paper presented in ECSA meetings.

Tucker, Emma (1996). 'Brussels Bid for Merger Powers Fails'. *Financial Times*, 15 November.

——(1997). 'Brussels to Get Wider Power on Vetting Mergers'. *Financial Times*, 25 April.

Türk, Alexander (2000). 'Appendix Two: Comment on the Commission Proposal by Alexander Türk', in Mads Andenas and Alexander Türk (eds), *Delegated Legislation and the Role of Committees in the EC*. Boston: Kluwer Law International.

Tuohy, William (1986). 'West Germans in a Froth over "Purity of Beer" Ruling due from European Court'. *Los Angeles Times*, 1 November.

Valentine, Donald Graham (1954). *The Court of Justice of the European Coal and Steel Community*. Gravenhage: Martinus Nijhoff.

Van Schendelen, M. P. C. M. (1996). 'EC Committees: Influence Counts More than Legal Powers', in Robin H. Pedlar and Guenther F. Schaefer (eds), *Shaping European Law and Policy: The Role of Committees and Comitology in the Political Process*. Maastricht: European Institute of Public Administration.

Verdun, Amy (1998). 'The Institutional Design of EMU: A Democratic Deficit?' *Journal of Public Policy*, 18: 107–32.

Vogel, David (1995). *Trading Up: Consumer and Environmental Regulation in a Global Economy*. Cambridge, MA: Harvard University Press.

Vos, Ellen (1997). 'The Rise of Committees'. *European Law Journal*, 3: 210–29.

——(1999). *Institutional Frameworks of Community Health and Safety Legislation: Committees, Agencies, and Private Bodies*. Oxford: Hart Publishing.

Wallace, Helen (2000). 'The Institutional Setting: Five Variations on a Theme', in Helen Wallace and William Wallace (eds), *Policy-making in the European Union*. New York: Oxford University Press.

——, Caporaso, James A., Scharpf, Fritz W., and Moravcsik, Andrew (1999). 'Review Section Symposium: The Choice for Europe: Social Purpose and State Power from Messina to Maastricht'. *Journal of European Public Policy*, 6: 155–79.

Waltz, Kenneth (1979). *Theory of International Politics*. Reading, MA: Addison-Wesley.

Wapner, Paul (1996). *Environmental Activism and World Civic Politics*. Albany: SUNY Press.

Ward, Angela (2000). *Judicial Review and the Rights of Private Parties in EC Law*. New York: Oxford University Press.

Wastell, David and Kirkbride, Julie (1996). 'Ministers Face Personal Lawsuits on 48-Hour Week'. *Daily Telegraph*, 13 July.

Weatherill, Stephen (1996). 'After *Keck*: Some Thoughts on How to Clarify the Clarification'. *Common Market Law Review*, 33: 885–906.

—— and Beaumont, Paul (1999). *EC Law: The Essential Guide to the Legal Workings of the European Community* (3rd edn). New York: Penguin Books.

Webber, Douglas (1998). 'High Midnight in Brussels: An Analysis of the September 1993 Council Meeting on the Uruguay Round'. *Journal of European Public Policy*, 5: 578–94.

Weigall, David and Stirk, Peter (eds) (1992). *The Origins and Development of the European Community*. New York: St Martin's Press.

Weiler, J. H. H. (1981). 'The Community Legal System: The Dual Character of Supranationalism', in Frances G. Jacobs, *Yearbook of European Law*, 1: 257–306. Oxford: Clarendon Press.

——(1991). 'The Transformation of Europe'. *Yale Law Journal*, 100: 2403–83.

——(1993a). 'Neither Unity Nor Three Pillars—The Trinity Structure of the Treaty on European Union', in Joerg Monar, Werner Ungerer, and Wolfgang Wessels (eds), *The Maastricht Treaty on European Union*. Brussels: European Interuniversity Press.

——(1993b). 'Journey to an Unknown Destination: A Retrospective and Prospective of the European Court of Justice in the Arena of Political Integration'. *Journal of Common Market Studies*, 31: 417–46.

——(1994). 'A Quiet Revolution: The European Court of Justice and its Interlocutors'. *Comparative Political Studies*, 24: 510–34.

——(1995). 'Does Europe Need a Constitution? Reflections on Demos, Telos, and the German Maastricht Decision'. *European Law Journal*, 1: 219–58.

Weingast, Barry R. and Marshall, William J. (1988). 'The Industrial Organization of Congress: Or Why Legislatures, Like Firms, Are Not Organized as Markets'. *Journal of Political Economy*, 96: 132–63.

—— and Moran, Mark (1983). 'Bureaucratic Discretion or Congressional Control? Regulatory Policy-Making by the Federal Trade Commission'. *Journal of Political Economy*, 91: 765–800.

Wendt, Alexander (1999). *Social Theory of International Politics*. New York: Cambridge University Press.

Wessels, Wolfgang (1998). 'Comitology: Fusion in Action. Politico-administrative trends in the EU System'. *Journal of European Public Policy*, 5: 209–34.

West, William (1995). *Controlling the Bureaucracy: Institutional Constraints in Theory and Practice*. Armonk, NY: M. E. Sharpe.

Westlake, Martin (1994). *The Commission and the Parliament: Partners and Rivals in the European Policy-Making Process*. London: Butterworths.

White, Eric L. (1989). 'In Search of the Limits to Article 30'. *Common Market Law Review*, 26: 235–80.

Whiteford, Elaine A. (1996). 'Occupational Pensions and European Law: Clarity at Last?', in Tamara K. Hervey and David O'Keeffe (eds), *Sex Equality Law in the European Union*. New York: John Wiley and Sons.

Wilks, S. and McGowan, L. (1995). 'Disarming the Commission: The Debate over a European Cartel Office'. *Journal of Common Market Studies*, 32: 259–73.

Williams, Shirley (1991). 'Sovereignty and Accountability in the European Community', in Robert O. Keohane and Stanley Hoffmann (eds), *The New European Community*. Boulder, CO: Westview Press.

Williamson, Oliver (1985). *The Economic Institutions of Capitalism: Firms, Markets, Regional Contracting*. New York: Free Press.

Wolf, Julie (1991). 'Europe: Power Play in Brussels'. *Guardian*, 18 October.

——(1992). 'Brittan Wins Battle over Vetting Power'. *Guardian*, 5 February.

Wood, B. Dan. (1988). 'Principals, Bureaucrats, and Responsiveness in Clean Air Enforcement'. *American Political Science Review*, 82: 213–34.

——and Milne, Seamus (1996). 'Tories Will Fight "Stupid" 48-Hour Week'. *Manchester Guardian Weekly*, 24 March.

——and Waterman, Richard (1991). 'The Dynamics of Political Control of the Bureaucracy'. *American Political Science Review*, 85: 801–28.

————(1993). 'The Dynamics of Political-Bureaucratic Adaptation'. *American Journal of Political Science*, 37: 497–528.

Woolcock, Stephen (2000). 'European Trade Policy: Global Pressures and Domestic Constraints', in Helen Wallace and William Wallace (eds), *Policy-Making in the European Union*. New York: Oxford University Press.

——and Hodges, M. (1996). 'EU Policy and the Uruguay Round', in Helen Wallace and William Wallace (eds), *Policy-making in the European Union*. Oxford: Oxford University Press.

Woolley, John (1993). 'Conflict Among Regulators and the Hypothesis of Congressional Dominance'. *Journal of Politics*, 55: 92–114.

Yataganas, Xénophon A. (2001). 'Delegation of Regulatory Authority in the European Union: The Relevance of the American Model of Independent Agencies'. Harvard Jean Monnet Working Paper 2001/3; www.jeanmonnetprogram.org/papers/01/010301.html.

Young, Oran (1999). 'Comment on Andrew Moravcsik, "A New Statecraft? Supranational Entrepreneurs and International Cooperation"'. *International Organization*, 53: 805–9.

Yuill, D., Allen, K., Bachtler, J., Clement, K., and Wishlade, F. (eds) (1993). *European Regional Incentives (1993–1994)*. Glasgow: University of Strathclyde.

Zürn, Michael (2000). 'Democratic Governance Beyond the Nation-State', in Michael Th. Greven and Louis Pauly (eds), *Democracy Beyond the State? The European Dilemma and the Emerging Global Order*. Lanham, MD: Rowman and Littlefield.

Zysman, John and Sandholtz, Wayne (1989). '1992: Recasting the European Bargain'. *World Politics*, 41: 1–30.

INDEX